6 00

American Principles
and Issues

American Principles and Issues

* *

The National Purpose

* * * *

Edited by
Oscar Handlin

Professor of History
Harvard University

Holt, Rinehart and Winston, Inc.
New York

Library of Congress Catalog Card Number: 61-10827

23430-0111

Editor's Introduction

In the spring of 1960, the editors of *Life* asked a group of distinguished Americans to consider the problem of American national purpose. The Republic, having become great, seemed to have lost sight of the visions that had animated it in its youth. All over the land people were asking what the United States ought to do with its greatness. *Life* thought that serious consideration of the issues might illuminate some of the basic problems of our times. Each of the contributors invited to do so by *Life* independently wrote an essay outlining the situation as it seemed to him at the opening of the seventh decade of the twentieth century. The papers were published in *Life* and in *The New York Times;* and they form the core of this volume.

Such an enterprise was altogether appropriate at this juncture in American history. The great war that had ended in 1945 had not brought peace. Instead, it had opened into a long period of disturbance both within the United States and in the relationship of the country to the rest of the world.

Year after year, Americans found their way of life challenged by a foreign enemy, strong in military power and armed with an ideology which constituted the most serious threat to the nation since its establishment. At the same time, great internal changes called for painful readjustments in the character and values of American society. The result was a pervasive sense of insecurity and doubt, at home and abroad.

Under such conditions it was enormously stimulating to inquire just what the American experience had been and was likely to be in the future. Such an inquiry might help trace the guidelines that would better equip Americans to deal with the problems of the future.

Efforts to define a communal purpose were by no means new in America. As far back as the seventeenth century,

21611

some settlers had perceived a distinctive character in the
civilization they were building in the New World. And at
each point of crisis in the history of the nation thoughtful
men groped for a definition of that distinctiveness in order
to be able to meet immediate issues in the light of long-
term principles. The necessity for doing so was compelling
for people aware that the American universe was not as
fixed and unalterable as that of the Old World. Here the
absence of rigid, inherited institutions and the availability
of space seemed to offer man an opportunity to make a new
beginning. He was not bound simply to accept the past as
given; by the exercise of his will, he could shape the society
he created according to patterns that he considered desirable and that obliged him to reflect upon what was desirable. The quest for purpose was therefore a continuing
theme in the development of American culture.

To some extent, the first challenge was that of making
something of the opportunities for material well-being
that an unexploited continent seemed to offer. Here an
abundance of resources, and above all, of land, promised a
release from the bonds of scarcity which had long confined
Europeans. For a long time Americans wrestled with the
implications of being a people of relative plenty. The accessibility of wealth meant that men were not to be fixed
in the stations into which they had been born and opened
up the possibility of improvement through mobility. That
was undoubtedly connected with the emphasis on success
and individual achievement that played so important a
part in shaping American attitudes. But the accessibility of
material goods also raised troubling questions about the
part they should play in the life of the whole society.

The problems of individualism were particularly grave
in a society in which culture was not as rigidly controlled
as in Europe. No class was dominant enough to control the
developing culture of the United States. Nor did patterns
inherited from the Old World have weight enough to restrict its evolution. Ideas and forms of expression were free
to mirror the interests and tastes of the common man. Art,
literature, and the style of life could not simply follow
traditional folk patterns or the tastes of a dominant class,
as in Europe; American culture had to serve quite different
needs and often seemed tainted by mediocrity and vulgarity. But judged by its own standards, it displayed great
achievements as well as manifest shortcomings.

The emphasis upon success and upon individualism often
raised problems about the relationship between public

means and private ends. In the Old World great leaders and powerful groups were able to shape policy and to control legislation toward their own goals. But the looser organization of American society made it difficult to formulate clearly the objectives toward which the whole community could strive. On the other hand, Americans were not anarchists; they wished their government to take positive steps to serve their common needs, but to do so in ways that did not infringe upon their rights as individuals. This problem was, of course, complicated by the democratic framework in which Americans were compelled to act. Widespread acceptance of necessity for ruling with the consent of the governed not only shaped the political institutions of the nation, but also set limits upon the ways in which common ends could be defined. Democracy also posed the necessity for public debate by which all problems were considered in open discussion.

The ethnic diversity of the American people was a further stimulant to such discussion. In a society in which everyone was an immigrant, in which people were constantly in motion so that few died in the place of their birth, it was not possible to take for granted a uniformity of inherited habits and attitudes. The juxtaposition of various heritages frequently raised questions that compelled men to consider the purposes and goals of their society. The variety of population drawn from every end of Europe, Africa, and Asia also compelled them to grapple with fundamental problems of how men of different cultures learned to live together and what their relationships should be in a free society.

Through the whole course of their history, deeply held assumptions as to freedom and human rights also narrowed the range of alternatives open to Americans. While the exact definition of these privileges changed from time to time, the conviction that the state was not all-powerful protected the individual within certain spheres against interference either by government or by other persons and had a marked influence upon the thinking of Americans about the purpose of their national experience.

Finally, Americans never forgot that they were part of a wider world. Even though many of them were immigrants who had fled from their old homes out of discontent with the conditions that they left behind, they did not conceive that their own destiny was isolated from that of the rest of the world. In the seventeenth and eighteenth centuries there was an acute awareness of the links of the New World to the Old; and as the Republic grew in strength after the Revolution, there was a constant expectation that it would play a prominent part in world affairs. In the twentieth century, the increase of national power and the contraction of distances made that role ever more significant. The national purpose was therefore meaningful not only for the people who lived within the territorial limits of the United States, but for all mankind. Consciousness of those implications added gravity to all considerations of what the national purpose should be.

In the volume that follows, an effort has been made to add depth to the material in the *Life* symposium. Each of the ten essays touches on some of the themes connected with the idea of national purpose, although from a variety of points of view. Each is presented as it was written. Each essay leads into a selection of important documents from the American past organized into a convenient unit for discussion. The documents do not necessarily agree with the position set forth in the essay; they aim rather to provide a broad basis for understanding the general problem. The materials have been chosen from a wide variety of sources, from public documents, philosophical analyses, poetry and fiction, for the implications of the conception of national purpose have permeated all these forms. The selections emanate from every period of American history, but the criterion of inclusion has been their relevance to present-day understanding of the problems of the immediate future.

Cambridge, Mass.   O. H.
January, 1961

Acknowledgments

I am very grateful to the following authors and publishers for permission to use selections from copyright materials which they control: the American Jewish Committee; James Baldwin; John A. Brittain; E. E. Cummings; Justice William O. Douglas; John Dos Passos; *Fortune* Magazine; Harcourt, Brace and World, Inc.; Harper & Brothers; Holt, Rinehart and Winston, Inc.; Miami University Press; Jewish Publication Society of America; Alfred A. Knopf, Inc.; James Laughlin; The Macmillan Company; New Directions; New University Thought; David Riesman; Random House, Inc.; Dean Eugene V. Rostow; and Simon and Schuster, Inc.

In the course of compiling this work I have had, as always, the devoted collaboration of Mary F. Handlin; and I profited from many helpful suggestions from Professor Philip A. Young of the Pennsylvania State University.

The manuscript was prepared with the assistance of Evelyn R. Bender and Janice Y. Shapiro.

O. H.

Statement by Henry R. Luce

More than anything else, the people of America are asking
for a clear sense of National Purpose.

In 1776 Thomas Jefferson wrote the Declaration of Independence. It said what the people of the colonies wanted
and why. Without that Declaration, the United States of
America might never have come into existence. For it took
the words of the Declaration to unite a majority of the
colonists in a clear purpose, involving a most difficult and
painful struggle.

First the Declaration. Then Valley Forge. Then Victory.
Then the Constitution. And today, from those foundations,
the greatest nation in the world.

But what now shall Americans *do* with the greatness of
their nation? And is it great enough? And is it great in the
right way?

From all over the land, there is evidence that this is
what Americans are worrying about. A group of citizens
may begin by talking about the price of eggs or the merits
of education but they end by asking each other: What are
we trying to do, over-all? Where are we trying to get? What
is the National Purpose of the U.S.A.?

Some leaders say we should "sacrifice" more than we do;
we should work harder, pay higher taxes. And one American answer is: Okay, but for what? By sacrificing and by
working and by paying, what is it we expect to achieve?

Peace? Perhaps Peace is the No. 1 Purpose, but what kind
of Peace—and, even, what do we do with Peace when we
have it or if we get it?

Peace, of course, Peace in Freedom. But Freedom to do
what? And be what?

To these questions of American purpose, *Life* recently
asked ten thoughtful Americans to address themselves.

These articles, now brought together in this book, are
offered as a summons, of some urgency, to a national debate.

HENRY R. LUCE,
Editor-in-Chief
Life

Contents

III   MATERIAL WELL-BEING

IV   SUCCESS AND INDIVIDUALISM

V   THE CULTURE OF THE COMMON MAN

VI   PUBLIC MEANS AND PRIVATE ENDS

VII   Democracy and the Consent of the Governed

VIII   Equality in a Melting Pot of People

IX   FREEDOM AND HUMAN RIGHTS

X   AMERICA AND THE WIDER WORLD

****

The Confrontation of 1960

The election of 1960, coming at a crisis in American affairs as serious as any in the history of the nation, elicited significant statements on national purpose from the two major candidates. Shortly after their nominations, each felt called upon to consider the general problem and to express publicly his own attitudes toward it. As significant as the differences between the two statements was the fact that both responded to a consciousness of the need for some expression of views on the issue.

John Fitzgerald Kennedy, the nominee of the Democratic party, was born in Brookline, Massachusetts, in 1917. A member of a family prominent in politics and business, he was educated at Harvard University and served with distinction in the Navy during the war. Shortly after the peace he entered public life and acted as a member of Congress between 1947 and 1953. In 1953 he was elected to the Senate, of which he was a forceful member when he was nominated in 1960. He was the author of *Why England Slept* (1945) and of *Profiles in Courage* (1956), which won the Pulitzer Prize in biography.

Richard Milhouse Nixon was born in Yorba Linda, California, in 1913. Educated at Whittier College and Duke University, he entered upon the practice of law in Whittier, California, in 1937. He remained there until the war, when, after a brief period of service with the Office of Emergency Management in 1942, he entered the Navy. After the peace, he became active in politics, serving as a member of the House of Representatives in the Eightieth and Eighty-first Congresses. He became Senator from California in 1951, and in the following year he was nominated and elected to the Vice-Presidency of the United States.

President John F. Kennedy

In all recorded history, probably the sagest bit of advice ever offered man was the ancient admonition to "know thyself." As with individuals, so with nations. Just as a man who realizes that his life has gone off course can regain his bearings only through the strictest self-scrutiny, so a whole people, become aware that things have somehow gone wrong, can right matters only by a rigidly honest look at its core of collective being, its national purpose.

Thus, while on the one hand the fact that we have felt the urge to debate our national purpose signalizes our arrival at a potential crisis point, on the other hand the fact that we have entered into the debate willingly, indeed with gusto, bodes well for the eventual outcome.

Among our overindulgences of the past decade has been the lavish use of a kind of cloudy rhetoric that only befogs the truth. Yet basically we Americans prefer plain talk and common sense. It is these we must apply if we are to "know ourselves" again.

The facets of this debate on national purpose are many. Other than to agree that the whole subject vitally needs airing, the debaters are split a dozen ways as to which aspect of it demands greatest emphasis. Some prefer to dwell on what has happened to our national purpose—whether irrevocably lost, permanently strayed or temporarily sidetracked; others on why what has happened has happened; others on what can be done by way of remedy or retrieve. Above all, the debate turns on precisely what this "purpose" is that, momentarily or forever, has gone from our midst.

The distinguished contributors to previous instalments of this LIFE series have offered a variety of definitions of our national purpose, all of them valid. From this it can be seen that no one word or catch phrase will suffice to pinpoint it. Our national purpose is resident, obviously, in the magnificent principles of the Declaration of Independence and of the Constitution and Bill of Rights. It also plainly appears in the writings of Jefferson, Madison and Hamilton, in the words of Jackson and Lincoln, in the works of Emerson and Whitman, in the opinions of Marshall and Holmes, in Wilson's New Freedom and Franklin D. Roosevelt's Four

Freedoms. In common, all of these pulse with a sense of idealistic aspiration, of the struggle for a more perfect Union, of the effort to build the good society as well as the good life here and in the rest of the world.

There is, I think, still another way to describe our national purpose. This definition, while almost a literal one, is nevertheless not a narrow one. It is that our national purpose consists of the combined purposefulness of each of us *when we are at our moral best*: striving, risking, choosing, making decisions, engaging in a pursuit of happiness that is strenuous, heroic, exciting and exalted. When we do so as individuals, we make a nation that, in Jefferson's words, will always be "in the full tide of successful experiment."

Such a definition, because it implies a constant, restless, confident questing, neither precludes nor outmodes, but rather complements, the expression of national purpose set forth in our Declaration, our Constitution, and in the words of our great Presidents, jurists and writers. The purpose they envisioned can, indeed, never be outmoded, because it has never been and can never be fully achieved. It will always be somewhere just out of reach, a challenge to further aspiring, struggling, striving and searching. Quest has always been the dominant note of our history, whether a quest for national independence; a quest for personal liberty and economic opportunity on a new continent from which the rest of mankind could take heart and hope; a quest for more land, more knowledge, more dignity; a quest for more effective democracy; a quest for a world of free and pacific nations.

It should be said at once that no nation has a corner on striving and aspiring any more than on virtue and compassion. Thus our national purpose finds echo in the minds of men of good intent everywhere. But our purpose may differ from others in the particular background against which it evolved, and by three fundamental facts about us:

First, Americans, more than other peoples, have since independence cherished a strong sense of destiny.

Second, we have always been optimists about our national future. Down through the decades we have had our indentured servants, our slaves and Simon Legrees, our sweated immigrants, our Okies, our depressed and discouraged folk of many stripes. But we have been unfailingly confident of winning through all obstacles to realize our dream.

Third, Americans have always been willing to experiment. With no feudal inheritance, with little dead weight of caste or tradition, we have ever been in the mood for bold adventure. Our forefathers would not have tossed aside old associations and crossed the seas without it. New frontiers have always seemed unfolding on our horizon.

With these basic considerations, and because of them, the pace of change in this land has been faster than anywhere else on the globe. The change has been less noisy and melodramatic than in Russia or

China, among others, for since 1865 it has lacked any real elements of violence. We believe in progress by evolution, not revolution. But for precisely this reason the progress has been deeper, saner and more continuously rapid. In our energy, our resourcefulness and our powers of organization, we can assert that the United States has been and is the most dynamic nation in history.

Since this is so, why then our current widespread sense of staleness, of frustration; why the gnawing feeling that we may have lost our way? In my mind there are two broad answers.

One is that the very abundance which our dynamism has created has weaned and wooed us from the tough condition in which, heretofore, we have approached whatever it is we have had to do. A man with extra fat will look doubtfully on attempting the four-minute mile; a nation replete with goods and services, confident that "there's more where that came from," may feel less ardor for questing.

The second answer is that we have, of late, lacked the leadership we require—human frailty being what it is—to remind us of our national purpose, to direct its shaping for current ends, to spur us to new efforts, to encourage and, if need be, to exhort.

In his stirring speech at Queen's Hall in London seeking World War I volunteers, David Lloyd George, soon to be Britain's Prime Minister, described a snug valley in his native Wales. Nestled between the mountains and the sea, shielded from the storms and stresses of the outside world, that little valley offered its inhabitants a placid and sheltered life. But on occasion, Lloyd George recalled, the young men of the valley would refuse to stay put. They would climb its highest hill to be inspired by the majestic peaks in the distance, to have their energies sharpened by the mountain breezes.

Too many Americans in the 1950s, I believe, have been living too much of the time in such a valley. We have felt contented and complacent and comfortable. Now it is time once again to climb to the hilltop, to be reinvigorated and reinspired by those faraway peaks, the principles that are vital to our national greatness, that underlie our national purpose, that foster our "American dream."

Whether we see them or not, those peaks never change. Whether we remember it or not, their meaning never diminishes.

Thus the task that lies ahead is not to create a new national purpose, but to try to recapture the old one. This is no call to retrogression, for this purpose, born 184 years ago, will be as noble and as fresh 184 years hence—and beyond.

It is those same old slogans and same old solutions, surrounding the national purpose, that we must guard against. The old ways will not do. They cannot do. The Census Bureau predicts that, if the present curve of growth continues, our population will reach 260 million in only 20 years. When we think of how this increase alone will clothe all our problems in growing urgency, we know that when we once again seize hold of our purpose, we will have to do so with new ideas and new vigor.

Where and how do we apply our national purpose to the challenges of 1960?

Survival is often listed as the major challenge today, and certainly other issues are overshadowed by the one issue that could render the rest moot. But although our physical safety as a nation is more imperiled than ever before in our history, survival alone is insufficient as an expression of national purpose. Mere physical survival, at the cost of our way of life, would be worth little; more importantly, survival alone is hardly an aspiration worthy of a great nation. The nobleman who, when asked what he did in the French Revolution, replied, "I survived," may have been hailed for his wit but for little else.

We remember too seldom that survival is threatened not only by ever more awesome weapons of death and destruction but also by a lack of aim and aspiration. Outside the walls of every nation that has grown fat and overly fond of itself has always lurked a lean and hungry enemy.

Competition with that enemy is today deemed by some to be our major challenge; but it, too, reflects our national purpose inadequately. We are, indeed, in competition with the Soviets, and to a large extent our hopes for the future rest on our comparative efforts in economic growth, in the arms race, in scientific achievement, in aid to other nations, in propaganda, in prestige and in a host of other fields.

But we will err tragically if we make competition with the Communists an end in itself. Whatever we do in the name of that competition— improving our race relations, expanding our economy, helping new nations, exploring outer space and all the rest—we ought to be doing anyway, for its own sake, whether competition exists or not.

Peace is humanity's deepest longing, and with the failure to achieve it all other aspirations fail too. In acclaiming it as the major expression of our national purpose, however, we must know what sort of peace we mean. Certainly the unjust peace of subjugation, the uneasy peace of cold war or the fruitless peace of an interval between hot wars is far from a goal that will satisfy.

Prosperity, like peace, is desired by all, and our political orators have traditionally held out the goal of personal and national economic well-being as a primary American aim. But the good life falls short as an indicator of national purpose unless it goes hand in hand with the good society. Even in material terms, prosperity is not enough when there is no equal opportunity to share in it; when economic progress means over-crowded cities, abandoned farms, technological unemployment, polluted air and water, and littered parks and countrysides; when those too young to earn are denied their chance to learn; when those no longer earning live out their lives in lonely degradation.

No single one of these four challenges—survival, competition, peace, prosperity—sums up our national purpose today. The creation of a more perfect Union requires the pursuit of a whole series of ideals, ideals which can never be fully attained, but the eternal quest for which embodies the American National Purpose:

The fulfillment of every individual's dignity and potential.

The perfection of the democratic process.

The education of every individual to his capacity.

The elimination of ignorance, prejudice, hate and the squalor in which crime is bred.

The elimination of slums, poverty and hunger.

Protection against the economic catastrophes of illness, disability and unemployment.

The achievement of a constantly expanding economy, without inflation or dislocation, either in the factory or on the farm.

The conquest of dread diseases.

The enrichment of American culture.

The attainment of world peace and disarmament, based on world law and order, on the mutual respect of free peoples and on a world economy in which there are no "have-not" or "under-developed" nations.

A dream? Of course—the American dream. No candidate for office, unless he were foolish or deceitful, would *promise* its fulfillment. But we are in urgent need of public men who will *work* toward its fulfillment, guiding, directing and encouraging the popular impetus toward that end.

That this impetus exists is beyond question. We are not a people in panic or despair. We have not "gone over the hill" of history. We have simply, and fortuitously, begun to recognize that somehow we have gotten off the track, and that to get back on we will need stern effort, spirited leadership and common sacrifice.

If we are to recharge our sense of national purpose, we should accept no invitations to relax on a patent mattress stuffed with woolly illusions labeled peace, prosperity and normalcy. We should congratulate ourselves not for our country's past glories and present accumulations but for our opportunities for further toil and risk. Rather than take satisfaction in goals already reached, we should be contrite about the goals unreached. We ought not to look for excuses in the budget, but for justifications in the dizzying rush of events and in the harsh realities of our time.

For these are harsh times. The future will not be easier. Our responsibilities will not lessen. Our enemies will not weaken. We must demonstrate that we can meet our responsibility as a free society—that we can by voluntary means match their ruthless exploitation of human, natural and material resources—that freedom can not only compete and survive but prevail and flourish.

It is not enough to debate "What is the meaning of America?" Each of us must also decide "What does it mean to be an American?" Upon us destiny has lavished special favors of liberty and opportunity—and it therefore has demanded of us special efforts, particularly in times such as these.

It requires each one of us to be a little more decent, alert, intelligent, compassionate and resolute in our daily lives—that we exercise our civic duties, whether paying taxes or electing Presidents, with an extra pride and care—that we use our freedom of choice to pursue our own destiny in a manner that advances the national destiny, in the work we produce, the subjects we study, the positions we seek, the languages we learn, the complaints we voice, the leaders we follow, the inconveniences we endure.

If a dark corner of Africa needs technicians—if a troubled spot in Asia needs language specialists—if a Soviet threat in Berlin requires patience and determination—if the space race requires better schools—we must and can demonstrate that the dedicated efforts of free men can meet these needs better than the efforts of totalitarian compulsion.

Every American must take far more seriously than he has in the past decade his responsibility for achieving and maintaining a democratic society of a truly model kind, worthy to be the champion of freedom throughout the world.

We Americans must again commit ourselves to great ends. We must resume our searching, surging, questing. Then, assuredly, we will come nearer the vision of John Adams of Massachusetts, who, in 1813, assured his friend Thomas Jefferson that our republic would some day "introduce the perfection of man."

Richard M. Nixon

It is particularly appropriate that *Life* has stimulated a comprehensive re-examination of our national purpose at a time when the American people are making some important decisions about their future, as they are in the election of a new President.

A common denominator of agreement among the eminent contributors to this series is that the nation has mounted insufficient response to the Communist challenge to free society.

We can all agree that we have never faced a more formidable challenge. Yet contrary to some of the other viewpoints which have been presented, it is my belief that never has the American purpose been more clear.

For me the discussion has served the very useful function of pointing up the difference between interest and purpose. Some of those who have participated seem to have been talking mostly about interests; others were truly dealing with the more elusive thing which we can recognize as purpose.

That there is a difference between the two was recognized by a man who was caught up in one of the several re-examinations of our national purpose which have already taken place in this century. Woodrow Wilson noted prophetically just before the struggle over the League of Nations, "Interest does not bind men together. Interest separates men." Only purpose, Wilson said, can unite men.

Since we are now engaged in a national political campaign, it is well to keep in mind this difference between interest and purpose. In the Wilsonian sense an interest is an end peculiar to a group or individual. It is the kind of end sought by what we call an "interest group." It is not an end that recommends itself for general adoption; it sets no goal that can unite a whole people. Such a goal Wilson called purpose.

Too often we wage our political campaigns and evaluate our national posture in terms of interests. Too often the parties put forth platforms, and the candidates make campaign promises, which seek a mere compromise of conflicting interests, which propose some "splitting of the difference." Would it not be more in keeping with our best tradition if we sought a larger purpose within which our separate interests could be united in a more elevated conception of our destiny? Fundamentally, purpose must be examined in terms of what an entire people can regard as the ends of human existence and their relation to the external universe and to God.

The first problem in re-examining national purpose, then, would be to separate interest from purpose. The second would be to distinguish purpose from fulfillment.

If our purpose, as I believe it does, comes from a higher authority than ourselves, we still retain the responsibility. It rests with us, as men, and as a nation, whether we will or will not fulfill our purpose. From this point on when I speak of national purpose I will mean both the purpose that should unite us and the dedication of mind and spirit necessary to achieve it.

Life's editor-in-chief said before a Senate committee recently, "The founding purpose of the United States was to make men free, and to enable them to be free and to preach the gospel of freedom to themselves and to all men. The purpose has withstood all manner of trial and tribulation, stress and strain."

While I concur that this has proved to be the American purpose reduced to its purest terms, we should remind ourselves that it was not unmistakably so at the time. At the very least we should differentiate between the stated purpose and the processes of fulfillment which are revealed in the continuing thread of our history. Capability, as well as intent to fulfill purpose, is and always has been part of this unfolding destiny.

Stated in the more practical terms which then obtained, the founding purpose was to establish in the new land a society founded on principles of equality under God, dedicated to the general welfare and the blessings of liberty. These were the stated purposes written into the charter documents by the Founding Fathers—philosophers whose collective wisdom under stress we find so worthy of emulation today.

But while Jefferson said we act not "for ourselves alone, but for the whole human race," we know that the English colonies struggling for survival between the wilderness and the sea—a sea open to the warships of predatory monarchies—had not the capability to make *all* men free. We also know that the founders did not even have the intent to make *all* men free because they established the United States, partially at least, as a slave society.

Moreover the founders suffered agonizing uncertainties and soul-searching doubts as they went about the fulfillment of the great purpose, of which we can now see that they were seized. As late as the year 1774 so well informed a man as Benjamin Franklin could say in all seriousness that he "never had heard in any conversation from any person, drunk or sober, the least expression of a wish for a separation" from England.

We now know that even as Franklin said these words, the American sense of purpose was running at full tide. In no time, as we reckon these things, independence had been declared and a war to confirm it was in progress.

Today we look back to the author of the Declaration of Independence as a man truly aware of the purpose that was flowing around him. Yet at the time even he was writing, in his "Notes on Virginia," in almost the exact vein of several of these modern essays on national purpose: "From the conclusion of this war we shall be going downhill. It will not then be necessary to resort every moment to the people for support. . . . They will forget themselves but in the sole faculty of making money, and will never think of uniting to effect a due respect for their rights."

The people did unite. They did rise above their material self-interest. The Constitution was written and adopted including, in the end, the Bill of Rights.

Fifty years later the Americans were speaking of a manifest destiny. The new nation had begun to be stirred by the technological revolution which has changed the world. The age of Jackson brought the rise to prominence of the common man, politically and economically. The word "democracy" was becoming respectable. The U.S. could feel its muscle, and its face was turned westward.

But again, not all saw it so. One particularly prominent essayist of the time saw a serious absence of purpose and a dangerous national tendency to materialism. Americans, Emerson wrote, spent their money on trifles and lost themselves in seeking "after fine garment, handsome apartment, access to public houses and places of amusements." He detested what he called the mediocrity which he saw about him and wanted us to be "away with this hurrah of the masses."

There was a difficulty about democracy, but it was not the chasing after fine garments and handsome apartments. It was the revelation of a fundamental conflict in the constitution.

As the westward movement continued, the ever-present, overriding question was, shall the new territory be free or slave? By the middle of the nineteenth century this unresolved question of purpose clearly threatened to destroy the American dream.

The issue was irreconcilable. William Lloyd Garrison and the anti-slavery society held, "The right to enjoy liberty is inalienable. . . . Every man has a right to his own body—to the products of his own labor—to the protection of law—and to the common advantages of society."

Against them Calhoun argued: "It is a great and dangerous error to suppose that all people are equally entitled to liberty. It is a reward . . . reserved for the intelligent, the patriotic, the virtuous and deserving;—and not a boon to be bestowed on [those incapable] either of appreciating or of enjoying it."

From the national dialogue one would conclude the American purpose was muddy and confused.

A sure grasp of the right seemed to fail even Lincoln, who was obliged to confess as the slavery issue was joined, "if all earthly power were given me, I should not know what to do as to the existing Constitution."

Slowly, reluctantly, but nonetheless inexorably, the answer came to him. He declared the Negro slaves emancipated.

It might have been said, as the Civil War ended and the bitter Reconstruction began, that the national purpose was finally to make all Americans free, and by example, to encourage the spread of freedom on earth. But not yet could it be said that America was ready to *act* to make all men free.

With the obstruction of slavery removed, the nation exploded again to the westward—over the continental divide to the western ocean. The expansion was coupled with industrialization. For the next three decades our people pursued their separate but converging interests with a vigor unparalleled in history.

Opportunity was the watchword in America and its sound exerted a pull on the entire Western world.

The poet's inscription for the Statue of Liberty ("Give me your tired, your poor") truly represented an invitation which was heard round the world. They came, by the hundreds, by the thousands, ultimately by the millions: Irish, Germans, Italians, Scandinavians, Poles, Slavs and many others.

The preoccupation with the western expansion, with the industrialization, increased.

Our political men fell under the influence of the spell of economic conquest. The public dialogue became strongly flavored with arguments—for example, about the survival of the fittest—that bore little resemblance to the purpose of making men free.

America abruptly entered the twentieth century on a new tack. If we had lost our national purpose, we seemed to have found it again. The public dialogue began to accentuate again the voices addressed to the general welfare and the blessings of liberty, to government by law and not by men, to faith in government by the people.

Theodore Roosevelt became the man of the hour by denouncing the malefactors of great wealth and by reinforcing his words with actions to restrain their arrogance.

"The only safe course," he warned, "to follow in this great American democracy, is to provide for making the popular judgment really effective. When this is done, then it is our duty to see that the people, having the full power, realize their heavy responsibility for exercising that power aright."

The surge of annexation ended and the U.S. became the first Western power, of those which had tasted its fruits, to renounce colonialism.

A voice speaking again with the ringing tones of freedom suddenly echoed over the world.

"The world must be made safe for democracy. Its peace must be planted upon the tested foundations of political liberty. . . . But the right is more precious than peace, and we shall fight for the things which we have always carried nearest our hearts—for democracy, for the right of those who submit to authority to have a voice in their own governments, for the rights and liberties of small nations, for a universal domination of right by such a concert of free peoples as shall bring peace and safety to all nations and make the world itself at last free. . . . America is privileged to spend her blood and her might for the principles that gave her birth."

Those words from Wilson's war message of April, 1917—which pointed a new direction toward fulfillment of the American purpose to make *all* men free—were often mocked in the disillusioned '20's and '30's. But they proved to be fully valid in the fourth and fifth decades of the century when the always recurring assaults on freedom came from across the Rhine in 1940 and Yalu in 1950.

The American resolve to spend her might for freedom has been even more recently tested and not yet has it been found to waver. Nor, I predict, will it ever be, so far as any of us living can foresee.

In my opinion we are definitely and demonstrably a young country. We can, I am confident, put aside for this century, as far as America is concerned, Professor Toynbee's image of a dead civilization which has only its artifacts, covered with jungle vine or sand blasted in the desert sun, to recall it.

We have the vigor and imagination of youth. We are ready to go ahead and explore new approaches. We are a society of individuals. Our institutions project outward from people, not downward to people. The individual initiates, society imitates. The individual follows his endless curiosity, society builds roads that follow his footprints.

Our institutions are the creations of individuals and groups of individuals. They are not ordered into existence by the state. We have no state socialism. We have no state religion. We have no state aristocracy. Our schools—whether they be public or private—remain enterprises shared by men and women actively interested in them.

Our businesses—commercial, industrial, agricultural and professional— number more than 10 million, 10 million separate ventures which voluntarily serve society and are voluntarily accepted by society. Our capitalists are not the few but the many. There are more than 12½ million shareholders in American business, more of them women than men. Many of our larger corporations have, in fact, more shareholders than employes.

There are in addition, tens of millions of *indirect* capitalists. Every person taking out an insurance policy, contributing to a pension plan, or putting his money in a bank is indirectly investing in America.

We are also a nation of *land* capitalists—we have no landed aristocracy. More than 60% of American families own their own homes.

Our technology is surging ahead so fast that it is hard to perceive just what breakthrough in industrial productivity the immediate years ahead will bring, what 10 years will bring, or 15, or 20. Let those who blithely tell us what the gross national product of the U.S. or the U.S.S.R. will be in 1965, 1970, or 1975 ponder the evidence recently submitted by the Stanford Research Institute to the Senate Foreign Relations Committee.

The institute reminded us that even the most sophisticated predictions can go sadly awry. For example, a report to the National Resources Committee in 1937 tried to anticipate "the kinds of new inventions which may affect living and working conditions in America in the next . . . 25 years" —or by 1962. In this report most of the major technological developments between 1937 and now were completely unforeseen—despite the fact that many of the nation's then leading scientists and engineers had been consulted in its preparation.

The 1937 report, for instance, anticipated certain developments in vitamins and synthetic drugs but was silent on antibiotics. There was a long section on power but not a single gazer into the future envisioned atomic energy. Communications was treated at length but there was no hint of radar. Aircraft speeds of 240 miles at 20,000 feet were predicted—but on condition that the problem of cabin-pressurization could be solved. Jet-propulsion was not even mentioned.

It has been argued in some of the essays on national purpose, just as Emerson argued in the last century and Jefferson argued in the century before, that America is threatened by preoccupation with materialism and that we suffer a major cultural crisis. There is little doubt that our level of appreciation for art and literature leaves much to be desired, but it is my sincere conviction we are only at the beginning of our cultural thrust.

So far, our unique achievement has been the political achievement. We still have to equal the contributions to the fine arts, to philosophy, and to unlocking the fundamental secrets of the universe which have been our heritage from the older societies. But I suggest that the greatest American achievements in these fields lie ahead. Even now we see all about us—in art gallery, in symphony hall, in scientific laboratory—new creative activity in every branch of human aspiration. And all our accomplishments, along with those of other times and countries, are immediately made available to all Americans through our unrivaled channels of print and electronics.

We cannot yet determine the full implications of the effect of massive cultural exposure on national taste and creativity. There is no previous example.

More important, in my judgment, than any of these other descriptions of our society, is that we are openly prepared to share it with the world. We are, in this respect, comparable to the society which generated the creativity of the Hellenic civilization.

As Pericles said of his beloved Athens, "We throw open our city to the world, and never by alien acts exclude foreigners from any opportunity of learning or observing, although the eyes of an enemy may occasionally profit by our liberality; trusting less in system and policy than to the native spirit of our citizens."

Finally, I believe we often fail to see the full dimensions of our nation's purpose. In my opinion the truth is that the American purpose has continued to broaden as the country has matured and our capabilities have grown. We can see the process in retrospect, in the painful separation from England, in the establishment of government of the people, in the bloody eradication of slavery, in the great expansion and technological adaptation, in the renunciation of conquest, in the willingness to fight for freedom anywhere in the world.

I have a deep conviction that the American purpose is running strong in the 1960s.

I am struck by the fact that in the 15 years since the Communist challenge emerged in full force out of the ashes of World War II, the American people have been the principal effective force to keep it from overrunning the world. They have levied upon themselves the immense sum of $565 billion to preserve the security of the free world and contain the military threat of Communism. American forces have stood guard along the frontiers of Communism around the world in numbers never before sent forth by a nation for the general security.

If there have been moments of doubt and reversal, we should remember that the American nation has dealt with a threat to freedom more virulent than any which has existed in human history and continues to deal with this threat day by day. I doubt that a greater dedication, with or without the urgency of open warfare, can be found in our own history or in that of any other people.

So much for what we are and what we have done to fulfill our national purpose.

It can never be said that we have done enough while Communist power exists in such magnitude as to threaten the total end of freedom and of humanity itself.

Several of the contributors to this series have called for action to strengthen the American purpose so that we may more adequately meet this threat.

Dr. Graham called upon the American people as individuals to look particularly to their fitness, their courage, and their moral strength. I know of no better place to begin and I truly hope his message has been heard.

Mr. Gardner, in an eloquent plea for the pursuit of excellence, says, "When we raise our sights, strive for excellence and dedicate ourselves to the highest goals of our society, we are enrolling in an ancient and meaningful cause: the age-long struggle of man to realize the best that is in him."

Certainly he and Dr. Graham have supplied ringing answers to the question: "What can I do?"

I believe that we should also take special account of General Sarnoff's call for "an unequivocal decision" to win the cold war and his point that news of this be plainly told to the world.

Mr. Luce, in his own statement on national purpose, delivered as testimony to the Senate Committee on Government Operations, accepted General Sarnoff's proposition as his own, with an amendment. In the atomic age, he suggested, no nation capable of launching a war of annihilation can be presented with the alternative of unconditional surrender. He proposed a more limited aim: severance of the state power of Russia and China from the mission of their present rulers to Communize the world.

We all know that the struggle with Communism must be fought without atomic war. Mr. Khrushchev himself knows that, though he has yet to convince his Chinese partner, Chairman Mao, who openly has foreseen a Communist victory, and more probably a Chinese Communist victory, from a war of general annihilation. Khrushchev in this instance is right and Mao is wrong. No one, not even the Chinese nation, will survive a general atomic war.

It is, therefore, essential to the American purpose that atomic war must be prevented. I know of only two ways this can be assured: by the maintenance on our part of invulnerable military strength, or by honest disarmament. Until the latter is within our grasp, we cannot temporize with the former.

It is essential to the American purpose that Communism shall not be permitted to spread.

These are negative aspects of our national purpose to which not only most Americans, but most of the free world will subscribe. They are, as Wilson said, purposes which unite men.

Beyond this, and insofar as God grants us power to see these things, I believe we are even now witnessing a further broadening of national purpose for achievement of affirmative goals which will unite us.

Since the end of World War II the core of American foreign policy has been support of the United Nations. Immediately second have been our efforts, still widely debated among us, to give strong economic support to the free nations. We have gone to the relief of distressed populations, rehabilitated the shattered economies of our allies and former enemies alike.

We have assisted the technological adaptation of the emergent societies. In all of these programs one can find self-interest. In fact, they have often been defended as such by their hard-presssed supporters in Congress. It could be argued that we have merely been stimulated by the Communist challenge. I prefer, as an American, to think these things would have come if Communism had never spread beyond the pages of Marx and Engels.

Moreover, it is my belief that there is something more fundamental here than interest. We have already converted more than $78 billion from our own uses for these efforts, and they are certain to continue.

Most of us know instinctively that there is no more important human event occurring today than the revolution of expectations among the peoples of newly emerging nations, representing a third of the human race and uncommitted as between the free world and the Communist tyranny.

It is my firm belief that it is America's national purpose to extend the goals of the preamble of our Constitution to our relations with all men. At this point I should like to repeat these propositions:

Form a more perfect union.

Establish justice.

Insure domestic tranquillity.

Provide for the common defense.

Promote the general welfare.

Secure the blessings of liberty for ourselves and posterity.

Four of these six goals Communism purports to offer mankind. That is why their cause has wide appeal. In place of two of them, justice and liberty, they demand a social discipline enforced by tyrannical state power.

I am as certain as I am certain of anything in life that these propositions were not conceived in the minds of men solely or unaided, and that they are inseparable. I am also certain that the inseparability applies not to ourselves alone but to all mankind.

I believe that the inseparability of these propositions from human destiny is the American purpose and that it will prevail.

I

* *

The American Mission

JOHN K. JESSUP

is chief editorial writer of *Life* magazine.

He was born in Rochester, New York, in 1907. He was graduated from Yale University in 1928, taught English there, and served as assistant editor of the *Yale Alumni Weekly*. He was an advertising copywriter until he joined Time, Inc., in 1935, as a writer for *Fortune* magazine.

In 1940 he was transferred to *Time* magazine. When Time, Inc., formed a committee in 1942 to study the postwar outlook, Mr. Jessup was named its chairman. He was responsible for the preparation of reports published periodically during World War II as a supplement to *Fortune*.

He became chief editorial writer for *Life* in 1944. From 1948 to 1951 he served in other capacities for Time, Inc., then returned to *Life* as chief editorial writer.

John K. Jessup ✳✳✳ A Noble
Framework for a Great Debate

"The critical weakness of our society is that for the time being our people do not have great purposes which they are united in wanting to achieve. The public mood of the country is defensive, to hold on and to conserve, not to push forward and to create. We talk about ourselves these days as if we were a completed society, one which has achieved its purposes, and has no further great business to transact. . . ."

So wrote Columnist Walter Lippmann a few months ago. It is a disturbing charge for three reasons. First, Lippmann is not alone in making it. The same complaint is heard, with varying emphasis, from many other critics and leaders of opinion, and also, according to a recent survey of *Life's* correspondents, from many an average anonymous American as well. Some of them speak like Lippmann of our lost or mislaid national purpose or purposes; others use an older phrase, "the American dream." Thus William Faulkner: "What happened to the American dream? We dozed, and it abandoned us. And in that vacuum now there sound no longer the strong loud voices . . . speaking in mutual unification of one hope and will." As though he also felt something missing, the President himself has appointed a Commission on National Goals "to develop a broad outline of national objectives and programs for the next decade and longer." So much palpable concern, in quarters high and low, suggests that the vacuum of purpose may be a real one.

Second, the charge is disturbing because if it is true it is new. The U.S. has hitherto been a country associated with great purpose. If that purpose is now absent, we are not what we were. Is there not a connection between the rise of nations and great purposes, between the loss of purpose and their decline? A U.S. without a purpose, or no greater purpose than "Don't rock the boat," may well be a U.S. in decline.

Third, the world needs a purposeful America. Even if the U.S. could ever be a "completed society," to use Lippmann's phrase, the world is

21

not. Mankind has much further "great business to transact"—if not with the active leadership of the U.S., then without it, and probably with the leadership of Communism.

It may be argued that Lippmann's charge, even if true, is irrelevant. Does the U.S. really need a self-conscious purpose in the world? Is not a democracy its own *raison d'être,* and survival the whole of its duty? Many feel that only individuals, not nations, are capable of high purposes; and that the proper role of the American nation is simply to provide the political framework in which each American citizen defines and conducts his own private "pursuit of happiness," nobly or ignobly, to suit himself. Yet this theory of a passive role for the nation has not satisfied the growing uneasiness. "Why are many Americans fearful that we have lost our sense of national purpose?" asks Adlai Stevenson. "Why is there a slackness about public problems and a wholesale retreat to the joys of private life?"

If America is in fact an eldery, *status quo* nation, it has had one of the briefest runs for its money in the history of great nations, and its early senescence will have belied more prophecies and grander promises than any nation ever made. During most of its brief history America has been bursting with confidence in its own unlimited destiny. A French visitor in the 1840s asked one of these confident spokesmen, Senator Lewis Cass of Michigan, "If such is the youth of the republic, what will be its old age?" Replied the senator, "Sir, it will have no old age." Cass's bold prophecy is already proved doubtful by the fact that so few Americans feel like repeating it today.

Thus there appears to be a real vacuum in the national will, or at least the widespread fear that such a vacuum exists. Does the U.S. lack a national purpose? Does it need a national purpose in the world? If so, what should that purpose be?

The present article is a résumé of what earlier generations have felt about the American national purpose, together with a few remarks on the new historical conditions that may have affected these beliefs. How far are the older beliefs relevant to the problems that face our country now, in this strange era of Communism, megaton weaponry, fractured empires, mushrooming sovereignties and continuing moral, social, and technical revolution? The answers hinted at in this introduction are not offered as definitive. Fuller answers will be presented subsequently by leaders of opinion.

The motivating beliefs of a nation are to be sought in its deeds and illuminated by the words of its leaders, its spokesmen, and its key documents. Deeds and words do not always match, but in America they have matched often enough to show a pattern to those who look for one. Thus when Roger Williams expounded the *principles* of religious liberty and democracy, his authority did not run beyond colonial Rhode Island; but the practical *experience* of mutual accommodation among the sects in other colonies eventually established religious liberty as part of the American political creed. Thus, too, township self-government and the common law, which helped to make the Constitution workable, were the slow deposit of English and colonial experience rather than the decree of towering prophets or statesmen. But on occasion sudden flashes of great documentary lightning have also illuminated our beliefs. The greatest of these was, of course, the Declaration of Independence on July 4, 1776.

The Declaration turned what had just a few months before been an Anglo-American family quarrel into a defiance of all tyranny everywhere. Colonial loyalty to the English crown, the dominant American sentiment of 1775, was transformed into national loyalty to the cause of political freedom for the human race.

Thomas Jefferson achieved his masterpiece not by taking an opinion poll, nor yet by sucking the words from his thumb. In writing the Declaration he borrowed some current political ideas from England, from Virginia, from Massachusetts, from Tom Paine, and from other sources. He carefully listed the colonists' particular grievances against George III. But above all he related the cause of American independence to certain timeless beliefs about the nature of man, society, and government.

Men are created with equal and inalienable rights—all men everywhere. The chief purpose of any government is to secure these rights, and its just power comes only from the consent of the governed. Although this news took decades to spread and has yet to penetrate everywhere, all other theories of government were doomed by this Declaration and the American independence that followed it. Tom Paine did not exaggerate: "Despotism felt a shock, and man began to contemplate redress." The Declaration went round the Western world, adding an important stimulus to the revolution in France, the independence of Latin America, the national movements in Germany, Italy, Greece, and eastern Europe, and eventually to be reflected in the political reformation of England itself.

Small wonder, then, that in America the Declaration became the focus of that sense of special destiny and vocation which most vocal Americans had long associated with their country. Just as the Puritans had felt akin to the Israelites, chosen by God for a "holy experiment" in rule by conscience on new soil, so George Washington's generation felt themselves to be the vanguard of a new political dispensation. They were a watershed in human history, agents of what John Adams had called "a grand scheme and design in Providence for the illumination and emancipation of the slavish part of mankind all over the earth."

Added Adams: "The institutions now made in America will not wholly wear out for thousands of years. It is therefore of the last importance that they should be right." In this self-conscious spirit was our Constitution written. It was to be *the* test of the basic question whether men, as Alexander Hamilton put it, can achieve good government by "reflection and choice," or whether they must always be governed by "accident and force."

The Constitution was not a universal document in the same sense as the Declaration. It was a working document for Americans, not for Laplanders or Chinese. It has nevertheless proved an adequate political franchise for Americans while they subdued a continent, added 37 new states, fought seven wars and changed from an agricultural federal republic into an industrialized democratic nation. We have seen fit to amend the Constitution 22 times but not to change a word of the preamble, which is a summary statement of what the founders thought to be the true purposes of government—any government. Here are those purposes: "To form a more perfect Union, establish justice, insure domestic tranquillity, provide for the common defense, promote the general welfare, and secure the blessings of liberty."

These purposes, and the principle of strong but limited government under law which imbues it, have made the Constitution a focus of American patriotic reverence second only to the Declaration. It is a much stronger focus of loyalty, for example, than the American land, for all this land's purple majesty and beloved rocks and rills. An English visitor in 1837 remarked on the transient place-sense of this migratory people: "Give the American his institutions, and he cares little where you place him." Said Hawthorne, "We have so much country that we have really no country at all." The land has been an inestimable stimulus to effort and to wealth, but the system that enabled every man to take up his pursuit of wealth and happiness has been the most valued part of the whole. The American system has always been held to be far wider than American geography. As Walt Whitman said, repeating the idea in poem after poem, "O America, because you build for mankind I build for you."

By Whitman's time the U.S., like its great poet, was taking pride in the title of "democracy," a word the Founding Fathers had not much liked. Our 19th Century legislation—from free schools and no-jail-for-debt to the Homestead Act, not to mention the emancipation of slaves—maintained an egalitarian bent. Its purpose and effect were to widen the suffrage and enlarge the opportunities of the average man. John Locke had made the amount of its emigration a test of whether a country is truly governed by consent or not. Waves of immigration, visibly assimilated, were evidence that America was the most consent-governed country in the world. As one not untypical immigrant wrote home: "Here a highway to honor, wealth and renown is open to all." Our national mission was to exemplify the success of free self-government, to let our democratic light so shine before men that they could see its good works and become democrats too. Many did, including most of Europe.

The first internationally recognized American historian, George Bancroft, saw American democracy as the highest revelation of God's purpose in history and the consummation of all previous civilizations. "In the fulness of time," he wrote, "a republic arose in the wilderness of America. Thousands of years had passed away before this child of the ages could be born . . . from her the human race drew hope." This viewpoint, which today sounds primitive or jingoistic, was as self-evident to many nine-teenth-century Americans as the rights of man were to those of the 18th. Both were vindicated by continuing success. Indeed, the American experiment was succeeding in so many directions that the sense of national purpose, though no less intense, became somewhat diffuse. Patriotism became identified with practically every virtue except patience. Thus Emerson: "I wish to see America a benefactor such as no country ever was . . . the office of America is to liberate, to abolish kingcraft, priestcraft, castle, monopoly, to pull down the gallows, to burn up the bloody statute-book, to take in the immigrant, to open the doors of the sea and the fields of the earth." In the swelling tide of immigration and expansion he also foresaw the advent of "a new race, a new religion, a new state, a new literature."

By the end of the nineteenth-century there were at least four great causes which America could be said to exemplify and which many Americans were eager to urge on the human race. These were:

1) *Democracy*. Bancroft called it "practical Christianity" and said: "The duty of America is to secure the culture and the happiness of the masses by their reliance on themselves." The people's voice was the voice of God, and of progress and of civilization as well.

2) *Individual liberty*. The wisdom of the Founding Fathers in making the free individual the cornerstone of our institutions was proved by his accomplishments. The individual was especially credited with our economic feats and therefore not begrudged his unequal rewards through the free enterprise system. He was the agent of that conquest of poverty which America had anticipated since colonial times.

3) *"Pluralism."* This became the scholar's word for our harmonious diversity of races, creeds, and conditions. Scientist-Author E. E. Slosson was to define America as "the finest of all the fine arts, the art of getting along peaceably with all sorts and conditions of men." Our pluralistic laboratory proved the beneficence of the federal system, crowning our good with brotherhood from sea to shining sea. Since federalism had shown that it could govern and harmonize a continent, why not a world?

4) *Morality*. The universe is moral and "civilization depends on morality," said Emerson. Our system was assumed to be in closer touch than others with what Seward called "a higher law than the Constitu-tion." The old Stephen Decatur formula, "our country, right or wrong," was offensive to intellectual patriots like Senator Carl Schurz, who amended it thus: "Our country . . . when right, to be kept right; when wrong, to be put right." Kept or set right by reliable methods, the vocal conscience of responsible citizens manifested itself through free institu-tions.

These four diverse national purposes could get somewhat out of alignment. Such was the case when Theodore Roosevelt came on the scene. Creative individualism had made it seem that America's dominant purpose—as it seems to many today—was merely to get rich. T.R., a great teacher as well as politican, used the White House as a pulpit to stir the national conscience to higher aims than the amassing of wealth. He preached the responsibility of the individual citizen, the social necessity of personal character, the central role of righteousness in democracy. He attacked that optimistic fatalism which assumed the country could always, in a contemporary's words, "slide down hill into the valley of fulfillment" and warned that the rights of men had to be freshly earned every day. He reasserted America's championship of popular rights. He told us that "the history of America is now the central feature of the history of the world." He sought to put U.S. foreign policy in the central position in that history, a position it was soon to occupy in fact.

American foreign policy before Teddy Roosevelt was sometimes summarized as "the Monroe Doctrine and the Golden Rule." Both were thoroughly consistent with American beliefs. If the Monroe Doctrine seems too defensive today, it was for a century defiant of half the globe. It aimed to keep European autocracy out of Latin America as well as to allow the spread of democracy through our own territorial expansion. It was not just the "manifest destiny" of continental geography, but also democratic idealism that carried our flag to California, Hawaii, and the Philippines. It was George Bancroft himself who, as acting Secretary of War, gave the order that sent U.S. troops into Texas in 1846—just as young T.R., as Assistant Secretary of the Navy, sent Commodore Dewey into Manila Bay in 1898.

Preoccupation with our own hemisphere did not always blind us to the cause of freedom and democracy elsewhere. National revolutionaries like Kossuth in Hungary, freely admitting American inspiration, could also count on at least unofficial American support. Commodore Perry in opening Japan, John Hay in proclaiming the Open Door against colonialism in China, Captain Mahan in his lectures at the Naval War College—all were prophets of the fact that American interests were becoming as global as the American cause.

In 1909 the Monroe Doctrine was reanalyzed by Herbert Croly, author of *The Promise of American Life,* which greatly influenced T.R.'s thinking. Now that Europe was democratized, Croly argued, Europe's interests and America's could no longer be considered "essentially incompatible," as some interpreters of the Doctrine had maintained. A time was coming when we would have to assume a wider and more active role. George Washington, in his Farewell Address, had enjoined us to avoid foreign entanglements and "give to mankind the magnanimous and too novel example of a people always guided by an exalted justice and benevolence." These words, said Croly, had been more honored in the letter than in the spirit. The time was coming when we should *seek* allies in order to build democracy into "a world system." In such a system, peace would inevitably depend on "the righteous use of superior force," and America's force would be needed on that righteous side.

Croly's contemporary patriots, however, were happier setting a no-longer-so-novel example than leading a magnanimous crusade. They responded more to the idea of a happy American destiny than to a clear American purpose. To Woodrow Wilson fell the sad task of proving the unreality of this distinction and of testing the American devotion to righteousness in a great European war. His war message of April 2, 1917, linked our destiny with that of democracy all over the world:

"The world must be made safe for democracy. Its peace must be planted upon the tested foundations of political liberty. . . , civilization itself seeming to be in the balance. But the right is more precious than peace, and we shall fight for the things which we have always carried nearest our hearts—for democracy, for the right of those who submit to authority to have a voice in their own governments, for the rights and liberties of small nations, for a universal dominion of right by such a concert of free peoples as shall bring peace and safety to all nations and make the world itself at last free. . . . America is privileged to spend her blood and her might for the princples that gave her birth. . . ."

The "concert of free peoples" eventually became the Wilson-inspired League of Nations. The League failed for various reasons, but one of them was surely the failure of follow-through in America's political will. Another and even greater war, another and even more "pluralistic" league called the United Nations, and the Wilson-era failure has at least been patched up. Said Franklin Roosevelt in 1945: "We have learned that we cannot live alone, at peace; that our own well-being is dependent upon the well-being of other nations far away."

The Preamble and the stated Purposes of the U.N. contain many statements in which Americans can take pride, since they could never have been written had not America long preached and exemplified them—most notably the declaration of "equal rights of men and women and of nations large and small." Yet this declaration is made hypocritical by the nature of the U.N.'s membership, which includes Communist states and thus severs the cause of peace from its anchor in freedom and principle. The word "righteousness," which to Wilson as to T.R. was synonymous with the higher patriotism, was not popularized by F.D.R., is not used in the U.N. charter, and is seldom heard in its debates.

Wilson's war message was in many ways the last great documentary link between modern America and "the principles that gave her birth." Its echoes of the Declaration of Independence are not mere rhetoric. Those echoes had been enriched for Wilson's generation by the memory of our most profound national experience, the Civil War, and our greatest spokesman of national purpose, Abraham Lincoln.

Lincoln's first show of "stubborn grandeur," said Carl Sandburg, was in the passionate seriousness with which he took the words of the Declaration. To him it was a charter of political truth for "augmenting the happiness and value of life to all people of all colors everywhere." Because slavery was incompatible with the Declaration, the Declaration was the real issue of the Civil War. But this issue had been so long evaded and compromised that Lincoln could exploit it only within the larger cause of saving the Union. Thus political and military necessities robbed the words of his Emancipation Proclamation of great documentary lightning, but the deed was as "fundamental and astounding" as anything he said. Forced into the Constitution by war, by conscience, and by the Declaration, the Proclamation was what Whitman called "by far the greatest revolutionary step in the history of the U.S."

Lincoln's greatness was more than verbal. It lay in the resolution with which he preserved the idea of union through our most tragic crisis. Such resolution could be sustained only by faith in "the proposition that all men are created equal." The national purpose that Lincoln stated for the union was that free government of the people, by the people, and for the people should not perish from the earth.

Since Lincoln's time government by the people has been broadened step by step and deepened here and abroad with a cumulative effect scarcely less revolutionary than the Emancipation Proclamation itself. The abstraction for which Lincoln fought is now operative in more than half the world. Scores of new nations have been born since World War I because of the conviction that men should govern themselves, and the 1960 crop will be at least a half dozen more in Africa alone. Yet the popularity of Lincoln's abstraction has not made democracy any safer. On the contrary, some of the nations for whose freedom we fought under Wilson and Franklin Roosevelt, notably in eastern Europe and the Far East, have long since succumbed to ancient tyranny in its newest and most insidious guise, Communism. In all countries the new tyranny, like the old, is still abetted by ignorance and poverty, and in the poorer ones by a widespread belief that freedom and morality are luxuries—"first the grub, then the morals." Meanwhile in America, suffused in real luxuries, freedom and morality are taken for granted as casually as bread.

This does not mean that the U.S. has altogether forsaken its traditional purposes in foreign affairs. They have guided our reactions to many new and puzzling challenges, such generally creditable reactions as the Marshall Plan, the North Atlantic treaty, the defense of Korea, the upholding of the U.N. in the Suez and other crises, the spending of billions for alliances and aid. At vast expense but with fair success, the U.S. has contained Communism since 1949. We have defended the chance of many nations to choose freedom and establish self-government, from Guatemala to Vietnam.

But at other times and places we have failed to defend this right. From

Hungary in 1956 the appeal to American principles for American help was so direct and unmistakable that many Americans, in our government's blank failure to respond, thought they heard the snapping of a great cord to the most precious part of our past. To others this sound was muffled by the very scope and complexity of the challenge, for tyranny is only one of the conditions of human life that wears a new, confusing, and very non-eighteenth-century mask.

The whole order of organized power has changed. The once worthy title of "nation" may now denote either a monster or a pygmy state. Both weaponry and economics have made nonsense of long-established boundaries between nations. Strange new alignments seem to be forming, one perhaps being an alignment of races. The scientific and technical revolution, which has already overthrown the social structure of some very old nations, may have overnight changes in store for many others, either from within their own laboratories or from some point in outer space. As for what Communism has done to international politics, in the words of a recent Rockefeller Brothers Fund report, "The chessboard itself may be said to have disappeared."

Nation states may no longer be the most meaningful integers of creative political thought. No existing state is or can be safe for democracy or freedom. Whatever may be hoped or feared from regional or racial alignments, any lasting political purpose must take the whole great globe for its arena. Nor is it just the Ghanaian, or the American, whose chance at happiness is threatened by technology. Human nature itself is threatened by dehumanization. A great political purpose today must have something to say about human nature, how to keep it as human and as rational as may be.

Such are the fantastic new conditions in which our old beliefs must find a home, a grave, or a toehold. How can we best adapt our beliefs to the conditions? What purposes may rightfully be considered today?

Survival. Sensible patriots have proposed that our true cause today is sheer national survival. They say that this is important enough, and doubtful enough, to engage our full attention. Biology tells us that survival is a primary concern. Yet if survival by military means is meant, modern weapons are two-edged. Our present strategy of nuclear deterrence, if ever tested, could so reduce our population that its survivors, the bearers of our beliefs about liberty and self-government, might prefer to live elsewhere. On the other hand, since America is now the world's chief home and hope of freedom, a refusal to defend it could demoralize the cause of freedom for a thousand years. From this dilemma the only escape is to perceive that survival is not an adequate goal.

What is, then? No single goal, perhaps. A great power's foreign policy cannot be reduced to a phrase. The Council on Foreign Relations, analyzing our "Basic Aims" for the Senate Foreign Relations Committee, made a multiple recommendation: that while maintaining our negative policy of resisting and containing Communism, we must at the same time do much more to anticipate "the world's other problems," and try to link the non-Communist nations more closely through more and better institutions of law and order, security, economic development, freedom, and peace. A large order!—but not necessarily an inspiring one. Although the U.S. has virtually unlimited responsibilities, can it respond to all alarms everywhere in the free world at once?

Self-government. The one principle that Americans have preached most consistently since their own founding is that men can govern themselves in freedom under law, and that all of them deserve a chance to try. Perhaps this simple message is too 18th Century for the world's needs today, or America's complex relation to it. But the millions who have not yet had their chance seldom say so. Self-government is clearly a central purpose for many peoples of the world.

Moral Law. Democracy, though we have treasured it, is not the highest value known to man. Indeed, it is only because enough Americans have had still higher allegiances that we have made democracy work.

America's public love affair with righteousness, for example, was not confined to the speeches of T.R. It began with the Mayflower Compact, whose ultimate purpose was the quest of God's truth. The same quest underlay our insistence on religious freedom, and the assumption of a moral order in the universe underlies much of our constitutional law. Said John Marshall, the great interpreter of the Constitution: "There are principles of abstract justice which the Creator of all things has impressed on the mind of his creature man, and which are admitted to regulate in great degree the right of civilized nations." Our very right to self-government is derived from "the Laws of Nature and of Nature's God," and to its harmony with these laws democracy owes its moral sanction.

If this moral order of the universe exists in fact—if there is such a thing as the Natural Law in which our Founding Fathers trusted—then it is surely the highest of man's political purposes to contrive his human institutions in conformity with this order, while realizing that all human institutions are subject to constant change. No more challenging task faces American leaders and intellectuals, if they believe in natural law, than to find its mundane applications in this revolutionary age. Certainly there resides in every human breast a natural instinct for justice, which experience has refined into the world's systems of law. A world that needs peace, which is the work of justice, needs clearer codifications of its sense of justice—*i.e.*, more and better national and international law.

But those of us who make World Law our national purpose must be sure the positive laws that we champion enjoy maximum consent. For example, by throwing its economic weight around, the U.S. can do much to promote free enterprise and freer trade in the non-Communist world. But it could do this better with less friction if Americans should produce a new definition of the right to property, which John Locke and our

Founding Fathers considered basic to liberty. Such a definition would have to appear in harmony with natural justice to farmers and workers as well as to businessmen in all industrialized societies.

Private Purposes. Many Americans will approve the above-mentioned purposes and still deny that they should be avowed by the nation or its government. A consensus of private purposes can give shape and direction to our national life without getting into formal policy at all. Yet "in the fatness of these pursy times" our private purposes do not add up to anything so firm. As one Air Force lieutenant wrote to *Time,* "What America stands for is making money, and as the society approaches affluence, its members are left to stew in their own ennui."

As monarchies were said to live by honor, so republics live by virtue. Yet republics have no public means of supplying a lack of virtue in the sovereign people. The public educational system can set and inculcate standards of the mind, and with this aim the Rockefeller Brothers Fund proposed to raise these standards, calling its report on our schools *The Pursuit of Excellence.* Even the citizen who thinks that virtue is old-fashioned, or that it is none of the state's business, can perhaps subscribe to excellence as a public purpose, and in a context of intellectual excellence, moral excellence (which must always be an individual purpose and achievement) may have a better chance. As T.R. used to say, a patriot will make the most of himself. If enough do, so will the nation.

Is There an American Mission?

God has predestined, mankind expects, great things from our race; and great things we feel in our souls.

—Herman Melville
"White-Jacket"

Almost from the start, Americans were convinced that there was some special purpose to their coming to the New World; and they remained persuaded that it was not by chance that they were able to form here the kind of society they did. It was part of their psychology as migrants that they had to answer a question that did not trouble more stable men. Why had they been selected to undertake the difficult tasks of moving from one civilization to another? The search for an answer constantly stimulated them to inquire why their culture was different from that of Europe. And since much that existed around them was not simply the inherited product of centuries of history, but the work of their own hands, they had frequently to wonder why they had acted as they did.

Often Americans drew upon the idea of a distinctive mission to describe the purpose of their national experience. It was not simply blind accident that had permitted the New World to remain empty while awaiting their coming, but rather some larger providential scheme of things that reserved for them a unique opportunity to create a unique society. God had charged them with the task of founding a city upon a hill that would be a model for the emulation of men everywhere.

Selections from two colonial writers illustrate this theme. John Winthrop (1588–1649) was a leading spirit in the Puritan migration to New England and for many years Governor of the Massachusetts Bay Colony; aboard the ship that bore him to the New World he reflected on the necessity for acting with purpose in the hazardous enterprise on which he had embarked (1). Edward Johnson (1598-1672) was also an early migrant to Massachusetts and prominent in local affairs. His "Wonder-working Providence," written between 1650 and 1653, was an effort to show that a providential design had worked itself out in the early settlement of the colonies (2).

The most exciting elaborations of the conception of mission came during the Revolutionary generation. The radical step of separation from England and the creation of a Republican government seemed to contemporaries signs not only of the appearance of a new nation but also of a new kind of man. Michel Guillaume Jean de Crèvecoeur (1735–1813) was born in France and settled in Canada at an early age. After the close of the French and Indian War he moved to the English colonies and there wrote his "Letters from an American Farmer." A hopeful man writing in an optimistic era, he saw a vision of the potentialities of American life at the point when the new nation was just acquiring a fresh consciousness of its own identity (3).

The success of the Revolution evoked an outburst of patriotic statements that continued to emphasize the conception of mission, now in terms of the destiny of America to pioneer in establishing the forms of a free society. The poet and journalist, Philip M. Freneau (1752–1832) was a young man when the war began and was deeply moved by these sentiments. He had not yet entered upon his active career as a political journalist when, just before the end of the war, he set forth a broad vision of the mission of the new nation in the extract here presented (4). Thomas Jefferson (1743–1826), whose words in the Declaration of Independence had already expressed the ideas that animated his countrymen in their struggle against England, continued later to reflect upon the problem. In his first Inaugural Address in 1801, after a bitter party battle, he called upon his fellow citizens to take up the tasks of national development in a constructive and positive attitude (5).

In the early nineteenth century, the idea of mission continued to be probed from a variety of points of view. The historian George Bancroft (1800–91), who was also an active Jacksonian politician, pondered the matters in the introductory pages of his great "History of the United States"; he was convinced, as many of his predecessors had been, that the subjects of his story were charged with a mission of providential importance.

Significantly, one of the most moving evocations of that conception came just after the middle of the nineteenth century from Carl Schurz (1829–1906), a German immigrant. Schurz was already moved by the vision of America as the land of hope before he crossed the ocean. Speaking on the eve of the Civil

War, while the Know-Nothing party challenged the role of the foreign-born in the society, he attempted to put into words a conception of national destiny centering in the potentialities of freedom and opportunity. His oration on true Americanism earned widespread attention (7). Schurz's eloquence was expansive and diffuse, although it held his audience. But the most moving summation of the significance of the American experience came from Abraham Lincoln (1809–65) at the crisis of the Civil War. The phrases of his Gettysburg Address (8) have become part of the total American heritage.

Toward the end of the nineteenth century, when industrialization, urbanization, and imperialism transformed the society of the United States, it became more difficult to describe the national mission in similar terms. In our own century the acceleration in the rate of change made those difficulties correspondingly more complex. In the 1880's, it was still possible to write confidently as did Josiah Strong (1847–1916), the Congregational minister and social reformer, of the triumphal destiny of the country (9). But one could no longer be sure whether that optimism expressed a clear vision of generally accepted goals or whether it rested on familiar slogans no longer related to reality. At the end of the nineteenth century even as farsighted a thinker as Woodrow Wilson (1856–1924), in the conclusion of his "History of the American People," gave the idea a formulation that in retrospect seems only partial and distorted (10). In our day, a thoughtful student of the social sciences, David Riesman (1909–), has set forth some of the intricacies of the problem in challenging terms (11). It remains yet to be seen whether the idea of mission can still have significance in the 1960's.

1. JOHN WINTHROP, *A City on a Hill, 1630**

The work we have in hand, it is by a mutual consent through a special overruling Providence . . . to seek out a place of cohabitation and consortship under a due form of government both civil and ecclesiastical. In such cases as this the care of the public must oversway all private respects, by which not only conscience, but mere civil policy doth bind us; for it is a true rule that particular estates cannot exist in the ruin of the public. . . .

The end is to improve our lives to do more service to the Lord . . . that ourselves and posterity may be the better preserved from the common corruptions of this evil world to serve the Lord and work out our salvation under the power and purity of his holy ordinances. . . .

The means whereby this must be effected, they are twofold, a conformity with the work and end we aim at. These we see are extraordinary, therefore we must not content ourselves with usual ordinary means. Whatsoever we did or ought to have done when we lived in England, the same must we do and more also where we go. That which the most in their churches maintain as a truth in profession only we must bring into familiar and constant prac-

* John Winthrop, "A Model of Christian Charity" (written on the "Arabella," 1630), *Winthrop Papers* (Boston: Massachusetts Historical Society, 1931), II, 292–95.

tice. . . . We must love brotherly without dissimulation, we must love one another with a pure heart fervently, we must bear one another's burthens, we must not look only on our own things, but also on the things of our brethren. Neither must we think that the Lord will bear with such failings at our hands as he doth from those among whom we have lived. . . .

When God gives a special commission he looks to have it strictly observed in every article. . . . Thus stands the cause between God and us. We are entered into a covenant with him for this work. We have taken out a commission. The Lord hath given us leave to draw our own articles; we have professed to enterprise these actions upon these and these ends. We have hereupon besought him of favor and blessing. Now if the Lord shall please to hear us and bring us in peace to the place we desire, then hath he ratified this covenant and settled our commission [and] will expect a strict performance of the articles contained in it. But if we shall neglect the observation of these articles . . . , the Lord will surely break out in wrath against us, be revenged of such a perjured people, and make us know the

price of the breach of such a covenant.

Now the only way to avoid this shipwreck and to provide for our posterity is to follow the council of Micah, to do justly, to love mercy, to walk humbly with our God. . . . We must be knit together in this work as one man, we must entertain each other in brotherly affection, we must be willing to abridge ourselves of our superfluities, for the supply of others' necessities. . . . We must . . . labor and suffer together, always having before our eyes our commission and community in the work. . . . So shall we keep the unity of the spirit in the bond of peace, the Lord will be our God and delight to dwell among us as his own people and will command a blessing upon us in all our ways, that we shall see much more of his wisdom, power, goodness and truth than formerly we have been acquainted with. We shall find that the God of Israel is among us, when ten of us shall be able to resist a thousand of our enemies, when he shall make this a praise and a glory, that men shall say of succeeding plantations: the Lord make it like that of New England. For we must consider that we shall be as a city upon a hill, the eyes of all people are upon us.

2. EDWARD JOHNSON, *A Wonder-Working Providence, 1654*[*]

Those honored persons who were now in places of government, having the propagation of the churches of Christ in their eye, labored by all means to make room for inhabitants, knowing well that where the dead carcass is, thither will the eagles resort. But herein they were much opposed by certain persons, whose greedy desire

for land much hindered the work for a time. . . . And let such take notice how these were cured of this distemper; some were taken away by death, and then to be sure they had land enough; others fearing poverty and famishment, supposing the present scarcity would never be turned into plenty, removed themselves away, and so never

---

[*] Edward Johnson, *Wonder-Working Providence 1628–1651* (1654) (J. F. Jameson, ed.: New York, 1910) , pp. 58–61, 77–78, 85, 187, 198–202.

beheld the great good the Lord hath done for His people.

But the valiant of the Lord waited with patience, and in the miss of beer supplied themselves with water, even the most honored as well as others, contentedly rejoicing in a cup of cold water, blessing the Lord that had given them the taste of that living water.

The women once a day, as the tide gave way, resorted to the mussels and clam banks . . . where they daily gathered their families' food with much heavenly discourse of the provisions Christ had formerly made for many thousands of His followers in the wilderness. Quoth one, "My husband hath traveled as far as Plymouth" (which is near forty miles) "and hath with great toil brought a little corn home with him, and before that is spent the Lord will assuredly provide." Quoth the other, "Our last peck of meal is now in the oven at home a baking, and many of our godly neighbors have quite spent all, and we owe one loaf of that little we have." . . . And as they were encouraging one another in Christ's careful providing for them, they lift up their eyes and saw two ships coming in, and presently this news came to their ears, that they were come from Ireland full of victuals; now their poor hearts were not so much refreshed in regard of the food they saw they were like to have, as their souls rejoiced in that Christ would now manifest Himself to be the commissary general of this His army, and that He should honor them so far as to be poor sutlers for His camp. . . .

The winter's frost being extracted forth the earth, they fell to tearing up the roots and bushes with their hoes; even such men as scarce ever set hand to labor before, men of good birth and breeding, but coming through the strength of Christ to war their warfare, readily rush through all difficulties. Cutting down of the woods, they en-

close corn fields, the Lord having mitigated their labors by the Indians' frequent firing of the woods . . . which makes them thin of timber in many places, like our parks in England. The chiefest corn they planted before they had plows was Indian grain, whose increase is very much beyond all other, to the great refreshing of the poor servants of Christ in their low beginnings. . . .

[In 1638], although the estates of these pilgrim people were much wasted, yet seeing the benefit that would accrue to the churches of Christ and civil government, by the Lord's blessing, upon learning, they began to erect a college, the Lord by His provident hand giving His approbation to the work, in sending over a faithful and godly servant of His, the Reverend Mr. John Harvard, who, joining with the people of Christ at Charlestown, suddenly after departed this life, and gave near a thousand pound toward this work; wherefore the government thought it meet to call it Harvard College in remembrance of him. . . .

And verily, had not the Lord been pleased to furnish New England with means for the attainment of learning, the work would have been carried on very heavily, and the hearts of godly parents would have vanished away with heaviness for their poor children, whom they must have left in a desolate wilderness, destitute of the means of grace.

It being a work . . . past the reach of a poor pilgrim people, who had expended the greatest part of their estates on a long voyage, . . . knowing likewise, that young students could make but a poor progress in learning, by looking on the bare walls of their chambers, . . . amidst all these difficulties, it was thought meet learning should plead for itself, and . . . plod out a way to live. . . . Upon these resolutions, to work they go, and with thankful acknowledgment, readily take up all lawful means as they come to hand.

For place they fix their eye upon New-Town, which to tell their posterity whence they came, is now called Cambridge, and withal to make the whole world understand, that spiritual learning was the thing they chiefly desired . . . they chose this place, being then under the orthodox and soul-flourishing ministry of Mr. Thomas Shepheard. . . . The situation of this college is very pleasant, at the end of a spacious plain, more like a bowling green than a wilderness, near a fair navigable river, environed with many neighboring towns of note, being so near, that their houses join with her suburbs. . . . It hath the conveniences of a fair hall, comfortable studies and a good library, given by the liberal hand of some magistrates and ministers, with others. . . . The government hath endeavored to grant them all the privileges fit for a college, and accordingly the governor and magistrates, together with the president of the college . . . have a continual care of ordering all matters for the good of the whole. This college hath brought forth, and nursed up very hopeful plants, to the supplying some churches here. . . .

And now all you whose affections are taken with wonderful matters (attend) and you that think Christ hath forgotten his poor despised people (behold) and all you that hopefully long for Christ's appearing to confound antiChrist (consider). And rejoice all ye His churches the world throughout, for the Lamb is preparing His bride. And oh, ye the ancient beloved of Christ, whom He of old led by the hand from Egypt to Canaan, through that great and terrible wilderness, look here. Behold Him whom you have pierced, preparing to pierce your hearts with His Wonder-working Prov-

idence, and to provoke you by this little handful of His people to look on Him, and mourn. Yet let no man think these few weak worms would restrain the wonderful works of Christ, as only to themselves, but the quite contrary, these [are] but the porch of His glorious building in hand. . . .

The winter is past, the rain is changed and gone. Come out of the holes of the secret places; fear not because your number is but small. Gather into churches, and let Christ be your king. Ye presbytery, lord it not over them or any churches, but feed every one, that one flock over which Christ hath made you overseers. And ye people of Christ give your presbytery double honors, that they with you may keep the watch of the Lord over His churches. Ye Dutch, come out of your hodge-podge; the great mingle-mangle of religion among you hath caused the churches of Christ to increase so little with you, standing at a stay like corn among weeds. Oh, ye French! fear not the great swarms of locusts, nor the croaking frogs in your land; Christ is reaching out the hand to you; look what He hath done for these English. . . . Ye Germans that have had such a bloody bickering, Christ is now coming to your aid; then cast off your loose and careless kind of reformation, gather into churches and keep them pure, that Christ may delight to dwell among you. Oh Italy! the seat and center of the beast, Christ will now pick out a people from among you for Himself; see here what wonders He works in a little time. Oh! ye Spaniards and Portugalls, Christ will show you the abominations of that beastly whore who hath made your nations drunk with the wine of her fornication. Dread not that cruel murderous inquisition, for Christ is now making inquisition for them. . . .

Finally, oh all ye nations of the world, behold, great is the work of the glorious King of Heaven and Earth hath in hand; beware of neglecting the call of Christ. And you the seed of Israel both less and more, the rattling of your dead bones together is at hand. . . . If Christ hath done such great things for these low shrubs, what will His most admirable, excellent and wonderful work for you be, but as the resurrection from the dead, when all the miraculous acts of His wonderful power showed upon Pharaoh for your forefathers' deliverance shall be swallowed up with those far greater works that Christ shall show for your deliverance upon the whole world; by fires and blood destroying both Pope and Turk, when you shall see great smoke and flames ascending up on high, of that great whore. . . . Then oh! you people of Israel gather together as one man, and grow together as one tree. . . . For Christ the great King of all the earth is now going forth in His great wrath and terrible indignation to avenge the blood of His saints . . . ; and now for the great and bloody battle of Gog and Magog, rivers of blood, and up to the horse-bridles, even the blood of those [who] have drunk blood so long. Oh! dreadful day, when the patience and long-suffering of Christ that hath lasted so many hundreds of years, shall end. What wonderous works are now suddenly to be wrought for the accomplishment of these things!

Then judge all you . . . whether these poor New England people, be not the forerunners of Christ's army, and the marvelous providences which you shall now hear, be not the very finger of God, and whether the Lord hath not sent this people to preach in this wilderness, and to proclaim to all nations, the near approach of the most wonderful works that ever the sons of men saw.

Will you not believe that a nation can be born in a day? Here is a work come very near it. But if you will believe you shall see far greater things than these, and that in very little time.

3. CRÈVECOEUR, *Letters from an American Farmer, 1782**

I wish I could be acquainted with the feelings and thoughts which must agitate the heart and present themselves to the mind of an enlightened Englishman when he first lands on this continent. He must greatly rejoice that he lived at a time to see this fair country discovered and settled. He must necessarily feel a share of national pride when he views the chain of settlements which embellishes these extended shores. When he says to himself, this is the work of my countrymen who, when convulsed by factions, afflicted by a variety of miseries and wants, restless and impatient, took refuge here. They brought along with them their national genius, to which they principally owe what liberty they enjoy and what substance they possess. Here he sees the industry of his native country displayed in a new manner, and traces, in their works, the embryos of all the arts, sciences, and ingenuity which flourish in Europe. Here he beholds fair cities, substantial villages, extensive fields, an immense country filled with decent houses, good roads,

* M. G. St. Jean de Crèvecoeur, *Letters from an American Farmer* (London, 1782), pp. 45 ff.

orchards, meadows, and bridges, where a hundred years ago all was wild, woody, and uncultivated! What a train of pleasing ideas this fair spectacle must suggest! It is a prospect which must inspire a good citizen with the most heartfelt pleasure!

The difficulty consists in the manner of viewing so extensive a scene. He is arrived on a new continent; a modern society offers itself to his contemplation, different from what he had hitherto seen. It is not composed, as in Europe, of great lords who possess everything, and of a herd of people who have nothing. Here are no aristocratic families, no courts, no kings, no bishops, no ecclesiastical dominion, no invisible power giving to a few a very visible one, no great manufacturers employing thousands, no great refinements of luxury. The rich and the poor are not so far removed from each other as they are in Europe. Some few towns excepted, we are all tillers of the earth, from Nova Scotia to West Florida. We are a people of cultivators, scattered over an immense territory, communicating with each other by means of good roads and navigable rivers, united by the silken bands of mild government, all respecting the laws, without dreading their power, because they are equitable. We are all animated with the spirit of an industry which is unfettered and unrestrained, because each person works for himself.

If he travels through our rural districts, the stranger views not the hostile castle and the haughty mansion contrasted with the clay-built hut and miserable cabin, where cattle and men help to keep each other warm, and dwell in meanness, smoke, and indigence. A pleasing uniformity of decent competence appears throughout our habitations. The meanest of our log houses is a dry and comfortable habitation. Lawyer or merchant are the fairest titles our towns afford; that of a farmer is the only appellation of the rural inhabitants of our country. It must take some time ere he can reconcile himself to our dictionary, which is but short in words of dignity and names of honor. There, on a Sunday, he sees a congregation of respectable farmers and their wives, all clad in neat homespun, well-mounted, or riding in their own humble wagons. There is not among them an esquire, saving the unlettered magistrate. There he sees a parson as simple as his flock, a farmer who does not riot on the labor of others. We have no princes, for whom we toil, starve, and bleed. We are the most perfect society now existing in the world. Here man is free as he ought to be.

The next wish of this traveler will be to know whence came all these people? They are a mixture of English, Scotch, Irish, French, Dutch, Germans, and Swedes. From this promiscuous breed, that race now called Americans have arisen. In this great American asylum the poor of Europe have by some means met together, and in consequence of various causes. To what purpose should they ask one another what countrymen they are? Alas, two-thirds of them had no country. Can a wretch, who wanders about, who works and starves, whose life is a continual scene of sore affliction or pinching penury; can that man call England or any other kingdom his country, a country that had no bread for him, whose fields produced him no harvest; who met with nothing but the frowns of the rich, the severity of the laws, with jails and punishments; who owned not a single foot of the extensive surface of this planet? No! Urged by a variety of motives, here they came. Everything has tended to regenerate them: new laws, a new mode of living, a new social system. Here they are become men. In Europe they were so many useless plants, wanting vegetative mold and refreshing showers. They withered; and were mowed down by want, hunger, and war. But now, by the power of transplantation, like all other plants, they have taken root and flourished! Formerly they were not numbered in any civil lists of their country, except in those of the poor; here they rank as citizens.

By what invisible power has this surprising metamorphosis been performed? By that of the laws and that of the people's industry. The laws, the indulgent laws, protect them as they arrive, stamping on them the symbol of adoption. They receive ample rewards for their labors; these accumulated rewards procure them lands; those lands confer on them the title of freemen; and to that title every benefit is affixed which men can possibly require. This is the great operation daily performed by our laws. Whence proceed these laws? From our government. Whence that government? It is derived from the original genius and the strong desire of the people ratified and confirmed by the crown.

What attachment can a poor European emigrant have for a country where he had nothing? The knowledge of the language, the love of a few kindred as poor as himself, were the only cords that tied him. His country is now that which gives him land, bread, protection, and consequence. "Ubi panis ibi patria" is the motto of all emigrants. He is either a European, or the descendant of a European; hence that strange mixture of blood which you will find in no other country. I could point out to you a man whose grandfather was an Englishman, whose wife was Dutch, whose son married a French woman, and whose present four sons have now four wives of different nations. *He* is an American, who, leaving behind him all his ancient prejudices and manners, receives new ones from the new mode of life he has embraced, the new government he obeys, and the new rank he holds. He becomes an American by being received in the broad lap of our great alma mater. Here individuals of all nations are melted into a new race of men, whose labors and posterity will one day cause great changes in the world. Americans are the western pilgrims who are carrying along with them that great mass of arts, sciences, vigor, and industry which began long since in the east. They will finish the great circle.

The Americans were once scattered all over Europe. Here they are incorporated into one of the finest systems of population which has ever appeared, and which will hereafter become distinct by the power of the different climates they inhabit. The American is a new man, who acts upon new principles; he must therefore entertain new ideas and form new opinions. From involuntary idleness, servile dependence, penury, and useless labor, he has passed to toils of a very different nature, rewarded by ample subsistence —This is an American.

British America is divided into many provinces, forming a large association, scattered along a coast of 1500 miles extent and about 200 wide. This society I would fain examine, at least such as it appears in the middle provinces; if it does not afford that variety of tinges and gradations which may be observed in Europe, we have colors peculiar to ourselves. For instance, it is natural to conceive that those who live near the sea must be very different from those who live in the woods; the intermediate space will afford a separate and distinct class.

Those who live near the sea feed more on fish than on flesh. They often encounter the sea, that boisterous element. This renders them more bold and enterprising; this leads them to neglect the confined occupations of the land. They see and converse with a variety of people. Their intercourse with mankind becomes extensive. The sea inspires them with a love of traffic, a desire of transporting produce from one place to another; and leads them to a variety of resources which supply the place of labor.

Those who inhabit the middle settlements, by far the most numerous, must be very different. The simple cultivation of the earth purifies them; but the indulgences of the government, the soft remonstrances of religion, the rank of independent freeholders, must necessarily inspire them with sentiments very little known in Europe among a people of the same class. What do I say? Europe has no such class of men. The early knowledge they acquire, the early bargains they make, give them a great degree of sagacity. As freemen they will be litigious. Pride and obstinacy are often the cause of law-suits; the nature of our laws and governments may be another. As citizens, it is easy to imagine that they will carefully read the newspapers, enter into every political disquisition, freely blame or censure governors and others. As farmers, they will be careful and anxious to get as much as they can, because what they get is their own. As northern men, they will love the cheerful cup. As Christians, religion curbs them not in their opinions; the general indulgence leaves every one to think for himself in spiritual matters. The law inspects our actions; our thoughts are left to God. Industry, good living, selfishness, litigiousness, country politics, the pride of freemen, religious indifference, are their characteristics. If you recede still farther from the sea, you will come into more modern settlements; they exhibit the same strong lineaments in a ruder appearance. Religion seems to have still less influence, and manners are still less improved.

Now we arrive near the great woods, near the last inhabited districts. There men seem to be placed still farther beyond the reach of government, which, in some measure, leaves them to themselves. How can it pervade every corner, as they were driven there by misfortunes, necessity of beginnings, desire of acquiring large tracts of land, idleness, frequent want of economy, ancient debts. The reunion of such people does not afford a very pleasing spectacle. When discord, want of unity and friendship, and either drunkenness or idleness prevail in such remote districts, contention, inactivity, and wretchedness must ensue. There are not the same remedies to these evils as in a long-established community. The few magistrates they have are, in general, little better than the rest. They are often in a perfect state of war: that of man against man, sometimes decided by blows, sometimes by means of the law; that of man against every wild inhabitant of these venerable woods, of which they are come to dispossess them. There men appear to be no better than carnivorous animals, of a superior rank, living on the flesh of wild animals when they can catch them, and when they are not able, subsisting on grain.

He who would wish to see America in its proper light, and have a true idea of its feeble beginnings and barbarous rudiments, must visit our extended line of frontiers, where the last settlers dwell, and where he may see the first labors of settlement, the mode of clearing the earth, in all their different appearances. There, remote from the power of example and check of shame, many families exhibit the most hideous parts of our society. They are a kind of forlorn hope, preceding, by ten or twelve years, the most respectable army of veterans which come after them. In that space, prosperity will polish some, vice and law will drive off the rest, who, uniting again with others like themselves, will recede still farther, making room for more industrious people, who will finish their improvements, convert the log house into a convenient habitation, and, rejoicing that the first heavy labors are finished, will change, in a few years, that hitherto-barbarous country into a fine, fertile, well-regulated, district. Such is our progress, such is the march of the Europeans toward the interior parts of this continent.

It is with men as it is with the plants and animals that grow and live in the forests. They are entirely different from those that live in the plains. By living in or near the woods, their actions are regulated by the wildness of the neighborhood. The deer often come to eat their grain, the wolves to destroy their sheep, the bears to kill their hogs, the foxes to catch their poultry. This surrounding hostility immediately puts the gun into their hands. They watch these animals; they kill some; and thus, by defending their property, they soon become professed hunters. This is the progress. Once hunters, farewell to the plough. The chase renders them ferocious, gloomy, and unsocial. A hunter wants no neighbors; he rather hates them, because he dreads the competition. In a little time their success in the woods makes them neglect their tillage. They trust to the natural fecundity of the earth, and therefore do little. Carelessness in fencing often exposes what little they sow to destruction. They are not at home to watch. In order, therefore, to make up the deficiency, they go oftener to the woods.

That new mode of life brings along with it a new set of manners, which I cannot easily describe. These new manners, being grafted on the old stock, produce a strange sort of lawless profligacy, the impressions of which are indelible. The manners of the Indian natives are respectable compared with this European medley. Wives and children live in sloth and inactivity, and, having no proper pursuits, you may judge what education the latter receive. Their tender minds have nothing else to contemplate but the example of their parents; like them they grow up a mongrel breed, half-civilized, half-savage, except nature stamps on them some constitutional propensities.

To all these reasons you must add their lonely situation, and you cannot imagine what an effect on manners the great distances they live from each other has! Consider one of the last settlements in its first view. Of what is it composed? Europeans, who have not that sufficient share of knowledge they ought to have in order to prosper; people who have suddenly passed from oppression, dread of government, and fear of laws, into the unlimited freedom of the woods. This sudden change must have a very great effect on most men, and on that class particularly. Eating of wild meat, whatever you may think, tends to alter their temper, though all the proof I can adduce is that I have seen it; and, having no place of worship to resort to, what little society this might afford is denied them. Is it then surprising to see men, thus situated, immersed in great and heavy labors, degenerate a little? It is rather a wonder the effect is not more diffusive.

The Moravians and the Quakers are the only instances in exception to what I have advanced. The first never settle singly; it is a colony of the society which emigrates. They carry with them their forms, worship, rules, and decency. The others never begin so hard; they are always able to buy improvements, in which there is a great advantage, for by that time the country is recovered from its first barbarity. Thus, our bad people are those who are half cultivators and half hunters; and the worst of them are those who have degenerated altogether into the hunting state. As old plough-men and new men of the woods, as Europeans and new-made Indians, they contract the vices of both. They adopt the moroseness and feroc-ity of a native, without his mild-ness or even his industry at home. Hunting is but a licentious idle life, and, if it does not always pervert good disposition, yet, when it is united with bad luck, it leads to want. Want stimu-lates that propensity to rapacity and injustice, too natural to needy men, which is the fatal gradation. After this explanation of the effects which follow by living in the woods, shall we yet vainly flatter ourselves with the hope of converting the Indians? We should rather begin with converting our back settlers.

Europe contains hardly any other distinctions but lords and tenants; this fair country alone is settled by free-holders, the possessors of the soil they cultivate, members of the government they obey, and the framers of their own laws, by means of their representa-tives. Our distance from Europe, far from diminishing, rather adds to our usefulness and consequence as men and subjects. Had our forefathers re-mained there, they would only have crowded it, and perhaps prolonged those convulsions which had shaken it for so long. Every industrious Euro-pean, who transports himself here, may be compared to a sprout growing at the foot of a great tree; it enjoys and draws but a little portion of sap; wrench it from the parent roots, trans-plant it, and it will become a tree bearing fruit also. It is here, then, that the idle may be employed, the useless become useful, and the poor become rich. But by riches I do not mean gold and silver; we have but little of those metals. I mean a better sort of wealth: cleared lands, cattle, good houses, good clothes, and an increase of people to enjoy them.

There is no wonder that this country has so many charms, and presents to Europeans so many temptations to remain in it. A traveler in Europe becomes a stranger as soon as he quits his own kingdom; but it is otherwise here. We know, properly speaking, no strangers. This is every person's coun-try; the variety of our soils, situations, climates, governments, and produce, has something which must please every-body. No sooner does a European arrive, no matter of what condition, than his eyes are opened upon the fair prospect. When in England, he was a mere Englishman; here he stands on a larger portion of the globe. He does not find, as in Europe, a crowded soci-ety, where every place is overstocked; he does not feel that perpetual colli-sion of parties, that difficulty of begin-ning, that contention which oversets so many. There is room for everybody in America. Has he any particular talent or industry, he exerts it in order to procure a livelihood, and it succeeds. I do not mean that everyone who comes will grow rich in a little time; no, but he may procure an easy, decent maintenance by his industry. Instead of starving he will be fed, instead of being idle he will have employment; and these are riches enough for such men as come over here. The rich stay in Europe; it is only the middling and poor that emigrate. It is no wonder that the European, who has lived here a few years, is desirous to remain; Europe, with all its pomp, is not to be compared with this continent for men of middle stations or laborers.

A European, when he first arrives, seems limited in his intentions as well as in his views; but he very suddenly alters his scale; two hundred miles formerly appeared a very great dis-tance, it is now but a trifle; he no sooner breathes our air than he forms schemes, and embarks in designs he never would have thought of in his own country. There the plenitude of society confines many useful ideas, and often extinguishes the most laudable schemes which here ripen into maturity. Thus Europeans become Americans.

But how is this accomplished in that crowd of low indigent people who flock here every year from all parts of Europe? I will tell you: they no sooner arrive than they immediately feel the good effects of that plenty of provisions we possess; they fare on our best food, and are kindly entertained; their talents, character, and peculiar industry are immediately inquired into; they find countrymen everywhere disseminated, let them come from whatever part of Europe. Let me select one as an epitome of the rest. He is hired, he goes to work, and works moderately; instead of being employed by a haughty person he finds himself with his equal, placed at the substantial table of the farmer, or else at an inferior one as good; his wages are high, his bed is not like that bed of sorrow on which he used to lie. If he behaves with propriety, and is faithful, he is caressed, and becomes as it were a member of the family. He begins to feel the effects of a sort of resurrection; hitherto he had not lived, but simply vegetated; he now feels himself a man, because he is treated as such. Judge what an alteration there must arise in the mind and the thoughts of this man; he begins to forget his former servitude and dependence. His heart involuntarily swells and glows; this first swell inspires him

with those new thoughts which constitute an American.

He looks around and sees many a prosperous person, who, but a few years before, was as poor as himself. This encourages him much; he begins to form some little scheme, the first, alas, he ever formed in his life. If he is wise, he thus spends two or three years, in which time he acquires knowledge, the use of tools, the modes of working the lands, felling trees, and so on. This prepares the foundation of a good name, the most useful acquisition he can make. He is encouraged, he has gained friends; he is advised and directed, he feels bold, he purchases some land; he gives all the money he has brought over, as well as what he has earned, and trusts to the God of harvests for the discharge of the rest. His good name procures him credit; he is now possessed of the deed, conveying to him and his posterity the fee simple and absolute property of two-hundred acres of land, situated on such a river. What an epoch in this man's life! He is become a freeholder, from perhaps a German boor; he is now an American, a Pennsylvanian, an English subject. He is naturalized, his name is enrolled with those of the other citizens of the province. Instead of being a vagrant, he has a place of residence; he is called the inhabitant of such a county, or of such a district, and for the first time in his life counts for something; for hitherto he had been a cipher.

4. PHILIP FRENEAU, *The Greatness of America, 1782**

It is not easy to conceive what will be the greatness and importance of

North America in a century or two . . . if the present fabric of Nature is up-

* Philip Freneau, "Philosopher of the Forest, X" in *Miscellaneous Works* (Philadelphia, 1788), pp. 364–67.

held, and the people retain those bold
and manly sentiments of freedom,
which actuate them at this day. Agriculture, the basis of a nation's greatness, will here, most probably, be
advanced to its summit of perfection;
and its attendant, commerce, will so
agreeably and usefully employ mankind, that wars will be forgotten;
nations, by a free intercourse with this
vast and fertile continent, . . . will
again become brothers . . . and no
longer treat each other as savages and
monsters. The iron generation will
verge to decay, and those days of felicity advance which have been so often
wished for by all good men, and which
are so beautifully described by the
prophetic sages of ancient times. . . .

It is a standing rule in philosophy,
that Nature does nothing in vain. A
potent nation, now at war with these
republics, has proclaimed her resolution to lay waste what she cannot reclaim by conquest, and schemes are
projected to oblige such to re-emigrate
to Europe as shall escape the fury of
the destroyers. But if this new world
was not to become at some time or
another the receptacle of numerous
civilized nations, from one extremity
to the other, for what visible purpose
could Nature have formed these vast
lakes in the bosom of her infant empire . . . ? These lakes having, severally,
a communication with each other, and
lastly with the Atlantic Ocean, towards
the northeast; approaching also very
near, by the west, to several of the
navigable branches of the Mississippi,
from an easy communication through
a long tract of country, the intercourse
between the various parts of which
would, in future times, at least for the
purposes of commerce, be extremely
difficult and laborious, were it not for
this continuation of waters, that for
ages have been waiting to receive the

barque of traffic, urged forward by the
sail or the stroke of the springy oar; as
the soil bordering thereon has no less
impatiently expected the operations of
the industrious plough.

During a very considerable part of
the year, the southwest wind blows
unremittedly on the face of this serpen-
tine river, the Ohio; and even at other
times, the current of air is more prevalent in that direction than in any
other, which being directly opposed to
the course of the stream, moving at the
rate of one mile hourly, is it not evident that Providence, Nature, or Fate,
has so ordered this matter, that the
commercial vessels hereafter sailing
northward thereon may have favorable
gales to make an answerable progress
against a current that is still contrary
and the same, and that those bound
to the south may have the assistance
of the ebbing stream to combat the
adverse winds with more advantage.—
It would carry me far beyond the
bounds of a short essay, to point out
every particular, indicating the future
importance of this newly discovered
country; and it is really astonishing,
as I intimated before, that a nation
endued with the divine gift of reason,
if they would exercise that gift, should
at this day entertain a serious thought
of reducing, by force of arms, this immense continent to their absolute sway;
a continent beholding two hemispheres,
abounding with a hardy and active race
of inhabitants, producing everything
within itself proper for its own maintenance and defense; a continent extending through such a number of
degrees of latitude and longitude, from
the limits of the torrid zone, the circle
of the northern tropic, to those frozen
streams and icy mountains, where,
chilled with the extreme rigors of
perpetual winter, Nature seems to have
lost her vegetative powers.

5. THOMAS JEFFERSON, *First Inaugural Address, 1801**

Called upon to undertake the duties of the first executive office of our country, I avail myself of the presence of that portion of my fellow citizens which is here assembled, to express my grateful thanks for the favor with which they have been pleased to look toward me, to declare a sincere consciousness that the task is above my talents, and that I approach it with those anxious and awful presentiments which the greatness of the charge and the weakness of my powers so justly inspire. A rising nation, spread over a wide and fruitful land, traversing all the seas with the rich productions of their industry, engaged in commerce with nations who feel power and forget right, advancing rapidly to destinies beyond the reach of mortal eye—when I contemplate these transcendent objects, and see the honor, the happiness, and the hopes of this beloved country committed to the issue and the auspices of this day, I shrink from the contemplation, and humble myself before the magnitude of the understaking. Utterly indeed, should I despair, did not the presence of many whom I here see remind me, that in the other high authorities provided by our constitution, I shall find resources of wisdom, of virtue, and of zeal, on which to rely under all difficulties. To you, then, gentlemen, who are charged with the sovereign functions of legislation, and to those associated with you, I look with encouragement for that guidance and support which may enable us to steer with safety the vessel in which we are all embarked amidst the conflicting elements of a troubled world.

During the contest of opinion through which we have passed, the animation of discussions and of exertions has sometimes worn an aspect which might impose on strangers unused to think freely and to speak and to write what they think; but this being now decided by the voice of the nation, announced according to the rules of the constitution, all will, of course, arrange themselves under the will of the law, and unite in common efforts for the common good. All, too, will bear in mind this sacred principle, that though the will of the majority is in all cases to prevail, that will, to be rightful, must be reasonable; that the minority possess their equal rights, which equal laws must protect, and to violate which would be oppression. Let us, then, fellow citizens, unite with one heart and one mind. Let us restore to social intercourse that harmony and affection without which liberty and even life itself are but dreary things. And let us reflect that having banished from our land that religious intolerance under which mankind so long bled and suffered, we have yet gained little if we countenance a political intolerance as despotic, as wicked, and capable of as bitter and bloody persecutions. During the throes and convulsions of the ancient world, during the agonizing spasms of infuriated man, seeking through blood and slaughter his long-lost liberty, it was not wonderful that the agitations of the billows should reach even this distant and peaceful shore; that this should be more felt and feared by some and less by others, and should divide opinions as to measures of safety. But every difference of opinion is not a dif-

* J. D. Richardson, ed., *Messages and Papers of the Presidents* (New York, 1896), I, 321–24.

ference of principle. We have called by different names brethren of the same principle. We are all republicans —we are all federalists. If there be any among us who would wish to dissolve this Union or to change its republican form, let them stand undisturbed as monuments of the safety with which error of opinion may be tolerated where reason is left free to combat it. I know, indeed, that some honest men fear that a republican government cannot be strong; that this government is not strong enough. But would the honest patriot, in the full tide of successful experiment, abandon a government which has so far kept us free and firm, on the theoretic and visionary fear that this government, the world's best hope, may by possibility want energy to preserve itself? I trust not. I believe this, on the contrary, the strongest government on earth. I believe it is the only one where every man, at the call of the law, would fly to the standard of the law, and would meet invasions of the public order as his own personal concern. Sometimes it is said that man cannot be trusted with the government of himself. Can he, then, be trusted with the government of others? Or have we found angels in the forms of kings to govern him? Let history answer this question.

Let us, then, with courage and confidence pursue our own federal and republican principles, our attachment to our union and representative government. Kindly separated by nature and a wide ocean from the exterminating havoc of one quarter of the globe; too high-minded to endure the degradations of the others; possessing a chosen country, with room enough for our descendants to the hundredth and thousandth generation; entertaining a due sense of our equal right to the use of our own faculties, to the acquisitions of our industry, to honor and confidence from our fellow citizens, result-

ing not from birth but from our actions and their sense of them; enlightened by a benign religion, professed, indeed, and practiced in various forms, yet all of them inculcating honesty, truth, temperance, gratitude, and the love of man; acknowledging and adoring an overruling Providence, which by all its dispensations proves that it delights in the happiness of man here and his greater happiness hereafter; with all these blessings, what more is necessary to make us a happy and a prosperous people? Still one thing more, fellow citizens—a wise and frugal government, which shall restrain men from injuring one another, shall leave them otherwise free to regulate their own pursuits of industry and improvement, and shall not take from the mouth of labor the bread it has earned. This is the sum of good government, and this is necessary to close the circle of our felicities.

About to enter, fellow citizens, on the exercise of duties which comprehend everything dear and valuable to you, it is proper that you should understand what I deem the essential principles of our government, and consequently those which ought to shape its administration. I will compress them within the narrowest compass they will bear, stating the general principle, but not all its limitations. Equal and exact justice to all men, of whatever state or persuasion, religious or political; peace, commerce, and honest friendship, with all nations—entangling alliances with none; the support of the state governments in all their rights, as the most competent administrations for our domestic concerns and the surest bulwarks against anti-republican tendencies; the preservation of the general government in its whole constitutional vigor, as the sheet anchor of our peace at home and safety abroad; a jealous care of the right of election by the people—a mild and safe corrective of abuses which are lopped by the sword of the revolution where peaceable remedies are unprovided; absolute acquiescence in the decisions of the majority—the vital principle of republics, from which there is no appeal but to force, the vital principle and immediate parent of despotism; a well-disciplined militia—our best reliance in peace and for the first moments of war, till regulars may relieve them; the supremacy of the civil over the military authority; economy in the public expense, that labor may be lightly burdened; the honest payment of our debts and sacred preservation of the public faith; encouragement of agriculture, and of commerce as its handmaid; the diffusion of information and the arraignment of all abuses at the bar of public reason; freedom of religion; freedom of the press, and freedom of person under the protection of the habeas corpus; and trial by juries impartially selected—these principles form the bright constellation which has gone before us, and guided our steps through an age of revolution and reformation. The wisdom of our sages and the blood of our heroes have been devoted to their attainment. They should be the creed of our political faith—the text of civil instruction—the touchstone by which to try the services of those we trust; and should we wander from them in moments of error or alarm, let us hasten to retrace our steps and to regain the road which alone leads to peace, liberty, and safety.

I repair, then, fellow citizens, to the post you have assigned me. With experience enough in subordinate offices to have seen the difficulties of this, the greatest of all, I have learned to expect that it will rarely fall to the lot of imperfect man to retire from this station with the reputation and the favor which bring him into it. Without pretensions to that high confidence reposed in our first and greatest revolutionary character, whose preeminent services had entitled him to the first place in his country's love, and destined for him the fairest page in the volume of faithful history, I ask so much confidence only as may give firmness and effect to the legal administration of your affairs. I shall often go wrong through defect of judgment. When right, I shall often be thought wrong by those whose positions will not command a view of the whole ground. I ask your indulgence for my own errors, which will never be intentional; and your support against the errors of others, who may condemn what they would not if seen in all its parts. The approbation implied by your suffrage is a consolation to me for the past; and my future solicitude will be to retain the good opinion of those who have bestowed it in advance, to conciliate that of others by doing them all the good in my power, and to be instrumental to the happiness and freedom of all.

Relying, then, on the patronage of your good will, I advance with obedience to the work, ready to retire from it whenever you become sensible how much better choice it is in your power to make. And may that Infinite Power which rules the destinies of the universe, lead our councils to what is best, and give them a favorable issue for your peace and prosperity.

6. GEORGE BANCROFT, *History of the United States, 1834**

The United States of America constitute an essential portion of a great political system, embracing all the civilized nations of the earth. At a period when the force of moral opinion is rapidly increasing, they have the precedence in the practice and the defence of the equal rights of man. The sovereignty of the people is here a conceded axiom, and the laws, established upon that basis, are cherished with faithful patriotism. While the nations of Europe aspire after change, our constitution engages the fond admiration of the people, by which it has been established. Prosperity follows the execution of even justice; invention is quickened by the freedom of competition; and labor rewarded with sure and unexampled returns. Domestic peace is maintained without the aid of a military establishment; public sentiment permits the existence of but few standing troops, and those only along the seaboard and on the frontiers. A gallant navy protects our commerce, which spreads its banners on every sea, and extends its enterprise to every clime. Our diplomatic relations connect us on terms of equality and honest friendship with the chief powers of the world; while we avoid entangling participation in their intrigues, their passions, and their wars. Our national resources are developed by an earnest culture of the arts of peace. Every man may enjoy the fruits of his industry; every mind is free to publish its convictions. Our government, by its organization, is necessarily identified with the interests of the people, and relies exclusively on their attachment for its durability and support. Even the enemies of the state, if there are any among us, have liberty to express their opinions undisturbed; and are safely tolerated, where reason is left free to combat their errors. Nor is the constitution a dead letter, unalterably fixed: it has the capacity for improvement; adopting whatever changes time and the public will may require, and safe from decay, so long as that will retains its energy. New states are forming in the wilderness; canals, intersecting our plains and crossing our highlands, open numerous channels to internal commerce; manufactures prosper along our watercourses; the use of steam on our rivers and railroads annihilates distance by the acceleration of speed. Our wealth and population, already giving us a place in the first rank of nations, are so rapidly cumulative, that the former is increased fourfold, and the latter is doubled, in every period of twenty-two or twenty-three years. There is no national debt; the community is opulent; the government economical; and the public treasury full. Religion, neither persecuted nor paid by the state, is sustained by the regard for public morals and the convictions of an enlightened faith. Intelligence is diffused with unparalleled universality; a free press teems with the choicest productions of all nations and ages. There are more daily journals in the United States than in the world beside. A public document of general interest is, within a month, reproduced in at least a million of copies, and is brought within the reach of every freeman in the country. An immense concourse of emigrants of the most various lineage is perpetually crowding to our shores; and the principles of liberty, uniting all interests by the operation

---

* George Bancroft, *History of the United States* (Boston, 1834), I, 1–3.

of equal laws, blend the discordant elements into harmonious union. Other governments are convulsed by the innovations and reforms of neighboring states; our constitution, fixed in the affections of the people, from whose choice it has sprung, neutralizes the influence of foreign principles, and fearlessly opens an asylum to the virtuous, the unfortunate, and the oppressed of every nation.

And yet it is but little more than two centuries since the oldest of our states received its first permanent colony. Before that time the whole territory was an unproductive waste. Throughout its wide extent the arts had not erected a monument. Its only inhabitants were a few scattered tribes of feeble barbarians, destitute of commerce and of political connection. The axe and the ploughshare were unknown. The soil, which had been gathering fertility from the repose of centuries, was lavishing its strength in magnificent but useless vegetation. In the view of civilization the immense domain was a solitude.

It is the object of the present work to explain how the change in the condition of our land has been brought about; and, as the fortunes of a nation are not under the control of blind destiny, to follow the steps by which a favoring Providence, calling our institutions into being, has conducted the country to its present happiness and glory.

7. CARL SCHURZ, *True Americanism, 1859**

It is one of the earliest recollections of my boyhood, that one summer night our whole village was stirred up by an uncommon occurrence. I say our village, for I was born not far from that beautiful spot where the Rhine rolls his green waters out of the wonderful gate of the Seven Mountains. . . . That night our neighbors were pressing around a few wagons covered with linen sheets and loaded with household utensils. . . . One of our neighboring families was moving far away across a great water, and it was said that they would never again return. And I saw silent tears trickling down weather-beaten cheeks, and the hands of rough peasants firmly pressing each other, and some of the men and women hardly able to speak when they nodded to one another a last farewell. At last the train started into motion, they gave three cheers for *America,* and then in the first gray dawn of the morning I saw them wending their way over the hill until they disappeared in the shadow of the forest. And I heard many a man say, how happy he would be if he could go with them to that great and free country, where a man could be himself.

That was the first time that I heard of America, and my childish imagination took possession of a land covered partly with majestic trees, partly with flowery prairies, immeasurable to the eye, and intersected with large rivers and broad lakes—a land where everybody could do what he thought best, and where nobody need be poor, because everybody was free.

And later, when I was old enough to read, and descriptions of this country and books on American history fell into my hands, the offspring of my imagination acquired the colors of

* A speech delivered in Boston, April 18, 1859. The full text may be found in Carl Schurz, *Speeches, Correspondence and Political Papers* (Frederic Bancroft, ed.; New York, 1913), I, 48–72.

reality, and I began to exercise my brain with the thought of what man might be and become when left perfectly free to himself. And still later, when ripening into manhood, I looked up from my school-books into the stir and bustle of the world, and the trumpet-tones of struggling humanity struck my ear and thrilled my heart, and I saw my nation shake her chains in order to burst them, and I heard a gigantic, universal shout for Liberty rising up to the skies; and at last, after having struggled manfully and drenched the earth of Fatherland with the blood of thousands of noble beings, I saw that nation crushed down again, not only by overwhelming armies, but by the dead weight of customs and institutions and notions and prejudices which past centuries had heaped upon them, and which a moment of enthusiasm, however sublime, could not destroy; then I consoled an almost despondent heart with the idea of a youthful people and of original institutions clearing the way for an untrammeled development of the ideal nature of man. Then I turned my eyes instinctively across the Atlantic Ocean, and America and Americanism, as I fancied them, appeared to me as the last depositories of the hopes of all true friends of humanity.

I say all this, not as though I indulged in the presumptuous delusion that my personal feelings and experience would be of any interest to you, but in order to show you what America is to the thousands of thinking men in the old world, who, disappointed in their fondest hopes and depressed by the saddest experience, cling with their last remnant of confidence in human nature, to the last spot on earth where man is free to follow the road to attainable perfection, and where, unbiased by the disastrous influence of traditional notions, customs, and institutions, he acts on his own responsibility.

They ask themselves: Was it but a wild delusion when we thought that man has the faculty to be free and to govern himself? Have we been fighting, were we ready to die, for a mere phantom, for a mere product of a morbid imagination? This question downtrodden humanity cries out into the world, and from this country it expects an answer.

As its advocate I speak to you. I will speak of Americanism as the great representative of the reformatory age, as the great champion of the dignity of human nature, as the great repository of the last hopes of suffering mankind. I will speak of the ideal mission of this country and of this people.

You may tell me that these views are visionary, that the destiny of this country is less exalted, that the American people are less great than I think they are or ought to be. I answer, ideals are like stars; you will not succeed in touching them with your hands. But like the sea-faring man on the desert of waters, you choose them as your guides, and following them you will reach your destiny. I invite you to ascend with me the watchtower of history, overlooking the grand panorama of the development of human affairs, in which the American Republic stands in so bold and prominent relief.

He who reviews the past of this country in connection with the history of the world besides, cannot fail to discover a wonderful coincidence of great events and fortunate circumstances, which were destined to produce everlasting results, unless recklessly thrown away by imbecile generations.

Look back with me four or five centuries. The dark period of the middle ages is drawing near its close. The accidental explosion of that mysterious black powder, discovered by an obscure German monk, is the first flash of lightning preluding that gigantic thunderstorm which is to shatter the edifice of feudal society to pieces. The invention of gunpowder strips the feudal lord of his prestige as a *warrior;* another discovery is to strip him of his prestige as a *man!* Gutenberg, another obscure German, invents the printing-press, and as gunpowder blows the castles of the small feudal tyrants into the air, so the formidable artillery of printed letters batters down the citadels of ignorance and superstition. Soul and body take up arms and prepare themselves for the great battle of the Reformation. Now the mighty volcano of the German mind bursts the crust of indolence which has covered it. Luther's triumphant thunder rattles against the holy see of Rome. The world is ablaze, all the elements of society are rising up in boiling commotion—two ages are battling against each other.

This is the time when the regeneration of the old world is to take place. But the old order of things, fortified in customs and prejudices and deeply-rooted institutions, does not surrender at the first blast of trumpets. The grand but fearful struggle of the reformatory movement plunges all Europe into endless confusion. The very wheel of progress seems to grind and crush one generation after another. The ideas which concerned the highest and most sacred relations of humanity seem at the same time to call into their service the basest and most violent passions of the human heart, and in all Europe the wars of great principles degenerate into wars of general devastation.

But, meanwhile, a new country has opened its boundless fields to those great ideas, for the realization of which the Old World seems no longer to be wide enough. It is as though the earth herself had taken part in the general revolution, and had thrown up from her sea-covered womb a new battleground for the spirit of the new era. That is America. Not only the inven-

tion of gunpowder and of the printing-press, but also the discovery of America, inaugurates the modern age.

There is the new and immense continent. The most restless and enterprising elements of European society direct their looks towards it. First, the greediness of the gold-hunting adventurer pounces upon the new conquest; but, his inordinate appetites being disappointed, he gradually abandons the field to men in whose hearts the future of the new world is sleeping, unborn.

While the coast of Virginia is settled by a motley immigration, led and ruled by men of ideas and enterprise, the sturdiest champions of principle descend upon the stony shores of New England. While the Southern colonies are settled under the auspices of lordly merchants and proprietaries, original democracy plants its stern banner upon Plymouth Rock. Mercantile speculation, aristocratic ambition, and stern virtue that seeks freedom and nothing but freedom, lead the most different classes of people, different in origin, habits and persuasion, upon the virgin soil, and entrust to them the task of realizing the great principles of the age. Nor is this privilege confined to one nationality alone. While the Anglo-Saxon takes possession of New England, Virginia, and Pennsylvania, the Frenchman plants his colonies on the soil of French Florida and the interior of the continent; the Hollander locates New Netherlands on the banks of the Hudson; the Swede, led there by the great mind of Oxenstiern, occupies the banks of the Delaware; the Spaniard maintains himself in peninsular Florida, and a numerous immigration of Germans, who follow the call of religious freedom, and of Irishmen, gradually flowing in, scatters itself all over this vast extent of country. Soon all the social and national elements of the civilized world are represented in the new land. Every people, every creed, every class of society has contributed its share to that wonderful mixture out of which is to grow the great nation of the new world. It is true, the Anglo-Saxon establishes and maintains his ascendancy, but without absolutely absorbing the other national elements. They modify each other, and their peculiar characteristics are to be blended together by the all-assimilating power of freedom. This is the origin of the American nationality, which did not spring from one family, one tribe, one country, but incorporates the vigorous elements of all civilized nations on earth.

This fact is not without great importance. It is an essential link in the chain of historical development. The student of history cannot fail to notice that when new periods of civilization break upon humanity, the people of the earth cannot maintain their national relations. New ideas are to be carried out by young nations. From time to time, violent, irresistible hurricanes sweep over the world, blowing the most different elements of the human family together, which by mingling reinvigorate each other, and the general confusion then becomes the starting-point of a new period of progress. Nations which have long subsisted exclusively on their own resources will gradually lose their original vigor, and die the death of decrepitude. But mankind becomes young again by its different elements being shaken together, by race crossing race and mind penetrating mind. . . .

Thus, I say, was founded the colony of free humanity on virgin soil. The youthful elements which constitute [the] people of the New World cannot submit to rules which are not of their own making; they must throw off the fetters which bind them to an old decrepit order of things. They resolve to enter the great family of nations as an independent member. And in the colony of free humanity, whose mother-country is the world, they establish *the Republic of equal rights, where the title of manhood is the title to citizenship*. My friends, if I had a thousand tongues, and a voice strong as the thunder of heaven, they would not be sufficient to impress upon your minds forcibly enough the greatness of this idea, the overshadowing glory of this result. This was the dream of the truest friends of man from the beginning; for this the noblest blood of martyrs has been shed; for this has mankind waded through seas of blood and tears. There it is now; there it stands, the noble fabric in all the splendor of reality. . . .

Sir, I wish the words of the Declaration of Independence "that all men are created free and equal, and are endowed with certain inalienable rights," were inscribed upon every gate-post within the limits of this Republic. From this principle the Revolutionary Fathers derived their claim to independence; upon this they founded the institutions of this country, and the whole structure was to be the living incarnation of this idea. This principle contains the programme of our political existence. It is the most progressive, and at the same time the most conservative one; the most progressive, for it takes even the lowliest members of the human family out of their degradation, and inspires them with the elevating consciousness of equal human dignity; the most conservative, for it makes a common cause of individual rights. From the equality of rights springs identity of our highest interests; you cannot subvert your neighbor's rights without striking a dangerous blow at your own. And when the rights of one cannot be infringed without finding a ready defense in all others who defend their own rights in defending his, then, and only then, are the rights of all safe against the usurpations of governmental authority.

This general identity of interests is the only thing that can guarantee the stability of democratic institutions. Equality of rights, embodied in general self-government, is the great moral element of true democracy; it is the only reliable safety-valve in the machinery of modern society. There is the solid foundation of our system of government; there is our mission; there is our greatness; there is our safety; there, and nowhere else! This is true Americanism, and to this I pay the tribute of my devotion.

Shall I point out to you the consequences of a deviation from this principle? Look at the slave States. There is a class of men who are deprived of their natural rights. But this is not the only deplorable feature of that peculiar organization of society. Equally deplorable is it, that there is another class of men who keep the former in subjection. That there are slaves is bad; but almost worse is it, that there are masters. Are not the masters freemen? No, sir! Where is their liberty of the press? Where is their liberty of speech? Where is the man among them who dares to advocate openly principles not in strict accordance with the ruling system? They speak of a republican form of government—they speak of democracy, but the despotic spirit of slavery and mastership combined pervades their whole political life like a liquid poison. They do not dare to be free, lest the spirit of liberty become contagious. The system of slavery has enslaved them all, master as well as slave. What is the cause of all this? It is that you cannot deny one class of society the full measure of their natural rights without imposing restraints upon your own liberty. If you want to be free, there is but one way: it is to guarantee an equally full measure of liberty to all your neighbors. There is no other. . . .

It is an old dodge of the advocates of despotism throughout the world, that the people who are not experienced in self-government are not fit for the exercise of self-government, and must first be educated under the rule of a superior authority. But at the same time the advocates of despotism will never offer them an opportunity to acquire experience in self-government, lest they suddenly become fit for its independent exercise. To this treacherous sophistry the fathers of this republic opposed the noble doctrine, that liberty is the best school for liberty, and that self-government cannot be learned but by practicing it. This, sir, is a truly American idea; this is true Americanism, and to this I pay the tribute of my devotion.

You object that some people do not understand their own interests? There is nothing that, in the course of time, will make a man better understand his interests than the independent management of his own affairs on his own responsibility. You object that people are ignorant? There is no better schoolmaster in the world than self-government, independently exercised. You object that people have no just idea of their duties as citizens? There is no other source from which they can derive a just notion of their duties, than the enjoyment of the rights from which they arise. You object that people are misled by their religious prejudices, and by the intrigues of the Roman hierarchy? Since when have the enlightened citizens of this Republic lost their faith in the final invincibility of truth? Since when have they forgotten that if the Roman or any other church plants the seed of superstition, liberty sows broadcast the seed of enlightenment? Do they no longer believe in the invincible spirit of inquiry, which characterizes the reformatory age? If the struggle be fair, can the victory be doubtful? As to religious fanaticism, it will prosper under oppression; it will feed on persecution; it will grow strong by proscription; but it is powerless against genuine democracy. It may indulge in short-lived freaks of passion, or in wily intrigues, but it will die of itself, for its lungs are not adapted to breathe the atmosphere of liberty. It is like the shark of the sea: drag him into the air, and the monster will perhaps struggle fearfully and frighten timid people with the powerful blows of his tail, and the terrible array of his teeth, but leave him quietly to die and he will die. But engage with him in a hand-to-hand struggle even then, and the last of his convulsions may fatally punish your rash attempt. Against fanaticism genuine democracy wields an irresistible weapon—it is *Toleration*. Toleration will not strike down the fanatic, but it will quietly and gently disarm him. But fight fanaticism *with* fanaticism, and you will restore it to its own congenial element. It is like Antæus, who gained strength when touching his native earth.

Whoever reads the history of this country calmly and thoroughly, cannot but discover that religious liberty is slowly but steadily rooting out the elements of superstition, and even of prejudice. It has dissolved the war of sects, of which persecution was characteristic, into a contest of abstract opinions, which creates convictions without oppressing men. By recognizing perfect freedom of inquiry, it will engender among men of different belief that mutual respect of true convictions which makes inquiry earnest and discussion fair. It will recognize as supremely inviolable, what Roger Williams, one of the most luminous stars of the American sky, called the sanctity of conscience. Read your history, and add the thousands and thousands of Romanists and their offspring together, who, from the first establishment of the colonies, gradually came to this country, and the sum will amount to many millions; compare that number with the number of Romanists who are now here, and you will find that millions are missing. Where are they? You did not kill them; you did not drive them away; they did not perish as the victims of persecution. But where are they? The peaceable working of the great principles which called this Republic into existence, has gradually and silently absorbed them. True Americanism, toleration, the equality of rights, has absorbed their prejudices, and will peaceably absorb everything that is not consistent with the victorious spirit of our institutions.

Oh, sir, there is a wonderful vitality in true democracy founded upon the equality of rights. There is an inexhaustible power of resistance in that system of government, which makes the protection of individual rights a matter of common interest. If preserved in its purity, there is no warfare of opinions which can endanger it—there is no conspiracy of despotic aspirations that can destroy it. But if not preserved in its purity! There are dangers which only blindness can not see, and which only stubborn party prejudice will not see. . . .

Liberty, sir, is like a spirited housewife; she will have her whims, she will be somewhat unruly sometimes, and, like so many husbands, you cannot always have it all your own way. She may spoil your favorite dish sometimes; but will you, therefore, at once smash her china, break her kettles and shut her out from the kitchen? Let her practice, let her try again and again, and even when she makes a mistake, encourage her with a benignant smile, and your broth will be right after a while. But meddle with her concerns, tease her, bore her, and your little squabbles, spirited as she is, will ultimately result in a divorce. What then? It is one of Jefferson's wisest words that "he would much rather be exposed to the inconveniences arising from too much liberty, than to those arising from too small a degree of it." It is a matter of historical experience, that nothing that is wrong in principle can be right in practice. People are apt to delude themselves on that point; but the ultimate result will always prove the truth of the maxim. A violation of equal rights can never serve to maintain institutions which are founded upon equal rights. A contrary policy is not only pusillanimous and small, but it is senseless. It reminds me of the soldier who, for fear of being shot in battle, committed suicide on the march; or of the man who would cut off his foot, because he had a corn on his toe. It is that ridiculous policy of premature despair, which commences to throw the freight overboard when there is a suspicious cloud in the sky.

Another danger for the safety of our institutions, and perhaps the most formidable one, arises from the general propensity of political parties and public men to act on a policy of mere expediency, and to sacrifice principle to local and temporary success. And here, sir, let me address a solemn appeal to the consciences of those with whom I am proud to struggle side by side against human thraldom.

You hate kingcraft, and you would sacrifice your fortunes and your lives in order to prevent its establishment on the soil of this Republic. But let me tell you that the rule of political parties which sacrifice principle to expediency, is no less dangerous, no less disastrous, no less aggressive, of no less despotic a nature, than the rule of monarchs. Do not indulge in the delusion, that in order to make a government fair and liberal, the only thing necessary is to make it elective. When a political party in power, however liberal their principles may be, have

once adopted the policy of knocking down their opponents instead of voting them down, there is an end of justice and equal rights. The history of the world shows no example of a more arbitrary despotism, than that exercised by the party which ruled the National Assembly of France in the bloodiest days of the great French Revolution. I will not discuss here what might have been done, and what not, in those times of a fearful crisis; but I will say that they tried to establish liberty by means of despotism, and that in her gigantic struggle against the united monarchs of Europe, revolutionary France won the victory, but lost her liberty.

Remember the shout of indignation that went all over the Northern States when we heard that the border ruffians of Kansas had crowded the free-State men away from the polls and had not allowed them to vote. That indignation was just, not only because the men thus terrorized were free-State men and friends of liberty, but because they were deprived of their right of suffrage, and because the government of that territory was placed on the basis of force, instead of equal rights. Sir, if ever the party of liberty should use their local predominance for the purpose of disarming their opponents instead of convincing them, they will but follow the example set by the ruffians of Kansas, although legislative enactments may be a genteeler weapon than the revolver and bowie knife. They may perhaps achieve some petty local success, they may gain some small temporary advantage, but they will help to introduce a system of action into our politics which will gradually undermine the very foundations upon which our republican edifice rests. Of all the dangers and difficulties that beset us, there is none more horrible than the hideous monster, whose name is "Proscription for opinion's sake." I am an anti-slavery man, and I have a right to my opinion in South Carolina just as well as in Massachusetts. My neighbor is a pro-slavery man; I may be sorry for it, but I solemnly acknowledge his right to his opinion in Massachusetts as well as in South Carolina. You tell me, that for my opinion they would mob me in South Carolina? Sir, there is the difference between South Carolina and Massachusetts. There is the difference between an anti-slavery man, who is a freeman, and a slaveholder, who is himself a slave.

Our present issues will pass away. The slavery question will be settled, liberty will be triumphant and other matters of difference will divide the political parties of this country. What if we, in our struggle against slavery, had removed the solid basis of equal rights, on which such new matters of difference may be peaceably settled? What if we had based the institutions of this country upon a difference of rights between different classes of people? What if, in destroying the generality of natural rights, we had resolved them into privileges? There is a thing which stands above the command of the most ingenious of politicians: *it is the logic of things and events*. It cannot be turned and twisted by artificial arrangements and delusive settlements; it will go its own way with the steady step of fate. It will force you . . . to choose between two social organizations, one of which is founded upon privilege, and the other upon the doctrine of equal rights. . . .

Sir, I was to speak on Republicanism at the West, and so I did. This *is* Western Republicanism. These are its principles, and I am proud to say its principles are its policy. These are the ideas which have rallied around the banner of liberty not only the natives of the soil, but an innumerable host of Germans, Scandinavians, Scotchmen,

Frenchmen, and a goodly number of Irishmen, also. And here I tell you, those are mistaken who believe that the Irish heart is devoid of those noble impulses which will lead him to the side of justice, where he sees his own rights respected and unendangered. Under this banner, all the languages of civilized mankind are spoken, every creed is protected, every right is sacred. There stands every element of Western society, with enthusiasm for a great cause, with confidence in each other, with honor to themselves. This is the banner floating over the glorious valley which stretches from the western slope of the Alleghenies to the Rocky Mountains—that Valley of Jehoshaphat where the nations of the world assemble to celebrate the resurrection of human freedom. The inscription on that banner is not "Opposition to the Democratic party for the sake of placing a new set of men into office"; for this battle-cry of speculators our hearts have no response. Nor is it "Restriction of slavery and restriction of the right of suffrage," for this—believe my words, I entreat you—this would be the signal of deserved, inevitable, and disgraceful defeat. But the inscription is "Liberty and equal rights, common to all as the air of Heaven—Liberty and equal rights, one and inseparable!"

With this banner we stand before the world. In this sign—in this sign alone, and no other—there is victory. And thus, sir, we mean to realize the great cosmopolitan idea, upon which the existence of the American nation rests. Thus we mean to fulfill the great mission of true Americanism—thus we mean to answer the anxious question of down-trodden humanity—"Has *man* the faculty to be free and to govern himself?" The answer is a triumphant "Aye," thundering into the ears of the despots of the Old World that "a man is a man for all that"; proclaiming to the oppressed that they are held in subjection on false pretences; cheering the hearts of the despondent friends of man with consolation and renewed confidence.

This is true Americanism, clasping mankind to its great heart. Under its banner we march; let the world follow.

8. ABRAHAN LINCOLN, *Gettysburg Address, 1863**

Fourscore and seven years ago our fathers brought forth on this continent a new nation, conceived in liberty, and dedicated to the proposition that all men are created equal.

Now we are engaged in a great civil war, testing whether that nation or any nation so conceived and so dedicated, can long endure. We are met on a great battlefield of that war. We have come to dedicate a portion of that field as a final resting-place for those who here gave their lives that that nation might live. It is altogether fitting and proper that we should do this.

But, in a larger sense, we cannot dedicate—we cannot consecrate—we cannot hallow—this ground. The brave men, living and dead, who struggled here, have consecrated it far above our poor power to add or detract. The world will little note nor long remember what we say here, but it can never forget what they did here. It is for us, the living, rather, to be dedicated here to the unfinished work which they who fought here have thus far so nobly advanced. It is rather for us to be here dedicated to the great task remaining before us—that from these honored dead we take increased devotion to that cause for which they gave the last full measure of devotion; that we here highly resolve that these dead shall not have died in vain that this nation, under God, shall have a new birth of freedom; and that government of the people, by the people, for the people, shall not perish from the earth.

* "Address at the Dedication of the Gettysburg Cemetery, November 19, 1863," in Abraham Lincoln, *Complete Works* (J. G. Nicolay and John Hay, eds.; New York, 1905), IX, 209–10.

9. JOSIAH STRONG, *Our Country, 1885**

Every race which has deeply impressed itself on the human family has been the representative of some great idea—one or more—which has given direction to the nation's life and form to its civilization. Among the Egyptians this seminal idea was life, among the Persians it was light, among the Hebrews it was purity, among the Greeks it was beauty, among the Romans it was law. The Anglo-Saxon is the representative of two great ideas, which are closely related. One of them is that of civil liberty. Nearly all of the civil liberty in the world is enjoyed by Anglo-Saxons: the English, the British colonists, and the people of the United States. To some, like the Swiss, it is permitted by the sufferance of their neighbors; others, like the French, have experimented with it; but, in modern times, the peoples whose love of liberty

* Josiah Strong, *Our Country* (New York, 1885), chap. 13.

has won it, and whose genius for self-government has preserved it, have been Anglo-Saxons. The noblest races have always been lovers of liberty. That love ran strong in early German blood, and has profoundly influenced the institutions of all the branches of the great German family; but it was left for the Anglo-Saxon branch fully to recognize the right of the individual to himself, and formally to declare it the foundation stone of government.

The other great idea of which the Anglo-Saxon is the exponent is that of a pure *spiritual* Christianity. It was no accident that the great reformation of the sixteenth century originated among a Teutonic, rather than a Latin people. It was the fire of liberty burning in the Saxon heart that flamed up against the absolutism of the Pope. Speaking roughly, the peoples of Europe which are Celtic are Catholic, and those which are Teutonic are Protestant; and where the Teutonic race was purest, there Protestantism spread with the greatest rapidity. . . .

It is not necessary to argue to those for whom I write that the two great needs of mankind, that all men may be lifted into the light of the highest Christian civilization, are, first, a pure, spiritual Christianity, and, second, civil liberty. Without controversy, these are the forces, which in the past, have contributed most to the elevation of the human race, and they must continue to be, in the future, the most efficient ministers to its progress. It follows, then, that the Anglo-Saxon, as the great representative of these two ideas, the depositary of these two greatest blessings, sustains peculiar relations to the world's future, is divinely commissioned to be, in a peculiar sense, his brother's keeper. Add to this the fact of his rapidly increasing strength in modern times, and we have well nigh a demonstration of his destiny. In 1700 this race numbered less than 6,000,000

souls. In 1800, Anglo-Saxons (I use the term somewhat broadly to include all English-speaking peoples) had increased to about 20,500,000, and in 1880 they numbered nearly 100,000,000, having multiplied almost five-fold in eighty years. At the end of the reign of Charles II the English colonists in America numbered 200,000. During these two hundred years, our population has increased two hundred and fifty-fold. And the expansion of this race has been no less remarkable than its multiplication. In one century the United States has increased its territory ten-fold, while the enormous acquisition of foreign territory by Great Britain—and chiefly within the last hundred years—is wholly unparalleled in history. This mighty Anglo-Saxon race, though comprising one one-fifteenth part of mankind, now rules more than one-third of the earth's surface, and more than one-fourth of its people. And if this race, while growing from 6,000,000 to 100,000,000, thus gained possession of a third portion of the earth, is it to be supposed that when it numbers 1,000,000,000, it will lose the disposition, or lack the power to extend its sway?

This race is multiplying not only more rapidly than any other European race, but far more rapidly than *all* the races of continental Europe. There is no exact knowledge of the population of Europe early in the century; we know, however, that the increase on the continent during the ten years from 1870 to 1880, was 6.89 per cent. If this rate of increase is sustained for a century (and it is more likely to fall, as Europe becomes more crowded), the population on the continent in 1980 will be 534,000,000; while the one Anglo-Saxon race, if it should multiply for a hundred years as it increased from 1870 to 1880, would, in 1980, number 1,343,000,000 souls; but we cannot reasonably expect this ratio of increase to be sustained so long. What, then, will be the probable numbers of this race a hundred years hence? In attempting to answer this question, several things must be borne in mind. Heretofore, the great causes which have operated to check the growth of population in the world have been war, famine, and pestilence; but, among civilized peoples, these causes are becoming constantly less operative. Paradoxical as it seems, the invention of more destructive weapons of war renders war less destructive; commerce and wealth have removed the fear of famine, the pestilence is being brought more and more under control by medical skill and sanitary science. Moreover, Anglo-Saxons, with the exception of the people of Great Britain, who now compose only a little more than one-third of this race, are much less exposed to these checks upon growth than the races of Europe. Again, Europe is crowded, and is constantly becoming more so, which will tend to reduce continually the ratio of increase; while nearly two-thirds of the Anglo-Saxons occupy lands which invite almost unlimited expansion—the United States, Canada, Australia, and South Africa. Again, emigration from Europe, which is certain to increase, is chiefly into Anglo-Saxon countries; while these foreign elements exert a modifying influence on the Anglo-Saxon stock, their descendants are certain to be Anglo-Saxonized. From 1870 to 1880, Germany lost 987,000 inhabitants by emigration; in one generation, their children will be counted Anglo-Saxons. This race has been undergoing an unparalleled expansion during the eighteenth and nineteenth centuries, and the conditions for its continued growth are singularly favorable. . . .

There can be no reasonable doubt that North America is to be the great home of the Anglo-Saxon, the principal seat of his power, the center of his life and influence. Not only does it constitute seven-elevenths of his possessions, but his empire is unsevered, while the remaining four-elevenths are fragmentary and scattered over the earth. Australia will have a great population; but its disadvantages, as compared with North America, are too manifest to need mention. Our continent has room and resources and climate, it lies in the pathway of the nations, it belongs to the zone of power, and already, among Anglo-Saxons, do we lead in population and wealth. . . . England can hardly hope to maintain her relative importance among Anglo-Saxon peoples when her "pretty island" is the home of only one-twentieth part of that race. With the wider distribution of wealth, and increasing facilities of intercourse, intelligence and influence are less centralized, and peoples become more homogeneous; and the more nearly homogeneous people are, the more do *numbers tell*. America is to have the great preponderance of numbers and of wealth, and by the logic of events will follow the scepter of controlling influence. This will be but the consummation of a movement as old as civilization—a result to which men have looked forward for centuries. John Adams records that nothing was "more ancient in his memory than the observation that arts, sciences and empire had traveled westward; and in conversation it was always added that their next leap would be over the Atlantic into America." He recalled a couplet that had been "inscribed, or rather drilled, into a rock on the shore of Monument Bay in our old colony of Plymouth:

The Eastern Nations sink, their glory ends,
And empire rises where the sun descends."

The brilliant Galiani, who foresaw a future in which Europe should be ruled by America, wrote, during the Revolutionary War, "I will wager in favor of America, for the reason merely physical, that for 5,000 years genius has turned opposite to the diurnal motion, and traveled from the East to the West." Count d'Aranda, after signing the Treaty of Paris of 1773, as the representative of Spain, wrote his king: "This Federal Republic is born a pigmy. . . . a day will come when it will be a giant, even a colossus formidable in these countries."

Adam Smith, in his "Wealth of Nations," predicts the transfer of empire from Europe to America. The traveler, Burnaby, found, in the middle of the last century, that an idea had "entered into the minds of the generality of mankind, that empire is traveling westward; and every one is looking forward with eager and impatient expectation to that destined moment when America is to give the law to the rest of the world." Charles Sumner wrote of the "coming time when the whole continent, with all its various states, shall be a Plural Unit, with one Constitution, one Liberty and one Destiny," and when "the national example will be more puissant than army or navy for the conquest of the world." It surely needs no prophet's eye to see that the civilization of the *United States* is to be the civilization of America, and that the future of the continent is ours. In 1880, the United States was the home of more than one-half of the Anglo-Saxon race; and, if the computations already given, are correct, a much larger proportion will be here a hundred years hence. It has been shown that we have room for at least a thousand millions. According to recent figures, there is in France a population of 180.88 to the square mile; in Germany, 216.62; in England and Wales, 428.67; in Belgium, 481.71; in the United States—not including Alaska—16.88. If our population were as dense as that of France, we should have, this side of Alaska,

537,000,000; if as dense as that of Germany, 643,000,000; if as dense as that of England and Wales, 1,173,000,000; if as dense as that of Belgium, 1,430,000,000.

But we are to have not only the larger portion of the Anglo-Saxon race for generations to come, we may reasonably expect to develop the highest type of Anglo-Saxon civilization. If human progress follows a law of development, if

Time's noblest offspring is the last,

our civilization should be the noblest; for we are

The heirs of all the ages in the foremost files of time,

and not only do we occupy the latitude of power, but *our land is the last to be occupied in that latitude.* There is no other virgin soil in the North Temperate Zone. If the consummation of human progress is not to be looked for here, if there is yet to flower a higher civilization, where is the soil that is to produce it? Whipple says: "There has never been a great migration that did not result in a new form of national genius." Our national genius is Anglo-Saxon, but not English, its distinctive type is the result of a finer nervous organization, which is certainly being developed in this country. "The history of the world's progress from savagery to barbarism, from barbarism to civilization, and, in civilization, from the lower degrees toward the higher, is the history of increase in average longevity, corresponding to, and accompanied by, increase of nervousness. Mankind has grown to be at once more delicate and more enduring, more sensitive to weariness and yet more patient of toil, impressible, but capable of bearing powerful irritation; we are woven of finer fiber, which, though apparently frail, yet outlasts the coarser, as rich and costly garments oftentimes wear better than those of rougher workmanship." The roots of civilization are the nerves; and other things being equal, the finest nervous organization will produce the highest civilization. Heretofore, war has been almost the chief occupation of strong races. . . . The mission of the Anglo-Saxon has been largely that of the soldier; but the world is making progress, we are leaving behind the barbarism of war; as civilization advances, it will learn less of war, and concern itself more with the arts of peace, and for these the massive battle-ax must be wrought into tools of finer temper. The physical changes accompanied by mental, which are taking place in the people of the United States, are apparently to adapt men to the demands of a higher civilization. . . .

There is abundant reason to believe that the Anglo-Saxon race is to be, is, indeed, already becoming, more effective here than in the mother country. The marked superiority of this race is due, in large measure, to its highly mixed origin. . . . "History repeats itself"; but, as the wheels of history are the chariot wheels of the Almighty, there is, with every revolution, an onward movement toward the goal of his eternal purposes. There is here a new commingling of races; and, while the largest injections of foreign blood are substantially the same elements that constituted the original Anglo-Saxon admixture, so that we may infer the general type will be preserved, there are strains of other bloods being added, which, if Mr. Emerson's remark is true, that "the best nations are those most widely related," may be expected to improve the stock, and aid it to a higher destiny. If the dangers of immigration, which have been pointed out, can be successfully met for the next few years, until it has passed its climax, it may be expected to add value to the amalgam which will constitute the new Anglo-Saxon race of the New World. Concerning our future, Herbert Spen-cer says: "One great result is, I think, tolerably clear. From biological truths it is to be inferred that the eventual mixture of the allied varieties of the Aryan race, forming the population, will produce a more powerful type of man than has hitherto existed, and a type of man more plastic, more adaptable, more capable of undergoing the modifications needful for complete social life. I think, whatever difficulties they may have to surmount, and whatever tribulations they may have to pass through, the Americans may reasonably look forward to a time when they will have produced a civilization grander than any the world has known."

It may be easily shown, and is of no small significance, that the two great ideas of which the Anglo-Saxon is the exponent are having a fuller development in the United States than in Great Britain. There the union of Church and State tends strongly to paralyze some of the members of the body of Christ. Here there is no such influence to destroy spiritual life and power. Here, also, has been evolved the form of government consistent with the largest possible civil liberty. Furthermore, it is significant that the marked characteristics of this race are being here emphasized most. Among the most striking features of the Anglo-Saxon is his money-making power—a power of increasing importance in the widening commerce of the world's future. We have seen, in a preceding chapter, that, although England is by far the richest nation of Europe, we have already outstripped her in the race after wealth, and we have only begun the development of our vast resources.

Again, another marked characteristic of the Anglo-Saxon is what may be called an instinct or genius for colonizing. His unequaled energy, his indomitable perseverance, and his personal independence, made him a pioneer. He excels all others in pushing his way into new countries. It was those in whom this tendency was strongest that came to America, and this inherited tendency has been further developed by the westward sweep of successive generations across the continent. So noticeable has this characteristic become that English visitors remark it. Charles Dickens once said that the typical American would hesitate to enter heaven unless assured that he could go further west.

Again, nothing more manifestly distinguishes the Anglo-Saxon than his intense and persistent energy; and he is developing in the United States an energy which, in eager activity and effectiveness, is peculiarly American. This is due partly to the fact that Americans are much better fed than Europeans, and partly to the undeveloped resources of a new country, but more largely to our climate, which acts as a constant stimulus. Ten years after the landing of the Pilgrims, the Rev. Francis Higginson, a good observer, wrote: "A sup of New England air is better than a whole flagon of English ale." Thus early had the stimulating effect of our climate been noted. Moreover, our social institutions are stimulating. In Europe the various ranks of society are, like the strata of the earth, fixed and fossilized. There can be no great change without a terrible upheaval, a social earthquake. Here society is like the waters of the sea, mobile; as General Garfield said, and so signally illustrated in his own experience, that which is at the bottom to-day may one day flash on the crest of the highest wave. Every one is free to become whatever he can make of himself; free to transform himself from a rail-splitter or a tanner or a canal-boy, into the nation's President. Our aristocracy, unlike that of Europe, is open to all comers. Wealth, position, influence, are prizes offered for energy; and every farmer's boy, every apprentice and clerk, every friendless and penniless immigrant, is free to enter the lists. Thus many causes co-operate to produce here the most forceful and tremendous energy in the world.

What is the significance of such facts? These tendencies infold the future; they are the mighty alphabet with which God writes his prophecies. May we not, by a careful laying together of the letters, spell out something of his meaning? It seems to me that God, with infinite wisdom and skill, is training the Anglo-Saxon race for an hour sure to come in the world's future. Heretofore there has always been in the history of the world a comparatively unoccupied land westward, into which the crowded countries of the East have poured their surplus populations. But the widening waves of migration, which millenniums ago rolled east and west from the valley of the Euphrates meet to-day on our Pacific coast. There are no more new worlds. The unoccupied arable lands of the earth are limited, and will soon be taken. The time is coming when the pressure of population on the means of subsistence will be felt here as it is now felt in Europe and Asia. Then will the world enter upon a new stage of its history—*the final competition of races, for which the Anglo-Saxon is being schooled.* Long before the thousand millions are here, the mighty *centrifugal* tendency, inherent in this stock and strengthened in the United States, will assert itself. Then this race of unequaled energy, with all the majesty of numbers and the might of wealth behind it—the representative, let us hope, of the largest liberty, the purest Christianity, the highest civilization—having developed peculiarly aggressive traits calculated to impress its institutions upon mankind, will spread itself over the earth. If I read not amiss, this powerful race will move down upon Mexico, down upon Central and South

America, out upon the islands of the sea, over upon Africa and beyond. And can any one doubt that the result of this competition of races will be the "survival of the fittest"? "Any people," says Dr. Bushnell, "that is physiologically advanced in culture, though it be only in a degree beyond another which is mingled with it on strictly equal terms, is sure to live down and finally live out its inferior. Nothing can save the inferior race but a ready and pliant assimilation. Whether the feebler and more abject races are going to be regenerated and raised up, is already very much of a question. What if it should be God's plan to people the world with better and finer material? Certain it is, whatever expectations we may indulge, that there is a tremendous overbearing surge of power in the Christian nations, which, if the others are not speedily raised to some vastly higher capacity, will inevitably submerge and bury them forever. . . ." To this result no war of extermination is needful; the contest is not one of arms, but of vitality and of civilization. "At the present day," says Mr. Darwin, "civilized nations are everywhere supplanting barbarous nations, excepting where the climate opposes a deadly barrier; and they succeed mainly, though not exclusively, through their arts, which are the products of the intellect?" . . . Bring savages into contact with our civilization, and its destructive forces become operative at once, while years are necessary to render effective the saving influences of Christian instruction. Moreover, the pioneer wave of our civilization carries with it more scum than salt. Where there is one missionary, there are hundreds of miners or traders or adventurers ready to debauch the native. Whether the extinction of inferior races before the advancing Anglo-Saxon seems to the reader sad or otherwise, it certainly appears probable. I know of nothing

except climatic conditions to prevent this race from populating Africa as it has peopled North America. And those portions of Africa which are unfavorable to Anglo-Saxon life are less extensive than was once supposed. The Dutch Boers, after two centuries of life there, are as hardy as any race on earth. The Anglo-Saxon has established himself in climates totally diverse—Canada, South Africa, and India—and, through several generations, has preserved his essential race characteristics. He is not, of course, superior to climatic influences; but, even in warm climates, he is likely to retain his aggressive vigor long enough to supplant races already enfeebled. Thus, in what Dr. Bushnell calls "the out-populating power of the Christian stock," may be found God's final and complete solution of the dark problem of heathenism among many inferior peoples.

Some of the stronger races, doubtless, may be able to preserve their integrity; but, in order to compete with the Anglo-Saxon, they will probably be forced to adopt his methods and instruments, his civilization and his religion. Significant movements are now in progress among them. While the Christian religion was never more vital, or its hold upon the Anglo-Saxon mind stronger, there is taking place among the nations a wide-spread intellectual revolt against traditional beliefs. "In every corner of the world," said Mr. Froude, "there is the same phenomenon of the decay of established religions. . . . Among Mohammedans, Jews, Buddhists, Brahmins, traditionary creeds are losing their hold. An intellectual revolution is sweeping over the world, breaking down established opinions, dissolving foundations on which historical faiths have been built up." The contact of Christian with heathen nations is awaking the latter to new life. Old superstitions are loosening their grasp. The dead crust of fossil faiths is being shattered by the movements of life underneath. In Catholic countries, Catholicism is losing its influence over educated minds, and in some cases the masses have already lost all faith in it. Thus, while on this continent God is training the Anglo-Saxon race for its mission, a complemental work has been in progress in the great world beyond. God has two hands. Not only is he preparing in our civilization the die with which to stamp the nations, but, by what Southey called the "timing of Providence," he is preparing mankind to receive our impress.

Is there room for reasonable doubt that this race, unless devitalized by alcohol and tobacco, is destined to dispossess many weaker races, assimilate others and mold the remainder, until, in a very true and important sense, it has Anglo-Saxonized mankind? Already "the English language, saturated with Christian ideas, gathering up into itself the best thought of all the ages, is the great agent of Christian civilization throughout the world; at this moment affecting the destinies and molding the character of half the human race." Jacob Grimm, the German philologist, said of this language: "It seems chosen, like its people, to rule in future times in a still greater degree in all the corners of the earth." He predicted, indeed, that the language of Shakespeare would eventually become the language of mankind. Is not Tennyson's noble prophecy to find its fulfillment in Anglo-Saxondom's extending its dominion and influence—

Till the war-drum throbs no longer,
　　and the battle flags are furl'd
In the Parliament of man, the Federation of the world.

In my own mind, there is no doubt that the Anglo-Saxon is to exercise the commanding influence in the world's future; but the exact nature of that influence is, as yet, undetermined. How far his civilization will be materialistic and atheistic, and how long it will take thoroughly to Christianize and sweeten it, how rapidly he will hasten the coming of the kingdom wherein dwelleth righteousness, or how many ages he may retard it, is still uncertain; but *it is now being swiftly determined.* Let us weld together in a chain the various links of our logic which we have endeavored to forge. Is it manifest that the Anglo-Saxon holds in his hands the destinies of mankind for ages to come? Is it evident that the United States is to be the home of this race, the principal seat of his power, the great center of his influence? Is it true . . . that the great West is to dominate the nation's future? Has it been shown . . . that this generation is to determine the character, and hence the destiny, of the West? Then may God open the eyes of this generation! . . . "Remember that from yonder heights forty centuries look down on you." Men of this generation, from the pyramid top of opportunity on which God has set us, *we look down on forty centuries!* We stretch our hand into the future with power to mold the destinies of unborn millions.

We are living, we are dwelling,
　　in a grand and awful time,
In an age on ages telling—
　　To be living is sublime!

Notwithstanding the great perils which threaten it, I cannot think our civilization will perish; but I believe it is fully in the hands of the Christians of the United States, during the next fifteen or twenty years to hasten or retard the coming of Christ's kingdom in the world by hundreds, and perhaps thousands, of years. We of this generation and nation occupy the Gibraltar of the ages which commands the world's future.

10. WOODROW WILSON, *The American Situation in 1900**

It was interesting to note with how changed an aspect the government stood upon the threshold of a new century. The President seemed again to be always in the foreground, as if the first days of the government were to be repeated,—that first quarter of a century in which it was making good its right to exist and to act as an independent power among the nations of the world. Now, full grown, it was to take a place of leadership.

The closing year of the century (1900) witnessed a great upheaval of revolutionary forces in China. Insurgent bands filled the country, the very capital itself, in protest against the presence and the growing influence of the foreigner, and particularly the occupation of new ports of entry by Russia, England, and Germany,—the dowager empress, the real mistress of the kingdom, acting as their ally. The very legations at Peking were invested in deadly siege by the insurgents; and America, with the other nations whose representatives were threatened, sent troops to their relief.

America played her new part with conspicuous success. Her voice told for peace, conciliation, justice, and yet for a firm vindication of sovereign rights, at every turn of the difficult business; her troops were among the first to withdraw, to the Philippines, when their presence became unnecessary; the world noted a calm poise of judgment, a steady confidence as if of conscious power in the utterances of the American Secretary of State; the new functions of America in the East were plain enough for all to see.

The old landmarks of politics within the United States themselves seemed, meanwhile, submerged. The southern States were readjusting their elective suffrage so as to exclude the illiterate Negroes and so in part undo the mischief of reconstruction; and yet the rest of the country withheld its hand from interference. Sections began to draw together with a new understanding of one another. Parties were turning to the new days to come and to the common efforts of peace. Statesmen knew that it was to be their task to release the energies of the country for the great day of trade and of manufacture which was to change the face of the world: to ease the processes of labor, govern capital in the interest of those who were its indispensable servants in pushing the great industries of the country to their final value and perfection, and make law the instrument, not of justice merely, but also of social progress.

* Woodrow Wilson, *A History of the American People* (New York, 1902), V, 299–300.

11. DAVID RIESMAN, *The Search for Challenge, 1960**

I want to discuss the problem of discovering challenge in what Galbraith calls the "affluent society," challenge when the older challenges based

* David Riesman, "The Search for Challenge," *New University Thought*, I (1960), 3–15; also in *Merrill-Palmer Quarterly*, VI (1960), 218–34. Reprinted by permission of the author.

on the subsistent society and the struggle for sheer survival are no longer imperative. One of the perspectives I want to use is cross-cultural, and we shall look at an anthropological example. Another is historical, and we shall look at ourselves as we were in an earlier day—this, too, is cross-cultural. The third perspective is genetic, in which I shall ask what sorts of challenges are requisite at what stages of one's own life cycle. This is a vast topic. I don't bring to it the erudition of a Toynbee or an Alfred Kroeber, but on the contrary I shall bring to it some observations and free associations in the hope of stimulating further thinking.

Periodically throughout Western history men have imagined that collective as well as individual life could be better, or at least less bad. In times of chaos and of war they dreamed of social stability and hierarchy, as Plato did in *The Republic,* or as Sir Thomas More did in his *Utopia.* Myths of heaven refracted the popular weariness of toil, short life, illness and social disorganization. Periodically, too, men could be mobilized for revolt against plainly oppressive conditions, once these conditions had lightened enough to make them seem less than divinely given. For the ills that have plagued man have been such nightmares that men at all but the lowest levels of brutishness could grasp the possibility of being less badly off, once they *were* less badly off. Today, however, we are faced with a paradox: the United States and a few other rich countries have caught up with many Utopian ideals while at the same time literal belief in heaven has almost vanished. In this country people suffer less from nightmarish misery than from the more subtle disorders previously buried by the harsh struggle for existence.

We can seen an analogue to this development in the short career of psychoanalytic therapy, which is about 50 years old. When Freud began, patients came to him who were suffering from hysteria, from paralyzed arms, from inability to talk, from obvious symptoms. By helping them internalize what they had externalized, that is, what they had (so to speak) thrown into an arm, it was relatively easy and even speedy to cure them. Today, in contrast, one sees such cases only, for instance in this country, among immigrant Poles in Pittsburgh or among rural southerners in West Virginia. Many therapists go through their entire lives without ever seeing such a case. People come to analysis today who do not suffer from an external subsistence problem, from a paralysis. Their limbs work and their sexual organs work, but somehow life doesn't live up to its billing for them; they carry on an unrepressed interior dialogue, but it bores them. Often, I might add, all they do is include the analyst in the dialogue and bore him. They need, usually without knowing it, a new vision and not merely a new way of talking about themselves; in fact, I was talking the other day with an analyst who said that patients talked today, as was no surprise, very freely indeed about any of the things that in Freud's day they would have considered private and intimate.

Yet, as we all know, most of the rest of the world would trade places any day with the rich American and trade its miseries for his neuroses. An ironic instance are the Manus whom Margaret Mead revisited several years ago, twenty-five years after her first field trip in 1928. When she had first been there the Manus had been a Stone Age people; then had come World War II and their island had been a staging area for American troops. When she arrived, the Manus had just finished throwing out a Catholic mission on the ground that the mission was trying to get them to adjust slowly to the ways of the West, whereas they wanted to take over the distance to modernity in one big jump. They thought the white people in the mission were patronizing them, holding out on them, trying to ration the blessings of industrial society. You can imagine the position of the mission which was saying in effect, "It isn't just so wonderful to be Westernized, and take it easy." For the Manus the effort to act like Americans was a heroic challenge; one, in fact, which produced a revolutionary leader, Paliau, a man of enormous strength and determination. For him, it was a new religion to become Americanized.

The Manus, like many South Pacific peoples, had had their craze of cargo cults in which traditional objects had been thrown in the ocean in the fond belief that planes or boats would come, piled high with the white man's goods, if only the Manus would propitiate the cargo by appropriate action. Even where the cargo cult does not take such open and violent form, it exists. A few years ago I met a Burmese doctor who had come to the University of Chicago to study technological change. I asked him why he, a gentle and speculative man, had left his homeland on such a quest; and he replied that once the peasants in the rice fields had seen American movies and Cadillacs they would never be quiet again until they had them too. In his book *The Passing of Traditional Society,* Daniel Lerner discusses interviews which were done a few years ago in seven countries of the Middle East. In these the theme that life in America is more modern and, hence, better comes up again and again— whatever the political hostilities towards America, one finds this lure among Egyptians and Syrians and others who are politically, ideologically,

violently antagonistic to America and yet admire it. The dream of America— the dream of plenty—is shared by people at all levels, and it is also rejected on religious and traditional grounds by many who are obviously and plainly influenced by it. The conflicts are only about the rate of speed with which one should move to plenty and the mode, and the Malthusian handicaps and how they are to be overcome, and the values to be reintegrated by doing so. And all this is new and exciting to peoples to whom it happens, but it is not new to the West—we have had it.

In fact, we can today in some considerable degree measure the backwardness of a social class or a nation by the extent to which America provides it with a model of Utopia. For the intellectuals of Europe and of India, for instance, America is more to be feared than admired, distrusted than copied. The collapse of the image of America as a vision of Jeffersonian equality and of orderly democracy has been enormously rapid and is not merely the result of Communist propaganda. One factor is the shutting off of immigration after the first World War, which doused the hopes of millions of south Europeans and Levantines that they might find a personal Utopia in the United States; and in these interviews of Professor Lerner's one finds this also coming up again and again—people who have uncles in America from Syria or Turkey and who would like to come here and can't.

The more vociferous Americans themselves, moreover, in desperate search of a self-justifying ideology, have been tempted to identify *the* American way with their own tendentious misinterpretations of our economy as one of free enterprise, or to boast of American technological virtuosity or of the workingman's standard of living. This last might appear to appeal to workingmen in some places, but it does not appeal to the elites whose own frustrated materialism is all too well acted out on their behalf by strident Americans.

I have in the last years talked to a good many non-Americans who, like the Burmese doctor, are visiting this country in the hope of hastening the economic development of their own land, and they have gone home again with an ambivalent feeling: can they reduce poverty, cut the birth rate, start cumulative economic growth, all without arriving at the American destiny—that is, arriving at the place we are now, from which the next steps are opaque—once the novelty wears off?

I would be giving the wrong impression if I were understood to contend that there is no Utopianism in present-day America. There are first of all many conservative people, maybe some here, who find in the American past an adequate image for the future: they contend that if only we balanced our budgets, spanked our kids, worked hard and uncomplainingly, tore down all the teachers colleges—all would be well. And there are many others who find in the huge distance we still have to travel towards economic, and especially towards racial equality, enough challenge for their lifetimes—and in a sense it is enough. Likewise, the effort of the Communist bloc to overtake America has given still other Americans of both major parties the short-run aims of a coach whose all too confident team has lost a game—the feeling that with a little discipline and locker-room talk, along with better scouting and recruiting for scientists, all will be recouped. Perhaps the major benefit thus provided for Americans is the renewed conviction that there is a game and that winning it can give meaning to life. In my opinion none of these, not even the generous one of getting rid of the

residues of inequality, is sufficient to mobilize social energies to take the next obscure steps in American life that would bring us a measure of international security and more adequate social goals for an age of plenty.

In this situation many of the most sensitive and truly disinterested young people have given up the larger societal goals to pursue what I might call the Utopianism of private life. It is in the family first of all, and beyond that in the circle of friends and neighbors, that one looks for Jeffersonian simplicity, an idyll of decency, generosity, and sensibility. Much of the confusion in current discussion is due to failure to distinguish between the high quality of these personal goals of young people and the low quality of our social aims. That is, if one is looking at the texture of individual life in America, this country is harboring, despite all surrounding miasmas, extraordinarily fine enclaves whose tone, though not ascetic, has something in common with the outlook of Utopian colonies in the last century, or with Hopi pueblos, or with the spirit of some of our great 19th Century dissidents, whether Melville or Whitman, William James or Bellamy. In many past epochs of cultural greatness the dichotomy between an avant-garde few and the brutalized many was taken for granted and would occasionally perpetuate itself for long periods. But in the United States today the contrast between the private Utopianism that I have spoken of and the general low level of vision in the general population and in its political activities seems to my mind both less tolerable and less viable for the long term. With the growth of interdependence within and between nations, private virtues, if they do not actually become public vices, become almost irrelevant—beautiful gardens at the mercy of fall-out. I don't expect every young person to take part in the development of a more inclusive Utopia than "familism," but I would like to see a better proportion achieved between private and public visions; indeed, I believe that private life would be enriched and in a way become more meaningful if the two spheres were both more forcefully cultivated.

When I spent a summer in the Soviet Union twenty-seven years ago, I met many eager young Communists who had enthusiastically junked all private aims in the communal enterprise of "building socialism." Amid a Philistine culture made desolate with slogans, they *were* building socialism in an all too literal sense, *i.e,* they were building dams, railroads, factories, and machine tractor stations and Communist Party apparatus. They brought to their work the zeal of pioneers and, as a blueprint for their own activities, the model of American industrial achievement. At the Stalingrad tractor plant, then barely beginning to produce, I saw fanatical young Stakhanovites (and I guess the term "Stakhanovite" is unknown to many undergraduates today; that is a kind of Russian version of an Eagle Scout) working with tremendous zeal in the midst of a mass of sullen peasants, new to industry and by no means reconciled to its restrictions. I had gone over with a group of American students, some of whom found this spectacle in contrast to the America of the depression marvelously exhilarating. It was a battle with simple rules and clear goals, or so it seemed, and, in fact, the reports from Stalingrad in *Pravda* and *Isvestia* were couched in the language of battle—so many tractors had been turned out that week on the Stalingrad front, or there were that many defeats in the battle for electrification, and so on. I thought then, and I still think now, that the tasks confronting Americans are more

exhilarating but also more problematical. It would be child's play for us to build the Turk-Sib Railway or the Dneprostroi dam, although, as I shall indicate later, every child should have this opportunity. We have to make our own model of the future as we go, in a situation which is new historically.

It is at this point that the Communists have done us an immense and possibly fatal disservice by so largely discrediting secular Utopias at the very time when religion no longer offers an illuminating other-worldly Utopia but has also become an adjunct to private life. While it is helpful for people to realize that fanaticism in pursuit of Utopian goals is a danger, allowing people to express their worst impulses while defeating their best hopes, the reaction among contemporary non-Communist intellectuals has gone much too far. Today the most influential Utopian writings are satiric anti-Utopias such as *Brave New World* or *1984,* which extrapolate, in the former case largely from the United States and in the latter largely from the Soviet Union, to their visions of a more total despair.

The Poles and for a time the Hungarians who rose against the terror could express in the writings of students and intellectuals a kind of minimum-decency platform—humane and sensible, but Utopian only in contrast to Stalinism. They have been like hysterics recovering from paralysis in the early days of psychoanalysis; and as the hysterics, once cured, could continue to operate on the moral capital of Victorianism, so these Polish and Hungarian revisionists can draw on the moral capital of pre-war Social Democracy; hence can project into the future their recall of the slightly less gruesome past, just as heaven is often the retroactive image of a childhood Eden.

As I have said, however, we Americans have caught up with our future at the very historical moment when the Communist example has done much to dampen Utopian thinking; such thinking, I need hardly say to you, is never easy. All literature shows that writers can more readily picture terrors than delights. For one thing, as Margaret Mead pointed out, we can all empathize with terrors, whereas delights, if they go beyond platitude, differentiate us. I have been struck all my life with how difficult it is for people—even storytellers and artists—to imagine nonexistent things: to imagine, for instance, nonexistent animals; they can only put parts together which are already available and come up with a centaur or a unicorn, much as science fiction for the most part is more science than fiction. Now that we can draw on the world storehouse of cultures through our knowledge of anthropology and history we can in imagination make unicorns, *i.e.,* fit pieces of culture together, but we find it hard to invent new ones.

And yet on the whole, social science, while enabling us to draw on a far wider spectrum of human experience than any one culture has ever had available to it, may have contributed to the decline of Utopian thinking. To free themselves from moralism and the kind of shallow evolutionism one can find in Herbert Spencer, social scientists in our time largely have eschewed either looking at evolution or engaging in prophecy. Somebody asked me recently whether sociologists weren't "do-gooders" and I said I was afraid that that was a thing of the past. The most frequent device for saving thought and conscience here is to say that the social scientist when he makes proposals for change, rather than presenting limited alternatives to a powerful decision-maker, is simply a citizen. As a scientist that is not his business. And science increasingly has become his business, and a business carried on in a business-like way, making measurements and keeping up with what is euphemistically called "the literature." Utopianism reappears in disguised forms, to be sure, as for instance in the belief that if vaster sums were spent on the sciences, prediction and control could take the place of prophecy; there is also the narrower Utopian hope that if each subdivision of science pursues its private aims, some later ecumenical movement may reunite the scattered findings within a grand scheme. (The very largeness of the branches of social science in so vast a country as this means that men can live their whole intellectual lives within the boundaries of a single subdiscipline.) Moreover, as more and more people go to college and more and more people teach those who go to college, intellectuals are increasingly becoming attached to universities; and this is an ambivalent trend in the light of the experience of the past that many of the most seminal ideas have come from outside the academy. And social science, like other intellectual activities, has been steadily democratized, in the sense that its concepts and findings are regarded as valid only if they can be taught to any competent graduate student. Thus, analysis of social wholes, entire cultures, which remains something of an art, is not a game at which any number can play and it tends to be deprecated and hence postponed until that quite distant and hardly foreseeable day when it can be handled in terms available to anybody. Thinking, that is, about a whole society is not something that can readily be democratized. And as for Utopian thinking, most of us after childhood form categorical images of our society and, while aided by images of hell we can imagine things being worse, we cannot imagine them being significantly better.

In addition, although the first explorations into social science often made men hopeful, as they made Condorcet or Marx hopeful (although not Malthus), later immersion tends to make people less hopeful, for it destroys the illusion that the masses have noble dreams which the capitalists or the bureaucrats repress. It shows how immense and how far-reaching are the changes in men's hopes and desires that would be necessary for the creation of a better world: we do not stand outside the portals of heaven only because some vested interests bar the way. And market research is frequently interpreted in such a way as to confirm the status quo; it makes, when conducted by politicians, things that might be worth doing "politically impossible." Let me take a trivial illustration: we go to people for instance and ask them if they would like a small car, and they say "no," or they say "yes" in such a way as to mean "no." Then we proceed to make many big cars, thus changing the visual landscape and people's expectations of what a car looks like and thus prove that people don't like small cars. Even so, a change in circumstances, let us say a slight recession, can show how evanescent was the earlier preference, especially among educated people who, having gone to college, have opinions and tastes which fluctuate more rapidly than do those of lesser learning. And, of course, market and public opinion research often can serve, if well done, to show that people no longer believe what they are supposed to believe and this can be emancipating.

Nevertheless, it seems to me that over-all the tendency of the effect on us of increasing knowledge of man is to curb radical departures of thought

in the social sphere, less I think because of McCarthyite opposition than because we ourselves want to feel we are sensible, calm, well-organized people. The great achievement of the physical sciences, in my judgment, is not their ability to codify and measure—this is a detail, though important —but their ability to go beyond common or even uncommon sense to hold ideas—like the concept of the wavicle —which are paradoxical or contradictory and which bear no relation to daily sense experience. (It would be better, on second thought, to speak not of daily sense experience but rather of our cultural and linguistic codification of reality: those categorical imperatives which result from our specific and historical way of seeing as well as from perspectives framed by the human condition as such.) . . . .

I want to mention one example of approaching Utopia through the techniques of social science—an example that, I fear, shows how little these techniques can contribute at present. I have in mind a recent study done at The University of Michigan for the Michigan Bell Telephone Company in which a group of articulate adults were invited to let their imaginations roam free, and to tell trained interviewers what sort of things they would like to see in the "world of tomorrow." Out of 126 interviews, mainly with well-educated respondents, there were, in fact, few suggestions which were at all visionary. Respondents want a machine which will bring them the morning newspaper from the doorstep. They want conveyor-belt highways and drive-in supermarkets and automatic car controls. They want a personal air-conditioning unit inside their clothes. (This reminded me of Aldous Huxley's novel *Antic Hay*.) Or they want a machine which will bring them any sight, sound, smell, or climate they choose without having to go out to find it. They want to be able to bring back fond memories at will, and to erase annoyances at will. One wants a device to look a doctor over without going to his office, another a device to make it easy to complain to a supercilious sales person, or another a gadget to allow one safely and anonymously to bawl out somebody. One wistfully asks, and here is one of the few quasi-political suggestions, for some means of making suggestions to the legislative government (that's his term) and still another says, "I want to be able to visit relatives and friends without missing church." One wants "more variety in my daily living—a surprise every day."

If such wishes can be called Utopian at all, they are once more very private; they are seldom connected with any plan for the development of the individual's powers, let alone any plan for society more extensive than that of the person who wanted whole cities covered with plastic to keep out the weather. Many of the suggestions represent what I have sometimes called the cult of effortlessness. I speak of it as a cult, for I don't believe that most Americans not presently overworked seek this nirvana with steady passion. But it is striking that in the interviews, and perhaps reflecting their relaxed form, no one seems to wish for obstacles, for challenges, for things that take time and require effort. . . .

Colleges are sometimes criticized as breeding discontented intellectuals who are too good for this world, whether "this world" is the graduate school to which they go on or a career in business or the professions. But I would be much happier if more colleges put more of this kind of pressure on later life to live up to college; that is, if more people got out of college who

insisted that the world live up to the expectations created by college. I think one reason such insistence is muted is that people, once in a job and in a marriage, have no financial leeway to make a radical break and therefore the criticisms they might otherwise make simply don't occur to them; and this again goes back to my thought that if one had a period of compulsory service doing such work as building mountains, one could then later in life have a claim on society on the basis of that service. Now, actually, our society is rich enough so that we don't need that basis, we don't need it, that is, economically although we do need it psychologically or politically. Today, if people find their job undemanding, their temptation is not to seek for a demanding job or to struggle politically for a world in which jobs are more demanding and more interesting and in which industry and the professions do less in the way of stockpiling talent than they now do. Rather I think people flee into what I have called the Utopianism of private life, of domesticity. The trouble with this is that it puts too much of a burden on domesticity, because if one wants to live at the height of the times in work, one has to in leisure and vice versa.

To return to the beginning, it comes as a surprise to Americans that when we are faced with plenty we still find problems no less grave. It still takes nine months to produce a baby; it still takes time to develop anything worth while, whether this be a painting or a friendship or a talent or an interest. Walt Whitman wrote: "It is provided in the essence of things that from any fruition of success, no matter what, shall come forth something to make a greater struggle necessary."

II

* * * * * * * * * * * * * * * * * * * *

The Malleability of the
American Universe

William Franklin Graham

is the evangelist and Baptist minister better known as Billy Graham.

He was born in Charlotte, North Carolina, in 1918. He received a Bachelor of Arts degree from Wheaton College in 1943, a Bachelor of Theology from the Florida Bible Seminary in 1940, and a Doctor of Divinity from Kings College in 1948.

Dr. Graham was president of a small interdenominational school in Minneapolis from 1947 to 1951. He has conducted nation-wide campaigns since 1946 and has made seven trips to Europe since World War II.

He is the author of *Calling Youth to Christ,* published in 1947; *Revival in Our Times,* 1950; *America's Hour of Decision,* 1951; *Korean Diary,* 1953, and *Peace With God,* 1953.

He has also written a daily newspaper column, produced religious films, and appeared on radio and television.

Billy Graham ✳✳✳✳ Men Must Be Changed Before a Nation Can

A few months ago I played golf with a man who looked and acted as though he enjoyed perfect health. Today he is dead. In spite of outward appearance he had a virulent form of cancer which within a short time took his life.

I am convinced that regardless of the outward appearance of prosperity within the corporate life of America today there is present a form of moral and spiritual cancer which could ultimately lead to the country's destruction unless the disease is treated promptly and the trend reversed.

Many thoughtful Americans are disturbed because as a nation we seem bereft of a sense of purpose. We have the mood and stance of a people who have "arrived" and have nowhere else to go.

We have achieved an affluence unprecedented in our history.

Some of our most outstanding citizens are warning us with statements that are reminiscent of the flaming prophets of old who prophesied the doom of nations that refused to change their moral course. George F. Kennan, the historian and former American ambassador to Russia, recently said, "If you ask me whether a country—with no highly developed sense of national purpose, with the overwhelming accent of life on personal comfort, with a dearth of public services and a surfeit of privately sold gadgetry, with insufficient social discipline even to keep its major industries functioning without grievous interruption—if you ask me whether such a country has, over the long run, good chances of competing with a purposeful, serious and disciplined society such as that of the Soviet Union, I must say that the answer is No."

Many American leaders have serious doubts concerning the nation's moral and spiritual capability to match the challenge of a dedicated, disciplined Communism. I am convinced that unless we heed the warning, unless we bring Americans back to an awareness of God's moral laws, unless a moral fiber is put back into the structure of our nation, we are headed for national disaster.

No patient is willing to take the doctor's medicine until he has heard the diagnosis, and no one should try to prescribe a national purpose for America until he has listened to her heart. It has been my privilege to travel and preach in nearly all the states of the country for ten years. I have talked personally with thousands of Americans from every walk of life. My own feeling is that the heart of America is still basically sound but that the blood stream is being poisoned with the toxins of modern life.

History has many examples of nations that "arrived" and then fell due to overconfidence, internal decay, or neglect of the ideals and philosophies that had made them great. America is in desperate need of a moral and spiritual transfusion that will cause her to recapture some of the strength and idealism that made us the greatest nation in the world.

First, we need to recapture the strength of individualism. Mass-produced machinery has given rise to the mass-produced man. We are inclined to think like the Joneses, dress like the Joneses, build houses like the Joneses, and talk like the Joneses. We have become status conscious and have built for ourselves sets of status symbols.

A few weeks ago, in a visit to the Holy Land, I followed in the steps of some of the great nonconformists of the Bible, men such as Elijah, Amos, Micah. I stood on top of Mount Carmel, overlooking the beautiful Israeli city of Haifa, and prayed, "Lord, help me not to be a conformist." Psychologists tell us that we are shaped by heredity and by environment. The prophets of Israel were a part of their environment, yet they were not shaped by it. They reacted *against* it. They had the courage to stand for moral right—alone if necessary. We need men who will live up to their idealism and who refuse to be moral copycats.

Second, we need to recapture the spirit of '76. While we encourage nationalism for ambitious smaller nations abroad, we discourage it at home. Patriotism in America seems to be "old hat." If a man gets out and waves the American flag, he is now "suspect" or called a "reactionary." We applaud the nationalistic demonstrations in other countries. Perhaps we need a few demonstrations for America. The Soviet Communist party recently published 97 slogans for May Day with the accent on complete liquidation of colonialism and a production drive to overtake the United States. Where are the American slogans? Commander Vincent J. Lonergan, a Roman Catholic chaplain, warned participants at the White House Conference on Children and Youth recently that "far too many of [our youth] have been led to believe that patriotism is a phony virtue, that military service is an intolerable burden to be avoided as a plague; or if imposed upon them, to be carried out grudgingly, without pride, without honor. It is extremely important that we imbue our young people with the spirit of intelligent sacrifice that is our heritage as Americans." What a heartening thing it would be to see the people of America making the spirit of '76 the spirit of 1960.

Third, we need to recapture hardness and discipline in our national life. Our excessive allotment of leisure in an affluent society is making dullards out of us. Thousands of our young men are not even able to pass the army physical exam. We play too much and work too little. We overeat, overdrink, oversex, and overplay, but few of us are ever over-exercised. We have become surfeited in this land of plenty. Our sedentary way of life has brought an alarming rash of coronaries and related ill-nesses. We may be the richest people in the world, but we are far from being the sturdiest.

The Bible warns, "Woe to them that are at ease in Zion." We need to recapture the love and dedication of hard work.

Fourth, we must recapture the courage of our fathers. The chairman of the history department of one of our great universities recently con-fided in me, "We have become a nation of cowards." I challenged him on this statement, but his arguments were convincing. The great courage that once was so characteristic of America and Americans seems to be going. Many of our military leaders are deeply concerned about the dis-appearance of the will to fight for what we believe. We seem to be content to sit within the security of our homes and watch the brave Western heroes on television doing the things that inwardly we wish we had the courage to do. What boldness we may have is vicarious and reflected in the fictional acts on the screen. We are content to live in a world of fantasy and cringe at the thought of becoming personally involved with life. We are so intent on saving our own skins that we are in danger of losing our souls.

We have become reluctant to follow a course that isn't popular, even if deep inside we know it is right. If the odds are ten to one in our favor we will take a stand, but if there is any appreciable risk involved in standing up for what we know to be right, we'll play it safe. Woodrow Wilson said, "I would a great deal rather lose in a cause that I know someday will triumph than triumph in a cause that I know someday will lose." We have played the flip side of that record and said, "I won't buck the tide of popular opinion, for I would rather be liked than to be right." This is the sort of devastating fear that eats at the heart of a people and robs them of a sense of individual and national purpose.

Fifth, we must recapture the American challenge. William James fifty years ago observed that America needs "a moral equivalent of war" to challenge it. The rise of the Beatniks is at least partially a pitiful attempt to find a challenge. Robert Lindner, the late Baltimore psychoanalyst, wrote the book *Rebel without a Cause.* Lindner found that American youth feel that they are so surrounded by conformity that they rebel for the sake of rebelling. This is the psychological basis of much of our teen-age delinquency. We need a challenge such as our forefathers had when they transformed this wilderness into a civilized nation. While the chal-lenge of the present hour may take different forms, I believe it is even greater than what the early Americans faced.

What is the American challenge? What is our reason for existence? There are a thousand challenges that should stir our emotions and demand the dedication of every fiber of our being. Some of them may be:

The challenge to be on the side of the little people of the world, the hungry, the homeless, the friendless, the oppressed, the discriminated against, the captives, and those who live in countries where there is no freedom.

The challenge to throw political expediency to the wind if necessary and do what we know is morally right because it is right.

The challenge of sharing our immense wealth with others.

The challenge of electing men with moral courage to high office who will be ruthless with the gangsters that operate on such a wide scale throughout the nation.

The challenge of selling the American dream and ideals to the world.

The challenge of humility to admit our failures, to repent of our sins and to serve God unashamedly.

The challenge of solving the world-wide problems of ignorance, disease, and poverty.

The challenge of finding the individual peace and joy that is so lacking in the "good life" of modern America.

The challenge of contentment with what we have, remembering the words of the Apostle Paul, "I have learned that in whatsover state I find myself therewith to be content."

America still has a glorious future if we rise to the challenges, opportunities, and responsibilities of the hour. If we fail, may God help us!

Sixth, we must recapture our moral strength and our faith in God. Some recent surveys of American life have been alarming and discouraging. We now know that cheating is accepted practice in our society. Morals have become irrelevant or relative—no longer are there moral absolutes. Success at any price is our maxim. We excuse our immorality by saying, "Everybody is doing it." Many of our modern educators have decreed that we are what we are because of external pressures and that each of us is a victim of environment or inherent tendencies and that we cannot help what we are. This is totally contrary to the teachings of Holy Scripture. The Bible teaches that we are responsible for our moral choices.

We cannot possibly exist if we reject the time-honored moral absolutes of the Ten Commandments and the Sermon on the Mount. The Scripture says, "Righteousness exalteth a nation, but sin is a reproach to any people."

The nation is no longer shocked at exposés. Our conscience is being hardened and the Scriptures warn against a hardening conscience. "We live today," says Dr. Robert E. Fitch in *Christianity and Crisis,* "in an age when ethics is becoming obsolete. It is superseded by science, deleted by psychology, dismissed as emotive by philosophy: it is drowned in compassion, evaporates into aesthetics and retreats before relativism. . . . The usual moral distinctions are simply drowned in a maudlin emotion in which we have more feeling for the murderer than for the murdered, for the adulterer than for the betrayed; and in which we gradually begin to believe that the really guilty party, the one who somehow caused it all, is the victim, not the perpetrator, of the crime."

America is said to have the highest per capita boredom of any spot on earth. We have tried to fill ourselves with science and education, with better living and pleasure, with the many other things we thought we wanted, but we are still empty and bored. Why are we empty? Because the Creator made us for Himself, and we shall never find completeness and fullness apart from fellowship with Him. Jesus told us long ago that "man shall not live by bread alone," but we have paid no heed. We have gone on stuffing ourselves with bread of every description—except the bread Christ offered. We are desperately weary of the emptiness and boredom within. We are confused by the prejudice, hatred, greed, and lust that are within us. We seem to be caught in quicksand: we want out of our human dilemma but are powerless. The American genius has enabled us to change everything but ourselves.

It is absolutely impossible to change society and reverse the moral trend unless we ourselves are changed from the inside out. Man needs transformation or conversion. Unless we Americans are willing to accept humbly the diagnosis of the Book upon which our culture was largely founded—and to accept its remedy—we are going to continue along the road to disaster and ruin. No nation in history has had a greater opportunity than America. Because our privileges have been greater, our responsibilities are greater. Thus, a Holy God requires more of the American people than of any nation in the history of the world with the possible exception of Israel. Our only way to moral reform is through repentance of our sins and a return to God.

Confronted with the evidences of spiritual and moral decay on every hand, we now find ourselves more frequently looking for relief from the consequences of our waywardness rather than to the cause and cure of the desperate situation in which we find ourselves. In the Old Testament we read, "If my people, which are called by my name, shall humble themselves, and pray, and seek my face, and turn from their wicked ways; then will I hear from heaven, and will forgive their sin, and will heal their land." Here is a formula of God's own making, a way by which a nation may return to a right relationship with Him. But I repeat, it is men who must be changed before a nation can be changed.

I am not so naïve as to believe that all personal and national problems would be solved if all men should have this transformation. But in Christ the personal problem of sin, which is the "root cause" of many of our problems, would be answered. A new atmosphere could be created as we approach the complicated social and political problems of our corporate life. We would then have the inner strength, courage, and ability to cope with these problems. America can rise no higher than the individuals who walk her streets, conduct her business, teach her young people, make her homes, and attend her churches. It is these individuals who must be changed. As compelling as are the great social needs of our nation and of the world, these can only be met as individuals are themselves. It was to make new men and women that Christ came into the world.

Can Man Alter the Universe?

Americans were frequently compelled to consider the question that troubles Billy Graham, whether man can change society without first transforming himself through a religious conversion. The answers they have given have depended upon their views of the nature of the universe and of the efficacy of man's will to operate upon it.

In the seventeenth century the settlers in the New World were impressed, as were other Europeans, with the relative helplessness of human beings before God's power. How little was man capable of altering the world in which he lived if his very fate on earth, and for eternity, were predetermined by an all-powerful God. An extreme of this negative conception was set forth by Michael Wigglesworth in the section of "The Day of Doom" (1662) which considered the awful question of infant damnation (1). Wigglesworth (1631–1705) came to Massachusetts as a boy, studied at Harvard, and became a minister in Malden, Massachusetts. His poem was widely reprinted and its popularity testified to the widespread diffusion of his point of view.

This attitude gave way in the eighteenth century to a growing sense of man's capacity for altering the universe about him, which now came to be regarded as beneficent, reasonable, and subject to indefinite improvement. The success of the Revolution which identified patriotism with progress strengthened this optimistic faith. Joel Barlow (1754–1812) expressed these ideas in an epic poem which first appeared as "The Vision of Columbus" in 1787 and which was published in its final form as "The Columbiad" in 1807. In this work, Columbus, on the eve of his discovery, seeks enlightenment from a guiding spirit who traces the regular progress of mankind from its origins and anticipates that America will provide the ground for the culmination of the process of continual improvement (2).

In the first half of the nineteenth century the prospects for progress and for the indefinite improvement of mankind seemed unlimited. The advance in science and the application of intelligence to the problems of human life promised a hopeful generation of Americans that they could transform the world about them, and in doing so, that the nature of man himself could improve. These hopes found expression in thriving reform movements and also in the speculations of persuasive writers.

The most forceful debate of the issue came in New England, where religious and social conditions lent a special impetus to the reform impulse. William Ellery Channing (1780–1842), the well-known Unitarian divine, was representative of many hopeful men in his comments on the future. Addressing himself to the subject of a national literature, he was drawn into an extended hopeful discussion of human improvement (3). A little later the young lawyer and politician Charles Sumner (1811–74), who was just beginning the career that would lead him to the United States Senate, gave voice to the leading assumptions of his day in an address in 1848 to the Phi Beta Kappa Society of Union College (4). And the well-known poet Henry Wadsworth Longfellow (1807–82), commenting on the way in which old forms must give way to new ones, also implied that progress was inevitable (5).

There were significant forebodings even in these years that all would not go as well as the optimists imagined. In the South, the specter of the slavery question led many to wonder whether or not the reformers were realistic in their appraisal of the situation. More important, Nathaniel Hawthorne (1804–64), a thoughtful novelist, doubted that human nature was as thoroughly subject to manipulation as his contemporaries seemed to think. In the theme of a moving short story he embedded a penetrating criticism of the assumption that man through his own will could effect whatever change he wished (6).

In the latter half of the nineteenth century, however, the predominant mood remained optimistic despite the torment of the Civil War. Such poets as Walt Whitman (1819–92) and Emily Dickinson (1830–86) in different ways spoke of the continued capacity of man to improve himself through education (7) and to achieve great things through the exercise of his own will (8).

Forebodings as to the future acquired greater point after the opening of the twentieth century. The question had by then already been raised, whether the nation has reached or was approaching the end of its resources. George Perkins Marsh (1801–82), a lawyer, diplomat, and erudite scholar, in "Man and Nature" (1864) had pointed out that man could not simply be heedless of the harmonies and balances in the natural world (9). Now a widespread conservation movement argued that progress in the past had only been a factor of temporary opportunities for exploitation. Once those were exhausted, man would have to accept intractable limits to his ability to do what he liked .

On the other hand, there remained faith that planning and the ingenuity of invention compensate for the attrition of resources and permit further progress. Thus John Dos Passos (1896–   ), the novelist, in a sketch of Charles Steinmetz celebrated the power of inventive genius (10). President Franklin D. Roosevelt (1882–1945) summed up these hopes and fears in the Commonwealth Club Address of 1933 in which he set forth the dangers that the future might hold and yet expressed the determination to deal with its problems (11).

1. MICHAEL WIGGLESWORTH, from
The Day of Doom, 1662 *

Before his Throne a Trump is Blown,
    Proclaiming th' Day of Doom:
Forthwith he cries, *Ye Dead arise,*
    and unto Judgment come.
No sooner said, but 'tis obey'd;
    Sepulchers open'd are:
Dead Bodies all rise at his call,
    and's mighty power declare. . . .

Then to the Bar, all they drew near
    Who dy'd in Infancy,
And never had or good or bad
    effected pers'nally,
But from the womb unto the tomb
    were straightway carried,
(Or at the last e're they transgrest)
    who thus began to plead:

If for our own transgression,
    or disobedience,
We here did stand at thy left-hand
    just were the Recompence:
But *Adam's* guilt our souls hath spilt,
    his fault is charg'd on us;
And that alone hath overthrown
    and utterly undone us.

Not we, but he, ate of the Tree,
    whose fruit was interdicted:
Yet on us all of his sad Fall,
    the punishment's inflicted.
How could we sin that had not been,
    or how is his sin our,
Without consent, which to prevent,
    we never had a pow'r?

O great Creator, why was our Nature
    depraved and forlorn?
Why so defil'd and made so vild
    whilst we were yet unborn?
If it be just, and needs we must
    transgressors reck'ned be,
Thy Mercy, Lord, to us afford,
    which sinners hath set free.

Behold we see *Adam* set free,
    and sav'd from his trespass,
Whose sinful Fall hath spilt us all,
    and brought us to this pass.

Canst thou deny us once to try,
    or Grace to us to tender,
When he finds grace before thy face,
    that was the chief offender?

Then answered the Judge most dread,
    God doth such doom forbid,
That men should die eternally
    for what they never did.
But what you call old *Adam's* Fall,
    and only his Trespass,
You can amiss to call it his,
    both his and yours it was.

He was design'd of all Mankind
    to be a publick Head,
A common Root, whence all should
        shoot,
    and stood in all their stead.
He stood and fell, did ill or well,
    not for himself alone,
But for you all, who now his Fall
    and trespass would disown.

If he had stood, then all his brood
    had been established.
In Gods true love, never to move,
    nor once awry to tread:
Then all his Race, my Father's Grace,
    should have enjoy'd for ever,
And wicked Sprights by subtile sleights
    could them have harmed never.

Would you have griev'd to have
        receiv'd
    through *Adam* so much good,
As had been your for evermore,
    if he at first had stood?
Would you have said, we ne'r obey'd,
    nor did thy Laws regard;
It ill befits with benefits,
    us, Lord, to so reward?

Since then to share in his welfare,
    you could have been content,
You may with reason share in his
        treason,
    and in the punishment.

* Michael Wigglesworth, *The Day of Doom* (K. B. Murdock, ed.; New York, 1929) is
the best edition of the full text.

Hence you were born in state forlorn,
  with Natures so depraved;
Death was your due, because that you
  had thus your selves behaved.

You think if we had been as he,
  whom God did so betrust,
We to our cost would ne'er have lost
  all for a paltry Lust.
Had you been made in *Adam's* stead,
  you would like things have wrought,
And so into the self-same wo,
  yourselves and yours have brought.

I may deny you once to try,
  or Grace to you to tender,
Though he finds Grace before my face
  who was the chief offender;
Else should my Grace cease to be
    Grace;
  for it would not be free,
If to release whom I should please
  I have no libertee.

If upon one what's due to none
  I frankly shall bestow,
And on the rest shall not think best
  compassions skirt to throw,
Whom injure I? will you envy
  and grudge at others' weal?
Or me accuse, who do refuse
  your selves to help and heal?

Am I alone of what's my own,
  no Master or no Lord?
And if I am, how can you claim
  what I to some afford?
Will you demand Grace at my hand,
  and challenge what is mine?
Will you teach me whom to set free,
  and thus my Grace confine?

You sinners are, and such a share
  as sinners may expect,
Such you shall have; for I do save
  none but mine own Elect.
Yet to compare your sin with their,
  who liv'd a longer time,
I do confess yours is much less,
  though every sin's a crime.

A crime it is, therefore in bliss
  you may not hope to dwell;
But unto you I shall allow
  the easiest room in Hell.
The glorious King thus answering,
  they cease, and plead no longer:
Their Consciences must needs confess
  his Reasons are the stronger. . . .

2. JOEL BARLOW, from *The Columbiad, 1807**

[The guiding spirit outlines the stages of past progress for Columbus:]

One vast creation, lately borne abroad,
Cheers the young nations like a nurturing god. . . .
Tis the prolific Press; whose tablet, fraught
By graphic Genius with his painted thought,
Flings forth by millions the prodigious birth
And in a moment stocks the astonisht earth.
    Genius, enamor'd of his fruitful bride,
Assumes new force and elevates his pride.
No more, recumbent o'er his finger'd style,
He plods whole years each copy to compile. . . .
But bold and buoyant, with his sister Fame,
He strides o'er earth, holds high his ardent flame,
Calls up Discovery with her tube and scroll
And points the trembling magnet to the pole.

* Joel Barlow, *The Columbiad* (Paris, 1813), pp. 326–62.

Hence the brave Lusitanians stretch the sail,
Scorn guiding stars and tame the midsea gale;
And hence thy prow deprest the boreal wain,
Rear'd adverse heavens, a second earth to gain,
Ran down old Night, her western curtain thirl'd
And snatcht from swaddling shades an infant world.
    Rome, Athens, Memphis, Tyre! had you but known
This glorious triad, now familiar grown,
The Press, the Magnet faithful to its pole,
And earth's own movement round her stedfast goal;
Ne'er had your science from that splendid height,
Sunk in her strength nor seen succeeding night.
Her own utility had forced her sway,
All nations caught the fast extending ray,
Nature thro all her kingdoms oped the road,
Resign'd her secrets and her wealth bestow'd;
Her moral codes a like dominion rear'd,
Freedom been born and folly disappear'd,
War and his monsters sunk beneath her ban
And left the world to reason and to man.
    But now behold him bend his broader way,
Lift keener eyes and drink diviner day.
All systems scrutinize, their truths unfold,
Prove well the recent, well revise the old,
Reject all mystery and define with force
The point he aims at in his laboring course,—
To know these elements, learn how they wind,
Their wondrous webs of matter and of mind,
What springs, what guides organic life requires,
To move, rule, rein its ever changing gyres,
Improve and utilize each opening birth
And aid the labors of this nurturing earth.
But chief their moral soul he learns to trace,
That stronger chain which links and leads the race;
Which forms and sanctions every social tie
And blinds or clears their intellectual eye.
He strips that soul from every filmy shade
That schools had caught, that oracles had made,
Relumes her visual nerve, develops strong
The rules of right, the subtle shifts of wrong;
Of civil power draws clear the sacred line,
Gives to just government its right divine,
Forms, varies, fashions, as his lights increase,
Till earth is fill'd with happiness and peace.
    Already taught, thou knowest the fame that waits
His rising seat in thy confederate states:
There stands the model, thence he long shall draw
His forms of policy, his traits of law;
Each land shall imitate, each nation join
The well based brotherhood, the league divine,
Extend its empire with the circling sun,
And band the peopled globe within its federal zone.
    As thus he spoke, returning tears of joy
Suffused the Hero's cheek and pearl'd his eye:
Unveil, said he, my friend, and stretch once more

Beneath my view that heaven-illumined shore;
Let me behold her silver beams expand
To lead all nations, lighten every land,
Instruct the total race and teach at last
Their toils to lessen and their chains to cast,
Trace and attain the purpose of their birth
And hold in peace this heritage of earth.
The Seraph smiled consent; the Hero's eye
Watcht for the daybeam round the changing sky. . . .

[The guiding spirit then outlines the stages of future progress:]

First of his future stages, thou shalt see
His trade unfetter'd and his ocean free.
From thy young states the code consoling springs
To strip from vulture War his naval wings;
In views so just all Europe's powers combine,
And earth's full voice approves the vast design.
Tho still her inland realms the combat wage
And hold in lingering broils the unsettled age,
Yet no rude shocks that shake the crimson plain
Shall more disturb the labors of the main;
The main that spread so wide his travell'd way,
Liberal as air, impartial as the day,
That all thy race the common wealth might share,
Exchange their fruits and fill their treasures there,
Their speech assimilate, their counsels blend,
Till mutual interest fix the mutual friend.
Now see, my son, the destined hour advance;
Safe in their leagues commercial navies dance,
Leave their curst cannon on the quay-built strand
And like the stars of heaven a fearless course command.
The Hero lookt; beneath his wondering eyes
Gay streamers lengthen round the seas and skies;
The countless nations open all their stores,
Load every wave and crowd the lively shores;
Bright sails in mingling mazes streak the air,
And commerce triumphs o'er the rage of war.
From Baltic streams, from Elba's opening side,
From Rhine's long course and Texel's laboring tide,
From Gaul, from Albion, tired of fruitless fight,
From green Hibernia, clothed in recent light,
Hispania's strand that two broad oceans lave,
From Senegal and Gambia's golden wave,
Tago the rich and Douro's viny shores,
The sweet Canaries and the soft Azores,
Commingling barks their mutual banners hail
And drink by turns the same distending gale.
Thro Calpe's strait that leads the Midland main,
From Adria, Pontus, Nile's resurgent reign,
The sails look forth and wave their bandrols high
And ask their breezes from a broader sky.
Where Asia's isles and utmost shorelands bend,
Like rising suns the sheeted masts ascend;
Coast after coast their flowing flags unrol,
From Deimen's rocks to Zembla's ice-propt pole,

Where Behren's pass collapsing worlds divides,
Where California breaks the billowy tides,
Peruvian streams their golden margins boast,
Or Chili bluffs or Plata flats the coast.
Where, clothed in splendor, his Atlantic way
Spreads the blue borders of Hesperian day,
From all his havens, with majestic sweep,
The swiftest boldest daughters of the deep
Swarm forth before him; till the cloudlike train
From pole to pole o'ersheet the whitening main.
   Where Grecian states in even balance hung
And warm'd with jealous fires the patriot's tongue,
The exclusive ardor cherisht in the breast
Love to one land and Hatred to the rest.
And where the flames of civil discord rage,
And Roman arms with Roman arms engage,
The mime of virtue rises still the same
To build a Cesar's as a Pompey's name.
   But now no more the patriotic mind,
To narrow views and local laws confined,
Gainst neighboring lands directs the public rage,
Plods for a clan or counsels for an age;
But soars to loftier thoughts and reaches far
Beyond the power, beyond the wish of war;
For realms and ages forms the general aim,
Makes patriot views and moral views the same,
Works with enlighten'd zeal, to see combined
The strength and happiness of humankind.
   Long had Columbus with delighted eyes
Markt all the changes that around him rise,
Lived thro descending ages as they roll
And feasted still the still expanding soul;
When now the peopled regions swell more near,
And a mixt noise tumultuous stuns his ear.
At first, like heavy thunders roll'd in air,
Or the rude shock of cannonading war,
Or waves resounding on the craggy shore,
Hoarse roll'd the loud-toned undulating roar.
But soon the sounds like human voices rise,
All nations pouring undistinguisht cries;
Till more distinct the wide concussion grown
Rolls forth at times an accent like his own.
By turns the tongues assimilating blend,
And smoother idioms over earth ascend;
Mingling and softening still in every gale,
O'er discord's din, harmonious tones prevail.
At last a simple universal sound
Winds thro the welkin, soothes the world around,
From echoing shores in swelling strain replies
And moves melodious o'er the warbling skies,
   Such wild commotions as he heard and view'd,
In fixt astonishment the Hero stood
And thus besought the Guide: Celestial friend,
What good to man can these dread scenes intend? . . .
Tell then, my Seer, if future earthquakes sleep,

Closed in the conscious caverns of the deep,
Waiting the day of vengeance, when to roll
And rock the rending pillars of the pole.
Or tell if aught more dreadful to my race
In these dark signs they heavenly wisdom trace;
And why the loud discordance melts again
In the smooth glidings of a tuneful strain.

The guardian god replied: Thy fears give o'er;
War's hosted hounds shall havoc earth no more;
No sore distress these signal sounds foredoom,
But give the pledge of peaceful years to come;
The tongues of nations here their accents blend,
Till one pure language thro the world extend.

Thou knowst the tale of Babel; how the skies
Fear'd for their safety as they felt him rise,
Sent unknown jargons mid the laboring bands,
Confused their converse and unnerved their hands,
Dispersed the bickering tribes and drove them far
From peaceful toil to violence and war;
Bade kings arise with bloody flags unfurl'd,
Bade pride and conquest wander o'er the world,
Taught adverse creeds, commutual hatreds bred,
Till holy homicide the climes o'erspread.
—For that fine apologue, with mystic strain,
Gave like the rest of a golden age (50) to man,
Ascribed perfection to his infant state,
Science unsought and all his arts innate;
Supposed the experience of the growing race
Must lead him retrograde and cramp his pace,
Obscure his vision as his lights increast
And sink him from an angel to a beast.

Tis thus the teachers of despotic sway
Strive in all times to blot his inward day,
To keep him curb'd nor let him lift his eyes
To see where happiness, where misery lies.
They lead him blind, and o'er each newborn light
Cast their own shadows, renovate the night,
Crush every art that might the mind expand
And plant with demons every desert land;
That, fixt in straiten'd bounds, their lust of power
May ravage still and still the race devour.
An easy prey the hoodwinkt hordes remain,
And oceans roll and shores extend in vain.

Long have they reign'd; till now the race at last
Shake off their manacles, their blinders cast,
O'errule the crimes their fraudful foes produce,
By ways unseen to serve the happiest use,
Tempt the wide wave, probe every yielding soil,
Fill with their fruits the hardy hand of toil,
Unite their forces, wheel the conquering car,
Deal mutual death, but civilize by war.

Dear bought the experiment and hard the strife
Of social man, that rear'd his arts to life.
His passions wild that agitate the mind,
His reason calm, their watchful guide design'd,

While yet unreconciled, his march restrain,
Mislead the judgment and betray the man.
Fear, his first passion, long maintain'd the sway,
Long shrouded in its glooms the mental ray,
Shook, curb'd, controll'd his intellectual force
And bore him wild thro many a devious course.
Long had his Reason, with experienced eye,
Perused the book of earth and scaled the sky,
Led fancy, memory, foresight in her train,
And o'er creation stretcht her vast domain;
Yet would that rival Fear her strength appal;
In that one conflict always sure to fall,
Mild Reason shunn'd the foe she could not brave,
Renounced her empire and remained a slave.
But deathless, tho debased, she still could find
Some beams of truth to pour upon the mind;
And tho she dared no moral code to scan,
Thro physic forms she learnt to lead the man;
To strengthen thus his opening orbs of sight
And nerve and clear them for a stronger light.
That stronger light, from nature's double codes,
Now springs expanding and his doubts explodes;
All nations catch it, all their tongues combine
To hail the human morn and greet the day divine.
At this blest period, when the total race
Shall speak one language and all truths embrace,
Instruction clear a speedier course shall find,
And open earlier on the infant mind.
No foreign terms shall crowd with barbarous rules
The dull unmeaning pageantry of schools;
Nor dark authorities nor names unknown
Fill the learn'd head with ignorance not its own;
But wisdom's eye with beams unclouded shine,
And simplest rules her native charms define;
One living language, one unborrow'd dress
Her boldest flights with fullest force express;
Triumphant virtue, in the garb of truth,
Win a pure passage to the heart of youth,
Pervade all climes where suns or oceans roll
And warm the world with one great moral soul,
To see, facilitate, attain the scope
Of all their labor and of all their hope. . . .
Thus heard Columbus, eager to behold
The famed Apocalypse its years unfold; . . .
Eager he lookt. Another train of years
Had roll'd unseen and brighten'd still their spheres;
Earth more resplendent in the floods of day
Assumed new smiles and flusht around him lay.
Green swell the mountains, calm the oceans roll,
Fresh beams of beauty kindle round the pole;
Thro all the range where shores and seas extend,
In tenfold pomp the works of peace ascend.
Robed in the bloom of spring's eternal year,
And ripe with fruits the same glad fields appear;
O'er hills and vales perennial gardens run,

Cities unwall'd stand sparkling to the sun;
The streams all freighted from the bounteous plain
Swell with the load and labor to the main,
Whose stormless waves command a steadier gale
And prop the pinions of a bolder sail:
Sway'd with the floating weight each ocean toils,
And joyous nature's full perfection smiles.

   Fill'd with unfolding fate, the vision'd age
Now leads its actors on a broader stage;
When clothed majestic in the robes of state,
Moved by one voice, in general congress meet
The legates of all empires. Twas the place
Where man first sought to socialize his race;
Ere yet beguiled, the dark delirious hordes
Began to fight for altars and for lords;
Nile washes still the soil and feels once more
The works of wisdom press his peopled shore.

   In this mid site, this monumental clime,
Rear'd by all realms to brave the wrecks of time
A spacious dome swells up, commodious great,
The last resort, the unchanging scene of state.
On rocks of adamant the walls ascend,
Tall columns heave and sky-like arches bend;
Bright o'er the golden roofs the glittering spires
Far in the concave meet the solar fires;
Four blazing fronts, with gates unfolding high,
Look with immortal splendor round the sky.
Hither the delegated sires ascend,
And all the cares of every clime attend.

   As the blest guardian guides, to whom was given
To light the suns and steer the stars of heaven,
(When one great cosmogyre has proved their spheres,
And time well taught them how to wind their years)
Shall meet in general council; call'd to state
The laws and labors that their charge await;
To learn, to teach, to settle how to hold
Their course more glorious, as their lights unfold:
From all the bounds of space (the mandate known)
They wing their passage to the eternal throne;
Each thro his far dim sky illumes the road
And sails and centres tow'rd the mount of God;
There, in mid universe, their seats to rear,
Exchange their counsels and their works compare:
So, from all tracts of earth, this gathering throng
In ships and chariots shape their course along,
Reach with unwonted speed the place assign'd
To hear and give the counsels of mankind.

   South of the sacred mansion, first resort
The assembled sires, and pass the spacious court.
Here in his porch earth's figured Genius stands,
Truth's mighty mirror poising in his hands;
Graved on the pedestal and chased in gold,
Man's noblest arts their symbol forms unfold,
His tillage and his trade; with all the store
Of wondrous fabrics and of useful lore:

Labors that fashion to his sovereign sway
Earth's total powers, her soil and air and sea;
Force them to yield their fruits at his known call,
And bear his mandates round the rolling ball.
Beneath the footstool all destructive things,
The mask of priesthood and the mace of kings,
Lie trampled in the dust; for here at last
Fraud, folly, error all their emblems cast.
Each envoy here unloads his wearied hand
Of some old idol from his native land;
One flings a pagod on the mingled heap,
One lays a crescent, one a cross to sleep;
Swords, sceptres, mitres, crowns and globes and stars,
Codes of false fame and stimulants to wars
Sink in the settling mass; since guile began,
These are the agents of the woes of man.
    Now the full concourse, where the arches bend,
Pour thro by thousands and their seats ascend.
Far as the centred eye can range around,
Or the deep trumpet's solemn voice resound,
Long rows of reverend sires sublime extend,
And cares of worlds on every brow suspend.
High in the front, for soundest wisdom known,
A sire elect in peerless grandeur shone;
He open'd calm the universal cause
To give each realm its limit and its laws,
Bid the last breath of tired contention cease
And bind all regions in the leagues of peace;
Till one confederate, condependent sway
Spread with the sun and bound the walks of day,
One centred system, one all ruling soul
Live thro the parts and regulate the whole.
    Here then, said Hesper, with a blissful smile,
Behold the fruits of thy long years of toil.
To yon bright borders of Atlantic day
Thy swelling pinions led the trackless way
And taught mankind such useful deeds to dare,
To trace new seas and happy nations rear;
Till by fraternal hands their sails unfurl'd
Have waved at last in union o'er the world.
    Then let thy stedfast soul no more complain
Of dangers braved and griefs endured in vain,
Of courts insidious, envy's poison'd stings,
The loss of empire and the frown of kings;
While these broad views thy better thoughts compose
To spurn the malice of insulting foes;
And all the joys descending ages gain
Repay thy labors and remove thy pain.

3. WILLIAM ELLERY CHANNING, *On National Literature, 1830**

The question which we most solicitously ask about this country is, what race of men it is likely to produce. We consider its liberty of value only as far as it favors the growth of men. What is liberty? The removal of restraint from human powers. Its benefit is that it opens new fields for action and a wider range for the mind. The only freedom worth possessing is that which gives enlargement to a people's energy, intellect, and virtues. The savage makes his boast of freedom. But what is its worth? Free as he is, he continues for ages in the same ignorance, leads the same comfortless life, sees the same untamed wilderness spread around him. He is indeed free from what he calls the yoke of civil institutions. But other and worse chains bind him. The very privation of civil government is in effect a chain; for, by withholding protection from property, it virtually shackles the arm of industry, and forbids exertion for the melioration of his lot. Progress, the growth of power, is the end and boon of liberty; and, without this, a people may have the name, but want the substance and spirit of freedom.

We are the more earnest in enlarging on these views because we feel that our attachment to our country must be very much proportioned to what we deem its tendency to form a generous race of men. We pretend not to have thrown off national feeling; but we have some stronger feelings. We love our country much, but mankind more. As men and Christians, our first desire is to see the improvement of human nature. We desire to see the soul of man wiser, firmer, nobler, more conscious of its imperishable treasures,

more beneficent and powerful, more alive to its connection with God, more able to use pleasure and prosperity aright, and more victorious over poverty, adversity, and pain. In our survey of our own and other countries, the great question which comes to us is this, Where and under what institutions are men most likely to advance? . . . What nation possesses, in its history, its traditions, its government, its religion, its manners, its pursuits, its relations to other communities, and especially in its private and public means of education, the instruments and pledges of a more resolute virtue and devotion to truth than we now witness? Such a nation, be it where it may, will engage our warmest interest. We love our country, but not blindly. In all nations we recognize one great family, and our chief wish for our native land is that it may take the first rank among the lights and benefactors of the human race.

These views will explain the vast importance which we attach to a national literature. By this, as we have said, we understand the expression of a nation's mind in writing. It is the action of the most gifted understandings on the community. It throws into circulation through a wide sphere the most quickening and beautiful thoughts which have grown up in men of laborious study or creative genius. It is a much higher work than the communication of a gifted intellect in discourse. It is the mind giving to multitudes, whom no voice can reach, its compressed and selected thoughts in the most lucid order and attractive forms which it is capable of inventing. In other words, literature

* William Ellery Channing, *Works* (Boston, 1843), I, 246–80.

is the concentration of intellect for the purpose of spreading itself abroad and multiplying its energy.

Such being the nature of literature, it is plainly among the most powerful methods of exalting the character of a nation, of forming a better race of men; in truth, we apprehend that it may claim the first rank among the means of improvement. We know nothing so fitted to the advancement of society as to bring its higher minds to bear upon the multitude; as to establish close connections between the more or less gifted; as to spread far and wide the light which springs up in meditative, profound, and sublime understandings. It is the ordinance of God, and one of his most benevolent laws, that the human race should be carried forward by impulses which originate in a few minds, perhaps in an individual; and in this way the most interesting relations and dependencies of life are framed. When a great truth is to be revealed, it does not flash at once on the race, but dawns and brightens on a superior understanding, from which it is to emanate and to illuminate future ages. On the faithfulness of great minds to this awful function, the progress and happiness of men chiefly depend. . . .

The quickening influences of literature need not be urged on those who are familiar with the history of modern Europe, and who of course know the spring given to the human mind by the revival of ancient learning. Through their writings the great men of antiquity have exercised a sovereignty over these later ages not enjoyed in their own. It is more important to observe that the influence of literature is perpetually increasing; for, through the press and the spread of education, its sphere is indefinitely enlarged. Reading, once the privilege of a few, is now the occupation of multitudes, and is to become one of the chief gratifications of all. Books penetrate everywhere, and some of the works of genius find their way to obscure dwellings which, a little while ago, seemed barred against all intellectual light. Writing is now the mightiest instrument on earth. Through this the mind has acquired a kind of omnipresence. To literature we then look as the chief means of forming a better race of human beings. To superior minds, which may act through this, we look for the impulses by which their country is to be carried forward. We would teach them that they are the depositaries of the highest power on earth, and that on them the best hopes of society rest.

We are aware that some may think that we are exalting intellectual above moral and religious influence. They may tell us that the teaching of moral and religious truth, not by philosophers and boasters of wisdom, but by the comparatively weak and foolish, is the great means of renovating the world. This truth we indeed regard as "the power of God unto salvation." But let none imagine that its chosen temple is an uncultivated mind, and that it selects, as its chief organs, the lips of the unlearned. Religious and moral truth is indeed appointed to carry forward mankind, but not as conceived and expounded by narrow minds, not as darkened by the ignorant, not as debased by the superstitious, not as subtilized by the visionary, not as thundered out by the intolerant fanatic, not as turned into a driveling cant by the hypocrite. Like all other truths, it requires for its full reception and powerful communication a free and vigorous intellect. Indeed, its grandeur and infinite connections demand a more earnest and various use of our faculties than any other subject. As a single illustration of this remark, we may observe that all moral and religious truth may be reduced to one great and central thought, perfection of mind, a thought which comprehends all that is glorious in the Divine nature, and which reveals to us the end and happiness of our own existence. This perfection has as yet only dawned on the most gifted human beings, and the great purpose of our present and future existence is to enlarge our conceptions of it without end, and to embody and make them manifest in character and life. And is this sublime thought to grow within us, to refine itself from error and impure mixture, to receive perpetual accessions of brightness from the study of God, man, and nature, and especially to be communicated powerfully to others, without the vigorous exertion of our intellectual nature? Religion has been wronged by nothing more than by being separated from intellect, than by being removed from the province of reason and free research into that of mystery and authority, of impulse and feeling. Hence it is that the prevalent forms or exhibitions of Christianity are comparatively inert, and that most which is written on the subject is of little or no worth. Christianity was given not to contradict and degrade the rational nature, but to call it forth, to enlarge its range and its powers. It admits of endless development. It is the last truth which should remain stationary. It ought to be so explored and so expressed as to take the highest place in a nation's literature, as to exalt and purify all other literature. From these remarks it will be seen that the efficacy which we have ascribed to literary or intellectual influence in the work of human improvement is consistent with the supreme importance of moral and religious truth.

If we have succeeded in conveying the impressions which we have aimed to make, our readers are now prepared to inquire with interest into the condition and prospects of literature among ourselves. Do we possess, indeed, what may be called a national literature? Have we produced eminent writers in the various departments of intellectual effort? Are our chief resources of instruction and literary enjoyment furnished from ourselves? We regret that the reply to these questions is so obvious. The few standard works which we have produced, and which promise to live, can hardly, by any courtesy, be denominated a national literature. On this point, if marks and proofs of our real condition were needed, we should find them in the current apologies for our deficiencies. Our writers are accustomed to plead in our excuse our youth, the necessities of a newly settled country, and the direction of our best talents to practical life. Be the pleas sufficient or not, one thing they prove, and that is, our consciousness of having failed to make important contributions to the interests of the intellect. We have few names to place by the side of the great names in science and literature on the other side of the ocean. We want those lights which make a country conspicuous at a distance. . . .

We are accustomed to console ourselves for the absence of a commanding literature by urging our superiority to other nations in our institutions for the diffusion of elementary knowledge through all classes of the community. We have here just cause for boasting, though perhaps less than we imagine. That there are gross deficiencies in our common schools, and that the amount of knowledge which they communicate, when compared with the time spent in its acquisition, is lamentably small, the community begin to feel. There is a crying need for a higher and more quickening kind of instruction than the laboring part of society have yet received, and we rejoice that the cry begins to be heard. But, allowing our elementary institutions to be ever so perfect, we confess that they do not satisfy us. We want something more. A dead level of intellect, even if it should rise above what is common in other nations, would not answer our wishes and hopes for our country. We want great minds to be formed among us, —minds which shall be felt afar, and through which we may act on the world. We want the human intellect to do its utmost here. We want this people to obtain a claim on the gratitude of the human race by adding strength to the foundation, and fulness and splendor to the development of moral and religious truth; by originality of thought, by discoveries of science, and by contributions to the refining pleasures of taste and imagination.

With these views, we do and must lament that, however we surpass other nations in providing for and spreading elementary instruction, we fall behind many in provision for the liberal training of the intellect, for forming great scholars, for communicating that profound knowledge, and that thirst for higher truths, which can alone originate a commanding literature. The truth ought to be known. There is among us much superficial knowledge, but little severe, persevering research; little of that consuming passion for new truth which makes outward things worthless; little resolute devotion to a high intellectual culture. . . .

We boast of our political institutions, and receive our chief teachings, books, impressions, from the school of monarchy. True, we labor under disadvantages. But, if our liberty deserves the praise which it receives, it is more than a balance for these. We believe that it is. We believe that it does open to us an indefinite intellectual progress. Did we not so regard it, we should value it little. If heredi-

tary governments minister most to the growth of the mind, it were better to restore them than to cling to a barren freedom. Let us not expose liberty to this reproach. Let us prove, by more generous provisions for the diffusion of elementary knowledge, for the training of great minds, and for the joint culture of the moral and intellectual powers, that we are more and more instructed by freedom in the worth and greatness of human nature, and in the obligation of contributing to its strength and glory.

We have spoken of the condition of our literature. We now proceed to the consideration of the causes which obstruct its advancement; and we are immediately struck by one so prevalent as to deserve distinct notice. We refer to the common doctrine that we need, in this country, useful knowledge rather than profound, extensive, and elegant literature, and that this last, if we covet it, may be imported from abroad in such variety and abundance as to save us the necessity of producing it among ourselves. How far are these opinions just? This question we purpose to answer.

That useful knowledge should receive our first and chief care we mean not to dispute. . . . We . . . prize, as highly as any, useful knowledge. But by this we mean knowledge which answers and ministers to our complex and various nature; we mean that which is useful, not only to the animal man, but to the intellectual, moral, and religious man,—useful to a being of spiritual faculties, whose happiness is to be found in their free and harmonious exercise. We grant that there is primary necessity for that information and skill by which subsistence is earned and life is preserved; for it is plain that we must live in order to act and improve. But life is the means; action and improvement the end; and who will deny that the noblest utility belongs to that knowledge by which the chief purpose of our creation is accomplished? According to these views, a people should honor and cultivate, as unspeakably useful, that literature which corresponds to and calls forth the highest faculties; which expresses and communicates energy of thought, fruitfulness of invention, force of moral purpose, a thirst for the true, and a delight in the beautiful. According to these views we attach special importance to those branches of literature which relate to human nature, and which give it a consciousness of its own powers. History has a noble use, for it shows us human beings in various and opposite conditions, in their strength and weakness, in their progress and relapses, and thus reveals the causes and means by which the happiness and virtue of the race may be enlarged. Poetry is useful, by touching deep springs in the human soul; by giving voice to its more delicate feelings; by breathing out and making more intelligible the sympathy which subsists between the mind and the outward universe; by creating beautiful forms of manifestations for great moral truths. Above all, that higher philosophy, which treats of the intellectual and moral constitution of man, of the foundation of knowledge, of duty, of perfection, of our relations to the spiritual world, and especially to God,—this has a usefulness so peculiar as to throw other departments of knowledge into obscurity; and a people among whom this does not find honor has little ground to boast of its superiority to uncivilized tribes. It will be seen from these remarks that utility with us has a broad meaning. In truth, we are slow to condemn as useless any researches or discoveries of original and strong minds, even when we discern in them no bearing on any interests of mankind; for all truth is of a prolific nature, and has

connections not immediately perceived; and it may be that what we call vain speculations may, at no distant period, link themselves with some new facts or theories, and guide a profound thinker to the most important results. The ancient mathematician, when absorbed in solitary thought, little imagined that his theorems, after the lapse of ages, were to be applied by the mind of Newton to the solution of the mysteries of the universe, and not only to guide the astronomer through the heavens, but the navigator through the pathless ocean. For ourselves, we incline to hope much from truths which are particularly decried as useless; for the noblest and most useful truth is of an abstract or universal nature: and yet the abstract, though susceptible of infinite application, is generally, as we know, opposed to the practical.

We maintain that a people which has any serious purpose of taking a place among improved communities should studiously promote within itself every variety of intellectual exertion. It should resolve strenuously to be surpassed by none. It should feel that mind is the creative power through which all the resources of nature are to be turned to account, and by which a people is to spread its influence, and establish the noblest form of empire. It should train within itself men able to understand and to use whatever is thought and discovered over the whole earth. The whole mass of human knowledge should exist among a people not in neglected libraries, but in its higher minds. Among its most cherished institutions should be those which will ensure to it ripe scholars, explorers of ancient learning, profound historians and mathematicians, intellectual laborers devoted to physical and moral science, and to the creation of a refined and beautiful literature. . . .

We now proceed to an argument in favor of native literature which, if less obvious, is, we believe, not less sound than those now already adduced. We have hitherto spoken of literature as the expression, the communication of the higher minds in a community. We now add that it does much more than is commonly supposed to *form* such minds, so that without it a people wants one of the chief means of educating or perfecting talent and genius. One of the great laws of our nature, and a law singularly important to social beings, is that the intellect enlarges and strengthens itself by expressing worthily its best views. In this as in other respects it is more blessed to give than to receive. Superior minds are formed, not merely by solitary thought, but almost as much by communication. Great thoughts are never fully possessed till he who has conceived them has given them fit utterance. One of the noblest and most invigorating labors of genius is to clothe its conceptions in clear and glorious forms, to give them existence in other souls. Thus literature creates, as well as manifests, intellectual power, and without it the highest minds will never be summoned to the most invigorating action.

We doubt whether a man ever brings his faculties to bear with their whole force on a subject until he writes upon it for the instruction or gratification of others. To place it clearly before others, he feels the necessity of viewing it more vividly himself. By attempting to seize his thoughts and fix them in an enduring form, he finds them vague and unsatisfactory to a degree which he did not suspect, and toils for a precision and harmony of views of which he had never before felt the need. He places his subject in new lights,—submits it to a searching analysis, compares and connects with it his various

knowledge, seeks for it new illustrations and analogies, weighs objections, and through these processes often arrives at higher truths than he at first aimed to illustrate. . . .

If we confine ourselves simply to the consideration of style, we shall have reason to think that a people among whom this is neglected wants one important intellectual aid. In this great power is exerted, and by exertion increased. To the multitude, indeed, language seems so natural an instrument that to use it with clearness and energy seems no great effort. It is framed, they think, to the writer's hand, and so continually employed as to need little thought or skill. But in nothing is the creative power of a gifted writer seen more than in his style. True, his words may be found in the dictionary. But there they lie disjointed and dead. What a wonderful life does he breathe into them by compacting them into his sentences! Perhaps he uses no term which has not yet been hackneyed by ordinary writers; and yet with these vulgar materials what miracles does he achieve! What a world of thought does he condense into a phrase! By new combinations of common words what delicate hues or what a blaze of light does he pour over his subject! Power of style depends very little on the structure or copiousness of the language which the writer of genius employs, but chiefly, if not wholly, on his own mind. The words arranged in his dictionary are no more fitted to depict his thoughts than the block of marble in the sculptor's shop to show forth the conceptions which are dawning in his mind. Both are inert materials. The power which pervades them comes from the soul; and the same creative energy is manifested in the production of a noble style as in extracting beautiful forms from lifeless stone. How unfaithful, then, is a nation to its own intellect in which grace and force of style receive no culture! . . .

We come now to our last—and what we deem a weighty—argument in favor of a native literature. We desire and would cherish it, because we hope from it important aids to the cause of truth and human nature. We believe that a literature springing up in this new soil would bear new fruits, and, in some respects, more precious fruits than are elsewhere produced. We know that our hopes may be set down to the account of that national vanity which, with too much reason, is placed by foreigners among our besetting sins. But we speak from calm and deliberate conviction. We are inclined to believe that, as a people, we occupy a position from which the great subjects of literature may be viewed more justly than from those which most other nations hold. Undoubtedly we labor under disadvantages. We want the literary apparatus of Europe,—her libraries, her universities, her learned institutions, her race of professed scholars, her spots consecrated by the memory of sages, and a thousand stirring associations which hover over ancient nurseries of learning. But the mind is not a local power. Its spring is within itself, and under the inspiration of liberal and high feeling it may attain and worthily express nobler truth than outward helps could reveal.

The great distinction of our country is, that we enjoy some peculiar advantages for understanding our own nature. Man is the great subject of literature, and juster and profounder views of man may be expected here than elsewhere. In Europe political and artificial distinctions have, more or less, triumphed over and obscured our common nature. In Europe we meet kings, nobles, priests, peasants. How much rarer is it to meet *men;* by which we mean human beings conscious of their own nature, and conscious of the utter worthlessness of all outward distinctions compared with what is treasured up in their own souls. Man does not value himself as man. It is for his blood, his rank, or some artificial distinction, and not for the attributes of humanity, that he holds himself in respect. The institutions of the Old World all tend to throw obscurity over what we most need to know, and that is, the worth and claims of a human being. We know that great improvements in this respect are going on abroad. Still, the many are too often postponed to the few. The mass of men are regarded as instruments to work with, as materials to be shaped for the use of their superiors. That consciousness of our own nature which contains, as a germ, all nobler thoughts, which teaches us at once self-respect and respect for others, and which binds us to God by filial sentiment and hope, —this has been repressed, kept down by establishments founded in force; and literature, in all its departments, bears, we think, the traces of this inward degradation. We conceive that our position favors a juster and profounder estimate of human nature. We mean not to boast, but there are fewer obstructions to that moral consciousness, that consciousness of humanity, of which we have spoken. Man is not hidden from us by so many disguises as in the Old World. The essential equality of all human beings, founded on the possession of a spiritual, progressive, immortal nature, is, we hope, better understood; and nothing more than this single conviction is needed to work the mightiest changes in every province of human life and of human thought.

We have stated what seems to us our most important distinction. But our position has other advantages. The mere circumstance of its being a new one gives reason to hope for some new intellectual activity, some fresher views of nature and life. We are not borne down by the weight of antiquated institutions, time-hallowed abuses, and the remnants of feudal barbarism. The absence of a religious establishment is an immense gain, as far as originality of mind is in question; for an establishment, however advantageous in other respects, is, by its nature, hostile to discovery and progress. To keep the mind where it is, to fasten the notions of one age on all future time, is its aim and proper business; and if it happened, as has generally been the case, to grow up in an age of strife and passion, when, as history demonstrates, the church was overrun with error, it cannot but perpetuate darkness and mental bondage. Among us, intellect, though far from being free, has broken some of the chains of other countries, and is more likely, we conceive, to propose to itself its legitimate object, truth,—everlasting and universal truth.

We have no thought of speaking contemptuously of the literature of the Old World. It is our daily nutriment. We feel our debt to be immense to the glorious company of pure and wise minds which in foreign lands have bequeathed us in writing their choicest thoughts and holiest feelings. Still, we feel that all existing literature has been produced under influences which have necessarily mixed with it much error and corruption; and that the whole of it ought to pass, and must pass, under rigorous review. For example, we think that the history of the human race is to be rewritten. Men imbued with the prejudices which thrive under aristocracies and state religions cannot understand it. Past ages, with their great events and great men, are to undergo, we think, a new trial, and yield new results. It is plain that history is already viewed under new aspects, and we believe that the true principles for studying and writing it are to be unfolded here, at least as rapidly as in other countries. It seems to us that in literature an immense work is yet to be done. The most interesting questions to mankind are yet in debate. Great principles are yet to be settled in criticism, in morals, in politics; and, above all, the true character of religion is to be rescued from the disguises and corruptions of ages. We want a reformation. We want a literature in which genius will pay supreme, if not undivided, homage to truth and virtue; in which the childish admiration of what has been called greatness will give place to a wise moral judgment, which will breathe reverence for the mind and elevating thoughts of God. The part which this country is to bear in this great intellectual reform we presume not to predict. We feel, however, that, if true to itself, it will have the glory and happiness of giving new impulses to the human mind. This is our cherished hope. We should have no heart to encourage native literature, did we not hope that it would become instinct with a new spirit. We cannot admit the thought that this country is to be only a repetition of the Old World. We delight to believe that God, in the fulness of time, has brought a new continent to light, in order that the human mind should move here with a new freedom, should frame new social institutions, should explore new paths and reap new harvests. We are accustomed to estimate nations by their creative energies; and we shall blush for our country if, in circumstances so peculiar, original, and creative, it shall satisfy itself with a passive reception and mechanical reiteration of the thoughts of strangers.

We have now completed our remarks on the importance of a native literature. The next great topic is the means of producing it. And here our limits forbid us to enlarge; yet we cannot pass it over in silence. A primary and essential means of the improvement of our literature is, that, as a people, we should feel its value, should desire it, should demand it, should encourage it, and should give it a hearty welcome. It will come if called for; and, under this conviction, we have now labored to create a want for it in the community. We say that we must call for it, by which we mean not merely that we must invite it by good wishes and kind words, but must make liberal provision for intellectual education. We must enlarge our literary institutions, secure more extensive and profound teaching, and furnish helps and resources to men of superior talent for continued laborious research. As yet intellectual labor, devoted to a thorough investigation and a full development of great subjects, is almost unknown among us; and without it we shall certainly rear few lasting monuments of thought. We boast of our primary schools. We want universities worthy of the name, where a man of genius and literary zeal may possess himself of all that is yet known, and may strengthen himself by intercourse with kindred minds. We know it will be said that we cannot afford these. But it is not so. We are rich enough for ostentation, for intemperance, for luxury. We can lavish millions on fashion, on furniture, on dress, on our palaces, on our pleasures; but we have nothing to spend for the mind. Where lies our poverty? In the purse or in the soul?

We have spoken of improved institutions as essential to an improved literature. We beg, however, not to be misunderstood, as if these were invested with a creating power, or would necessarily yield the results which we desire. They are the means, not causes, of advancement. Literature depends on individual genius, and this, though

fostered, cannot be created by outward helps. No human mechanism can produce original thought. After all the attempts to explain by education the varieties of intellect, we are compelled to believe that minds, like all the other products of nature, have original and indestructible differences, that they are not exempted from that great and beautiful law which joins with strong resemblances as strong diversities; and, of consequence, we believe that the men who are to be the lights of the world bring with them their commission and power from God. Still, whilst institutions cannot create, they may and do unfold genius; and, for want of them, great minds often slumber or run to waste, whilst a still larger class, who want genius, but possess admirable powers, fail of that culture through which they might enjoy and approach their more gifted brethren.

A people, as we have said, are to give aid to literature by founding wise and enlarged institutions. They may do much more. They may exert a nobler patronage. By cherishing in their own breasts the love of truth, virtue, and freedom, they may do much to nurse and kindle genius in its favored possessors. There is a constant reaction between a community and the great minds which spring up within it, and they form one another. In truth, great minds are developed more by the spirit and character of the people to which they belong than by all other causes. Thus a free spirit, a thirst for new and higher knowledge in a community, does infinitely more for literature than the most splendid benefactions under despotism. A nation under any powerful excitement becomes fruitful of talent. Among a people called to discuss great questions, to contend for great interests, to make great sacrifices for the public weal, we always find new and unsuspected energies of thought brought out. A mercenary, selfish, luxurious, sensual people, toiling only to secure the pleasures of sloth, will often communicate their own softness and baseness to the superior minds which dwell among them. In this impure atmosphere the celestial spark burns dim; and well will it be if God's great gift of genius be not impiously prostituted to lust and crime.

In conformity with the views now stated, we believe that literature is to be carried forward, here and elsewhere, chiefly by some new and powerful impulses communicated to society; and it is a question naturally suggested by this discussion from what impulse, principle, excitement, the highest action of the mind may now be expected. When we look back, we see that literature has been originated and modified by a variety of principles,—by patriotism and national feeling, by reverence for antiquity, by the spirit of innovation, by enthusiasm, by scepticism, by the passion for fame, by romantic love, and by political and religious convulsions. Now we do not expect from these causes any higher action of the mind than they have yet produced. Perhaps most of them have spent their force. The very improvements of society seem to forbid the manifestation of their former energy. For example, the patriotism of antiquity and the sexual love of chivalrous ages, which inspired so much of the old literature, are now seen to be feverish and vicious excesses of natural principles, and have gone, we trust, never to return.

Are we asked, then, to what impulse or power we look for a higher literature than has yet existed? We answer, To a new action or development of the religious principle. This remark will probably surprise not a few of our readers. It seems to us that the energy with which this principle is to act on the intellect is hardly suspected. Men identify religion with superstition, with fanaticism, with the common forms of Christianity; and seeing it arrayed against intellect, leagued with oppression, fettering inquiry, and incapable of being blended with the sacred dictates of reason and conscience, they see in its progress only new encroachments on free and enlightened thinking. Still, man's relation to God is the great quickening truth, throwing all other truths into insignificance, and a truth which, however obscured and paralyzed by the many errors which ignorance and fraud have hitherto linked with it, has ever been a chief spring of human improvement. We look to it as the true life of the intellect. No man can be just to himself—can comprehend his own existence, can put forth all his powers with an heroic confidence, can deserve to be the guide and inspirer of other minds—till he has risen to communion with the Supreme Mind; till he feels his filial connection with the Universal Parent; till he regards himself as the recipient and minister of the Infinite Spirit; till he feels his consecration to the ends which religion unfolds; till he rises above human opinion, and is moved by a higher impulse than fame.

From these remarks it will be seen that our chief hopes of an improved literature rest on our hopes of an improved religion. From the prevalent theology which has come down to us from the dark ages, we hope nothing. It has done its best. All that can grow up under its sad shade has already been brought forth. It wraps the Divine nature and human nature in impenetrable gloom. It overlays Christianity with technical, arbitrary dogmas. True faith is of another lineage. It comes from the same source with reason, conscience, and our best affections, and is in harmony with them all. True faith is essentially a moral conviction; a confidence in the reality and immutableness of moral distinctions; a confidence in disinterested virtue or in spiritual excellence as the supreme good; a confidence in God as its fountain and Almighty Friend, and in Jesus Christ as having lived and died to breathe .it into the soul; a confidence in its power, triumphs, and immortality; a confidence through which outward changes, obstructions, disasters, sufferings, are overcome, or rather made instruments of perfection. Such a faith, unfolded freely and powerfully, must "work mightily" on the intellect as well as on practice. By revealing to us the supreme purpose of the Creator, it places us, as it were, in the centre of the universe, from which the harmonies, true relations, and brightest aspect of things are discerned. It unites calmness and enthusiasm, and the concord of these seemingly hostile elements is essential to the full and healthy action of the creative powers of the soul. It opens the eye to beauty and the heart to love. Literature, under this influence, will become more ingenuous and single-hearted; will penetrate farther into the soul; will find new interpretations of nature and life; will breathe a martyr's love of truth, tempered with a never-failing charity; and, whilst sympathizing with all human suffering, will still be pervaded by a healthful cheerfulness, and will often break forth in tones of irrepressible joy, responsive to that happiness which fills God's universe. . . .

We have now finished our remarks on the importance and means of an improved literature among ourselves. Are we asked what we hope in this particular? We answer, Much. We see reasons for anticipating an increased and more efficient direction of talent to this object. But on these we cannot enlarge. There is, however, one ground of expectation to which we will call a moment's attention. We apprehend that literature is to make progress through an important change in society, which civilization and good institutions are making more and more apparent. It seems to us that, through these causes, political life is less and less regarded as the only or chief sphere for superior minds, and that influence and honor are more and more accumulated in the hands of literary and thinking men. Of consequence, more and more of the intellect of communities is to be drawn to literature. The distinction between antiquity and the present times, in respect to the importance attached to political life, seems to us striking; and it is not an accidental difference, but founded on permanent causes which are to operate with increased power. In ancient times everything, abroad and at home, threw men upon the public, and generated an intense thirst for political power. On the contrary, the improvement of later periods inclines men to give importance to literature. For example, the instability of the ancient republics, the unsettled relations of different classes of society, the power of demagogues and orators, the intensity of factions, the want of moral and religious restraints, the want of some regular organ for expressing the public mind, the want of precedents and precise laws for the courts of justice, —these and other circumstances gave to the ancient citizen a feeling as if revolutions and convulsions were inseparable from society, turned his mind with unremitting anxiety to public affairs, and made a participation of political power an important, if not an essential, means of personal safety. Again, the ancient citizen had no home, in our sense of the word. He lived in the market, the forum, the place of general resort, and of course his attention was very much engrossed by affairs of state. Again, religion, which now more than all things throws a man upon himself, was in ancient times a public concern, and turned men to political life. The religion of the heart and closet was unknown. The relation of the gods to particular states was their most prominent attribute; and, to conciliate their favor to the community, the chief end of worship. Accordingly, religion consisted chiefly in public and national rites. In Rome the highest men in the state presided at the altar, and, adding to their other titles that of Supreme Pontiff, performed the most solemn functions of the priesthood. Thus the whole strength of the religious principle was turned into political channels. The gods were thought to sustain no higher office than a political one, and of consequence this was esteemed the most glorious for men. Once more, in ancient times political rank was vastly more efficient, whether for good or for evil, than at present, and of consequence was the object of a more insatiable ambition. It was almost the only way of access to the multitude. The public man held a sway over opinion, over his country, perhaps over foreign states, now unknown. It is the influence of the press and of good institutions to reduce the importance of the man of office. In proportion as private individuals can act on the public mind; in proportion as a people read, think, and have the means of express-ing and enforcing their opinions; in proportion as laws become fixed, known, and sanctioned by the moral sense of the community; in proportion as the interest of the state, the principles of administration, and all public measures are subjected to free and familiar discussion,—government becomes a secondary influence. The power passes into the hands of those who think, write, and spread their minds far and wide. Accordingly, literature is to become more and more the instrument of swaying men, of doing good, of achieving fame. The contrast between ancient and modern times in the particulars now stated is too obvious to need illustration, and our great inference is equally clear. The vast improvements which in the course of ages have taken place in social order, in domestic life, in religion, in knowledge, all conspire to one result, all tend to introduce other and higher influences than political power, and to give to that form of intellectual effort which we call literature dominion over human affairs. Thus truth, we apprehend, is more and more felt; and from its influence, joined with our peculiar condition and free institutions, we hope for our country the happiness and glory of a pure, deep, rich, beautiful, and ennobling literature.

4. Charles Sumner, *The Law of Human Progress, 1848**

My subject is The Law of Human Progress. In selecting this theme, I would not minister to the pride or gratulation of the Present, nor would I furnish motives for indifference or repose. Rather would I teach how small is the Present and all it con-tains, compared with the Future, and how duties increase with the grandeur upon which we enter, while we derive new encouragement from knowledge of the law which is our support and guide.

The subject is vast as it is interesting

* Charles Sumner, "The Law of Human Progress. Oration before the Phi Beta Kappa Society of Union College, Schenectady, July 25, 1848," *Works* (Boston, 1870), II, 89 ff.

and important. It might well occupy a volume, rather than a brief discourse. In unfolding it, I shall speak *first* of the history of this law, as seen in its origin, gradual development, and recognition,—and *next* of its character, conditions, and limitations, with the duties it enjoins and the encouragements it affords.

And, first, of its history. The recognition of this law has been reserved for comparatively recent times. Like other general laws governing the courses of Nature, it was unknown to Antiquity. The ignorance and prejudice which then prevailed with regard to the earth, the heavenly bodies, and their relations to the universe, found fit companionship with the wild speculations concerning the Human Family. The ignorant live only in the Present, whether of time or place. What they see and observe bounds their knowledge. Thus to the early Greek the heavens were upborne by the mountains, and the sun traversed daily in fiery chariot from east to west. So things seemed to him. But the true Destiny of the Human Family was as little comprehended.

Man, in his origin and history, was surrounded with fable; nor was there any correct idea of the principles determining the succession of events. Revolutions of states were referred sometimes to chance, sometimes to certain innate elements of decay. . . .

As modern civilization gradually unfolded itself amidst the multiplying generations of men, they witnessed the successive manifestations of power,—but perceived no Law. They looked upon the imposing procession of events, but did not discern the rule which guided the mighty series. Ascending from triumph to triumph, they saw dominion extended by the discoveries of intrepid navigators,—saw learning strengthened by the studies of accomplished scholars,—saw

universities opening their portals to ingenuous youth in all corners of the land, from Aberdeen and Copenhagen to Toledo and Ferrara,—saw Art put forth new graces in the painting of Raffaelle, new grandeur in the painting, the sculpture, and the architecture of Michel Angelo,—caught the strains of poets, no longer cramped by ancient idioms, but flowing sweetly in the language learned at a mother's knee,—received the manifold revelations of science in geometry, mathematics, astronomy,—beheld the barbarism of the barbarous Art of War changed and refined, though barbarous still, by the invention of gun-powder, —witnessed knowledge of all kinds springing to unwonted power through the marvellous agency of the printing-press . . . and yet all these things, the harmonious expression of *progressive* energies belonging to Man, token of an untiring advance, earnest of a mightier Future, seemed to teach no certain lesson.

The key to this advance had not been found. It was not seen that the constant desire for improvement implanted in man, with the constant effort consequent thereon in a life susceptible of indefinite Progress, caused, naturally, under the laws of a beneficent God, an indefinite advance,— that the evil passions of individuals, or of masses, while retarding, could not permanently restrain this divine impulse,—and that each generation, by irresistible necessity, added to the accumulations of the Past, and in this way prepared a higher Future. . . .

To the eighteenth century belongs the honor—signal honor I venture to call it—of first distinctly acknowledging and enunciating that Law of Human Progress, which, though preached in Judea eighteen hundred years ago, failed to be received by men,—nay, still fails to be received by men. Writers in our own age, of much ability and unexampled hardihood, while adopting this fundamental law, proceed to arraign existing institutions of society. My present purpose does not require me to consider these, whether for censure or praise,—abounding as they do in evil, abounding as they do in good. It is my single aim to trace the gradual development and final establishment of that great law which teaches that "there is a good time coming,"—a Future even on earth, to arouse the hopes, the aspirations, and the energies of Man.

The way is now prepared to consider the character, conditions, and limitations of this law, the duties it enjoins, and the encouragements it affords.

Let me state the law as I understand it. Man, as an individual, is capable of indefinite improvement. Societies and nations, which are but aggregations of men, and, finally, the Human Family, or collective Humanity, are capable of indefinite improvement. And this is the destiny of man, of societies, of nations, and of the Human Family. . . .

There are revolutions in history seeming on a superficial view inconsistent with this law. From early childhood attention is directed to Greece and Rome; and we are sometimes taught that these two powers reached heights which subsequent nations cannot hope to equal, much less surpass. I would not disparage the triumphs of the ancient mind. The eloquence, the poetry, the philosophy, the art, of Athens still survive, and bear no mean sway upon earth. Rome, too, yet lives in her jurisprudence, which, next after Christianity, has exerted a paramount influence over the laws of modern communities.

But exalted as these productions may be, it is impossible not to perceive that something of their present importance is derived from the early period when

they appeared, something from the unquestioning and high-flown admiration of them transmitted through successive generations until it became a habit, and something also from the disposition, still prevalent, to elevate Antiquity at the expense of subsequent ages. Without undertaking to decide if the genius of Antiquity, as displayed by individuals, can justly claim supremacy, it would be easy to show that the ancient plane of civilization never reached our common level. The people were ignorant, vicious, and poor, or degraded to abject slavery,—itself the sum of all injustice and all vice. Even the most illustrious characters, whose names still shine from that distant night, were little more than splendid barbarians. Architecture, sculpture, painting, and vases of exquisite perfection attest an appreciation of beauty in form; but our masters in these things were strangers to the useful arts, as to the comforts and virtues of home. Abounding in what to us are luxuries, they had not what to us are necessaries.

Without knowledge there can be no sure Progress. Vice and barbarism are the inseparable companions of ignorance. Nor is it too much to say, that, except in rare instances, the highest virtue is attained only through intelligence. This is natural; for to do right, we must first understand what is right. But the people of Greece and Rome, even in the brilliant days of Pericles and Augustus, could not arrive at this knowledge. The sublime teachings of Plato and Socrates—calculated in many respects to promote the best interests of the race—were limited in influence to a small company of listeners, or to the few who could obtain a copy of the costly manuscripts in which they were preserved. Thus the knowledge and virtue acquired by individuals were not diffused in their own age or secured to posterity.

Now, at last, through an agency all

unknown to Antiquity, knowledge of every kind has become general and permanent. It can no longer be confined to a select circle. It cannot be crushed by tyranny, or lost by neglect. It is immortal as the soul from which it proceeds. This alone renders all relapse into barbarism impossible, while it affords an unquestionable distinction between ancient and modern times. The Press, watchful with more than the hundred eyes of Argus, strong with more than the hundred arms of Briareus, not only guards all the conquests of civilization, but leads the way to future triumphs. . . .

In receiving this law, two conditions of Humanity are recognized: first, its unity or solidarity; and, secondly, its indefinite duration upon earth. And now of these in their order.

1. It is true, doubtless, that there are various races of men; but there is but one great Human Family, in which Caucasian, Ethiopian, Chinese, and Indian are all brothers, children of *one* Father, and heirs to *one* happiness. Though variously endowed, they are all tending in the same direction; nor can the light obtained by one be withheld from any. The ether discovery in Boston will soothe pain hereafter in Africa and in Asia, in Abyssinia and in China. So are we all knit together, that words of wisdom and truth, which first sway the hearts of the American people, may help to elevate benighted tribes of the most distant regions. The vexed question of modern science, whether these races proceeded originally from one stock, does not interfere with the sublime revelation of Christianity, the Brotherhood of Man. In the light of science and of religion, Humanity is an organism, complex, but still one,—throbbing with one life, animated by one soul, every part sympathizing with every other part, and the whole advancing in one indefinite career of Progress.

2. And what is the measure of this career? It is common to speak of the long life already passed by man on earth; but how brief and trivial is this, compared with the countless ages before him! According to received chronology, six thousand years have not yet elapsed since his creation. But the science of Geology, that unimpeached interpreter of the Past, now demonstrates (and here the geology of New York furnishes important evidence), that, anterior to the commencement of human history, this globe had endured for ages upon ages, baffling human calculation and imagination. . . .

Thus we stand now between two infinities,—the infinity of the Past, and the infinity of the Future; and the infinity of the Future is equal to the infinity of the Past. In comparison with these untold spaces before and after, what, indeed, are the six thousand years of human history? In the contemplation of Man, what littleness! what grandeur! how diminutive in the creation! how brief his recorded history! and yet how vast in hopes! how majestic and transcendent in the Future! . . .

Admitting the Unity of Mankind, and an Indefinite Future on earth, it becomes easy to anticipate triumphs which else were impossible. Few will question that Man, as an individual, is capable of indefinite improvement, so long as he lives. This capacity is inborn. None so poor as not to possess it. Even the idiot, so abject in condition, is found at last to be within the sphere of education. Circumstances alone are required to call this capacity into action; and in proportion as knowledge, virtue, and religion prevail in a community will that sacred atmosphere be diffused under whose genial influence the most forlorn may grow into forms of unimagined strength and beauty. This capacity for indefinite improvement, which belongs to the individual, must belong also to society; for society does not die, and through the improvement of its individuals has the assurance of its own advance. It is immortal on earth, and will gather constantly new and richer fruits from the teeming generations, as they stretch through unknown time. To Chinese vision the period of the present may seem barren, but it is sure to yield its contribution to the indefinite accumulations which are the token of an indefinite Progress.

Tables speak sometimes as words cannot. From statistics of life, as recorded by Science, we learn the capacity for progress in the Human Family; the testimony is authentic, as it is interesting. A little more than two centuries have passed since Descartes predicted that improvement in human health which these figures exhibit. Could this seer of Science revisit the scene of his comprehensive labors and divine aspirations, he might well be astonished to learn how, in the lapse of so short a period in the life of Humanity, his glowing anticipations have been fulfilled. . . . Even the conqueror Death has been slowly driven back, and his inevitable triumph postponed. . . .

Glancing at the cradle of nations and races risen to grandeur, and observing the wretchedness by which they were originally surrounded, we learn that no lot is removed from the influence of this law. The Feejee Islander, the Bushman, the Hottentot, the Congo negro, is not too low for its care. No terms of imagined "finality" can arrest it. The polished Briton, whose civilization we now admire, traces his long-descended lineage from one of those painted barbarians whose degradation still lives in the pages of Julius Caesar. Slowly, and by degrees, he has reached the height where he now

stands; but this is no "finality." The improvement of the Past is the earnest of yet further improvement in the long ages of the Future. And who can doubt, that, in the lapse of time, as the Christian Law is gradually fulfilled, the elevation of the Briton will be shared by all his fellow-men?

The tokens of improvement may appear at a special period, in a limited circle only, among the people, favored of God, enjoying peculiar benefits of commerce and Christianity; but the happy influence cannot be narrowed to any time, place, or people. Every victory over evil redounds to the benefit of all. Every discovery, every humane thought, every truth, when declared, is a conquest of which the whole Human Family are partakers, extending by so much their dominion, while it lessens by so much the sphere of future struggle and trial. Thus, while Nature is always the same, the power of Man is ever increasing. Each day gives him some new advantage. The mountains have not diminished in size; but Man has overcome the barriers they interpose. The winds and waves are not less capricious now than when they first beat upon the ancient Silurian rocks; but the steamboat.

"Against the wind, against the tide,
  Now steadies on with upright keel."

The distance between two points on the surface of the globe is the same to-day as when the continents were upheaved from their ocean-bed; but the art of man triumphs over such separation, and distant people commune together. Much remains to be done; but the Creator did not speak in vain, when he blessed his earliest children, and bade them "multiply, and replenish the earth, and *subdue it.*"

There will be triumphs nobler than

any over inanimate Nature. Man himself will be subdued,—subdued to abhorrence of vice, injustice, violence,— subdued to the sweet charities of life,— subdued to all the requirements of duty,—subdued, according to the Law of Human Progress, to the recognition of that Gospel Law of Human Brotherhood, by the side of which the first is only as the scaffolding upon the sacred temple. To labor for this end was man sent forth into the world,—not in the listlessness of idle perfections, but endowed with infinite capacities, inspired by infinite desires, and commanded to strive perpetually after excellence, amidst the encouragements of hope, the promises of final success, and the inexpressible delights from its pursuit. Thus does the Law of Human Progress

"assert eternal Providence,
And justify the ways of God to men,"

by showing Evil no longer a gloomy mystery, binding the world in everlasting thrall, but an accident, under benign Power destined to be surely subdued, as the Human Family press on to the promised goal of happiness.

While recognizing Humanity as progressive, it is important to consider a condition or limitation which may justly temper the ardors of the reformer. Nothing is accomplished except by time and exertion. Nature abhors violence and suddenness. Nature does everything slowly and by degrees. It takes time for the seed to grow into "the bright consummate flower." It is many years before the slender shoot grows into the tree. It is slowly that we pass from infancy and imbecility to manhood and strength. Arrived at this stage, we are still subject to the same condition of Nature. A new temperature or a sudden stroke of light may shock us. Our frames are not made for extremes; so that death

may come, according to the poet's conceit, "in aromatic pain."

Gradual change is a necessary condition of the Law of Progress. It is only, according to the poetical phrase of Tacitus, *per intervalla ac spiramenta temporum,* "by intervals and breathings of time," that we can hope to make a sure advance. Men grow and are trained in knowledge and virtue; but they cannot be compelled into this path. This consideration teaches candor and charity towards all who do not yet see the truth as we do. It admonishes us also, while keeping the eye steadfast on the good we seek, to moderate our expectations, and be content when the day of triumph is postponed, for it cannot be always. . . .

Let us, then, be of good cheer. From the great Law of Progress we derive at once our duties and our encouragements. Humanity has ever advanced, urged by instincts and necessities implanted by God,—thwarted sometimes by obstacles, causing it for a time, a moment only in the immensity of ages, to deviate from its true line, or seem to retreat, but still ever onward. At last we know the law of this movement; we fasten our eyes upon that star, unobserved in the earlier ages, which lights the way to the Future, opening into vistas of infinite variety and extension. Amidst the disappointments which attend individual exertions, amidst the universal agitations which now surround us, let us recognize this law, let us follow this star, confident that whatever is just, whatever is humane, whatever is good, whatever is true, according to an immutable ordinance of Providence, in the sure light of the Future, must prevail. With this faith, we place our hands, as those of little children, in the great hand of God. He will guide and sustain us—through pains and perils it may be—in the path of Progress. . . .

Go forth, then, my country, "conquering and to conquer!"—not by brutal violence, not by force of arms, not, oh! not on dishonest fields of blood,—but in the majesty of Peace, Justice, Freedom, by the irresistible might of Christian Institutions!

5. HENRY WADSWORTH LONGFELLOW, *The Bells of San Blas, 1882**

What say the Bells of San Blas
To the ships that southward pass
 From the harbor of Mazatlan?
To them it is nothing more
Than the sound of surf on the shore,—
 Nothing more to master or man.

But to me, a dreamer of dreams,
To whom what is and what seems,
 Are often one and the same,—
The Bells of San Blas to me
Have a strange, wild melody,
 And are something more than a
  name.

For bells are the voice of the church;
They have tones that touch and search
 The hearts of young and old;
One sound to all, yet each
Lends a meaning to their speech,
 And the meaning is manifold.

They are a voice of the Past,
Of an age that is fading fast,
 Of a power austere and grand,
When the flag of Spain unfurled
Its folds o'er this western world,
 And the Priest was lord of the
  land.

The chapel that once looked down
On the little seaport town
 Has crumbled into the dust;
And on oaken beams below
The bells swing to and fro,
 And are green with mould and
  rust.

"Is, then, the old faith dead,"
They say, "and in its stead
 Is some new faith proclaimed,
That we are forced to remain
Naked to sun and rain,
 Unsheltered and ashamed?

"Once in our tower aloof,
We rang over wall and roof
 Our warnings and our complaints;
And round about us there
The white doves filled the air,
 Like the white souls of the saints.

"The saints! Ah, have they grown
Forgetful of their own?
 Are they asleep, or dead,
That open to the sky
Their ruined Missions lie,
 No longer tenanted?

"Oh, bring us back once more
The vanished days of yore,
 When the world with faith was
  filled;
Bring back the fervid zeal,
The hearts of fire and steel,
 The hands that believe and build.

"Then from our tower again
We will send over land and main
 Our voices of command,
Like exiled kings who return
To their thrones, and the people learn
 That the Priest is lord of the
  land!"

O Bells of San Blas, in vain
Ye call back the Past again!
 The Past is deaf to your prayer!
Out of the shadows of night
The world rolls into light;
 It is daybreak everywhere.

* Henry Wadsworth Longfellow, *Poetical Works* (Boston, 1884), p. 411.

6. NATHANIEL HAWTHORNE,
*Earth's Holocaust, 1844**

Once upon a time—but whether in the time past or time to come is a matter of little or no moment—this wide world had become so overburdened with an accumulation of wornout trumpery that the inhabitants determined to rid themselves of it by a general bonfire. The site fixed upon at the representation of the insurance companies, and as being as central a spot as any other on the globe, was one of the broadest prairies of the West, where no human habitation would be endangered by the flames, and where a vast assemblage of spectators might commodiously admire the show. Having a taste for sights of this kind, and imagining, likewise, that the illumination of the bonfire might reveal some profundity of moral truth heretofore hidden in mist or darkness, I made it convenient to journey thither and be present. At my arrival, although the heap of condemned rubbish was as yet comparatively small, the torch had already been applied. Amid that boundless plain, in the dusk of the evening, like a far off star alone in the firmament, there was merely visible one tremulous gleam, whence none could have anticipated so fierce a blaze as was destined to ensue. With every moment, however, there came foot travellers, women holding up their aprons, men on horseback, wheelbarrows, lumbering baggage wagons, and other vehicles, great and small, and from far and near laden with articles that were judged fit for nothing but to be burned.

"What materials have been used to kindle the flame?" inquired I of a by-stander; for I was desirous of knowing the whole process of the affair from beginning to end.

The person whom I addressed was a grave man, fifty years old or thereabout, who had evidently come thither as a looker on. He struck me immediately as having weighed for himself the true value of life and its circumstances, and therefore as feeling little personal interest in whatever judgment the world might form of them. Before answering my question, he looked me in the face by the kindling light of the fire.

"Oh, some very dry combustibles," replied he, "and extremely suitable to the purpose—no other, in fact, than yesterday's newspapers, last month's magazines, and last year's withered leaves. Here now comes some antiquated trash that will take fire like a handful of shavings."

As he spoke some rough-looking men advanced to the verge of the bonfire, and threw in, as it appeared, all the rubbish of the herald's office—the blazonry of coat armor, the crests and devices of illustrious families, pedigrees that extended back, like lines of light, into the mist of the dark ages, together with stars, garters, and embroidered collars, each of which, as paltry a bawble as it might appear to the uninstructed eyes, had once possessed vast significance, and was still, in truth, reckoned among the most precious of moral or material facts by the worshippers of the gorgeous past. Mingled with this confused heap, which was tossed into the flames by armfuls at once, were innumerable badges of knighthood, comprising those of all the European sovereignties, and Napole-

* Nathaniel Hawthorne, "Earth's Holocaust," *Graham's Magazine*, May, 1844. Reprinted in *Mosses from an Old Manse* (1846).

on's decoration of the Legion of Honor, the ribbons of which were entangled with those of the ancient order of St. Louis. There, too, were the medals of our own Society of Cincinnati, by means of which, as history tells us, an order of hereditary knights came near being constituted out of the king quellers of the revolution. And besides, there were the patents of nobility of German counts and barons, Spanish grandees, and English peers, from the worm-eaten instruments signed by William the Conqueror down to the brand new parchment of the latest lord who has received his honors from the fair hand of Victoria.

At sight of the dense volumes of smoke, mingled with vivid jets of flame, that gushed and eddied forth from this immense pile of earthly distinctions, the multitude of plebeian spectators set up a joyous shout, and clapped their hands with an emphasis that made the welkin echo. That was their moment of triumph, achieved, after long ages, over creatures of the same clay and the same spiritual infirmities, who had dared to assume the privileges due only to Heaven's better workmanship. But now there rushed towards the blazing heap a grayhaired man, of stately presence, wearing a coat, from the breast of which a star, or other badge of rank, seemed to have been forcibly wrenched away. He had not the tokens of intellectual power in his face; but still there was the demeanor, the habitual and almost native dignity, of one who had been born to the idea of his own social superiority, and had never felt it questioned till that moment.

"People," cried he, gazing at the ruin of what was dearest to his eyes with grief and wonder, but nevertheless with a degree of stateliness,—"people, what have you done? This fire is consuming all that marked your advance from barbarism, or that could have prevented your relapse thither. We,

the men of the privileged orders, were those who kept alive from age to age the old chivalrous spirit; the gentle and generous thought; the higher, the purer, the more refined and delicate life. With the nobles, too, you cast off the poet, the painter, the sculptor— all the beautiful arts; for we were their patrons, and created the atmosphere in which they flourish. In abolishing the majestic distinctions of rank, society loses not only its grace, but its steadfastness"—

More he would doubtless have spoken; but here there arose an outcry, sportive, contemptuous, and indignant, that altogether drowned the appeal of the fallen nobleman, insomuch that, casting one look of despair at his own half-burned pedigree, he shrunk back into the crowd, glad to shelter himself under his new-found insignificance.

"Let him thank his stars that we have not flung him into the same fire!" shouted a rude figure, spurning the embers with his foot. "And henceforth let no man dare to show a piece of musty parchment as his warrant for lording it over his fellows. If he have strength of arm, well and good; it is one species of superiority. If he have wit, wisdom, courage, force of character, let these attributes do for him what they may; but from this day forward no mortal must hope for place and consideration by reckoning up the mouldy bones of his ancestors. That nonsense is done away."

"And in good time," remarked the grave observer by my side, in a low voice, however, "if no worse nonsense comes in its place; but, at all events, this species of nonsense has fairly lived out its life."

There was little space to muse or moralize over the embers of this time-honored rubbish; for, before it was half burned out, there came another multitude from beyond the sea, bearing the purple robes of royalty, and the crowns, globes, and sceptres of emperors and kings. All these had been condemned as useless baubles, playthings at best, fit only for the infancy of the world, or rods to govern and chastise it in its nonage, but with which universal manhood at its full-grown stature could no longer brook to be insulted. Into such contempt had these regal insignia now fallen that the gilded crown and tinselled robes of the player king from Drury Lane Theatre had been thrown in among the rest, doubtless as a mockery of his brother monarchs on the great stage of the world. It was a strange sight to discern the crown jewels of England glowing and flashing in the midst of the fire. Some of them had been delivered down from the time of the Saxon princes; others were purchased with vast revenues, or perchance ravished from the dead brows of the native potentates of Hindostan; and the whole now blazed with a dazzling lustre, as if a star had fallen in that spot and been shattered into fragments. The splendor of the ruined monarchy had no reflection save in those inestimable precious stones. But enough on this subject. It were but tedious to describe how the Emperor of Austria's mantle was converted to tinder, and how the posts and pillars of the French throne became a heap of coals, which it was impossible to distinguish from those of any other wood. Let me add, however, that I noticed one of the exiled Poles stirring up the bonfire with the Czar of Russia's sceptre, which he afterwards flung into the flames.

"The smell of singed garments is quite intolerable here," observed my new acquaintance, as the breeze enveloped us in the smoke of a royal wardrobe. "Let us get to windward and see what they are doing on the other side of the bonfire."

We accordingly passed around, and were just in time to witness the arrival of a vast procession of Washingtonians,—as the votaries of temperance call themselves nowadays,— accompanied by thousands of the Irish disciples of Father Mathew, with that great apostle at their head. They brought a rich contribution to the bonfire—being nothing less than all the hogsheads and barrels of liquor in the world, which they rolled before them across the prairie.

"Now, my children," cried Father Mathew, when they reached the verge of the fire, "one shove more, and the work is done. And now let us stand off, and see Satan deal with his own liquor."

Accordingly, having placed their wooden vessels within reach of the flames, the procession stood off at a safe distance, and soon beheld them burst into a blaze that reached the clouds and threatened to set the sky itself on fire. And well it might: for here was the whole world's stock of spirituous liquors, which, instead of kindling a frenzied light in the eyes of individual topers as of yore, soared upwards with a bewildering gleam that startled all mankind. It was the aggregate of that fierce fire which would otherwise have scorched the hearts of millions. Meantime numberless bottles of precious wine were flung into the blaze, which lapped up the contents as if it loved them, and grew, like other drunkards, the merrier and fiercer for what it quaffed. Never again will the insatiable thirst of the fire fiend be so pampered. Here were the treasures of famous bon vivants— liquors that had been tossed on the ocean, and mellowed in the sun, and hoarded long in the recesses of the earth—the pale, the gold, the ruddy juice of whatever vineyards were most delicate—the entire vintage of Tokay— all mingling in one stream with the vile fluids of the common pothouse, and contributing to heighten the selfsame blaze. And while it rose in a gigantic spire that seemed to wave against the arch of the firmament and combine itself with the light of stars, the multitude gave a shout as if the broad earth were exulting in its deliverance from the curse of ages.

But the joy was not universal. Many deemed that human life would be gloomier than ever when that brief illumination should sink down. While the reformers were at work, I overheard muttered expostulations from several respectable gentlemen with red noses and wearing gouty shoes; and a ragged worthy, whose face looked like a hearth where the fire is burned out, now expressed his discontent more openly and boldly.

"What is this world good for," said the last toper, "now that we can never be jolly any more? What is to comfort the poor man in sorrow and perplexity? How is he to keep his heart warm against the cold winds of this cheerless earth? And what do you propose to give him in exchange for the solace that you take away? How are old friends to sit together by the fireside without a cheerful glass between them? A plague upon your reformation! It is a sad world, a cold world, a selfish world, a low world, not worth an honest fellow's living in, now that good fellowship is gone forever!"

This harangue excited great mirth among the bystanders; but, preposterous as was the sentiment, I could not help commiserating the forlorn condition of the last toper, whose boon companions had dwindled away from his side, leaving the poor fellow without a soul to countenance him in sipping his liquor, nor indeed any liquor to sip. Not that this was quite the true state of the case; for I had observed him at a critical moment filch a bottle of fourth-proof brandy that fell beside the bonfire and hide it in his pocket.

The spirituous and fermented liquors being thus disposed of, the zeal of the reformers next induced them to replenish the fire with all the boxes of tea and bags of coffee in the world. And now came the planters of Virginia, bringing their crops of tobacco. These, being cast upon the heap of inutility, aggregated it to the size of a mountain, and incensed the atmosphere with such potent fragrance that methought we should never draw pure breath again. The present sacrifice seemed to startle the lovers of the weed more than any that they had hitherto witnessed.

"Well, they've put my pipe out," said an old gentleman, flinging it into the flames in a pet. "What is this world coming to? Everything rich and racy—all the spice of life—is to be condemned as useless. Now that they have kindled the bonfire, if these nonsensical reformers would fling themselves into it, all would be well enough!"

"Be patient," responded a stanch conservative; "it will come to that in the end. They will first fling us in, and finally themselves."

From the general and systematic measures of reform I now turned to consider the individual contributions to this memorable bonfire. In many instances these were of a very amusing character. One poor fellow threw in his empty purse, and another a bundle of counterfeit or insolvable bank notes. Fashionable ladies threw in their last season's bonnets, together with heaps of ribbons, yellow lace, and much other half-worn milliner's ware, all of which proved even more evanescent in the fire than it had been in the fashion. A multitude of lovers of both sexes—discarded maids or bachelors and couples mutually weary of one another—tossed in bundles of perfumed letters and enamored sonnets. A hack politician, being deprived of bread by the loss of office, threw in his teeth, which happened to be false ones. The Rev. Sidney Smith—having voyaged across the Atlantic for that sole purpose—came up to the bonfire with a bitter grin and threw in certain repudiated bonds, fortified though they were with the broad seal of a sovereign state. A little boy of five years old, in the premature manliness of the present epoch, threw in his playthings; a college graduate his diploma; an apothecary, ruined by the spread of homoeopathy, his whole stock of drugs and medicines; a physician his library; a parson his old sermons; and a fine gentleman of the old school his code of manners, which he had formerly written down for the benefit of the next generation. A widow, resolving on a second marriage, slyly threw in her dead husband's miniature. A young man, jilted by his mistress, would willingly have flung his own desperate heart into the flames, but could find no means to wrench it out of his bosom. An American author, whose works were neglected by the public, threw his pen and paper into the bonfire, and betook himself to some less discouraging occupation. It somewhat startled me to overhear a number of ladies, highly respectable in appearance, proposing to fling their gowns and petticoats into the flames, and assume the garb, together with the manners, duties, offices, and responsibilities, of the opposite sex.

What favor was accorded to this scheme I am unable to say, my attention being suddenly drawn to a poor, deceived, and half-delirious girl, who, exclaiming that she was the most worthless thing alive or dead, attempted to cast herself into the fire amid all that wrecked and broken trumpery of the world. A good man, however, ran to her rescue.

"Patience, my poor girl!" said he, as he drew her back from the fierce embrace of the destroying angel. "Be patient, and abide Heaven's will. So long as you possess a living soul, all may be restored to its first freshness. These things of matter and creations of human fantasy are fit for nothing but to be burned when once they have had their day; but your day is eternity!"

"Yes," said the wretched girl, whose frenzy seemed now to have sunk down into deep despondency,—"yes, and the sunshine is blotted out of it!"

It was now rumored among the spectators that all the weapons and munitions of war were to be thrown into the bonfire, with the exception of the world's stock of gunpowder, which, as the safest mode of disposing of it, had already been drowned in the sea. This intelligence seemed to awaken great diversity of opinion. The hopeful philanthropist esteemed it a token that the millennium was already come; while persons of another stamp, in whose view mankind was a breed of bulldogs, prophesied that all the old stoutness, fervor, nobleness, generosity, and magnanimity of the race would disappear,—these qualities, as they affirmed, requiring blood for their nourishment. They comforted themselves, however, in the belief that the proposed abolition of war was impracticable for any length of time together.

Be that as it might, numberless great guns, whose thunder had long been the voice of battle,—the artillery of the Armada, the battering trains of Marlborough, and the adverse cannon of Napoleon and Wellington,—were trundled into the midst of the fire. By the continual addition of dry combustibles, it had now waxed so intense that neither brass nor iron could withstand it. It was wonderful to behold how these terrible instruments of slaughter melted away like playthings of wax. Then the armies of the earth wheeled around the mighty furnace, with their military music playing triumphant marches, and flung in their muskets and swords. The standard-bearers, likewise, cast one look upward at their banners, all tattered with shot holes and inscribed with the names of victorious fields; and, giving them a last flourish on the breeze, they lowered them into the flame, which snatched them upward in its rush towards the clouds. This ceremony being over, the world was left without a single weapon in its hands,—except possibly a few old king's arms and rusty swords, and other trophies of the Revolution in some of our state armories. And now the drums were beaten and the trumpets brayed all together, as a prelude to the proclamation of universal and eternal peace and the announcement that glory was no longer to be won by blood, but that it would henceforth be the contention of the human race to work out the greatest mutual good, and that beneficence, in the future annals of the earth, would claim the praise of valor. The blessed tidings were accordingly promulgated, and caused infinite rejoicings among those who had stood aghast at the horror and absurdity of war.

But I saw a grim smile pass over the seared visage of a stately old commander,—by his warworn figure and rich military dress, he might have been one of Napoleon's famous marshals,—who, with the rest of the world's soldiery, had just flung away the sword that had been familiar to his right hand for half a century.

"Ay! ay!" grumbled he. "Let them proclaim what they please; but, in the end, we shall find that all this foolery has only made more work for the armorers and cannon founders."

"Why, sir," exclaimed I, in astonishment, "do you imagine that the human race will ever so far return on the steps of its past madness as to weld another sword or cast another cannon?"

"There will be no need," observed, with a sneer, one who neither felt benevolence nor had faith in it. "When Cain wished to slay his brother, he was at no loss for a weapon."

"We shall see," replied the veteran commander. "If I am mistaken, so much the better; but in my opinion, without pretending to philosophize about the matter, the necessity of war lies far deeper than these honest gentlemen suppose. What! is there a field for all the petty disputes of individuals? and shall there be no great law court for the settlement of national difficulties? The battle field is the only court where such suits can be tried."

"You forget, general," rejoined I, "that, in this advanced stage of civilization, Reason and Philanthropy combined will constitute just such a tribunal as is requisite."

"Ah, I had forgotten that, indeed!" said the old warrior, as he limped away.

The fire was now to be replenished with materials that had hitherto been considered of even greater importance to the well being of society than the warlike munitions which we had already seen consumed. A body of reformers had travelled all over the earth in quest of the machinery by which the different nations were accustomed to inflict the punishment of death. A shudder passed through the multitude as these ghastly emblems were dragged forward. Even the flames seemed at first to shrink away, displaying the shape and murderous contrivance of each in a full blaze of light, which of itself was sufficient to convince mankind of the long and deadly error of human law. Those old implements of cruelty; those horrible monsters of mechanism; those inventions which seemed to demand something worse than man's natural heart to contrive, and which had lurked in the dusky nooks of ancient prisons, the subject of terror-stricken legend,—were now brought forth to view. Headsmen's axes, with the rust of noble and royal blood upon them, and a vast collection of halters that had choked the breath of plebeian victims, were thrown in together. A shout greeted the arrival of the guillotine, which was thrust forward on the same wheels that had borne it from one to another of the blood-stained streets of Paris. But the loudest roar of applause went up, telling the distant sky of triumph of the earth's redemption, when the gallows made its appearance. An ill-looking fellow, however, rushed forward, and, putting himself in the path of the reformers, bellowed hoarsely, and fought with brute fury to stay their progress.

It was little matter of surprise, perhaps, that the executioner should thus do his best to vindicate and uphold the machinery by which he himself had his livelihood and worthier individuals their death; but it deserved special note that men of a far different sphere —even of that consecrated class in whose guardianship the world is apt to trust its benevolence—were found to take the hangman's view of the question.

"Stay, my brethren!" cried one of them. "You are misled by a false philanthropy; you know not what you do. The gallows is a Heaven-ordained instrument. Bear it back, then, reverently, and set it up in its old place, else the world will fall to speedy ruin and desolation!"

"Onward! onward!" shouted a leader in the reform. "Into the flames with the accursed instrument of man's blood policy! How can human law inculcate benevolence and love while it persists in setting up the gallows as its chief symbol? One heave more, good friends, and the world will be redeemed from its greatest error."

A thousand hands, that nevertheless loathed the touch, now lent their assistance, and thrust the ominous burden far, far into the centre of the raging furnace. There its fatal and abhorred image was beheld, first black, then a red coal, then ashes.

"That was well done!" exclaimed I.

"Yes, it was well done," replied, but with less enthusiasm than I expected, the thoughtful observer who was still at my side; "well done, if the world be good enough for the measure. Death, however, is an idea that cannot easily be dispensed with in any condition between the primal innocence and that other purity and perfection which perchance we are destined to attain after travelling round the full circle; but, at all events, it is well that the experiment should now be tried."

"Too cold! too cold!" impatiently exclaimed the young and ardent leader in this triumph. "Let the heart have its voice here as well as the intellect. And as for ripeness, and as for progress, let mankind always do the highest, kindest, noblest thing that, at any given period, it has attained the perception of; and surely that thing cannot be wrong nor wrongly timed."

I know not whether it were the excitement of the scene, or whether the good people around the bonfire were really growing more enlightened every instant; but they now proceeded to measures in the full length of which I was hardly prepared to keep them company. For instance, some threw their marriage certificates into the flames, and declared themselves candidates for a higher, holier, and more comprehensive union than that which had subsisted from the birth of time under the form of the connubial tie. Others hastened to the vaults of banks and to the coffers of the rich,—all of which were open to the first comer on this fated occasion,—and brought entire bales of paper money to enliven the blaze, and tons of coin to be melted down by its intensity. Henceforth, they said, universal benevolence, uncoined and exhaustless, was to be the golden currency of the world. At this intelligence the bankers and speculators in the stocks grew pale, and a pickpocket, who had reaped a rich harvest among the crowd, fell down in a deadly fainting fit. A few men of business burned their daybooks and ledgers, the notes and obligations of their creditors, and all other evidences of debts due to themselves; while perhaps a somewhat larger number satisfied their zeal for reform with the sacrifice of any uncomfortable recollection of their own indebtment. There was then a cry that the period was arrived when the title deeds of landed property should be given to the flames, and the whole soil of the earth revert to the public, from whom it had been wrongfully abstracted and most unequally distributed among individuals. Another party demanded that all written constitutions, set forms of government, legislative acts, statute books, and everything else on which human invention had endeavored to stamp its arbitrary laws, should at once be destroyed, leaving the consummated world as free as the man first created.

Whether any ultimate action was taken with regard to these propositions is beyond my knowledge; for, just then, some matters were in progress that concerned my sympathies more nearly.

"See! see! What heaps of books and pamphlets!" cried a fellow, who did not seem to be a lover of literature. "Now we shall have a glorious blaze!"

"That's just the thing!" said a modern philosopher. "Now we shall get rid of the weight of dead men's thought, which has hitherto pressed so heavily on the living intellect that it has been incompetent to any effectual self-exer-

tion. Well done, my lads! Into the fire with them! Now you are enlightening the world indeed!"

"But what is to become of the trade?" cried a frantic bookseller.

"Oh, by all means, let them accompany their merchandise," coolly observed an author. "It will be a noble funeral pile!"

The truth was, that the human race had now reached a stage of progress so far beyond what the wisest and wittiest men of former ages had ever dreamed of that it would have been a manifest absurdity to allow the earth to be any longer encumbered with their poor achievements in the literary line. Accordingly a thorough and searching investigation had swept the booksellers' shops, hawkers' stands, public, and private libraries, and even the little bookshelf by the country fireside, and had brought the world's entire mass of printed paper, bound or in sheets, 'o swell the already mountain bulk of our illustrious bonfire. Thick, heavy folios, containing the labors of lexicographers, commentators, and encyclopedists, where flung in, and falling among the embers with a leaden thump, smouldered away to ashes like rotten wood. The small, richly gilt French tomes of the last age, with the hundred volumes of Voltaire among them, went off in a brilliant shower of sparkles and little jets of flame; while the current literature of the same nation burned red and blue, and threw an infernal light over the visages of the spectators, converting them all to the aspect of party-colored fiends. A collection of German stories emitted a scent of brimstone. The English standard authors made excellent fuel, generally exhibiting the properties of sound oak logs. Milton's works, in particular, sent up a powerful blaze, gradually reddening into a coal, which promised to endure longer than almost any other material of the pile. From Shakespeare there gushed a flame of such marvellous splendor that men shaded their eyes as against the sun's meridian glory; nor even when the works of his own elucidators were flung upon him did he cease to flash forth a dazzling radiance from beneath the ponderous heap. It is my belief that he is blazing as fervidly as ever.

"Could a poet but light a lamp at that glorious flame," remarked I, "he might then consume the midnight oil to some good purpose."

"That is the very thing which modern poets have been too apt to do, or at least to attempt," answered a critic. "The chief benefit to be expected from this conflagration of past literature undoubtedly is, that writers will henceforth be compelled to light their lamps at the sun or stars."

"If they can reach so high," said I; "but that task requires a giant, who may afterwards distribute the light among inferior men. It is not every one that can steal the fire from heaven like Prometheus; but, when once he had done the deed, a thousand hearths were kindled by it."

It amazed me much to observe how indefinite was the proportion between the physical mass of any given author and the property of brilliant and long-continued combustion. For instance, there was not a quarto volume of the last century—nor, indeed, of the present—that could compete in that particular with a child's little gilt-covered book, containing Mother Goose's Melodies. The Life and Death of Tom Thumb outlasted the biography of Marlborough. An epic, indeed a dozen of them, was converted to white ashes before the single sheet of an old ballad was half consumed. In more than one case, too, when volumes of applauded verse proved incapable of anything better than a stifling smoke, an unregarded ditty of some nameless bard—

perchance in the corner of a newspaper—soared up among the stars with a flame as brilliant as their own. Speaking of the properties of flame, methought Shelley's poetry emitted a purer light than almost any other productions of his day, contrasting beautifully with the fitful and lurid gleams and gushes of black vapor that flashed and eddied from the volumes of Lord Byron. As for Tom Moore, some of his songs diffused an odor like a burning pastil.

I felt particular interest in watching the combustion of American authors, and scrupulously noted by my watch the precise number of moments that changed most of them from shabbily-printed books to indistinguishable ashes. It would be invidious, however, if not perilous, to betray these awful secrets; so that I shall content myself with observing that it was not invariably the writer most frequent in the public mouth that made the most splendid appearance in the bonfire. I especially remember that a great deal of excellent inflammability was exhibited in a thin volume of poems by Ellery Channing; although, to speak the truth, there were certain portions that hissed and spluttered in a very disagreeable fashion. A curious phenomenon occurred in reference to several writers, native as well as foreign. Their books, though of highly respectable figure, instead of bursting into a blaze, or even smouldering out their substance in smoke, suddenly melted away in a manner that proved them to be ice.

If it be no lack of modesty to mention my own works, it must here be confessed that I looked for them with fatherly interest, but in vain. Too probably they were changed to vapor by the first action of the heat; at best, I can only hope that, in their quiet way, they contributed a glimmering spark or two to the splendor of the evening.

"Alas! and woe is me!" thus bemoaned himself a heavy-looking gentleman in green spectacles. "The world is utterly ruined, and there is nothing to live for any longer. The business of my life is snatched from me. Not a volume to be had for love or money!"

"This," remarked the sedate observer beside me, "is a bookworm— one of those men who are born to gnaw dead thoughts. His clothes, you see, are covered with the dust of libraries. He has no inward fountain of ideas; and, in good earnest, now that the old stock is abolished, I do not see what is to become of the poor fellow. Have you no word of comfort for him?"

"My dear sir," said I to the desperate bookworm, "is not Nature better than a book? Is not the human heart deeper than any system of philosophy? Is not life replete with more instruction than past observers have found it possible to write down in maxims? Be of good cheer. The great book of Time is still spread wide open before us; and, if we read it aright, it will be to us a volume of eternal truth."

"Oh, my books, my books, my precious printed books!" reiterated the forlorn bookworm. "My only reality was a bound volume; and now they will not leave me even a shadowy pamphlet!"

In fact, the last remnant of the literature of all the ages was now descending upon the blazing heap in the shape of a cloud of pamphlets from the press of the New World. These likewise were consumed in the twinkling of an eye, leaving the earth, for the first time since the days of Cadmus, free from the plague of letters—an enviable field for the authors of the next generation.

"Well, and does anything remain to be done?" inquired I somewhat anxiously. "Unless we set fire to the earth itself, and then leap boldly off into infinite space, I know not that we can carry reform to any farther point."

"You are vastly mistaken, my good friend," said the observer. "Believe me, the fire will not be allowed to settle down without the addition of fuel that will startle many persons who have lent a willing hand thus far."

Nevertheless there appeared to be a relaxation of effort for a little time, during which, probably, the leaders of the movement were considering what should be done next. In the interval, a philosopher threw his theory into the flames,—a sacrifice which, by those who knew how to estimate it, was pronounced the most remarkable that had yet been made. The combustion, however, was by no means brilliant. Some indefatigable people, scorning to take a moment's ease, now employed themselves in collecting all the withered leaves and fallen boughs of the forest, and thereby recruited the bonfire to a greater height than ever. But this was mere by-play.

"Here comes the fresh fuel that I spoke of," said my companion.

To my astonishment, the persons who now advanced into the vacant space around the mountain fire bore surplices and other priestly garments, mitres, crosiers, and a confusion of Popish and Protestant emblems, with which it seemed their purpose to consummate the great act of faith. Crosses from the spires of old cathedrals were cast upon the heap with as little remorse as if the reverence of centuries, passing in long array beneath the lofty towers, had not looked up to them as the holiest of symbols. The font in which infants were consecrated to God, the sacramental vessels whence piety received the hallowed draught, were given to the same destruction. Perhaps it most nearly touched my heart to see among these devoted relics fragments of the humble communion tables and undecorated pulpits which I recognized as having been torn from the meeting-houses of New England. Those simple edifices might have been permitted to retain all of sacred embellishment that their Puritan founders had bestowed, even though the mighty structure of St. Peter's had sent its spoils to the fire of this terrible sacrifice. Yet I felt that these were but the externals of religion, and might most safely be relinquished by spirits that best knew their deep significance.

"All is well," said I, cheerfully. "The woodpaths shall be the aisles of our cathedral,—the firmament itself shall be its ceiling. What needs an earthly roof between the Deity and his worshippers? Our faith can well afford to lose all the drapery that even the holiest men have thrown around it, and be only the more sublime in its simplicity."

"True," said my companion; "but will they pause here?"

The doubt implied in his question was well founded. In the general destruction of books already described, a holy volume, that stood apart from the catalogue of human literature, and yet, in one sense, was at its head, had been spared. But the Titan of innovation,—angel or fiend, double in his nature, and capable of deeds befitting both characters,—at first shaking down only the old and rotten shapes of things, had now, as it appeared, laid his terrible hand upon the main pillars which supported the whole edifice of our moral and spiritual state. The inhabitants of the earth had grown too enlightened to define their faith within a form of words, or to limit the spiritual by any analogy to our material existence. Truths which the heavens trembled at were now but a fable of the world's infancy. Therefore, as the final sacrifice of human error, what else remained to be thrown upon the embers of that awful pile except the book

which, though a celestial revelation to past ages, was but a voice from a lower sphere as regarded the present race of man? It was done! Upon the blazing heap of falsehood and wornout truth —things that the earth had never needed, or had ceased to need, or had grown childishly weary of—fell the ponderous church Bible, the great old volume that had lain so long on the cushion of the pulpit, and whence the pastor's solemn voice had given holy utterance on so many a Sabbath day. There, likewise, fell the family Bible, which the long-buried patriarch had read to his children,—in prosperity or sorrow, by the fireside and in the summer shade of trees,—and had bequeathed downward as the heirloom of generations. There fell the bosom Bible, the little volume that had been the soul's friend of some sorely-tried child of dust, who thence took courage, whether his trial were for life or death, steadfastly confronting both in the strong assurance of immortality.

All these were flung into the fierce and riotous blaze; and then a mighty wind came roaring across the plain with a desolate howl, as if it were the angry lamentation of the earth for the loss of heaven's sunshine; and it shook the gigantic pyramid of flame and scattered the cinders of half-consumed abominations around upon the spectators.

"This is terrible!" said I, feeling that my cheek grew pale, and seeing a like change in the visages about me.

"Be of good courage yet," answered the man with whom I had so often spoken. He continued to gaze steadily at the spectacle with a singular calmness, as if it concerned him merely as an observer. "Be of good courage, nor yet exult too much; for there is far less both of good and evil in the effect of this bonfire than the world might be willing to believe."

"How can that be?" exclaimed I, impatiently. "Has it not consumed everything? Has it not swallowed up or melted down every human or divine appendage of our mortal state that had substance enough to be acted on by fire? Will there be anything left us to-morrow morning better or worse than a heap of embers and ashes?"

"Assuredly there will," said my grave friend. "Come hither to-morrow morning, or whenever the combustible portion of the pile shall be quite burned out, and you will find among the ashes everything really valuable that you have seen cast into the flames. Trust me, the world of to-morrow will again enrich itself with the gold and diamonds which have been cast off by the world of to-day. Not a truth is destroyed nor buried so deep among the ashes but it will be raked up at last."

This was a strange assurance. Yet I felt inclined to credit it, the more especially as I beheld among the wallowing flames a copy of the Holy Scriptures, the pages of which, instead of being blackened into tinder, only assumed a more dazzling whiteness as the finger marks of human imperfection were purified away. Certain marginal notes and commentaries, it is true, yielded to the intensity of the fiery test, but without detriment to the smallest syllable that had flamed from the pen of inspiration.

"Yes; there is the proof of what you say," answered I, turning to the observer; "but if only what is evil can feel the action of the fire, then, surely, the conflagration has been of inestimable utility. Yet, if I understand aright, you intimate a doubt whether the world's expectation of benefit would be realized by it."

"Listen to the talk of these worthies," said he, pointing to a group in front of the blazing pile; "possibly they may teach you something useful without intending it."

The persons whom he indicated consisted of that brutal and most earthy figure who had stood forth so furiously in defence of the gallows,—the hangman, in short,—together with the last thief and the last murderer, all three of whom were clustered about the last toper. The latter was liberally passing the brandy bottle, which he had rescued from the general destruction of wines and spirits. This little convivial party seemed at the lowest pitch of despondency, as considering that the purified world must needs be utterly unlike the sphere that they had hitherto known, and therefore but a strange and desolate abode for gentlemen of their kidney.

"The best counsel for all of us is," remarked the hangman, "that, as soon as we have finished the last drop of liquor, I help you, my three friends, to a comfortable end upon the nearest tree, and then hang myself on the same bough. This is no world for us any longer."

"Poh, poh, my good fellows!" said a dark-complexioned personage, who now joined the group,—his complexion was indeed fearfully dark, and his eyes glowed with a redder light than that of the bonfire; "be not so cast down, my dear friends; you shall see good days yet. There's one thing that these wiseacres have forgotten to throw into the fire, and without which all the rest of the conflagration is just nothing at all; yes, though they had burned the earth itself to a cinder."

"And what may that be?" eagerly demanded the last murderer.

"What but the human heart itself?" said the dark-visaged stranger, with a portentous grin. "And, unless they hit upon some method of purifying that foul cavern, forth from it will reissue all the shapes of wrong and misery—the same old shapes or worse ones—which they have taken such a vast deal of trouble to consume to ashes. I have stood by this livelong night and laughed in my sleeve at the whole business. Oh, take my word for it, it will be the old world yet!"

This brief conversation supplied me with a theme for lengthened thought. How sad a truth, if true it were, that man's age-long endeavor for perfection had served only to render him the mockery of the evil principle, from the fatal circumstances of an error at the very root of the matter! The heart, the heart,—there was the little yet boundless sphere wherein existed the original wrong of which the crime and misery of this outward world were merely types. Purify that inward sphere, and the many shapes of evil that haunt the outward, and which now seem almost our only realities, will turn to shadowy phantoms and vanish of their own accord; but if we go no deeper than the intellect, and strive, with merely that feeble instrument, to discern and rectify what is wrong, our whole accomplishment will be a dream, so unsubstantial that it matters little whether the bonfire, which I have so faithfully described, were what we choose to call a real event and a flame that would scorch the finger, or only a phosphoric radiance and a parable of my own brain.

7. WALT WHITMAN, *An Old Man's Thought of School, 1874**

An old man's thought of school,
An old man gathering youthful memories and blooms that youth itself cannot,

Now only do I know you,
O fair auroral skies—O morning dew upon the grass!

And these I see, these sparkling eyes,
These stores of mystic meaning, these young lives,
Building, equipping like a fleet of ships, immortal ships,
Soon to sail out over the measureless seas,
On the soul's voyage.

Only a lot of boys and girls?
Only the tiresome spelling, writing, ciphering classes?
Only a public school?

Ah more, infinitely more;
(As George Fox rais'd his warning cry, "Is it this pile of brick and mortar, these
    dead floors, windows, rails, you call the church?
Why this is not the church at all—the church is living, ever living souls.")

And you America,
Cast you the real reckoning for your present?
The lights and shadows of your future, good or evil?
To girlhood, boyhood look, the teacher and the school.

* Written for the inauguration of a public school at Camden, New Jersey. In Walt Whitman, *Complete Writings* (New York, 1902), II, 173.

8. Emily Dickinson, *Aspiration, 1870**

We never know how high we are
Till we are asked to rise
And then if we are true to plan
Our statures touch the skies—

The Heroism we recite
Would be a normal thing
Did not ourselves the Cubits warp
For fear to be a King—

* Emily Dickinson, *Poems* (Boston, 1896), p. 27.

9. George Perkins Marsh, *Man and Nature, 1864, 1885**

Destructiveness of Man

Man has too long forgotten that the earth was given to him for usufruct alone, not for consumption, still less for profligate waste. Nature has provided against the absolute destruction of any of her elementary matter, the raw material of her works; the thunderbolt and the tornado, the most convulsive throes of even the volcano and the earthquake, being only phenomena of decomposition and recomposition. But she has left it within the power of man irreparably to derange the combinations of inorganic matter and of organic life, which through the night of aeons she had been proportioning and balancing, to prepare the earth for his habitation, when in the fullness of time his Creator should call him forth to enter into its possession.

Apart from the hostile influence of man, the organic and the inorganic world are, as I have remarked, bound together by such mutual relations and adaptations as secure, if not the absolute permanence and equilibrium of both, a long continuance of the established conditions of each at any given time and place, or at least, a very slow and gradual succession of changes in those conditions. But man is every-where a disturbing agent. Wherever he plants his foot, the harmonies of nature are turned to discords. The proportions and accommodations which insured the stability of existing arrangements are overthrown. Indigenous vegetable and animal species are extirpated, and supplanted by others of foreign origin, spontaneous production is forbidden or restricted, and the face of the earth is either laid bare or covered with a new and reluctant growth of vegetable forms and with alien tribes of animal life. These intentional changes and substitutions constitute, indeed, great revolutions; but vast as is their magnitude and importance, they are, as we shall see, insignificant in comparison with the contingent and unsought results which have flowed from them.

The fact that, of all organic beings, man alone is to be regarded as essentially a destructive power, and that he wields energies to resist which Nature—that nature whom all material life and all inorganic substance obey —is wholly impotent, tends to prove that, though living in physical nature, he is not of her, that he is of more exalted parentage, and belongs to a higher order of existences, than those

* The original work, *Man and Nature*, was published in 1864. The present selection is taken from the revision: George P. Marsh, *The Earth as Modified by Human Action* (New York, 1885), pp. 33–47.

which are born of her womb and live in blind submission to her dictates.

There are, indeed, brute destroyers, beasts and birds and insects of prey— all animal life feeds upon, and, of course, destroys other life,—but this destruction is balanced by compensations. It is, in fact, the very means by which the existence of one tribe of animals or of vegetables is secured against being smothered by the encroachments of another; and the reproductive powers of species which serve as the food of others are always proportioned to the demand they are destined to supply. Man pursues his victims with reckless destructiveness; and while the sacrifice of life by the lower animals is limited by the cravings of appetite, he unsparingly persecutes, even to extirpation, thousands of organic forms which he can not consume.

The earth was not, in its natural condition, completely adapted to the use of man, but only to the sustenance of wild animals and wild vegetation. These live, multiply their kind in just proportion, and attain their perfect measure of strength and beauty, without producing or requiring any important change in the natural arrangements of surface or in each other's spontaneous tendencies, except such mutual repression of excessive increase as may prevent the extirpation of one species by the encroachments of another. In short, without man, lower animal and spontaneous vegetable life would have been practically constant in type, distribution, and proportion, and the physical geography of the earth would have remained undisturbed for indefinite periods, and been subject to revolution only from slow development, from possible unknown cosmical causes, or from geological action.

But man, the domestic animals that serve him, the field and garden plants the products of which supply him with food and clothing, can not subsist and

rise to the full development of their higher properties, unless brute and unconscious nature be effectually combated, and, in a great degree, vanquished by human art. Hence, a certain measure of transformation of terrestrial surface, of suppression of natural, and stimulation of artificially modified productivity becomes necessary. This measure man has unfortunately exceeded. He has felled the forests whose network of fibrous roots bound the mould to the rocky skeleton of the earth; but had he allowed here and there a belt of woodland to reproduce itself by spontaneous propagation, most of the mischiefs which his reckless destruction of the natural protection of the soil has occasioned would have been averted. He has broken up the mountain reservoirs, the percolation of whose waters through unseen channels supplied the fountains that refreshed his cattle and fertilized his fields; but he has neglected to maintain the cisterns and the canals of irrigation which a wise antiquity had constructed to neutralize the consequences of its own imprudence. While he has torn the thin glebe which confined the light earth of extensive plains, and has destroyed the fringe of semi-aquatic plants which skirted the coast and checked the drifting of the sea sand, he has failed to prevent the spreading of the dunes by clothing them with artificially propagated vegetation. He has ruthlessly warred on all the tribes of animated nature whose spoil he could convert to his own uses, and he has not protected the birds which prey on the insects most destructive to his own harvests.

Purely untutored humanity, it is true, interferes comparatively little with the arrangements of nature, and the destructive agency of man becomes more and more energetic and unsparing as he advances in civilization, until the impoverishment, with which his exhaustion of the natural resources of the soil is threatening him, at last awakens him to the necessity of preserving what is left, if not of restoring what has been wantonly wasted. The wandering savage grows no cultivated vegetable, fells no forest, and extirpates no useful plant, no noxious weed. If his skill in the chase enables him to entrap numbers of the animals on which he feeds, he compensates this loss by destroying also the lion, the tiger, the wolf, the otter, the seal, and the eagle, thus indirectly protecting the feebler quadrupeds and fish and fowls, which would otherwise become the booty of beasts and bird of prey. But with stationary life, or at latest with the pastoral state, man at once commences an almost indiscriminate warfare upon all the forms of animal and vegetable existence around him, and as he advances in civilization, he gradually eradicates or transforms every spontaneous product of the soil he occupies.

Human and Brute Action Compared

It is maintained by authorities as high as any known to modern science, that the action of man upon nature, though greater in *degree,* does not differ in *kind* from that of wild animals. It is perhaps impossible to establish a radical distinction *in genere* between the two classes of effects, but there is an essential difference between the motive of action which calls out the energies of civilized man and the mere appetite which controls the life of the beast. The action of man, indeed, is frequently followed by unforeseen and undesired results, yet it is nevertheless guided by a self-conscious will aiming as often at secondary and remote as at immediate objects. The wild animal, on the other hand, acts instinctively, and, so far as we are able to perceive, always with a view to single and direct purposes. The backwoodsman and the beaver alike fell trees; the man, that he

may convert the forest into an olive grove that will mature its fruit only for a succeeeding generation; the beaver, that he may feed upon the bark of the trees or use them in the construction of his habitation. The action of brutes upon the material world is slow and gradual, and usually limited, in any case, to a narrow extent of territory. Nature is allowed time and opportunity to set her restorative powers at work, and the destructive animal has hardly retired from the field of his ravages before nature has repaired the damages occasioned by his operations. In fact, he is expelled from the scene by the very efforts which she makes for the restoration of her dominion. Man, on the contrary, extends his action over vast spaces, his revolutions are swift and radical, and his devastations are, for an almost incalculable time after he has withdrawn the arm that gave the blow, irreparable.

The form of geographical surface, and very probably the climate, of a given country, depend much on the character of the vegetable life belonging to it. Man had, by domestication, greatly changed the habits and properties of the plants he rears; he has, by voluntary selection, immensely modified the forms and qualities of the animated creatures that serve him; and he has, at the same time, completely rooted out many forms of animal if not of vegetable being. What is there in the influence of brute life that corresponds to this? We have no reason to believe that, in that portion of the American continent which, though peopled by many tribes of quadruped and fowl, remained uninhabited by man or thinly occupied by purely savage tribes, any sensible geographical change had occurred within twenty centuries before the epoch of discovery and colonization, while, during the same period, man had changed millions of square miles, in the fairest and most fertile regions of the Old World, into the barrenest deserts.

The ravages committed by man subvert the relations and destroy the balance which nature had established between her organized and her inorganic creations, and she avenges herself upon the intruder, by letting loose upon her defaced provinces destructive energies hitherto kept in check by organic forces destined to be his best auxiliaries, but which he has unwisely dispersed and driven from the field of action. When the forest is gone, the great reservoir of moisture stored up in its vegetable mould is evaporated, and returns only in deluges of rain to wash away the parched dust into which that mould has been converted. The well-wooded and humid hills are turned to ridges of dry rock, which encumber the low grounds and choke the watercourses with the débris, and—except in countries favored with an equable distribution of rain through the seasons, and a moderate and regular inclination of surface—the whole earth, unless rescued by human art from the physical degradation to which it tends, becomes an assemblage of bald mountains, of barren, turfless hills, and of swampy and malarious plains. There are parts of Asia Minor, of Northern Africa, of Greece, and even of Alpine Europe, where the operation of causes set in action by man has brought the face of the earth to desolation almost as complete as that of the moon; and though, within that brief space of time which we call "the historical period," they are known to have been covered with luxuriant woods, verdant pastures, and fertile meadows, they are now too far deteriorated to be reclaimable by man, nor can they become again fitted for human use, except through great geological changes, or other mysterious influences or agencies of which we have no present knowledge and over which we have no prospective control. The earth is fast becoming an unfit home for its noblest inhabitant, and another era of equal human crime and human improvidence, and of like duration with that through which traces of that crime and improvidence extend, would reduce it to such a condition of impoverished productiveness, of shattered surface, of climatic excess, as to threaten the depravation, barbarism, and perhaps even extinction of the species.

Physical Improvement

True, there is a partial reverse to this picture. On narrow theatres, new forests have been planted; inundations of flowing streams restrained by heavy walls of masonry and other constructions; torrents compelled to aid, by depositing the slime with which they are charged, in filling up lowlands, and raising the level of morasses which their own overflows had created; ground submerged by the encroachments of the ocean, or exposed to be covered by its tides, has been rescued from its dominion by diking; swamps and even lakes have been drained, and their beds brought within the domain of agricultural industry; drifting coast dunes have been checked and made productive by plantation; seas and inland waters have been repeopled with fish, and even the sands of the Sahara have been fertilized by artesian fountains. These achievements are more glorious than the proudest triumphs of war, but, thus far, they give but faint hope that we shall yet make full atonement for our spendthrift waste of the bounties of nature.

Limits of Human Power

It is, on the one hand, rash and unphilosophical to attempt to set limits to the ultimate power of man over inorganic nature, and it is unprofitable, on the other, to speculate on what may be accomplished by the discovery of now unknown and unimagined natural forces, or even by the invention of new arts and new processes. But since we have seen aerostation, the motive power of elastic vapors, the wonders of modern telegraphy, the destructive explosiveness of gunpowder, of nitro-glycerine, and even of a substance so harmless, unresisting, and inert as cotton, there is little in the way of mechanical achievement which seems hopelessly impossible, and it is hard to restrain the imagination from wandering forward a couple of generations to an epoch when our descendants shall have advanced as far beyond us in physical conquest, as we have marched beyond the trophies erected by our grandfathers. There are, nevertheless, in actual practice, limits to the efficiency of the forces which we are now able to bring into the field, and we must admit that, for the present, the agencies known to man and controlled by him are inadequate to the reducing of great Alpine precipices to such slopes as would enable them to support a vegetable clothing, or to the covering of large extents of denuded rock with earth, and planting upon them a forest growth. Yet among the mysteries which science is hereafter to reveal, there may be still undiscovered methods of accomplishing even grander wonders than these. Mechanical philosophers have suggested the possibility of accumulating and treasuring up for human use some of the greater natural forces, which the action of the elements puts forth with such astonishing energy. Could we gather, and bind, and make subservient to our control, the power which a West Indian hurricane exerts through a small area in one continuous blast, or the momentum expended by the waves, in a tempestuous winter, upon the breakwater at Cherbourg, or the lifting power of the tide, for a month, at the head of the Bay of Fundy, or the pressure of a square mile of sea water at the depth of five thousand fathoms, or a moment of the might of an earthquake or a volcano, our age—which moves no mountains and casts them into the sea by faith alone—might hope to scarp the rugged walls of the Alps and Pyrenees and Mount Taurus, robe them once more in a vegetation as rich as that of their pristine woods, and turn their wasting torrents into refreshing streams.

The recent discoveries of, if not new laws, at least of new relations between electrical energy and other natural forces and objects, and the various inventions for rendering this energy available for human uses, open a prospect of vast addition to the powers hitherto wielded by man. It is too soon even to conjecture by what limits these powers are conditioned, but it would seem that there is every reason to expect that man's most splendid achievements hitherto, in the conquest of Nature, will soon be eclipsed by new and more brilliant victories of mind over matter.

Could this Old World, which man has overthrown, be rebuilded, could human cunning rescue its wasted hillsides and its deserted plains from solitude or mere nomade occupation, from barrenness, from nakedness, and from insalubrity, and restore the ancient fertility and healthfulness of the Etruscan sea coast, the Campagna and the Pontine marshes, of Calabria, of Sicily, of the Peloponnesus and insular and continental Greece, of Asia Minor, of the slopes of Lebanon and Hermon, of Palestine, of the Syrian desert, of Mesopotamia and the delta of the Euphrates, of the Cyrenaica, of Africa proper, Numidia and Mauritania, the thronging millions of Europe might still find room on the Eastern continent, and the main current of emigration be turned towards the rising instead of the setting sun.

But changes like these must await not only great political and moral revolutions in the governments and peoples by whom those regions are now possessed, but, especially, a command of pecuniary and of mechanical means not at present enjoyed by those nations, and a more advanced and generally diffused knowledge of the processes by which the amelioration of soil and climate is possible than now anywhere exists. Until such circumstances shall conspire to favor the work of geographical regeneration, the countries I have mentioned, with here and there a local exception, will continue to sink into yet deeper desolation, and in the meantime the American continent, Southern Africa, Australia, New Zealand, and the smaller oceanic islands, will be almost the only theatres where man is engaged, on a great scale, in transforming the face of nature.

10. JOHN DOS PASSOS, *Proteus, 1930**

Steinmetz was a hunchback
son of a hunchback lithographer.

He was born in Breslau in 1865, graduated with highest honors at seventeen from the Breslau Gymnasium, went to the University of Breslau to study Mathematics;

mathematics to Steinmetz was muscular strength and long walks over the hills and the kiss of a girl in love and big evenings spent swilling beer with your friends;

on his broken back he felt the top-heavy weight of society the way workingmen felt it on their straight backs, the way poor students felt it, was a member of a socialist club, editor of a paper called *The People's Voice.*

Bismarck was sitting in Berlin like a big paperweight to keep the new Germany feudal, to hold down the empire for his bosses the Hohenzollerns.

Steinmetz had to run off to Zurich for fear of going to jail; at Zurich his mathematics woke up all the professors at the Polytechnic;

but Europe in the eighties was no place for a penniless German student with a broken back and a big head filled with symbolic calculus and wonder about electricity that is mathematics made power
and a socialist at that.

With a Danish friend he sailed for America steerage on an old French line boat *La Champagne,*

lived in Brooklyn at first and commuted to Yonkers where he had a twelvedollar a week job with Rudolph Eichemeyer who was a German exile from fortyeight an inventor and electrician and owner of a factory where he made hatmaking machinery and electrical generators.

In Yonkers he worked out the theory of the Third Harmonics
and the law of hysteresis which states in a formula the hundredfold relations between the metallic heat, density, frequency when the poles change places in the core of a magnet under an alternating current.

It is Steinmetz's law of hysteresis that makes possible all the transformers that crouch in little boxes and gableroofed houses in all the hightension lines all over everywhere. The mathematical

* John Dos Passos, *The 42nd Parallel* (New York: Harper & Brothers, 1930), pp. 332–35. Copyright by John Dos Passos, 1930, 1932, 1936; renewed 1958, 1960, and used with his permission.

symbols of Steinmetz's law are the patterns of all transformers everywhere.

In eighteen ninetytwo when Eichemeyer sold out to the corporation that was to form General Electric, Steinmetz was entered in the contract along with other valuable apparatus. All his life Steinmetz was a piece of apparatus belonging to General Electric.

First his laboratory was at Lynn, then it was moved and the little hunchback with it to Schenectady, the electric city.

General Electric humored him, let him be a socialist, let him keep a greenhouseful of cactuses lit up by mercury lights, let him have alligators, talking crows and a gila monster for pets and the publicity department talked up the wizard, the medicine man who knew the symbols that opened up the doors of Ali Baba's cave.

Steinmetz jotted a formula on his cuff and next morning a thousand new powerplants had sprung up and the dynamos sang dollars and the silence of the transformers was all dollars,

and the publicity department poured oily stories into the ears of the American public every Sunday and Steinmetz became the little parlor magician,

who made a toy thunderstorm in his laboratory and made all the toy trains run on time and the meat stay cold in the icebox and the lamp in the parlor

and the great lighthouses and the searchlights and the revolving beams of light that guide airplanes at night towards Chicago, New York, St. Louis, Los Angeles,

and they let him be a socialist and believe that human society could be improved the way you can improve a dynamo and they let him be pro-German and write a letter offering his services to Lenin because mathematicians are so impractical who make up formulas by which you can build powerplants, factories, subway systems, light, heat, air, sunshine but not human relations that affect the stockholders' money and the directors' salaries.

Steinmetz was a famous magician and he talked to Edison tapping with the Morse code on Edison's knee

because Edison was so very deaf

and he went out West

to make speeches that nobody understood

and he talked to Bryan about God on a railroad train

and all the reporters stood round while he and Einstein

met face to face,

but they couldn't catch what they said

and Steinmetz was the most valuable piece of apparatus General Electric had until he wore out and died.

11. FRANKLIN D. ROOSEVELT, *Commonwealth Club Address, 1932**

I want to speak not of politics but of Government. I want to speak not of parties, but of universal principles. They are not political, except in that larger sense in which a great American once expressed a definition of politics,

that nothing in all of human life is foreign to the science of politics.

I do want to give you, however, a recollection of a long life spent for a large part in public office. Some of my conclusions and observations have been

* From *The Public Papers and Addresses of Franklin D. Roosevelt* (New York, 1938). Copyright 1938 by Franklin Delano Roosevelt. Printed by permission of Random House, Inc.

deeply accentuated in these past few weeks. I have traveled far—from Albany to the Golden Gate. I have seen many people, and heard many things, and today, when in a sense my journey has reached the half-way mark, I am glad of the opportunity to discuss with you what it all means to me.

Sometimes, my friends, particularly in years such as these, the hand of discouragement falls upon us. It seems that things are in a rut, fixed, settled, that the world has grown old and tired and very much out of joint. This is the mood of depression, of dire and weary depression.

But then we look around us in America, and everything tells us that we are wrong. America is new. It is in the process of change and development. It has the great potentialities of youth, and particularly is this true of the great West, and of this coast, and of California.

I would not have you feel that I regard this as in any sense a new community. I have traveled in many parts of the world, but never have I felt the arresting thought of the change and development more than here, where the old, mystic East would seem to be near us, where the currents of life and thought and commerce of the whole world meet us. This factor alone is sufficient to cause man to stop and think of the deeper meaning of things, when he stands in this community.

But more than that, I appreciate that the membership of this club consists of men who are thinking in terms beyond the immediate present, beyond their own immediate tasks, beyond their own individual interests. I want to invite you, therefore, to consider with me in the large, some of the relationships of Government and economic life that go deeply into our daily lives, our happiness, our future and our security.

The issue of Government has always been whether individual men and women will have to serve some system of Government or economics, or whether a system of Government and economics exists to serve individual men and women. This question has persistently dominated the discussion of Government for many generations. On questions relating to these things men have differed, and for time immemorial it is probable that honest men will continue to differ.

The final word belongs to no man; yet we can still believe in change and progress. Democracy, as a dear old friend of mine in Indiana, Meredith Nicholson, has called it, is a quest, a never-ending seeking for better things, and in the seeking for these things and the striving for them, there are many roads to follow. But, if we map the course of these roads, we find that there are only two general directions.

When we look about us, we are likely to forget how hard people have worked to win the privilege of Government. The growth of the national Governments of Europe was a struggle for the development of a centralized force in the Nation, strong enough to impose peace upon ruling barons. In many instances the victory of the central Government, the creation of a strong central Government, was a haven of refuge to the individual. The people preferred the master far away to the exploitation and cruelty of the smaller master near at hand.

But the creators of national Government were perforce ruthless men. They were often cruel in their methods, but they did strive steadily toward something that society needed and very much wanted, a strong central State able to keep the peace, to stamp out civil war, to put the unruly nobleman in his place, and to permit the bulk of individuals to live safely. The man of ruthless force had his place in developing a pioneer country, just as he did in fixing the power of the central Government in the development of Nations. Society paid him well for his services and its development. When the development among the Nations of Europe, however, had been completed, ambition and ruthlessness, having served their term, tended to overstep their mark.

There came a growing feeling that Government was conducted for the benefit of a few who thrived unduly at the expense of all. The people sought a balancing—a limiting force. There came gradually, through town councils, trade guilds, national parliaments, by constitution and by popular participation and control, limitations on arbitrary power.

Another factor that tended to limit the power of those who ruled, was the rise of the ethical conception that a ruler bore a responsibility for the welfare of his subjects.

The American colonies were born in this struggle. The American Revolution was a turning point in it. After the Revolution the struggle continued and shaped itself in the public life of the country. There were those who because they had seen the confusion which attended the years of war for American independence surrendered to the belief that popular Government was essentially dangerous and essentially unworkable. They were honest people, my friends, and we cannot deny that their experience had warranted some measure of fear. The most brilliant, honest and able exponent of this point of view was Hamilton. He was too impatient of slow-moving methods. Fundamentally he believed that the safety of the republic lay in the autocratic strength of its Government, that the destiny of individuals was to serve that Government, and that fundamentally a great and strong group of central institutions, guided by a small group of able and public-spirited citizens, could best direct all Government.

But Mr. Jefferson, in the summer of 1776, after drafting the Declaration of Independence turned his mind to the same problem and took a different view. He did not deceive himself with outward forms. Government to him was a means to an end, not an end in itself; it might be either a refuge and a help or a threat and a danger, depending on the circumstances. We find him carefully analyzing the society for which he was to organize a Government. "We have no paupers. The great mass of our population is of laborers, our rich who cannot live without labor, either manual or professional, being few and of moderate wealth. Most of the laboring class possess property, cultivate their own lands, have families and from the demand for their labor, are enabled to exact from the rich and the competent such prices as enable them to feed abundantly, clothe above mere decency, to labor moderately and raise their families."

These people, he considered, had two sets of rights, those of "personal competency" and those involved in acquiring and possessing property. By "personal competency" he meant the right of free thinking, freedom of forming and expressing opinions, and freedom of personal living, each man according to his own lights. To insure the first set of rights, a Government must so order its functions as not to interfere with the individual. But even Jefferson realized that the exercise of the property rights might so interfere with the rights of the individual that the Government, without whose assistance the property rights could not exist, must intervene, not to destroy individualism, but to protect it.

You are familiar with the great political duel which followed; and how Hamilton, and his friends, building toward a dominant centralized power were at length defeated in the great election of 1800, by Mr. Jefferson's party. Out of that duel came the two parties, Republican and Democratic, as we know them today.

So began, in American political life, the new day, the day of the individual against the system, the day in which individualism was made the great watchword of American life. The happiest of economic conditions made that day long and splendid. On the Western frontier, land was substantially free. No one, who did not shirk the task of earning a living, was entirely without opportunity to do so. Depressions could, and did, come and go; but they could not alter the fundamental fact that most of the people lived partly by selling their labor and partly by extracting their livelihood from the soil, so that starvation and dislocation were practically impossible. At the very worst there was always the possibility of climbing into a covered wagon and moving west where the untilled prairies afforded a haven for men to whom the East did not provide a place. So great were our natural resources that we could offer this relief not only to our own people, but to the distressed of all the world; we could invite immigration from Europe, and welcome it with open arms. Traditionally, when a depression came a new section of land was opened in the West; and even our temporary misfortune served our manifest destiny.

It was in the middle of the nineteenth century that a new force was released and a new dream created. The force was what is called the industrial revolution, the advance of steam and machinery and the rise of the forerunners of the modern industrial plant. The dream was the dream of an economic machine, able to raise the standard of living for everyone; to bring luxury within the reach of the humblest; to annihilate distance by steam power and later by electricity, and to release everyone from the drudgery of the heaviest manual toil. It was to be expected that this would necessarily affect Government. Heretofore, Government had merely been called upon to produce conditions within which people could live happily, labor peacefully, and rest secure. Now it was called upon to aid in the consummation of this new dream. There was, however, a shadow over the dream. To be made real, it required use of the talents of men of tremendous will and tremendous ambition, since by no other force could the problems of financing and engineering and new developments be brought to a consummation.

So manifest were the advantages of the machine age, however, that the United States fearlessly, cheerfully, and, I think, rightly, accepted the bitter with the sweet. It was thought that no price was too high to pay for the advantages which we could draw from a finished industrial system. The history of the last half century is accordingly in large measure a history of a group of financial Titans, whose methods were not scrutinized with too much care, and who were honored in proportion as they produced the results, irrespective of the means they used. The financiers who pushed the railroads to the Pacific were always ruthless, often wasteful, and frequently corrupt; but they did build railroads, and we have them today. It has been estimated that the American investor paid for the American railway system more than three times over in the process; but despite this fact the net advantage was to the United States. As long as we had free land; as long as population was growing by leaps and bounds; as long as our industrial plants were insufficient to supply our own needs, society chose to give the ambitious man free play and unlimited reward provided only that he produced the economic plant so much desired.

During this period of expansion,

there was equal opportunity for all and the business of Government was not to interfere but to assist in the development of industry. This was done at the request of business men themselves. The tariff was originally imposed for the purpose of "fostering our infant industry," a phrase I think the older among you will remember as a political issue not so long ago. The railroads were subsidized, sometimes by grants of money, oftener by grants of land; some of the most valuable oil lands in the United States were granted to assist the financing of the railroad which pushed through the Southwest. A nascent merchant marine was assisted by grants of money, or by mail subsidies, so that our steam shipping might ply the seven seas. Some of my friends tell me that they do not want the Government in business. With this I agree; but I wonder whether they realize the implications of the past. For while it has been American doctrine that the Government must not go into business in competition with private enterprises, still it has been traditional, particularly in Republican administrations, for business to ask the Government to put at private disposal all kinds of Government assistance. The same man who tells you that he does not want to see the Government interfere in business— and he means it, and has plenty of good reasons for saying so—is the first to go to Washington and ask the Government for a prohibitory tariff on his product. When things get just bad enough, as they did two years ago, he will go with equal speed to the United States Government and ask for a loan; and the Reconstruction Finance Corporation is the outcome of it. Each group has sought protection from the Government for its own special interests, without realizing that the function of Government must be to favor no small group at the expense of its duty to protect the rights of personal freedom and of private property of all its citizens.

In retrospect we can now see that the turn of the tide came with the turn of the century. We were reaching our last frontier; there was no more free land and our industrial combinations had become great uncontrolled and irresponsible units of power within the State. Clear-sighted men saw with fear the danger that opportunity would no longer be equal; that the growing corporation, like the feudal baron of old, might threaten the economic freedom of individuals to earn a living. In that hour, our anti-trust laws were born. The cry was raised against the great corporations. Theodore Roosevelt, the first great Republican Progressive, fought a Presidential campaign on the issue of "trust busting" and talked freely about malefactors of great wealth. If the Government had a policy it was rather to turn the clock back, to destroy the large combinations and to return to the time when every man owned his individual small business.

This was impossible; Theodore Roosevelt, abandoning the idea of "trust busting," was forced to work out a difference between "good" trusts and "bad" trusts. The Supreme Court set forth the famous "rule of reason" by which it seems to have meant that a concentration of industrial power was permissible if the method by which it got its power, and the use it made of that power, were reasonable.

Woodrow Wilson, elected in 1912, saw the situation more clearly. Where Jefferson had feared the encroachment of political power on the lives of individuals, Wilson knew that the new power was financial. He saw, in the highly centralized economic system, the despot of the twentieth century, on whom great masses of individuals relied for their safety and their livelihood, and whose irresponsibility and greed (if they were not controlled) would reduce them to starvation and penury. The concentration of financial power had not proceeded so far in 1912 as it has today; but it had grown far enough for Mr. Wilson to realize fully its implications. It is interesting, now, to read his speeches. What is called "radical" today (and I have reason to know whereof I speak) is mild compared to the campaign of Mr. Wilson. "No man can deny," he said, "that the lines of endeavor have more and more narrowed and stiffened; no man who knows anything about the development of industry in this country can have failed to observe that the larger kinds of credit are more and more difficult to obtain unless you obtain them upon terms of uniting your efforts with those who already control the industry of the country, and nobody can fail to observe that every man who tries to set himself up in competition with any process of manufacture which has taken place under the control of large combinations of capital will presently find himself either squeezed out or obliged to sell and allow himself to be absorbed." Had there been no World War—had Mr. Wilson been able to devote eight years to domestic instead of to international affairs—we might have had a wholly different situation at the present time. However, the then distant roar of European cannon, growing ever louder, forced him to abandon the study of this issue. The problem he saw so clearly is left with us as a legacy; and no one of us on either side of the political controversy can deny that it is a matter of grave concern to the Government.

A glance at the situation today only too clearly indicates that equality of opportunity as we have known it no longer exists. Our industrial plant is built; the problem just now is whether under existing conditions it is not over-built. Our last frontier has long since been reached, and there is practically no more free land. More than half of our people do not live on the farms or on lands and cannot derive a living by cultivating their own property. There is no safety valve in the form of a Western prairie to which those thrown out of work by the Eastern economic machines can go for a new start. We are not able to invite the immigration from Europe to share our endless plenty. We are now providing a drab living for our own people.

Our system of constantly rising tariffs has at last reacted against us to the point of closing our Canadian frontier on the north, our European markets on the east, many of our Latin-American markets to the south, and a goodly proportion of our Pacific markets on the west, through the retaliatory tariffs of those countries. It has forced many of our great industrial institutions which exported their surplus production to such countries, to establish plants in such countries, within the tariff walls. This has resulted in the reduction of the operation of their American plants, and opportunity for employment.

Just as freedom to farm has ceased, so also the opportunity in business has narrowed. It still is true that men can start small enterprises, trusting to native shrewdness and ability to keep abreast of competitors; but area after area has been preempted altogether by the great corporations, and even in the fields which still have no great concerns, the small man starts under a handicap. The unfeeling statistics of the past three decades show that the independent business man is running a losing race. Perhaps he is forced to the wall; perhaps he cannot command credit; perhaps he is "squeezed out," in Mr. Wilson's words, by highly organized corporate competitors, as your corner grocery man can tell you. Recently a careful study was made of the concentration of business in the United

States. It showed that our economic life was dominated by some six hundred odd corporations who controlled two-thirds of American industry. Ten million small business men divided the other third. More striking still, it appeared that if the process of concentration goes on at the same rate, at the end of another century we shall have all American industry controlled by a dozen corporations, and run by perhaps a hundred men. Put plainly, we are steering a steady course toward economic oligarchy, if we are not there already.

Clearly, all this calls for a reappraisal of values. A mere builder of more industrial plants, a creator of more railroad systems, an organizer of more corporations, is as likely to be a danger as a help. The day of the great promoter or the financial Titan, to whom we granted anything if only he would build, or develop, is over. Our task now is not discovery or exploitation of natural resources, or necessarily producing more goods. It is the soberer, less dramatic business of administering resources and plants already in hand, of seeking to restablish foreign markets for our surplus production, of meeting the problem of underconsumption, of adjusting production to consumption, of distributing wealth and products more equitably, of adapting existing economic organizations to the service of the people. The day of enlightened administration has come.

Just as in older times the central Government was first a haven of refuge, and then a threat, so now in a closer economic system the central and ambitious financial unit is no longer a servant of national desire, but a danger. I would draw the parallel one step farther. We did not think because national Government had become a threat in the 18th century that therefore we should abandon the principle of national Government. Nor today should we abandon the principle of

strong economic units called corporations, merely because their power is susceptible of easy abuse. In other times we dealt with the problem of an unduly central Government by modifying it gradually into a constitutional democratic Government. So today we are modifying and controlling our economic units.

As I see it, the task of Government in its relation to business is to assist the development of an economic declaration of rights, an economic constitutional order. This is the common task of statesman and business man. It is the minimum requirement of a more permanently safe order of things.

Happily, the times indicate that to create such an order not only is the proper policy of Government, but it is the only line of safety for our economic structures as well. We know, now, that these economic units cannot exist unless prosperity is uniform, that is, unless purchasing power is well distributed throughout every group in the Nation. That is why even the most selfish of corporations for its own interest would be glad to see wages restored and unemployment ended and to bring the Western farmer back to his accustomed level of prosperity and to assure a permanent safety to both groups. That is why some enlightened industries themselves endeavor to limit the freedom of action of each man and business group within the industry in the common interest of all; why business men everywhere are asking a form of organization which will bring the scheme of things into balance, even though it may in some measure qualify the freedom of action of individual units within the business.

The exposition need not further be elaborated. It is brief and incomplete, but you will be able to expand it in terms of your own business or occupation without difficulty. I think everyone who has actually entered the economic struggle—which means everyone who was not born to safe wealth—knows in his own experience and his own life that we have now to apply the earlier concepts of American Government to the conditions of today.

The Declaration of Independence discusses the problem of Government in terms of a contract. Government is a relation of give and take, a contract, perforce, if we would follow the thinking out of which it grew. Under such a contract rulers were accorded power, and the people consented to that power on consideration that they be accorded certain rights. The task of statesmanship has always been the re-definition of these rights in terms of a changing and growing social order. New conditions impose new requirements upon Government and those who conduct Government.

I held, for example, in proceedings before me as Governor, the purpose of which was the removal of the Sheriff of New York, that under modern conditions it was not enough for a public official merely to evade the legal terms of official wrong-doing. He owed a positive duty as well. I said in substance that if he had acquired large sums of money, he was when accused required to explain the sources of such wealth. To that extent this wealth was colored with a public interest. I said that in financial matters, public servants should, even beyond private citizens, be held to a stern and uncompromising rectitude.

I feel that we are coming to a view through the drift of our legislation and our public thinking in the past quarter century that private economic power is, to enlarge an old phrase, a public trust as well. I hold that continued enjoyment of that power by any individual or group must depend upon the fulfillment of that trust. The men who have reached the summit of American business life know this best; happily, many of these urge the binding quality of this greater social contract.

The terms of that contract are as old as the Republic, and as new as the new economic order.

Every man has a right to life; and this means that he has also the right to make a comfortable living. He may by sloth or crime decline to exercise that right; but it may not be denied him. We have no actual famine or dearth; our industrial and agricultural mechanism can produce enough and to spare. Our Government formal and informal, political and economic, owes to everyone an avenue to possess himself of a portion of that plenty sufficient for his needs, through his own work.

Every man has a right to his own property; which means a right to be assured, to the fullest extent attainable, in the safety of his savings. By no other means can men carry the burdens of those parts of life which, in the nature of things, afford no chance of labor; childhood, sickness, old age. In all thought of property, this right is paramount; all other property rights must yield to it. If, in accord with this principle, we must restrict the operations of the speculator, the manipulator, even the financier, I believe we must accept the restriction as needful, not to hamper individualism but to protect it.

These two requirements must be satisfied, in the main, by individuals who claim and hold control of the great industrial and financial combinations which dominate so large a part of our industrial life. They have undertaken to be, not business men, but princes of property. I am not prepared to say that the system which produces them is wrong. I am very clear that they must fearlessly and competently assume the responsibility which goes with the power. So many enlightened business men know this that the statement would be little more than a platitude, were it not for an added implication.

This implication is, briefly, that the

responsible heads of finance and industry, instead of acting each for himself, must work together to achieve the common end. They must, where necessary, sacrifice this or that private advantage; and in reciprocal self-denial must seek a general advantage. It is here that formal Government—political Government, if you choose—comes in. Whenever in the pursuit of this objective the lone wolf, the unethical competitor, the reckless promoter, the Ishmael or Insull whose hand is against every man's, declines to join in achieving an end recognized as being for the public welfare, and threatens to drag the industry back to a state of anarchy, the Government may properly be asked to apply restraint. Likewise, should the group ever use its collective power contrary to the public welfare, the Government must be swift to enter and protect the public interest.

The Government should assume the function of economic regulation only as a last resort, to be tried only when private initiative, inspired by high responsibility, with such assistance and balance as Government can give, has finally failed. As yet there has been no final failure, because there has been no attempt; and I decline to assume that this Nation is unable to meet the situation.

The final term of the high contract was for liberty and the pursuit of happiness. We have learned a great deal of both in the past century. We know that individual liberty and individual happiness mean nothing unless both are ordered in the sense that one man's meat is not another man's poison. We know that the old "rights of personal competency," the right to read, to think, to speak, to choose and live a mode of life, must be respected at all hazards. We know that liberty to do anything which deprives others of those elemental rights is outside the protection of any compact; and that

Government in this regard is the maintenance of a balance, within which every individual may have a place if he will take it; in which every individual may find safety if he wishes it; in which every individual may attain such power as his ability permits, consistent with his assuming the accompanying responsibility.

All this is a long, slow task. Nothing is more striking than the simple innocence of the men who insist, whenever an objective is present, on the prompt production of a patent scheme guaranteed to produce a result. Human endeavor is not so simple as that. Government includes the art of formulating a policy, and using the political technique to attain so much of that policy as will receive general support; persuading, leading, sacrificing, teaching always, because the greatest duty of a statesman is to educate. But in the matters of which I have spoken, we are learning rapidly, in a severe school. The lessons so learned must not be forgotten, even in the mental lethargy of a speculative upturn. We must build toward the time when a major depression cannot occur again; and if this means sacrificing the easy profits of inflationist booms, then let them go; and good riddance.

Faith in America, faith in our tradition of personal responsibility, faith in our institutions, faith in ourselves demand that we recognize the new terms of the old social contract. We shall fulfill them, as we fulfilled the obligation of the apparent Utopia which Jefferson imagined for us in 1776, and which Jefferson, Roosevelt, and Wilson sought to bring to realization. We must do so, lest a rising tide of misery, engendered by our common failure, engulf us all. But failure is not an American habit; and in the strength of great hope we must all shoulder our common load.

III

****

Material Well-Being

JAMES RESTON

was born in Clydebank, Scotland, in 1909.

His parents brought him to the United States the following year, but he returned to Scotland for some of his early schooling and then came back to this country in 1920. He attended public schools in Dayton, Ohio, and graduated from the University of Illinois in 1932.

After holding a number of news and publicity jobs in the Middle West, he joined The Associated Press in 1934 as a sports writer in New York. Three years later the agency sent him to London where he covered the diplomatic activity preceding the outbreak of World War II. In 1939 he joined the London Bureau of the New York *Times* and spent most of the war years in London and Washington. He became the Washington correspondent of the *Times* in 1953.

Mr. Reston won the Pulitzer Prize for his news dispatches in 1944 and 1956. He now writes an editorial page column three times a week in addition to his news reporting.

James Reston ✳✳✳✳ Our History Suggests a Remedy

If it is true that America needs and lacks a sense of purpose, the history of the nation suggests a remedy.

For if George Washington had waited for the doubters to develop a sense of purpose in the 18th century, he'd still be crossing the Delaware. In fact, most of the great political crises of the American past have been resolved, not by the zeal and purpose of the people, but usually by the will power or obstinacy of their leaders.

No doubt the massive thirst of a long-tormented majority brought back 3.2 beer, but the plain fact is that in most other emergencies, a resolute minority has usually prevailed over an easy-going or wobbly majority whose primary purpose was to be left alone.

John Adams estimated that one-third of the population was against the American Revolution, one-third for it, and one-third indifferent. And this is the way it has usually been.

Some far-sighted character like Thomas Jefferson or Teddy Roosevelt was always buying Louisiana or the Panama Canal when nobody was looking, and writers have always been grumbling, mainly to each other, about the feebleness of the national will.

The main difference between today's lamentations and those of the past is that the language is milder and the pay better. Thomas Paine, roaring about America's mulish indifference in 1775, makes today's orators sound complacent. And even Ralph Waldo Emerson, who was really a pretty cheery fellow, could wail in 1847:

"Alas for America, the air is loaded with poppy, with imbecility, with dispersion and sloth. . . . Eager, solicitous, hungry, rabid, busy-bodied America: catch thy breath and correct thyself."

Thus, criticism of the American people for lack of purpose is not new. What is new is that leaders now seem to think they must follow the nation instead of leading it. What is new is that a hostile coalition of nations now has the military power to destroy the Republic. The margin of error granted to us in past wars and crises has vanished. What could be won before with partial effort, late starts, feeble alliances, and mediocre administration can no longer be won in a contest with the Communists.

It is not that they are so efficient but that they are so purposeful. They are all working on the main target and we are not. Life, tyranny, and the pursuit of Capitalists is the Russian way of life. They have obliterated the difference between war and peace. They are always at war, all of them, women as well as men—teachers, philosophers, scientists, engineers, lady discus throwers, airmen, and three or four million foot soldiers.

None of this need trouble us very much except for *their* national purpose, which is simply to replace our system of individual freedom with their system of state control wherever they can, including regions vital to our security such as Germany, Japan, and even Cuba.

I must say they have been very frank about it. They have given us timely if not fair warning. They are directing all the energies of all their people to that goal. They are not arguing about the conflict between private interests and the national interest. They have simply eliminated private interest. They have put everybody to work on "burying" capitalism, and since our national purpose, among other things, is to avoid being buried, this creates an awkward and even nasty situation.

How, then, shall we approach the problem? I was brought up on the Church of Scotland's shorter catechism, the first question of which is: "What is the chief end of man?"

Accordingly, I am all for self-direction and self-criticism. Nevertheless, I have my doubts about the imminence of any self-induced renaissance or epoch of austerity.

When I consider attacking the problem through the people, I think of Harry Ashmore's old story about the man who acquired a reputation for training mules with honeyed words and kindness. Hearing about this remarkable achievement, the Society for the Prevention of Cruelty to Animals dispatched a lady emissary to present the mule-trainer with a medal.

Upon arrival, she asked for a demonstration. The trainer obligingly trotted out a young mule, reached for a long two-by-four, and clouted the beast over the head. As the mule struggled back to his feet, the good lady exclaimed in horror, "Good heavens, man, I thought you trained these animals with kindness!"

"I do, ma'am," he replied, "but first I got to git the critters' attention."

I don't know how just anybody gets the attention of 180 million people these days. They are engaged in the pursuit of happiness, which, incidentally, the Declaration of Independence spells with a capital "H," and to be frank about it, I suspect that public debates on the national purpose give them a pain.

It will not, I think, be wise to underestimate America's current resistance to exhortations from the preachers, professors, columnists, and editorial writers of the nation. For unless I miss my guess, the Americano, *circa* 1960, is in no mood to rush off on his own initiative to "emancipate the human race," or to set any new records as the greatest benefactor of all time, or engage in any of the other crusades mapped out for him in Cambridge, Mass.

He may do many of these things because he is honest enough to know that he doesn't know all the facts of this dangerous and complicated era, but he is not likely to set out to do them because of his own "reflection and reason" or the arguments of talkers or writers he seldom sees.

Accordingly, we must, I think, start with the national leadership, partly because this is the engine that has pulled us out of the mud before, and partly because this is an election year, when we will be picking a President, probably for most of the nineteen sixties.

The President of the United States is the one man who can get the attention of the American people. If he says the nation is in trouble, they will listen to him. If he addresses himself to their doubts and questions, they will hear him out. If he presents programs and legislation to do what he thinks is necessary for the safety of the Republic and explains and keeps explaining why these are essential, he may very well prevail.

All the magazine articles on the national purpose, all the reports by all the foundations on all our manifold weaknesses, all the speeches by Adlai Stevenson, Jack Kennedy, Lyndon Johnson, and Stuart Symington on the wickedness of the Republicans, all the exhortations to return to the faith of our fathers—all are nothing compared to serious programs eloquently expressed and strongly pushed by a determined president of the United States.

"His is the only national voice in affairs," wrote Woodrow Wilson. "Let him once win the admiration and confidence of the country and no other single force can withstand him, no combination of forces will easily overpower him. His position takes the imagination of the country. . . . His is the vital place of action in the system. . . ."

Of course, he has to act. He cannot ask for half-measures and run away. But once he expresses the national need, once he decides to try to remove rather than to perpetuate the illusions of the past, then his specific remedies will affect the spirit and direction of the nation.

I remember when the Marshall Plan for Europe was devised in Washington. It was perfectly obvious that the sickness of the European economy was creating a crisis of great magnitude, and the bare bones of a four-year plan, costing perhaps as much as $20,000,000,000, were worked out and approved by President Truman.

I printed a long story about it one Sunday in the New York *Times,* and by 10 o'clock that morning, the late Senator Arthur H. Vandenberg of Michigan, then Chairman of the Foreign Relations Committee, called me at home and said: "You must be out of your senses. No administration would dare to come to the Senate with a proposal like that."

Yet once the lead was taken and the need documented, Senator Vandenberg ended up as a key supporter of what almost everybody agrees was the most far-sighted piece of legislation since the war.

I do not underestimate the task. I agree with much that has been said in these essays about the slackness of our society, but I find the present mood understandable, perhaps inevitable, under the circumstances, and not without hope.

At the end of the last war, the American people made a genuine effort to clear the wreckage and understand the new situation. They went through the biggest geography and history lesson in their history, always with the false optimism that they were dealing with a temporary situation that would eventually go away.

Instead of going away, the problem became larger and more complex: after Europe, it was the Middle East; after the Middle East, the Far East; after the Far East, Africa; after Africa, outer space; and after outer space a lot of inner tensions over U-2, me too, inflation, deflation, rising cost of living, balance of payments, nuclear testing, sputniks, luniks and a lot of other things that everybody seemed to be differing about.

There was no panic about any of this. The people merely turned from what they did not understand to what they did understand. They turned inward from the world to the community and the family. In the 15 years of the atomic age, they increased the population of the nation by more than 40,000,000, which is not the action of a frightened people, and which is interesting when you think that the entire population of the country at the start of the Civil War 100 years ago was only 31,000,000.

A distinction has to be made, I think, between the façade of America and the other more genuine America. There is, of course, this big obvious clattering America of Hollywood and Madison Avenue and Washington, but there is also the outer, quieter America, which has either kept its religious faith or at least held on to the morality derived from religious tradition.

I do not wish to glorify the multitude. Much can be said about the dubious effects on the American character of very early marriage, easy credit, cheap booze, cheaper TV, low education standards, and job security even for sloppy work.

Nevertheless, there is more concern for the outside world, more interest in its problems, more generosity, and more resourcefulness in this society than in any free society I know anything about.

If it is true, as I believe, that this generation of Americans is doing less than it could, it is also true that it has done everything it was asked to do. It may be more concerned about its private interests than about the public interest, but if a man is offered a choice between a Cadillac and a swift kick in the pants, we should not be surprised if he doesn't bend over.

What has it been asked to do that it has not done?

It was asked to restore the broken economy of Europe, and it helped bring that continent, within a decade, to the highest level of prosperity in history.

It was asked to accept high taxation and military conscription to police the world, and it has done so from the North Cape of Norway to Japan and Korea.

It was asked to keep a standing army of a quarter of a million men in Western Europe and it has done so for 15 years, with scarcely a murmur of protest from a single American politician.

It was asked to abandon its tradition of isolation, and it took on more responsibilities involving more risks—in Korea and elsewhere—than the British ever did at the height of their imperial power

These are not the acts of a slack and decadent people. There is nothing in the record of free peoples to compare with it. This is not a static society. The problem is merely that the pace of history has outrun the pace of change. Ideas and policies have lagged behind events, so that by the time policies were formulated, debated, and put in force, the situations they were intended to remedy had changed.

Thus, in a torrent of change, in a revolution of science, a social revolution at home and an unprecedented political revolution in Asia, Africa, and Latin America, it is scarcely surprising that there is a crisis of understanding in the nation. This is all the more true because there has been a serious weakening of the ties between the men of ideas and the men of politics in this country during the last decade.

"Our slow world," wrote Woodrow Wilson in 1890, "spends its time catching up with the ideas of its best minds. It would seem that in almost every generation men are born who embody the projected consciousness of their time and people.

"Their thought runs forward apace into the regions whither the race is advancing, but where it will not for many a weary day arrive. . . . The new thoughts of one age are the commonplaces of the next.

"The men who act stand nearer to the mass than the men who write; and it is in their hands that new thought gets its translation into the crude language of deeds. . . ."

It cannot be said that the men of ideas in the country have not performed in these last few years their traditional tasks. They have observed the convulsions of our time and let their minds run ahead to the logical consequences for the nation.

I cannot remember a time when there has been more purposeful thought on contemporary problems in the universities and foundations than now. Their reports and conclusions would fill a good-sized library, but the alliance between them and the White House has been feeble, and somehow it must be restored.

What, then, can be done?

We can, at least, look at the world as it is instead of the world as we would like it to be. In the 43 years since the Soviet revolution—of which 25 have been devoted to establishing their regime and fighting the last world war—they have brought their industrial production to about 45% of ours.

Since the war, their rate of growth has been between 9 and 10% while ours has been in the neighborhood of 3%. They are having trouble with their agricultural production, but if they and we both continue at the present rates of growth, the experts figure they will have approximately as much effective industrial production as the United States in 1975.

On the face of it, this may not worry the American people, but it is perfectly obvious that the trend is running against us in this field, and that, as former Secretary of State Dean Acheson says, the likelihood is that Moscow will do three things with this new production: (1) increase their military capabilities; (2) increase their resources for economic penetration in the underdeveloped nations; and (3) by a combination of these two, demonstrate to the uncommitted countries of the world that the Soviet Union is the country of spectacular growth, and that the Communist system is the way to lift new countries in a short time into the new scientific age.

It is this latter point, rather than the threat of nuclear war against the United States, that concerns most students of the problem.

The Russians have already increased their exports to underdeveloped countries to about $3 million. They have five thousand people administering these programs. And they are directing them primarily in six countries of considerable political importance to the U.S.S.R.

It is much harder to understand the threat of this kind of economic penetration than it is to understand the threat of indirect Communist aggression, as, for example, in Korea. But the threat is there just the same.

Since the last war, 1.2 billion people have changed their form of government in the world, and 800 million of these have achieved independence for the first time. These new nations are determined to be industrialized, ready or not. Hunger and pestilence are not new in the world, but the 2 billion hungry people are less willing to tolerate hunger and pestilence now that they know something can be done about it.

How these new governments develop, in freedom or by the quicker way of state control, may very well determine, not only the climate of freedom in the world, but the balance of power as well.

Thus the primary problem of foreign affairs may very well be, not the East-West problem we hear so much about, but what Sir Oliver Frank calls the North-South problem: whether the nations of the South, in Africa, Asia, and Latin America, develop along the lines of the free industrialized nations of the north, or the state-controlled methods of the two large Communist northern states of the Soviet Union and China.

We have tended to make several assumptions about this: that most nations wanted to develop like the United States, that knowledge cannot develop except in a climate of freedom, and that the Western powers could deal with the underdeveloped nations without interfering much with present concepts of sovereignty or commercial practice.

All these assumptions are now under challenge. The Soviet Union has shown that spectacular scientific progress can be made in a closed society. Cuba, to take only one example close at hand, has not only indicated contempt for the American system of free enterprise but is now organizing its whole society under state control.

The problem is not that the Soviet Union produces better engineers than the United States—though it certainly produces more—but that it can direct its engineers into these new countries or anywhere else that helps promote the purpose of the state.

As Dean McGeorge Bundy of Harvard has pointed out:

"It may be that we are at the edge of a time in which authoritarian societies, controlling and using this new investment, the human mind, will be able to produce revolutions in power and in growth as remarkable to us as our own revolution, the industrial and technological revolution of the last 150 years, is remarkable today to the people who inhabit the world of rising expectations.

"To me, this hazardous possibility that centralized control of technology and of science behind it may lead to a new order of growth, of power, and of change in the hands of people with a high degree of political purpose and centralized and ruthless control . . . seems to be the real danger in the growth of Soviet and Chinese power."

My conclusions about all this mysterious sociology and economics are unoriginal, vague, and even modest. All I know about the "rate of growth" is what happened to three boys of my own in the last 23 years, and even that is a little confusing. It would be pleasant to think, however, that all this concern in the nation among serious men about the higher rate of growth in the U.S.S.R. was seriously discussed and not dismissed as another left-wing trick to increase the size of government or elect some Democrat.

First, therefore, an honest debate on the issue might not be a bad idea. Maybe we cannot do everything everywhere. Maybe after 125 years of isolation and a generation of internationalism, somebody should call out once more to America: "Catch thy breath and correct thyself."

But anyway, a revival of honest plain talk in the country wouldn't do any harm.

Second, in the face of the clear facts, anything less than the highest possible standard of education for the children of America is obviously a disgrace. We cannot punch kids out like cookies and drop them into slots, and wouldn't if we could; but we ought to be able to spend more money on their education than we do on all that sexy advertising.

Third, offhand, I would guess we were kidding ourselves in thinking we could do this job with the kind of people now working on it overseas or that we could do it without far more cooperation and coordination among the allies.

If the main war now is the battle in the underdeveloped areas, why not offer talented young men of draft age the option of using their brains in a civilian service in Indochina rather than sentencing them to Army KP in Hoboken?

It is not fair or accurate to say that the voluntary system cannot compete with the directed system in recruiting men for service in the under-developed areas, for no really imaginative effort has been made to attract the volunteers.

Thus, wherever you look it is hard to escape the conclusion that our response is unequal to the threat. We are in what Professor Walt Whitman Rostow of the Massachusetts Institute of Technology calls one of those "neurotic fixations of history." These are periods when nations are confronted by radically new situations but hang on to old policies that are increasingly divorced from reality.

This is what George III of England did when confronted by what he called the "rebellion" of the American colonies, what Edward VIII did when he hung on to Wally Simpson, what Stanley Baldwin did when he refused to rearm Britain in the face of Hitler's challenge, and what the United States did when it clung to isolation after the rise of Nazi Germany.

Isolation is now gone, but the hangover of the old habits of the days of isolation remain; in our assumptions that we can meet the Soviet challenge with the same school system, the same political patronage system, the same attitudes toward politics and the public service, and the same old chestnut about private interests inevitably serving the public interest.

It is not so much that we have lost our way forward but that we have lost our way home. This is the country of freedom, youth, experimentation, and innovation; of pioneers and missionaries and adventurers.

If you ask whether we can meet the Soviet challenge by concentrating on our private interests instead of on the public interest, by losing a great many of our best young brains in poor schools before they ever get to the college level, by not using our intelligent women when the Russians are using theirs, by not making a genuine effort to get our best brains into the most effective jobs to serve the nation, why I'm bound to say that the answer is "no."

I believe, however, that there is still a lot of spunk and spirit in this country that can be brought by free methods into the service of the nation, provided presidential power is used to clarify where the nation stands.

The first national purpose is to know who we are and what we stand for; it would be an impertinence to try to improve on the second paragraph of the Declaration of Independence as a guide to the problem.

"We hold these truths to be self-evident," it says in the first sentence.

It thereupon lists, as if they were the indisputable facts of last Sunday's American League batting averages, a whole catalogue of wonderful things that are not only not "self-evident" in 1960, but are actually in violent dispute among men all over the world, including quite a few in our own country.

"All men are created equal," it says, and, of course, this is just the trouble, for you can get an argument on that one anywhere in the province of Georgia, U.S.S.R., or the state of Georgia, U.S.A.

In the minds of the Founding Fathers, the moral idea came before the political, and the latter was merely an expression of the former. This, too, was apparently the idea Matthew Arnold had in mind when he came to this country before the turn of the century and discussed our national purpose in New York.

He made two points:

"We must hold fast to the austere but true doctrine," he said, "as to what really governs politics, overrides with an inexorable fatality the combinations of so-called politicians, and saves or destroys states.

"Having in mind things true, things elevated, things just, things pure, things amiable, things of good report: having these in mind, studying and loving these, is what saves states."

However, the old gentleman, when writing these exuberant sentences, had no illusion about their being put into force by the majority. These moral concepts would prevail, he said, only as they were upheld by "the remnant" of leaders and thinkers who loved wisdom, for the majority, he insisted, was full of "prosperities, idolatries, oppression, luxury, pleasures, and careless women. . . . That shall come to nought and pass away."

"The remnant" in America of those who love wisdom and have the ability to compete with any nation in the world is very large. It has greatly increased as the population of the nation has increased, but it needs to be brought to bear on the great purposes of the nation more than it is today, and this is obviously one task of presidential leadership.

Meanwhile, there is no cause to despair over the evidence of disorder and menace, for in all the golden ages of history, disorder and hazard have existed alongside vitality and creativeness.

"Surely our age shares many characteristics with the earlier golden times," Caryl P. Haskins, President of the Carnegie Institution of Washington, has written. "Theirs is the wide feeling of insecurity, the deeplying anxiety, the sense of confusion, not unlike the earlier times in general character. . . .

"But there is likewise the same intense concern with new ideas and new concepts, the same eagerness for widened vistas of understanding. . . ."

What Mr. Haskins did not say was that these golden ages were also periods of great leaders who knew how to bring ideas and politics together, and this seems to me to be the heart of our present problem.

The Problems of a People of Plenty

The nation itself, with all its so-called internal improvements, which, by the way, are all external and superficial, is . . . an unwieldy and overgrown establishment, cluttered with furniture and tripped up by its own traps, ruined by luxury and heedless expense, by want of calculation and a worthy aim, as the million households in the land; and the only cure for it, as for them, is in a rigid economy, a stern and more than Spartan simplicity of life and elevation of purpose.

—Henry Thoreau,
"Walden"

The concealed premise in James Reston's essay is the assumption that Americans can live up to the challenge of their times if only they wish to do so and are properly led. He has faith that there are untapped reserves of idealism in the United States that need only be properly used to be effective. He thus points indirectly to the problem of the place that the pursuit of material well-being should occupy in the national culture. For the idealism to which this author appeals may call for sacrifices for which our pursuit of personal prosperity has not prepared us.

Believing, as they generally did, that their country had a distinctive role in human development and that they could make of the world what they wished, Americans were frequently tempted to interpret their task in the concrete terms of individual wealth. Europe was bound to a life of scarcity, poverty, and lack of opportunity; by contrast, the New World was a land of abundance, riches, and endless opportunities for gain. From the belief in the desirability of change and in the ability to transform the universe, it was logically easy to move to the faith that the goal of the acquisition of goods was self-sufficient and adequate in itself.

Many of the expansive conditions of American life tended to sustain these beliefs. The fact that all Americans were immigrants or the descendants of immigrants created a vivid contrast between the old homes they had been compelled to leave and their new ones. The fact that Americans for almost three centuries lived on a frontier, in which large amounts of free land offered a boundless challenge, heightened that tendency to consider economic opportunity limitless. Americans were readily inclined to think of themselves as a people of plenty and to think also that the attainment of plenty was an end in itself.

These themes emerge very early in American history. The very first immigrants in the seventeenth century wrote optimistic accounts of the economic conditions of the settlements to persuade others of the superiority of conditions in the New World. The Reverend Francis Higginson (1586–1630), for instance, described Massachusetts in 1630 as a land of milk and honey (1). Ironically, he died of tuberculosis within a year, but the output of such promotional literature continued unabated.

The debate over the relative advantages of conditions in the Old and the New World extended on through the whole colonial period. In his "Notes on

Virginia," (1785) Thomas Jefferson (1743–1826) still found it necessary to argue that nature had a beneficent aspect in America (2). But after the success of the Revolution and the opening of the Great West this argument was no longer heard; the fact seemed self-evident as the nation grew in territorial extent and in economic strength.

Indeed, as the eighteenth century drew to a close the emphasis in the discussion shifted. Influential Americans were now also explaining that manufacturing, by adding to the wealth of the nation, would help it to solve its basic problems. One of the most forceful expressions of that point of view came in the report of Alexander Hamilton (1757–1804) on manufactures (3). Hamilton was in a strategic position to advance his ideas on the importance of economic development, for after his services in the Revolution and in the Constitutional Convention he had become Secretary of the Treasury and was responsible for laying out the fiscal policies of the new Republic.

In the nineteenth century, the problem assumed another form. There was then no denying the facts of abundance. But there were grounds for raising questions about the effects on the spirit of man of the concern with material things. The New England writers influenced by Transcendentalism were particularly troubled by these aspects of the issue. Ralph Waldo Emerson (1803–82), whom conscience had led out of the Unitarian ministry, in an ode inscribed to W. H. Channing commented forcefully on the power of idealism and on the littleness of materialism (4). Even more shocking to the contemporaries was the denial by Henry David Thoreau (1817–62) of the utility of man's effort to amass worldly goods. In "Walden" this author attempted to demonstrate that a life of solitude and self-denial was more conducive to personal satisfaction than the pursuit of wealth (5). And in an acid short story, Herman Melville (1819–91) pointed to the damaging effects of the industrial environment upon the human beings compelled to live in it (6).

Yet, the underlying faith of Americans in the worth of the struggle for wealth was not fundamentally altered. The questions that Emerson, Thoreau, and Melville raised were deeply troubling, but they did not shake the conviction that the way to happiness was through the pursuit of abundance. Through the rest of the nineteenth century, and on into the twentieth, that faith survived intact. The attainment of material plenty was still regarded as a means of dissolving personal, national, and social difficulties.

Thus, on one level Walt Whitman (1819–92) explained the satisfactions that came to men out of the performance of their jobs (7). On another level, Andrew Carnegie (1835–1919), himself an immigrant who began as a poor boy and earned a great fortune, in "Triumphant Democracy" celebrated the superiority of the United States in terms of its ability to achieve abundance (8). And Henry W. Grady (1850–89), southern editor and orator, expressed the hope that a New South dedicated to the acquisition of wealth, would escape the dilemmas created by its past. Confronting the immense social problems of his region after the Civil War, Grady envisioned a radical change in its society to make it more thoroughly American in its devotion to industry and the quest for material gain (9).

The same faith has endured to our own day; even in 1960 the dominant domestic issue in American politics seemed to be whether the country could increase its productivity as rapidly as before. And many citizens continued to believe that all the difficulties of foreign policy would vanish if only other nations could achieve an abundance comparable to that of the United States.

1. Francis Higginson, *The New World's Abundance, 1630*[*]

New-England . . . is a land of divers and sundry sorts. . . . At *Charles* River is as fat black earth as can be seen anywhere; and in other places you have a clay soil, in other gravel, in other sandy, as it is all about our plantation at Salem. . . .

The form of the earth here . . . is neither too flat in the plainness, nor too high in hills, but partakes of both in a mediocrity, and fit for pasture, or for plow or meadow ground, as men please to employ it. Though all the country be as it were a thick wood for the general, yet in divers places there is much ground cleared by the *Indians,* especially about the plantation. And I am told that about three miles from us a man may stand upon a little hilly place and see divers thousands of acres of ground as good as needs be, and not a tree in the same. It is thought here is good clay to make brick and tiles and earthen pots as needs to be. . . . For stone here is plenty of slate . . . and limestone, freestone, and smoothstone, and ironstone, and marblestone also in such store that we have great rocks of it, and a harbor hard by. . . .

The fertility of the soil is to be admired at, as appeareth in the abundance of grass that groweth everywhere both very thick, very long and very high. . . . It is scarce to be believed how our kine and goats, horses, and hogs do thrive and prosper here and like well of this country.

In our plantation we have already a quart of milk for a penny; but the abundant increase of corn proves this country to be a wonderment. Thirty, forty, fifty, sixty, are ordinary here; yea Joseph's increase in Egypt is outstripped here with us. Our planters hope to have more than a hundred fold this year, and all this while I am in compass; what will you say of two hundred fold and upwards? . . . Little children here by setting of corn may earn much more than their own maintenance. . . .

This country abounds naturally with store of roots of great variety and good to eat. Our turnips, parsnips and carrots are here both bigger and sweeter than is ordinarily to be found in *England*. Here are also stores of pumpkins, cucumbers, and other things of that nature . . . also mulberries, plums, raspberries, currants, chestnuts, filberts, walnuts, smallnuts, hurtleberries and hawes of whitethorne near as good as our cherries in England, they grow in plenty here.

For wood there is no better in the world I think, here being four sorts of oak, differing both in the leaf, timber, and color,—all excellent good. There

[*] Francis Higginson, *New-England's Plantation. Or, a Short and True Description of the Commodities and Discommodities of That Countrey. Written by a Reverend Divine Now There Resident* (London, 1630).

is also good ash, elm, willow, beech, sassafras, birch, juniper, cypress, cedar, spruce, pine and fir that will yield abundance of turpentine, pitch, tar, masts and other materials for building both ships and houses. . . .

New England has water enough, both salt and fresh, . . . there are abundance of islands along the shore, some full of wood and mast to feed swine and others clear of wood and fruitful to bear corn. . . . The abundance of sea fish are almost beyond belief and sure I should scarce have believed it excepting I had seen it with mine own eyes. I saw great store of whales, . . . and such abundance of mackerel that it would astonish one to behold, likewise cod fish . . . are plentifully taken. There is a fish called a bass, a most sweet and wholesome fish as ever I did eat. It is all together as good as our fresh salmon. . . . Of this fish our fishers take many hundreds together, which I have seen lying on the shore to my admiration; yea, their nets ordinarily take more than they are able to hale to land, and for want of boats and men they are constrained to let as many go after they have taken them. . . . Besides there is probability that the country is of an excellent temper for the making of salt, for since our coming our fishermen have brought home very good salt which they found candied by the standing of the sea water and the heat of the sun upon a rock by the sea shore. . . . Thus we see both land and sea abound with store of blessings for the comfortable sustenance of man's life in *New England*.

The temper of the air of New England is one special thing that commends this place. Experience has manifested that there is hardly a more healthful place to be found in the world and agrees better with our English bodies. Many that have been weak and sickly in Old England by coming hither have been thoroughly healed and grown healthful and strong. For here is an extraordinarily clear and dry air and is of the most healing nature to all such as are of a cold, melancholy, phlegmatic, rheumatic temper of body. None can more truly speak hereof by their own experience than myself. My friends that knew me can well tell how very sickly I have been and continually in physic, being much troubled with a tormenting pain . . . ; but since I came hither on this voyage, I thank God I have had perfect health, and free from pain and vomitings, having the stomach to digest the hardest and coarsest fare who before could not eat finest meat. . . . I that have not gone without a cap for many years together, neither durst leave off the same, have now cast away my cap, and wear none at all in the day time. And whereas before times I clothed myself with double clothes and thick waistcoats to keep me warm even in the summertime, I do now go as thin clad as any, only wearing a light stuff cassock upon my shirt. . . . Besides I have one of my children that was formerly most lamentably handled with sore breaking out on both his hands and feet of the king's evil, but since he came hither he is very well. . . . And therefore I think it is a wise course for all cold complections to come to take physic in *New England*. For a sup of *New England's* air is better than a whole draft of *Old England's* ale. . . .

Fowls of the air are plentiful here and of all sorts as we have in England. . . . Here are likewise abundance of turkeys often killed in the woods, far greater than our English turkeys and exceedingly fat, sweet, and fleshy, for here they have abundance of feeding all the year long. . . . In winter time this country does abound with wild geese, wild ducks, and other sea fowl, that a great part of winter the planters have eaten nothing but roast meat of these divers fowls which they have killed. . . .

Though it be here something cold in the winter, yet here we have plenty of fire to warm us and that a great deal

cheaper than they sell billots and fagots in *London*. Nay all *Europe* is not able to afford to make so great fires as *New England*. A poor servant here that is to possess but fifty acres of land may afford to give more wood for timber and fire. . . . than many noblemen in England.

2. THOMAS JEFFERSON, *Notes on Virginia, 1785**

Hitherto I have considered this hypothesis [that the New World is naturally inferior to the Old] as applied to brute animals only, and not in its extension to the man of America, whether aboriginal or transplanted. It is the opinion of Monsieur de Buffon that the former furnishes no exception to it. . . .

An afflicting picture, indeed, which, for the honor of human nature, I am glad to believe has no original. Of the Indian of South America I know nothing; for I would not honor with the appellation of knowledge, what I derive from the fables published of them. These I believe to be just as true as the fables of Æsop. This belief is founded on what I have seen of man, white, red, and black, and what has been written of him by authors, enlightened themselves, and writing amidst an enlightened people. The Indian of North America being more within our reach, I can speak of him somewhat from my own knowledge, but more from the information of others better acquainted with him, and on whose truth and judgment I can rely. From these sources I am able to say, in contradiction to this representation, that he is neither more defective in ardor, nor more impotent with his female, than the white reduced to the

same diet and exercise; that he is brave, when an enterprise depends on bravery; education with him making the point of honor consist in the destruction of an enemy by stratagem, and in the preservation of his own person free from injury; or, perhaps, this is nature, while it is education which teaches us to honor force more than finesse; that he will defend himself against a host of enemies, always choosing to be killed, rather than to surrender, though it be to the whites, who he knows will treat him well; that in other situations, also, he meets death with more deliberation, and endures tortures with a firmness unknown almost to religious enthusiasm with us; that he is affectionate to his children, careful of them, and indulgent in the extreme; that his affections comprehend his other connections, weakening, as with us, from circle to circle, as they recede from the centre; that his friendships are strong and faithful to the uttermost extremity; that his sensibility is keen, even the warriors weeping most bitterly on the loss of their children, though in general they endeavor to appear superior to human events; that his vivacity and activity of mind is equal to ours in the same situation; hence his eagerness for

* Thomas Jefferson, *Notes on the State of Virginia Written in 1781 . . . Enlarged in . . . 1782, for the Use of a Foreigner of Distinction* . . . (Paris, 1785), pp. 61–70.

hunting, and for games of chance. The women are submitted to unjust drudgery. This I believe is the case with every barbarous people. With such, force is law. The stronger sex therefore imposes on the weaker. It is civilization alone which replaces women in the enjoyment of their natural equality. That first teaches us to subdue the selfish passions, and to respect those rights in others which we value in ourselves. Were we in equal barbarism, our females would be equal drudges. The man with them is less strong than the man with us, but their women stronger than ours; and both for the same obvious reason; because our man and their woman is habituated to labor and formed by it. With both races the sex which is indulged with ease is the least athletic. An Indian man is small in the hand and wrist, for the same reason for which a sailor is large and strong in the arms and shoulders, and a porter in the legs and thighs. They raise fewer children than we do. The causes of this are to be found, not in a difference of nature, but of circumstance. The women very frequently attending the men in their parties of war and of hunting, child-bearing becomes extremely inconvenient to them. It is said, therefore, that they have learned the practice of procuring abortion by the use of some vegetable; and that it even extends to prevent conception for a considerable time after. During these parties they are exposed to numerous hazards, to excessive exertions, to the greatest extremities of hunger. Even at their homes the nation depends for food, through a certain part of every year, on the gleanings of the forest; that is, they experience a famine once in every year. With all animals, if the female be illy fed, or not fed at all, her young perish; and if both male and female be reduced to like want, generation becomes less active, less productive. To the obstacles, then, of want and

hazard, which nature has opposed to the multiplication of wild animals, for the purpose of restraining their numbers within certain bounds, those of labour and of voluntary abortion are added with the Indian. No wonder, then, if they multiply less than we do. Where food is regularly supplied, a single farm will show more of cattle, than a whole country of forests can of buffalos. The same Indian women, when married to white traders, who feed them and their children plentifully and regularly, who exempt them from excessive drudgery, who keep them stationary and unexposed to accident, produce and raise as many children as the white women. Instances are known, under these circumstances, of their rearing a dozen children. An inhuman practice once prevailed in this country, of making slaves of Indians. It is a fact well known with us, that the Indian women so enslaved produced and raised as numerous families as either the whites or blacks among whom they lived. It has been said that Indians have less hair than the whites, except on the head. But this is a fact of which fair proof can scarcely be had. With them it is disgraceful to be hairy on the body. They say it likens them to hogs. They therefore pluck the hair as fast as it appears. But the traders who marry their women, and prevail on them to discontinue this practice, say, that nature is the same with them as with the whites. Nor, if the fact be true, is the consequence necessary which has been drawn from it. Negroes have notoriously less hair than the whites; yet they are more ardent. But if cold and moisture be the agents of nature for diminishing the races of animals, how comes she all at once to suspend their operation as to the physical man of the new world, whom the Count acknowledges to be "á peu près même stature que l'homme de notre monde," and to let loose their influence on his moral faculties? How has this "combination of the elements and other physical causes, so contrary to the enlargement of animal nature in this new world, these obstacles to the development and formation of great germs," been arrested and suspended, so as to permit the human body to acquire its just dimensions, and by what inconceivable process has their action been directed on his mind alone? To judge of the truth of this, to form a just estimate of their genius and mental powers, more facts are wanting, and great allowance to be made for those circumstances of their situation which call for a display of particular talents only. This done, we shall probably find that they are formed in mind as well as body, on the same module with the "Homo sapiens Europaeus." The principles of their society forbidding all compulsion, they are to be led to duty and to enterprise by personal influence and persuasion. Hence eloquence in council, bravery and address in war, become the foundations of all consequence with them. To these acquirements all their faculties are directed. Of their bravery and address in war we have multiplied proofs, because we have been the subjects on which they were exercised. Of their eminence in oratory we have fewer examples, because it is displayed chiefly in their own councils. Some, however, we have, of a very superior lustre. I may challenge the whole orations of Demosthenes and Cicero, and of any more eminent orator, if Europe has furnished any more eminent, to produce a single passage, superior to the speech of Logan, a Mingo chief, to Lord Dunmore, when governor of this state. And as a testimony of their talents in this line, I beg leave to introduce it, first stating the incidents necessary for understanding it. In the spring of the year 1774, a robbery and murder were committed on an inhabitant of the frontiers of Virginia, by two Indians of the Shawnee tribe. The neighboring whites, according to their custom, undertook to punish this outrage in a summary way. Col. Cresap, a man infamous for the many murders he had committed on those much injured people, collected a party and proceded down the Kanhaway in quest of vengeance. Unfortunately a canoe of women and children, with one man only, was seen coming from the opposite shore, unarmed, and unsuspecting an hostile attack from the whites. Cresap and his party concealed themselves on the bank of the river, and the moment the canoe reached the shore, singled out their objects, and at one fire, killed every person in it. This happened to be the family of Logan, who had long been distinguished as a friend of the whites. This unworthy return provoked his vengeance. He accordingly signalized himself in the war which ensued. In the autumn of the same year a decisive battle was fought at the mouth of the Great Kanhaway, between the collected forces of the Shawanees, Mingoes and Delawares, and a detachment of the Virginia militia. The Indians were defeated and sued for peace. Logan, however, disdained to be seen among the suppliants. But lest the sincerity of a treaty should be distrusted, from which so distinguished a chief absented himself, he sent, by a messenger, the following speech, to be delivered to Lord Dunmore.

"I appeal to any white man to say, if ever he entered Logan's cabin hungry, and he gave him not meat; if ever he came cold and naked, and he clothed him not. During the course of the last long and bloody war Logan remained idle in his cabin, an advocate for peace. Such was my love for the whites, that my countrymen pointed as they passed, and said, 'Logan is the friend of white men.' I had even thought to have lived with you, but for the injuries of one man. Colonel Cresap, the last spring in cold blood, and unprovoked, murdered all the relations of Logan, not sparing even my women and children. There runs not a drop of my blood in the veins of any living creature. This called on me for revenge: I have sought it: I have killed many: I have fully glutted my vengeance: for my country I rejoice at the beams of peace. But do not harbour a thought that mine is the joy of fear. Logan never felt fear. He will not turn on his heel to save his life. Who is there to mourn for Logan?—Not one."

Before we condemn the Indians of this continent as wanting genius, we must consider that letters have not yet been introduced among them. Were we to compare them in their present state with the Europeans north of the Alps, when the Roman arms and arts first crossed those mountains, the comparison would be unequal, because, at that time, those parts of Europe were swarming with numbers: because numbers produce emulation and multiply the chances of improvement, and one improvement begets another. Yet I may safely ask, how many good poets, how many able mathematicians, how many great inventors, in arts or sciences, had Europe, North of the Alps, then produced? And it was sixteen centuries after this before a Newton could be formed. I do not mean to deny that there are varieties in the race of man, distinguished by their powers both of body and mind. I believe there are, as I see to be the case in the races of other animals. I only mean to suggest a doubt, whether the bulk and faculties of animals depend on the side of the Atlantic on which their food happens to grow, or which furnishes the elements of which they are compounded? Whether nature has enlisted herself as a Cis- or Trans-Atlantic partisan? I am induced to sus-

pect there has been more eloquence than sound reasoning displayed in support of this theory; that it is one of those cases where the judgment has been seduced by a glowing pen; and whilst I render every tribute of honor and esteem to the celebrated Zoologist, who has added, and is still adding, so many precious things to the treasures of science, I must doubt whether in this instance he has not cherished error also by lending her for a moment his vivid imagination and bewitching language.

So far the Count de Buffon has carried this new theory of the tendency of nature to belittle her productions on this side of the Atlantic. Its application to the race of whites transplanted from Europe, remained for the Abbé Raynal. "On doit être etonné (he says) que l'Amerique n'ait pas encore produit un bon poëte, un habile mathematicien, un homme de génie dans un seul art, ou seule science." 7. Hist. Philos. p. 92, ed. Maestricht, 1774. "America has not yet produced one good poet." When we shall have existed as a people as long as the Greeks did before they produced a Homer, the Romans a Virgil, the French a Racine and Voltaire, the English a Shakespeare and Milton, should this reproach be still true, we will inquire from what unfriendly causes it has proceeded, that the other countries of Europe and quarters of the earth shall not have inscribed any name in the roll of poets. But neither has America produced "one able mathematician, one man of genius in a single art or a single science." In war we have produced a Washington, whose memory will be adored while liberty shall have votaries, whose name will triumph over time, and will in future ages assume its just station among the most celebrated worthies of the world, when that wretched philosophy shall be forgotten which would have arranged him among the degeneracies of nature. In Physics we have produced a Franklin, than whom no one of the present age has made more important discoveries, nor has enriched philosophy with more, or more ingenious solutions of the phenomena of nature. We have supposed Mr. Rittenhouse second to no astronomer living; that in genius he must be the first, because he is self taught. As an artist he has exhibited as great a proof of mechanical genius as the world has ever produced. He has not indeed made a world; but he has by imitation approached nearer its Maker than any man who has lived from the creation to this day. As in philosophy and war, so in government, in oratory, in painting, in the plastic art, we might show that America, though but a child of yesterday, has already given hopeful proofs of genius, as well as of the nobler kinds, which arouse the best feelings of man, which call him into action, which substantiate his freedom, and conduct him to happiness, as of the subordinate, which serve to amuse him only. We therefore suppose, that this reproach is as unjust as it is unkind; and that, of the geniuses which adorn the present age, America contributes its full share. For comparing it with those countries where genius is most cultivated, where are the most excellent models for art, and scaffold-

ings for the attainment of science, as France and England for instance, we calculate thus. The United States contains three millions of inhabitants; France twenty millions; and the British islands ten. We produce a Washington, a Franklin, a Rittenhouse. France then should have half a dozen in each of these lines, and Great Britain half that number, equally eminent. It may be true the France has: we are but just becoming acquainted with her, and our acquaintance so far gives us high ideas of the genius of her inhabitants. It would be injuring too many of them to name particularly a Voltaire, a Buffon, the constellation of Encyclopedists, the Abbé Raynal himself, etc. etc. We therefore have reason to believe she can produce her full quota of genius. The present war having so long cut off all communication with Great Britain, we are not able to make a fair estimate of the state of science in that country. The spirit in which she wages war, is the only sample before our eyes, and that does not seem the legitimate offspring either of science or of civilization. The sun of her glory is fast descending to the horizon. Her Philosophy has crossed the Channel, her freedom the Atlantic, and herself seems passing to that awful dissolution whose issue is not given human foresight to scan.

3. ALEXANDER HAMILTON, *Report on Manufactures, 1791**

The expendiency of encouraging manufactures in the United States, which was not long since deemed very questionable, appears at this time to be pretty generally admitted. The embarrassments which have obstructed the progress of our external trade, have led to serious reflections on the necessity of enlarging the sphere of our domestic commerce. The restrictive regulations, which, in foreign markets, abridge the vent of the increasing sur-

* Alexander Hamilton, *Works* (Henry Cabot Lodge, ed.; New York, 1904), Vol. IV.

plus of our agricultural produce, serve to beget an earnest desire, that a more extensive demand for that surplus may be created at home; and the complete success which has rewarded manufacturing enterprise, in some valuable branches, conspiring with the promising symptoms which attend some less mature essays in others, justify a hope, that the obstacles to the growth of this species of industry are less formidable than they were apprehended to be; and that it is not difficult to find, in its further extension, a full indemnification for any external disadvantages, which are or may be experienced, as well as an accession of resources, favorable to national independence and safety. . . .

It is now proper to proceed a step further, and to enumerate the principal circumstances from which it may be inferred that manufacturing establishments not only occasion a positive augmentation of the produce and revenue of the society, but that they contribute essentially to rendering them greater than they could possibly be without such establishments. These circumstances are:

1. The division of labor.

2. An extension of the use of machinery.

3. Additional employment to classes of the community not ordinarily engaged in the business.

4. The promoting of emigration from foreign countries.

5. The furnishing greater scope for the diversity of talents and dispositions, which discriminate men from each other.

6. The affording a more ample and various field for enterprise.

7. The creating, in some instances, a new, and securing, in all, a more certain and steady demand for the surplus produce of the soil.

Each of these circumstances has a considerable influence upon the total mass of industrious effort in a community; together, they add to it a degree of energy and effect which is not easily conceived. Some comments upon each of them, in the order in which they have been stated, may serve to explain their importance.

1. As to the division of labor.

It has justly been observed that there is scarcely anything of greater moment in the economy of a nation than the proper division of labor. The separation of occupations causes each to be carried to a much greater perfection than it could possible acquire if they were blended. This arises principally from three circumstances:

1st. The greater skill and dexterity naturally resulting from a constant and undivided application to a single object. It is evident that these properties must increase in proportion to the separation and simplification of objects, and the steadiness of the attention devoted to each; and must be less in proportion to the complication of objects, and the number among which the attention is distracted.

2nd. The economy of time, by avoiding the loss of it, incident to a frequent transistion from one operation to another of a different nature. This depends on various circumstances; the transition itself, the orderly disposition of the implements, machines, and materials employed in the operation to be relinquished, the preparatory steps to the commencement of a new one, the interruption of the impulse which the mind of a workman acquires from being engaged in a particular operation, the distractions, hesitations and reluctances which attend the passage from one kind of business to another.

3rd. An extension of the use of machinery. A man occupied on a single object will have it more in his power, and will be more naturally led to exert his imagination, in devising methods to facilitate and abridge labor, than if he were perplexed by a variety of independent and dissimilar operations. Besides this, the fabrication of machines, in numerous instances, becoming itself a distinct trade, the artist who follows it has all the advantages which have been enumerated for improvement in his particular art; and, in both ways, the invention and application of machinery are extended.

And from these causes united, the mere separation of the occupation of the cultivator from that of the artificer, has the effect of augmenting the productive powers of labor, and with them, the total mass of the produce or revenue of a country. In this single view of the subject, therefore, the utility of artificers or manufacturers, towards promoting an increase of productive industry, is apparent.

2. *As to an extension of the use of machinery, a point which, though partly anticipated, requires to be placed in one or two additional lights.*

The employment of machinery forms an item of great importance in the general mass of national industry. It is an artificial force brought in aid of the natural force of man;, and, to all the purposes of labor, is an increase of hands, an accession of strength, unencumbered too by the expense of maintaining the laborer. May it not, therefore, be fairly inferred that those occupations which give the greatest scope to the use of this auxiliary contribute most to the general stock of industrious effort, and, in consequence, to the general product of industry?

It shall be taken for granted, and the truth of the position referred to observation, that manufacturing pursuits are susceptible, in a greater degree, of the application of machinery, than those of agriculture. If so, all the difference is lost to a community which, instead of manufacturing for itself, procures the fabrics requisite to its supply from other countries. The substitution of foreign for domestic manufactures is a transfer to foreign nations of the advantages accruing from the employment of machinery, in the modes in which it is capable of being employed with most utility and to the greatest extent.

The cotton-mill, invented in England, within the last twenty years, is a signal illustration of the general proposition which has been just advanced. In consequence of it, all the different processes for spinning cotton are performed by means of machines, which are put in motion by water, and attended chiefly by women and children—and by a smaller number of persons, in the whole, than are requisite in the ordinary mode of spinning. And it is an advantage of great moment, that the operations of this mill continue with convenience during the night as well as through the day. The prodigious effect of such a machine is easily conceived. To this invention is to be attributed, essentially, the immense progress which has been so suddenly made in Great Britain in the various fabrics of cotton.

3. *As to the additional employment of classes of the community not originally engaged in the particular business.*

This is not among the least valuable of the names by which manufacturing institutions contribute to augment the general stock of industry and production. In places where these institutions prevail, besides the persons regularly engaged in them, they afford occasional and extra employment to industrious individuals and families, who are willing to devote the leisure resulting from the intermissions of their ordinary pursuits to collateral labors, as a resource for multiplying their acquisitions or their enjoyments. The husbandman himself experiences a new source of profit and support from the increased industry of his wife and daughters, invited and stimulated by the demands of the neighboring manufactories.

Besides this advantage of occasional employment to classes having different occupations, there is another, of a nature allied to it and of a similar tendency. This is the employment of persons who would otherwise be idle, and in many cases a burthen on the community, either from the bias of temper, habit, infirmity of body, or some other cause, indisposing or disqualifying them for the toils of the country. It is worthy of particular remark that, in general, women and children are rendered more useful, and the latter more early useful, by manufacturing establishments, than they would otherwise be. Of the number of persons employed in the cotton manufactories of Great Britain, it is computed that four-sevenths, nearly, are women and children, of whom the greater proportion are children, and many of them of a tender age.

And thus it appears to be one of the attributes of manufactures, and one of no small consequence, to give occasion to the exertion of a greater quantity of industry, even by the same number of persons, where they happen to prevail, than would exist if there were no such establishments.

4. As to the promoting of immigration from foreign countries.

Men reluctantly quit one course of occupation and livelihood for another, unless invited to it by very apparent and proximate advantages. Many who would go from one country to another, if they had a prospect of continuing with more benefit the callings to which they have been educated, will often not be tempted to change their situation by the hope of doing better in some other way. Manufacturers who,

listening to the powerful invitations of a better price for their fabrics or their labor, of greater cheapness of provisions, and raw materials, or an exemption from the chief part of the taxes, burthens and restraints which they endure in the Old World, of greater personal independence and consequence, under the operation of a more equal government, and of what is far more precious than mere religious toleration, a perfect equality of religious privileges, would probably flock from Europe to the United States, to pursue their own trades or professions, if they were once made sensible of the advantages they would enjoy, and were inspired with an assurance of encouragement and employment, will, with difficulty, be induced to transplant themselves, with a view to becoming cultivators of land.

If it be true, then, that it is the interest of the United States to open every possible avenue to emigration from abroad, it affords a weighty argument for the encouragement of manufactures; which, for the reasons just assigned, will have the strongest tendency to multiply the inducements to it.

Here is perceived an important resource, not only for extending the population, and with it the useful and productive labor of the country, but likewise for the prosecution of manufactures, without deducting from the number of hands which might otherwise be drawn to tillage, and even for the indemnification of agriculture for such as might happen to be diverted from it. Many, whom manufacturing views would induce to emigrate, would afterwards yield to the temptation which the particular situation of this country holds out to agricultural pursuits. And while agriculture would, in other respects, derive many signal and unmingled advantages from the growth of manufactures, it is a problem whether it would gain or lose, as to the article or the number of persons employed in carrying it on.

5. *As to the furnishing greater scope for the diversity of talents and dispositions, which discriminate men from each other.*

This is a much more powerful means of augmenting the fund of national industry than may at first sight appear. It is a just observation, that minds of the strongest and most active powers for their proper objects fall below mediocrity, and labor without effect if confined to uncongenial pursuits. And it is thence to be inferred, that the results of human exertion may be immensely increased by diversifying its objects. When all the different kinds of industry obtain in a community, each individual can find his proper element, and can call into activity the whole vigor of his nature. And the community is benefited by the services of its respective members, in the manner in which each can serve it with most effect.

If there be anything in a remark often to be met with, namely, that there is, in the genius of the people of this country, a peculiar aptitude for mechanic improvements, it would operate as a forcible reason for giving opportunities to the exercise of that species of talent, by the propagation of manufactures.

6. *As to the affording a more ample and various field for enterprise.*

This is also of greater consequence in the general scale of national exertion than might, perhaps, on a superficial view, be supposed, and has effects not altogether dissimilar from those of the circumstances last noticed. To cherish and stimulate the activity of the human mind, by multiplying the objects of enterprise, is not among the least considerable of the expedients by which the wealth of a nation may be promoted. Even things in themselves not positively advantageous sometimes become so, by their tendency to provoke exertion. Every new scene which is opened to the busy nature of man to rouse and exert itself, is the addition of a new energy to the general stock of effort.

The spirit of enterprise, useful and prolific as it is, must necessarily be contracted or expanded in proportion to the simplicity or variety of the occupations and productions which are to be found in a society. It must be less in a nation of mere cultivators than in a nation of cultivators and merchants; less in a nation of cultivators and merchants than in a nation of cultivators, artificers, and merchants.

7. *As to the creating, in some instances, a new, and securing, in all, a more certain and steady demand for the surplus produce of the soil.*

This is among the most important of the circumstances which have been indicated. It is a principal means by which the establishment of manufactures contributes to an augmentation of the produce or revenue of a country, and has an immediate and direct relation to the prosperity of agriculture.

It is evident that the exertions of the husbandman will be steady or fluctuating, vigorous or feeble, in proportion to the steadiness or fluctuation, adequateness or inadequateness of the markets on which he must depend for the vent of the surplus which may be produced by his labor; and that such surplus, in the ordinary course of things, will be greater or less in the same proportion. For the purpose of this vent, a domestic market is greatly to be preferred to a foreign one; because it is, in the nature of things, far more to be relied upon.

4. Ralph Waldo Emerson, *Ode to W. H. Channing, 1847**

Though loath to grieve
The evil time's sole patriot,
I cannot leave
My honied thought
For the priest's cant,
Or statesman's rant.

If I refuse
My study for their politique,
Which at the best is trick,
The angry Muse
Puts confusion in my brain.

But who is he that prates
Of the culture of mankind,
Of better arts and life?
Go, blindworm, go,
Behold the famous States
Harrying Mexico
With rifle and with knife!

Or who, with accent bolder,
Dare praise the freedom-loving
    mountaineer?
I found by thee, O rushing Contoocook!
And in thy valleys, Agiochook!
The jackals of the Negro-holder.

The God who made New Hampshire
Taunted the lofty land
With little men;
Small bat and wren
House in the oak:
If earth-fire cleave
The upheaved land, and bury the folk,
The southern crocodile would grieve.
Virtue palters; Right is hence;

Freedom praised, but hid;
Funeral eloquence
Rattles the coffin-lid.

What boots thy zeal,
O glowing friend,
That would indignant rend
The northland from the south?
Wherefore? to what good end?
Boston Bay and Bunker Hill
Would serve things still;
Things are of the snake.

The horseman serves the horse,
The neatherd serves the neat,
The merchant serves the purse,
The eater serves his meat;
'Tis the day of the chattel
Web to weave, and corn to grind,
Things are in the saddle,
And ride mankind.
There are two laws discrete,
Not reconciled,
Law for man, and law for thing;
The last builds town and fleet,
But it runs wild,
And doth the man unking.

'Tis fit the forest fall,
The steep be graded,
The mountain tunnelled,
The sand shaded,

The orchard planted,
The glebe tilled,
The prairie granted,
The steamer built.

Let man serve law for man;
Live for friendship, live for love,
For truth's and harmony's behoof;
The state may follow how it can,
As Olympus follows Jove.

Yet do not I implore
The wrinkled shopman to my sounding
    woods,
Nor bid the unwilling senator
Ask votes of thrushes in the solitudes.
Every one to his chosen work;
Foolish hands may mix and mar;
Wise and sure the issues are.
Round they roll till dark is light,
Sex to sex, and even to odd;
The over-god
Who marries Right to Might,
Who peoples, unpeoples,
He who exterminates
Races by stronger races,
Black by white faces,
Knows to bring honey

* Ralph Waldo Emerson, *Works* (Boston, 1895), IX, 71–74.

Out of the lion;
Grafts gentlest scion
On pirate and Turk.

The Cossack eats Poland,
Like stolen fruit;
Her last noble is ruined,

Her last poet mute:
Straight, into double band
The victors divide;
Half for freedom strike and stand;
The astonished Muse finds thousands
at her side.

5. Henry D. Thoreau, *The Economy of Walden, 1849**

Talk of a divinity in man! Look at the teamster on the highway, wending to market by day or night; does any divinity stir within him? His highest duty to fodder and water his horses! What is his destiny to him compared with the shipping interests? Does not he drive for Squire Make-a-stir? How godlike, how immortal, is he? See how he cowers and sneaks, how vaguely all the day he fears, not being immortal nor divine, but the slave and prisoner of his own opinion of himself, a fame won by his own deeds. Public opinion is a weak tyrant compared with our own private opinion. What a man thinks of himself, that it is which determines, or rather indicates, his fate. Self-emancipation even in the West Indian provinces of the fancy and imagination,—what Wilberforce is there to bring that about? Think, also, of the ladies of the land weaving toilet cushions against the last day, not to betray too green an interest in their fates! As if you could kill time without injuring eternity.

The mass of men lead lives of quiet desperation. What is called resignation is confirmed desperation. From the desperate city you go into the desperate country, and have to console yourself with the bravery of minks and muskrats. A stereotyped but unconscious despair is concealed even under what are called the games and amuse-ments of mankind. There is no play in them, for this comes after work. But it is а characteristic of wisdom not to do desperate things.

When we consider what, to use the words of the catechism, is the chief end of man, and what are the true necessaries and means of life, it appears as if men had deliberately chosen the common mode of living because they preferred it to any other. Yet they honestly think there is no choice left. But alert and healthy natures remember that the sun rose clear. It is never too late to give up our prejudices. No way of thinking or doing, however ancient, can be trusted without proof. What everybody echoes or in silence passes by as true to-day may turn out to be falsehood to-morrow, mere smoke of opinion, which some had trusted for a cloud that would sprinkle fertilizing rain on their fields. What old people say you cannot do, you try and find that you can. Old deeds for old people, and new deeds for new. Old people did not know enough once, perchance, to fetch fresh fuel to keep the fire a-going; new people put a little dry wood under a pot, and are whirled round the globe with the speed of birds, in a way to kill old people, as the phrase is. Age is no better, hardly so well, qualified for an instructor as youth, for it has not profited so much as it has lost. One

* Henry D. Thoreau, *Walden; or, Life in the Woods* (Boston, 1889) I, 14–28.

may almost doubt if the wisest man has learned anything of absolute value by living. Practically, the old have no very important advice to give the young, their own experience has been so partial, and their lives have been such miserable failures, for private reasons, as they must believe; and it may be that they have some faith left which belies that experience, and they are only less young than they were. I have lived some thirty years on this planet, and I have yet to hear the first syllable of valuable or even earnest advice from my seniors. They have told me nothing, and probably cannot tell me anything to the purpose. Here is life, an experiment to a great extent untried by me; but it does not avail me that they have tried it. If I have any experience which I think valuable, I am sure to reflect that this my Mentors said nothing about.

One farmer says to me, "You cannot live on vegetable food solely, for it furnishes nothing to make bones with"; and so he religiously devotes a part of his day to supplying his system with the raw material of bones; walking all the while he talks behind his oxen, which, with vegetable-made bones, jerk him and his lumbering plow along in spite of every obstacle. Some things are really necessaries of life in some circles, the most helpless and diseased, which in others are luxuries merely, and in others still are entirely unknown.

The whole ground of human life seems to some to have been gone over by their predecessors, both the heights and the valleys, and all things to have been cared for. According to Evelyn, "the wise Solomon prescribed ordinances for the very distances of trees; and the Roman praetors have decided how often you may go into your neighbor's land to gather the acorns which fall on it without trespass, and what share belongs to that neighbor." Hippocrates has even left directions how we should cut our nails; that is, even with the ends of the fingers, neither shorter nor longer. Undoubtedly the very tedium and ennui which presume to have exhausted the variety and the joys of life are as old as Adam. But man's capacities have never been measured; nor are we to judge of what he can do by any precedents, so little has been tried. Whatever have been thy failures hitherto, "be not afflicted, my child, for who shall assign to thee what thou hast left undone?"

We might try our lives by a thousand simple tests; as, for instance, that the same sun which ripens my beans illumines at once a system of earths like ours. If I had remembered this it would have prevented some mistakes. This was not the light in which I hoed them. The stars are the apexes of what wonderful triangles! What distant and different beings in the various mansions of the universe are contemplating the same one at the same moment! Nature and human life are as various as our several constitutions. Who shall say what prospect life offers to another? Could a greater miracle take place than for us to look through each other's eyes for an instant? We should live in all the ages of the world in an hour; ay, in all the worlds of the ages. History, Poetry, Mythology! —I know of no reading of another's experience so startling and informing as this would be.

The greater part of what my neighbors call good I believe in my soul to be bad, and if I repent of anything, it is very likely to be my good behavior. What demon possessed me that I behaved so well? You may say the wisest thing you can, old man,—you who have lived seventy years, not without honor of a kind,—I hear an irresistible voice which invites me away from all that. One generation abandons the enterprises of another like stranded vessels.

I think that we may safely trust a good deal more than we do. We may waive just so much care of ourselves as we honestly bestow elsewhere. Nature is as well adapted to our weakness as to our strength. The incessant anxiety and strain of some is a well-nigh incurable form of disease. We are made to exaggerate the importance of what work we do; and yet how much is not done by us! or, what if we had been taken sick? How vigilant we are! determined not to live by faith if we can avoid it; all the day long on the alert, at night we unwillingly say our prayers and commit ourselves to uncertainties. So thoroughly and sincerely are we compelled to live, reverencing our life, and denying the possibility of change. This is the only way, we say; but there are as many ways as there can be drawn radii from one centre. All change is a miracle to contemplate; but it is a miracle which is taking place every instant. Confucius said, "To know that we know what we know, and that we do not know what we do not know, that is true knowledge." When one man has reduced a fact of the imagination to be a fact to his understanding, I foresee that all men will at length establish their lives on that basis.

Let us consider for a moment what most of the trouble and anxiety which I have referred to is about, and how much it is necessary that we be troubled, or at least careful. It would be some advantage to live a primitive and frontier life, though in the midst of an outward civilization, if only to learn what are the gross necessaries of life and what methods have been taken to obtain them; or even to look over the old day-books of the merchants, to see what it was that men most commonly bought at the stores, what they stored, that is, what are the grossest groceries. For the improvements of ages have had but little influence on the essential laws of man's existence: as our skeletons, probably, are not to be distinguished from those of our ancestors.

By the words, *necessary of life,* I mean whatever, of all that man obtains by his own exertions, has been from the first, or from long use has become, so important to human life that few, if any, whether from savageness, or poverty, or philosophy, ever attempt to do without it. To many creatures there is in this sense but one necessary of life, Food. To the bison of the prairie it is a few inches of palatable grass, with water to drink; unless he seeks the Shelter of the forest or the mountain's shadow. None of the brute creation requires more than Food and Shelter. The necessaries of life for man in this climate may, accurately enough, be distributed under the several heads of Food, Shelter, Clothing, and Fuel; for not till we have secured these are we prepared to entertain the true problems of life with freedom and a prospect of success. Man has invented, not only houses, but clothes and cooked food; and possibly from the accidental discovery of the warmth of fire, and the consequent use of it, at first a luxury, arose the present necessity to sit by it. We observe cats and dogs acquiring the same second nature. By proper Shelter and Clothing we legitimately retain our own internal heat; but with an excess of these, or of Fuel, that is, with an external heat greater than our own internal, may not cookery properly be said to begin? Darwin, the naturalist, says of the inhabitants of Tierra del Fuego, that while his own party, who were well clothed and sitting close to a fire, were far from too warm, these naked savages, who were farther off, were observed, to his great surprise, "to be streaming with perspiration at undergoing such a roasting." So, we are told, the New Hollander goes naked with impunity, while the European shivers in his clothes. Is it impossible to combine the hardiness of these savages with the intellectualness of the civilized man? According to Liebig, man's body is a stove, and food the fuel which keeps up the internal combustion in the lungs. In cold weather we eat more, in warm less. The animal heat is the result of a slow combustion, and disease and death take place when this is too rapid; or for want of fuel, or from some defect in the draught, the fire goes out. Of course the vital heat is not to be confounded with fire; but so much for analogy. It appears, therefore, from the above list, that the expression, *animal life,* is nearly synonymous with the expression, *animal heat;* for while Food may be regarded as the Fuel which keeps up to the fire within us,— and Fuel serves only to prepare that Food or to increase the warmth of our bodies by addition from without, —Shelter and Clothing also serve only to retain the *heat* thus generated and absorbed.

The grand necessity, then, for our bodies, is to keep warm, to keep the vital heat in us. What pains we accordingly take, not only with our Food, and Clothing, and Shelter, but with our beds, which are our nightclothes, robbing the nests and breasts of birds to prepare this shelter within a shelter, as the mole has its bed of grass and leaves at the end of its burrow! The poor man is wont to complain that this is a cold world; and to cold, no less physical than social, we refer directly a great part of our ails. The summer, in some climates, makes possible to man a sort of Elysian life. Fuel, except to cook his Food, is then unnecessary; the sun is his fire, and many of the fruits are sufficiently cooked by its rays; while Food gen-

erally is more various, and more easily obtained, and Clothing and Shelter are wholly or half unnecessary. At the present day, and in this country, as I find by my own experience, a few implements, a knife, an axe, a spade, a wheelbarrow, etc., and for the studious, lamplight, stationery, and access to a few books, rank next to necessaries, and can all be obtained at a trifling cost. Yet some, not wise, go to the other side of the globe, to barbarous and unhealthy regions, and devote themselves to trade for ten or twenty years, in order that they may live,— that is, keep comfortably warm,—and die in New England at last. The luxuriously rich are not simply kept comfortably warm, but unnaturally hot; as I implied before, they are cooked, of course *à la mode.*

Most of the luxuries, and many of the so-called comforts of life, are not only not indispensable, but positive hindrances to the elevation of mankind. With respect to luxuries and comforts, the wisest have ever lived a more simple and meagre life than the poor. The ancient philosophers, Chinese, Hindoo, Persian, and Greek, were a class than which none has been poorer in outward riches, none so rich in inward. We know not much about them. It is remarkable that *we* know so much of them as we do. The same is true of the more modern reformers and benefactors of their race. None can be an impartial or wise observer of human life but from the vantage ground of what *we* should call voluntary poverty. Of a life of luxury the fruit is luxury, whether in agriculture, or commerce, or literature, or art. There are nowadays professors of philosophy, but not philosophers. Yet it is admirable to profess because it was once admirable to live. To be a philosopher is not merely to have subtle thoughts, nor even to found a school, but so to love wisdom as to live according to its dictates, a life of simplicity, independence, magnanimity, and trust. It is to solve some of the problems of life, not only theoretically, but practically. The success of great scholars and thinkers is commonly a courtier-like success, not kingly, not manly. They make shift to live merely by conformity, practically as their fathers did, and are in no sense the progenitors of a nobler race of men. But why do men degenerate ever? What makes families run out? What is the nature of the luxury which enervates and destroys nations? Are we sure that there is none of it in our own lives? The philosopher is in advance of his age even in the outward form of his life. He is not fed, sheltered, clothed, warmed, like his contemporaries. How can a man be a philosopher and not maintain his vital heat by better methods than other men?

When a man is warmed by the several modes which I have described, what does he want next? Surely not more warmth of the same kind, as more and richer food, larger and more splendid houses, finer and more abundant clothing, more numerous, incessant, and hotter fires, and the like. When he has obtained those things which are necessary to life, there is another alternative than to obtain the superfluities; and that is, to adventure on life now, his vacation from humbler toil having commenced. The soil, it appears, is suited to the seed, for it has sent its radicle downward, and it may now send its shoot upward also with confidence. Why has man rooted himself thus firmly in the earth, but that he may rise in the same proportion into the heavens above?—for the nobler plants are valued for the fruit they bear at last in the air and light, far from the ground, and are not treated like the humbler esculents, which, though they may be biennials, are cultivated only till they have perfected their root, and often cut down at top for this purpose, so that most would not know them in their flowering season.

I do not mean to prescribe rules to strong and valiant natures, who will mind their own affairs whether in heaven or hell, and perchance build more magnificently and spend more lavishly than the richest, without ever impoverishing themselves, not knowing how they live,—if, indeed, there are any such, as has been dreamed; nor to those who find their encouragement and inspiration in precisely the present condition of things, and cherish it with the fondness and enthusiasm of lovers,—and, to some extent, I reckon myself in this number; I do not speak to those who are well employed, in whatever circumstances, and they know whether they are well employed or not; —but mainly to the mass of men who are discontented, and idly complaining of the hardness of their lot or of the times, when they might improve them. There are some who complain most energetically and inconsolably of any, because they are, as they say, doing their duty. I also have in my mind that seemingly wealthy, but most terribly impoverished class of all, who have accumulated dross, but know not how to use it, or get rid of it, and thus have forged their own golden or silver fetters.

6. HERMAN MELVILLE, *The Tartarus of Maids, 1855**

Not far from the bottom of the Dungeon stands a large whitewashed building, relieved, like some great white sepulchre, against the sullen background of mountainside firs, and other hardy evergreens, inaccessibly rising in grim terraces for some two thousand feet.

The building is a paper-mill.

Having embarked on a large scale in the seedman's business (so extensively and broadcast, indeed, that at length my seeds were distributed through all the Eastern and Northern States, and even fell into the far soil of Missouri and the Carolinas), the demand for paper at my place became so great, that the expenditure soon amounted to a most important item in the general account. It need hardly be hinted how paper comes into use with seedsmen, as envelopes. These are mostly made of yellowish paper, folded square; and when filled, are all but flat, and being stamped, and superscribed with the nature of the seeds contained, assume not a little the appearance of business letters ready for the mail. Of these small envelopes I used an incredible quantity—several hundreds of thousands in a year. For a time I had purchased my paper from the wholesale dealers in a neighboring town. For economy's sake, and partly for the adventure of the trip, I now resolved to cross the mountains, some sixty miles, and order my future paper at the Devil's Dungeon paper-mill ..

At first I could not discover the paper-mill.

The whole hollow gleamed with the white, except, here and there, where a pinnacle of granite showed one wind-swept angle bare. The mountains stood pinned in shrouds—a pass of Alpine corpses. Where stands the mill? Suddenly a whirling, humming sound broke upon my ear. I looked, and there, like an arrested avalanche, lay the large whitewashed factory. It was subordinately surrounded by a cluster of other and smaller buildings, some of which, from their cheap, blank air, great length, gregarious windows, and comfortless expression no doubt were boarding-houses of the operatives. A snow-white hamlet amidst the snows. Various rude, irregular squares and courts resulted from the somewhat picturesque clusterings of these buildings, owing to the broken, rocky nature of the ground, which forbade all method in their relative arrangement. Several narrow lanes and alleys, too, partly blocked with snow fallen from the roof, cut up the hamlet in all directions.

When, turning from the travelled highway, jingling with bells of numerous farmers—who, availing themselves of the fine sleighing, were dragging their wood to market—and frequently diversified with swift cutters dashing from inn to inn of the scattered villages—when, I say, turning from that bustling main-road, I by degrees wound into the Mad Maid's Bellows'-pipe, and saw the grim Black Notch beyond, then something latent, as well as something obvious in the time and scene, strangely brought back to my mind my first sight of dark and grimy Temple Bar. And when Black, my horse, went darting through the Notch, perilously

* Herman Melville, "Paradise of Bachelors and Tartarus of Maids," *Harper's New Monthly Magazine*, April, 1855.

grazing its rocky wall, I remembered being in a runaway London omnibus, which in much the same sort of style, though by no means at an equal rate, dashed through the ancient arch of Wren. Though the two objects did by no means completely correspond, yet this partial inadequacy but served to tinge the similitude not less with the vividness than the disorder of a dream. So that, when upon reining up at the protruding rock I at last caught sight of the quaint groupings of the factory-buildings, and with the travelled high-way and the Notch behind, found myself all alone, silently and privily steal-ing through deep-cloven passages into this sequestered spot, and saw the long, high-gabled main factory edifice, with a rude tower—for hoisting heavy boxes —at one end, standing among its crowded outbuildings and boarding-houses, as the Temple Church amidst the surrounding offices and dormitories, and when the marvellous retirement of this mysterious mountain nook fas-tened its whole spell upon me, then, what memory lacked, all tributary imagination furnished, and I said to myself, "This is the very counterpart of the Paradise of Bachelors, but snowed upon, and frost-painted to a sepulchre."

Dismounting, and warily picking my way down the dangerous declivity—horse and man both sliding now and then upon the icy ledges—at length I drove, or the blast drove me, into the largest square, before one side of the main edifice. Piercingly and shrilly the shotted blast blew by the corner; and redly and demoniacally boiled Blood River at one side. A long wood-pile, of many scores of cords, all glit-tering in mail of crusted ice, stood crosswise in the square. A row of horse-posts, their north sides plastered with adhesive snow, flanked the factory wall. The bleak frost packed and paved the square as with some ringing metal.

The inverted similitude recurred—"The sweet, tranquil Temple garden, with the Thames bordering its green beds," strangely meditated I.

But where are the gay bachelors?

Then, as I and my horse stood shiv-ering in the wind-spray, a girl ran from a neighboring dormitory door, and throwing her thin apron over her bare head, made for the opposite building.

"One moment, my girl; is there no shed hereabouts which I may drive into?"

Pausing, she turned upon me a face pale with work, and blue with cold; an eye supernatural with unrelated misery.

"Nay," faltered I, "I mistook you. Go on; I want nothing."

Leading my horse close to the door from which she had come, I knocked. Another pale, blue girl appeared, shiv-ering in the doorway as, to prevent the blast, she jealously held the door ajar.

"Nay, I mistake again. In God's name shut the door. But hold, is there no man about?"

That moment a dark-complexioned, well-wrapped personage passed, mak-ing for the factory door, and spying him coming, the girl rapidly closed the other one.

"Is there no horse-shed here, sir?"

"Yonder, the wood-shed," he replied, and disappeared inside the factory.

With much ado I managed to wedge in horse and pung between the scat-tered piles of wood all sawn and split. Then, blanketing my horse, and piling my buffalo on the blanket's top, and tucking in its edges well around the breast-band and breeching, so that the wind might not strip him bare, I tied him fast, and ran lamely for the fac-tory door, stiff with frost, and cumbered with my driver's dreadnaught.

Immediately I found myself standing in a spacious place, intolerably lighted by long rows of windows, focusing inward the snowy scene without.

At rows of blank-looking counters sat rows of blank-looking girls, with blank, white folders in their blank hands, all blankly folding blank paper.

In one corner stood some huge frame of ponderous iron, with a vertical thing like a piston periodically rising and falling upon a heavy wooden block. Before it—its tame minister—stood a tall girl, feeding the iron animal with half-quires of rose-hued note-paper, which, at every downward dab of the piston-like machine, received in the corner the impress of a wreath of roses. I looked from the rosy paper to the pallid cheek, but said nothing.

Seated before a long apparatus, strung with long, slender strings like any harp, another girl was feeding it with foolscap sheets, which, so soon as they curiously travelled from her on the cords, were withdrawn at the opposite end of the machine by a second girl. They came to the first girl blank; they went to the second girl ruled.

I looked upon the first girl's brow, and saw it was young and fair; I looked upon the second girl's brow, and saw it was ruled and wrinkled. Then, as I still looked, the two—for some small variety to the monotony—changed places; and where had stood the young, fair brow, now stood the ruled and wrinkled one.

Perched high upon a narrow platform, and still higher upon a high stool crowning it, sat another figure serving some other iron animal; while below the platform sat her mate in some sort of reciprocal attendance.

Not a syllable was breathed. Nothing was heard but the low, steady, overruling hum of the iron animals. The human voice was banished from the spot. Machinery—that vaunted slave of humanity—here stood menially served by human beings, who served mutely and cringingly as the slave serves the Sultan. The girls did not so much seem accessory wheels to the general machinery as mere cogs to the wheels.

All this scene around me was instantaneously taken in at one sweeping glance—even before I had proceeded to unwind the heavy fur tippet from around my neck. But as soon as this fell from me the dark-complexioned man, standing close by, raised a sudden cry, and seizing my arm, dragged me out into the open air, and without pausing for a word instantly caught up some congealed snow and began rubbing both my cheeks

"Two white spots like the whites of your eyes," he said; "man, your cheeks are frozen."

"That may well be," muttered I; "'tis some wonder the frost of the Devil's Dungeon strikes in no deeper. Rub away."

Soon a horrible, tearing pain caught at my reviving cheeks. Two gaunt blood-hounds, one on each side, seemed mumbling them. I seemed Actaeon.

Presently, when all was over, I re-entered the factory, made known my business, concluded it satisfactorily, and then begged to be conducted throughout the place to view it.

"Cupid is the boy for that," said the dark-complexioned man. "Cupid!" and by this odd fancy-name calling a dimpled, red-cheeked, spirited-looking, forward little fellow, who was rather impudently, I thought, gliding about among the passive-looking girls—like a goldfish through hueless waves—yet doing nothing in particular that I could see, the man bade him lead the stranger through the edifice.

"Come first and see the water-wheel," said this lively lad, with the air of boyishly-brisk importance.

Quitting the folding-room, we crossed some damp, cold boards, and stood beneath a great wet shed, incessantly showering with foam, like the green barnacled bow of some East India-man .n a gale. Round and round here went the enormous revolutions of the dark colossal water-wheel, grim with its one immutable purpose.

"This sets our whole machinery a-going, sir; in every part of all these buildings; where the girls work and all."

I looked, and saw that the turbid waters of Blood River had not changed their hue by coming under the use of man.

"You make only blank paper; no printing of any sort, I suppose? All blank paper, don't you?"

"Certainly; what else should a paper-factory make?"

The lad here looked at me as if suspicious of my common-sense.

"Oh, to be sure!" said I, confused and stammering; "it only struck me as so strange that red waters should turn out pale chee—paper, I mean."

He took me up a wet and rickety stair to a great light room, furnished with no visible thing but rude, manger-like receptacles running all round its sides; and up to these mangers, like so many mares haltered to the rack, stood rows of girls. Before each was vertically thrust up a long, glittering scythe, immovably fixed at bottom to the manger-edge. The curve of the scythe, and its having no snath to it, made it look exactly like a sword. To and fro, across the sharp edge, the girls forever dragged long strips of rags, washed white, picked from baskets at one side; thus ripping asunder every seam, and converting the tatters almost into lint. The air swam with the fine, poisonous particles, which from all sides darted, subtilely, as motes in sunbeams, into the lungs.

"This is the rag-room," coughed the boy.

"You find it rather stifling here," coughed I, in answer; "but the girls don't cough."

"Oh, they are used to it."

"Where do you get such hosts of rags?" picking up a handful from a basket.

"Some from the country round about; some from far over sea—Leghorn and London."

" 'Tis not unlikely, then," murmured I, "that among these heaps of rags there may be some old shirts, gathered from the dormitories of the Paradise of Bachelors. But the buttons are all dropped off. Pray, my lad, do you ever find any bachelor's buttons hereabouts?"

"None grow in this part of the country. The Devil's Dungeon is no place for flowers."

"Oh! you mean the *flowers* so called —the Bachelor's Buttons?"

"And was not that what you asked about? Or did you mean the gold bosom-buttons of our boss, Old Bach, as our whispering girls all call him?"

"The man, then, I saw below is a bachelor, is he?"

"Oh yes, he's a Bach."

"The edges of those swords, they are turned outward from the girls, if I see right; but their rags and fingers fly so, I cannot distinctly see"

"Turned outward."

Yes, murmured I to myself; I see it now; turned outward; and each erected sword is so borne, edge outward, before each girl. If my reading fails me not, just so, of old, condemned state-prisoners went from the hall of judgment to their doom: an officer before, bearing a sword, its edge turned outward, in significance of their fatal sentence. So, through consumptive pallors of this blank, raggy life, go these white girls to death.

"Those scythes look very sharp," again turning toward the boy.

"Yes; they have to keep them so. Look!"

That moment two of the girls, dropping their rags, plied each a whetstone up and down the sword-blade. My unaccustomed blood curdled at the sharp shriek of the tormented steel.

Their own executioners; themselves whetting the very swords that slay them, meditated I.

"What makes those girls so sheet-white, my lad?"

"Why"—with a roguish twinkle, pure ignorant drollery, not-knowing heartlessness—"I suppose the handling of such white bits of sheets all the time makes them so sheety."

"Let us leave the rag-room now, my lad."

More tragical and more inscrutably mysterious than any mystic sight, human or machine, throughout the factory, was the strange innocence of cruel-heartedness in this usage-hardened boy.

"And now," said he, cheerily, "I suppose you want to see our great machine, which cost us twelve thousand dollars only last autumn. That's the machine that makes the paper, too. This way, sir."

Following him, I crossed a large, bespattered place, with two great round vats in it, full of a white, wet, woolly-looking stuff, not unlike the albuminous part of an egg, soft-boiled.

"There," said Cupid, tapping the vats carelessly, "these are the first beginnings of the paper; this white pulp you see. Look how it swims bubbling round and round, moved by the paddle here. From hence it pours from both vats into that one common channel yonder; and so goes, mixed up and leisurely, to the great machine. And now for that."

He led me into a room, stifling with a strange, blood-like, abdominal heat, as if here, true enough, were being finally developed the germinous particles lately seen.

Before me, rolled out like some long Eastern manuscript, lay stretched one continuous length of iron framework—multitudinous and mystical, with all sorts of rollers, wheels, and cylinders, in slowly-measured and unceasing motion.

"Here first comes the pulp now," said Cupid, pointing to the nighest end of the machine. "See; first it pours out and spreads itself upon this wide, sloping board; and then—look—slides, thin and quivering, beneath the first roller there. Follow on now, and see it as it slides from under that to the next cylinder. There; see how it becomes just a very little less pulpy now. One step more, and it grows still more to some slight consistence. Still another cylinder, and it is so knitted—though as yet mere dragon-fly wing—that it forms an airbridge here, like a suspended cobweb, between two more separated rollers; and flowing over the last one, and under again, and doubling about there out of sight for a minute among all those mixed cylinders you indistinctly see, it reappears here, looking now at last a little less like pulp and more like paper, but still quite delicate and defective yet awhile. But—a little further onward, sir, if you please—here now, at this further point, it puts on something of a real look, as if it might turn out to be something you might possibly handle in the end. But it's not yet done, sir. Good way to travel yet, and plenty more of cylinders must roll it."

"Bless my soul!" said I, amazed at the elongation, interminable convolutions, and deliberate slowness of the machine; "it must take a long time for the pulp to pass from end to end, and come out paper."

"Oh, not so long," smiled the precocious lad, with a superior and patronising air; "only nine minutes. But look; you may try it for yourself. Have you a bit of paper? Ah! here's a bit on the floor. Now mark that with any word you please, and let me dab it on here, and we'll see how long before it comes out at the other end."

"Well, let me see," said I taking out my pencil; "come, I'll mark it with your name."

Bidding me take out my watch, Cupid adroitly dropped the inscribed slip on an exposed part of the incipient mass.

Instantly my eye marked the second-hand on my dial-plate.

Slowly I followed the slip, inch by inch; sometimes pausing for full half a minute as it disappeared beneath inscrutable groups of the lower cylinders, but only gradually to emerge again; and so, on, and on, and on—inch by inch; now in open sight, sliding along like a freckle on the quivering sheet; and then again wholly vanished; and so, on, and on, and on—inch by inch; all the time the main sheet growing more and more to final firmness—when, suddenly, I saw a sort of paper-fall, not wholly unlike a water-fall; a scissory sound smote my ear, as of some cord being snapped; and down dropped an unfolded sheet of perfect foolscap, with my "Cupid" half faded out of it, and still moist and warm.

My travels were at an end, for here was the end of the machine.

"Well, how long was it?" said Cupid. "Nine minutes to a second," replied I, watch in hand.

"I told you so."

For a moment a curious emotion filled me, not wholly unlike that which one might experience at the fulfillment of some mysterious prophecy. But how absurd, thought I again; the thing is a mere machine, the essence of which is which is unvarying punctuality and precision.

Previously absorbed by the wheels and cylinders, my attention was now directed to a sad-looking woman standing by.

"That is rather an elderly person so silently tending the machine-end here. She would not seem wholly used to it either."

"Oh," knowingly whispered Cupid, through the din, "she only came last week. She was a nurse formerly. But the business is poor in these parts, and she's left it. But look at the paper she is piling there."

"Ay, foolscap," handling the piles of moist, warm sheets, which continually were being delivered into the woman's waiting hands. "Don't you turn out anything but foolscap at this machine?"

"Oh, sometimes, but not often, we turn out finer work—cream-laid and royal sheets, we call them. But foolscap being in chief demand, we turn out foolscap most."

It was very curious. Looking at that blank paper continually dropping, dropping, dropping, my mind ran on in wonderings of those strange uses to which those thousand sheets eventually would be put. All sorts of writings would be writ on those now vacant things—sermons, lawyers' briefs, physicians' prescriptions, love-letters, marriage certificates, bills of divorce, registers of births, death-warrants, and so on, without end. Then, recurring back to them as they here lay all blank, I could not but bethink me of that celebrated comparison of John Locke, who, in demonstration of his theory that man had no innate ideas, compared the human mind at birth to a sheet of blank paper; something destined to be scribbled on, but what sort of characters no soul might tell.

Pacing slowly to and fro along the involved machine, still humming with its play, I was struck as well by the inevitability as the evolvement-power in all its motions.

"Does that thin cobweb there," said I, pointing to the sheet in its more imperfect stage, "does that never tear or break? It is marvellous fragile, and yet this machine it passes through is so mighty."

"It never is known to tear a hair's point."

"Does it never stop—get clogged?"

"No. It *must* go. The machinery makes it go just *so*; just that very way, and at that very pace you there plainly *see* it go. The pulp can't help going."

Something of awe now stole over me, as I gazed upon this inflexible iron animal. Always, more or less, machinery of this ponderous, elaborate sort strikes, in some moods, strange dread into the human heart, as some living, panting Behemoth might. But what made the thing I saw so specially terrible to me was the metallic necessity, the unbudging fatality which governed it. Though, here and there, I could not follow the thin, gauzy veil of pulp in the course of its more mysterious or entirely invisible advance, yet it was indubitable that, at those points where it eluded me, it still marched on in unvarying docility to the autocratic cunning of the machine. A fascination fastened on me. I stood spellbound and wandering in my soul. Before my eyes—there, passing in slow procession along the wheeling cylinders, I seemed to see, glued to the pallid incipience of the pulp, the yet more pallid faces of all the pallid girls I had eyed that heavy day. Slowly, mournfully, beseechingly, yet unresistingly, they gleamed along, their agony dimly outlined on the imperfect paper, like the print of the tormented face on the handkerchief of Saint Veronica.

"Halloa! the heat of the room is too much for you," cried Cupid, staring at me.

"No—I am rather chill, if anything."

"Come out, sir—out—out," and, with the protecting air of a careful father, the precocious lad hurried me outside.

In a few moments, feeling revived a little, I went into the folding-room —the first room I had entered, and where the desk for transacting business stood, surrounded by the blank counters and blank girls engaged at them.

"Cupid here had led me a strange tour," said I to the dark-complexioned man before mentioned, whom I had ere this discovered not only to be an old bachelor, but also the principal proprietor. "Yours is a most wonderful factory. Your great machine is a miracle of inscrutable intricacy."

"Yes, all our visitors think it so. But we don't have many. We are in a very out-of-the-way corner here. Few inhabitants, too. Most of our girls come from far-off villages."

"The girls," echoed I, glancing round at their silent forms. "Why is it, sir, that in most factories, female operatives, of whatever age, are indiscriminately called girls, never women?"

"Oh! as to that—why, I suppose, the fact of their being generally unmarried —that's the reason, I should think. But it never struck me before. For our factory here, we will not have married women; they are apt to be off-and-on too much. We want none but steady workers: twelve hours to the day, day after day, through the three hundred and sixty-five days, excepting Sundays, Thanksgiving, and Fast-days. That's our rule. And so, having no married women, what females we have are rightly enough called girls."

"Then these are all maids," said I, while some pained homage to their pale virginity made me involuntarily bow.

"All maids."

Again the strange emotion filled me.

"Your cheeks look whitish yet, sir," said the man, gazing at me narrowly. "You must be careful going home. Do they pain you at all now? It's a bad sign, if they do."

"No doubt, sir," answered I, "when once I have got out of the Devil's

Dungeon, I shall feel them mending."

"Ah, yes; the winter air in valleys, or gorges, or any sunken place, is far colder and more bitter than elsewhere. You would hardly believe it now, but it is colder here than at the top of Woedolor Mountain."

"I dare say it is, sir. But time presses me; I must depart."

With that, remuffling myself in dreadnaught and tippet, thrusting my hands into my huge sealskin mittens, I sallied out into the nipping air, and found poor Black, my horse, all cringing and doubled up with the cold.

Soon, wrapped in furs and meditations, I ascended from the Devil's Dungeon.

At the Black Notch I paused, and once more bethought me of Temple Bar. Then, shooting through the pass, all alone with inscrutable nature, I exclaimed—Oh! Paradise of Bachelors! and oh! Tartarus of Maids!

7. WALT WHITMAN, *I Hear America Singing, 1867**

I hear America singing, the varied carols I hear,
Those of mechanics, each one singing his as it should be blithe and strong,
The carpenter singing his as he measures his plank or beam,
The mason singing his as he makes ready for work, or leaves off work,
The boatman singing what belongs to him in his boat, the deck-hand singing on
    the steamboat deck,
The shoemaker singing as he sits on his bench, the hatter singing as he stands,
The wood-cutter's song, the ploughboy's on his way in the morning, or at noon
    intermission or at sundown,
The delicious singing of the mother, or of the young wife at work, or of the girl
    sewing or washing,
Each singing what belongs to him or her and to none else,
The day what belongs to the day—at night the party of young fellows, robust,
    friendly,
Singing with open mouths their strong melodious songs.

* Walt Whitman, *Complete Writings* (New York, 1902), I, 13.

8. ANDREW CARNEGIE, *Triumphant Democracy, 1893**

The settlement of a country usually follows a natural order or sequence. The first settlers, finding land abundant and cheap, engage in pastoral pursuits, pasturing their herds over broad tracts of land. As settlement increases, there succeeds a conflict between herdsmen and farmers, which the latter inevitably win, and the community becomes agricultural; the herdsman removes with his flocks to the frontier. In this, the agricultural stage, the vast body of the population is widely distributed over the country; towns and villages are

* Andrew Carnegie, *Triumphant Democracy: Sixty Years' March of the Republic* (New York, 1893), pp. 139 ff.

small and of trifling importance. As settlement increases, little by little trade and commerce, then manufactures, grow in importance, and towns and cities multiply. The last stage which the world has yet seen is that in which the greater proportion of the population has become massed in towns and cities, engaged in manufactures and trade, agriculture occupying a secondary position.

Certain parts of the Republic have passed through these changes, while others present various stages of progress in this succession. The northeastern part has become very largely a manufacturing section. The States of the upper Mississippi and the Ohio valleys are now transferring their allegiance from King Agriculture to King Manufacture. The Southern States as a whole are still firm in their adherence to King Cotton, although several States are going rapidly into manufacturing. The States and Territories of the far West are either still in the pastoral, or are passing from that to the agricultural, stage.

The occupations of the people have therefore greatly changed in the past century with the changes in industries. The introduction of machinery has greatly affected their occupations. A century, nay, half a century ago, those engaged in manufactures were skilled mechanics. Each man had his trade. The man who made shoes was a shoemaker. The man who worked in iron was a blacksmith, There were wheelwrights, watchmakers, cabinetmakers, upholsterers, and so on through a long list of well-defined trades. These trades to-day are almost obliterated. In the place of manual skill we have machines which do almost everything but think. Shoes, clothing, furniture, articles of iron and steel and other metals are made by machines, and in the place of the skilled workman there is a machine tender whose duty is simply to watch

the machine and see that it does its work properly.

The same man may be able, without long special training, to manage any one of a dozen different kinds of machines, and thus successively superintend anything from the making of a suit of clothes to a bicycle, or from a watch to a locomotive.

Great specialization has taken place. The vast majority of men engaged in mechanical pursuits are no longer skilled mechanics in the old sense. They are now skilled in attending machines, or in performing one special part of a process. Thus, in watchmaking, for instance, in the Waltham factory 1,519 operations are necessary to complete a watch; 686 operatives work, and 503 machines are used on each watch. The change from the old hand work to the present machine-made watch was made in 1854. There are 2,954 names upon the pay-roll, divided as follows: Tool makers, 165; machine tenders, 1,983; assemblers, 532; office help, 100; sweepers, watchmen, and pipers, 47; carpenters, painters, and masons, 21; the remainder superintendents, foremen, and assistants.

All this is not to the disadvantage of the workman. Although skill in all branches of his craft is no longer in demand, his earnings are higher than ever before, and his hours of labor fewer; and although one machine doing the work of a hundred men requires but one man to manage it, the other ninety-nine are not thrown out of employment. The cheapening of the product, nearly all of which goes to the consumer, increases the demand to such an extent that the hundred men are still employed in producing while the entire community lives better at less expense.

This brings us to another very important point, viz.: that, by the aid of machinery, we are vastly more effective than a century, or even a generation, ago. It is no exaggeration to say that each man produces, with the aid of machines, from ten to one hundred times as much as he could a century ago—a striking proof of the value of science to every-day life. The human brain has evolved these machines, which make every man worth a hundred men of old in productive capacity. It measures, also, the relative value of brain work as compared with manual labor —of brain *versus* muscle.

The occupations of the people of half a century ago appear strangely primitive when contrasted with those of present times. Indeed, the difference is more like that of five centuries than of five decades. Take as an example the shoe manufacture at Lynn, Massachusetts. Sixty years ago a visitor to this village would have heard the beat of many hammers issuing from small wooden sheds erected against the sides of the houses. These were the sounds of the disciples of St. Crispin working away, with last upon knee, and making perhaps one pair of shoes per day. During the summer the same men became farmers or fishermen, and the village ceased to resound with the shoemakers' hammers. The present city of Lynn, with fifty-five thousand inhabitants, has numerous fine buildings of great height and length, which are the lineal descendants of the little wooden sheds of fifty years ago. In these, boots and shoes are made by the million, and with hardly any handling by the sons of St. Crispin. Machines now do all the cutting, the hammering, and the sewing. Massachusetts is the shoe State par excellence. According to Mulhall, in 1835, there were in the State thirty thousand more bootmakers than in 1880, yet in the latter year the factories produced more than they did in 1835. Thus the boot and shoe machinery more than equalled the labor of an army of thirty thousand men.

Changes equally great took place in the nature of work in textile industries. In 1830, woollen, linen, and cotton manufactures were largely conducted in the household. In Hinton's "Topography of the United States" we read that "many thousands of families spin, and make up their own clothing, sheets, table-linen, etc. They purchase cotton yarn, and have it frequently mixed with their linen and woollen; blankets, quilts, or coverlets, in short, nearly all articles of domestic use, are chiefly made in the family. It is supposed that two-thirds of all the clothing, linen, blankets, etc., of those inhabitants who reside in the interior of the country are of household manufacture. It is the same in the interior with both soap and candles." But many forces were at work revolutionizing the industrial methods of the day. The steam-engine was gradually replacing the water-wheel, or supplementing it when winter bound fast the rivers, thereby insuring to employees regularity of work in factories, and releasing manufacturers from the incubus of idle capital during half the year. Railroads and canals were rapidly increasing the facilities for distributing the products of manufacturing centres. Great improvements in machinery placed manual labor more and more at a discount. Thus, in 1834, a spindle would spin on an average from one-sixth to one-third more than it did a few years previous. Indeed, it was said, in 1834, "that a person could spin more than double the weight of yarn in a given time than he could in 1829." And so there resulted a complete change in the manner of life of the people. Instead of working with the old-fashioned spinning-wheel in country farm-houses, or the hand-loom in the rural cottage, spinners and weavers gathered together in large towns. And here we have one cause of the great growth of towns as compared with the country, which has been referred to in a previous chapter.

A large proportion of the people

sixty years ago were engaged in agriculture, another pursuit in which mechanical appliances have since worked a complete revolution. The transformation is shown with startling vividness by two extracts:

"Among new inventions to increase the pauperism of England, we observe a portable steam threshing-machine."—*New York Evening Star,* August, 1834.

"Dr. Glin, of California, has forty-five thousand acres under wheat. On this farm is used an improved kind of machinery; each machine can cut, thresh, winnow, and bag sixty acres of wheat in a day."—*Mulhall's Progress of the World,* p. 499 (date, 1880).

In view of such a contrast we hardly need the assurance of Mr. H. Murray, who, writing in 1834, says: "Agriculture is in its infancy in the United States." The statement which follows is also interesting: "The country," he adds, "is covered with dense dark woods. Even the State of New York is still three-fourths forest." Since that period the expansion of agriculture has been phenomenal. The farms of America equal the entire territory of the United Kingdom, France, Belgium, Germany, Austria, Hungary, and Portugal. The corn fields equal the extent of England, Scotland, and Belgium; while the grain fields generally would overlap Spain. The cotton fields cover an area larger than Holland, and twice as large as Belgium. The rice fields, sugar, and tobacco plantations would also form kingdoms of no insignificant size. And such is the state of advancement reached by American agriculturists, that Mulhall estimates that one farmer like Dr. Glin or Mr. Dalrymple, with a field of wheat covering a hundred square miles, can raise as much grain with four hundred farm servants as five thousand peasant proprietors in France.

Notwithstanding this, it is pleasing to know that not even with the advantage here implied are these gigantic farms able to maintain the struggle against the smaller farms owned and cultivated by families. The average size of farms continues to decrease. It is the same in Old England; during this period of agricultural depression it is found that the large farmers fail, and that those who till small areas by the labor of the family, without having to employ other labor, are better able to withstand low prices for products.

The Republic to-day is, as it ever was, a nation of workers. The idlers are few—much fewer than in any other great nation. A continent lies before the American, awaiting development. The rewards of labor are high; and prizes are to be won in every pursuit. The family which strikes out boldly for the West, settles upon the soil, and expends its labor upon it, may confidently look forward to reach independent circumstances long before old age. The mechanic with skill and energy rises first to foremanship and ultimately to a partnership or business of his own. As the country fills, these prizes naturally become more and more difficult to secure; but the very knowledge of this acts as an additional incentive, and impels men to "make hay while the sun shines."

The American works much harder than the Briton. His application is greater; his hours are longer; his holidays fewer. Until recently, a leisure class has scarcely been known; and even now a man who is not engaged in some useful occupation lacks one claim to the respect of his fellows. The American must do something. Even if disposed to be idle, he is forced to join the army of toilers from sheer impossibility to find suitable companions for idle hours. One conversant with the mother and child lands is particularly struck with the difference between Britons and Americans in this regard. If a party of educated and agreeable gentlemen are wanted to join in a pleasure excursion, twenty are available in Britain to one in this high-pressure America. The American has always so much to do. Even when the family leaves home in the summer, the man returns to town every few days to hammer away at something. The English gentleman, on the contrary, seems always to have a few days he can call his own for pleasure. Ladies are equally available upon both sides of the ferry. The American woman seems to have quite as much leisure as her English sister. We must not fail to note, however, the signs of change which begin to appear. A small number of the best men of this generation, especially in the Eastern cities, having inherited fortunes, now devote themselves to public work, not necessarily political, as a Briton would infer, and discard the lower ambition of adding more to that which is enough. The roughest and most pressing work, that of clearing and settling the land, has been done to a great extent; and the evidences of refinement and elevation are now patent everywhere. It is thus that a free society evolves that which is fitted for its highest ends. . . .

From all sides . . . comes positive proof of the fact that labor in the Republic is receiving more and more of the combined earnings of capital and labor. The United States presents a strange spectacle to the nations of the earth to-day. In all other lands labor is not fully employed. Throughout the length and breadth of the Republic it is fully employed. There is no man, able and willing to work, under the Stars and Stripes to-day, who cannot find work at wages which would seem to the wage earners of other lands to assure a small fortune for old age. . . .

The American workingman is steadier than his fellow in Britain—much more sober and possessed of higher tastes. Among his amusements is found scarcely a trace of the ruder practices of British manufacturing districts, such as cock-fighting, badger-baiting, dog-fighting, prize-fighting. Wife-beating is scarcely ever heard of, and drunkenness is quite rare. The manufacturer in America considers it cause for instant dismissal, and is able to act, and does act, upon this theory, thereby ensuring a standard of sobriety throughout the works. During all my experience among workingmen I have rarely seen a native American workman under the influence of liquor, and I have never known of any serious inconvenience or loss of time in any works resulting from the intemperance of the men. Even on the Fourth of July the blast-furnaces are run with accustomed regularity, and if the "glorious Fourth" be passed successfully, all other temptations are naturally harmless. It is upon Independence Day, if upon any day in the calendar, that the laboring citizen feels impelled to give vent to his feelings in violent demonstrations of irrepressible joy.

The Irishman was formerly the common laborer in mills and mines, but he has long since risen in the scale and become the skilled workman, paid by the piece or ton. The Hungarian and Italian have taken his place at the foot of the ladder, and upon these the mining and manufacturing and railroad employer is now forced to depend for the lowest class of work performed by pick and shovel. The native American workman is the mechanic, foreman, and manager—expert, skilful, inventive, fairminded, intelligent, sober, and lawabiding, the model workman and the model citizen. Such is the result of his training: a class of which any country would be proud, but which no other country can yet boast.

9. Henry W. Grady, *Industry to Draw the Nation Together, 1889**

Far to the south, Mr. President, separated from this section by a line, once defined in irrepressible difference, once traced in fratricidal blood, and now, thank God, but a vanishing shadow, lies the fairest and richest domain of this earth. It is the home of a brave and hospitable people. There, is centered all that can please or prosper mankind. A perfect climate above a fertile soil, yields to the husbandman every product of the temperate zone. There, by night the cotton whitens beneath the stars, and by day the wheat locks the sunshine in its bearded sheaf. In the same field the clover steals the fragrance of the wind, and the tobacco catches the quick aroma of the rains. There, are mountains stored with exhaustless treasures; forests, vast and primeval, and rivers that, tumbling or loitering, run wanton to the sea. Of the three essential items of all industries—cotton, iron, and wool—that region has easy control. In cotton, a fixed monopoly—in iron, proven supremacy—in timber, the reserve supply of the Republic. From this assured and permanent advantage, against which artificial conditions cannot much longer prevail, has grown an amazing system of industries. Not maintained by human contrivance of tariff or capital, afar off from the fullest and cheapest source of supply, but resting in Divine assurance, within touch of field and mine and forest—not set amid costly farms from which competition has driven the farmer in despair, but amid cheap and sunny lands, rich with agriculture, to which neither season nor soil has set a limit—this system of industries is mounting to a splendor that shall dazzle and illumine the world.

That, sir, is the picture and the promise of my home—a land better and fairer than I have told you, and yet but fit setting, in its material excellence, for the loyal and gentle quality of its citizenship. Against that, sir, we have New England, recruiting the Republic from its sturdy loins, shaking from its overcrowded hives new swarms of workers and touching this land all over with its energy and its courage. And yet, while in the El Dorado of which I have told you, but fifteen percent of lands are cultivated, its mines scarcely touched and its population so scant that, were it set equi-distant, the sound of the human voice could not be heard from Virginia to Texas—while on the threshold of nearly every house in New England stands a son, seeking with troubled eyes some new land to which to carry his modest patrimony, the strange fact remains that in 1880 the South had fewer Northern-born citizens than she had in 1870—fewer in '70 than in '60. Why is this? Why is it, sir, though the sectional line be now but a mist that the breath may dispel, fewer men of the North have crossed it over to the South than when it was crimson with the best blood of the Republic, or even when the slaveholder stood guard every inch of its way?

There can be but one answer. It is the very problem we are now to consider. The key that opens that problem will unlock to the world the fairer half of this Republic, and free the halted feet of thousands whose eyes are already kindled with its beauty. Better than this, it will open the hearts of brothers for thirty years estranged, and clasp in lasting comradeship a million hands now withheld in doubt. Nothing, sir,

* Henry W. Grady, "A Speech before the Boston Merchants Association," in *Life and Labors of Henry W. Grady, His Speeches, Writings, Etc.* (New York, 1890), pp. 248 ff.

but this problem, and the suspicions it breeds, hinders a clear understanding and a perfect union. Nothing else stands between us and such love as bound Georgia and Massachusetts at Valley Forge and Yorktown, chastened by the sacrifices at Manassas and Gettysburg, and illumined with the coming of better work and a nobler destiny than was ever wrought with the sword or sought at the cannon's mouth.

If this does not invite your patient hearing to-night—hear one thing more. My people, your brothers in the South —brothers in blood, in destiny, in all that is best in our past and future—are so beset with this problem that their very existence depends upon its right solution. Nor are they wholly to blame for its presence. The slave-ships of the Republic sailed from your ports—the slaves worked in our fields. You will not defend the traffic, nor I the institution. But I do hereby declare that in its wise and humane administration, in lifting the slave to heights of which he had not dreamed in his savage home, and giving him a happiness he has not yet found in freedom—our fathers left their sons a saving and excellent heritage. In the storm of war this institution was lost. I thank God as heartily as you do that human slavery is gone forever from the American soil.

But the freedman remains. With him a problem without precedent or parallel. Note its appalling conditions. Two utterly dissimilar races on the same soil —with equal political and civil rights— almost equal in numbers, but terribly unequal in intelligence and responsibility—each pledged against fusion—one for a century in servitude to the other, and freed at last by a desolating war— the experiment sought by neither, but approached by both with doubt—these are the conditions. Under these, adverse at every point, we are required to carry these two races in peace and honor to the end. Never, sir, has such a task been given to mortal stewardship. Never before in this Republic has the white race divided on the rights of an alien race. The red man was cut down as a weed, because he hindered the way of the American citizen. The yellow man was shut out of this Republic because he is an alien and inferior. The red man was owner of the land—the yellow man highly civilized and assimilable—but they hindered both sections and are gone!

But the black man, affecting but one section, is clothed with every privilege of government and pinned to the soil, and my people commanded to make good at any hazard and at any cost, his full and equal heirship of American privilege and prosperity. It matters not that wherever the whites and blacks have touched, in any era or any clime, there has been irreconcilable violence. It matters not that no two races, however similar, have lived anywhere at any time on the same soil with equal rights in peace. In spite of these things we are commanded to make good this change of American policy which has not perhaps changed American prejudice—to make certain here what has elsewhere been impossible between whites and blacks—and to reverse, under the very worst conditions, the universal verdict of racial history. And driven, sir, to this superhuman task with an impatience that brooks no delay, a rigor that accepts no excuse, and a suspicion that discourages frankness and sincerity. We do not shrink from this trial. It is so interwoven with our industrial fabric that we cannot disentangle it if we would—so bound up in our honorable obligation to the world, that we would not if we could. Can we solve it? The God who gave it into our hands, He alone can know. But this the weakest and wisest of us do know; we can not solve it with less than your tolerant and patient sympathy—with less than the knowledge that the blood that runs in your veins is our blood—and that when we have done our best, whether the issue be lost or won, we shall feel your strong arms about us and hear the beating of your approving hearts.

The resolute, clear-headed, broad-minded men of the South—the men whose genius made glorious every page of the first seventy years of American history—whose courage and fortitude you tested in five years of the fiercest war—whose energy has made bricks without straw and spread splendor amid the ashes of their war-wasted homes—these men wear this problem in their hearts and their brains, by day and by night. They realize, as you cannot, what this problem means—what they owe to this kindly and dependent race—the measure of their debt to the world in whose despite they defended and maintained slavery. And though their feet are hindered in its undergrowth and their march encumbered with its burdens, they have lost neither the patience from which comes clearness nor the faith from which comes courage. Nor, sir, when in passionate moments is disclosed to them that vague and awful shadow, with its lurid abysses and its crimson stains, into which I pray God they may never go, are they struck with more of apprehension than is needed to complete their consecration!

Such is the temper of my people. But what of the problem itself? Mr. President, we need not go one step further unless you concede right here the people I speak for are as honest, as sensible, and as just as your people, seeking as earnestly as you would in their place, rightly to solve the problem that touches them at every vital point. If you insist that they are ruffians, blindly striving with bludgeon and shotgun to plunder and oppress a race, then I shall sacrifice my self-respect and tax your patience in vain. But admit that they are men of common sense and common honesty—wisely modifying an environment they cannot wholly disregard—guiding and controlling as best they can the vicious and irresponsible of either race—compensating error with frankness and retrieving in patience what they lose in passion—and conscious all the time that wrong means ruin,—admit this, and we may reach an understanding to-night.

The President of the United States [Harrison] in his late message to Congress, discussing the plea that the South should be left to solve this problem, asks: "Are they at work upon it? What solution do they offer? When will the black man cast a free ballot? When will he have the civil rights that are his?" I shall not here protest against the partisanry that, for the first time in our history in time of peace, has stamped with the great seal of our government a stigma upon the people of a great and loyal section, though I gratefully remember that the great dead soldier, who held the helm of state for the eight stormy years of reconstruction, never found need for such a step; and though there is no personal sacrifice I would not make to remove this cruel and unjust imputation on my people from the archives of my country!

But, sir, backed by a record on every page of which is progress, I venture to make earnest and respectful answer to the questions that are asked. I bespeak your patience, while with vigorous plainness of speech, seeking your judgment rather than your applause, I proceed step by step. We give to the world this year a crop of 7,500,000 bales of cotton, worth $45,000,000, and its cash equivalent in grain, grasses, and fruit. This enormous crop could not have come from the hands of sullen and discontented labor. It comes from peaceful fields, in which laughter and gossip rise above the hum of industry and contentment runs with the singing plow.

It is claimed that this ignorant labor is defrauded of its just hire. I present the tax-books of Georgia, which show that the Negro, 25 years ago a slave, has in Georgia alone $10,000,000 of assessed property, worth twice that much. Does not that record honor him and vindicate his neighbors? What people, penniless, illiterate, has done so well? For every Afro-American agitator, stirring the strife in which alone he prospers, I can show you a thousand Negroes, happy in their cabin homes, tilling their own land by day, and at night taking from the lips of their children the helpful message their State sends them from the schoolhouse door. And the schoolhouse itself bears testimony. In Georgia we added last year $250,000 to the school fund, making a total of more than $1,000,000—and this in the face of prejudice not yet conquered—of the fact that the whites are assessed for $368,000,000, the blacks for $10,000,000, and yet 49 per cent of the beneficiaries are black children—and in the doubt of many wise men if education helps, or can help, our problem. Charleston, with her taxable values cut half in two since 1860, pays more in proportion for public schools than Boston. Although it is easier to give much out of much than little out of little, the South with one-seventh of the taxable property of the country, with relatively larger debt, having received only one-twelfth as much public land, and having back of its tax-books none of the half billion of bonds that enrich the North—and though it pays annually $26,000,000 to your section as pensions —yet gives nearly one-sixth of the public school fund. The South since 1865 has spent $122,000,000 in education, and this year is pledged to $37,000,000 for State and city schools, although the blacks, paying one-thirtieth of the taxes, get nearly one-half of the fund.

Go into our fields and see whites and blacks working side by side, on our buildings in the same squad, in our shops at the same forge. Often the blacks crowd the whites from work, or lower wages by greater need or simpler habits, and yet are permitted because

we want to bar them from no avenue in which their feet are fitted to tread. They could not there be elected orators of the white universities, as they have been here, but they do enter there a hundred useful trades that are closed against them here. We hold it better and wiser to tend the weeds in the garden than to water the exotic in the window. In the South, there are Negro lawyers, teachers, editors, dentists, doctors, preachers, multiplying with the increasing ability of their race to support them. In villages and towns they have their military companies equipped from the armories of the State, their churches and societies built and supported largely by their neighbors. What is the testimony of the courts? In penal legislation we have steadily reduced felonies to misdemeanors, and have led the world in mitigating punishment for crime, that we might save, as far as possible, this dependent race from its own weakness. In our penitentiary record 60 percent of the prosecutors are Negroes, and in every court the Negro criminal strikes the colored juror, that white men may judge his case. In the North, one Negro in every 466 is in jail —in the South only one in 1,865. In the North the percentage of Negro prisoners is six times as great as native whites —in the South, only four times as great. If prejudice wrongs him in Southern courts, the record shows it to be deeper in Northern courts.

I assert here, and a bar as intelligent and upright as the bar of Massachusetts will solemnly indorse my assertion, that in the Southern courts, from highest to lowest, pleading for life, liberty, or property, the Negro has distinct advantage because he is a Negro, apt to be overreached, oppressed—and that this advantage reaches from the juror in making his verdict to the judge in measuring his sentence. Now, Mr. President, can it be seriously maintained that we are terrorizing the people from whose willing hands come every year $1,000,-000,000 of farm crops? Or have robbed a people, who twenty-five years from unrewarded slavery have amassed in one State $20,000,000 of property? Or that we intend to oppress the people we are arming every day? Or deceive them when we are educating them to the utmost limit of our ability? Or outlaw them when we work side by side with them? Or re-enslave them under legal forms when for their benefit we have even imprudently narrowed the limit of felonies and mitigated the severity of law? My fellow countrymen, as you yourself may sometimes have to appeal to the bar of human judgment for justice and for right, give to my people to-night the fair and unanswerable conclusion of these incontestible facts. . . .

When will the black cast a free ballot? When ignorance anywhere is not dominated by the will of the intelligent; when the laborer anywhere casts a vote unhindered by his boss; when the vote of the poor anywhere is not influenced by the power of the rich; when the strong and the steadfast do not everywhere control the suffrage of the weak and shiftless—then and not till then will the ballot of the Negro be free. The white people of the South are banded, Mr. President, not in prejudice against the blacks—not in sectional estrangement, not in the hope of political dominion—but in a deep and abiding necessity. Here is this vast ignorant and purchasable vote—clannish, credulous, impulsive, and passionate—tempting every art of the demagogue, but insensible to the appeal of the statesman. Wrongly started, in that it was led into alienation from its neighbor and taught to rely on the protection of an outside force, it cannot be merged and lost in the two great parties through logical currents, for it lacks political conviction and even that information on which conviction must be

based. It must remain a faction—strong enough in every community to control on the slightest division of the whites. Under that division it becomes the prey of the cunning and unscrupulous of both parties. Its credulity is imposed on, its patience inflamed, its cupidity tempted, its impulses misdirected—and even its superstition made to play its part in a campaign in which every interest of society is jeopardized and every approach to the ballot box debauched. It is against such campaigns as this—the folly and the bitterness and the danger of which every Southern community has drunk deeply—that the white people of the South are banded together. Just as you in Massachusetts would be banded if 300,000 black men—not one in a hundred able to read his ballot—banded in a race instinct, holding against you the memory of a century of slavery, taught by your late conquerors to distrust and oppose you, had already travestied legislation from your state house, and in every species of folly or villainy had wasted your substance and exhausted your credit. . . .

I regret, sir, that my section, hindered with this problem, stands in seeming estrangement to the North. If, sir, any man will point out to me a path down which the white people of the South divided may walk in peace and honor, I will take that path though I take it alone—for at the end, and nowhere else, I fear, is to be found the full prosperity of my section and the full restoration of this Union. But, sir, if the Negro had not been enfranchised, the South would have been divided and the Republic united. What solution, then, can we offer for this problem? Time alone can disclose it to us. We simply report progress and ask your patience. If the problem be solved at all —and I firmly believe it will, though nowhere else has it been—it will be solved by the people most deeply bound in interest, most deeply pledged in honor to its solution. I had rather see my people render back this question rightly solved than to see them gather all the spoils over which the faction has contended since Catiline conspired and Caesar fought.

Meantime we treat the Negro fairly, measuring to him justice in the fullness the strong should give to the weak, and leading him in the steadfast ways of citizenship that he may not longer be the prey of the unscrupulous and the sport of the thoughtless. We open to him every pursuit in which he can prosper, and seek to broaden his training and capacity. We seek to hold his confidence and friendship, and to pin him to the soil with ownership, that he may catch in the fire of his own hearthstone that sense of responsibility the shiftless can never know. And we gather him into that alliance of intelligence and responsibility that, though it now runs close to racial lines, welcomes the responsible and intelligent of any race. By this course, confirmed in our judgment and justified in the progress already made, we hope to progress slowly but surely to the end.

The love we feel for that race you cannot measure nor comprehend. As I attest it here, the spirit of my old black mammy from her home up there looks down to bless, and through the tumult of this night steals the sweet music of her croonings as thirty years ago she held me in her black arms and led me smiling into sleep. . . .

Whatever the future may hold for them—whether they plod along in the servitude from which they have never been lifted since the Cyrenian was laid hold upon by the Roman soldiers and made to bear the cross of the fainting Christ—whether they find homes again in Africa, and thus hasten the prophecy of the psalmist who said: "And suddenly Ethiopa shall hold out her hands unto God"—whether, forever dislocated and separated, they remain a weak people

beset by stronger, and exist as the Turk, who lives in the jealousy rather than in the conscience of Europe—or whether in this miraculous Republic they break through the caste of twenty centuries and, belying universal history, reach the full stature of citizenship, and in peace maintain it—we shall give them uttermost justice and abiding friendship. And whatever we do, into whatever seeming estrangement we may be driven, nothing shall disturb the love we bear this Republic, or mitigate our consecration to its service.

I stand here, Mr. President, to profess no new loyalty. When General Lee, whose heart was the temple of our hopes and whose arm was clothed with our strength, renewed his allegiance to the government at Appomattox, he spoke from a heart too great to be false, and he spoke for every honest man from Maryland to Texas. From that day to this, Hamilcar has nowhere in the South sworn young Hannibal to hatred and vengeance—but everywhere to loyalty and to love. Witness the soldier standing at the base of a Confederate monument above the graves of his comrades, his empty sleeve tossing in the April wind, adjuring the young men about him to serve as honest and loyal citizens the government against which their fathers fought. This message, delivered from that sacred presence, has gone home to the hearts of my fellows! And, sir, I declare here, if physical courage be always equal to human aspiration, that they would die, sir, if need be, to restore this Republic their fathers fought to dissolve!

Such, Mr. President, is this problem as we see it; such is the temper in which we approach it; such the progress made. What do we ask of you? First, patience; out of this alone can come perfect work. Second, confidence; in this alone can you judge fairly. Third, sympathy; in this you can help us best. Fourth, give us your sons as hostages. When you plant your capital in millions send your sons that they may help know how true are our hearts and help swell the Anglo-Saxon current until it can carry without danger this black infusion. Fifth, loyalty to the Republic—for there is sectionalism in loyalty as in estrangement. This hour little needs the loyalty that is loyal to one section and yet holds the other in enduring suspicion and estrangement. Give us the broad and perfect loyalty that loves and trusts Georgia alike with Massachusetts—that knows no South, no North, no East, no West; but endears with equal and patriotic love every foot of our soil, every State of our Union.

A mighty duty, sir, and a mighty inspiration impels every one of us tonight to lose in patriotic consecration whatever estranges, whatever divides. We, sir, are Americans—and we fight for human liberty. The uplifting force of the American idea is under every throne on earth. France, Brazil—these are our victories. To redeem the earth from kingcraft and oppression—this is our mission. And we shall not fail. God has sown in our soil the seed of this millennial harvest, and he will not lay the sickle to the ripening crop until his full and perfect day has come. Our history, sir, has been a constant and expanding miracle from Plymouth Rock and Jamestown all the way—aye, even from the hour when, from the voiceless and trackless ocean, a new world rose to the sight of the inspired sailor.

As we approach the fourth centennial of that stupendous day—when the Old World will come to marvel and to learn, amid our gathered treasures—let us resolve to crown the miracles of our past with the spectacle of a Republic compact, united, indissoluble in the bonds of love—loving from the lakes to the Gulf—the wounds of war healed in every heart as on every hill—serene and resplendent at the summit of human achievement and earthly glory—blazing out the path, and making clear the way up which all the nations of the earth must come in God's appointed time.

IV

* *

Success and Individualism

DAVID SARNOFF

board chairman of the Radio Corporation of America, was born in Russia in 1891.

He came to this country in 1900 and six years later started work as an office boy for the Marconi Wireless Telegraph Company. In 1909 he became manager of the Marconi station at Sea Gate, Brooklyn, and later served as a wireless operator for the Marconi company.

Mr. Sarnoff became commercial manager for RCA when it absorbed Marconi in 1919. He became general manager and vice-president of RCA in 1922.

Meantime he had studied electrical engineering at Pratt Institute in Brooklyn. He received the degree of Doctor of Science from St. Lawrence University in 1927. He has been RCA chairman since 1947.

Mr. Sarnoff served in the Army and was made a brigadier general in the Reserve in 1944.

David Sarnoff ✻✻✻✻ Turn the Cold War Tide in America's Favor

The unfolding American debate on national purpose carries the disquieting implication that our traditional purposes, though they served the nation well in the past, have somehow been outmoded if not wholly invalidated. This I do not believe to be true. I am convinced, on the contrary, that these time-tested purposes, rooted in the nation's whole history, are more compelling than ever before. More, they are indispensable in enabling the U.S. to meet the paramount challenge of this epoch: the struggle between Communism and freedom. If revitalized, redefined for our times, and translated into great decisions, they could turn the tide of conflict in our favor.

The need now, as I see it, is not for tailor-made new purposes but for a renewed understanding and dedication to old purposes—raised to a dimension adequate for this fateful period. The need is for firm and inspiring positions commensurate with the immense perils facing our country and the human race.

The Communists, whatever their tactics in a given period, have never deviated from *their* purpose. It has been openly proclaimed from Lenin's day down to Khrushchev's and Mao Tse-tung's. It is, in the words of the official Moscow magazine *Kommunist,* "implacable struggle" looking to "the inevitable end of capitalism and the total triumph of Communism." Such a challenge can be met and frustrated only with a purpose of equal scope.

Five years ago I submitted a memorandum to the White House sketching a Program for a Political Offensive against World Communism. "For Moscow," it said, "the real alternative to a nuclear showdown is not 'peace' but political-psychological warfare of a magnitude to weaken, demoralize, chip away and ultimately take over what remains of the free world." The memorandum therefore urged that we renounce all delusions of easy solutions and compromises; that instead we mount a

189

political counterstrategy as massive, as intensive, and as clear about its ultimate goals as the strategy of the enemy himself.

Events in the intervening years and intensified Communist pressures today have, if anything, fortified this point of view. The essence of my proposed program, for which I claim no originality, was—and still is—an unequivocal decision to fight the so-called cold war with a will and on a scale for complete victory.

The decision would have to be communicated to the entire world as boldly and energetically as the Communists communicate their intentions. Our message to humankind must be that America has decided, irrevocably, to win the cold war and thereby to cancel out the destructive power of Soviet-based Communism. A national commitment of this scope, I submit, would be consistent with American instincts and experience, a restatement of historic purposes in contemporary terms.

The nature of those purposes has been sufficiently defined by the editors in the introductory article to this series. It is explicit in basic American documents, beginning with the Declaration of Independence of which Thomas Jefferson could say, "We are acting for all mankind."

It is implicit in the widespread assertion—presented by some as an accusation—that our foreign policies have been "idealistic." Through the generations Americans have always thought of themselves as being in the vanguard of freedom. They cherished the image of their country as the citadel of democracy and morality and a living defiance to despotism anywhere.

The Rockefeller Brothers Fund Report on U.S. Foreign Policy—prepared by a panel of which I was a member and published last year—put it this way: "The United States at its best has always seen its national life as an experiment in liberty . . . [Americans] have known that the hopes of the world were, in some measure, bound up with their success. . . . Whenever [the United States] has wielded effective power in the world, its ideals and its moral convictions have played a vital part in its decisions. Whenever, on the contrary, the United States has tried to act without moral conviction, or in ways that went counter to its basic beliefs, it has found itself inhibited and has ultimately had to rechart its course. . . . Ideas and ideals are thus to the United States an essential element of reality."

This is why expediency and appeasement, solutions that condemn other peoples to enslavement, failure to react to international crimes violate the deepest instincts of the American people. Why is there such a pervasive skepticism about our historic purposes and such a widespread search for substitutes? Why the shrinking from lofty goals for all mankind in favor of the safe, the compromising, or mere survival?

The easy answer—that it is all due to the advent of terrible new weapons—will hardly do. The calendar refutes it: the retreat began before those weapons were forged and grew more panicky during the time when

America had a monopoly on the atom bomb. It was precisely in the years before Soviet Russia produced the bomb that Communism scored its greatest gains, and it did so almost always by the default of the free world. The Soviet advantages were not military and technological but political and psychological.

The true answer, as I see it, is related to the ever-rising costs of idealism in terms of the sacrifices and the hazards involved. The trouble is not that the older purposes have become irrelevant but that they have become too relevant. I mean that the time when America could serve passively as an example or inspiration to other nations has run out. Today, professions of principle have serious consequences: they must be implemented in policy and action. To say it in slang, the time has come to put up or shut up.

As far as the contest with Communism is concerned we had "shut up," quite literally. We had curbed our tongues for fear of offending the delicate sensibilities of those who daily offend *us*. Few democratic leaders dare to speak as uninhibitedly about the coming doom of the Communist empire as Khrushchev and Mao-Tse-tung regularly speak about our impending doom. Our opponents defy, denounce, and challenge, while we plead and propitiate. We have left the vocabulary of confidence and victory to the other side, contenting ourselves with such solacing and temporizing words as accommodation, *modus vivendi*, relaxed tensions, and coexistence.

This semantic timidity, of course, is merely a symptom and a minor one. The all-encompassing malady is a loss of nerve, marked by depleted self-esteem and purpose. It has impelled us, whenever we have been faced with a choice of interpretations on some aspect of the Communist affliction, to choose the more agreeable one, the one more conducive to complacency and less likely to tax our courage. With rare exceptions the choice has turned out to be the wrong and often the disastrous one, regardless of the political parties in power in this country and in the free world.

Thus in the 1930s we eagerly found assurance in Stalin's talk about "socialism in one country." Later we relaxed in the cozy conviction that the Chinese Communists were simply "agrarian reformers." We prefer to believe in the "evolution" of Communism, though there has not been the slightest revision of ultimate Communist goals. We seek a comforting answer to our prayers in tensions between Moscow and Peking, though these are strictly within the framework of their unshakable alliance against the West, no more significant than Anglo-American tension within our alliance.

A familiar gambit is to list Communism as just one item in a long inventory of problems. But if the Sino-Soviet bloc wins world dominion, the other problems will cease to matter: they will have been solved for the free world in about the way that death solves all bodily ills.

In the debate on National Purpose we find at least one area of virtually unanimous agreement. It is that sheer survival, in the elementary physical sense, is not enough. A nation that thinks and acts exclusively for self-preservation cannot, in the present-day world, preserve itself. The posture, even if it were desired or desirable, has been turned into an anachronism by the surge of science and technology. The world has become too small for physical, economic, or political isolationism. The polarization of forces dueling for supremacy has gone too far to permit the survival of an island of humanism in a sea of dehumanized totalitarianism. No single nation can survive unless the civilization of which it is part survives.

Our civilization, too, cannot remain isolated, confined to a delimited segment of the earth and indifferent to the humanity beyond those limits. The world cannot be frozen in its present patterns. In this period of great flux and of intermeshed revolutions, static and passive arrangements are doomed to disruption. If the area of freedom is not expanded, then assuredly it will continue to contract.

Despite this, "survival of the free world"—side by side with an unfree world—has been and remains the maximum goal of Western diplomacy. Not the weakening and eventual defeat of Communism but a lasting accommodation seems to mark the farthest reach of hope. It is scarcely a vision to inspire confidence or zeal, and in any case it is utterly utopian, because two parties are needed to make an accommodation.

The best analysis of Communist strategy that I know is in a recent book called *Protracted Conflict* by Dr. Robert Strausz-Hupé of the University of Pennsylvania and three associates. The book's title is a phrase used by Mao Tse-tung. The Communist plan, say the authors, is protracted in time and space and in the limitless variety of its techniques and weapons, and the weapons can even include "the final and total knockout punch." Short of surrender, the authors see for our world no alternative but a many-sided, continuous, long-range counteroffensive.

Such a policy would reject all illusions of an enduring truce, let alone a negotiated division of the globe. The historic contest will be with us for a long, long time. We may delay, maneuver, bargain, and compromise, but it will be so much flailing of water unless all such moves become for us—as they have always been for the enemy—calculated holding actions geared to long-range objectives, means not ends, tactics not strategy.

Whatever we do or fail to do in the years and decades ahead, we shall be forced to take great risks and make great sacrifices. These cannot be evaded even by piecemeal surrenders. In fact, if Americans and other free peoples are to understand and accept these costs and exertions, there must be some rational relation between the magnitude of the goal and the magnitude of the burdens it imposes.

This means that in the conflict with Communism we must become the dynamic challenger rather than remain the inert target of challenge. Only then can freedom regain the initiative. Only then will we have a global goal to match that of Communism, and the incentive to apply the full weight of our brains, energies, and resources to its achievement. The great decision, once made and communicated to all concerned, will dictate its appropriate program of policy and action. The strategy will shape the necessary tactics.

Even the things we are now doing and must continue to do will become more relevant and more effective when geared to a conscious ultimate goal. Military and economic aid to our allies, to underdeveloped areas, and to neutral nations will cease to be hit-or-miss improvisations. They will be integral elements of an affirmative program. Propaganda, cultural exchanges, diplomatic moves, summit meetings will all acquire for us—as they always have for the Communists—dimensions of purpose beyond their limited immediate effects.

Before the Soviet Union attained its present technological stature, America's paramount problem appeared to be the struggle for men's minds. Today it is dangerous to concentrate on any one facet of the conflict. I think of the image in terms of a table with four legs, military, political, economic, and psychological. The significance of the last three is self-evident, since they relate to activities short of all-out war. But the "military leg" must not be underrated.

The present approximate balance of terror presents a false appearance of stability. But it may be upset. And if we relax in this area it will be upset. The enemy is constantly probing our vitality and resolution. Any one of these probes may lead to the brink of war and possibly to war itself. No matter how often we repeat that war is "unthinkable" it remains possible. War may be touched off by accident, or it may come because the Communist high command considers itself ready to deliver the "final and total knockout punch." The maintenance of adequate military power, both offensive and defensive, is therefore of paramount importance. Whether it is ever used or not, moreover, it is the indispensable shield for all other types of action in the protracted conflict.

A strategy for victory in the cold war would, however, begin with a complete reappraisal of present efforts. It would aim to seize the initiative in every possible arena of competition. Not merely the expansion of present projects and the addition of new ones would be considered but how to give each of them a clear role within the framework of the over-all objective.

It would not reject courses of action simply because they are unconventional. We would no longer disdain to use against the enemy some of the weapons used against us. Having finally acknowledged that the struggle is decisive and therefore as real as a "real" war, we would not hesitate to fight fire with fire.

American ingenuity would be called upon to evolve devices and techniques to exploit weaknesses and vulnerabilities in the Communist world, to keep the enemy constantly off balance, to impose upon him problems and crises instead of always waiting to counteract crises of his making. By all the instruments of communication and through the loud-speakers of events, we would aim to saturate the Communist world with reminders that we intend to keep alive the memory of human dignity, the hatred of injustice, the hope of liberation, and the courage needed for resistance.

Debates in the United Nations and at diplomatic conferences would be made sounding boards for our views as well as for theirs. No allusion to "colonialism" would be permitted to pass without our throwing the limelight on Red imperialism and on the principles of self-determination.

Thus the Communist world, rather than ours, would tend increasingly to become the principal battlefield of ideological and political conflict. The immunity their world has so long enjoyed would be shattered.

A bill to establish a Freedom Academy for training cold war specialists —what a *Life* editorial called a Political West Point—is before Congress. Whatever the merits or demerits of this particular bill, it is in line with a commitment to victory. Various proposals have been made for setting up a Liberation Force, a volunteer formation drawn largely from among refugees from captive nations and ready to serve in emergencies. That, too, is in line with a strategy for victory. Official and private agencies of other kinds would be generated by focused strategic thinking in offensive rather than defensive terms. And a new department of Cabinet rank could and should be established to plan and coordinate all cold war activities.

Certainly this new approach would call for substantial sacrifices in material terms. But the notion that it would require a deep cut in American living standards underestimates the wealth and productive genius of our country. The more demanding sacrifices, indeed, would be in the psychological and moral domains. Our people, in short, would have to renounce complacency, euphoria, and illusion; they would have to embrace the grim but inspiring realities of our epoch.

The ultimate rise of a world order under law is dictated by the logic of devastating weaponry, the conquest of space, and modern communications. What remains to be settled is whether it will be an order rooted in freedom or in universal tyranny.

I do not doubt that we have what it takes to assure that it will be an order that we may cherish. The Western concepts of open societies, of liberty under law, of government by the consent of the governed, of the supremacy of the individual rather than the state—these are far closer to the natural aspirations of man than the anthill concepts of Communism. In any equal propaganda contest, what these Western concepts have brought in human well-being will become obvious and irresistible to the majority of mankind.

In my 1955 Memorandum to the White House I wrote: "Once that decision is made, some of the means for implementing it will become self-evident; others will be explored and developed under the impetus of a clear-cut goal. Agreement on the problem must come before agreement on the solution." But Abraham Lincoln said it better a century ago: "Determine that the thing can and shall be done, and then we shall find the way."

How Far Can the Individual Stand Alone?

Do the feasters gluttonous feast?
Do the corpulent sleepers sleep? have they lock'd and bolted doors?
Still be ours the diet hard, and the blanket on the ground,
Pioneers! O pioneers!

—Walt Whitman
"Pioneers! O Pioneers!"

David Sarnoff's essay sounds a call for idealism and for substantial sacrifice to permit the nation to assume the offensive in the struggle for men's minds that will occupy the 1960's. It is appropriate that this challenge should come from a self-made man whose success was earned in business. For often, in the past, it seemed that a preoccupation with personal success excessively absorbed the attentions of Americans. A society not bound by restraints inherited from the past was frequently tempted to exaggerate the role of the individual in shaping his own destiny. Since everything was susceptible of change for the better, and since improvement was measurable in terms of material well-being, it was easy to conclude that what man became depended not on the conditions about him but on his ability and on the exercise of his own will.

All the conditions of American life tended to locate the responsibility for his fate upon the individual himself. The deep strain of Calvinism that ran through American thought minimized the importance of intermediaries between man and God and taught each person to look to himself for the salvation of his soul. More generally, the weakness of established institutions and the transitory character of all social life in the United States encouraged the emphasis upon self-reliance and self-defined standards of conduct.

Even in the seventeenth century, therefore, Americans were likely to measure men by their external success. Thereafter the opportunities of the frontier, of an expanding society, and of industrialism further located the responsibility for achievement upon the rugged individualism of each person. But it was significant that the reiterations of this point of view never altogether obscured the consciousness that the individual was also subject to some broader obligations.

In the eighteenth and early nineteenth centuries there was confidence that a balance would be struck between individual opportunity and social responsibility. Benjamin Franklin (1706–90) earned much of his early popularity by his skill in phrasing aphorisms which pointed out that success was there for the striving (1). On the other hand, Amos Lawrence (1786–1852), a successful merchant in Boston, in letters and in his diary expressed a clear consciousness of the obligations that rested upon him as the steward of wealth bestowed by God (2). It was his duty not only to accumulate riches but also to use them in ways that justified his success.

By the early nineteenth century, however, social changes in the United States had already revealed to some Americans the inadequacies of the conception of individualism. Thomas Skidmore (?–1832), for instance, spoke for many artisans who found their opportunities blocked off by the growth of industry. He denied that wealth was a reflection of individual worth and, asserting that every man had a right to property, looked back nostalgically to an earlier age of abundance (3). Somewhat later, Ralph Waldo Emerson (1803–82) in a subtle poem expressed his doubts about the limited value of individual success (4).

In the middle of the nineteenth century, however, the dominant view in American life still stressed the necessity of struggling for successes as a means of asserting man's individuality. Freeman Hunt (1804–58), the editor of a widely read business magazine, had no doubts on this point when he edited a series of lives of great merchants to illustrate it (5). And William Graham Sumner (1840–1910), a professor of sociology at Yale University, brushed aside all social consideration by arguing the pre-eminent value of laissez faire as a means of releasing individual energies (6). Using a somewhat different phraseology, Russell Conwell (1843–1925), in a widely popular lecture entitled "Acres of Diamonds," emphasized that it was the duty of man to pursue the success available to all who sought it (7).

In the twentieth century, the doubts grew greater. Frederick Jackson Turner (1861–1932), the distinguished historian, who had already pointed to the significance of the passing of the frontier, now explained that the conception of individualism had been related to a temporary circumstance of American life and that it would thereafter be necessary to create a new setting within which to preserve the old ideals (8). Furthermore, while individualism was tolerable as long as it fell within accepted norms, it was not so readily accepted when it led men to question the dominant values of their times as did Thorstein Veblen. In a sketch of that critic of American society, John Dos Passos (1896–) explained some of the difficulties in attempting to assert an individuality which was not that of the mass of men (9).

The crisis in this aspect of American thinking came as a result of the Great Depression of 1929 and of the changes in American society that followed the end of World War II. It was still possible for men of an older generation, such as President Herbert Hoover (1874–), to speak of the virtues of rugged individualism (10). But a younger critic like Kenneth Fearing (1902–) viewed these phrases as merely hollow shams. And in an age which seemed to emphasize the conformity of the organization man, it was difficult to say what individualism now meant or in what sphere it still was an important personal or social objective (11).

1. BENJAMIN FRANKLIN, *Advice to a Young Tradesman, 1748**

To my Friend, A. B.:

As you have desired it of me, I write the following hints, which have been of service to me, and may, if observed, be so to you.

Remember, that *time* is money. He that can earn ten shillings a day by his labour, and goes abroad, or sits idle, one half of that day, though he spends but sixpence during his diversion or idleness, ought not to reckon *that* the only expense; he has really spent, or rather thrown away, five shillings besides.

Remember, that *credit* is money. If a man lets his money lie in my hands after it is due, he gives me the interest, or so much as I can make of it during that time. This amounts to a considerable sum where a man has good and large credit, and makes good use of it.

Remember, that money is of the prolific, generating nature. Money can beget money, and its offspring can beget more, and so on. Five shillings turned is six, turned again it is seven and three-pence, and so on till it becomes an hundred pounds. The more there is of it, the more it produces every turning, so that the profits rise quicker and quicker. He that kills a breeding sow, destroys all her offspring to the thousandth generation. He that murders a crown, destroys all that it might have produced, even scores of pounds.

Remember, that six pounds a year is but a groat a day. For this little sum (which may be daily wasted either in time or expense unperceived) a man of credit may, on his own security, have the constant possession and use of an hundred pounds. So much in stock, briskly turned by an industrious man, produces great advantage.

Remember this saying, *The good paymaster is lord of another man's purse.* He that is known to pay punctually and exactly to the time he promises, may at any time, and on any occasion, raise all the money his friends can spare. This is sometimes of great use. After industry and frugality, nothing contributes more to the raising of a young man in the world than punctuality and justice in all his dealings; therefore never keep borrowed money an hour beyond the time you promised, lest a disappointment shut up your friend's purse for ever.

The most trifling actions that affect a man's credit are to be regarded. The sound of your hammer at five in the morning, or nine at night, heard by a creditor, makes him easy six months longer; but, if he sees you at a billiard-table, or hears your voice at a tavern, when you should be at work, he sends for his money the next day; demands it, before he can receive it, in a lump.

It shows, besides, that you are mindful of what you owe; it makes you appear a careful as well as an honest man, and that still increases your credit.

Beware of thinking all your own that you possess, and of living accordingly. It is a mistake that many people who have credit fall into. To prevent this, keep an exact account for some time, both of your expenses and your income. If you take the pains at first to mention particulars, it will have this good effect: you will discover how wonderfully small, trifling expenses mount up to large sums, and will discern what might have been, and may for the future be saved, without occasioning any great inconvenience.

In short, the way to wealth, if you

* Benjamin Franklin, *Writings* (Albert Henry Smyth, ed.; New York, 1905), II, 370–72.

desire it, is as plain as the way to market. It depends chiefly on two words, *industry* and *frugality;* that is, waste neither *time* nor *money,* but make the best use of both. Without industry and frugality nothing will do, and with them every thing. He that gets all he can honestly, and saves all he gets (necessary expenses excepted), will certainly become *rich,* if that Being who governs the world, to whom all should look for a blessing on their honest endeavors, doth not, in his wise providence, otherwise determine.

An Old Tradesman

2. Amos Lawrence, *Reflections of a Boston Merchant, 1837–38**

Letter to his mother, December 17, 1837:

This day completes thirty years since my commencing business, with the hope of acquiring no very definite amount of property, or having in my mind any anticipation of ever enjoying a tithe of that consideration my friends and the public are disposed to award me at this time. In looking back to that period, and reviewing the events as they come along, I can see the good hand of God in all my experience; and acknowledge, with deep humiliation, my want of gratitude and proper return for all his mercies. May each day I live impress me more deeply with a sense of duty, and find me better prepared to answer his call, and account for my stewardship! The changes in our family have been perhaps no greater than usual in other families in that period, excepting in the matter of the eminent success that has attended our efforts of a worldly nature. This worldly success is the great cause of our danger in its uses, and may prove a snare, unless we strive to keep constantly in mind, that to whom much is given, of him will much be required. I feel my own deficiencies, and lament them; but am encouraged and rewarded by the enjoyment, in a high degree, of all my well-meant efforts for the good of those around me. In short, I feel as though I can still do a little to advance the cause of human happiness while I remain here. My maxim is, that I ought to "work while the day lasts; for the night of death will soon overtake me, when I can no more work." I continue to mend in strength, and feel at times the buoyancy of early days. It is now raining in torrents, keeping us all within doors. I have been at work with gimlet, saw, fore-plane, and hammer, thus securing a good share of exercise without leaving my chamber.

Extracts from his diary, January 1, 1838:

Bless the Lord, O my soul! and forget not all his benefits; for he has restored my life twice during the past year, when I was apparently dead, and has permitted me to live, and see and enjoy much, and has surrounded me with blessings that call for thankfulness. The possession of my mind, the intercourse with beloved friends, the opportunity of performing some labor as his steward (although imperfectly done), all call upon me for thanksgiving and praise. The violent revulsion in the business of the country during the past year has been

* Amos Lawrence, *Extracts from the Diary and Correspondence* (Boston, 1855), pp. 141–45.

ruinous to many; but, so far as my own interests are concerned, has been less than I anticipated. My property remains much as it was a year ago. Something beyond my income has been disposed of; and I have no debts against me, either as a partner in the firm or individually. Everything is in better form for settlement than at any former period, and I hope to feel ready to depart whenever called.

Letter to his son, January 1, 1838:

I give you this little book, that you may write in it how much money you receive, and how you use it. It is of much importance, in forming your early character, to have correct habits, and a strict regard to truth in all you do. For this purpose, I advise you never to cheat yourself by making a false entry in this book. If you spend money for an object you would not willingly have known, you will be more likely to avoid doing the same thing again if you call it by its right name here, remembering always that there is *One* who cannot be deceived, and that *He* requires his children to render an account of all their doings at last. I pray God so to guide and direct you that, when your stewardship here is ended, he may say to you that the talents intrusted to your care have been faithfully employed.

Letter to his sister, December 28, 1838:

It is thirty-one years this week since I commenced business on my own account, and the prospects were as gloomy at that period for its successful pursuits as at any time since; but I never had any doubt or misgiving as to my success, for I then had no more wants than my means would justify. The habits then formed, and since confirmed and strengthened by use, have been the foundation of my good name, good fortune, and present happy condition. At that time (when you know I used to visit you as often as I could, by riding in the night until I sometimes encroached upon the earliest hour of the Sabbath before reaching my beloved home, to be at my business at the dawn of day on Monday morning), my gains were more than my expenses; thus strengthening and encouraging me in the steady pursuit of those objects I had in view as a beginner. From that time to this, I am not aware of ever desiring or acquiring any great amount by a single operation, or of taking any part of the property of any other man and mingling it with my own, where I had a legal right to do so. I have had such uniform success as to make my fidelity a matter of deep concern to myself; and my prayer to God is, that I may be found to have acted a uniform part, and receive the joyful "Well done," which is substantial wealth, that no man can take away. If my experience could be made available by my successors, I sometimes feel that it would be a guaranty that they would keep in the best path; but, as they are to be fitted by discipline for the journey, it is perhaps a vain thing for me to allow any doubts to rest upon my mind that *that* discipline is not for their highest good. The pleasures of memory have never been more highly enjoyed than during the period of my last sickness. They solaced my pains, and supported me through numerous fainting fits, growing out of the surgical treatment I have endured. I would ask you, my dear sister, if a merciful Parent has not stretched forth his hand almost visibly to support me through this trying scene, by scattering in my path these flowers and fruits so freely as almost to make me forget bodily pains; and bless him for what is past, and trust that what is future will be the means of making me a better man.

3. THOMAS SKIDMORE, *The Right to Property, 1829**

If a man were to ask me, to what I would compare the unequal distribution of property which prevails in the world, and has ever prevailed, I would say, that it reminds me of a large party of gentlemen, who should have a common right to dine at one and the same public table; a part of whom should arrive first, sit down and eat what they chose; and then, because the remaining part came later to dinner, should undertake to monopolize the whole; and deprive them of the opportunity of satisfying their hunger, but upon terms such as those who had feasted, should be pleased to prescribe.

Such, now, is the actual condition of the whole human race. Those who have gone before us, have been the first to sit down to the table, and to enjoy themselves, without interruption, from those who came afterwards; and not content with this enjoyment, they have disposed of the whole dinner, in such a manner, that nine-tenths of the beings that now people this globe, have not wherewith to dine, but upon terms such as these first monopolizers, or those to whom they pretend they have conferred their own power as successors, shall choose to dictate. It is, as if, after dining till they were satisfied, a general scramble ensued, for what remained on the table; and those who succeeded in filling their pockets and other receptacles, with provisions, should have something to give to their children; but those who should have the misfortune to get none, or having got it, should lose it again, through fraud, calamity, or force, should have none for theirs, to the latest generation.

Such is the exact resemblance of the present order of things. Ye proud and rich possessors of the earth, look at this, and see if it be not so; and being so, and seeing that it is in your power to consent to a more *honorable* method of obtaining title to possession; say, if ye will not do so? I do not ask you, because it is in your power to confer any favor by giving such consent; for, this community, and every other, whenever they shall understand their rights, will have power enough in their own hands to do what they shall think fit, without seeking for any acquisition from you; but because it will be more agreeable to your own true happiness, to give such consent freely; than, with the ill, but unavailing grace of reluctance. . . .

Before I approach the termination of this work, it may not be amiss, that we ask ourselves, how has it happened, that wealth, or in other words, possession, has succeeded in making itself so unequal in the world as it appears. . . . To ascertain, we must go to those countries, in whose first settlement conquest had no agency; and when we have arrived there, we must ascend to the earliest age of the people who inhabit it. What shall we find there? . . .

At that early age, we may understand a great extent of country before us. We may understand, also, that there were very few people. We may consider them ignorant and helpless. Their resources of subsistence would be the fruits and roots of trees; animals and fish; and their clothing, as far as they might have any, would be, perhaps, the skins of the beasts they had killed for food. Habitation they would have none; or if any, it would be for rest, a cave, or a hollow

---

* Thomas Skidmore, *The Rights of Man to Property! Being a Proposition to Make It Equal among the Adults of the Present Generation* (New York, 1829).

tree, or the recess of some superimpending rock. If, in process of time, they should learn, as they would, that the animals on which they subsist, might be rendered docile and tractable, it would lead them to discover that those which they now take in the chase, with great labor and difficulty, and frequently at great intervals of time, producing great distress from hunger; might be bred up in a domestic way; and they would adopt the practice. This change would lead them from the state of hunters, to that of shepherds. At first, these would locate themselves no where. They would ramble about for food: and as there is supposed to be a great superabundance of territory, and but few people, there would be no objection, because there would be no collision of interest; and, therefore, there would arise no investigation of rights. . . .

They did not, at this stage of their existence, inquire   why one should have a larger flock than another; or why one shepherd dying, a certain person, or persons, rather than any other person, or persons, should become the owner of it. All had enough for their own simple wants, and this was sufficient to render inquiry unnecessary. . . .

In progress of time it was discovered, that these flocks could be raised with less labor and risk, if *cultivation* were added to their store of resources. But this required a *permanent* location. It called upon the shepherd to fix upon some place. In this there would be no difficulty. For inasmuch as territory is very abundant, and population thin, there is room enough, and more than enough, for all. Why should they differ? Differ they did not; and not differing, no inquiry was made, why *this* location should belong to *one* rather than to another. . . .

During all this time, population increases slowly. Deaths happen. Parents more or less keep their children around them. When the former die, as there is

little wealth anywhere, little or no inquiry is started, as to whose are the flocks that the father possessed? Probably none at all. Land is abundant everywhere; and all have opportunity to have flocks of their own, and to cultivate, little as they may do, fields of their own. The children are, therefore, left in possession.

Nor, if two shepherds immediately adjacent to each other, should die, at the same time, one having, it may be, five children, and the other only one; would inquiry arise why the one child should have the flocks of the one father, and the five children have only the flocks of the other father? In general among all such nations, and I believe, always, hospitality prevails, to a great extent, and if need should arise, for the numerous family to receive of the flocks of the richer son, hospitality would afford it. Besides, land still greatly abounding, new locations would be taken, new flocks reared, and new fields cultivated; without any investigation of their actual original rights.

I said, fields would be cultivated; but the tillage they would undergo, would hardly deserve the name of cultivation. Every thing would be extremely rude. Nor, in most cases, would those fields have any fences. The locations would be *without lines* or *limits*. There would be no boundaries, for the simple reason that there is yet more of soil than any of them want. If fence be made at all, at this period, it is such, perhaps, as that which may be sufficient to inclose their flocks, and keep them from straying, while their owner sleeps.

The handicraft arts would begin to make some progress. Accidental circumstances would give some much more taste and skill, in their prosecution, than others could acquire. This superior taste and skill would be turned to account, to supply the wants of their possessor. He would look less to land, and the ordinary resources, than others are obliged to do. He would soon become indifferent, more or less, to the possession of the soil. By imitation, too, his children and associates would, more or less, adopt his mode of life, and acquire similar facility in the same pursuits. If they did not, they still could get land as much as they might want.

In this way, society advances in numbers. The arts also advance in number, perfection, and the population engaged in them; and still there is land enough for all, and more. But they find it in their common interest to divide, almost without knowing that they have done so, their occupations. Still the principle prevails, and gains strength, that whoever is near the dying man, at and about the latter part of his life, succeeds to his possessions. Nor is there yet any great harm in it: for there would be very little alteration produced for the common benefit, if the attendants upon the dying man, (being generally his children,) should abandon his location, and take another. For as yet there is more land than any and all want.

The children of those, too, who pursue handicraft trades, succeed to the possession of their father's effects; because the principle is seen to be similar; and because it is perceived, that they will better understand the use of them; and can better employ them in the satisfaction of the wants of others.

In the course of time, however, land is taken up so much, that there begins to arise some inquiry as to the *extent* of rights; none, however, as it regards the rights themselves. Long established custom having sanctioned the latest, as well as the earliest locations, it does not occur to them, to go back to periods of times anterior to their first fixation. All they conceive they have to do, is to assign *limits* or *boundaries* to such locations, as they now find them; and this, of course, is done, by what may be called the public authority. They lose sight of that original question, which they would have had to discuss, if instead of coming through this long and tedious process, it may be, of some thousand years, to their present condition, in point of numbers, and knowledge; they had just arrived, for the first time, to the possession of the territory they now occupy. In the latter event, they would have to inquire, why this location, rather than another, should belong to this man; . . . these are questions, now, *which they do not discuss;* and for the simple reason, there is no subject requiring their interposition, but that of *boundaries* or *limits,* to each man's possessions. As yet there is land, there is property enough for all; and therefore, again, they do not inquire about their rights.

At the same time, too, that limits are assigned to these locations, they are made transmissible, like ordinary personal property; and probably now, or before this time, money is invented.

Here a great change takes place. Population continues to increase; and now they can find no more unsettled land. Of if they can, they must go farther for it, than they are disposed, or are able to afford the means necessary. Sooner than do this, they prefer to enter into a treaty with him or those who have, and may spare. For the first time, the land-holder begins to feel that he has power. He tastes the advantage of it; and his thirst increases for more. Here, then, has avarice begun. Nor could it begin, until some human being was found, out of whose distress, arising in consequence of *his wanting possessions, such as his fellows enjoy,* the sweets of another's labor, were to be extracted.

Necessity arising from a deprivation of their natural and original right to property, compels many to make a treaty, whereby they surrender a portion; a small portion, at first, it is true, of their labor. Numbers continue to increase, but the land itself does not increase. Greater and greater exactions are made, till, at last, they become so great that more cannot be given; for more is not in being to be given. Still population increases yet more; and men, needy and wretched; finding that they cannot obtain the means of supporting life, but by engaging in the interest of some large possessor, who has cause of quarrel with another, *he consents;* and thus do we see the origin of the soldier. And so does this state of things continue to increase, in inflicting misery and wretchedness upon the race, till it arrives at the condition in which we now see mankind suffering.

In all principles of the rights of property which are thus seen to have been almost insensibly adopted, *there is not one which has been adopted on any consideration, correct or otherwise, of its own merits.* Usage has done every thing. Custom, practice, habit, has made all the law; and made it at times, and under circumstances, in which it was of *no consequence to the generation then being,* whether the *principles involved* in the custom, were good in themselves, or not; whether they would be productive of immense injury or not, when they should come to have a dense population to act upon; whether they were consistent with the rigid rights of their own generation, or not; whether they preserved the rights of posterity, or sacrificed them with a most unsparing hand. To them, it was all the same, whether they had good principles, or bad, *or none at all.* And the latter was the fact. For it is not to be said that any *principle* prevails, where no investigation is had, of the effects which the practice, whatever it may be, will produce, when carried out to the fullest extent.

Thus, in detail, do we see, how the present state of things has had its origin. In the origin of the soldier, the material of conquest, do we see also, the origin of every other miserable and dependent human being. And when conquest has once created for itself an existence; how frightfully rapid does it transfer into its own keeping, as it were,

the whole property of the globe. Look at the early history of this country, and see how vast are the possessions that owe their origin more or less, to this source. Look, also, at South America. Is there any legitimacy of title in all this? And now, that suffrage, and the printing press, have come to the redemption of man's rights; shall not man undo the wrongs of the sword? Shall he not correct those errors that gave the sword its existence and its power? Shall not man, now, even at this late date, when myriads of millions have gone to their graves, without ever having once enjoyed their rights; shall not man, now, rise in the majesty of his strength, and claim that which as much belongs to him, as does his life and liberty?

Let it not be said, that man is yet unfit to enjoy these rights. Who, or what is it, that has made him so? Is it not the very evil of which I am speaking, *if it be anything?* And is it to be said that man is to be made fit, by keeping him under the operation of the same cause that has made him otherwise? Besides, why should it be said, that man's right to property, in the light in which I present it, his real and true right, is more to be kept from his possession and enjoyment, than a right in the same person even, to property coming to him in the ordinary way? No man, now, undertakes to say, that an heir at law, as now the law is among us, shall not come into possession of a legacy, because people whoever they may be, choose to say he is unfit to receive it. Even if he be truly unfit, he nevertheless receives it, by way of guardian or trustee. . . .

But not to treat these frivolous pretexts either with a levity or a severity unbecoming our subject, it would be easy, I think, to show, in any age, and particularly the present, that the poor and the middling classes, those whose condition would be benefited by the adoption of the system recommended in this work, are *now* possessed of higher intellectual, and better moral acquirements and habits, than belong to those whom we call rich. And the proof is, as it regards the comparison of *knowledge,* both theoretical and practical, between the two parties, that if, this day, their opportunities of displaying it, were made equal, by making property equal, those who now fill the lower ranks in life, would live better and happier, on the same amount of exertion, than those who fill the higher. This, then, I take it, is evidence of the fact. For if knowledge be not that which enables us thus to live better and happier, I have yet to learn in what it consists. Any knowledge of a character different from this, I apprehend, is not worth having, and deserves to be considered as either worthless or hostile to human happiness. He, therefore, is surely no friend to the race, who, on any such unfounded pretence, as that of unfitness, want of knowledge, etc. etc. objects to the *immediate* enjoyment, by the numerous class of whom I am speaking, of their right of property, as well as of every other right. And as to the question of comparative *morality* of the two classes, every one knows that the poorer is the most virtuous.

Besides, how ridiculously absurd must those political physicians appear, who shall oppose, or attempt to *postpone* such enjoyment of their rights by the great mass of the people, until they shall receive as the phrase is, the benefit of education. If they be sincere in their belief that such education is so very indispensable as a previous step to this enjoyment; and that the people are not now sufficiently instructed, let me ask them how, under present circumstances, is it ever *possible* to give it? Is a family, where both parents and children are suffering daily, in their animal wants; where excessive toil is required to obtain the little they enjoy; where the unkind and the unfriendly passions, generated by such a wretched condition of things, reign with full sway; is such a family in a situation to receive instruction? Even if the children *attend* public institutions of education, as punctually as may be wished, where is that equality of rank and condition, as well between their parents as between themselves, which is so necessary to banish even from among children, those envious remarks on dress, etc. etc. which now render our public schools in a measure abortive? Political dreamers! Reformers, if ye prefer that I should call you so! Feed first the hungry; clothe first the naked, or ill-clad; provide comfortable homes for all; by hewing down colossal estates among us, and equalizing all property; take care that the animal wants be supplied first; that even the *apprehension* of want be banished; and then will you have a good field and good subjects for education. Then will instruction be conveyed without obstacle; for the wants, the unsatisfied wants of the body will not interfere with it. In the mean time, let all remember, that those who undertake to *hold back* the people from their rights of property, as shown in this Work, until *education,* as they call it, can first be communicated, (though as already shown, they now know more of all that is valuable among men, than those who attempt to teach them,) either do not understand themselves, or pursue the course they *are* pursuing, for the purpose of diverting the people from the possession of these rights; that they may be held in bondage, even yet longer. It becomes the people to consider, and reflect, how far it is proper for them, *to suffer* themselves to be thus *decoyed* out of the enjoyment of their rights, even for a single hour, by any such fallacious pretexts. And fallacious they must undoubtedly appear, since the entire accomplishment of all that I have marked out in this work, as well the form of government it exhibits, as the method of bringing it into existence, is a matter as plain as that of the equal division of an estate, which the father of twelve children may have left, without a will, and therefore left to them all equally. These, although not one of them could read or write a letter or understand any thing of what is called science in all its thousand branches, could nevertheless divide it among them with the most equal and impartial justice. It would be the veriest nonsense to talk first of lecturing these heirs into knowledge; if you please, into the knowledge of Astronomy, Chemistry, Botany, Anatomy, Medicine, Painting, Sculpture, Mathematics, etc. etc. etc., knowledge which has no kind of necessary connection with any correct understanding of our rights, before giving them their property; but not more so, than it is now to say, that the people are not fit to have *their* property given to *them,* until they have first gone through a course of education.

The truth is, all men are fitted for the enjoyment of their rights, when they know what they are. And *until* that time, they do not desire them. They languish in misery and wretchedness; every new day being a new day of sorrow to them, when they do not perceive them; and seem rather disposed to charge their evil condition to some "bad luck," as they call it; to some imaginary decree of destiny; to some superstitious interference with their happiness; than to any possession by others of property which belongs to *them.* Thus is it the case with the poor and the rich, passing now in review before us. The former does not imagine that it is the latter which renders his life miserable and wretched. He does not conceive that it is he who fills his cup with bitterness, and visits himself and his family with the afflictions of slavery. "Still, slavery, still thou art a bitter draught; and though thousands have been made to drink of thee," without knowing that thou comest in the shape of the rich man, holding in his hands that property which belongs to his fellow-men; "still thou art not the less bitter on that account." So would Sterne have said, and so say I. . . . .

I approach, then, the close of this Work. I hasten to commit it to the hands, the heads and the hearts of those for whose benefit it is written. It is to them that I look, for the *power* necessary, to bring the system it recommends into existence. If they shall think I have so far understood myself, and the subject I have undertaken to discuss, as to have perceived, and marked out the path that leads them to the enjoyment of their rights, their interests and their happiness, IT WILL BE FOR THOSE WHO ARE SUFFERING THE EVILS, of which I have endeavored to point out the causes and the remedies, TO LEAD THE WAY. Those who are enjoying the sweets of the labor of others, will have no hearts to feel for the misery which the present system occasions. And the first throe of pain, which they *will* feel, will be that of *alarm,* that they are soon to be ordered to riot on the toils of others no more for ever! But those who *suffer,* will feel no cause of alarm. The very intensity of their sufferings, since now they understand their origin and cure, will add double vigor to their exertions to recover their rights. But let them understand, that much is to be done, to accomplish this recovery. IT IS TO BE THE RESULT OF THE COMBINED EXERTIONS, OF GREAT NUMBERS OF MEN. These, by no means, *now* understand their true situation; but when they do, they will be ready and willing to do what belongs to their happiness. If, then, there be truth; if there be reason; if there be force of argument, in the work which I thus commit to the hands of those for whose benefit it is written; let them read; let it be read; let it be conversed about, in the hearing of those whose *interest* it is, to hear whatever of truth, of reason, and argument it may contain; and *as often,* too, as there may be opportunity. Let them awake to a *knowledge* of their rights, and how they may be obtained, and they will not be slow (since it will *then* be so easy) to reclaim them.

Let the poor and middling classes understand that their oppressions come from the overgrown wealth that exists among them, on the one hand, and from entire destitution on the other; and that as this overgrown wealth is continually augmenting its possessions, in a rapid ratio, the public sufferings are continually augmenting also; and must continue to augment, until the equal and unalienable rights of the people shall order otherwise. Let the parent reflect, if he be now a man of toil, that his children must be, ninety-nine cases in a hundred, slaves, *and worse,* to some rich proprietor; and that there is no alternative, but the change proposed. Let him not cheat himself with empty pretensions; for, *he who commands the property of a State, or even an inordinate portion of it,* HAS THE LIBERTY AND THE HAPPINESS OF ITS CITIZENS IN HIS OWN KEEPING.

4. RALPH WALDO EMERSON, *Hamatreya, 1847* *

Bulkeley, Hunt, Willard, Hosmer,
Meriam, Flint,
Possessed the land which rendered to
their toil
Hay, corn, roots, hemp, flax, apples,
wool and wood.
Each of these landlords walked amidst
his farm,
Saying, " 'Tis mine, my children's and
my name's.
How sweet the west wind sounds in
my own trees!
How graceful climb those shadows on
my hill!
I fancy these pure waters and the flags
Know me, as does my dog: we
sympathize;
And, I affirm, my actions smack of the
soil."

Where are these men? Asleep beneath
their grounds:
And strangers, fond as they, their
furrows plough.
Earth laughs in flowers, to see her
boastful boys
Earth-proud, proud of the earth which
is not theirs;
Who steer the plough, but cannot steer
their feet
Clear of the grave. . . .

Ah! the hot owner sees not Death, who
adds
Him to his land, a lump of mold the
more.
Hear what the Earth says:

EARTH-SONG

"Mine and yours;
Mine, not yours.
Earth endures;
Stars abide—
Shine down in the old sea;
Old are the shores;
But where are old men?
I who have seen much,
Such have I never seen.

"The lawyer's deed
Ran sure,
In tail,
To them, and to their heirs
Who shall succeed,
Without fail,
Forevermore.

Here is the land,
Shaggy with wood,
With its old valley,
Mound and flood.
But the heritors?
Fled like the flood's foam.

* Ralph Waldo Emerson, *Works* (Boston, 1895), IX, 35.

The lawyer, and the laws,
And the kingdom,
Clean swept herefrom.

"They called me theirs,
Who so controlled me;
Yet every one
Wished to stay, and is gone,

How am I theirs,
If they cannot hold me,
But I hold them?"

When I heard the Earth-song,
I was no longer brave;
My avarice cooled
Like lust in the chill of the grave.

5. FREEMAN HUNT, *Worth and Wealth, 1857**

Self-reliance, to the merchant, and indeed to all who would succeed in the accomplishment of a laudable purpose or pursuit, is indispensable. It was this trait, perhaps, more than any other, that enabled an Astor, a Girard, a Gray, in our own country, to work out for themselves vast fortunes—to accumulate millions. An eminent writer has somewhere said, if our young men miscarry in their first enterprise, they lose all heart. If the young merchant fails, men say he is ruined. If the finest genius studies in one of our colleges, and is not installed in an office in one year afterwards, it seems to his friends and to himself that he is right in being disheartened, and in complaining the rest of his life. A sturdy Yankee who in turn tries all the professions, who teams it, farms it, peddles, keeps a school, preaches, edits a newspaper, goes to Congress, buys a township, and so forth, in successive years, and always, like a cat, falls on his feet, is worth a hundred of these city dolls. He walks abreast with his days, and feels no shame in not studying a profession, for he does not postpone his life, but lives already. He has not one chance! Let a stoic arise who shall reveal the resources of man, and tell men they are not leaning willows, but can and must detach themselves; that,

with the exercise of self-trust, new powers shall appear . . . ; and that the moment he acts from himself, tossing the laws, the books' idolatries and customs, out of the window, we pity him no more, but thank him and revere him—and that teacher shall restore the life of man to splendor, and make his name dear to all history. It is easy to see that a greater self-reliance—a new respect for the divinity in man—must work a revolution in all the offices and relations of men: in their religion; in their education; in their pursuits; their modes of living; their association; in their property; in their speculative views.

A man of business should be able to fix his attention on details, and be ready to give every kind of argument a hearing. This will not encumber him, for he must have been practised beforehand in the exercise of his intellect, and be strong in principles. One man collects materials together, and there they remain, a shapeless heap; another, possessed of method, can arrange what he has collected; but such a man as I would describe, by the aid of principles, goes farther, and builds with his materials.

He should be courageous. The courage, however, required in civil affairs, is that which belongs rather to the

* Freeman Hunt, *Worth and Wealth; a Collection of Maxims, Morals and Miscellanies for Merchants and Men of Business* (New York, 1857), pp. 82–83, 103–5, 120, 503–4.

able commander than the mere soldier. But any kind of courage is serviceable.

Besides a stout heart, he should have a patient temperament, and a vigorous but disciplined imagination; and then he will plan boldly, and with large extent of view, execute calmly, and not be stretching out his hand for things not yet within his grasp. He will let opportunities grow before his eyes until they are ripe to be seized. He will think steadily over possible failure, in order to provide a remedy or a retreat. There will be the strength of repose about him.

He must have a deep sense of responsibility. He must believe in the power and vitality of truth, and in all he does or says, should be anxious to express as much truth as possible.

His feeling of responsibility and love of truth will almost inevitably endow him with diligence, accuracy and discreetness—those commonplace requisites for a good man of business, without which all the rest may never come to be "translated into action." . . .

Almost every merchant has been rich, or at least prosperous, at some point of his life; and if he is poor now, he can see very well how he might have avoided the disaster which overthrew his hopes. He will probably see that his misfortunes arose from neglecting some of the following rules:—

Be industrious. Everybody knows that industry is the fundamental virtue in the man of business. But it is not every sort of industry which tends to wealth. Many men work hard to do a great deal of business, and, after all, make less money than they would if they did less. Industry should be expended in seeing to all the details of business— in the careful finishing up of each separate undertaking, and in the maintenance of such a system will keep everything under control.

Be economical. This rule, also, is familiar to everybody. Economy is a virtue to be practiced every hour in a great city. It is to be practised in pence as much as in pounds. A shilling a day saved, amounts to an estate in the course of a life. Economy is especially important in the outset of life, until the foundations of an estate are laid. Many men are poor all their days, because, when their necessary expenses were small, they did not seize the opportunity to save a small capital, which would have changed their fortunes for the whole of their lives.

Stick to the business in which you are regularly employed. Let speculators make their thousands in a year or day; mind your own regular trade, never turning from it to the right hand or the left. If you are a merchant, a professional man, or a mechanic, never buy lots or stocks unless you have surplus money which you wish to invest. Your own business you understand as well as other men; but other people's business you do not understand. Let your business be some one which is useful to the community. All such occupations possess the elements of profits in themselves, while mere speculation has no such element.

Never take great hazards. Such hazards are seldom well balanced by the prospects of profit; and if they were, the habit of mind which is induced is unfavorable, and generally the result is bad. To keep what you have, should be the first rule; to get what you can fairly, the second.

Do not be in a hurry to get rich. Gradual gains are the only natural gains, and they who are in haste to be rich, break over sound rules, fall into temptations and distress of various sorts, and generally fail of their object. There is no use in getting rich suddenly. The man who keeps his business under his control, and saves something from year to year, is always rich. At any rate, he possesses the highest enjoyment which riches are able to afford.

Never do business for the sake of doing it, and being counted a great merchant. There is often more money to be made by a small business than a large one; and that business will in the end be most respectable which is most successful. Do not get deeply in debt; but so manage as always, if possible, to have your financial position easy, so that you can turn any way you please.

Do not love money extravagantly. We speak here merely with reference to getting rich. In morals, the inordinate love of money is one of the most degrading vices. But the extravagant desire of accumulation induces an eagerness, many times, which is imprudent, and so misses its object from too much haste to grasp it. . . .

Success in life mainly depends upon perseverance. When a man has determined to follow a certain line of business, he must at the same time resolve to persevere until success crowns his efforts. He must never be cast down by the difficulties which may beset his path—for whoever conquers difficulty, conquers a weakness of his own frail nature likewise. How many men have commenced business under the most favorable auspices, and yet when a cloud has momentarily overshadowed their path, have lost all command over themselves and fled before the temporary gloom, instead of persevering on until the cloud has been dispersed, and sunshine once more smiled upon their efforts. Others, more fickle, have thought their business, in some minor departments, unworthy of their perseverance and energy, and forgetting the golden maxim that, "whatever is worth doing is worth doing well," have ceased to persevere in small matters, until sloth has entered deeply into

their minds, and their whole business greatly neglected.

We are too apt to attribute success in business to good fortune, instead of great perseverance. This is a great evil, and should be eschewed, as it leads many to suppose that Dame Fortune will do that for them which they are unwilling to do for themselves.

The history of every great success in business is the history of great perseverance. By perseverance the mind is strengthened and invigorated, and the difficulty that once seemed so formidable is a second time surmounted with ease and confidence.

Energy and great perseverance are never thrown away on a good cause, or left unrewarded; and to every man of business, perseverance should be his motto, and then he may look with confidence to fortune as his reward. . . .

There is a class of men whose patronage of art has been princely in its munificence, as their wealth has equalled that of princes, whose interests have become a chief concern of statesmen, and have involved the issues of peace and war; whose affairs afford a leading subject of the legislation of States, and fill the largest space in the volumes of modern jurists. This class has produced men who have combined a vast comprehensiveness with a most minute grasp of details, and whose force of mind and will in other situations would have commanded armies and ruled States; they are men whose plans and combinations take in every continent, and the islands and the waters of every sea; whose pursuits, though peaceful, occupy people enough to fill armies and man navies; who have placed science and invention under contribution, and made use of their most ingenious instruments and marvellous discoveries in aid of their enterprises; who are covering continents with railroads and oceans with steamships; who can boast the magnificence of the Medici, and the philanthropy of Gresham and of Amos Lawrence; and whose zeal for science and zeal for philanthropy have penetrated to the highest latitude of the Arctic seas, ever reached by civilized man, in the ships of Grinnell.

Modern scholars have seen the important bearing of the history of commerce upon the history of the world; have seen, rather,—as who, in this most commercial of all eras, can fail to see?—how large a chapter it forms in the history of the world, although crowded out of the space it ought to fill by the wars and crimes which destroy what it creates. Hume was among the first to call attention to this branch of historical inquiry, and Heeren has investigated with much learning the commerce of the ancients. If we were in possession of lives of the great merchants of antiquity, what light would they not throw upon the origin of States, the foundation of cities, and inventions and discoveries, of which we now do not even know the dates?

Trade planted Tyre, Carthage, Marseilles, London, and all the Ionic colonies of Greece. Plato was for a while a merchant; Herodotus, they say, was a merchant. Trade was honorable at Athens, as among all nations of original and vigorous thought; when we find discredit attached to it, it is among nations of a secondary and less original civilization, like the Romans.

But if commerce forms so large a chapter in the history of the world, what would the history of America be if commerce and men of commerce were left out? Trade discovered America in the vessels of adventurers, seeking new channels to the old marts of India; trade planted the American colonies, and made them flourish, even in New England, say what we please about Plymouth Rock; our colonial growth was the growth of trade—revolution and independence were the results of measures of trade and commercial legislation, although they undoubtedly involved the first principles of free government: the history of the country, its politics and policy, has ever since turned chiefly upon questions of trade and of finance, sailor's rights, protection, banks, and cotton.

6. WILLIAM GRAHAM SUMNER, *Fallacies of the Times, 1894**

The passion for dealing with social questions is one of the marks of our time. Every man gets some experience of, and makes some observations on social affairs. Except matters of health, probably none have such general interest as matters of society. Except matters of health, none are so much afflicted by dogmatism and crude speculation as those which appertain to society. The amateurs in social science always ask: What shall we do? What shall we do with Neighbor A? What shall we do for Neighbor B? What shall we make Neighbor A do for Neighbor B? It is a fine thing to be planning and discussing broad and general theories of wide application. The amateurs always plan to use the individual for some constructive and inferential social purpose, or to use the society for some constructive and inferential individual purpose. For A to sit down and think, What shall I do? is commonplace; but

* William Graham Sumner, *What Social Classes Owe to Each Other* (New York, 1883), pp. 112–22.

to think what B ought to do is interesting, romantic, moral, self-flattering, and public-spirited all at once. It satisfies a great number of human weaknesses at once. To go on and plan what a whole class of people ought to do is to feel one's self a power on earth, to win a public position, to clothe one's self in dignity. Hence we have an unlimited supply of reformers, philanthropists, humanitarians, and would-be managers-in-general of society.

Every man and woman in society has one big duty. That is, to take care of his or her own self. This is a social duty. For, fortunately, the matter stands so that the duty of making the best of one's self individually is not a separate thing from the duty of filling one's place in society, but the two are one, and the latter is accomplished when the former is done. The common notion, however, seems to be that one has a duty to society, as a special and separate thing, and that this duty consists in considering and deciding what other people ought to do. Now, the man who can do anything for or about anybody else than himself is fit to be head of a family; and when he becomes head of a family he has duties to his wife and his children, in addition to the former big duty. Then, again, any man who can take care of himself and his family is in a very exceptional position, if he does not find in his immediate surroundings people who need his care and have some sort of a personal claim upon him. If, now, he is able to fulfil all this, and to take care of anybody outside his family and his dependents, he must have a surplus of energy, wisdom, and moral virtue beyond what he needs for his own business. No man has this; for a family is a charge which is capable of infinite development, and no man could suffice to the full measure of duty for which a family may draw upon him. Neither can a man give to society so advantageous an employment of his services, whatever they are, in any other way as by spending them on his family. Upon this, however, I will not insist. I recur to the observation that a man who proposes to take care of other people must have himself and his family taken care of, after some sort of a fashion, and must have an as yet unexhausted store of energy.

The danger of minding other people's business is twofold. First, there is the danger that a man may leave his own business unattended to; and, second, there is the danger of an impertinent interference with another's affairs. The "friends of humanity" almost always run into both dangers. I am one of humanity, and I do not want any volunteer friends. I regard friendship as mutual, and I want to have my say about it. I suppose that other components of humanity feel in the same way about it. If so, they must regard any one who assumes the *rôle* of a friend of humanity as impertinent. The reference of the friend of humanity back to his own business is obviously the next step.

Yet we are constantly annoyed, and the legislatures are kept constantly busy, by the people who have made up their minds that it is wise and conducive to happiness to live in a certain way, and who want to compel everybody else to live in their way. Some people have decided to spend Sunday in a certain way, and they want laws passed to make other people spend Sunday in the same way. Some people have resolved to be teetotalers, and they want a law passed to make everybody else a teetotaler. Some people have resolved to eschew luxury, and they want taxes laid to make others eschew luxury. The taxing power is especially something after which the reformer's fingers always itches. Sometimes there is an element of self-interest in the proposed reformation, as when a publisher wanted a duty imposed on books, to keep Americans from reading books, which would unsettle their Americanism: and when artists wanted a tax laid on pictures, to save Americans from buying bad paintings.

I make no reference here to the giving and taking of counsel and aid between man and man: of that I shall say something in the last chapter. The very sacredness of the relation in which two men stand to one another when one of them rescues the other from vice separates that relation from any connection with the work of the social busybody, the professional philanthropist, and the empirical legislator.

The amateur social doctors are like the amateur physicians—they always begin with the question of *remedies,* and they go at this without any diagnosis or any knowledge of the anatomy or physiology of society. They never have any doubt of the efficacy of their remedies. They never take account of any ulterior effects which may be apprehended from the remedy itself. It generally troubles them not a whit that their remedy implies a complete reconstruction of society, or even a reconstitution of human nature. Against all such social quackery the obvious injunction to the quacks is, to mind their own business.

The social doctors enjoy the satisfaction of feeling themselves to be more moral or more enlightened than their fellow-men. They are able to see what other men ought to do when the other men do not see it. An examination of the work of the social doctors, however, shows that they are only more ignorant and more presumptuous than other people. We have a great many social difficulties and hardships to contend with. Poverty, pain, disease, and misfortune surround our existence. We fight against them all the time. The individual is a centre of hopes, affections, desires, and sufferings. When he

dies, life changes its form, but does not cease. That means that the person—the centre of all the hopes, affections, etc.—after struggling as long as he can, is sure to succumb at last. We would, therefore, as far as the hardships of the human lot are concerned, go on struggling to the best of our ability against them but for the social doctors, and we would endure what we could not cure. But we have inherited a vast number of social ills which never came from Nature. They are the complicated products of all the tinkering, muddling, and blundering of social doctors in the past. These products of social quackery are now buttressed by habit, fashion, prejudice, platitudinarian thinking, and new quackery in political economy and social science. It is a fact worth noticing, just when there seems to be a revival of faith in legislative agencies, that our States are generally providing against the experienced evils of overlegislation by ordering that the Legislature shall sit only every other year. During the hard times, when Congress had a real chance to make or mar the public welfare, the final adjournment of that body was hailed year after year with cries of relief from a great anxiety. The greatest reforms which could now be accomplished would consist in undoing the work of statesmen in the past, and the greatest difficulty in the way of reform is to find out how to undo their work without injury to what is natural and sound. All this mischief has been done by men who sat down to consider the problem (as I heard an apprentice of theirs once express it), What kind of a society do we want to make? When they had settled this question *a priori* to their satisfaction, they set to work to make their ideal society, and to-day we suffer the consequences. Human society tries hard to adapt itself to any conditions in which it finds itself, and we have been warped and distorted until we have got used to it, as the foot adapts itself to an ill-made boot. Next, we have come to think that that is the right way for things to be; and it is true that a change to a sound and normal condition would for a time hurt us, as a man whose foot has been distorted would suffer if he tried to wear a well-shaped boot. Finally, we have produced a lot of economists and social philosophers who have invented sophisms for fitting our thinking to the distorted facts.

Society, therefore, does not need any care or supervision. If we can acquire a science of society, based on observation of phenomena and study of forces, we may hope to gain some ground slowly toward the elimination of old errors and the re-establishment of a sound and natural social order. Whatever we gain that way will be by growth, never in the world by any reconstruction of society on the plan of some enthusiastic social architect. The latter is only repeating the old error over again, and postponing all our chances of real improvement. Society needs first of all to be freed from these meddlers—that is, to be let alone. Here we are, then, once more back at the old doctrine— *Laissez faire.* Let us translate it into blunt English, and it will read, Mind your own business. It is nothing but the doctrine of liberty. Let every man be happy in his own way. If his sphere of action and interest impinges on that of any other man, there will have to be compromise and adjustment. Wait for the occasion. Do not attempt to generalize those interferences or to plan for them *a priori*. We have a body of laws and institutions which have grown up as occasion has occurred for adjusting rights. Let the same process go on. Practise the utmost reserve possible in your interferences even of this kind, and by no means seize occasion for interfering with natural adjustments. Try first long and patiently whether the natural adjustment will not come about through the play of interests and the voluntary concessions of the parties.

I have said that we have an empirical political economy and social science to fit the distortions of our society. The test of empiricism in this matter is the attitude which one takes up toward *laissez faire*. It no doubt wounds the vanity of a philosopher who is just ready with a new solution of the universe to be told to mind his own business. So he goes on to tell us that if we think that we shall, by being let alone, attain to perfect happiness on earth, we are mistaken. The half-way men—the professional socialists—join him. They solemnly shake their heads, and tell us that he is right—that letting us alone will never secure us perfect happiness. Under all this lies the familiar logical fallacy, never expressed, but really the point of the whole, that we *shall* get perfect happiness if we put ourselves in the hands of the world-reformer. We never supposed that *laissez faire* would give us perfect happiness. We have left perfect happiness entirely out of our account. If the social doctors will mind their own business, we shall have no troubles but what belong to Nature. Those we will endure or combat as we can. What we desire is, that the friends of humanity should cease to add to them. Our disposition toward the ills which our fellow-man inflicts on us through malice or meddling is quite different from our disposition toward the ills which are inherent in the conditions of human life.

To mind one's own business is a purely negative and unproductive injunction, but, taking social matters as they are just now, it is a sociological principle of the first importance. There might be developed a grand philosophy on the basis of minding one's own business.

7. Russell Conwell, *Acres of Diamonds, 1890**

I say again that the opportunity to get rich, to attain unto great wealth, is . . . within the reach of almost every man and woman who hears me speak tonight, and I mean just what I say. . . . I have come to tell you . . . that the men and women sitting here, who found it difficult perhaps to buy a ticket to this lecture or gathering tonight, have within their reach "acres of diamonds," opportunities to get largely wealthy. There never was a place on earth more adapted than the city of Philadelphia today, and never in the history of the world did a poor man without capital have such an opportunity to get rich quickly and honestly as he has now in our city. . . . Unless some of you get richer for what I am saying tonight my time is wasted.

I say that you ought to get rich, and it is your duty to get rich. How many of my pious brethren say to me, "Do you, a Christian minister, spend your time going up and down the country advising young people to get rich, to get money?" "Yes, of course I do." They say, "Isn't that awful! Why don't you preach the gospel instead of preaching about man's making money?" "Because to make money honestly is to preach the gospel." That is the reason. The men who get rich may be the most honest men you find in the community.

"Oh," but says some young man here tonight, "I have been told all my life that if a person has money he is very dishonest and dishonorable and mean and contemptible." My friend, that is the reason why you have none, because you have that idea of people. The foundation of your faith is altogether false. Let me say here clearly, and say it briefly . . . ninety-eight out of one hundred of the rich men of America are honest. That is why they are rich. That is why they are trusted with money. That is why they carry on great enterprises and find plenty of people to work with them. . . .

Money is power, and you ought to be reasonably ambitious to have it. You ought because you could do more good with it than you could without it. Money printed your Bible, money builds your churches, money sends your missionaries, and money pays your preachers. . . .

I say, then, you ought to have money. If you can honestly attain unto riches in Philadelphia, it is your Christian and godly duty to do so. It is an awful mistake of these pious people to think you must be awfully poor in order to be pious.

Some men say, "Don't you sympathize with the poor people?" Of course I do, or else I would not have been lecturing these years. I won't give in but what I sympathize with the poor, but the number of poor who are to be sympathized with is very small. To sympathize with a man whom God has punished for his sins, thus to help him when God would still continue a just punishment, is to do wrong, no doubt about it, and we do that more than we help those who are deserving. While we should sympathize with God's poor—that is, those who cannot help themselves—let us remember there is not a poor person in the United States who was not made poor by his own shortcomings, or by the shortcomings of someone else. It is all wrong to be poor, anyhow.

* R. H. Conwell, *Acres of Diamonds* (New York, 1915), pp. 17–21.

8. FREDERICK JACKSON TURNER, *The West and American Ideals, 1914**

Today we are looking with a shock upon a changed world. The National problem is no longer how to cut and burn away the vast screen of the dense and daunting forest; it is how to save and wisely use the remaining timber. It is no longer how to get the great spaces of fertile prairie land in humid zones out of the hands of the government into the hands of the pioneer; these lands have already passed into private possession. No longer is it a question of how to avoid or cross the Great Plains and the arid desert. It is a question of how to conquer those rejected lands by new method of farming and by cultivating new crops from seed collected by the government and by scientists from the cold, dry steppes of Siberia, the burning sands of Egypt, and the remote interior of China. It is a problem of how to bring the precious rills of water on to the alkali and sage brush. Population is increasing faster than the food supply.

New farm lands no longer increase decade after decade in areas equal to those of European states. While the ratio of increase of improved land declines, the value of farm lands rise and the price of food leaps upward, reversing the old ratio between the two. The cry of scientific farming and the conservation of natural resources replaces the cry of rapid conquest of the wilderness. We have so far won our national home, wrested from it its first rich treasures, and drawn to it the unfortunate of other lands, that we are already obliged to compare ourselves with settled states of the Old World. In place of our attitude of contemptuous indifference to the legislation of such countries as Germany and England, even Western States like Wisconsin send commissions to study their systems of taxation, workingmen's insurance, old age pensions and a great variety of other remedies for social ills.

If we look about the periphery of the nation, everywhere we see the indications that our world is changing. On the streets of Northeastern cities like New York and Boston, the faces which we meet are to a surprising extent those of Southeastern Europe. Puritan New England, which turned its capital into factories and mills and drew to its shores an army of cheap labor, governed these people for a time by a ruling class like an upper stratum between which and the lower strata there was no assimilation. There was no such evolution into an assimilated commonwealth as is seen in Middle Western agricultural States, where immigrant and old native stock came in together and built up a homogeneous society on the principle of give and take. But now the Northeastern coast finds its destiny, politically and economically, passing away from the descendants of the Puritans. It is the little Jewish boy, the Greek or the Sicilian, who takes the traveler through historic streets, now the home of these newer people to the Old North Church or to Paul Revere's house, or to Tea Wharf, and tells you in his strange patois the story of revolution against oppression.

Along the Southern Atlantic and the Gulf coast, in spite of the preservative influence of the negro, whose presence has always called out resistance

* Frederick Jackson Turner, *The Frontier in American History* (New York: Holt, Rinehart and Winston, Inc., 1920), pp. 293–310. Reprinted by permission.

to change on the part of the whites, the forces of social and industrial transformation are at work. The old tidewater aristocracy has surrendered to the up-country democrats. Along the line of the Alleghanies like an advancing column, the forces of Northern capital, textile and steel mills, year after year extend their invasion into the lower South. New Orleans, once the mistress of the commerce of the Mississippi Valley, is awakening to new dreams of world commerce. On the southern border, similar invasions of American capital have been entering Mexico. At the same time, the opening of the Panama Canal has completed the dream of the ages of the Straits of Anian between Atlantic and Pacific. Four hundred years ago, Balboa raised the flag of Spain at the edge of the Sea of the West and we are now preparing to celebrate both that anniversary, and the piercing of the continent. New relations have been created between Spanish America and the United States and the world is watching the mediation of Argentina, Brazil and Chile between the contending forces of Mexico and the Union. Once more alien national interests lie threatening at our borders, but we no longer appeal to the Monroe Doctrine and send our armies of frontiersmen to settle our concerns off-hand. We take council with European nations and with the sisterhood of South America, and propose a remedy of social reorganization in place of imperious will and force. Whether the effort will succeed or not, it is a significant indication that an old order is passing away, when such a solution is undertaken by a President of Scotch Presbyterian stock, born in the State of Virginia.

If we turn to the Northern border, where we are about to celebrate a century of peace with England, we see in progress, like a belated procession of our own history the spread of pioneers,

the opening of new wildernesses, the building of new cities, the growth of a new and mighty nation. That old American advance of the wheat farmer from the Connecticut to the Mohawk, and the Genesee, from the Great Valley of Pennsylvania to the Ohio Valley and the prairies of the Middle West, is now by its own momentum and under the stimulus of Canadian homesteads and the high price of wheat, carried across the national border to the once lone plains where the Hudson Bay dog trains crossed the desolate snows of the wild North Land. In the Pacific Northwest the era of construction has not ended, but it is so rapidly in progress that we can already see the closing of the age of the pioneer. Already Alaska beckons on the north, and pointing to her wealth of natural resources asks the nation on what new terms the new age will deal with her. Across the Pacific looms Asia, no longer a remote vision and a symbol of the unchanging, but borne as by mirage close to our shores and raising grave questions of the common destiny of the people of the ocean. The dreams of Benton and of Seward of a regenerated Orient, when the long march of westward civilization should complete its circle, seem almost to be in process of realization. The age of the Pacific Ocean begins, mysterious and unfathomable in its meaning for our own future.

Turning to view the interior, we see the same picture of change. When the Superintendent of the Census in 1890 declared the frontier line no longer traceable, the beginning of the rush into Oklahoma had just occurred. Here where the broken fragments of Indian nations from the East had been gathered and where the wilder tribes of the Southwest were being settled, came the rush of the land-hungry pioneer. Almost at a blow the old Indian territory passed away, populous cities came into being and it was not long before gushing oil wells made a new era of sudden wealth. The farm lands of the Middle West taken as free homesteads or bought for a mere pittance, have risen so in value that the original owners have in an increasing degree either sold them in order to reinvest in the newer cheap lands of the West, or have moved into the town and have left the tillage to tenant farmers. The growth of absentee ownership of the soil is producing a serious problem in the former centers of the Granger and the Populist. Along the Old Northwest the Great Lakes are becoming a new Mediterranean Sea joining the realms of wheat and iron ore, at one end with the coal and furnaces of the forks of the Ohio, where the most intense and wide-reaching center of industrial energy exists. City life like that of the East, manufactures and accumulated capital, seem to be reproducing in the center of the Republic the tendencies already so plain on the Atlantic Coast.

Across the Great Plains where buffalo and Indian held sway successive industrial waves are passing. The old free range gave place to the ranch, the ranch to the homestead and now in places in the arid lands the homestead is replaced by the ten or twenty acre irrigated fruit farm. The age of cheap land, cheap corn and wheat, and cheap cattle has gone forever. The federal government has undertaken vast paternal enterprises of reclamation of the desert.

In the Rocky Mountains where at the time of Civil War, the first important rushes of gold and silver mines carried the frontier backward on a march toward the east, the most amazing transformations have occurred. Here, where prospectors made new trails, and lived the wild free life of mountain men, here where the human spirit seemed likely to attain the largest measure of individual freedom, and

where fortune beckoned to the common man, have come revolutions wrought by the demand for organized industry and capital. In the regions where the popular tribunal and the free competitive life flourished, we have seen law and order break down in the unmitigated collision of great aggregations of capital, with each other and with organized socialistic labor. The Cripple Creek strikes, the contests at Butte, the Goldfield mobs, the recent Colorado fighting, all tell a similar story,—the solid impact of contending forces in regions where civic power and loyalty to the State have never fully developed. Like the Grand Cañon, where in dazzling light the huge geologic history is written so large that none may fail to read it, so in the Rocky Mountains the dangers of modern American industrial tendencies have been exposed.

As we crossed the Cascades on our way to Seattle, one of the passengers was moved to explain his feeling on the excellence of Puget Sound in contrast with the remaining visible Universe. He did it well in spite of irreverent interruptions from those fellow travelers who were unconverted children of the East, and at last he broke forth in passionate challenge, "Why should I not love Seattle! It took me from the slums of the Atlantic Coast, a poor Swedish boy with hardly fifteen dollars in my pocket. It gave me a home by the beautiful sea; it spread before my eyes a vision of snow-capped peaks and smiling fields; it brought abundance and a new life to me and my children and I love it, I love it! If I were a multi-millionaire I would charter freight cars and carry away from the crowded tenements and noisome alleys of the eastern cities and the Old World the toiling masses, and let them loose in our vast forests and ore-laden mountains to learn what life really is!" And my heart was stirred by his words and by the whirling spaces of woods and peaks through which we passed.

But as I looked and listened to this passionate outcry, I remembered the words of Talleyrand, the exiled Bishop of Autun, in Washington's administration. Looking down from an eminence not far from Philadelphia upon a wilderness which is now in the heart of that huge industrial society where population presses on the means of life, even the cold-blooded and cynical Talleyrand, gazing on those unpeopled hills and forests, kindled with the vision of coming clearings, the smiling farms and grazing herds that were to be, the populous towns that should be built, the newer and finer social organization that should there arise. And then I remembered the hall in Harvard's museum of social ethics through which I pass to my lecture room when I speak on the history of the Westward movement. That hall is covered with an exhibit of the work in Pittsburgh steel mills, and of the congested tenements. Its charts and diagrams tell of the long hours of work, the death rate, the relation of typhoid to the slums, the gathering of the poor of all Southeastern Europe to make a civilization at that center of American industrial energy and vast capital that is a social tragedy. As I enter my lecture room through that hall, I speak of the young Washington leading his Virginia frontiersmen to the magnificent forest at the forks of the Ohio. Where Braddock and his men, "carving a cross on the wilderness rim," were struck by the painted savages in the primeval woods, huge furnaces belch forth perpetual fires and Huns and Bulgars, Poles and Sicilians struggle for a chance to earn their daily bread, and live a brutal and degraded life. Irresistibly there rushed across my mind the memorable words of Huxley:

"Even the best of modern civilization appears to me to exhibit a condition of mankind which neither embodies any worthy ideal nor even possesses the merit of stability. I do not hesitate to express the opinion that, if there is no hope of a large improvement of the condition of the greater part of the human family; if it is true that the increase of knowledge, the winning of a greater dominion over Nature, which is its consequence, and the wealth which follows upon that dominion, are to make no difference in the extent and the intensity of Want, with its concomitant physical and moral degradation, among the masses of the people, I should hail the advent of some kindly comet, which would sweep the whole affair away, as a desirable consummation."

But if there is disillusion and shock and apprehension as we come to realize these changes, to strong men and women there is challenge and inspiration in them too. In place of old frontiers of wilderness, there are new frontiers of unwon fields of science, fruitful for the needs of the race; there are frontiers of better social domains yet unexplored. Let us hold to our attitude of faith and courage, and creative zeal. Let us dream as our fathers dreamt and let us make our dreams come true.

"Daughters of Time, the hypocritic days,
Muffled and dumb like barefoot dervishes,
And marching single in an endless file,
Bear diadems and fagots in their hands.
To each they offer gifts after his will
Bread, kingdoms, stars, and sky that hold them all.
I, in my pleachéd garden watched the pomp,
Forgot my morning wishes, hastily

Took a few herbs and apples and
the day
Turned and departed silent. I, too
late,
Under her solemn fillet, saw the
scorn!"

What were America's "morning
wishes"? From the beginning of that
long westward march of the American
people America has never been the
home of mere contented materialism.
It has continuously sought new ways
and dreamed of a perfected social type.

In the fifteenth century when men
dealt with the New World which Columbus found, the ideal of discovery
was dominant. Here was placed within
the reach of men whose ideas had been
bounded by the Atlantic, new realms
to be explored. America became the
land of European dreams, its Fortunate Islands were made real, where,
in the imagination of old Europe,
peace and happiness, as well as riches
and eternal youth, were to be found.
To Sir Edwin Sandys and his friends
of the London Company, Virginia offered an opportunity to erect the Republic for which they had longed in
vain in England. To the Puritans, New
England was the new land for freedom, wherein they might establish the
institutions of God, according to their
own faith. As the vision died away in
Virginia toward the close of the seventeenth century, it was taken up anew
by the fiery Bacon with his revolution
to establish a real democracy in place
of the rule of the planter aristocracy,
that formed along the coast. Hardly
had he been overthrown when in the
eighteenth century, the democratic
ideal was rejuvenated by the strong
frontiersmen, who pressed beyond the
New England Coast into the Berk-
shires and up the valleys of the Green
Mountains of Vermont, and by the
Scotch-Irish and German pioneers who
followed the Great Valley from Penn-

sylvania into the Upland South. In
both the Yankee frontiersmen and the
Scotch-Irish Presbyterians of the South,
the Calvinistic conception of the importance of the individual, bound by
free covenant to his fellow men and to
God, was a compelling influence, and
all their wilderness experience combined to emphasize the ideals of opening new ways, of giving freer play to
the individual, and of constructing
democratic society.

When the backwoodsmen crossed the
Alleghanies they put between themselves and the Atlantic Coast a barrier
which seemed to separate them from a
region already too much like the
Europe they had left, and as they followed the courses of the rivers that
flowed to the Mississippi, they called
themselves "Men of the Western
Waters," and their new home in the
Mississippi Valley was the "Western
World." Here, by the thirties, Jacksonian democracy flourished, strong in the
faith of the intrinsic excellence of the
common man, in his right to make his
own place in the world, and in his
capacity to share in government. But
while Jacksonian democracy demanded
these rights, it was also loyal to leadership as the very name implies. It was
ready to follow to the uttermost the
man in whom it placed its trust, whether the hero were frontier fighter or
president, and it even rebuked and
limited its own legislative representatives and recalled its senators when
they ran counter to their chosen executive. Jacksonian democracy was essentially rural. It was based on the good
fellowship and genuine social feeling of
the frontier, in which classes and inequalities of fortune played little part.
But it did not demand equality of condition, for there was abundance of
natural resources and the belief that
the self-made man had a right to his
success in the free competition which

western life afforded, was as prominent in their thought as was the love of democracy. On the other hand, they viewed governmental restraints with suspicion as a limitation on their right to work out their own individuality.

For the banking institutions and capitalists of the East they had an instinctive antipathy. Already they feared that the "money power" as Jackson called it, was planning to make hewers of wood and drawers of water of the common people.

In this view they found allies among the labor leaders of the East, who in the same period began their fight for better conditions of the wage earner. These Locofocos were the first Americans to demand fundamental social changes for the benefit of the workers in the cities. Like the Western pioneers, they protested against monopolies and special privilege But they also had a constructive policy, whereby society was to be kept democratic by free gifts of the public land, so that surplus labor might not bid against itself, but might find an outlet in the West. Thus to both the labor theorist and the practical pioneer, the existence of what seemed inexhaustible cheap land and unpossessed resources was the condition of democracy. In these years of the thirties and forties, Western democracy took on its distinctive form. Travelers like De Tocqueville and Harriet Martineau, came to study and to report it enthusiastically to Europe.

Side by side with this westward marching army of individualistic liberty-loving democratic backwoodsmen, went a more northern stream of pioneers, who cherished similar ideas, but added to them the desire to create new industrial centers, to build up factories, to build railroads, and to develop the country by founding cities and extending prosperity. They were ready to call upon legislatures to aid

in this, by subscriptions to stock, grants of franchises, promotion of banking and internal improvements. These were the Whig followers of that other Western leader, Henry Clay, and their early strength lay in the Ohio Valley, and particularly among the well-to-do. In the South their strength was found among the aristocracy of the Cotton Kingdom.

Both of these Western groups, Whigs and Democrats alike, had one common ideal: the desire to leave their children a better heritage than they themselves had received, and both were fired with devotion to the ideal of creating in this New World a home more worthy of mankind. Both were ready to break with the past, to boldly strike out new lines of social endeavor, and both believed in American expansion.

Before these tendencies had worked themselves out, three new forces entered. In the sudden extension of our boundaries to the Pacific Coast, which took place in the forties, the nation won so vast a domain that its resources seemed illimitable and its society seemed able to throw off all its maladies by the very presence of these vast new spaces. At the same period the great activity of railroad building to the Mississippi Valley occurred, making these lands available and diverting attention to the task of economic construction. The third influence was the slavery question which, becoming acute, shaped the American ideals and public discussion for nearly a generation. Viewed from one angle, this struggle involved the great question of national unity. From another it involved the question of the relations of labor and capital, democracy and aristocracy. It was not without significance that Abraham Lincoln became the very type of American pioneer democracy, the first adequate and elemental demonstration to the world that that democracy could produce a man who belonged to the ages.

After the war, new national energies were set loose, and new construction and development engaged the attention of the Westerners as they occupied prairies and Great Plains and mountains. Democracy and capitalistic development did not seem antagonistic.

With the passing of the frontier, Western social and political ideals took new form. Capital began to consolidate in even greater masses, and increasingly attempted to reduce to system and control the processes of industrial development. Labor with equal step organized its forces to destroy the old competitive system. It is not strange that the Western pioneers took alarm for their ideals of democracy as the outcome of the free struggle for the national resources became apparent. They espoused the cause of governmental activity.

It was a new gospel, for the Western radical became convinced that he must sacrifice his ideal of individualism and free competition in order to maintain his ideal of democracy. Under this conviction the Populist revised the pioneer conception of government He saw in government no longer something outside of him, but the people themselves shaping their own affairs. He demanded therefore an extension of the powers of governments in the interest of his historic ideal of democratic society. He demanded not only free silver, but the ownership of the agencies of communication and transportation, the income tax, the postal savings bank, the provision of means of credit for agriculture, the construction of more effective devices to express the will of the people, primary nominations, direct elections, initiative, referendum and recall. In a word, capital, labor, and the Western pioneer, all deserted the ideal of competitive individualism in order to organize their interests in more effective

combinations. The disappearance of the frontier, the closing of the era which was marked by the influence of the West as a form of society, brings with it new problems of social adjustment, new demands for considering our past ideals and our present needs.

Let us recall the conditions of the foreign relations along our borders, the dangers that wait us if we fail to unite in the solution of our domestic problems. Let us recall those internal evidences of the destruction of our old social order. If we take to heart this warning, we shall do well also to recount our historic ideals, to take stock of those purposes, and fundamental assumptions that have gone to make the American spirit and the meaning of America in world history.

First of all, there was the ideal of discovery, the courageous determination to break new paths, indifference to the dogma that because an institution or a condition exists, it must remain. All American experience has gone to the making of the spirit of innovation; it is in the blood and will not be repressed.

Then, there was the ideal of democracy, the ideal of a free self-directing people, responsive to leadership in the forming of programs and their execution, but insistent that the procedure should be that of free choice, not of compulsion.

But there was also the ideal of individualism. This democratic society was not a disciplined army, where all must keep step and where the collective interests destroyed individual will and work. Rather it was a mobile mass of freely circulating atoms, each seeking its own place and finding play for its own powers and for its own original initiative. We cannot lay too much stress upon this point, for it was at the very heart of the whole American movement. The world was to be made a better world by the example of a democracy in which there was freedom of the individual, in which there was the vitality and mobility productive of originality and variety.

Bearing in mind the far-reaching influence of the disappearance of unlimited resources open to all men for the taking, and considering the recoil of the common man when he saw the outcome of the competitive struggle for these resources as the supply came to its end over most of the nation, we can understand the reaction against individualism and in favor of drastic assertion of the powers of government. Legislation is taking the place of the free lands as the means of preserving the ideal of democracy. But at the same time it is endangering the other pioneer ideal of creative and competitive individualism. Both were essential and constituted what was best in America's contribution to history and to progress. Both must be preserved if the nation would be true to its past, and would fulfil its highest destiny. It would be a grave misfortune if these people so rich in experience, in self-confidence and aspiration, in creative genius, should turn to some Old World discipline of socialism or plutocracy, or despotic rule, whether by class or by dictator. Nor shall we be driven to these alternatives. Our ancient hopes, our courageous faith, our underlying good humor and love of fair play will triumph in the end. There will be give and take in all directions. There will be disinterested leadership, under loyalty to the best American ideals. Nowhere is this leadership more likely to arise than among the men trained in the Universities, aware of the promise of the past and the possibilities of the future. The times call for new ambitions and new motives.

In a most suggestive essay on the Problems of Modern Democracy, Mr. Godkin has said:

M. de Tocqueville and all his followers take it for granted that the great incentive to excellence, in all countries in which excellence is found, is the patronage and encouragement of an aristocracy; that democracy is generally content with mediocrity. But where is the proof of this? The incentive to exertion which is widest, most constant, and most powerful in its operations in all civilized countries, is the desire of distinction; and this may be composed either of love of fame or love of wealth or of both. In literary and artistic and scientific pursuits, sometimes the strongest influence is exerted by a love of the subject. But it may safely be said that no man has ever labored in any of the higher colleges to whom the applause and appreciation of his fellows was not one of the sweetest rewards of his exertions.

What is there we would ask, in the nature of democratic institutions, that should render this great spring of action powerless, that should deprive glory of all radiance, and put ambition to sleep? Is it not notorious, on the contrary, that one of the most marked peculiarities of democratic society, or of a society drifting toward democracy, is the fire of competition which rages in it, the fevered anxiety which possesses all its members to rise above the dead level to which the law is ever seeking to confine them, and by some brilliant stroke become something higher and more remarkable than their fellows? The secret of that great restlessness which is one of the most disagreeable accompaniments of life in democratic countries, is in fact due to the eagerness of everybody to grasp the prizes of which in aristocratic countries, only the few have much chance. And in no other society is success more worshiped, is distinction of any kind more widely flattered and caressed.

In democratic societies, in fact,

excellence is the first title to distinction; in aristocratic ones there are two or three others which are far stronger and which must be stronger or aristocracy could not exist. The moment you acknowledge that the highest social position ought to be the reward of the man who has the most talent, you make aristocratic institutions impossible.

All that was buoyant and creative in American life would be lost if we gave up the respect for distinct personality, and variety in genius, and came to the dead level of common standards. To be "socialized into an average" and placed "under the tutelage of the mass of us," as a recent writer has put it, would be an irreparable loss. Nor is it necessary in a democracy, as these words of Godkin well disclose. What is needed is the multiplication of motives for ambition and the opening of new lines of achievement for the strongest. As we turn from the task of the first rough conquest of the continent there lies before us a whole wealth of unexploited resources in

the realm of the spirit. Arts and letters, science and better social creation, loyalty and political service to the commonweal,—these and a thousand other directions of activity are open to the men, who formerly under the incentive of attaining distinction by amassing extraordinary wealth, saw success only in material display. Newer and finer careers will open to the ambitious when once public opinion shall award the laurels to those who rise above their fellows in these new fields of labor. It has not been the gold, but the getting of the gold, that has caught the imaginations of our captains of industry. Their real enjoyment lay not in the luxuries which wealth brought, but in the work of construction and in the place which society awarded them. A new era will come if schools and universities can only widen the intellectual horizon of the people, help to lay the foundations of a better industrial life, show them new goals for endeavor, inspire them with more varied and higher ideals.

9. JOHN DOS PASSOS, *The Bitter Drink, 1930**

Veblen,

a greyfaced shambling man lolling resentful at his desk with his cheek on his hand, in a low sarcastic mumble of intricate phrases subtly paying out the logical inescapable rope of matteroffact for a society to hang itself by,

dissecting out the century with a scalpel so keen, so comical, so exact that the professors and students ninetenths of the time didn't know it was there, and the magnates and the respected windbags and the applauded loudspeakers never knew it was there.

Veblen

asked too many questions, suffered

from a constitutional inability to say yes.

Socrates asked questions, drank down the bitter drink one night when the first cock crowed,

but Veblen

drank it in little sips through a long life in the stuffiness of classrooms, the dust of libraries, the staleness of cheap flats such as a poor instructor can afford. He fought the boys all right, pedantry, routine, timeservers at office desks, trustees, collegepresidents, the plump flunkies of the ruling businessmen, all the good jobs kept for yesmen, never enough money, every

* John Dos Passos, *The Big Money* (New York, 1934), pp. 93–105. Copyright by John Dos Passos, 1930, 1932, 1936; renewed 1958, 1960, and used with his permission.

broadening hope thwarted. Veblen drank the bitter drink all right.

The Veblens were a family of freeholding farmers.

The freeholders of the narrow Norwegian valleys were a stubborn hardworking people, farmers, dairymen, fishermen, rooted in their fathers' stony fields, in their old timbered farmsteads with carved gables they took their names from, in the upland pastures where they grazed the stock in summer.

During the early nineteenth century the towns grew; Norway filled up with landless men, storekeepers, sheriffs, moneylenders, bailiffs, notaries in black with stiff collars and briefcases full of foreclosures under their arms. Industries were coming in. The townsmen were beginning to get profits out of the country and to finagle the farmers out of the freedom of their narrow farms.

The meanspirited submitted as tenants, daylaborers; but the strong men went out of the country

as their fathers had gone out of the country centuries before when Harald the Fairhaired and St. Olaf hacked to pieces the liberties of the northern men, who had been each man lord of his own creek, to make Christians and serfs of them,

only in the old days it was Iceland, Greenland, Vineland the northmen had sailed west to; now it was America.

Both Thorstein Veblen's father's people and his mother's people had lost their farmsteads and with them the names that denoted them free men

Thomas Anderson for a while tried to make his living as a traveling carpenter and cabinetmaker, but in 1847 he and his wife, Kari Thorsteinsdatter, crossed in a whalingship from Bremen and went out to join friends in the Scandihoovian colonies round Milwaukee.

Next year his brother Haldor joined him.

They were hard workers; in another year they had saved up money to preempt a claim on 160 acres of uncleared land in Sheboygan County, Wisconsin; when they'd gotten that land part cleared they sold it and moved to an all-Norway colony in Manitowoc County, near Cato and a place named Valders after the valley they had all come from in the old country;

there in the house Thomas Anderson built with his own tools, the sixth of twelve children, Thorstein Veblen was born.

When Thorstein was eight years old, Thomas Anderson moved west again into the blacksoil prairies of Minnesota that the Sioux and the buffalo had only been driven off from a few years before. In the deed to the new farm Thomas Anderson took back the old farmstead name of Veblen.

He was a solid farmer, builder, a clever carpenter, the first man to import merino sheep and a mechanical reaper and binder; he was a man of standing in the group of Norway people farming the edge of the prairie, who kept their dialects, the manner of life of their narrow Norway valleys, their Lutheran pastors, their homemade clothes and cheese and bread, their suspicion and stubborn dislike of townsmen's ways.

The townspeople were Yankees mostly, smart to make two dollars grow where a dollar grew before, storekeepers, middlemen, speculators, moneylenders, with long heads for politics and mortgages; they despised the Scandihoovian dirtfarmers they lived off, whose daughters did their wives' kitchenwork.

The Norway people believed as their fathers had believed that there were only two callings for an honest man, farming or preaching.

Thorstein grew up a hulking lad with a reputation for laziness and wit. He hated the irk of everrepeated backbreaking chores round the farm. Reading he was happy. Carpentering he liked or running farmmachinery. The Lutheran pastors who came to the house noticed that his supple mind slid easily round the corners of their theology. It was hard to get farmwork out of him, he had a stinging tongue and was famous for the funny names he called people; his father decided to make a preacher out of him.

When he was seventeen he was sent for out of the field where he was working. His bag was already packed. The horses were hitched up. He was being sent to Carleton Academy in Northfield, to prepare for Carleton College.

As there were several young Veblens to be educated their father built them a house on a lot near the campus. Their food and clothes were sent to them from the farm. Cash money was something they never saw.

Thorstein spoke English with an accent. He had a constitutional inability to say yes. His mind was formed on the Norse sagas and on the matteroffact sense of his father's farming and the exact needs of carpenterwork and threshingmachines.

He could never take much interest in the theology, sociology, economics of Carleton College where they were busy trimming down the jagged dogmas of the old New England bibletaught traders to make stencils to hang on the walls of commissionmerchants' offices.

Veblen's collegeyears were the years when Darwin's assertions of growth and becoming were breaking the set molds of the Noah's Ark world,

when Ibsen's women were tearing down the portieres of the Victorian parlors,

and Marx's mighty machine was rigging the countinghouse's own logic to destroy the countinghouse.

When Veblen went home to the farm he talked about these things with his father, following him up and down at his plowing, starting an argument while they were waiting for a new load for the wheatthresher. Thomas Anderson had seen Norway and America; he had the squarebuilt mind of a carpenter and builder, and an understanding of tools and the treasured elaborated builtupseasonbyseason knowledge of a careful farmer,

a tough whetstone for the sharpening steel of young Thorstein's wits.

At Carleton College young Veblen was considered a brilliant unsound eccentric; nobody could understand why a boy of such attainments wouldn't settle down to the business of the day, which was to buttress property and profits with anything usable in the debris of Christian ethics and eighteenthcentury economics that cluttered the minds of collegeprofessors, and to reinforce the sacred, already shaky edifice with the new strong girderwork of science Herbert Spencer was throwing up for the benefit of the bosses.

People complained they never knew whether Veblen was joking or serious.

In 1880 Thorstein Veblen started to try to make his living by teaching. A year in an academy at Madison, Wisconsin, wasn't much of a success. Next year he and his brother Andrew started graduate work at Johns Hopkins. Johns Hopkins didn't suit, but boarding in an old Baltimore house with some ruined gentlewomen gave him a disdaining glimpse of an etiquette motheaten now but handed down through the lavish leisure of the slaveowning planters' mansions straight from the merry England of the landlord cavaliers.

(The valleyfarmers had always been scornful of outlanders' ways.)

He was more at home at Yale where in Noah Porter he found a New England roundhead granite against which his Norway granite rang in clear dissent. He took his Ph.D. there. But there was still some question as to what department of the academic world he could best make a living in.

He read Kant and wrote prize essays. But he couldn't get a job. Try as he could he couldn't get his mouth round the essential yes.

He went back to Minnesota with a certain intolerant knowledge of the amenities of the higher learning. To his slight Norwegian accent he'd added the broad a.

At home he loafed about the farm and tinkered with inventions of new machinery and read and talked theology and philosophy with his father. In the Scandihoovian colonies the price of wheat and the belief in God and St. Olaf were going down together. The farmers of the Northwest were starting their long losing fight against the parasite businessmen who were sucking them dry. There was a mortgage on the farm, interest on debts to pay, always fertilizer, new machines to buy to speed production to pump in a halfcentury the wealth out of the soil laid down in a million years of buffalograss. His brothers kept grumbling about this sardonic loafer who wouldn't earn his keep.

Back home he met again his college sweetheart, Ellen Rolfe, the niece of the president of Carleton College, a girl who had railroadmagnates and money in the family. People in Northfield were shocked when it came out that she was going to marry the drawling pernickety bookish badlydressed young Norwegian ne'erdowell.

Her family hatched a plan to get him a job as economist for the Santa Fe Railroad but at the wrong moment Ellen Rolfe's uncle lost control of the line. The young couple went to live at Stacyville where they did everything but earn a living. They read Latin and Greek and botanized in the woods and along the fences and in the roadside scrub. They boated on the river and Veblen started his translation of the *Laxdaelasaga*. They read *Looking Backward* and articles by Henry George. They looked at their world from the outside.

In '91 Veblen got together some money to go to Cornell to do postgraduate work. He turned up there in the office of the head of the economics department wearing a coonskin cap and grey corduroy trousers and said in his low sarcastic drawl, "I am Thorstein Veblen,"

but it was not until several years later, after he was established at the new University of Chicago that had grown up next to the World's Fair, and had published *The Theory of the Leisure Class,* put on the map by Howell's famous review, that the world of the higher learning knew who Thorstein Veblen was.

Even in Chicago as the brilliant young economist he lived pioneerfashion. (The valleyfarmers had always been scornful of outlanders' ways.) He kept his books in packingcases laid on their sides along the walls. His only extravagances were the Russian cigarettes he smoked and the red sash he sometimes sported. He was a man without smalltalk. When he lectured he put his cheek on his hand and mumbled out his long spiral sentences, reiterative like the eddas. His language was a mixture of mechanics' terms, scientific latinity, slang and Roget's Thesaurus. The other profs couldn't imagine why the girls fell for him so.

The girls fell for him so that Ellen Rolfe kept leaving him. He'd take summer trips abroad without his wife. There was a scandal about a girl on an ocean liner.

Tongues wagged so (Veblen was a man who never explained, who never could get his tongue around the essential yes; the valleyfarmers had always been scornful of the outlanders' ways, and their opinions) that his wife left him and went off to live alone on a timberclaim in Idaho and the president asked for his resignation.

Veblen went out to Idaho to get Ellen Rolfe to go with him to California when he succeeded in getting a job at a better salary at Leland Stanford, but in Palo Alto it was the same story as in Chicago. He suffered from woman trouble and the constitutional inability to say yes and an unnatural tendency to feel with the workingclass instead of with the profittakers. There were the same complaints that his courses were not constructive or attractive to big money bequests and didn't help his students to butter their bread, make Phi Beta Kappa, pick plums off the hierarchies of the academic grove. His wife left him for good. He wrote to a friend: "The president doesn't approve of my domestic arrangements; nor do I."

Talking about it he once said, "What is one to do if the woman moves in on you?"

He went back up to the shack in the Idaho woods.

Friends tried to get him an appointment to make studies in Crete, a chair at the University of Pekin, but always the boys, routine, businessmen's flunkeys in all the university offices . . . for the questioner the bitter drink.

His friend Davenport got him an appointment at the University of Missouri. At Columbia he lived like a hermit in the basement of the Davenports' house, helped with the work round the place, carpentered himself a table and chairs. He was already a bitter elderly man with a grey face covered with a net of fine wrinkles, a vandyke beard and yellow teeth. Few students could follow his courses. The college authorities were often surprised and somewhat chagrined that when visitors came from Europe it was always Veblen they wanted to meet.

These were the years he did most of his writing, trying out his ideas on his students, writing slowly at night in violet ink with a pen of his own designing. Whenever he published a book he had to put up a guarantee with the publishers. In *The Theory of Business Enterprise, The Instinct of Workmanship, The Vested Interests and the Common Man,*

he established a new diagram of a society dominated by monopoly capital,

etched in irony

the sabotage of production by business,

the sabotage of life by blind need for money profits,

pointed out the alternatives: a warlike society strangled by the bureaucracies of the monopolies forced by the law of diminishing returns to grind down more and more the common man for profits,

or a new matteroffact commonsense society dominated by the needs of the men and women who did the work and the incredibly vast possibilities for peace and plenty offered by the progress of technology.

These were the years of Debs's speeches, growing laborunions, the I.W.W. talk about industrial democracy: these years Veblen still held to the hope that the workingclass would take over the machine of production before monopoly had pushed the western nations down into the dark again.

War cut across all that: under the cover of the bunting of Woodrow Wilson's phrases the monopolies cracked down. American democracy was crushed.

The war at least offered Veblen an opportunity to break out of the airless greenhouse of academic life. He was offered a job with the Food Administration, he sent the Navy Department a device for catching submarines by trailing lengths of stout bindingwire. (Meanwhile the government found his books somewhat confusing. The postoffice was forbidding the mails to *Imperial Germany and the Industrial Revolution* while propaganda agencies were sending it out to make people hate the Huns. Educators were denouncing *The Nature of Peace* while Washington experts were clipping phrases out of it to add to the Wilsonian smokescreen.)

For the Food Administration Thorstein Veblen wrote two reports: in one he advocated granting the demands of the I.W.W. as a wartime measure and conciliating the workingclass instead of beating up and jailing all the honest leaders; in the other he pointed out that the Food Administration was a businessman's racket and was not aiming for the most efficient organization of the country as a producing machine. He suggested that, in the interests of the efficient prosecution of the war, the government step into the place of the middleman and furnish necessities to the farmers direct in return for raw materials;

but cutting out business was not at all the Administration's idea of making the world safe for democracy,

so Veblen had to resign from the Food Administration.

He signed the protests against the trial of the hundred and one wobblies in Chicago.

After the armistice he went to New York. In spite of all the oppression of the war years, the air was freshening. In Russia the great storm of revolt had broken, seemed to be sweeping west, in the strong gusts from the new world in the east the warsodden multitudes began to see again. At Versailles allies and enemies, magnates, generals, flunkey politicians were slamming the shutters against the storm, against the new, against hope. It was suddenly clear for a second in the thundering glare what war was about, what peace was about.

In America, in Europe, the old men won. The bankers in their offices took a deep breath, the bediamonded old ladies of the leisure class went back to clipping their coupons in the refined quiet of their safedeposit vaults,

the last puffs of the ozone of revolt went stale

in the whisper of speakeasy arguments.

Veblen wrote for the *Dial,*

lectured at the New School for Social Research.

He still had a hope that the engineers, the technicians, the nonprofiteers whose hands were on the switchboard might take up the fight where the workingclass had failed. He helped form the Technical Alliance. His last hope was the British general strike.

Was there no group of men bold enough to take charge of the magnificent machine before the pigeyed speculators and the yesmen at office desks irrevocably ruined it

and with it the hopes of four hundred years?

No one went to Veblen's lectures at the New School. With every article he wrote in the *Dial* the circulation dropped.

Harding's normalcy, the new era was beginning;

even Veblen made a small killing on the stockmarket.

He was an old man and lonely.

His second wife had gone to a sanitarium suffering from delusions of persecution.

There seemed no place for a masterless man.

Veblen went back out to Palo Alto to live in his shack in the tawny hills and observe from outside the last grabbing urges of the profit system taking on, as he put it, the systematized delusions of dementia praecox.

There he finished his translation of the *Laxdaelasaga.*

He was an old man. He was much alone. He let the woodrats take what they wanted from his larder. A skunk that hung round the shack was so tame he'd rub up against Veblen's leg like a cat.

He told a friend he'd sometimes hear in the stillness about him the voices of his boyhood talking Norwegian as clear as on the farm in Minnesota where he was raised. His friends found him harder than ever to

talk to, harder than ever to interest in anything. He was running down. The last sips of the bitter drink.

He died on August 3, 1929.

Among his papers a penciled note was found:

It is also my wish, in case of death, to be cremated if it can conveniently be done, as expeditiously and inexpensively as may be, without ritual or ceremony of any kind; that my ashes be thrown loose into the sea or into some sizable stream running into the sea; that no tombstone, slab, epitaph, effigy, tablet, inscription or monument of any name or nature, be set up to my memory or name in any place or at any time; that no obituary, memorial, portrait or biography of me, nor any letters written to or by me be printed or published, or in any way reproduced, copied or circulated;

but his memorial remains
riveted into the language:
the sharp clear prism of his mind.

10. HERBERT HOOVER, *Rugged Individualism, 1928**

During the war we necessarily turned to the Government to solve every difficult economic problem. The Government having absorbed every energy of our people for war, there was no other solution. For the preservation of the State the Federal Government became a centralized despotism which undertook unprecedented responsibilities, assumed autocratic powers, and took over the business of citizens. To a large degree we regimented our whole people temporarily into a socialistic state. However justified in time of war, if continued in peace time it would destroy not only

our American system but with it our progress and freedom as well.

When the war closed, the most vital of all issues both in our own country and throughout the world was whether Governments should continue their wartime ownership and operation of many instrumentalities of production and distribution. We were challenged with a peace-time choice between the American system of rugged individualism and a European philosophy of diametrically opposed doctrines—doctrines of paternalism and state socialism. The acceptance of these ideas would have meant the destruction of self-

* Herbert Hoover, "Rugged Individualism" as reported in *The New York Times,* October 23, 1928.

government through centralization of government. It would have meant the undermining of the individual initiative and enterprise through which our people have grown to unparalleled greatness.

The Republican Party from the beginning resolutely turned its face away from these ideas and these war practices. A Republican Congress cooperated with the Democratic Administration to demobilize many of our war activities. At that time the two parties were in accord upon that point. When the Republican Party came into full power it went at once resolutely back to our fundamental conception of the State and the rights and responsibilities of the individual. Thereby it restored confidence and hope in the American people, it freed and stimulated enterprise, it restored the Government to its position as an umpire instead of a player in the economic game. For these reasons the American people have gone forward in progress while the rest of the world has halted, and some countries have even gone backward. If any one will study the causes of retarded recuperation in Europe, he will find much of it due to the stifling of private initiative on one hand, and overloading of the Government with business on the other. . . .

Bureaucracy is ever desirous of spreading its influence and its power. You cannot extend the mastery of the Government over the daily working life of a people without at the same time making it the master of the people's souls and thoughts. Every expansion of Government in business means that Government in order to protect itself from the political consequences of its errors and wrongs is driven irresistibly without peace to greater and greater control of the nation's press and platform. Free speech does not live many hours after free industry and free commerce die.

It is a false liberalism that interprets itself into the Government operation of commercial business. Every step of bureaucratizing of the business of our country poisons the very roots of liberalism—that is, political equality, free spech, free assembly, free press, and equality of opportunity. It is the road not to more liberty but to less liberty. Liberalism should be found not striving to spread bureaucracy but striving to set bounds to it. True liberalism seeks all legitimate freedom, first in the confident belief that without such freedom the pursuit of all other blessings and benefits is vain. That belief is the foundation of all American progress, political as well as economic.

Liberalism is a force truly of the spirit, a force proceeding from the deep realization that economic freedom cannot be sacrificed if political freedom is to be preserved. Even if governmental conduct of business could give us more efficiency instead of less efficiency, the fundamental objection to it would remain unaltered and unabated. It would destroy political equality. It would increase rather than decrease abuse and corruption. It would stifle initiative and invention. It would undermine the development of leadership. It would cramp and cripple the mental and spiritual energies of our people. It would extinguish equality and opportunity. It would dry up the spirit of liberty and progress. For these reasons primarily it must be resisted. For a hundred and fifty years liberalism has found its true spirit in the American system, not in the European systems.

I do not wish to be misunderstood in this statement. I am defining a general policy. It does not mean that our Government is to part with one iota of its national resources without complete protection to the public interest. I have already stated that where the Government is engaged in public works for purposes of flood control, of navigation, of irrigation, of scientific research or national defense, or in pioneering a new art, it will at times necessarily produce power or commodities as a by-product. But they must be a by-product of the major purpose, not the major purpose itself.

Nor do I wish to be misinterpreted as believing that the United States is free-for-all and devil-take-the-hindmost. The very essence of equality of opportunity and of American individualism is that there shall be no domination by any group or combination in this Republic, whether it be business or political. On the contrary, it demands economic justice as well as political and social justice. It is no system of laissez faire.

I feel deeply on this subject because during the war I had some practical experience with governmental operation and control. I have witnessed not only at home but abroad the many failures of Government in business. I have seen its tyrannies, its injustices, its destructions of self-government, its undermining of the very instincts which carry our people forward to progress. I have witnessed the lack of advance, the lowered standards of living, the depressed spirits of people working under such a system. My objection is based not upon theory or upon a failure to recognize wrong or abuse, but I know the adoption of such methods would strike at the very roots of American life and would destroy the very basis of American progress.

Our people have the right to know whether we can continue to solve our great problems without abandonment of our American system. I know we can. We have demonstrated that our

system is responsive enough to meet any new and intricate development in our economic and business life. We have demonstrated that we can meet any economic problem and still maintain our democracy and master in its own house and that we can at the same time preserve equality of opportunity and individual freedom. . . .

And what have been the results of our American system? Our country has become the land of opportunity to those born without inheritance, not merely because of the wealth of its resources and industry, but because of this freedom of initiative and enterprise. Russia has natural resources equal to ours. Her people are equally industrious, but she has not had the blessings of 150 years of our form of government and of our social system.

By adherence to the principles of decentralized self-government, ordered liberty, equal opportunity, and freedom to the individual our American experiment in human welfare has yielded a degree of well-being unparalleled in all the world. It has come nearer to the abolition of poverty, to the abolition of fear of want, than humanity has ever reached before. Progress of the past seven years is the proof of it. This alone furnishes the answer to our opponents who ask us to introduce destructive elements into the system by which this has been accomplished.

Let us see what this system has done for us in our recent years of difficult and trying reconstruction and let us then solemnly ask ourselves if we now wish to abandon it.

As a nation we came out of the war with great losses. We made no profits from it. The apparent increases in wages were at that time fictitious. We were poorer as a nation when we emerged from the war. Yet during these last eight years we have recovered from these losses and increased our national income by over one-third, even if we discount the inflation of the dollar. That there has been a wide diffusion of our gain in wealth and income is marked by a hundred proofs. I know of no better test of the improved conditions of the average family than the combined increase in assets of life and industrial insurance, building and loan associations, and savings deposits. These are the savings banks of the average man. These agencies alone have in seven years increased by nearly 100 per cent to the gigantic sum of over fifty billions of dollars, or nearly one-sixth of our whole national wealth. We have increased in home ownership, we have expanded the investments of the average man.

In addition to these evidences of larger savings, our people are steadily increasing their spending for higher standards of living. Today there are almost nine automobiles for each ten families, where seven and a half years ago only enough automobiles were running to average less than four for each ten families. The slogan of progress is changing from the full dinner pail to the full garage. Our people have more to eat, better things to wear and better homes. We have even gained in elbow room, for the increase of residential floor space is over 25 per cent, with less than 10 per cent increase in our number of people. Wages have increased, the cost of living has decreased. The job to every man and woman has been made more secure. We have in this short period decreased the fear of poverty, the fear of unemployment, the fear of old age; and these are fears that are the greatest calamities of human kind.

11. KENNETH FEARING, *Dirge, 1935**

1-2-3 was the number he played but today the number came 3-2-1;
bought his Carbide at 30 and it went
to 29; had the favorite at Bowie
but the track was slow—

O, executive type, would you like to
drive a floating power, knee-
action, silk-upholstered six? Wed
a Hollywood star? Shoot the
course in 58? Draw to the ace,
king, jack?
O, fellow with a will who won't take
no, watch out for three cigarettes on the same, single match;
O, democratic voter born in August under Mars, beware of li-
quidated rails—

Denouement to denouement, he took
a personal pride in the certain,

certain way he lived his own,
private life,
but nevertheless, they shut off his
gas; nevertheless, the bank fore-
closed; nevertheless, the landlord called; nevertheless, the
radio broke,

And twelve o'clock arrived just once
too often,
just the same he wore one grey
tweed suit, bought one straw
hat, drank one straight Scotch,
walked one short step, took one
long look, drew one deep
breath,
just one too many,

And wow he died as wow he lived,
going whop to the office and blooie
home to sleep and biff got mar-

* Kenneth Fearing, *Poems* (New York, 1935), pp. 43–44. Reprinted with permission.

ried and bam had children and
oof got fired,
zowie did he live and zowie did he
die,

With who the hell are you at the corner of his casket, and where
the hell we going on the right-
hand silver knob, and who the
hell cares walking second from
the end with an American
Beauty wreath from why the
hell not,

Very much missed by the circulation
staff of the New York Evening
Post; deeply, deeply mourned
by the B.M.T.,

Wham, Mr. Roosevelt; pow, Sears Roe-
buck; awk, big dipper; bop,
summer rain;
bong, Mr., bong, Mr., bong, Mr.,
bong.

V

* *

The Culture of the
Common Man

CLINTON LAWRENCE ROSSITER 3D,

educator and author, is a widely recognized authority on political science and government.

He has been Professor of Government and chairman of the Department of Government at Cornell University since 1956. Among his books are *Constitutional Dictatorship,* published in 1948; *The Supreme Court and the Commander in Chief,* 1951; *Seedtime of the Republic,* 1953; *Conservatism in America,* 1955; *The First American Presidency,* 1956.

Professor Rossiter was born in Philadelphia in 1917. He received an A.B. from Cornell in 1939; an M.A. from Princeton in 1941, and a Ph.D. from Princeton in 1942.

He served as a Navy lieutenant in World War II, taught political science at Cornell from 1946 to 1954 and was a Guggenheim fellow in 1953–54.

Clinton Rossiter ✳✳✳ We Must
Show the Way to Enduring Peace

The United States is rightly numbered among those nations for which a benevolent sense of national purpose—or, as I prefer, of mission—has been a historical necessity. We have been, like the children of Israel, a "peculiar treasure." Upon us destiny has bestowed special favor; of us it has therefore asked special effort. Because men like Washington and Lincoln sensed this grand truth and acted consciously upon it, we have counted more heavily in history than our size and wealth, however majestic, would seem to have warranted. The world, we must think, would be in a far different and unhappier situation today if there had never been a United States.

If we think that, we must also think that it will be in a far different and unhappier situation in 25 or 50 or 100 years unless the United States survives and flourishes. We are, however, besieged with doubts about our capacity to flourish and perhaps even to survive. The sharpest doubt of all is compounded of two related suspicions: that we have lost the sense of mission of our early years, and yet that we need this sense more desperately than ever today.

We need it because we stand at one of those rare points in history when a nation must choose consciously between greatness and mediocrity. The United States may well go on for centuries as a territorial entity in which men and women can pursue reasonably useful and satisfying lives. Will it also be, as it has hitherto been, a unique civilization whose decline would be counted a major calamity in history? That is the choice we must now make. If we choose greatness, as surely we must, we choose effort—the kind of national effort that transcends the ordinary lives of men and commits them to the pursuit of a common purpose, that persuades them to sacrifice private indulgences to the public interest, that sends them on a search for leaders who call forth strengths rather than pander to weaknesses.

Such an effort must have its beginning in the minds and hearts of Americans, and take the form of a clear statement of the meaning and goals of a unique people. America will not flourish, not in the hot winds of this volcanic age, unless it can develop a profound, inspiring, benevolent sense of mission. While this is only the first short step to the grandeur to which we may still properly aspire, it is the kind that must be taken boldly before any other can be attempted.

One reason why we must take it boldly, or not bother to take it at all, is that it will not be easy. As an historian, I am bound to point out that this country stands on shaky historical and cultural ground from which to launch a new search for a national mission and then to pursue it. The sense of mission seems to spring most readily from the consciousness of a young nation, even of a nation in the making, and America, alas, is well into middle age.

In our youth we had a profound sense of national purpose, which we lost over the years of our rise to glory. The American mission that inspired every statesman from Washington through Lincoln called upon us to serve as a testament to freedom, to spread by our example the good news of personal liberty and popular government throughout the world. We did not lose our youthful sense of mission because it was childish or wicked or impossible in its demands upon us, rather because it had to be fulfilled in the course of time or be cast aside as a youthful extravagance. And it was in fact fulfilled nobly. For all its areas of blighted hope, the world today counts many constitutional democracies where once it counted only the United States.

Can a nation that has fulfilled the mission of its youth expect to find a second mission in its later years? And can a nation that has known the material success of ours shake loose from the clutch of self-indulgence? Once we were lean and hungry, a people "on the make," and we generated a sense of mission almost instinctively in order to survive and move ahead. Now we are fat and complacent, a people that "has it made," and we find it hard to rouse to the trumpet of sacrifice—even if anyone in authority were to blow it.

Still another hurdle in the path of our search for a new sense of national purpose is the cherished doctrine of American individualism, which has taught even the most dependent of us to look with suspicion on the community and its demands. The characteristic American, if such a man there be, is too much an individualist to listen comfortably to men who talk of a collective destiny. Out of the lives of millions of free, decent, duty-conscious individuals there may well arise, this American thinks, some greater purpose: progress for the human race, glory for God, the triumph of liberty. Yet essentially he is a man who, try as he might, can find no ultimate purpose in history that justifies an exaltation of the nation, no cosmic plan for America that gives special meaning to his life and thus calls for special sacrifice.

Finally, we are faced with the hard question: Who speaks for America? Who can state our mission in such a way that, if truthfully and eloquently stated, it will be accepted and acted upon by the American people? We have no Marx, no teacher revered as the First Source. We have no Pope, no God-touched prophet whose words command unique respect. To redirect the aspirations of an entire people is a monstrous task, especially if the people has always been encouraged to speak in a confusion of tongues and to listen with suspicion to the voices of its leaders. The machinery of freedom is not effectively geared to produce and disseminate the One Big Idea, even if it be the idea of freedom. If this country is ever to recapture a sense of national purpose, that purpose will have to be voiced by a line of plain-talking presidents and given a cutting edge in laws enacted by a series of tough-minded congresses. Then it will have to be put into daily practice by tens of thousands of dedicated administrators, teachers, ministers, editors, managers, and community leaders.

These are genuine difficulties, yet they need not prove insuperable, certainly not for a nation with the untapped resolve that ours still carries within it; and, in any case we are bound by every imperative of tradition, patriotism, and morality to make the attempt. Where, then, are we to find this idea, this new sense of national purpose, and what form are we to give it? The answer, I submit, lies waiting for discovery in the history and present condition of the American people.

The history is one of genuine achievement. Our failures have been shocking, but our triumphs have been earth-shaking. To have occupied a continent, created a new nation out of the surplus of other nations, built up a giant society based on individual liberty, maintained an effective government based on popular consent, led all nations in producing and distributing the fruits of technology, given unique dignity and fulfillment to the lives of ordinary men, and stood before the world as an example of the blessings of freedom are achievements of which we might well be more conscious and proud. Surely a nation that has just come from doing such deeds should be able to do others no less historic. Surely such a nation has no choice but to do them—or cease to be the nation it has always been.

The present condition, plainly, is one of growing uneasiness. We are sliding into a series of discontents to whose solution the energies of a consciously dedicated people may alone be equal. While I do not wish to sound too presumptuous or pat in my catalogue of these discontents, I can best describe the crisis of our age as a tangle of four separate yet curiously related crises: the crisis in race relations, the crisis in culture, the crisis of the community, and the crisis of peace and war— all of which are growing in intensity with each passing year.

The crisis in the relations of the white majority and the Negro minority in this country is the oldest, most puzzling, and most distressing with which we have ever been faced or may ever be. This situation is especially puzzling because of our contrasting success in dealing with many problems in the area of social relations that have been the despair and even the destruction of other societies. We took the lead in softening the impact of religious differences upon the delicate pattern of social harmony; we have made a mockery of Marx's insistence upon the universality of the class struggle; we have converted mobility from a threat to social stability into one of its stoutest supports. Yet always we have known that every claim for the fairness of our social order had to be footnoted "except for the Negroes."

If we can say anything for certain about American society in 1960, it is that the Negroes are no longer a footnote and we can no longer make them an exception. They are a powerful presence, 18 million Americans growing daily less content with the status and symbols of third-class citizenship. 18 million Americans with determined, conscience-stricken allies in the white majority. We must take it as a fact of history that we will have no peace in our minds nor self-esteem in our hearts until we have broadened the boundaries of American democracy to include the Negro (and, I might add, the Puerto Rican, the Indian, and the Asian), until we have built a system in which equal justice, equal respect, and equal opportunity are the patrimony of all Americans.

The crisis in American culture is perhaps more obvious to the schoolteacher than to the housewife, to the artist than to the salesman, to the egghead than to the hardhead. It is a crisis nonetheless, for surely no great nation can be said to be worth respecting or imitating if it has not achieved a high level of culture, and it is at least an arguable question whether this nation will ever achieve it.

I do not mean to ignore our genuine successes in the many fields of art and learning, nor to disparage those Americans who have won them for us. If we are not Athenians or Florentines, neither are we Philistines. Yet we lack a widespread popular respect for the fruits of art and learning and for those who produce them, and we have much too short a supply of first-class artists and intellectuals. More than that, no people in history has ever had to put up with so much vulgarity, cheapness, and ugliness in its surroundings. History has flung us an exciting challenge by making us the first of all nations in which men of every rank could display a measure of taste; we have responded by displaying bad taste on a massive scale—and by exporting some of the worst examples of this taste to countries all over the world. Let us be honest about it: we have the wealth and leisure and techniques to make a great culture an essential part of our lives, an inspiration to the world, and a monument for future generations—and we have not even come close to the mark. When will we come to realize that lives without culture are lives only half lived, that the arts can be introduced in a hundred subtle ways to enrich our daily comings and goings, and that there is no pride to match that of living in a country that is taken seriously by the world as a fountain of art and letters?

The crisis of the community is one that has burst upon us only in the past few years. I mean, of course, the steadily widening gap between the richness of our private lives and the poverty of our public services, between a standard of living inside our homes that is the highest in the world and a standard of living outside them that is fast becoming a national disgrace. The American economy is wonderfully constructed, technically and ideologically, to satisfy the demands of a rapidly growing population for food, clothing, entertainment, private transportation, labor-saving devices, luxuries, and much of its housing. It is only poorly constructed to do what so plainly needs to be done about the blight of our cities, the shortage of water and power, the disappearance of open space, the inadequacy of education, the need for recreational facilities, the high incidence of crime and delinquency, the crowding of the roads, the decay of the railroads, the ugliness of the sullied landscape, the pollution of the very air we breathe.

These public problems will never be handled in the style of a great nation until we rid our minds of threadbare prejudices about the role of government, value the things we buy with our taxes as highly as those we buy with what is left over after taxes, and distribute our richest treasure men and women of intelligence and character—more judiciously among the callings and professions. We lure far too many talented young people into advertising and far too few into city planning, far too many into car-dealing and far too few into teaching, far too many into high-priced private psychiatry and far too few into low-cost public health. The gross misuse of human resources is a situation that cries out for correction.

Looming above and aggravating all our other crises is the desperate situation of a world one-third uncertainly free, one-third aggressively totalitarian, one-third racked by poverty, hunger, envy, and the pangs of awakening nationalism. The first two of these mighty camps are so awesomely armed that they could destroy one another as going civilizations in a matter of hours. Around their peripheries we find points of frightening volatility, any one of them capable of triggering a war that would put an abrupt end to all speculations about the higher destiny of the American people.

Even if we can forestall the crisis of a war that will be worse than war, we are left deep in the crisis of a peace that is no peace. We pour an appalling amount of money, resources, skills, and energy into the development and production of weapons we pray to God we will never use. I am aware that much of the waste is imperative, that the menace of the Soviet Union has left us only a small range of choice in deciding how much of our total resources we should spend on national defense. I can, however, draw little comfort from the thought that we have done merely our duty to ourselves and to our allies. Sitting on the edge of an abyss costs a great deal in spiritual as well as material resources.

These are not the only major troubles that are plaguing this country today, but no other current problem, not even the much discussed crisis in morals, presents so urgent a challenge to a nation that has been great, remains great, and must now choose consciously whether it will be great in the future. These four problems are the unfinished business of American democracy; they are the tests of our determination to remain a notable civilization; they are the raw materials out of which we will spin the sense of national purpose we need so badly.

It is, I think, the last of these problems that presents this nation with its most fateful challenge to greatness. In the crisis of war and peace— in the yearning of mankind to be done with wars and rumors of wars and to build up the conditions of a secure and bountiful peace—we will find, if we are ever to find it at all, a renewed sense of national purpose, a second American mission. Several considerations make this choice as appealing as it is inevitable.

First, the challenge of peace looms above the others in present urgency and future import. No purpose of the American people could be more pressing than that of forestalling a savage war that all participants and spectators are certain to lose. The achievement of this purpose would give us first rank among all nations in the histories of the future; the refusal to conceive and act upon it would expose us to ridicule and shame. We brought ourselves, virtually unaided, to the center of the stage of history, and we will fail all mankind as well as ourselves if we do not act greatly upon it.

Second, this challenge seems much the best calculated to unite the American people. The unity of the nation in the face of vast centrifugal forces has been one of its most treasured possessions, and we are bound to consider it carefully as we make our historic choice of a second American mission. No other problem directs itself so immediately to every American; no other calls for sacrifices from every man and woman in due proportion; no other holds out a richer reward to every group and interest and section.

This is by no means to downgrade the vast benefits to be gained for the health and reputation of the United States in a forceful, imaginative pursuit of the other goals I have indicated. Indeed, we must pursue them steadily at peril of breaking faith with our historic commitment to liberty, justice, opportunity, and well-being. Yet they are also goals that may be reached more quickly by a nation committed to leadership in the search for enduring peace. Although history and circumstance both support our claim to such leadership, the claim will remain suspect to most nations of the world so long as we punish men of color for claiming the rights of other Americans, make trash our major cultural export, and starve the efforts of the community to serve our public needs. The search for peace incorporates, strengthens, and transcends the search for equity in race relations, quality in culture and balance in the political economy. All these searches must go forward together.

Finally, the challenge of peace calls upon us to deal not just with ourselves but with all mankind, and thus throws our self-awareness as a nation into sharpest focus. A sense of national purpose is at bottom a sense of international purpose, whether evil or benevolent in its influence upon the rest of the world. In the absence of any desire to influence the world, or even to do business with it, the quest for a sense of national purpose becomes an exercise in futility.

How then are we to frame our response as a nation to this greatest of challenges? What are we to consider our special role in the search of all nations for a peace that rewards them with freedom, security, justice, and opportunity? The answer, once again, stares us patiently in the face. To find it we need only look with fresh eyes at the poignant situation of a rich, proud, and successful nation in a world full of poor, bewildered, and aspiring nations.

All things considered, especially the psychological and ideological distance we had to travel from the aloofness of 1938 to the involvement of 1948, we have done remarkably well in honoring our obligations to this world. We have helped to keep the peace, we have spread our bounty widely. Yet the peace is fragile and costly, the bounty has made only a small dent in the sufferings of mankind. The time has surely come for a new American approach to the world outside. While the immediate pressure to adopt a new approach may result from the ubiquitous activities of the Soviet Union, the next great step to a peaceful world would seem, in any case, to be the special responsibility of the United States.

In my opinion, it has now become the destiny of this nation to lead the world prudently and pragmatically—step by step, pact by pact, concession by concession—through cooperation to confederacy to federation and at last to a government having power to enforce peace. There is little doubt that the world is moving fitfully in this direction, and the mightiest nation should show the way rather than drag its feet. This, surely, is the second American mission. While the process may and should take several generations—and may need a few small catastrophes to spur it onward—the ultimate goal and our responsibility for leading the way toward it must never be lost from sight. In the next century the world will achieve a peace of abundance and justice through law or become a vast basket of crabs in which the struggle for bare survival consumes the energies of all nations.

The second American mission will not be easy for us to go on, for we will have to redirect some of our deepest urges toward ends that our fathers would have found unthinkable. It will not be easy for us to complete, for we cannot be sure that mankind, even under the most prudent leadership and with the best of luck, will be spared the agonies of nuclear war. The fact that it calls for new ways of thinking and for calculated risks is, however, no reason not to enter upon it boldly.

Let us labor, then, in the world at large—in the United Nations, in the World Court, in conferences at Geneva, in the reach into space, in the dozen great ventures in which we have already begun to surrender some aspect of our pristine sovereignty—with this lofty purpose in mind. While we keep our defenses up, let us look with fresh eyes for ways to tear them down. While we pursue our present program of foreign aid, let us consider whether we are not in fact stingy to the point of absurdity. While we use force when force is the only workable means, let us remember that true leadership is largely an exercise in example and persuasion. We are called upon by history to guide the world, not to dominate it. And while we continue to cherish the fond belief that our country is a peculiar treasure, let us perceive that it is just such a country that may rise above its apparent self-interest in a grand attempt to secure the interest of humanity. To make such an attempt we must, like Jefferson and his colleagues, be aware that we are acting "not for ourselves alone, but for the whole human race."

A nation that has counted as a special force in history must strive to count again or reap the fruits of demoralization. Having once been great, we cannot endure to be mediocre. Like tens of millions of Americans, I live in grateful awareness of our past achievements. Like perhaps a few million less, I want to die—well, a half-century from now—knowing that we had gone on to even greater achievements. Above all, I want to die—and shouldn't all Americans?—suspecting that this country would be remembered and saluted down through the centuries for its services to "the whole human race."

How Far Do Higher Ideals Move the Materialistic American?

Professor Rossiter fears that the people of the United States are but poorly prepared for the great challenge that confronts them. The mediocrity that pervades their lives offers shaky ground for greatness; and their bad taste on a massive scale has come close to producing a crisis in their culture.

Professor Rossiter's comments touch upon a theme frequently reiterated in discussions of American culture. He thereby raises a series of important questions: are the lack of respect for the artist and the intellectual and the poor taste so frequently displayed in this country the necessary concomitants of a democratic culture?

These questions had already troubled Jefferson, who had attempted to justify his society on the grounds of its youth and newness (see above, page 152). But such pleas for time became ever less convincing as the nation grew in maturity. By the nineteenth century some troubled Americans were seriously wondering whether the sense of mission which drove their countrymen on toward material growth did not also lower their spiritual stature. Few were willing to admit, as some Europeans then charged, that the overwhelming concern with the abundance of goods tended to crush any impulse toward idealism or creativity in the arts. The judgment of such foreign observers as De Tocqueville that democracy and equality were themselves hostile to exceptional achievements ran counter to the most widely held convictions of the people of the United States. Yet it was hard to formulate an alternative explanation for the apparent poverty of American culture.

Perhaps, in their readiness to justify themselves, Americans too easily accepted the European view that culture was the expression of an orderly society led by an aristocracy. In the United States, where many men of many different origins mingled uneasily together, where society was constantly in transition, and where leadership was difficult to define, culture had another meaning. In the New World it expressed the ideas and emotions, not of fixed communities, but of masses of individuals who often lacked roots and were beset by numerous anxieties. Both the achievements and the deficiencies of American culture therefore must be measured by standards other than those of Europe.

The South Carolina historian David Ramsay (1749–1815) early gained an insight into this condition in his comments upon the cultural effects of the American Revolution. Noting the stimulating consequences of the liberation from European institutions, he expected a new and improved culture to flower as a result (1). These hopes continued high in the first half-century of the Republic. When Ralph Waldo Emerson (1803–82) delivered his address on The American Scholar in 1837 he still thought optimistically of the capacities for achievement of the free individual released from arbitrary external restraints (2).

Yet already by then there were signs that the culture of the common man was taking another, unanticipated form. The circus and the minstrel show were the most typical expressions of this period; and P. T. Barnum (1810–91), who successfully exploited these media, understood their relationship to the uneasiness and difficulties of American life, as he explained in the concluding pages of his autobiography (3).

In the latter part of the nineteenth century, there were still grounds for expecting that the Emersonian ideal would be achieved, although in a form appropriate to the particular conditions of American life. In a group of perceptive essays, the novelist W. D. Howells (1837–1920) examined the peculiar characteristics of American literature, in particular its relationship to the lives of the people which it mirrored and whom it served (4).

The whole problem became far more complex with the growing urbanization of American society toward the end of the century. The great cities became ever more important and offered a new context to the mass of individuals drawn into them. The internal migrants and the foreign-born immigrants remained isolated either as individuals or in tight ethnic communities, and had peculiar needs that the old forms could not readily supply. The noted social worker Jane Addams

(1860–1935) observed some of these people in the cultural wilderness of Chicago and sympathetically explained their cultural dilemmas (5). W. E. B. DuBois, the Negro writer (1868–   ) set forth the special connection between the spirituals of the black folk who were his subjects and their depressed place in American society (6).

These rather extreme cases illustrated the general problem of culture in the United States. Millions of Americans, many of them housed in the teeming cities, many of them immigrants and the children of immigrants, many of them scarcely literate, were not likely to read the placid novels or the short stories of respectable literature. Their emotional needs were to be satisfied in other ways, which genteel critics were hardly willing to recognize as culture at all. Vaudeville, the music hall, the yellow press, the comic strip, and, later, the movies provided them with authentic expressions of attitudes toward the life around them. In a sparkling essay, the poet E. E. Cummings (1894–   ) explained the meaning and the wide appeal of a comic strip, Krazy Kat (7). And the critic Gilbert Seldes (1893–   ) described the work of the greatest movie-maker of them all, Charles Chaplin (8). Both analyses establish a correspondence between the needs and the desires of the audience and the creative artists who satisfied them. This was popular art in its most effective period.

In more recent times, the rise of the mass media has destroyed the connection between the audience and the artist. In the great gaps left as a result there is only the vulgarity of synthetic satisfactions. Lonely isolated men no longer have the opportunity to understand or express themselves through their culture.

They conform, for want of any better models, to common patterns generated by unsatisfied wants. The poet Robinson Jeffers (1887–   ) early reflected upon the resultant threat to national ideals (9). Later, James Laughlin's (1914–   ) bitter poem pointed to the irrelevant trivialities of much of the culture transmitted by the mass media (10). Finally the scathing last chapter of Nathaniel West's (1906–40) novel, reveals the aimless, empty quality of the lives of many Americans driven into a heedless search for excitement and thrills by the lack of meaningful personal and social goals (11).

These accounts are, perhaps, exaggerated in their emphasis on the negative aspects of contemporary American culture. They neglect promising indications of the potential for more positive trends. But they certainly expose the genuine danger that a society which values individuality and which still lacks a firm traditional basis may find it difficult to define its own or its members' purpose in life.

1. DAVID RAMSAY, *The Revolution and the Minds of the Citizens, 1789**

The American Revolution, on the one hand, brought forth great vices; but on the other hand, it called forth many virtues, and gave occasion for the display of abilities which, but for that event, would have been lost to the world. When the war began, the Americans were a mass of husbandmen, merchants, mechanics, and fishermen; but the necessities of the country gave a spring to the active powers of the inhabitants, and set them on thinking, speaking, and acting, in a line far beyond that to which they had been accustomed. . . . In the years 1775 and 1776 the country being suddenly thrown into a situation that needed the abilities of all its sons, these generally took their places, each according to the bent of his inclination. As they severally pursued their objects with ardor, a vast expansion of the human mind speedily followed. This displayed itself in a variety of ways. It was found that the talents for great stations did not differ in kind, but only in degree, from those which were necessary for the proper discharge of the ordinary business of civil society. In the bustle that was occasioned by the war, few instances could be produced of any persons who made a figure, or who rendered essential services, but from among those who had given specimens of similar talents in their respective professions. . . . The great bulk of those, who were the active instruments of carrying on the revolution, were self-made, industrious men. These who by their own exertions, had established or laid a foundation for establishing personal independence, were most generally trusted, and most successfully employed in establishing that of their country. In these times of ac-

tion, classical education was found of less service than good natural parts, guided by common sense and sound judgment. . . .

The Americans knew but little of one another, previous to the revolution. Trade and business had brought the inhabitants of their seaports acquainted with each other, but the bulk of the people in the interior country were unacquainted with their fellow citizens. A continental army, and Congress composed of men from all the States, by freely mixing together, were assimilated into one mass. Individuals of both, mingling with the citizens, disseminated principles of union among them. Local prejudices abated. By frequent collision asperities were worn off, and a foundation was laid for the establishment of a nation, out of discordant materials. Intermarriages between men and women of different States were much more common than before the war, and became an additional cement to the union. Unreasonable jealousies had existed between the inhabitants of the eastern and of the southern States; but on becoming better acquainted with each other, these in a great measure subsided. A wiser policy prevailed. Men of liberal minds led the way in discouraging local distinctions, and the great body of the people, as soon as reason got the better of prejudice, found that their best interests would be most effectually promoted by such practices and sentiments as were favourable to union. Religious bigotry had broken in upon the peace of various sects, before the American war. This was kept up by partial establishments, and by a dread that the church of England through the power of the mother country, would be

* David Ramsay, *History of the American Revolution* (Philadelphia, 1789), II, 315–24.

made to triumph over all other denominations. These apprehensions were done away by the revolution. The different sects, having nothing to fear from each other, dismissed all religious controversy. A proposal for introducing bishops into America before the war had kindled a flame among the dissenters; but the revolution was no sooner accomplished, than a scheme for that purpose was perfected, with the consent and approbation of all those sects who had previously opposed it. Pulpits which had formerly been shut to worthy men, because their heads had not been consecrated by the imposition of the hands of a Bishop or of a Presbytery, have since the establishment of independence, been reciprocally opened to each other, whensoever the public convenience required it. The world will soon see the result of an experiment in politics, and be able to determine whether the happiness of society is increased by religious establishments, or diminished by the want of them.

Though schools and colleges were generally shut up during the war, yet many of the arts and sciences were promoted by it. The Geography of the United States before the revolution was but little known; but the marches of armies, and the operations of war, gave birth to many geographical enquiries and discoveries, which otherwise would not have been made. A passionate fondness for studies of this kind, and the growing importance of the country, excited one of its sons, the Rev. Mr. Morse, to travel through every State of the Union, and amass a fund of topographical knowledge, far exceeding any thing heretofore communicated to the public. The necessities of the States led to the study of Tactics, Fortification, Gunnery, and a variety of other arts connected with war, and diffused a knowledge of them among a peaceable people, who would otherwise have had no inducement to study them.

The abilities of ingenious men were directed to make farther improvements in the art of destroying an enemy. Among these, David Bushnell of Connecticut invented a machine for submarine navigation, which was found to answer the purpose of rowing horizontally, at any given depth under water, and of rising or sinking at pleasure. To this was attached a magazine of powder, and the whole was contrived in such a manner, as to make it practicable to blow up vessels by machinery under them. Mr. Bushnell also contrived sundry other curious machines for the annoyance of British shipping; but from accident they only succeeded in part. He destroyed one vessel in charge of Commodore Symonds, and a second one near the shore of Long-Island.

Surgery was one of the arts which was promoted by the war. From the want of hospitals and other aids, the medical men of America, had few opportunities of perfecting themselves in this art, the thorough knowledge of which can only be acquired by practice and observation. The melancholy events of battles, gave the American students an opportunity of seeing, and learning more in one day, than they could have acquired in years of peace. It was in the hospitals of the United States, that Dr. Rush first discovered the method of curing the lock jaw by bark and wine, added to other invigorating remedies, which has since been adopted with success in Europe, as well as in the United States.

The science of government, has been more generally diffused among the Americans by means of the revolution. The policy of Great Britain, in throwing them out of her protection, induced a necessity of establishing independent constitutions. This led to reading and reasoning on the subject. The many errors that were at first committed by unexperienced statesmen, have been a practical comment on the folly of unbalanced constitutions, and injudicious laws. The discussions concerning the new constitution, gave birth to much reasoning on the subject of government, and particularly to a series of letters signed Publius, but really the work of Alexander Hamilton, in which much political knowledge and wisdom were displayed, and which will long remain a monument of the strength and acuteness of the human understanding in investigating truth.

When Great Britain first began her encroachments on the colonies, there were few natives of America who had distinguished themselves as speakers or writers, but the controversy between the two countries multiplied their number.

The stamp act, which was to have taken place in 1765, employed the pens and tongues of many of the colonists, and by repeated exercise improved their ability to serve their country. The duties imposed in 1767, called forth the pen of John Dickinson, who in a series of letters signed a Pennsylvania Farmer, may be said to have sown the seeds of the revolution. For being universally read by the colonists, they universally enlightened them on the dangerous consequences, likely to result from their being taxed by the parliament of Great Britain.

In establishing American independence, the pen and the press had merit equal to that of the sword. As the war was the people's war, and was carried on without funds, the exertions of the army would have been insufficient to effect the revolution, unless the great body of the people had been prepared for it, and also kept in a constant disposition to oppose Great Britain. To rouse and unite the inhabitants, and to persuade them to patience for several years, under present sufferings, with the hope of obtaining remote advantages for their posterity, was a work of difficulty. This was effected in a great measure by the tongues and pens of the

well informed citizens, and on it depended the success of military operations. . . .

The early attention which had been paid to literature in New-England, was also eminently conducive to the success of the Americans in resisting Great Britain. The university of Cambridge was founded as early as 1636, and Yale college in 1700. It has been computed, that in the year the Boston port act was passed, there were in the four eastern colonies, upwards of two thousand graduates of their colleges dispersed through their several towns, who by their knowledge and abilities, were able to influence and direct the great body of the people to a proper line of conduct, for opposing the encroachments of Great Britain on their liberties. The colleges to the southward of New-England, except that of William and Mary in Virginia, were but of modern date; but they had been of a standing sufficiently long, to have trained for public service, a considerable number of the youth of the country. The college of New-Jersey, which was incorporated about 28 years before the revolution, had in that time educated upwards of 300 persons, who, with a few exceptions, were active and useful friends of independence. From the influence which knowledge had in securing and preserving the liberties of America, the present generation may trace the wise policy of their fathers, in erecting schools and colleges. They may also learn that it is their duty to found more, and support all such institutions. Without the advantages derived from these lights of this new world, the United States would probably have fallen in their unequal contest with Great Britain. Union which was essential to the success of their resistance, could scarcely have taken place, in the measures adopted by an ignorant multitude. Much less could wisdom in council, unity in system, or perseverance in the prosecution of a long and self denying war, be expected from an uninformed people. It is a well known fact, that persons unfriendly to the revolution, were always most numerous in those parts of the United States, which had either never been illuminated, or but faintly warmed by the rays of science. The uninformed and the misinformed constituted a great proportion of those Americans, who preferred the leading strings of the Parent State, though encroaching on their liberties, to a government of their own countrymen and fellow citizens.

As literature had in the first instance favoured the revolution, so in its turn, the revolution promoted literature. The study of eloquence and of the Belles Lettres, was more successfully prosecuted in America, after the disputes between Great Britain and her colonies began to be serious, than it ever had been before. The various orations, addresses, letters, dissertations, and other literary performances which the war made necessary, called forth abilities where they were, and excited the rising generation to study arts, which brought with them their own reward. Many incidents afforded materials for the favourites of the muses, to display their talents. Even burlesquing royal proclamations by parodies and doggerel poetry, had great effects on the minds of the people. A celebrated historian has remarked, that the song of Lillibullero forwarded the revolution of 1688 in England. It may be truly affirmed, that similar productions produced similar effects in America. Francis Hopkinson rendered essential service to his country by turning the artillery of wit and ridicule on the enemy. Philip Freneau laboured successfully in the same way. Royal proclamations and other productions which issued from royal printing presses were by the help of a warm imagination, arrayed in such dresses as rendered them truly ridiculous. Trumbull with a vein of original

Hudibrastic humour, diverted his countrymen so much with the follies of their enemies, that for a time they forgot the calamities of war. Humphries twined the literary with the military laurel, by superadding the fame of an elegant poet, to that of an accomplished officer. Barlow increased the fame of his country and of the distinguished actors in the revolution, by the bold design of an epic poem ably executed, on the idea that Columbus foresaw in vision, the scenes that were to be transacted on the theatre of the new world, which he had discovered. Dwight struck out in the same line, and at an early period of life finished, an elegant work entitled the conquest of Canaan, on a plan which has rarely been attempted. The principles of their mother tongue, were first unfolded to the Americans since the revolution, by their countryman Webster. Pursuing an unbeaten track, he has made discoveries in the genius and construction of the English language, which had escaped the researches of preceding philologists. These and a group of other literary characters have been brought into view by the revolution. It is remarkable, that of these, Connecticut has produced an unusual proportion. In that truly republican state, every thing conspires to adorn human nature with its highest honours.

From the later periods of the revolution till the present time, schools, colleges, societies and institutions for promoting literature, arts, manufactures, agriculture, and for extending human happiness, have been increased far beyond anything that ever took place before the declaration of independence. Every state in the union, has done more or less in this way, but Pennsylvania has done the most. The following institutions have been very lately founded in that state, and most of them in the time of the war or since the peace. An university in the city of Philadelphia; a college of physicians in the same place;

Dickinson college at Carlisle; Franklin college at Lancaster; the Protestant Episcopal academy in Philadelphia; academies at York-town, at Germantown, at Pittsburgh and Washington; and an academy in Philadelphia for young ladies; societies for promoting political enquiries; for the medical relief of the poor, under the title of the Philadelphia Dispensary; for the promoting the abolition of slavery, and the relief of free negroes unlawfully held in bondage; for propagating the gospel among the Indians, under the direction of the United Brethren; for the encouragement of manufactures and the useful arts; for alleviating the miseries of prisons. Such have been some of the beneficial effects, which have resulted from that expansion of the human mind, which has been produced by the revolution.

2. RALPH WALDO EMERSON, *The American Scholar, 1837**

The office of the scholar is to cheer, to raise, and to guide men by showing them facts amidst appearances. He plies the slow, unhonored, and unpaid task of observation. Flamsteed and Herschel, in their glazed observatories, may catalogue the stars with the praise of all men, and, the results being splendid and useful, honor is sure. But he, in his private observatory, cataloguing obscure and nebulous stars of the human mind, which as yet no man has thought of as such,—watching days and months sometimes for a few facts; correcting still his old records,—must relinquish display and immediate fame. In the long period of his preparation he must betray often an ignorance and shiftlessness in popular arts, incurring the disdain of the able who shoulder him aside. Long he must stammer in his speech; often forgo the living for the dead. Worse yet, he must accept—how often!—poverty and solitude. For the ease and pleasure of treading the old road, accepting the fashions, the education, the religion of society, he takes the cross of making his own, and, of course, the self-accusation, the faint heart, the frequent uncertainty and loss of time, which are the nettles and tangling vines in the way of the self-relying and self-directed; and the state of virtual hostility in which he seems to stand to society, and especially to educated society. For all this loss and scorn, what offset? He is to find consolation in exercising the highest functions of human nature. He is one who raises himself from private considerations, and breathes and lives on public and illustrious thoughts. He is the world's eye. He is the world's heart. He is to resist the vulgar prosperity that retrogrades ever to barbarism, by preserving and communicating heroic sentiments, noble biographies, melodious verse, and the conclusions of history. Whatsoever oracles the human heart, in all emergencies, in all solemn hours, has uttered as its commentary on the world of actions,—these he shall receive and impart. And whatsoever new verdict Reason from her inviolable seat pronounces on the passing men and events of to-day,—this he shall hear and promulgate.

These being his functions, it becomes him to feel all confidence in himself, and to defer never to the popular cry.

* Ralph Waldo Emerson, "The American Scholar." Oration before the Phi Beta Kappa Society, Cambridge, August 31, 1837; *Works* (Boston, 1883), I, 101–15.

He and he only knows the world. The world of any moment is the merest appearance. Some great decorum, some fetish of a government, some ephemeral trade, or war, or man, is cried up by half mankind and cried down by the other half, as if all depended on this particular up or down. The odds are that the whole question is not worth the poorest thought which the scholar has lost in listening to the controversy. Let him not quit his belief that a popgun is a popgun, though the ancient and honorable of the earth affirm it to be the crack of doom. In silence, in steadiness, in severe abstraction, let him hold by himself; add observation to observation, patient of neglect, patient of reproach, and bide his own time,— happy enough if he can satisfy himself alone that this day he has seen something truly. Success treads on every right step. For the instinct is sure, that prompts him to tell his brother what he thinks. He then learns that in going down into the secrets of his own mind he has descended into the secrets of all minds. He learns that he who has mastered any law in his private thoughts, is master to that extent of all men whose language he speaks, and of all into whose language his own can be translated. The poet, in utter solitude remembering his spontaneous thoughts and recording them, is found to have recorded that which men in crowded cities find true for them also. The orator distrusts at first the fitness of his frank confessions, his want of knowledge of the person he addresses, until he finds that he is the complement of his hearers; that they drink his words because he fulfils for them their own nature; the deeper he dives into his privatest, secretest presentiment, to his wonder he finds this is the most acceptable, most public, and universally true. The people delight in it; the better part of every man feels, This is my music; this is myself.

In self-trust all the virtues are comprehended. Free should the scholar be, —free and brave. Free even to the definition of freedom, "without any hindrance that does not arise out of his own constitution." Brave; for fear is a thing which a scholar by his very function puts behind him. Fear always springs from ignorance. It is a shame to him if his tranquillity, amid dangerous times, arise from the presumption that, like children and women, his is a protected class; or if he seek a temporary peace by the diversion of his thoughts from politics or vexed questions, hiding his head like an ostrich in the flowering bushes, peeping into microscopes, and turning rhymes, as a boy whistles to keep his courage up. So is the danger a danger still; so is the fear worse. Manlike let him turn and face it. Let him look into its eye and search its nature, inspect its origin,—see the whelping of this lion,—which lies no great way back; he will then find in himself a perfect comprehension of its nature and extent; he will have made his hands meet on the other side, and can henceforth defy it, and pass on superior. The world is his who can see through its pretension. What deafness, what stone-blind custom, what overgrown error you behold is there only by sufferance,—by your sufferance. See it to be a lie, and you have already dealt it its mortal blow. . . .

Men are become of no account. Men in history, men in the world of to-day are bugs, are spawn, and are called "the mass" and "the herd." In a century, in a millennium, one or two men; that is to say, one or two approximations to the right state of every man. All the rest behold in the hero or the poet their own green and crude being,—ripened; yes, and are content to be less, so *that* may attain to its full stature. What a testimony, full of grandeur, full of pity, is borne to the demands of his own nature, by the poor clansman, the poor partisan, who rejoices in the glory of his chief. The poor and the low find some amends to their immense moral capacity, for their acquiescence in a political and social inferiority. They are content to be brushed like flies from the path of a great person, so that justice shall be done by him to that common nature which it is the dearest desire of all to see enlarged and glorified. They sun themselves in the great man's light, and feel it to be their own element. They cast the dignity of man from their downtrod selves upon the shoulders of a hero, and will perish to add one drop of blood to make that great heart beat, those giant sinews combat and conquer. He lives for us, and we live in him.

Men such as they are, very naturally seek money or power; and power because it is as good as money,—the "spoils," so called, "of office." And why not? for they aspire to the highest, and this, in their sleep-walking, they dream is highest. Wake them, and they shall quit the false good, and leap to the true, and leave governments to clerks and desks. This revolution is to be wrought by the gradual domestication of the idea of Culture. The main enterprise of the world for splendor, for extent, is the upbuilding of a man. Here are the materials strewn along the ground. The private life of one man shall be a more illustrious monarchy, more formidable to its enemy, more sweet and serene in its influence to its friend, than any kingdom in history. For a man, rightly viewed, comprehendeth the particular natures of all men. Each philosopher, each bard, each actor has only done for me, as by a delegate, what one day I can do for myself. The books which once we valued more than the apple of the eye, we have quite exhausted. What is that but saying that we have come up with the point of view which the universal mind took through the eyes of one scribe; we

have been that man, and have passed on. First, one; then another; we drain all cisterns, and, waxing greater by all these supplies, we crave a better and more abundant food. The man has never lived that can feed us ever. The human mind cannot be enshrined in a person who shall set a barrier on any one side to this unbounded, unboundable empire. It is one central fire, which, flaming now out of the lips of Etna, lightens the capes of Sicily, and now out of the throat of Vesuvius, illuminates the towers and vineyards of Naples. It is one light which beams out of a thousand stars. It is one soul which animates all men.

But I have dwelt perhaps tediously upon this abstraction of the Scholar. I ought not to delay longer to add what I have to say of nearer reference to the time and to this country.

Historically, there is thought to be a difference in the ideas which predominate over successive epochs, and there are data for marking the genius of the Classic, of the Romantic, and now of the Reflective or Philosophical age. With the views I have intimated of the oneness or the identity of the mind through all individuals, I do not much dwell on these differences. In fact, I believe each individual passes through all three. The boy is a Greek; the youth, romantic; the adult, reflective. I deny not, however, that a revolution in the leading idea may be distinctly enough traced.

Our age is bewailed as the age of Introversion. Must that needs be evil? We, it seems, are critical; we are embarrassed with second thoughts; we cannot enjoy any thing for hankering to know whereof the pleasure consists; we are lined with eyes; we see with our feet; the time is infected with Hamlet's unhappiness,—

"Sicklied o'er with the pale cast of thought."

It is so bad then? Sight is the last thing to be pitied. Would we be blind? Do we fear lest we should outsee nature and God, and drink truth dry? I look upon the discontent of the literary class as a mere announcement of the fact that they find themselves not in the state of mind of their fathers, and regret the coming state as untried; as a boy dreads the water before he has learned that he can swim. If there is any period one would desire to be born in, is it not the age of Revolution; when the old and the new stand side by side and admit of being compared; when the energies of all men are searched by fear and by hope; when the historic glories of the old can be compensated by the rich possibilities of the new era? This time, like all times, is a very good one, if we but know what to do with it.

I read with some joy of the auspicious signs of the coming days, as they glimmer already through poetry and art, through philosophy and science, through church and state.

One of these signs is the fact that the same movement which effected the elevation of what was called the lowest class in the state, assumed in literature a very marked and as benign an aspect. Instead of the sublime and beautiful, the near, the low, the common, was explored and poetized. That which had been negligently trodden under foot by those who were harnessing and provisioning themselves for long journeys into far countries, is suddenly found to be richer than all foreign parts. The literature of the poor, the feelings of the child, the philosophy of the street, the meaning of household life, are the topics of the time. It is a great stride. It is a sign—is it not?—of new vigor when the extremities are made active, when currents of warm life run into the hands and the feet. I ask not for the great, the remote, the romantic; what is doing in Italy or Arabia; what is Greek art, or Provençal minstrelsy; I embrace the common, I explore and sit at the feet of the familiar, the low. Give me insight into to-day, and you may have the antique and future worlds. What would we really know the meaning of? The meal in the firkin; the milk in the pan; the ballad in the street; the news of the boat; the glance of the eye; the form and the gait of the body;—show me the ultimate reason of these matters; show me the sublime presence of the highest spiritual cause lurking, as always it does lurk, in these suburbs and extremities of nature; let me see every trifle bristling with the polarity that ranges it instantly on an eternal law; and the shop, the plough, and the ledger referred to the like cause by which light undulates and poets sing;—and the world lies no longer a dull miscellany and lumber-room, but has form and order; there is no trifle, there is no puzzle, but one design unites and animates the farthest pinnacle and the lowest trench.

This idea has inspired the genius of Goldsmith, Burns, Cowper, and, in a newer time, of Goethe, Wordsworth, and Carlyle. This idea they have differently followed and with various success. In contrast with their writing, the style of Pope, of Johnson, of Gibbon, looks cold and pedantic. This writing is blood-warm. Man is surprised to find that things near are not less beautiful and wondrous than things remote. The near explains the far. The drop is a small ocean. A man is related to all nature. This perception of the worth of the vulgar is fruitful in discoveries. Goethe, in this very thing the most modern of the moderns, has shown us, as none ever did, the genius of the ancients. . . .

Another sign of our times, also marked by an analogous political movement, is the new importance given to the single person. Every thing that tends to insulate the individual,—to surround him with barriers of natural respect, so that each man shall feel the world is his, and man shall treat with man as a sovereign state with a sovereign state, —tends to true union as well as greatness. "I learned," said the melancholy Pestalozzi, "that no man in God's wide earth is either willing or able to help any other man." Help must come from the bosom alone. The scholar is that man who must take up into himself all the ability of the time, all the contributions of the past, all the hopes of the future. He must be an university of knowledges. If there be one lesson more than another which should pierce his ear, it is: The world is nothing, the man is all; in yourself is the law of all nature, and you know not yet how a globule of sap ascends; in yourself slumbers the whole of Reason; it is for you to know all; it is for you to dare all. Mr. President and Gentlemen, this confidence in the unsearched might of man belongs, by all motives, by all prophecy, by all preparation, to the American Scholar. We have listened too long to the courtly muses of Europe. The spirit of the American freeman is already suspected to be timid, imitative, tame. Public and private avarice make the air we breathe thick and fat. The scholar is decent, indolent, complaisant. See already the tragic consequence. The mind of this country, taught to aim at low objects, eats upon itself. There is no work for any but the decorous and the complaisant. Young men of the fairest promise, who begin life upon our shores, inflated by the mountain winds, shined upon by all the stars of God, find the earth

below not in unison with these, but are hindered from action by the disgust which the principles on which business is managed inspire, and turn drudges, or die of disgust, some of them suicides. What is the remedy? They did not yet see, and thousands of young men as hopeful now crowding to the barriers for the career do not yet see, that if the single man plant himself indomitably on his instincts, and there abide, the huge world will come round to him. Patience,—patience; with the shades of all the good and great for company; and for solace the perspective of your own infinite life; and for work the study and the communication of principles, the making those instincts prevalent, the conversion of the world. Is it not the chief disgrace in the world, not to be an unit;—not to be reckoned one character;—not to yield that peculiar fruit which each man was created to bear, but to be reckoned in the gross, in the hundred, or the thousand, of the party, the section, to which we belong; and our opinion predicted geographically, as the north, or the south? Not so, brothers and friends,—please God, ours shall not be so. We will walk on our own feet; we will work with our own hands; we will speak our own minds. The study of letters shall be no longer a name for pity, for doubt, and for sensual indulgence. The dread of man and the love of man shall be a wall of defence and a wreath of joy around all. A nation of men will for the first time exist, because each believes himself inspired by the Divine Soul which also inspires all men.

3. P. T. Barnum, *Art and Happiness, 1855**

The great defect in our American civilization, it is generally acknowledged by observing and thoughtful men, is a severe and drudging practicalness—a practicalness which is not commendable, because it loses sight of the true aims of life, and concentrates itself upon dry and technical ideas of duty, and upon a sordid love of acquisition—leaving entirely out of view all those needful and proper relaxations and enjoyments which are interwoven through even the most humble conditions in other countries. If in the Catholic states of Europe there are too many holidays, with us the fault is on the other side: we have none at all. The consequence is, that with the most universal diffusion of the means of happiness ever known among any people, we are unhappy. Without ideality, "a primrose by the river's brim" does not arrest the attention of the American; the flower "a simple primrose is to him, and it is nothing more."

With their traditions and habits, our countrymen, of the middling classes, inherit in too great a degree a capacity only for the most valueless and irrational enjoyments, and their inclination to intemperance and kindred vices has repeatedly and most conclusively been shown to be a natural result of the lamentable deficiency among us of innocent and rational amusements. I am not going to set up as a philosopher, but the venerable and illustrious name of CHANNING—eminent alike for wisdom, benevolence, piety, and purity, for a private and public character unsurpassed in its elevation—may be adduced as earnestly and unqualifiedly supporting these views; and no higher authority, I conceive, has ever existed in this country upon morals and so-

ciety, and especially upon the difficult subject which he illustrated so admirably in the noblest production of his genius, the essay "On the Elevation of the Laboring Portion of the Community."

As a business man, undoubtedly, my prime object has been to put money in my purse. I succeeded beyond my most sanguine anticipations, and am satisfied. But what I have here said, will prepare the reader for what I conceive to be a just and altogether reasonable claim, that I have been a public benefactor, to an extent seldom paralleled in the histories of professed and professional philanthropists.

My travelling museums of natural history have been the largest and most interesting ever exhibited in the United States, and no author, or university even, has ever accomplished as much in the diffusion of a knowledge of the varied forms and classes of animal life. These, with my museums in New-York, Philadelphia, and Baltimore, have been one of the chief means by which I have instructed the masses.

For the elevation and refinement of musical taste in this country, it will not be denied that I have done more than any man living. By bringing Jenny Lind to the United States, I inaugurated a new era in the most beautiful and humanizing of all the fine arts, and gave to the cultivated and wealthy as well as to the middling classes a larger measure of enjoyment than has ever been derived from the enterprise of any other single individual.

I will not enter into a further recapitulation of the benefits I have conferred on my countrymen and

* P. T. Barnum, *The Life of P. T. Barnum* (New York, 1855), pp. 339–401.

countrywomen, as a minister to their instruction and happiness, while pursuing my main purpose of making money. The charges with which my claims in this respect will be met, are, simply, that I have *managed,* while my vocation has been that of a manager. It is granted. I have advertised my curiosities and my artists with all the ingenuity of which I was capable. My interests demanded that course, and it was my business to consult my interests in all legitimate ways. No one, however, for himself, can say that he ever paid for admission to one of my exhibitions more than his admission was worth to him. If a sight of my "Niagara Falls" was not worth twenty-five cents, the privilege of seeing the most extensive and valuable museum on this continent was worth double that sum to any one who was enticed into it by the advertisements of that ingenious contrivance. And I should like to see the moralist or the Christian who thinks my patron would have done as well with his money at the drinking den of any of the alternative places of buying entertainment.

4. W. D. HOWELLS, *American Ideals in Literature, 1891**

American novels generally . . . in their range and tendency . . . are admirable. I will not say they are all good, or that any of them is wholly good; but I find in nearly every one of them a disposition to regard our life without literary glasses so long thought desirable, and to see character, not as it is in other fiction, but as it abounds outside of all fiction. This disposition sometimes goes with poor enough performance, but in some of our novels it goes with performance that is excellent; and at any rate it is for the present more valuable than evenness of performance. It is what relates American fiction to the only living movement in imaginative literature, and distinguishes by a superior freshness and authenticity any group of American novels from a similarly accidental group of English novels, giving them the same good right to be as the like number of recent Russian novels, French novels, Spanish novels, Italian novels, Norwegian novels.

It is the difference of the American novelist's ideals from those of the English novelist that gives him his advantages, and seems to promise him the future. The love of the passionate and the heroic, as the Englishman has it, is such a crude and unwholesome thing, so deaf and blind to all the most delicate and important facts of art and life, so insensible to the subtle values in either that its presence or absence makes the whole difference, and enables one who is not obsessed by it to thank Heaven that he is not as that other man is.

There can be little question that many refinements of thought and spirit which every American is sensible of in the fiction of this continent, are necessarily lost upon our good kin beyond the seas, whose thumb-fingered apprehension requires something gross and palpable for its assurance of reality. This is not their fault, and I am not sure that it is wholly their misfortune: they are made so as not to miss what they do not find, and they are simply content without those subtleties of

** W. D. Howells, *Criticism and Fiction* (New York, 1891), pp. 123–40.*

life and character which it gives us so keen a pleasure to have noted in literature. If they perceive them at all it is as something vague and diaphanous, something that filmily wavers before their sense and teases them, much as the beings of an invisible world might mock one of our material frame by intimations of their presence. It is with reason, therefore, on the part of an Englishman, that Mr. Henley complains of our fiction as a shadow-land, though we find more and more in it the faithful report of our life, its motives and emotions, and all the comparatively etherealized passions and ideals that influence it.

In fact, the American who chooses to enjoy his birthright to the full, lives in a world wholly different from the Englishman's, and speaks (too often through his nose) another language: he breathes a rarefied and nimble air full of shining possibilities and radiant promises which the fog-and-soot-clogged lungs of those less-favored islanders struggle in vain to fill themselves with. But he ought to be modest in his advantage, and patient with the coughing and sputtering of his cousin who complains of finding himself in an exhausted receiver on plunging into one of our novels. To be quite just to the poor fellow, I have had some such experience as that myself in the atmosphere of some of our more attenuated romances.

Yet every now and then I read a book with perfect comfort and much exhilaration, whose scenes the average Englishman would gasp in. Nothing happens; that is, nobody murders or debauches anybody else; there is no arson or pillage of any sort; there is not a ghost, or a ravening beast, or a hair-breadth escape, or a shipwreck, or a monster of self-sacrifice, or a lady five thousand years old in the whole course of the story; "no promenade, no band of music, nossing!" as Mr. Du

Maurier's Frenchman said of the meet for a fox-hunt. Yet it is all alive with the keenest interest for those who enjoy the study of individual traits and general conditions as they make themselves known to American experience.

These conditions have been so favorable hitherto (though they are becoming always less so) that they easily account for the optimistic faith of our novel . . . . It used to be one of the disadvantages of the practice of romance in America, which Hawthorne more or less whimsically lamented, that there were so few shadows and inequalities in our broad level of prosperity; and it is one of the reflections suggested by Dostoïevsky's novel, The Crime and the Punishment, that whoever struck a note so profoundly tragic in American fiction would do a false and mistaken thing—as false and as mistaken in its way as dealing in American fiction with certain nudities which the Latin peoples seem to find edifying. Whatever their deserts, very few American novelists have been led out to be shot, or finally exiled to the rigors of a winter at Duluth; and in a land where journeymen carpenters and plumbers strike for four dollars a day the sum of hunger and cold is comparatively small, and the wrong from class to class has been almost inappreciable, though all this is changing for the worse. Our novelists, therefore, concern themselves with the more smiling aspects of life, which are the more American, and seek the universal in the individual rather than the social interests. It is worth while, even at the risk of being called commonplace, to be true to our well-to-do actualities; the very passions themselves seem to be softened and modified by conditions which formerly at least could not be said to wrong any one, to cramp endeavor, or to cross lawful desire. Sin and suffering and shame there must always be in the world, I suppose, but I believe that in this new world of ours it is still mainly from one to another one, and oftener still from one to one's self. We have death too in America, and a great deal of disagreeable and painful disease, which the multiplicity of our patent medicines does not seem to cure; but this is tragedy that comes in the very nature of things, and is not peculiarly American, as the large, cheerful average of health and success and happy life is. It will not do to boast, but it is well to be true to the facts, and to see that, apart from these purely mortal troubles, the race here has enjoyed conditions in which most of the ills that have darkened its annals might be averted by honest work and unselfish behavior.

Fine artists we have among us, and right-minded as far as they go; and we must not forget this at evil moments when it seems as if all the women had taken to writing hysterical improprieties, and some of the men were trying to be at least as hysterical in despair of being as improper. If we kept to the complexion of a certain school—which sadly needs a schoolmaster—we might very well be despondent; but, after all, that school is not representative of our conditions or our intentions. Other traits are much more characteristic of our life and our fiction. In most American novels, vivid and graphic as the best of them are, the people are segregated if not sequestered, and the scene is sparsely populated. The effect may be in instinctive response to the vacancy of our social life, and I shall not make haste to blame it. There are few places, few occasions among us, in which a novelist can get a large number of polite people together, or at least keep them together. Unless he carries a snap-camera his picture of them has no probability; they affect one like the figures perfunctorily associated in such deadly old engravings as that of "Washington Irving and his Friends." Perhaps it is for this reason that we excel in small pieces with three or four figures, or in studies of rustic communities, where there is propinquity if not society. Our grasp of more urbane life is feeble; most attempts to assemble it in our pictures are failures, possibly because it is too transitory, too intangible in its nature with us, to be truthfully represented as really existent.

I am not sure that the Americans have not brought the short story nearer perfection in the all-round sense than almost any other people, and for reasons very simple and near at hand. It might be argued from the national hurry and impatience that it was a literary form peculiarly adapted to the American temperament, but I suspect that its extraordinary development among us is owing much more to more tangible facts. The success of American magazines, which is nothing less than prodigious, is only commensurate with their excellence. Their sort of success is not only from the courage to decide what ought to please, but from the knowledge of what does please; and it is probable that, aside from the pictures, it is the short stories which please the readers of our best magazines. The serial novels they must have, of course; but rather more of course they must have short stories, and by operation of the law of supply and demand, the short stories, abundant in quantity and excellent in quality, are forthcoming because they are wanted. By another operation of the same law, which political economists have more recently taken account of, the demand follows the supply, and short stories are sought for because there is a proven ability to furnish them, and people read them willingly because they are usually very good. The art of writing them is now so disciplined and diffused with us that there is no lack either for the magazines or for the newspaper "syndicates" which deal in them almost to the exclusion of the serials. In other countries the *feuilleton* of the journals is a novel continued from day to day, but with us the papers, whether daily or weekly, now more rarely print novels, whether they get them at first hand from the writers, as a great many do, or through the syndicates, which purvey a vast variety of literary wares, chiefly for the Sunday editions of the city journals. In the country papers the short story takes the place of the chapters of a serial which used to be given.

An interesting fact in regard to the different varieties of the short story among us is that the sketches and studies by the women seem faithfuler and more realistic than those of the men, in proportion to their number. Their tendency is more distinctly in that direction, and there is a solidity, an honest observation, in the work of such women as Mrs. Cooke, Miss Murfree, Miss Wilkins, and Miss Jewett, which often leaves little to be desired. I should, upon the whole, be disposed to rank American short stories only below those of such Russian writers as I have read, and I should praise rather than blame their free use of our different local parlances, or "dialects," as people call them. I like this because I hope that our inherited English may be constantly freshened and revived from the native sources which our literary decentralization will help to keep open, and I will own that as I turn over novels coming from Philadelphia, from New Mexico, from Boston, from Tennessee, from rural New England, from New York, every local flavor of diction gives me courage and pleasure. M. Alphonse Daudet, in a conversation which Mr. H. H.

Boyesen has set down in a recently recorded interview with him, said, in speaking of Tourguéneff: "What a luxury it must be to have a great big untrodden barbaric language to wade into! We poor fellows who work in the language of an old civilization, we may sit and chisel our little verbal felicities, only to find in the end that it is a borrowed jewel we are polishing. The crown jewels of our French tongue have passed through the hands of so many generations of monarchs that it seems like presumption on the part of any late-born pretender to attempt to wear them."

This grief is, of course, a little whimsical, yet it has a certain measure of reason in it, and the same regret has been more seriously expressed by the Italian poet Aleardi:

Muse of an aged people, in the eve
Of fading civilization, I was born.
. . . Oh, fortunate,
My sisters, who in the heroic dawn
Of races sung! To them did destiny
    give
The virgin fire and chaste
    ingenuousness
Of their land's speech; and,
    reverenced, their hands
Ran over potent strings.

It will never do to allow that we are at such a desperate pass in English, but something of this divine despair we may feel too in thinking of "the spacious times of great Elizabeth," when the poets were trying the stops of the young language, and thrilling with the surprises of their own music. We may comfort ourselves, however, unless we prefer a luxury of grief by remembering that no language is ever old on the lips of those who speak it, no matter how decrepit it drops from the pen. We have only to leave our studies, editorial and other, and go into the shops and fields to find the "spacious times" again; and from the beginning Realism, before she had put on her capital letter, had divined this near-at-hand truth along with the rest. Mr. Lowell, almost the greatest and finest realist who ever wrought in verse, showed us that Elizabeth was still Queen where he heard Yankee farmers talk. One need not invite slang into the company of its betters, though perhaps slang has been dropping its "s" and becoming language ever since the world began, and is certainly sometimes delightful and forcible beyond the reach of the dictionary. I would not have any one go about for new words, but if one of them came aptly, not to reject its help. For our novelists to try to write Americanly, from any motive, would be a dismal error, but being born Americans, I would have them use "Americanisms" whenever these serve their turn; and when their characters speak, I should like to hear them speak true American, with all the varying Tennessean, Philadelphian, Bostonian, and New York accents. If we bother ourselves to write what the critics imagine to be "English," we shall be priggish and artificial, and still more so if we make our Americans talk "English." There is also this serious disadvantage about "English," that if we wrote the best "English" in the world, probably the English themselves would not know it, or, if they did, certainly would not own it. It has always been supposed by grammarians and purists that a language can be kept as they find it; but languages, while they live, are perpetually changing. God apparently meant them for the common people—whom Lincoln believed God liked because he had made so many of them; and the common people will use them freely as they use other gifts of God. On their lips our continental English will differ more and more from the insular English, and I believe that this is not deplorable, but desirable.

In fine, I would have our American novelists be as American as they unconsciously can. Matthew Arnold complained that he found no "distinction" in our life, and I would gladly persuade all artists intending greatness in any kind among us that the recognition of the fact pointed out by Mr. Arnold ought to be a source of inspiration to them, and not discouragement. We have been now some hundred years building up a state on the affirmation of the essential equality of men in their rights and duties, and whether we have been right or been wrong the gods have taken us at our word, and have responded to us with a civilization in which there is no "distinction" perceptible to the eye that loves and values it. Such beauty and such grandeur as we have is common beauty, common grandeur, or the beauty and grandeur in which the quality of solidarity so prevails that neither distinguishes itself to the disadvantage of anything else. It seems to me that these conditions invite the artist to the study and the appreciation of the common, and to the portrayal in every art of those finer and higher aspects which unite rather than sever humanity, if he would thrive in our new order of things. The talent that is robust enough to front the every-day world and catch the charm of its work-worn, care-worn, brave, kindly face, need not fear the encounter, though it seems terrible to the sort nurtured in the superstition of the romantic, the bizarre, the heroic, the distinguished, as the things alone worthy of painting or carving or writing. The arts must become democratic, and then we shall have the expression of America in art; and the reproach which Mr. Arnold was half right in making us shall have no justice in it any longer; we shall be "distinguished."

5. JANE ADDAMS, *Youth in the City, 1909**

Nothing is more certain than that each generation longs for a reassurance as to the value and charm of life, and is secretly afraid lest it lose its sense of the youth of the earth. This is doubtless one reason why it so passionately cherishes its poets and artists who have been able to explore for themselves and to reveal to others the perpetual springs of life's self-renewal.

And yet the average man cannot obtain this desired reassurance through literature, nor yet through glimpses of earth and sky. It can come to him only through the chance embodiment of joy and youth which life itself may throw in his way. It is doubtless true that for the mass of men the message is never so unchallenged and so invincible as when embodied in youth itself. One generation after another has depended upon its young to equip it with gaiety and enthusiasm, to persuade it that living is a pleasure, until men everywhere have anxiously provided channels through which this wine of life might flow, and be preserved for their delight. The classical city promoted play with careful solicitude, building the theater and stadium as it built the market place and the temple. The Greeks held their games so integral a part of religion and patriotism that they came to expect from their poets the highest utterances at the very moments when the sense of pleasure released the national life. In the medieval city the knights held their tourneys, the guilds their pageants, the people their dances, and the church made festival for its most cherished saints with gay street processions, and presented a drama in which no less a theme than the history of creation became a matter of thrilling interest. Only in the modern city have

men concluded that it is no longer necessary for the municipality to provide for the insatiable desire for play. In so far as they have acted upon this conclusion, they have entered upon a most difficult and dangerous experiment; and this at the very moment when the city has become distinctly industrial, and daily labor is continually more monotonous and subdivided. We forget how new the modern city is, and how short the span of time in which we have assumed that we can eliminate public provision for recreation.

A further difficulty lies in the fact that this industrialism has gathered together multitudes of eager young creatures from all quarters of the earth as a labor supply for the countless factories and workshops, upon which the present industrial city is based. Never before in civilization have such numbers of young girls been suddenly released from the protection of the home and permitted to walk unattended upon city streets and to work under alien roofs; for the first time they are being prized more for their labor power than for their innocence, their tender beauty, their ephemeral gaiety. Society cares more for the products they manufacture than for their immemorial ability to reaffirm the charm of existence. Never before have such numbers of young boys earned money independently of the family life, and felt themselves free to spend it as they choose in the midst of vice deliberately disguised as pleasure.

This stupid experiment of organizing work and failing to organize play has, of course, brought about a fine revenge. The love of pleasure will not be denied, and when it has turned into all sorts of malignant and vicious appetites, then

* Jane Addams, *The Spirit of Youth* (New York: Macmillan Company, 1909), 3–21. Reprinted by permission of John A. Brittain.

we, the middle aged, grow quite distracted and resort to all sorts of restrictive measures. We even try to dam up the sweet fountain itself because we are affrighted by these neglected streams; but almost worse than the restrictive measures is our apparent belief that the city itself has no obligation in the matter, an assumption upon which the modern city turns over to commercialism practically all the provisions for public recreation.

Quite as one set of men has organized the young people into industrial enterprises in order to profit from their toil, so another set of men and also of women, I am sorry to say, have entered the neglected field of recreation and have organized enterprises which make profit out of this invincible love of pleasure.

In every city arise so-called "places" —"gin palaces," they are called in fiction; in Chicago we euphemistically say merely "places,"—in which alcohol is dispensed, not to allay thirst, but, ostensibly to stimulate gaiety, it is sold really in order to empty pockets. Huge dance halls are opened to which hundreds of young people are attracted, many of whom stand wistfully outside a roped circle, for it requires five cents to procure within it for five minutes the sense of allurement and intoxication which is sold in lieu of innocent pleasure. These coarse and illicit merrymakings remind one of the unrestrained jollities of Restoration London, and they are indeed their direct descendants, properly commercialized, still confusing joy with lust, and gaiety with debauchery. Since the soldiers of Cromwell shut up the people's playhouses and destroyed their pleasure fields, the Anglo-Saxon city has turned over the provision for public recreation to the most evil-minded and the most unscrupulous members of the community. We see thousands of girls walking up and down the streets on a pleasant evening with no chance to catch a sight of pleasure even through a lighted window, save as these lurid places provide it. Apparently the modern city sees in these girls only two possibilities, both of them commercial: first, a chance to utilize by day their new and tender labor power in its factories and shops, and then another chance in the evening to extract from them their petty wages by pandering to their love of pleasure.

As these overworked girls stream along the street, the rest of us see only the self-conscious walk, the giggling speech, the preposterous clothing. And yet through the huge hat, with its wilderness of bedraggled feathers, the girl announces to the world that she is here. She demands attention to the fact of her existence, she states that she is ready to live, to take her place in the world. The most precious moment in human development is the young creature's assertion that he is unlike any other human being, and has an individual contribution to make to the world. The variation from the established type is at the root of all change, the only possible basis for progress, all that keeps life from growing unprofitably stale and repetitious.

Is it only the artists who really see these young creatures as they are—the artists who are themselves endowed with immortal youth? Is it our disregard of the artist's message which makes us so blind and so stupid, or are we so under the influence of our *Zeitgeist* that we can detect only commercial values in the young as well as in the old? It is as if our eyes were holden to the mystic beauty, the redemptive joy, the civic pride which these multitudes of young people might supply to our dingy towns.

The young creatures themselves piteously look all about them in order to find an adequate means of expression for their most precious message: One day a serious young man came to Hull-

House with his pretty young sister who, he explained, wanted to go somewhere every single evening, "although she could only give the flimsy excuse that the flat was too little and too stuffy to stay in." In the difficult rôle of elder brother, he had done his best, stating that he had taken her "to all the missions in the neighborhood, that she had had a chance to listen to some awful good sermons and to some elegant hymns, but that some way she did not seem to care for the society of the best Christian people." The little sister reddened painfully under this cruel indictment and could offer no word of excuse, but a curious thing happened to me. Perhaps it was the phrase "the best Christian people," perhaps it was the delicate color of her flushing cheeks and her swimming eyes, but certain it is, that instantly and vividly there appeared to my mind the delicately tinted piece of wall in a Roman catacomb where the early Christians, through a dozen devices of spring flowers, skipping lambs and a shepherd tenderly guiding the young, had indelibly written down that the Christian message is one of inexpressible joy. Who is responsible for forgetting this message delivered by the "best Christian people" two thousand years ago? Who is to blame that the lambs, the little ewe lambs, have been so caught upon the brambles?

But quite as the modern city wastes this most valuable moment in the life of the girl, and drives into all sorts of absurd and obscure expressions her love and yearning towards the world in which she forecasts her destiny, so it often drives the boy into gambling and drinking in order to find his adventure.
. . .

One of the most pathetic sights in the public dance halls of Chicago is a number of young men, obviously honest young fellows from the country, who stand about vainly hoping to make the acquaintance of some "nice girl." They look eagerly up and down the rows of girls, many of whom are drawn to the hall by the same keen desire for pleasure and social intercourse which the lonely young men themselves feel.

One Sunday night at twelve o'clock I had occasion to go into a large public dance hall. As I was standing by the rail looking for the girl I had come to find, a young man approached me and quite simply asked me to introduce him to some "nice girl," saying that he did not know any one there. On my replying that a public dance hall was not the best place in which to look for a nice girl, he said: "But I don't know any other place where there is a chance to meet any kind of girl. I'm awfully lonesome since I came to Chicago." And then he added rather defiantly: "Some nice girls do come here! It's one of the best halls in town." He was voicing the "bitter loneliness" that many city men remember to have experienced during the first years after they had "come up to town." Occasionally the right sort of man and girl meet each other in these dance halls and the romance with such a tawdry beginning ends happily and respectably. But, unfortunately, mingled with the respectable young men seeking to form the acquaintance of young women through the only channel which is available to them, are many young fellows of evil purpose, and among the girls who have left their lonely boarding houses or rigid homes for a "little fling" are likewise women who openly desire to make money from the young men whom they meet, and back of it all is the desire to profit by the sale of intoxicating and "doctored" drinks.

Perhaps never before have pleasures of the young and mature become so definitely separated as in the modern city. The public dance halls filled with frivolous and irresponsible young people in a feverish search for pleasure, are but a sorry substitute for the old dances on the village green in which all of the older people of the village participated. Chaperonage was not then a social duty but natural and inevitable, the whole courtship period was guarded by the conventions and restraint which were taken as a matter of course and had developed through years of publicity and simple propriety.

The only marvel is that the stupid attempt to put the fine old wine of traditional country life into the new bottles of the modern town does not lead to disaster oftener than it does, and that the wine so long remains pure and sparkling.

We cannot afford to be ungenerous to the city in which we live without suffering the penalty which lack of fair interpretation always entails. Let us know the modern city in its weakness and wickedness, and then seek to rectify and purify it until it shall be free at least from the grosser temptations which now beset the young people who are living in its tenement houses and working in its factories. The mass of these young people are possessed of good intentions and they are equipped with a certain understanding of city life. This itself could be made a most valuable social instrument toward securing innocent recreation and better social organization. They are already serving the city in so far as it is honeycombed with mutual benefit societies, with "pleasure clubs," with organizations connected with churches and factories which are filling a genuine social need. And yet the whole apparatus for supplying pleasure is wretchedly inadequate and full of danger to whomsoever may approach it. Who is responsible for its inadequacy and dangers? We certainly cannot expect the fathers and mothers who have come to the city from farms or who have emigrated from other lands to appreciate or rectify these dangers. We cannot expect the young people themselves to cling to conventions which are totally unsuited to modern city conditions, nor yet to be equal to the task of forming new conventions through which this more agglomerate social life may express itself. Above all we cannot hope that they will understand the emotional force which seizes them and which, when it does not find the traditional line of domesticity, serves as a cancer in the very tissues of society and as a disrupter of the securest social bonds. No attempt is made to treat the manifestations of this fundamental instinct with dignity or to give it possible social utility. The spontaneous joy, the clamor for pleasure, the desire of the young people to appear finer and better and altogether more lovely than they really are, the idealization not only of each other but of the whole earth which they regard but as a theater for their noble exploits, the unworldly ambitions, the romantic hopes, the make-believe world in which they live, if properly utilized, what might they not do to make our sordid cities more beautiful, more companionable? And yet at the present moment every city is full of young people who are utterly bewildered and uninstructed in regard to the basic experience which must inevitably come to them, and which has varied, remote, and indirect expressions.

Even those who may not agree with the authorities who claim that it is this fundamental sex susceptibility which suffuses the world with its deepest meaning and beauty, and furnishes the momentum towards all art, will perhaps permit me to quote the classical expressions of this view as set forth in that ancient and wonderful conversation between Socrates and the wise woman Diotima. Socrates asks: "What are they doing who show all this eagerness and heat which is called love? And what is the object they have in view? Answer me." Diotima replies: "I will teach you. The object which they have in view is birth in beauty, whether of body or soul. . . . For love, Socrates, is not as you imagine the love of the beautiful only . . . but the love of birth in beauty, because to the mortal creature generation is a sort of eternity and immortality."

To emphasize the eternal aspects of love is not of course an easy undertaking, even if we follow the clue afforded by the heart of every generous lover. His experience at least in certain moments tends to pull him on and out from the passion for one to an enthusiasm for that highest beauty and excellence of which the most perfect form is but an inadequate expression. Even the most loutish tenement-house youth vaguely feels this, and at least at rare intervals reveals it in his talk to his "girl." His memory unexpectedly brings hidden treasures to the surface of consciousness and he recalls the more delicate and tender experiences of his childhood and earlier youth. "I remember the time when my little sister died, that I rode out to the cemetery feeling that everybody in Chicago had moved away from the town to make room for that kid's funeral, everything was so darned lonesome and yet it was kind of peaceful too." Or, "I never had a chance to go into the country when I was a kid, but I remember one day when I had to deliver a package way out on the West Side, that I saw a flock of sheep in Douglas Park. I had never thought that a sheep could be anywhere but in a picture, and when I saw those big white spots on the green grass beginning to move and to turn into sheep, I felt exactly as if Saint Cecilia had come out of her frame over the organ and was walking in the park." Such moments come into the life of the most prosaic youth living in the most crowded quarters of the cities. What do we do to encourage and to solidify those moments, to make them come true in our dingy towns, to give them expression in forms of art?

We not only fail in this undertaking but even debase existing forms of art. We are informed by high authority that there is nothing in the environment to which youth so keenly responds as to music, and yet the streets, the vaudeville shows, the five-cent theaters are full of the most blatant and vulgar songs. The trivial and obscene words, the meaningless and flippant airs run through the heads of hundreds of young people for hours at a time while they are engaged in monotonous factory work. We totally ignore that ancient connection between music and morals which was so long insisted upon by philosophers as well as poets. The street music has quite broken away from all control, both of the educator and the patriot, and we have grown singularly careless in regard to its influence upon young people. Although we legislate against it in saloons because of its dangerous influence there, we constantly permit music on the street to incite that which should be controlled, to degrade that which should be exalted, to make sensuous that which might be lifted into the realm of the higher imagination.

Our attitude towards music is typical of our carelessness towards all those things which make for common joy and for the restraints of higher civilization on the streets. It is as if our cities had not yet developed a sense of responsibility in regard to the life of the streets, and continually forget that recreation is stronger than vice, and that recreation alone can stifle the lust for vice.

Perhaps we need to take a page from the philosophy of the Greeks to whom the world of fact was also the world of the ideal, and to whom the realization of what ought to be, involved not the destruction of what was, but merely its perfecting upon its own lines. To the Greeks virtue was not a hard conformity to a law felt as alien to the natural character, but a free expression of the inner life. To treat thus the fundamental susceptibility of sex which now so bewilders the street life and drives young people themselves into all sorts of difficulties, would mean to loosen it from the things of sense and to link it to the affairs of the imagination. It would mean to fit to this gross and heavy stuff the wings of the mind, to scatter from it "the clinging mud of banality and vulgarity," and to speed it on through our city streets amid spontaneous laughter, snatches of lyric song, the recovered forms of old dances, and the traditional rondels of merry games. It would thus bring charm and beauty to the prosaic city and connect it subtly with the arts of the past as well as with the vigor and renewed life of the future.

6. W. E. B. DuBois, *The Souls of Black Folk, 1903**

Little of beauty has America given the world save the rude grandeur God himself stamped on her bosom; the human spirit in this new world has expressed itself in vigor and ingenuity rather than in beauty. And so by fateful chance the Negro folk-song—the rhythmic cry of the slave—stands today not simply as the sole American music, but as the most beautiful expression of human experience born this side the seas. It has been neglected, it has been, and is, half despised, and above all it has been persistently mistaken and misunderstood; but notwithstanding, it still remains as the singular spiritual heritage of the nation and the greatest gift of the Negro people.

Away back in the thirties the melody of these slave songs stirred the nation, but the songs were soon half forgotten. Some, like "Near the lake where dropped the willow," passed into current airs and their source was forgotten; others were caricatured on the "minstrel" stage and their memory died away. Then in wartime came the singular Port Royal experiment after the capture of Hilton Head, and perhaps for the first time the North met the Southern slave face to face and heart to heart with no third witness. The Sea Islands of the Carolinas, where they met, were filled with a black folk of primitive type, touched and molded less by the world about them than any others outside the Black Belt. Their appearance was uncouth, their language funny, but their hearts were human and their singing stirred men with a mighty power. Thomas Wentworth Higginson hastened to tell of these songs, and Miss McKim and others urged upon the world their rare beauty. But the world listened only half credulously until the Fisk Jubilee Singers sang the slave songs so deeply into the world's heart that it can never wholly forget them again. . . .

What are these songs, and what do they mean? I know little of music and can say nothing in technical phrase, but I know something of men, and knowing them, I know that these songs are the articulate message of the slave to the world. They tell us in these eager days that life was joyous to the black slave, careless and happy.

* W. E. B. DuBois, *The Souls of Black Folk* (first published, 1903; reprinted New York, 1953), pp. 251–53, 257–59, 261–64.

I can easily believe this of some, of many. But not all the past South, though it rose from the dead, can gainsay the heart-touching witness of these songs. They are the music of an unhappy people, of the children of disappointment; they tell of death and suffering and unvoiced longing toward a truer world, of misty wanderings and hidden ways. . . .

The words that are left to us are not without interest, and, cleared of evident dross, they conceal much of real poetry and meaning beneath conventional theology and unmeaning rhapsody. Like all primitive folk, the slave stood near to Nature's heart. Life was a "rough and rolling sea" like the brown Atlantic of the Sea Islands; the "Wilderness" was the home of God, and the "lonesome valley" led to the way of life. "Winter'll soon be over," was the picture of life and death to a tropical imagination. The sudden wild thunder-storms of the South awed and impressed the Negroes,—at times the rumbling seemed to them "mournful," at times imperious:

"My Lord calls me,
He calls me by the thunder,
The trumpet sounds it in my soul."

The monotonous toil and exposure is painted in many words. One sees the ploughmen in the hot, moist furrow, singing:

"Dere's no rain to wet you,
Dere's no sun to burn you,
Oh, push along, believer,
I want to go home."

The bowed and bent old man cries, with thrice-repeated wail:

"O Lord, keep me from sinking down,"

and he rebukes the devil of doubt who can whisper:

"Jesus is dead and God's gone away."

Yet the soul-hunger is there, the restlessness of the savage, the wail of the wanderer. . . .

Over the inner thoughts of the slaves and their relations one with another the shadow of fear ever hung, so that we get but glimpses here and there, and also with them, eloquent omissions and silences. Mother and child are sung, but seldom father; fugitive and weary wanderer call for pity and affection, but there is little of wooing and wedding; the rocks and the mountains are well known, but home is unknown. Strange blending of love and helplessness sings through the refrain:

"Yonder's my ole mudder,
Been waggin' at de hill so long;
'Bout time she cross over,
Git home bime-by."

Elsewhere comes the cry of the "motherless" and the "Farewell, farewell, my only child." . . .

Through all the sorrow of the Sorrow Songs there breathes a hope—a faith in the ultimate justice of things. The minor cadences of despair change often to triumph and calm confidence. Sometimes it is faith in life, sometimes a faith in death, sometimes assurance of boundless justice in some fair world beyond. But whichever it is, the meaning is always clear: that sometime, somewhere, men will judge men by their souls and not by their skins. Is such a hope justified? Do the Sorrow Songs ring true? . . . .

Around us the history of the land has centered for thrice a hundred years; out of the nation's heart we have called all that was best to throttle and subdue all that was worst; fire and blood, prayer and sacrifice, have billowed over this people. and they have found peace only in the altars of the God of Right. Nor has our gift of the Spirit been merely passive. Actively we have woven ourselves with the very warp and woof of this nation,—we fought their battles, shared their sorrow, mingled our blood with theirs, and generation after generation have pleaded with a headstrong, careless people to despise not Justice, Mercy, and Truth, lest the nation be smitten with a curse. Our song, our toil, our cheer, and warning have been given to this nation in blood-brotherhood. Are not these gifts worth the giving? Is not this work and striving? Would America have been America without her Negro people?

Even so is the hope that sang in the songs of my fathers well sung. If somewhere in this whirl and chaos of things, there dwells Eternal Good, pitiful yet masterful, then anon in His good time America shall rend the Veil and the prisoned shall go free. Free, free as the sunshine trickling down the morning into these high windows of mine, free as yonder fresh young voices welling up to me from the caverns of brick and mortar below— swelling with song, instinct with life, tremulous treble and darkening bass. My children, my little children, are singing to the sunshine, and thus they sing:

"Let us cheer the weary traveler,
Cheer the weary traveler,
Let us cheer the weary traveler
Along the heavenly way."

And the traveler girds himself, and sets his face toward the Morning, and goes his way.

7. E. E. Cummings, *Krazy Kat*, 1946*

What concerns me fundamentally is a meteoric burlesk melodrama, born of the immemorial adage *love will find a way*. This frank frenzy (encouraged by a strictly irrational landscape in perpetual metamorphosis) generates three protagonists and a plot. Two of the protagonists are easily recognized as a cynical brick-throwing mouse and a sentimental policeman-dog. The third protagonist—whose ambiguous gender doesn't disguise the good news that here comes our heroine—may be described as a humbly poetic, gently clownlike, supremely innocent, and illimitably affectionate creature (slightly resembling a child's drawing of a cat, but gifted with the secret grace and obvious clumsiness of a penguin on terra firma) who is never so happy as when egoist-mouse, thwarting altruist-dog, hits her in the head with a brick. Dog hates mouse and worships "cat," mouse despises "cat" and hates dog, "cat" hates no one and loves mouse.

Ignatz Mouse and Offissa Pupp are opposite sides of the same coin. Is Offissa Pupp kind? Only in so far as Ignatz Mouse is cruel. If you're a two-fisted, spineless progressive (a mighty fashionable stance nowadays) Offissa Pupp, who forcefully asserts the will of socalled society, becomes a cosmic angel; while Ignatz Mouse, who forcefully defies society's socalled will by asserting his authentic own, becomes a demon of anarchy and a fiend of chaos. But if—whisper it—you're a 100% hidebound reactionary, the foot's in the other shoe. Ignatz Mouse then stands forth as a hero, pluckily strug-

* George Herriman, *Krazy Kat* (New York: Holt, Rinehart and Winston, Inc., 1946). Introduction by E. E. Cummings. Copyright, 1946, by E. E. Cummings and used with his permission.

gling to keep the flag of free-will flying; while Offissa Pupp assumes the monstrous mien of a Goliath, satanically bullying a tiny but indomitable David. Well, let's flip the coin—so: and lo! Offissa Pupp comes up. That makes Ignatz Mouse "tails." Now we have a hero whose heart has gone to his head and a villain whose head has gone to his heart.

This hero and this villain no more understand Krazy Kat than the mythical denizens of a two-dimensional intruder. The world of Offissa Pupp and Ignatz Mouse is a knowledgeable power-world, in terms of which our unknowledgeable heroine is powerlessness personified. The sensical law of this world is *might makes right;* the nonsensical law of our heroine is *love conquers all.* To put the oak in the acorn: Ignatz Mouse and Offissa Pupp (each completely convinced that his own particular brand of might makes right) are simple-minded—Krazy isn't —therefore, to Offissa Pupp and Ignatz Mouse, Krazy is. But if both our hero and our villain don't and can't understand our heroine, each of them can and each of them does misunderstand her differently. To our softheaded altruist, she is the adorably helpless incarnation of saintliness. To our hardhearted egoist, she is the puzzling indestructible embodiment of idiocy. The benevolent overdog sees her as an inspired weakling. The malevolent undermouse views her as a born target. Meanwhile Krazy Kat, through this double misunderstanding, fulfills her joyous destiny.

Let's make no mistake about Krazy. A lot of people "love" because, and a lot of people "love" although, and a few individuals love. Love is something illimitable; and a lot of people spend their limited lives trying to prevent anything illimitable from happening to them. Krazy, however, is not a lot of people. Krazy is herself. Krazy is illimitable—she loves. She loves in the only way anyone can love: illimitably. She isn't morbid and she isn't longsuffering; she doesn't "love" someone because he hurts her and she doesn't "love" someone although he hurts her. She doesn't, moreover, "love" someone who hurts her. Quite the contrary: she loves someone who gives her unmitigated joy. How? By always trying his limited worst to make her unlove him, and always failing—not that our heroine is insensitive (for a more sensitive heroine never existed), but that our villain's every effort to limit her love with his unlove ends by a transforming of his limitation into her illimitability. If you're going to pity anyone, the last anyone to pity is our loving heroine, Krazy Kat. You might better pity that doggedly idolatrous imbecile, our hero; who policemanfully strives to protect his idol from catastrophic desecration at the paws of our iconoclastic villain—never suspecting that this very desecration becomes, through our transcending heroine, a consecration; and that this consecration reveals the ultimate meaning of existence. But the person to really pity (if really pity you must) is Ignatz. Poor villain! All his malevolence turns to beneficence at contact with Krazy's head. By profaning the temple of altruism, alias law and order, he worships (entirely against his will) at the shrine of love.

I repeat: let's make no mistake about Krazy. Her helplessness, as we have just seen, is merely sensical—nonsensically she's a triumphant, not to say invincible, phenomenon. As for this invincible phenomenon's supposed idiocy, it doesn't even begin to fool nonsensical you and me. Life, to a lot of people, means either the triumph of mind over matter or the triumph of matter over mind; but you and I aren't a lot of people. We understand that, just as there is something—love

—infinitely more significant than brute force, there is something—wisdom—infinitely more significant than mental prowess. A remarkably developed intelligence impresses us about as much as sixteen-inch biceps. If we know anything, we know that a lot of people can learn knowledge (which is the same thing as unlearning ignorance) but that no one can learn wisdom. Wisdom, like love, is a spiritual gift. And Krazy happens to be extraordinarily gifted. She has not only the gift of love, but the gift of wisdom as well. Her unknowledgeable wisdom blossoms in almost every episode of our meteoric burlesk melodrama; the supreme blossom, perhaps, being a tribute to Offissa Pupp and Ignatz Mouse—who (as she observes) are playing a little game together. Right! The game they're playing, willy nilly, is the exciting democratic game of *cat loves mouse;* the game which a lot of highly moral people all over the socalled world consider uncivilized. I refer (of course) to those red-brown-and-black-shirted Puritans who want us all to scrap democracy and adopt their modernized version of *follow the leader*—a strictly ultraprogressive and superbenevolent affair which begins with the liquidation of Ignatz Mouse by Offissa Pupp. But (objects Krazy, in her innocent democratic way) Ignatz Mouse and Offissa Pupp are having fun. Right again! And—from the Puritan point of view—nothing could be worse. Fun, to Puritans, is something wicked: an invention of The Devil Himself. That's why all these superbenevolent collectivists are so hyperspinelessly keen on having us play their ultraprogressive game. The first superbenevolent rule of their ultraprogressive game is *thou shalt not play.*

If only the devilish game of democracy were exclusively concerned with such mindful matters as ignorance and knowledge, crime and punishment, cruelty and kindness, collectivists would really have something on the ball. But it so happens that democracy involves the spiritual values of wisdom, love, and joy. Democracy isn't democracy because or although Ignatz Mouse and Offissa Pupp are fighting a peaceful war. Democracy is democracy is so far as our villain and our hero—by having their fun, by playing their brutal little game—happen (despite their worst and best efforts) to be fulfilling our heroine's immeasurable destiny. Joy is her destiny: and joy comes through Ignatz—via Offissa Pupp; since it's our villain's loathing for law which gives him the strength of ten when he hurls his blissyielding brick. Let's not forget that. And let's be perfectly sure about something else. Even if Offissa Pupp should go crazy and start chasing Krazy, and even if Krazy should go crazy and start chasing Ignatz, and even if crazy Krazy should swallow crazy Ignatz and crazy Offissa Pupp should swallow crazy Krazy and it was the millennium—there'd still be the brick. And (having nothing else to swallow) Offissa Pupp would then swallow the brick. Whereupon, as the brick hit Krazy, Krazy would be happy.

Alas for sensical reformers! Never can they realize that penguins do fly; that Krazy's idiocy and helplessness in terms of a world—any world—are as nothing to the nth power, by comparison with a world's—any world's—helplessness and idiocy in terms of Krazy. Yet the truth of truths lies here and nowhere else. Always (no matter what's real) Krazy is no mere reality. She is a living ideal. She is a spiritual force, inhabiting a merely real world—and the realer a merely real world happens to be, the more this living ideal becomes herself. Hence—needless to add —the brick. Only if, and whenever, that kind reality (cruelly wielded by our heroic villain, Ignatz Mouse, in despite of our villainous hero, Offissa Pupp) smites Krazy—fairly and squarely—does the joyous symbol of Love Fulfilled appear above our triumphantly unknowledgeable heroine. And now do we understand the meaning of democracy? If we don't, a poet-painter called George Herriman most certainly cannot be blamed. Democracy, he tells us again and again and again, isn't some ultraprogressive myth of a superbenevolent World As Should Be. The meteoric burlesk melodrama of democracy is a struggle between society (Offissa Pupp) and the individual (Ignatz Mouse) over an ideal (our heroine) —a struggle from which, again and again and again, emerges one stupendous fact: namely, that the ideal of democracy fulfills herself only if, and whenever, society fails to suppress the individual.

Could anything possibly be clearer?

Nothing—unless it's the kindred fact that our illimitably affectionate Krazy has no connection with the oldfashioned heroine of common or garden melodrama. The prosaically "virtuous" puppet couldn't bat a decorously "innocent" eyelash without immediately provoking some utterly estimable Mr Righto to liquidate some perfectly wicked Mr Wrongo. In her hyperspineless puritanical simplicity, she desired nothing quite so much as an ultraprogressive and superbenevolent substitute for human nature. Democracy's merciful leading lady, on the other hand, is a fundamentally complex being who demands the whole mystery of life. Krazy Kat—who, with every mangled word and murdered gesture, translates a mangling and murdering world into Peace and Goodwill—is the only original and authentic revolutionary protagonist. All blood-and-thunder Worlds As Should Be cannot comprise this immeasurably generous heroine of the strictly unmitigated future.

She has no fear—even of a mouse.

8. Gilbert Seldes, *Charlie Chaplin*, 1924*

It amused me once, after seeing *The Pawnshop,* to write down exactly what had happened. Later I checked up the list, and I print it here. I believe that Chaplin is so great on the screen, his effect so complete, that few people are aware, afterward, of how much he has done. Nor can they be aware of how much of Chaplin's work is "in his own way"—even when he does something which another could have done he adds to it a touch of his own. I do not pretend that the following analysis is funny; it may be useful:

Charlot enters the pawnshop; it is evident that he is late. He compares his watch with the calendar pad hanging on the wall, and hastily begins to make up for lost time by entering the back room and going busily to work. He takes a duster out of a valise and meticulously dusts his walking-stick. Then proceeding to other objects, he fills the room with clouds of dust, and when he begins to dust the electric fan, looking at something else, the feathers are blown all over the room. He turns and sees the plucked butt of the duster—and carefully puts it away for to-morrow.

With the other assistant he takes a ladder and a bucket of water and goes out to polish the three balls and the shop sign. After some horseplay he

* Gilbert Seldes, *The Seven Lively Arts* (New York: Harper & Brothers, 1924), pp. 41–54, 361–65. Copyright, 1924, by Harper & Brothers.

rises to the top of the ladder and reaches over to polish the sign; the ladder sways, teeters, with Charlot on top of it. A policeman down the street looks aghast, and sways sympathetically with the ladder. Yet struggling to keep his balance, Charlot is intent on his work, and every time the ladder brings him near the sign he dabs frantically at it until he falls.

A quarrel with his fellow-worker follows. The man is caught between the rungs of the ladder, his arms imprisoned. Charlot calls a boy over to hold the other end of the ladder and begins a boxing match. Although his adversary is incapable of moving his arms, Charlot sidesteps, feints, and guards, leaping nimbly away from imaginary blows. The policeman interferes and both assistants run into the shop. By a toss of a coin Charlot is compelled to go back to fetch the bucket. He tiptoes behind the policeman, snatches the bucket, and with a wide swing and a swirling motion evades the policeman and returns. He is then caught by the boss in another fight and is discharged.

He makes a tragic appeal to be reinstated. He says he has eleven children, so high, and so high, and so high—until the fourth one is about a foot taller than himself. The boss relents only as Charlot's stricken figure is at the door. As he is pardoned, Charlot leaps upon the old boss, twining his legs around his abdomen; he is thrown off and surreptitiously kisses the old man's hand. He goes into the kitchen to help the daughter and passes dishes through the clothes wringer to dry them—passes a cup twice, as it seems not to be dry the first time. Then his hands. The jealous assistant provokes a fight; Charlot has a handful of dough and is about to throw it when the boss appears. With the same motion Charlot flings the dough into the wringer, passes it

through as a pie crust, seizes a pie plate, trims the crust over it, and goes out to work.

At the pawnshop counter pass a variety of human beings. Charlot is taken in by a sob story about a wedding ring; he tries to test the genuineness of goldfish by dropping acid on them. Sent to the back room, he takes his lunch out of the safe, gets into another fight, in which he is almost beating his rival to death when the girl enters. Charlot falls whimpering to the floor and is made much of. He returns to the counter and the episode of the clock begins.

A sinister figure enters, offering a clock in pawn. Charlot looks at it; then takes an auscultator and listens to its heart-beat; then taps it over crossed fingers for its pulmonary action; then taps it with a little hammer to see the quality, as with porcelain; then snaps his thumb on the bell. He takes an augur and bores a hole in it, then a can-opener, and when he has pried the lid off he smells the contents and with a disparaging gesture makes the owner smell them, too. He then does dentistry on it, with forceps; then plumbing. Finally he screws a jeweler's magnifying glass into his eye and hammers what is left in the clock, shakes out the contents, measures the mainspring from the tip of his nose to arm's length, like cloth, squirts oil on the debris to keep it quiet, and, lifting the man's hat from his head, sweeps the whole mess into it and returns it with a sad shake of the head.

A pearl-buyer has meanwhile come in and Charlot retraces his steps to the back room (carefully stepping over the buyer's hat) and begins to sweep. His broom becomes entangled with a piece of tape, which fights back and gets longer and longer. Suddenly Charlot begins to tight-rope upon it, balancing with the broom, and making a quick turn, coming forward for applause. A final quarrel with the other assistant ensues. As they are swarming round the legs of the kitchen table, the boss comes in and Charlot flees, leaps into a trunk, and is hidden. As the others enter the room, the pearl-buyer, who has stolen all the valuables, holds them up with a revolver. Charlot leaps from the trunk, fells the robber, and embraces the lovely maiden for a fade-out. All of this takes about thirty minutes. . . .

It is a miracle that there should arise in our time a figure wholly in the tradition of the great clowns—a tradition requiring creative energy, freshness, inventiveness, change—for neither the time nor the country in which Charlie works is exceptionally favourable to such a phenomenon. . . .

That he exists at all is due to the camera and to the selective genius of Mack Sennett. It is impossible to dissociate him entirely from the Keystone comedy where he began and worked wonders and learned much. The injustice of forgetting Sennett and the Keystone when thinking of Chaplin has undermined most of the intellectual appreciation of his work, for although he was the greatest of the Keystone comedians and passed far beyond them, the first *and decisive* phase of his popularity came while he was with them, and the Keystone touch remains in all his later work, often as its most precious element. It was the time of Charlie's actual contact with the American people, the movie-going populace before the days of the great moving pictures. He was the second man to be known widely by name— John Bunny was the first—and he achieved a fame which passed entirely by word of mouth into the category of the common myths and legends of America, as the name of Buffalo Bill had passed before. By the time the newspapers recognized the movie as

a source of circulation, Charlie was already a known quantity in the composition of the American mind and, what is equally significant, he had created the first *Charlot*. The French name which is and is not Charlie will serve for that figure on the screen, the created image which is, and at the same time is more than, Charlie Chaplin, and is less. Like every great artist in whatever medium, Charlie has created the mask of himself—many masks, in fact—and the first of these, the wanderer, came in the Keystone comedies. It was there he first detached himself from life and began to live in another world, with a specific rhythm of his own, as if the pulse-beat in him changed and was twice or half as fast as that of those who surrounded him. He created then that trajectory across the screen which is absolutely his own line of movement. No matter what the actual facts are, the curve he plots is always the same. It is of one who seems to enter from a corner of the screen, becomes entangled or involved in a force greater than himself as he advances upward and to the centre; there he spins like a marionette in a whirlpool, is flung from side to side, always in a parabola which seems centripetal until the madness of the action hurls him to refuge or compels him to flight at the opposite end of the screen. He wanders in, a stranger, an imposter, an anarchist; and passes again, buffeted, but unchanged.

The Keystone was the time of his wildest grotesquerie (after *Tillie's Punctured Romance,* to be sure), as if he needed, for a beginning, sharply to contrast his rhythm, his gait, his gesture, *mode,* with the actual world outside. His successes in this period were confined to those films in which the world intruded with all its natural crassness upon his detached existence. There was a film in which Charlie dreamed himself back into the Stone

Age and played the God of the Waters —wholly without success because he contrasted his fantasy with another fantasy in the same tempo, and could neither sink into nor stand apart from it. But in *His Night Out* the effect is perfect, and is intensified by the alternating coincidence and syncopation of rhythm in which Ben Turpin worked with him. Charlie's drunken line of march down a stairway was first followed in parallel and then in not-quite-parallel by Turpin; the degree of drunkenness was the same, then varied, then returned to identity; and the two, together, were always entirely apart from the actuality of bars and hotels and fountains and policemen which were properties in their existence. In this early day Charlie had already mastered his principles. He knew that the broad lines are funny and that the fragments—which are delicious—must "point" the main line of laughter. I recall, for example, an exquisite moment at the end of this film. Turpin is staggering down the street, dragging Charlie by the collar. Essentially the funny thing is that one drunkard should so gravely, so soberly, so obstinately take care of another and should convert himself into a policeman to do it; it is funny that they should be going nowhere, and go so doggedly. The lurching-forward body of Turpin, the singular angle formed with it by Charlie's body almost flat on the ground, added to the spectacle. And once as they went along Charlie's right hand fell to one side, and as idly as a girl plucks a water-lily from over the side of a canoe he plucked a daisy from the grass border of the path, and smelled it. The function of that gesture was to make everything that went before, and everything that came after, seem funnier; and it succeeded by creating another, incongruous image out of the picture before our eyes. The entire world, a moment earlier, had

been aslant and distorted and wholly male; it righted itself suddenly and created a soft idyll of tenderness. Nearly everything of Charlie is in that moment, and I know no better way to express its elusive quality than to say that as I sat watching the film a second time, about two hours later, the repetition of the gesture came with all the effect of surprise, although I had been wondering whether he could do it so perfectly again.

This was the Charlie whom little children came to know before any other and whose name they added to their prayers. He was then popular with the people; he was soon to become universally known and admired— the Charlie of *The Bank* and of *Shoulder Arms;* and finally he became "the great artist" in *The Kid*. The second period is pure development; the third is change; and the adherents of each join with the earlier enthusiasts to instruct and alarm their idol. No doubt the middle phase is the one which is richest in memory. It includes the masterpieces *A Dog's Life, The Pawnshop, The Vagabond, Easy Street,* as well as the two I have just mentioned, and, if I am not mistaken, the *genre* pictures like *The Floorwalker, The Fireman, The Immigrant,* and the fantastic *Cure*. To name these pictures is to call to mind their special scenes, the atmosphere in which they were played: the mock heroic of *The Bank* and its parody of passion; the unbelievable scene behind the curtain in *A Dog's Life;* Charlie as policeman in *Easy Street,* which had some beginnings of *The Kid;* Charlie left marking time alone after the squad had marched away in the film which made camp life supportable. Compare them with the very earliest films, *The Pile Driver* and the wheel-chairman film and so on: the later ones are richer in inventiveness, the texture is more solid, the emotions grow more complex, and the interweaving of tenderness and gravity with the fun becomes infinitely more deft. In essence it is the same figure—he is still a vagrant, an outsider; only now when he becomes entangled in the lives of other people he is a bit of a crusader, too. The accidental does not occur so frequently; the progress of each film is plotted in advance; there is a definite rise and fall as in *A Dog's Life,* where the climax is in the curtain scene toward which tends the first episode of the dog and from which the flight and the rustic idyll flow gently downward. The pace in the earlier pictures was more instinctive. In *The Count* the tempo is jerky; it moves from extreme to extreme. Yet one gets the sense of the impending flight beautifully when, at the close, Charlot as the bogus count has been shown up and is fleeing pell-mell through every room in the house; the whole movement grows tense; the rate of acceleration perceptibly heightens as Charlot slides in front of a vast birthday cake, pivots on his heel, and begins to play alternate pool and golf with the frosting, making every shot count like a machine gunner barricaded in a pill-box or a bandit in a deserted cabin.

It was foreordained that the improvised kind of comedy should give way to something more calculated, and in Charlie's case it is particularly futile to cry over spilled milk because for a long time he continued to give the *effect* of impromptu; his sudden movements and his finds in the way of unsuspected sources of fun are exceptional to this day. In *The Pawnshop* Charlie begins to sweep and catches in his broom the end of a long rope, which, instead of being swept away, keeps getting longer, actively fighting the broom. I have no way to prove it, but I am sure from the context that this is all he had originally had in mind to do with the scene. Suddenly the tape

on the floor creates something in his mind, and Charlie transforms the back room of the pawnshop into a circus, with himself walking the tight rope— a graceful, nimble balancing along the thin line of tape on the floor, the quick turn and coming forward, the conventional bow, arms flung out, smiling, to receive applause at the end. Again, as ever, he has created an imaginary scene out of the materials of the actual.

The plotting of these comedies did not destroy Charlie's inventiveness and made it possible for him to develop certain other of his characteristics. The moment the vagrant came to rest, the natural man appeared, the paradoxical creature who has the wisdom of simple souls and the incalculable strength of the weak. Charlie all through the middle period is at least half Tyl Eulenspiegl. It is another way for him to live apart from the world by assuming that the world actually means what it says, by taking every one of its conventional formulas, its polite phrases and idioms, with dreadful seriousness. He has created in Charlot a radical with an extraordinarily logical mind. Witness Charlot arriving late at the theatre and stepping on the toes of a whole row of people to his seat at the far end; the gravity of his expressions of regret is only matched by his humiliation when he discovers that he is, after all, in the wrong row and makes his way back again and all through the next row to his proper place. It is a careful exaggeration of the social fiction that when you apologize you can do anything to anyone. The same feeling underlies the characteristic moment when Charlot is fighting and suddenly stops, takes off his hat and coat, gives them to his opponent to hold, and then promptly knocks his obliging adversary down. Revisiting once an old Charlie, I saw him do this, and a few minutes later saw the same thing in a new Harold Lloyd; all there is to know of the difference between the two men was to be learned there; for Lloyd, who is a clever fellow, made it seem a smart trick so to catch his enemy off guard, while Chaplin made the moment equal to the conventional crossing of swords or the handshake before a prize fight. Similarly, the salutation with the hat takes seriously a social convention and carries it as far as it can go. In *Pay Day* Charlot arrives late to work and attempts to mollify the furious construction-gang boss by handing him an Easter lily.

The Kid was undoubtedly a beginning in "literature" for Charlie. I realize that in admitting this I am giving the whole case away, for in the opinion of certain critics the beginning of literature is the end of creative art. This attitude is not so familiar in America, but in France you hear the Charlot of *The Kid* spoken of as "theatre," as one who has ceased to be of the film entirely. I doubt if this is just. Like the one other great artist in America (George Herriman, with whom he is eminently in sympathy), Charlie has always had the Dickens touch, a thing which in its purity we do not otherwise discover in our art. Dickens himself is mixed; only a part of him is literature, and that not the best, nor is that part essentially the one which Charlie has imported to the screen. *The Kid* had some bad things in it: the story, the halo around the head of the unmarried mother, the quarrel with the authorities; it had an unnecessary amount of realism and its tempo was uncertain, for it was neither serious film nor Keystone. Yet it possessed moments of unbelievable intensity and touches of high imagination. The scenes in and outside the dosshouse were excellent and were old Charlie; the glazier's assistant was inventive and the training of Coogan to look like his foster-father was beautiful. Far above them stood the begin-

ning of the film: Charlot, in his usual polite rags, strolling down to his club after his breakfast (it would have been a grilled bone) and, avoiding slops as Villon did, twirling his cane, taking off his fingerless gloves to reach for his cigarette case (a sardine box), and selecting from the butts one of quality, *tamping it* to shake down the excess tobacco at the tip—all of this, as Mr. Herriman pointed out to me, was the creation of the society gentleman, the courageous refusal to be undermined by slums and poverty and rags. At the end of the film there was the vision of heaven: apotheosis of the long suffering of Charlot at the hands of the police, not only in *The Kid*—in a hundred films where he stood always against the authorities, always for his small independent freedom. The world in which even policemen have wings shatters, too; but something remains. The invincible Charlot, dazed by his dream, looking for wings on the actual policeman who is apparently taking him to jail, will not down. For as they start, a post comes between them, and Charlot, without the slightest effort to break away, too submissive to fight, still dodges back to walk round the post and so avoid bad luck. A moment later comes one of the highest points in Charlie's career. He is ushered into a limousine instead of a patrol wagon— it is the beginning of the happy ending. And as the motor starts he flashes at the spectators of his felicity a look of indescribable poignancy. It is frightened, it is hopeful, bewildered; it lasts a fraction of a second and is blurred by the plate glass of the car. I cannot hope to set down the quality of it, how it becomes a moment of unbearable intensity, and how one is breathless with suspense— and with adoration.

For, make no mistake, it is adoration, not less, that he deserves and has from us. He corresponds to our secret desires because he alone has passed beyond our categories, at one bound placing himself outside space and time. His escape from the world is complete and extraordinarily rapid, and what makes him more than a figure of romance is his immediate creation of another world. He has the vital energy, the composing and the functioning brain. This is what makes him aesthetically interesting, what will make him forever a school not only of acting, but of the whole creative process. The flow of his line always corresponds to the character and tempo; there is a definite relation between the melody and the orchestration he gives it. Beyond his technique—the style of his pieces—he has composition, because he creates anything but chaos in his separate world. "You might," wrote Mr. Stark Young, wise in everything but the choice of the person addressed, "you might really create in terms of the moving picture as you have already created in terms of character." As I have said, the surest way to be wrong about Charlie is to forget the Keystone. . . .

There is a future for him as for others, and it is quite possible that the future may not be as rich and as dear as the past. . . . If the literary side

conquers we shall have a great character actor and not a creator; we shall certainly not have again the image of riot and fun, the created personage, the annihilation of actuality; we may go so far as to . . . have a serious work of art. I hope this will not happen, because I do not believe that it is the necessary curve of Charlie's genius—it is the direction of worldly success, not in money, but in fame; it is not the curve of life at all. For the slowing-up of Charlie's physical energies and the deepening of his understanding may well restore to him his appreciation of those early monuments to laughter which are his greatest achievement. He stood then shod in absurdity, but with his feet on the earth. And he danced on the earth, an eternal figure of lightness and of the wisdom which knows that the earth was made to dance on. It was a green earth, excited with its own abundance and fruitfulness, and he possessed it entirely. For me he remains established in possession. As it spins under his feet he dances silently and with infinite grace upon it. It is as if in his whole life he had spoken only one word: "I am here *to-day*"—the beginning before time and the end without end of his wisdom and of his loveliness.

9. ROBINSON JEFFERS, *Shine, Perishing Republic, 1938**

While this America settles in the mould
   of its vulgarity, heavily thickening
   to empire,
And protest, only a bubble in the
   molten mass, pops and sighs out,
   and the mass hardens,

I sadly smiling remember that the
   flower fades to make fruit, the fruit
   rots to make earth.

Out of the mother; and through the
   spring exultances, ripeness and decadence; and home to the mother.

You making haste haste on decay: not
   blameworthy; life is good, be it
   stubbornly long or suddenly
A mortal splendor: meteors are not
   needed less than mountains: shine,
   perishing republic.

But for my children, I would have them
   keep their distance from the thickening center; corruption
Never has been compulsory, when the
   cities lie at the monster's feet there
   are left the mountains.

And boys, be in nothing so moderate as
   in love of man, a clever servant,
   insufferable master.
There is the trap that catches noblest
   spirits, that caught—they say—God,
   when he walked on earth.

10. JAMES LAUGHLIN, *Busy Day, 1948**

The cripple in the wheelchair
(who really isn't crippled up
at all) has shot & killed the

luscious lady who is fair but
false anonymous letters warn
Inspector Meadowes that this

crime is just the first Mac-
Teague the private eye cracks
wise and downs another drink

Hoppy the cub reporter with a
wooden leg meets in a mist the
lost and lonely girl with honey

in her voice yes friends dear
friends another golden day in
this most golden day is slip-

ping darkwards on its opiate
track don't wake good friends
don't stir the sound of pistol

shots is oh so soothing like
that muffled riffling of the
dollars piling up & up & up.

* James Laughlin, "Busy Day," from *A Small Book of Poems* (Norwalk, 1948). Copyright by New Directions and reprinted by their courtesy.

11. NATHANAEL WEST, *The Day of the Locust, 1939**

   When Tod reached the street, he saw a dozen great violet shafts of light moving across the evening sky in wide crazy sweeps. Whenever one of the fiery columns reached the lowest point of its arc, it hit for a moment the rose-colored domes and delicate minarets of Kahn's Persian Palace Theatre. The purpose of this display was to signal the world première of a new picture.

   Turning his back on the searchlights, he started in the opposite direction, toward Homer's place. Before he had gone very far, he saw a clock that read a quarter past six and changed his mind about going back just yet. He might as well let the poor fellow sleep for another hour and kill some time by looking at the crowds.

   When still a block from the theatre, he saw an enormous electric sign that hung over the middle of the street. In letters ten feet high he read that—

     "MR. KAHN A PLEASURE
       DOME DECREED"

   Although it was still several hours before the celebrities would arrive, thousands of people had already gathered. They stood facing the theatre with their backs toward the gutter in a thick line hundreds of feet long. A

* Nathanael West, *The Day of the Locust* (New York, 1939), chap. 27. Copyright 1949 by Nathanael West. Reprinted by permission of New Directions.

big squad of policemen was trying to keep a lane open between the front rank of the crowd and the façade of the theatre.

Tod entered the lane while the policeman guarding it was busy with a woman whose parcel had torn open, dropping oranges all over the place. Another policeman shouted for him to get the hell across the street, but he took a chance and kept going. They had enough to do without chasing him. He noticed how worried they looked and how careful they tried to be. If they had to arrest someone, they joked good-naturedly with the culprit, making light of it until they got him around the corner, then they whaled him with their clubs. Only so long as the man was actually part of the crowd did they have to be gentle.

Tod had walked only a short distance along the narrow lane when he began to get frightened. People shouted, commenting on his hat, his carriage, and his clothing. There was a continuous roar of catcalls, laughter, and yells, pierced occasionally by a scream. The scream was usually followed by a sudden movement in the dense mass and part of it would surge forward wherever the police line was weakest. As soon as that part was rammed back, the bulge would pop out somewhere else.

The police force would have to be doubled when the stars started to arrive. At the sight of their heroes and heroines, the crowd would turn demoniac. Some little gesture, either too pleasing or too offensive, would start it moving and then nothing but machine guns would stop it. Individually the purpose of its members might simply be to get a souvenir, but collectively it would grab and rend.

A young man with a portable microphone was describing the scene. His rapid, hysterical voice was like that of a revivalist preacher whipping his congregation toward the ecstasy of fits.

"What a crowd, folks! What a crowd! There must be ten thousand excited, screaming fans outside Kahn's Persian tonight. The police can't hold them. Here, listen to them roar."

He held the microphone out and those near it obligingly roared for him.

"Did you hear it? It's a bedlam, folks. A veritable bedlam! What excitement! Of all the premières I've attended, this is the most . . . the most . . . stupendous, folks. Can the police hold them? Can they? It doesn't look so, folks . . ."

Another squad of police came charging up. The sergeant pleaded with the announcer to stand further back so the people couldn't hear him. His men threw themselves at the crowd. It allowed itself to be hustled and shoved out of habit and because it lacked an objective. It tolerated the police, just as a bull elephant does when he allows a small boy to drive him with a light stick.

Tod could see very few people who looked tough, nor could he see any working men. The crowd was made up of the lower middle classes, every other person one of his torchbearers.

Just as he came near the end of the lane, it closed in front of him with a heave, and he had to fight his way through. Someone knocked his hat off and when he stooped to pick it up, someone kicked him. He whirled around angrily and found himself surrounded by people who were laughing at him. He knew enough to laugh with them. The crowd became sympathetic. A stout woman slapped him on the back, while a man handed him his hat, first brushing it carefully with his sleeve. Still another man shouted for a way to be cleared.

By a great deal of pushing and squirming, always trying to look as though he were enjoying himself, Tod finally managed to break into the open. After rearranging his clothes, he went over to a parking lot and sat down on the low retaining wall that ran along the front of it.

New groups, whole families, kept arriving. He could see a change come over them as soon as they had become part of the crowd. Until they reached the line, they looked diffident, almost furtive, but the moment they had become part of it, they turned arrogant and pugnacious. It was a mistake to think them harmless curiosity seekers. They were savage and bitter, especially the middle-aged and the old, and had been made so by boredom and disappointment.

All their lives they had slaved at some kind of dull, heavy labor, behind desks and counters, in the fields and at tedious machines of all sorts, saving their pennies and dreaming of the leisure that would be theirs when they had enough. Finally that day came. They could draw a weekly income of ten or fifteen dollars. Where else should they go but California, the land of sunshine and oranges?

Once there, they discovered that sunshine isn't enough. They get tired of oranges, even of avocado pears and passion fruit. Nothing happens. They don't know what to do with their time. They haven't the mental equipment for leisure, the money nor the physical equipment for pleasure. Did they slave so long just to go on an occasional Iowa picnic? What else is there? They watch the waves come in at Venice. There wasn't any ocean where most of them came from, but after you've seen one wave, you've seen them all. The same is true of the airplanes at Glendale. If only a plane would crash once in a while so that they could watch the passengers being consumed in a "holocaust of flame," as the newspapers put it. But the planes never crash.

Their boredom becomes more and more terrible. They realize that they've been tricked and burn with resentment. Every day of their lives they read the newspapers and went to the movies. Both fed them on lynchings, murder, sex crimes, explosions, wrecks, love nests, fires, miracles, revolutions, wars. This daily diet made sophisticates of them. The sun is a joke. Oranges can't titillate their jaded palates. Nothing can ever be violent enough to make taut their slack minds and bodies. They have been cheated and betrayed. They have slaved and saved for nothing.

Tod stood up. During the ten minutes he had been sitting on the wall, the crowd had grown thirty feet and he was afraid that his escape might be cut off if he loitered much longer. He crossed to the other side of the street and started back.

He was trying to figure what to do if he were unable to wake Homer when, suddenly he saw his head bobbing above the crowd. He hurried toward him. From his appearance, it was evident that there was something definitely wrong.

Homer walked more than ever like a badly made automaton and his features were set in a rigid, mechanical grin. He had his trousers on over his nightgown and part of it hung out of his open fly. In both of his hands were suitcases. With each step, he lurched to one side then the other, using the suitcases for balance weights.

Tod stopped directly in front of him, blocking his way.

"Where're you going?"

"Wayneville," he replied, using an extraordinary amount of jaw movement to get out this single word.

"That's fine. But you can't walk to the station from here. It's in Los Angeles."

Homer tried to get around him, but he caught his arm.

"We'll get a taxi. I'll go with you."

The cabs were all being routed around the block because of the preview. He explained this to Homer and tried to get him to walk to the corner.

"Come on, we're sure to get one on the next street."

Once Tod got him into a cab, he intended to tell the driver to go to the nearest hospital. But Homer wouldn't budge, no matter how hard he yanked and pleaded. People stopped to watch them, others turned their heads curiously. He decided to leave him and get a cab.

"I'll come right back," he said.

He couldn't tell from either Homer's eyes or expression whether he heard, for they both were empty of everything, even annoyance. At the corner he looked around and saw that Homer had started to cross the street, moving blindly. Brakes screeched and twice he was almost run over, but he didn't swerve or hurry. He moved in a straight diagonal. When he reached the other curb, he tried to get on the sidewalk at a point where the crowd was very thick and was shoved violently back. He made another attempt and this time a policeman grabbed him by the back of the neck and hustled him to the end of the line. When the policeman let go of him, he kept on walking as though nothing had happened.

Tod tried to get over to him, but was unable to cross until the traffic lights changed. When he reached the other side, he found Homer sitting on a bench, fifty or sixty feet from the outskirts of the crowd.

He put his arm around Homer's shoulder and suggested that they walk a few blocks further. When Homer didn't answer, he reached over to pick up one of the valises. Homer held on to it.

"I'll carry it for you," he said, tugging gently.

"Thief!"

Before Homer could repeat the shout, he jumped away. It would be extremely embarrassing if Homer shouted thief in front of a cop. He thought of phoning for an ambulance.

But then, after all, how could he be sure that Homer was crazy? He was sitting quietly on the bench, minding his own business.

Tod decided to wait, then try again to get him into a cab. The crowd was growing in size all the time, but it would be at least half an hour before it over-ran the bench. Before that happened, he would think of some plan. He moved a short distance away and stood with his back to a store window so that he could watch Homer without attracting attention.

About ten feet from where Homer was sitting grew a large eucalyptus tree and behind the trunk of the tree was a little boy. Tod saw him peer around it with great caution, then suddenly jerk his head back. A minute later he repeated the maneuver. At first Tod thought he was playing hide and seek, then noticed that he had a string in his hand which was attached to an old purse that lay in front of Homer's bench. Every once in a while the child would jerk the string, making the purse hop like a sluggish toad. Its torn lining hung from its iron mouth like a furry tongue and a few uncertain flies hovered over it.

Tod knew the game the child was playing. He used to play it himself when he was small. If Homer reached to pick up the purse, thinking there was money in it, he would yank it away and scream with laughter.

When Tod went over to the tree, he was surprised to discover that it was Adore Loomis, the kid who lived across the street from Homer. Tod tried to chase him, but he dodged around the tree, thumbing his nose. He gave up and went back to his original position. The moment he left, Adore got busy with his purse again. Homer wasn't paying any attention to the child, so Tod decided to let him alone.

Mrs. Loomis must be somewhere in the crowd, he thought. Tonight when she found Adore, she would give him a hiding. He had torn the pocket of his jacket and his Buster Brown collar was smeared with grease.

Adore had a nasty temper. The completeness with which Homer ignored both him and his pocketbook made him frantic. He gave up dancing it at the end of the string and approached the bench on tiptoes, making ferocious faces, yet ready to run at Homer's first move. He stopped when about four feet away and stuck his tongue out. Homer ignored him. He took another step forward and ran through a series of insulting gestures.

If Tod had known that the boy held a stone in his hand, he would have interfered. But he felt sure that Homer wouldn't hurt the child and was waiting to see if he wouldn't move because of his pestering. When Adore raised his arm, it was too late. The stone hit Homer in the face. The boy turned to flee, but tripped and fell. Before he could scramble away, Homer landed on his back with both feet, then jumped again.

Tod yelled for him to stop and tried to yank him away. He shoved Tod and went on using his heels. Tod hit him as hard as he could, first in the belly, then in the face. He ignored the blows and continued to stamp on the boy. Tod hit him again and again, then threw both arms around him and tried to pull him off. He couldn't budge him. He was like a stone column.

The next thing Tod knew, he was torn loose from Homer and sent to his knees by a blow in the back of the head that spun him sideways. The crowd in front of the theatre had charged. He was surrounded by churning legs and feet. He pulled himself erect by grabbing a man's coat, then let himself be carried along backwards in a long, curving swoop. He saw Homer rise above the mass for a moment, shoved against the sky, his jaw

hanging as though he wanted to scream but couldn't. A hand reached up and caught him by his open mouth and pulled him forward and down.

There was another dizzy rush. Tod closed his eyes and fought to keep upright. He was jostled about in a hacking cross surf of shoulders and backs, carried rapidly in one direction and then in the opposite. He kept pushing and hitting out at the people around him, trying to face in the direction he was going. Being carried backwards terrified him.

Using the eucalyptus tree as a landmark, he tried to work toward it by slipping sideways against the tide, pushing hard when carried away from it and riding the current when it moved toward his objective. He was within only a few feet of the tree when a sudden, driving rush carried him far past it. He struggled desperately for a moment, then gave up and let himself be swept along. He was the spearhead of a flying wedge when it collided with a mass going in the opposite direction. The impact turned him around. As the two forces ground against each other, he was turned again and again, like a grain between millstones. This didn't stop until he became part of the opposing force. The pressure continued to increase until he thought he must collapse. He was slowly being pushed into the air. Although relief for his cracking ribs could be gotten by continuing to rise, he fought to keep his feet on the ground. Not being able to touch was an even more dreadful sensation than being carried backwards.

There was another rush, shorter this time, and he found himself in a dead spot where the pressure was less and equal. He became conscious of a terrible pain in his left leg, just above the ankle, and tried to work it into a more comfortable position. He couldn't turn his body, but managed to get his head around. A very skinny boy, wearing a

Western Union cap, had his back wedged against his shoulder. The pain continued to grow and his whole leg as high as the groin throbbed. He finally got his left arm free and took the back of the boy's neck in his fingers. He twisted as hard as he could. The boy began to jump up and down in his clothes. He managed to straighten his elbow, by pushing at the back of the boy's head, and so turn half way around and free his leg. The pain didn't grow less.

There was another wild surge forward that ended in another dead spot. He now faced a young girl who was sobbing steadily. Her silk print dress had been torn down the front and her tiny brassiere hung from one strap. He tried by pressing back to give her room, but she moved with him every time he moved. Now and then, she would jerk violently and he wondered if she was going to have a fit. One of her thighs was between his legs. He struggled to get free of her, but she clung to him, moving with him and pressing against him.

She turned her head and said, "Stop, stop," to someone behind her.

He saw what the trouble was. An old man, wearing a Panama hat and horn-rimmed glasses, was hugging her. He had one of his hands inside her dress and was biting her neck.

Tod freed his right arm with a heave, reached over the girl and brought his fist down on the man's head. He couldn't hit very hard but managed to knock the man's hat off, also his glasses. The man tried to bury his face in the girl's shoulder, but Tod grabbed one of his ears and yanked. They started to move again. Tod held on to the ear as long as he could, hoping that it would come away in his hand. The girl managed to twist under his arm. A piece of her dress tore, but she was free of her attacker.

Another spasm passed through the mob and he was carried toward the curb. He fought toward a lamp-post, but he was swept by before he could grasp it. He saw another man catch the girl with the torn dress. She screamed for help. He tried to get to her, but was carried in the opposite direction. This rush also ended in a dead spot. Here his neighbors were all shorter than he was. He turned his head upward toward the sky and tried to pull some fresh air into his aching lungs, but it was all heavily tainted with sweat.

In this part of the mob no one was hysterical. In fact, most of the people seemed to be enjoying themselves. Near him was a stout woman with a man pressing hard against her from in front. His chin was on her shoulder, and his arms were around her. She paid no attention to him and went on talking to the woman at her side.

"The first thing I knew," Tod heard her say, "there was a rush and I was in the middle."

"Yeah. Somebody hollered, 'Here comes Gary Cooper,' and then wham!"

"That ain't it," said a little man wearing a cloth cap and pull-over sweater. "This is a riot you're in."

"Yeah," said a third woman, whose snaky gray hair was hanging over her face and shoulders. "A pervert attacked a child."

"He ought to be lynched."

Everybody agreed vehemently.

"I come from St. Louis," announced the stout woman, "and we had one of them pervert fellers in our neighborhood once. He ripped up a girl with a pair of scissors."

"He must have been crazy," said the man in the cap. "What kind of fun is that?"

Everybody laughed. The stout woman spoke to the man who was hugging her.

"Hey, you," she said. "I ain't no pillow."

The man smiled beatifically but didn't move. She laughed, making no effort to get out of his embrace.

"A fresh guy," she said.

The other woman laughed.

"Yeah," she said, "this is a regular free-for-all."

The man in the cap and sweater thought there was another laugh in his comment about the pervert.

"Ripping up a girl with scissors. That's the wrong tool."

He was right. They laughed even louder than the first time.

"You'd a done it different, eh, kid?" said a young man with a kidney-shaped head and waxed mustaches.

The two women laughed. This encouraged the man in the cap and he reached over and pinched the stout woman's friend. She squealed.

"Lay off that," she said good-naturedly.

"I was shoved," he said.

An ambulance siren screamed in the street. Its wailing moan started the crowd moving again and Tod was carried along in a slow, steady push. He closed his eyes and tried to protect his throbbing leg. This time, when the movement ended, he found himself with his back to the theatre wall. He kept his eyes closed and stood on his good leg. After what seemed like hours, the pack began to loosen and move again with a churning motion. It gathered momentum and rushed. He rode it until he was slammed against the base of an iron rail which fenced the driveway of the theatre from the street. He had the wind knocked out of him by the impact, but managed to cling to the rail. He held on desperately, fighting to keep from being sucked back. A woman caught him around the waist and tried to hang on. She was sobbing rhythmically. Tod felt his fingers slipping from the rail and kicked backwards as hard as he could. The woman let go.

Despite the agony in his leg, he was able to think clearly about his picture, "The Burning of Los Angeles." After his quarrel with Faye, he had worked on it continually to escape tormenting himself, and the way to it in his mind had become almost automatic.

As he stood on his good leg, clinging desperately to the iron rail, he could see all the rough charcoal strokes with which he had blocked it out on the big canvas. Across the top, parallel with the frame, he had drawn the burning city, a great bonfire of architectural styles, ranging from Egyptian to Cape Cod colonial. Through the center, winding from left to right, was a long hill street and down it, spilling into the middle foreground, came the mob carrying baseball bats and torches. For the faces of its members, he was using the innumerable sketches he had made of the people who come to California to die; the cultists of all sorts, economic as well as religious, the wave, airplane, funeral and preview watchers—all those poor devils who can only be stirred by the promise of miracles and then only to violence. A super "Dr. Know-All Pierce-All" had made the necessary promise and they were marching behind his banner in a great united front of screwballs and screwboxes to purify the land. No longer bored, they sang and danced joyously in the red light of the flames.

In the lower foreground, men and women fled wildly before the vanguard of the crusading mob. Among them were Faye, Harry, Homer, Claude and himself. Faye ran proudly, throwing her knees high. Harry stumbled along behind her, holding on to his beloved derby hat with both hands. Homer seemed to be falling out of the canvas, his face half-asleep, his big hands clawing the air in anguished pantomime. Claude turned his head as he ran to thumb his nose at his pursuers. Tod himself picked up a small stone to throw before continuing his flight.

He had almost forgotten both his leg and his predicament, and to make his escape still more complete he stood on a chair and worked at the flames in an upper corner of the canvas, modeling the tongues of fire so that they licked even more avidly at a corinthian column that held up the palmleaf roof of a nutburger stand.

He had finished one flame and was starting on another when he was brought back by someone shouting in his ear. He opened his eyes and saw a policeman trying to reach him from behind the rail to which he was clinging. He let go with his left hand and raised his arm. The policeman caught him by the wrist, but couldn't lift him. Tod was afraid to let go until another man came to aid the policeman and caught him by the back of his jacket. He let go of the rail and they hauled him up and over it.

When they saw that he couldn't stand, they let him down easily to the ground. He was in the theatre driveway. On the curb next to him sat a woman crying into her skirt. Along the wall were groups of other disheveled people. At the end of the driveway was an ambulance. A policeman asked him if he wanted to go to the hospital. He shook his head no. He then offered him a lift home. Tod had the presence of mind to give Claude's address.

He was carried through the exit to the back street and lifted into a police car. The siren began to scream and at first he thought he was making the noise himself. He felt his lips with his hands. They were clamped tight. He knew then it was the siren. For some reason this made him laugh and he began to imitate the siren as loudly as he could.

VI

* *

Public Means and Private Ends

ADLAI EWING STEVENSON

Democrat, was twice a candidate for the presidency, opposing Dwight D. Eisenhower, Republican.

Mr. Stevenson was born in Los Angeles in 1900. He received his Bachelor's degree from Princeton in 1922 and his Law degree from Northwestern University in 1926.

After practicing law in Chicago, he was assistant to the Secretary of the Navy from 1941 to 1944, assistant to the Secretary of State in 1945, and United States delegate to the United Nations General Assembly in 1946 and 1947.

He served as Governor of Illinois from 1949 to 1953.

Mr. Stevenson is trustee or director of various educational and philanthropic organizations. He is the author of *Call to Greatness,* published in 1954, and *What I Think,* 1956. In 1961 he became United States ambassador to the United Nations.

Adlai Stevenson ✳✳✳✳ Extend Our Vision . . . to All Mankind

It is not too difficult, I think, to state the classic goals and purposes of American society. We probably cannot improve on the definition offered by our Founding Fathers: "to form a more perfect union, establish justice, insure domestic tranquillity, provide for the common defence, promote the general welfare and secure the blessings of liberty." Add Tom Paine's words—"My country is the world; my countrymen are all mankind"—to give our goals universal application, and we have distilled the essence out of all the rhetoric about the freedom and democratic self-government for which we proudly stand.

But the difficulty is that aims in the abstract mean little. Communist double-talk—with "peace" meaning "cold war," "people's democracy" meaning dictatorship, and "liberation" meaning domination—is reminder enough that what gives depth and direction to national purpose is not phrase-making but the way a society actually behaves, its manner of realizing its aims, where it lays up its treasure, the dream it carries closest to its heart. A society, in short, is measured by what it does, and no grandiloquent rhetoric, no Fourth of July oratory, will make its purposes great if in fact they are small, or change them into a moving element in the world's passionate dialogue of destiny if they are meager and private and unconcerned.

We have therefore to look at our noble purpose of freedom—and surely no one would deny that it is the organizing principle of American life—in terms of the concrete, practical content which Americans give to the concept. As one might expect in a free society, we encounter at once that freedom itself has many meanings and has implied different things to different people at different times in our national life. In fact one can observe something of a rhythm in the nation's mood, a swing from one definition of freedom almost to its opposite, recurring regularly throughout the almost 200 years of our independent history.

The first mood reflects the *private* aspects of freedom—the right of men to choose their own ideas and pursuits, to be free from the arbitrary interventions of government, to "do what they like with their own." Many early immigrants were especially aware of this freedom in the economic sphere. They escaped the arbitrary restraints of governments in Europe and came to set their money and their wits to work in the new climate of enterprise. This sense of the link between "freedom" and private business has indeed been so strong that at some periods they have virtually been equated, as when Calvin Coolidge thus defined the American purpose: "The business of America is—business."

But equally freedom has had its *public* aspect as the organizing principle of a new kind of society. In the Declaration of Independence, the basic charter of the modern world, the picture is of a great civic order in which governments, deriving their authority from the consent of the governed, help to secure the inalienable pre-conditions of the good life— equality before the law and in human respect, life, liberty, and, most precious yet intangible of rights, the pursuit of happiness. This positive vision of society in which the public authority plays its essential part in bettering the lot of all citizens is as inherent as freedom itself in the vision of our founders and philosophers.

There is no inevitable contradiction between these public and private aspects of American society. Indeed, they are the essential poles of energy in a vigorous social order. Without individual decision and inventiveness, without widely dispersed centers of authority and responsibility, the social order grows rigid and centralized. Spontaneity withers before the killing frost of public conformity. Individual citizens with all their varied relationships—as parents, neighbors, churchgoers, workers, businessmen— are reduced to the single loyalties of party and state. In this century we are not likely to underestimate that risk. We have seen free societies destroyed in this way by totalitarians of both the right and the left.

Yet the pursuit of private interest and well-being does not, as the eighteenth century sometimes naïvely believed, automatically add up to the well-being of all. We cannot, like the poet Pope, believe that some divine ordering has bidden "self love and social be the same." They are not. The strong pursuit of *my* interest may override the vital interests of others, if nature, health, energy, and property have weighted the odds in my favor. Social evils pile up when little beyond unchecked private interest determines the pattern of society.

At best, the result is a "lobby" or "pressure group" state in which each organized group jostles for its own interests, at the expense of the weak, the isolated, or the unorganized. France under the Third and Fourth Republic had something of this quality—a republic of interests and buddies, not of principles and patriots.

At worst, the power and influence of the few can violate the fundamental rights and decencies of the many—as in the long survival of human slavery, and in the long resistance of industry to child labor laws and minimum wages. And in our own prosperous days, a new possibility has arisen—that the many can smugly overlook the squalor and misery of the few and tolerate, in the midst of unparalleled plenty, ugly slums, rural destitution, and second class citizenship.

It is the often mediocre and sometimes intolerable consequences of unchecked private interest that have led to the reassertion, at regular intervals in American history, of the primacy of public good. The concept of government as an evil to be reduced to the smallest possible proportions gives place to the idea—in keeping with the vision of the Founders—of government as a positive instrument designed to secure the well-being of all America's citizens. Sometimes, the swing occurs because evil has become so obtrusive that only vigorous public action can check it in time. The conviction that the spread of slavery endangered the Union itself helped to precipitate the Civil War. The demoralization of the entire economy after 1929 led to the experiments and reforms of Roosevelt's New Deal.

Sometimes the swing seems to occur in response to subtler promptings. Early in this century, for instance, under Theodore Roosevelt and Woodrow Wilson, it was not imminent social collapse but disgust at the smash and grab materialism which was devouring America that aroused people once more to demand the restatement of America's public purposes and a new vision of the common good.

Whatever the reasons for America's recurrent swing in emphasis from private interest to public responsibility, it has always had a significant *external* consequence. It has aroused both in America and in the world at large the sense, eloquently expressed by our greatest statesmen, that the American experiment has significance far beyond its own frontiers and is in some measure a portent for all mankind. The feeling of a new dawn for all humanity echoes through the great utterances and documents which are the foundation of the United States of America. In his time, the Declaration of Independence meant for Lincoln that victory in the war against slavery and disunion was indispensable to the survival of free government everywhere, and was the promise, too, that ultimately humanity's age-old burdens would be lifted from the shoulders of all mankind.

Still later Woodrow Wilson spoke of "making the world safe for democracy" and sought in his idea of the League of Nations to work out a pattern of free association under law for the emergent society of man. And from the reforming ferment of the New Deal followed the Atlantic Charter, American initiative in forming the United Nations, and the derivative new experiments in economic assistance, which, launched with the Marshall Plan, have opened a new phase in the effort to build a genuinely humane order in our neighborhood, the world.

Today I don't suppose anyone will deny that mankind is in acute need of a convincing working model of a free society. Never in human history has there been an epoch of such profound and sudden social upheaval on so universal a scale. Never has the working model of tyranny made such claims for its own effectiveness; never has monolithic discipline attacked so savagely what it calls the pretensions of the free way of life. The whole of human society has become plastic and malleable in the flames of social revolution. Human energies everywhere are seeking to run into new molds and the Communists universally claim that theirs alone is the truly effective system.

Thus there has never been a time when the *public* aspect of American liberty as the organizing principle of a great social order has needed to be more studied and stressed.

But what do we find? Never before in my lifetime—not even in the days of Harding and Coolidge—has the mystique of privacy seemed to me so pervasive. The face which we present to the world—especially through our mass circulation media—is the face of the individual or the family as a high consumption unit with minimal social links or responsibilities— father happily drinking his favorite beer, mother dreamily fondling soft garments newly rinsed in a marvel detergent, the children gaily calling from the new barbecue pit for a famous sauce for their steak. And, of course, a sleek new car is in the background.

No doubt many of the world's peoples want and mean to get a lot more of this. But it is not *all* they want, and they have to look hard to find the balancing picture of America's wider purposes and to learn that high private consumption is not our ultimate aim of life, nor our answer to all man's evils and disorders in a time of breath-taking social change. I think of the Psalmist's words: "And He gave them that which they lusted after, and sent leanness withal into their soul." High consumption is not spirit- ual growth. Nor is it the same as cultural growth. Gerald Johnson has used the phrase "America's high standard of low living." And all these good "things" do not solve the problems of urban decay and congestion. Behind the shining child in the advertisement lurks the juvenile delin- quent in the run-down slum. Nor does high consumption solve the sprawl of subdivisions which is gradually depriving us of either civilized urban living or uncluttered rural space. It does not guarantee America's chil- dren the teachers or the schools which should be their birthright. It does nothing to end the shame of racial discrimination. It does not counter the exorbitant cost of health, nor conserve the nation's precious reserves of land and water and wilderness.

The contrast between private opulence and public squalor on most of our panorama is now too obvious to be denied. Yet we still spend per capita almost as much on advertising to multiply the private wants of our people as we do in educating them to seek a fuller, wiser, and more satis- fying civic existence. Nor is this imbalance simply a matter of drift and the unmeant consequence of our fabulous new opportunities for wealth creation. It is in real measure the result of considered and deliberate government policy. Except for defense American public expenditure today is proportionately lower than it was in 1939. Moreover, it is lower than current levels in West Germany, Belgium, Britain, or Sweden—to take a European cross-section of capitalist economies. And while we raise a cheer at the comparison, let us also remember that it means a relative decline in support for such basic needs as schooling, research, health, small income housing, urban renewal, and all forms of public services—local, state, and federal—at a time when there has been steadily more income to spend on every private want, or unwant.

With the supermarket as our temple and the singing commercial as our litany, are we likely to fire the world with an irresistible vision of America's exalted purposes and inspiring way of life?

Even where public spending has been high—for defense and economic aid—our performance has been more defensive than indicative of freedom's positive purposes. We have stressed so much our aim of stopping Communism for our own security that self-interest has often contaminated our generous aid programs. And even in the vital field of military security the Administration's concern for the citizen as a private consumer rather than as a mature responsible American who will accept the unpleasant facts about his security, leaves one with the lurking doubt that budgetary considerations, rather than the stark needs of strategy, are determining our defense effort.

In short, at a time of universal social upheaval and challenge, our vision of our own society seems to be of limited social significance In the most public and civic of epochs—when the fate of nations and civilizations is the common theme of the world's discourse—we have drawn back and taken refuge in the joys of privacy. An air of disengagement and disinterest hangs over the most powerful and affluent society the world has ever known. Neither the turbulence of the world abroad nor the fatness and flatness of the world at home are moving us to more vital effort. We seem becalmed in a season of storm, drifting in a century of mighty dreams and great achievements. As an American I am disturbed.

John Adams said that at the time of the American Revolution never more than a third of the colonists really wanted independence. And probably even less cared to make the exertion independence demanded. A third were loyal to the King, and the rest were inert and uncommitted.

So the condition of our public discourse and individual freedom today is not one for despair or even much discouragement. And it is arguable that after the shocks and rigors of the 1930s and '40s, we as a nation needed a period of relaxation—though I would note that the Russians and the Chinese after far greater shocks have had no opportunity for a cozy nap. Now, however, we have had our rest, and I sense the stirring of a new vitality, possibly the beginning of that traditional swing of the political pendulum away from private pursuits to a concern for the nation's broader purposes, which has always provided the strong oscillating balance in our American experiment of freedom.

I am persuaded that the leaders and the parties which now speak clearly to the Americans of their social responsibilities, as well as their private wants, will command a more attentive hearing. I believe the old idea of America and its government as a positive instrument for the common weal is being restored once again after all the cheap sarcasm about "bureaucracy" and "creeping socialism." And if a change of mood and attitude toward our public needs and institutions is in fact on the way, I do not think there can be much question about the fields in which the new sense of responsibility must quickly go to work.

At home we must ask ourselves again what *quality* of life we want, both public and private, not simply as consumers and producers but as citizens of this great republic. Education and the arts is the starting point, for it is only here that the citizens of tomorrow can learn to demand and live a fuller life. A respect for excellence and a sense of discipline in the attainment of knowledge are virtues not just because the Russians pioneered the space age and photographed the dark side of the moon, but because the new society that technology is building demands a grasp and competence among the mass of citizens undreamed of in earlier civilizations.

By education and the arts we mean something more than better school buildings, higher teachers' salaries, and more scholarships for the intelligent. We mean a reorientation of our ideals and tastes, the strenuous stretching of mental and artistic talent, the exaltation of excellence above social approval, and of mental achievement above quick material success. We mean, in short, new standards of respect and reward for intellect and culture. And we mean more stable financing for basic research, more concern for advancing knowledge for its own sake. We mean cooperation with other communities of scholars and creative thinkers, as in the International Geophysical Year, in order that our pursuit of truth may be an adventure we share with all mankind. And we mean that the pursuit of truth in itself is the highest activity of man.

Here, then, in all its ramifications of expense, of standards, content, and opportunity is a top priority for a great new America and a national purpose few would dispute.

I would include not far below a reconsideration of our urban life. We are adding a city the size of Philadelphia to our population every year. From every large urban center the suburbs spread out and out, without shape or grace or any centered form of civic life. Many are so built that they are the slums of tomorrow. Meanwhile, town centers decay, racial divisions destroy harmony, commuters jam the city approaches, and a strange, half-life of divided families and Sunday fathers is growing up. If we accept both the fact of our rapid growth in population and the fact that most people will live in cities, we can begin a serious attack upon our congested, ugly, inconvenient metropolitan sprawls—creating the preconditions of a good urban life that could become a new model for an urbanizing world. In this vital field of future living the Russian contribution is meager, but we will find, as at Brasilia, that others are plunging forward ahead of us.

Restoration of compassion is a clumsy way to describe another great embracing national purpose. In the past, evils and miseries have been the driving force of majority discontent. But now for the first time in history, the engine of social progress has run out of the fuel of discontent. We have therefore to mobilize our imagination, our personal sense of indignity and outrage, if we are to act on the conviction that gross poverty, curable illness, racial indignity, mental disease, and suffering in old age are a disgrace amidst the surrounding luxuries, privileges, and indulgence of such a wealthy society as ours.

And here our top priorities must reach beyond our shores. For it is not chiefly in America or in the fortunate North Atlantic basin that the world's miseries are to be found. On the contrary, we confidently predict to ourselves a doubling and tripling of our high living standards. But in Asia, Africa, and Latin America live scores of millions who, on present forecasts, can equally confidently expect to fare steadily worse. This disparity in living standards between the rich and the poor is as great a threat to peace as the arms race, and narrowing the gap as imperative as arms control.

The purpose of our aid programs should therefore be designed not primarily to counter Communism—though it will do this too—but to create conditions of self-respect and self-sustaining growth in economies still behind the threshold of modernization. The needs are so staggering that to achieve this national purpose will demand not only the greatest intelligence, perseverance, and financial enterprise, private and public, but also a much broader cooperation and joint effort with other advanced nations than in the past. But if we accept this as fundamental American foreign policy, not on a year to year basis but for the next critical generation, we shall develop the perspective and staying power to reach real solutions, not doles, handouts, bad debts—and dislike.

And in doing so, we shall do more than set the processes of modernization in healthy motion. I believe that this is the chief way to us to extend our vision of "a more perfect union" to all mankind. It is a commonplace that in a world made one by science and the atom, the old national boundaries are dissolving, the old landmarks vanishing. We can't have privacy and the hydrogen bomb too. A workable human society has to be fashioned and we must start where we can—by setting up the institutions of a common economic life, by employing our wealth and wisdom to spark the growth of production in poorer lands, by working together with like-minded powers to establish the permanent patterns of a workable world economy. In this way we can hope to establish one of the two main preconditions of peaceful human society—economic solidarity and mutual help.

The other precondition of peace—and this, of all priorities is our highest—is our unwavering search for peace under law which, in our present context, means controlled and supervised disarmament. Only a disarmed world offers us security worth the name any longer.

I do not believe, even now, that the world accepts the idea that genuine disarmament is America's primary, public purpose. We talk of peace and our devotion to it. But there is far more hard, unremitting effort in the task than speeches or protestations or journeys—however distant. What seems to be lacking is sincere and sustained dedication to this goal and unwearying pursuit by our highest officers, military and civilian, in season and out. As it is now no major conference occurs without preliminary rumors of American indecision and even suggestions that our leaders are "dragging their feet." I would wish instead to see created an international atmosphere in which such forays as Mr. Khrushchev's speech on total disarmament at the United Nations would fall like a lead balloon from the certain knowledge all round the world that this and nothing less had been for years the public policy of the United States.

I believe that the American people are prepared to face the cost, the rigors, the efforts, and the challenge which are involved in recovering the public image of a great America. The cost in physical terms— in hard work, in discipline, in more taxes if need be—is hard to estimate precisely. Any arms control would release resources. Our growing national product will certainly provide wider margins out of which vital public expenditure could be met. But if the cost is higher than our present level of public spending, I frankly believe that education and health for our children, dignity and beauty in our civic lives, and security and well-being in the world at large, are more important than the "things" which might otherwise have priority.

But still more important is America's need to face squarely the *facts* about its situation. If freedom is really the organizing principle of our society, then we cannot forget that it is not illusion, propaganda, and sedatives, but truth, and truth alone, that makes us free. Under the influence of the politics of sedation and the techniques of salesmanship I believe that in recent years self-deceit has slackened our grip on reality. We have tended to shirk the difficult truth and accept the easy half-truth. Perhaps it is always that way; as the old humorist Josh Billings used to say: "As scarce as truth is, the supply is always greater than the demand."

But we know from our own lives that reality entails hard choices and disappointments: that it measures real achievement not in terms of luck but in terms of difficulties overcome. I don't believe our national life can follow any other pattern.

No preordained destiny decrees that America shall have all the breaks and soft options. Neither greatness nor even freedom lies that way. So we must surely return to the reality principle, to the bracing, invigorating, upland climate of truth itself. I think we are ready now to move forward into the rigors and glories of the new decade with open eyes, eager step, and firm purposes worthy of our great past.

How Can the Community Serve the Individual?

In urging the need to extend the vision of national purpose to serve all mankind, Adlai Stevenson touches upon a problem that has long troubled Americans. Freedom which, in one sense, liberated the individual also had a public aspect as the organizing principle of a new kind of society. But such a society, while dedicated to the service of private interest and well-being, demanded the occasional use of public instruments that might restrain the citizen. The necessity of harnessing the energy of a free society to satisfy needs that could only be achieved cooperatively might thus entail a restriction of individual liberty.

In traditional societies or in totalitarian regimes the problem did not exist. All the ends of the community were general; and therefore any means might be used to attain them, because the individual was only an instrument in the hands of the state. But in a free society which recognized that the ends of its actions were the preservation and furtherance of the individual's dignity and interests, it was more difficult to arrive at acceptable definitions of the extent to which public means were justified. For such a society was restrained by the consciousness that whatever means it used were to be directed toward private ends.

In the past, the individualism of Americans and the fragmented character of their society sometimes obscured the necessity of using such means. The jealousy of government power and the reluctance to permit its unrestrained exercise seemed to reduce the public role to the bare minimum of police and defense measures. At other times social crises induced a broad expansion of that role. Hence the protracted debate over the ways in which public means and private ends were to be reconciled in order best to fulfill the national purpose of the United States.

The earliest settlers had had no such dilemma, for they still expected to form coherent communities that would be capable of using wide powers toward generally recognized objectives. Thus the Mayflower Compact (1620), composed by the Pilgrims on the eve of their first landing, very clearly and very simply set forth the assumption that a body politic could further the ends of its members (1). But in the next century and a half, the growth and the fragmentation of American society along with the individualistic pressures of the frontier, pushed the necessity for communal action into the background. Only in the occasional writings of such men as John Woolman (1720–72), a Quaker schoolmaster and preacher in New Jersey, do we find assertions of a wider point of view. His eloquent plea for the poor in 1763 was widely read, and reminded many colonists of their communal obligations even to the oppressed Negroes (2).

The Revolution and the long debate over the future political structure of the nation gave an impetus to more considered views of what the community might do. Imbedded in the conception of the union was an emphasis upon the duty of common action, to which President George Washington (1732–99) was particularly sensitive. His Farewell Address (3) cautioned his fellow countrymen not to allow the differences among them to obscure that duty. Almost three decades later, when President John Quincy Adams (1767–1848) took office in 1825, his Inaugural Address still envisioned a wide range of activities that the government ought to carry forward on behalf of its citizens (4).

The temper of the times in the next fifty years complicated the whole problem. The need for new forms of communal action became more pressing. Yet territorial expansion, economic growth, and individualism, the dominant forces of the period, encouraged some men to focus upon their immediate interests and to treat government as no more than a device to protect and enlarge their own wealth. In response, some political leaders were disposed to resist by narrowing the role of the state. President Andrew Jackson (1767–1845), in his veto of the bill to recharter the Bank of the United States, thus attempted to limit government action to prevent it from becoming the tool of rapacious monopolists (5).

On the other hand, a variety of reformers kept pressing the government to act toward more general ends. Parke Godwin (1816–1904), a New York lawyer and journalist, saw the need for some considered regulation of the unrestrained tendencies of the economy (6). Dorothea Lynde Dix (1802–87), a teacher and nurse especially concerned with the problems of the insane, wished the state to further the health of its members (7). And Horace Mann (1796–1859), lawyer, congressman, and educator, envisioned a large role for the government in the school system (8). Thomas Wentworth Higginson (1823–1911), himself a minister, reformer, and soldier, summed up the character of such people in a good-natured essay which pointed to their zeal for action and their unwillingness to leave the individual alone (9).

In the last two decades of the nineteenth century, industrialization and urbanization created still more difficult problems with which the unaided individual was scarcely able to deal alone. The social critic Henry George (1839–97) traced the difficulties of his times to selfish monopolies of the natural resources of the nation (10); and Edward Bellamy (1850–98) argued the need for positive action by the community to serve the citizens who could not stand alone in industrial society (11).

In more recent times, the debate over the location of the line between communal and individual action has continued. But there has been a considerable degree of consensus that some forms of government action were essential. When in 1945, Vice-President Henry A. Wallace (1888–), exposed the need for government planning, he was regarded as an idealistic visionary (12). But in the next fifteen years, his proposals became government policy and are now scarcely subject to dispute. Indeed, within the organization of industry itself, the rugged individual is no longer as characteristic as he was in the nineteenth century. Instead, an ever more prominent role is being played by men who have moved up within the corporate bureaucracy. And the great corporations themselves now no longer act as if they were possessions of individual owners, but rather regard themselves as institutions with widespread responsibilities, as a perceptive article in *Fortune* pointed out (13).

The line between public means and private ends was thus always difficult to draw and changed frequently. But that the relationship between the two was important remained a constant in the thinking of Americans.

1. *Mayflower Compact, 1620**

IN THE NAME OF GOD, AMEN. We, whose names are underwritten, the loyal subjects of our dread Sovereign Lord King James, by the Grace of God, of Great Britain, France, and Ireland, King, Defender of the Faith, &c. Having undertaken for the glory of God and advancement of the Christian faith, and the honor of our king and country, a voyage to plant the first colony in the northern parts of Virginia; do by these presents, solemnly and mutually, in the presence of God and one another, convenant and combine ourselves together into a civil body politic, for our better ordering and preservation, and furtherance of the ends aforesaid: And by virtue hereof do enact, constitute, and frame, such just and equal laws, ordinances, acts, constitutions, and officers, from time to time, as shall be thought most meet and convenient for the general good of the colony; unto which we promise all due submission and obedience. IN WITNESS whereof we have hereunto subscribed our names at Cape Cod the eleventh of November. . . . Anno Domini, 1620.

* B. P. Poore, comp., *Federal and State Constitutions* (Washington, D.C., 1878), I, 931.

2. JOHN WOOLMAN, *A Plea for the Poor, 1769**

Men who have large possessions, and live in the spirit of charity, who carefully inspect the circumstance of those who occupy their estates, and, regardless of the customs of the times, regulate their demands agreeably to universal love: these by being righteous on a principle, do good to the poor without placing it as an act of bounty. Their example in avoiding superfluities tends to incite others to moderation; their goodness, in not exacting what the laws or customs would support them in, tends to open the channel to moderate labor in useful affairs, and to discourage those branches of business which have not their foundation in true wisdom.

To be busied in that which is but vanity, and serves only to please the unstable mind, tends to an alliance with those who promote that vanity, and is a snare in which many poor tradesmen are entangled.

To be employed in things connected with virtue, is most agreeable with the character and inclination of an honest man.

While industrious frugal people are borne down with poverty, and oppressed with too much labor in useful things, the way to apply money, without promoting pride and vanity, remains open to such who truly sympathize with them in their various difficulties. . . .

* John Woolman, "A Plea for the Poor; or a Word of Remembrance and Caution to the Rich," *Journal* (Philadelphia, 1837), pp. 324–27, 356–61.

The Creator of the earth is the owner of it. He gave us being thereon, and our nature requires nourishment, which is the produce of it. As he is kind and merciful we, as his creatures, while we live answerable to the design of our creation, are so far entitled to a convenient subsistence, that no man may justly deprive us of it.

By the agreements and contracts of our fathers and predecessors, and by doings and proceedings of our own, some claim a much greater share of this world than others: and while those possessions are faithfully improved to the good of the whole, it consists with equity. But he who with a view to self-exaltation, causeth some with their domestic animals to labor immoderately, and, with the moneys arising to him therefrom, employs others in the luxuries of life, acts contrary to the gracious designs of Him who is the true owner of the earth, nor can any possessions, either acquired or derived from ancestors, justify such conduct.

Goodness remains to be goodness, and the direction of pure wisdom is obligatory on all reasonable creatures: so that laws and customs are no further a standard for our proceedings, than as their foundation is in universal righteousness.

Though the poor occupy our estates by a bargain, to which they in their poor circumstances agreed; and we ask even less than a punctual fulfilling of their agreement; yet, if our views are to lay up riches, or to live in conformity to customs which have not their foundation in the Truth, and our demands are such as require greater toil, or application to business in them, than is consistent with pure love,—we invade their rights as inhabitants of that world, of which a good and gracious God is proprietor, under whom we are tenants.

Were all superfluities, and the desire of outward greatness laid aside, and the right use of things universally attended to, such a number of people might be employed in things useful, as that moderate labor, with the blessing of heaven, would answer all good purposes relating to people and their animals, and a sufficient number have time to attend on the proper affairs of civil society.

While our strength and spirits are lively, we go cheerfully through business. Either too much or too little action is tiresome; but a right portion is healthful to our bodies, and agreeable to an honest mind.

Where men have great estates, they stand in a place of trust. To have it in their power, without difficulty, to live in that fashion which occasions much labor, and at the same time, to confine themselves to that use of things prescribed by the Redeemer, and confirmed by his example, and the examples of many who lived in the early age of the Christian church, that they may more extensively relieve objects of charity;—for men who have great estates, to live thus, requires close attention to *Divine love*.

Our gracious Creator cares and provides for all his creatures: his tender mercies are over all his works. And so far as his love influences our minds, so far we become interested in his workmanship; and feel a desire to make use of every opportunity to lessen the distresses of the afflicted, and increase the happiness of the creation. Here we have a prospect of one common interest from which our own is inseparable; so that to turn all the treasures we possess into the channel of universal love, becomes the business of our lives.

Men of large estates, whose hearts are thus enlarged, are like fathers to the poor; and in looking over their brethren in distressed circumstances, and considering their own more easy condition, they find a field for humble meditation, and feel the strength of those obligations they are under, to be kind and tender-hearted toward them. Poor men eased of their burdens, and released from too close an application to business, are enabled to hire assistance, to provide well for their animals, and find time to perform those duties amongst their neighbors, which belong to a well guided social life.

When these reflect on the opportunity those had to oppress them, and consider the goodness of their conduct, they behold it lovely, and consistent with brotherhood. And, as the man whose mind is conformed to universal love, hath his trust settled in God, and finds a firm foundation to stand upon, in any changes or revolutions that happen amongst men; so also, the goodness of his conduct tends to spread a kind, benevolent disposition in the world. . . .

To keep Negroes as servants, till they are thirty years of age, and hold the profits of the last nine years of their labor as our own, on a supposition that they may some time be an expense to our estates, is a way of proceeding which appears to admit of improvement.

Reasons offered. *1st.* Men of mature age, who have walked orderly, and made no contract to serve, that they are entitled to freedom I expect is generally agreed to; and to make them serve as slaves nine years longer, may be to keep them slaves for term of Life. They may die before that age, and be no expense to us; and may leave Children to whom, with reason, they might in their last sickness, desire to give the monies they had earned after they had paid for their own education.

2d. The labor of a healthy, industrious Negro man for nine years, I suppose at a moderate computation, may not be less than fifty pounds . . . besides his diet and clothing. Now if this money be earned, either in the service of the man who educated him,

or laid by in yearly proportion under the care of the said man, and put out at a moderate interest for the Negroes use; and to be applied to his future necessities, or to such honest purposes as he by his last will might direct, this would appear to us a more brotherly way of proceeding, were we in the Negroes condition.

3d. Pure goodness tendeth to beget its own likeness, and where men are convinced that the conduct of those who have power over them is equitable, it naturally yields encouragement for them to provide against old age. The pure witness being reached, a care is thereby incited that they may not become a burden on the states of those whom they have found to be honest men, and true friends to them. But where men have labored without wages nine years longer than is common with other men amongst whom they dwell, and then set free; and at going off, are assured that those who so detained them are largely in their debt, but expect not to recover the debt except they become needy when unable to help themselves—such would naturally be induced to think this treatment unbrotherly; to think of the reasonableness of their wages being some time paid; to think that the state in which they labored might reasonably assist them in old age, and thus be tempted to decline from a wise application to business

4th. If I see a man want relief, and know he hath money in my hands which must some time be paid, with reasonable use, either to him, or to others by his direction, there appears in this case no temptation to withhold it at the time I saw that he wanted it; but if selfishness so far prevail in me, that I looked upon the money which I had in trust, with a desire to keep it from the true owner, and through the strength of desire, joined with expectation, at length so far consider it a part of my estate, as to apply it in promoting myself or my family in the world, and therewith entered into expenses which a humble follower of Christ might have shunned: here, by joining with one temptation there is great danger of falling into more, and of not attending to the wants of the man who had monies in my hands, with that care and diligence which I might have done, had the tempter found no entrance into my mind.

5th. If we righteously account for the monies which we have in security, with a reasonable use thereon, and frugally expend the whole in relieving the man who earned it; and more being wanted, the public refuseth to bear any part of the expense,—if our estates have not been benefited aforetime by the labors of his fathers nor ancestors:—this appears to be a case wherein the righteous suffer for the testimony of a good conscience; and from which, if faithfully attended to, they might in time, I trust, hope for relief.

The Negroes have been a suffering people; and we as a civil society are they by whom they have suffered. Now where persons have been injured, as to their outward substance, and died without having recompense, their children appear to have a right to that which was equitably due to and detained from their fathers.

Having thus far spoken of the Negroes as equally entitled to the benefit of their labor with us, I feel it on my mind to mention that debt which is due to many Negroes of the present age. Where men, within certain limits, are so formed into a society, as to become like a large body consisting of many members; here, whatever injuries are done to others not of this society, by members of this society,— if the society in whose power it is, doth not use all reasonable endeavors to execute justice and judgment, nor publicly disown those unrighteous proceedings,—the iniquities of individuals become chargeable on such civil society to which they remain united. And where persons have been injured, as to their outward substance, and died without having recompense, so that their children are kept out of that which was equitably due to their parents;—here such children appear to be justly entitled to receive recompense from that civil society under which their parents suffered.

My heart is affected with sorrow while I write on this subject, on account of the great injuries committed against these gentiles, and against their children born in that captivity which is an unrighteous captivity. Had the active members in civil society, when those injuries were first attempted, united in a firm opposition to those violent proceedings;—had others, in a selfish spirit, attempted the like afterwards, and met with a firm opposition, and been made to do justice to the injured persons, till the prospect of gain by such unrighteous proceedings appeared so doubtful that no further attempts had been made,—how much better it would have been for these American colonies and islands!

When the ancestors of these people were brought from Africa, some I believe bought those poor sufferers with intent to treat them kindly as slaves. They bought them as though those violent men had a right to sell them; but, I believe, without entering deep enough into the consideration of the nature and tendency of such a bargain, and the consequence of such proceedings. Others, I believe, bought them with views of outward ease and profit; and thus those violent men found people of reputation who purchased their booty, and built on that purchase as a foundation to exercise the authority of masters; and thus encouraged them in this horrible trade, till their proceedings were so far approved by civil society as to consider those men as members, without proceeding to punish them for their crimes. And hence, building on an unrighteous foundation, a veil was gradually drawn over a practice, very grievous and afflicting to great numbers of these gentiles, and most foreign to righteousness: and thus the face of things became so disguised, that under the most lamentable injustice, but few appeared to be alarmed at it, or zealously labored to have justice done to the sufferers and their posterity.

The poor Africans were people of a strange language, and not easy to converse with; and their situation as slaves, too generally destroyed that brotherly freedom which frequently subsists between us and inoffensive strangers.

In this adverse condition, how reasonable is it to suppose, that they would revolve in their distressed minds, the iniquities committed against them, and mourn without any to comfort them!

Though through gradual proceedings in unrighteousness, dimness hath come over many minds, yet the nature of things is not altered. Long oppression hath not made oppression consistent with brotherly love; nor length of time through several ages, made recompense to the posterity of those injured strangers. Many of them lived, and died without having their suffering cases heard, and determined according to equity. And under a degree of sorrow on account of the wantonness, the vanity and superfluity too common amongst us as a civil society, even while a heavy load of unrighteous proceedings lies upon us, do I now express these things, under a feeling of universal love, and with a fervent concern for the real interest of my fellow-members in society, as well as the interest of my fellow-creatures in general.

Suppose an inoffensive youth, forty years ago, was violently taken from Guinea, sold here as a slave, and labored hard till old age, and hath children who are now living. Though no sum may properly be mentioned as an equal reward for the total deprivation of liberty;—yet, if the sufferings of this man be computed at no more than fifty pounds, I expect candid men will suppose it within bounds, and that his children have an equitable right to it.

Fifty pounds, at three per cent, adding the interest to the principle once in ten years, appears in forty years to make upwards of one hundred and forty pounds.

Now when our minds are thoroughly divested of all prejudice in relation to the difference of color, and the Love of Christ, in which there is no partiality, prevails upon us, I believe it will appear that a heavy account lies against us as a civil society for oppressions committed against people who did not injure us; and that if the particular case of many individuals were fairly stated, it would appear that there was considerable due to them.

I conclude with the words of that Righteous Judge in Israel, Behold here I am: witness against me before the Lord, and before his anointed; whose ox have I taken? or whose ass have I taken? or whom have I defrauded? whom have I oppressed? or of whose hand have I received any bribe, to blind mine eyes therewith; and I will restore it to you. I Samuel xii. 3.

3. George Washington, *Farewell Address, 1796**

Friends and Fellow-Citizens:

The period for a new election of a citizen to administer the Executive Government of the United States being not far distant, and the time actually arrived when your thoughts must be employed in designating the person who is to be clothed with that important trust, it appears to me proper, especially as it may conduce to a more distinct expression of the public voice, that I should now apprise you of the resolution I have formed to decline being considered among the number of those out of whom a choice is to be made.

I beg you at the same time to do me the justice to be assured that this resolution has not been taken without a strict regard to all the considerations appertaining to the relation which binds a dutiful citizen to his country; and that in withdrawing the tender of service, which silence in my situation might imply, I am influenced by no diminution of zeal for your future interest, no deficiency of grateful respect for your past kindness, but am supported by a full conviction that the step is compatible with both. . . .

Here, perhaps, I ought to stop. But a solicitude for your welfare which can not end but with my life, and the apprehension of danger natural to that solicitude, urge me on an occasion like the present to offer to your solemn contemplation and to recommend to your frequent review some sentiments which are the result of much reflection, of no inconsiderable observation, and which appear to me all important to the permanency of your felicity as a people. These will be offered to you with the more freedom as you can only

see in them the disinterested warnings of a parting friend, who can possibly have no personal motive to bias his counsel. Nor can I forget as an encouragement to it your indulgent reception of my sentiments on a former and not dissimilar occasion.

Interwoven as is the love of liberty with every ligament of your hearts, no recommendation of mine is necessary to fortify or confirm the attachment.

The unity of government which constitutes you one people is also now dear to you. It is justly so, for it is a main pillar in the edifice of your real independence, the support of your tranquility at home, your peace abroad, of your safety, of your prosperity, of that very liberty which you so highly prize. But as it is easy to foresee that from different causes and from different quarters much pains will be taken, many artifices employed, to weaken in your minds the conviction of this truth, as this is the point in your political fortress against which the batteries of internal and external enemies will be most constantly and actively (though often covertly and insidiously) directed, it is of infinite moment that you should properly estimate the immense value of your national union to your collective and individual happiness; that you should cherish a cordial, habitual, and immovable attachment to it; accustoming yourselves to think and speak of it as of the palladium of your political safety and prosperity; watching for its preservation with jealous anxiety; discountenancing whatever may suggest even a suspicion that it can in any event be abandoned, and indignantly frowning upon the first dawning of every at-

* J. D. Richardson, *A Compilation of the Messages and Papers of the Presidents* (Washington, D.C., 1896–99), I, 221–23.

tempt to alienate any portion of our country from the rest or to enfeeble the sacred ties which now link together the various parts.

For this you have every inducement of sympathy and interest. Citizens by birth or choice of a common country, that country has a right to concentrate your affections. The name of American, which belongs to you in your national capacity, must always exalt the just pride of patriotism more than any appellation derived from local discriminations. With slight shades of difference, you have the same religion, manners, habits, and political principles. You have in a common cause fought and triumphed together. The independence and liberty you possess are the work of joint councils and joint efforts, of common dangers, sufferings, and successes.

But these considerations, however powerfully they address themselves to your sensibility, are greatly outweighed by those which apply more immediately to your interest. Here every portion of our country finds the most commanding motives for carefully guarding and preserving the union of the whole.

The *North,* in an unrestrained intercourse with the *South,* protected by the equal laws of a common government, finds in the productions of the latter great additional resources of maritime and commercial enterprise and precious materials of the manufacturing industry. The *South,* in the same intercourse, benefiting by the same agency of the *North,* sees its agriculture grow and its commerce expand. Turning partly into its own channels the seamen of the *North,* it finds its particular navigation invigorated; and while it contributes in different ways to nourish and increase the general mass of the national investigation, it looks forward to the protection of a maritime strength to

which itself is unequally adapted. The *East,* in a like intercourse with the *West,* already finds, and in the progressive improvement of interior communications by land and water will more and more find, a valuable vent for the commodities which it brings from abroad or manufactures at home. The *West* derives from the *East* supplies requisite to its growth and comfort, and what is perhaps of still greater consequence, it must of necessity owe the *secure* enjoyment of indispensable *outlets* for its own productions to the weight, influence, and the future maritime strength of the Atlantic side of the Union, directed by an indissoluble community of interest as *one nation.* Any other tenure by which the *West* can hold this essential advantage, whether derived from its own separate strength or from an apostate and unnatural connection with any foreign power, must be intrinsically precarious.

While, then, every part of our country thus feels an immediate and particular interest in union, all the parts combined can not fail to find in the united mass of means and efforts greater strength, greater resource, proportionably greater security from external danger, a less frequent interruption of their peace by foreign nations, and what is of inestimable value, they must derive from union an exemption from those broils and wars between themselves which so frequently afflict neighboring countries not tied together by the same governments, which their own rivalships alone would be sufficient to produce, but which opposite foreign alliances, attachments, and intrigues would stimulate and imbitter. Hence, likewise, they will avoid the necessity of those overgrown military establishments which, under any form of government, are inauspicious to liberty, and which are to be regarded as particularly hostile to republican liberty. In this sense it is that your union ought to be considered as a main prop of your liberty, and that the love of the one ought to endear to you the preservation of the other.

These considerations speak a persuasive language to every reflecting and virtuous mind, and exhibit the continuance of the union as a primary object of patriotic desire. Is there a doubt whether a common government can embrace so large a sphere? Let experience solve it. To listen to mere speculation in such a case were criminal. We are authorized to hope that a proper organization of the whole, with the auxiliary agency of governments for the respective subdivisions, will afford a happy issue to the experiment. It is well worth a fair and full experiment. With such powerful and obvious motives to union affecting all parts of our country, while experience shall not have demonstrated its impracticability, there will always be reason to distrust the patriotism of those who in any quarter may endeavor to weaken its bands. . . .

To the efficacy and permanency of your union a government for the whole is indispensable. No alliances, however strict, between the parts can be an adequate substitute. They must inevitably experience the infractions and interruptions which all alliances in all times have experienced. Sensible of this momentous truth, you have improved upon your first essay by the adoption of a Constitution of Government better calculated than your former for an intimate union and for the efficacious management of your common concerns. This Government, the offspring of our own choice, uninfluenced and unawed, adopted upon full investigation and mature deliberation, completely free in its principles, in the distribution of its powers, uniting security with energy, and containing within itself a provision for its own amendment, has a just claim to

your confidence and your support. Respect for its authority, compliance with its laws, acquiescence in its measures, are duties enjoined by the fundamental maxims of true liberty. The basis of our political systems is the right of the people to make and to alter their constitutions of government. But the constitution which at any time exists till changed by an explicit and authenic act of the whole people is sacredly obligatory upon all. The very idea of the power and the right of the people to establish government presupposes the duty of every individual to obey the established government. . . .

Toward the preservation of your Government and the permanency of your present happy state, it is requisite not only that you steadily discountenance irregular oppositions to its acknowledged authority, but also that you resist with care the spirit of innovation upon its principles, however specious the pretexts. One method of assault may be to effect in the forms of the Constitution alterations which will impair the energy of the system, and thus to undermine what can not be directly overthrown. In all the changes to which you may be invited remember that time and habit are at least as necessary to fix the true character of governments as of other human institutions; that experience is the surest standard by which to test the real tendency of the existing constitution of a country; that facility in changes upon the credit of mere hypothesis and opinion exposes to perpetual change, from the endless variety of hypothesis and opinion; and remember especially that for the efficient management of your common interests in a country so extensive as ours a government of as much vigor as is consistent with the perfect security of liberty is indispensable. Liberty itself will find in such a government, with powers properly distributed and adjusted, its surest guardian. It is, indeed, little else than a name where the government is too feeble to withstand the enterprises of faction, to confine each member of the society within the limits prescribed by the laws, and to maintain all in the secure and tranquil enjoyment of the rights of person and property. . . .

Of all the dispositions and habits which lead to political prosperity, religion and morality are indispensable supports. In vain would that man claim the tribute of patriotism who should labor to subvert these great pillars of human happiness—these firmest props of the duties of men and citizens. The mere politician, equally with the pious man, ought to respect and to cherish them. A volume could not trace all their connections with private and public felicity. Let it simply be asked, where is the security for property, for reputation, for life, if the sense of religious obligation *desert* the oaths which are the instruments of investigation in courts of justice? And let us with caution indulge the supposition that morality can be maintained without religion. Whatever may be conceded to the influence of refined education on minds of peculiar structure, reason and experience both forbid us to expect that national morality can prevail in exclusion of religious principle.

It is substantially true that virtue or morality is a necessary spring of popular government. The rule indeed extends with more or less force to every species of free government. Who that is a sincere friend to it can look with indifference upon attempts to shake the foundation of the fabric? Promote, then, as an object of primary importance, institutions for the general diffusion of knowledge. In proportion as the structure of a government gives force to public opinion, it is essential that public opinion should be enlightened.

As a very important source of strength and security, cherish public credit. One method of preserving it is to use it as sparingly as possible, avoiding occasions of expense by cultivating peace, but remembering also that timely disbursements to prepare for danger frequently prevent much greater disbursements to repel it; avoiding likewise the accumulation of debt, not only by shunning occasions of expense, but by vigorous exertions in time of peace to discharge the debts which unavoidable wars have occasioned, not ungenerously throwing upon posterity the burthen which we ourselves ought to bear. The execution of these maxims belongs to your representatives; but it is necessary that public opinion should cooperate. To facilitate to them the performance of their duty it is essential that you should practically bear in mind that toward the payment of debts there must be revenue; that to have revenue there must be taxes; that no taxes can be devised which are not more or less inconvenient and unpleasant; that the intrinsic embarrassment inseparable from the selection of the proper objects (which is always a choice of difficulties), ought to be a decisive motive for a candid construction of the conduct of the Government in making it, and for a spirit of acquiescence in the measures for obtaining revenue which the public exigencies may at any time dictate.

Observe good faith and justice toward all nations. Cultivate peace and harmony with all. Religion and morality enjoin this conduct. And can it be that good policy does not equally enjoin it? It will be worthy of a free, enlightened, and at no distant period a great nation to give to mankind the magnanimous and too novel example of a people always guided by an exalted justice and benevolence. Who can doubt that in the course of time and things the fruits of such a plan would richly repay any temporary advantages which might be lost by a steady adherence to it? Can it be that Providence has not connected the permanent felicity of a nation with its virtue? The experiment, at least, is recommended by every sentiment which ennobles human nature. Alas! is it rendered impossible by its vices?

In the execution of such a plan nothing is more essential than that permanent, inveterate antipathies against particular nations and passionate attachments for others should be excluded, and that in place of them just and amicable feelings toward all should be cultivated. The nation which indulges toward another an habitual hatred or an habitual fondness is in some degree a slave. It is a slave to its animosity or to its affection, either of which is sufficient to lead it astray from its duty and its interest. . . .

Excessive partiality for one foreign nation and excessive dislike for another cause those whom they actuate to see danger only on one side, and serve to veil and even second the arts of influence on the other. Real patriots who may resist the intrigues of the favorite are liable to become suspected and odious, while its tools and dupes usurp the applause and confidence of the people to surrender their interests.

The great rule of conduct for us in regard to foreign nations is, in extending our commercial relations to have with them as little *political* connection as possible. So far as we have already formed engagements let them be fulfilled with perfect good faith. Here let us stop.

Europe has a set of primary interests which to us have none or a very remote relation. Hence she must be engaged in frequent controversies, the causes of which are essentially foreign to our concerns. Hence, therefore, it must be unwise in us to implicate ourselves by artificial ties in the ordinary vicissitudes of her politics or the ordinary combinations and collisions of her friendships or enmities.

Our detached and distant situation invites and enables us to pursue a different course. If we remain one people, under an efficient government, the period is not far off when we may defy material injury from external annoyance; when we may take such an attitude as will cause the neutrality we may at any time resolve upon to be scrupulously respected; when belligerent nations, under the impossibility of making acquisitions upon us, will not lightly hazard the giving us provocation; when we may choose peace or war, as our interest, guided by justice, shall counsel.

Why forgo the advantages of so peculiar a situation? Why quit our own to stand upon foreign ground? Why, by interweaving our destiny with that of any part of Europe, entangle our peace and prosperity in the toils of European ambition, rivalship, interest, humor, or caprice?

It is our true policy to steer clear of permanent alliances with any portion of the foreign world, so far, I mean, as we are now at liberty to do it; for let me not be understood as capable of patronizing infidelity to existing engagements. I hold the maxim no less applicable to public than to private affairs that honesty is always the best policy. I repeat, therefore, let those engagements be observed in their genuine sense. But in my opinion it is unnecessary and would be unwise to extend them. . . .

Though in reviewing the incidents of my Administration I am unconscious of intentional error, I am nevertheless too sensible of my defects not to think it probable that I may have committed many errors. Whatever they may be, I fervently beseech the Almighty to avert or mitigate the evils to which they may tend. I shall also carry with me the hope that my country will never cease to view them with indulgence, and that, after forty-five years of my life dedicated to its service with an upright zeal, the faults of incompetent abilities will be consigned to oblivion, as myself must soon be to the mansions of rest.

Relying on its kindness in this as in other things, and actuated by that fervent love toward it which is so natural to a man who views in it the native soil of himself and his progenitors for several generations, I anticipate with pleasing expectation that retreat in which I promise myself to realize without alloy the sweet enjoyment of partaking in the midst of my fellow-citizens the benign influence of good laws under a free government—the ever-favorite object of my heart, and the happy reward, as I trust, of our mutual cares, labors, and dangers.

Go. Washington

4. John Quincy Adams, *Message to Congress, 1825** *

The great object of the institution of civil government is the improvement of the condition of those who are parties to the social compact, and no government, in whatever form constituted, can accomplish the lawful ends of its institution but in proportion as it improves the condition of those over whom it is established. Roads and canals, by multiplying and facilitating the communications and intercourse between distant regions and multitudes of men, are among the most important means of improvement. But moral, political, intellectual improvement are duties assigned by the Author of Our Existence to social no less than to individual man. For the fulfillment of those duties governments are invested with power, and to the attainment of the end—the progressive improvement of the condition of the governed—the exercise of delegated powers is a duty as sacred and indispensable as the usurpation of powers not granted is criminal and odious. Among the first, perhaps the very first, instrument for the improvement of the condition of men in knowledge, and to the acquisition of much of the knowledge adapted to the wants, the comforts, and enjoyments of human life public institutions and seminaries of learning are essential. So convinced of this was the first of my predecessors in this office, now first in the memory, as, living, he was first in the hearts, of our countrymen, that once and again in his addresses to the Congresses with whom he cooperated in the public service he earnestly recommended the establishment of seminaries of learning, to prepare for all the emergencies of peace and war—a national university and a military academy. With respect to the latter, had he lived to the present day, in turning his eyes to the institution at West Point he would have enjoyed the gratification of his most earnest wishes; but in surveying the city which has been honored with his name he would have seen the spot of earth which he had destined and bequeathed to the use and benefit of his country as the site for an university still bare and barren.

* Richardson, *Messages and Papers*, II, 311–14.

In assuming her station among the civilized nations of the earth it would seem that our country had contracted the engagement to contribute her share of mind, of labor, and of expense to the improvement of those parts of knowledge which lie beyond the reach of individual acquisition, and particularly to geographical and astronomical science. Looking back to the history only of the half century since the declaration of our independence, and observing the generous emulation with which the Governments of France, Great Britain, and Russia have devoted the genius, the intelligence, the treasures of their respective nations to the common improvement of the species in these branches of science, is it not incumbent upon us to inquire whether we are not bound by obligations of a high and honorable character to contribute our portion of energy and exertion to the common stock? The voyages of discovery prosecuted in the course of that time at the expense of those nations have not only redounded to their glory, but to the improvement of human knowledge. We have been partakers of that improvement and owe for it a sacred debt, not only of gratitude, but of equal or proportional exertion in the same common cause. Of the cost of these undertakings, if the mere expenditures of outfit, equipment, and completion of the expeditions were to be considered the only charges, it would be unworthy of a great and generous nation to take a second thought. One hundred expeditions of circumnavigation like those of Cook and La Pérouse would not burden the exchequer of the nation fitting them out so much as the ways and means of defraying a single campaign in war. But if we take into the account the lives of those benefactors of mankind of which their services in the cause of their species were the purchase, how shall the cost of those

heroic enterprises be estimated, and what compensation can be made to them or to their countries for them? Is it not by bearing them in affectionate remembrance? It is not still more by imitating their example—by enabling countrymen of our own to pursue the same career and to hazard their lives in the same cause?

In inviting the attention of Congress to the subject of internal improvements upon a view thus enlarged it is not my design to recommend the equipment of an expedition for circumnavigating the globe for purposes of scientific research and inquiry. We have objects of useful investigation nearer home, and to which our cares may be more beneficially applied. The interior of our own territories has yet been very imperfectly explored. Our coasts along many degrees of latitude upon the shores of the Pacific Ocean, though much frequented by our spirited commercial navigators, have been barely visited by our public ships. The River of the West, first fully discovered and navigated by a countryman of our own, still bears the name of the ship in which he ascended its waters, and claims the protection of our armed national flag at its mouth. With the establishment of a military post there or at some other point of that coast, recommended by my predecessor and already matured in the deliberations of the last Congress, I would suggest the expediency of connecting the equipment of a public ship for the exploration of the whole northwest coast of this continent.

The establishment of an uniform standard of weights and measures was one of the specific objects contemplated in the formation of our Constitution, and to fix that standard was one of the powers delegated by express terms in that instrument to Congress. The Governments of Great Britain and France have scarcely ceased to be occupied with inquiries and speculations on the same subject since the existence of our Constitution, and with them it has expanded into profound, laborious, and expensive researches into the figure of the earth and the comparative length of the pendulum vibrating seconds in various latitudes from the equator to the pole. These researches have resulted in the composition and publication of several works highly interesting to the cause of science. The experiments are yet in the process of performance. Some of them have recently been made on our own shores, within the walls of one of our own colleges, and partly by one of our own fellow-citizens. It would be honorable to our country if the sequel of the same experiments should be countenanced by the patronage of our Government, as they have hitherto been by those of France and Britain.

Connected with the establishment of an university, or separate from it, might be undertaken the erection of an astronomical observatory, with provision for the support of an astronomer, to be in constant attendance of observation upon the phenomena of the heavens, and for the periodical publication of his observations. It is with no feeling of pride as an American that the remark may be made that on the comparatively small territorial surface of Europe there are existing upward of 130 of these light-houses of the skies, while throughout the whole American hemisphere there is not one. If we reflect a moment upon the discoveries which in the last four centuries have been made in the physical contribution of the universe by the means of these buildings and of observers stationed in them, shall we doubt of their usefulness to every nation? And while scarcely a year passes over our heads without bringing some new astronomical discovery to light, which

we must fain receive at second hand from Europe, are we not cutting ourselves off from the means of returning light for light while we have neither observatory nor observer upon our half of the globe and the earth revolves in perpetual darkness to our unsearching eyes?

When, on the 25th of October, 1791, the first President of the United States announced to Congress the result of the first enumeration of the inhabitants of this Union, he informed them that the returns gave the pleasing assurance that the population of the United States bordered on 4,000,000 persons. At the distance of thirty years from that time the last enumeration, five years since completed, presented a population bordering upon 10,000,000. Perhaps of all the evidences of a prosperous and happy condition of human society the rapidity of the increase of population is the most unequivocal. But the demonstration of our prosperity rests not alone upon this indication. Our commerce, our wealth, and the extent of our territories have increased in corresponding proportions, and the number of independent communities associated in our Federal Union has since that time nearly doubled. The legislative representation of the States and people in the two Houses of Congress has grown with the growth of their constituent bodies. The House, which then consisted of 65 members, now numbers upward of 200. The Senate, which consisted of 26 members, has now 48. But the executive and, still more, the judiciary departments are yet in a great measure confined to their primitive organization, and are now not adequate to the urgent wants of a still growing community.

The naval armaments, which at an early period forced themselves upon the necessities of the Union, soon led to the establishment of a Department of the Navy. But the Departments of Foreign Affairs and of the Interior, which early after the formation of the Government had been united in one, continue so united to this time, to the unquestionable detriment of the public service. The multiplication of our relations with the nations and Governments of the Old World has kept pace with that of our population and commerce, while within the last ten years a new family of nations in our own hemisphere has arisen among the inhabitants of the earth, with whom our intercourse, commercial and political, would of itself furnish occupation to an active and industrious department. The constitution of the judiciary, experimental and imperfect as it was even in the infancy of our existing Government, is yet more inadequate to the administration of national justice at our present maturity. . . .

The laws relating to the administration of the Patent Office are deserving of much consideration and perhaps susceptible of some improvement. The grant of power to regulate the action of Congress upon this subject has specified both the end to be obtained and the means by which it is to be effected, "to promote the progress of science and useful arts by securing for limited times to authors and inventors the exclusive right to their respective writings and discoveries." If an honest pride might be indulged in the reflection that on the records of that office are already found inventions the usefulness of which has scarcely been transcended in the annals of human ingenuity, would not its exultation be allayed by the inquiry whether the laws effectively insured to the inventors the reward destined to them by the Constitution—even a limited term of exclusive right to their discoveries?

On the 24th of December, 1799, it was resolved by Congress that a mar-ble monument should be erected by the United States in the Capitol at the City of Washington; that the family of General Washington should be requested to permit his body to be deposited under it, and that the monument be so designed as to commemorate the great events of his military and political life. In reminding Congress of this resolution and that the monument contemplated by it remains yet without execution, I shall indulge only the remarks that the works at the Capitol are approaching completion; that the consent of the family, desired by the resolution, was requested and obtained; that a monument has been recently erected in this city over the remains of another distinguished patriot of the Revolution, and that a spot has been reserved within the walls where you are deliberating for the benefit of this and future ages, in which the mortal remains may be deposited of him whose spirit hovers over you and listens with delight to every act of the representatives of his nation which can tend to exalt and adorn his and their country.

The Constitution under which you are assembled is a charter of limited powers. After full and solemn deliberation upon all or any of the objects which, urged by an irresistible sense of my own duty, I have recommended to your attention should you come to the conclusion that, however desirable in themselves, the enactment of laws for effecting them would transcend the powers committed to you by that venerable instrument which we are all bound to support, let no consideration induce you to assume the exercise of powers not granted to you by the people. But if the power to exercise exclusive legislation in all cases whatsoever over the district of Columbia; if the power to lay and collect taxes, duties, imposts, and excises, to pay the debts and provide for the common defense and general welfare of the United States; if the power to regulate commerce with foreign nations and among the several States and with the Indian tribes, to fix the standard of weights and measures, to establish post-offices and post-roads, to declare war, to raise and support armies, to provide and maintain a navy, to dispose of and make all needful rules and regulations respecting the territory of other property belonging to the United States, and to make all laws which shall be necessary and proper for carrying these powers into execution—if these powers and others enumerated in the Constitution may be effectually brought into action by laws promoting the improvement of agriculture, commerce, and manufactures, the cultivation and encouragement of the mechanic and of the elegant arts, the advancement of literature, and the progress of the sciences, ornamental and profound, to refrain from exercising them for the benefit of the people themselves would be to hide in the earth the talent committed to our charge—would be treachery to the most sacred of trusts.

The spirit of improvement is abroad upon the earth. It stimulates the hearts and sharpens the faculties not of our fellow-citizens alone, but of the nations of Europe and of their rulers. While dwelling with pleasing satisfaction upon the superior excellence of our political institutions, let us not be unmindful that liberty is power; that the nation blessed with the largest portion of liberty must in proportion to its numbers be the most powerful nation upon earth, and that the tenure of power by man is, in the moral purposes of his Creator, upon condition that it shall be exercised to ends of beneficence, to improve the condition of himself and his fellowmen. While foreign nations less blessed with that freedom which is power than ourselves are advancing with gigantic strides in the career of public improvement, were we to slumber in indolence or fold up our arms and proclaim to the world that we are palsied by the will of our constituents, would it not be to cast away the bounties of Providence and doom ourselves to perpetual inferiority? In the course of the year now drawing to its close we have beheld, under the auspices and at the expense of one State of this Union, a new university unfolding its portals to the sons of science and holding up the torch of human improvement to eyes that seek the light. We have seen under the persevering and enlightened enterprise of another State the waters of our Western lakes mingle with those of the ocean. If undertakings like these have been accomplished in the compass of a few years by the authority of single members of our Confederation, can we, the representative authorities of the whole Union, fall behind our fellow-servants in the exercise of the trust committed to us for the benefit of our common sovereign by the accomplishment of works important to the whole and to which neither the authority nor the resources of any one State can be adequate?

Finally, fellow-citizens, I shall wait with cheering hope and faithful cooperation the result of your deliberations, assured that, without encroaching upon the powers reserved to the authorities of the respective States or to the people, you will, with a due sense of your obligations to your country and of the high responsibilities weighing upon yourselves, give efficacy to the means committed to you for the common good. And may He who searches the hearts of the children of men prosper your exertions to secure the blessings of peace and promote the highest welfare of our country.

5. ANDREW JACKSON, *Veto of the Bank Bill, 1832**

It is to be regretted that the rich and powerful too often bend the acts of government to their selfish purposes. Distinctions in society will always exist under every just government. Equality of talents, of education, or of wealth can not be produced by human institutions. In the full enjoyment of the gifts of Heaven and the fruits of superior industry, economy, and virtue, every man is equally entitled to protection by law; but when the laws undertake to add to these natural and just advantages artificial distinctions, to grant titles, gratuities, and exclusive privileges, to make the rich richer and the potent more powerful, the humble members of society—the farmers, mechanics, and laborers—who have neither the time nor the means of securing like favors to themselves, have a right to complain of the injustice of their Government. There are no necessary evils in government. Its evils exist only in its abuses. If it would confine itself to equal protection, and, as Heaven does its rains, shower its favors alike on the high and the low, the rich and the poor, it would be an unqualified blessing. In the act before me there seems to be a wide and unnecessary departure from these just principles.

Nor is our Government to be maintained or our Union preserved by invasions of the rights and powers of the several States. In thus attempting to make our General Government strong we make it weak. Its true strength consists in leaving individuals and States as much as possible to themselves—in making itself felt, not in its power, but in its beneficence; not in its control, but in its protection; not in binding the States more closely to the center, but leaving each to move unobstructed in its proper orbit.

Experience should teach us wisdom. Most of the difficulties our Government now encounters and most of the dangers which impend over our Union have sprung from an abandonment of the legitimate objects of Government by our national legislation, and the adoption of such principles as are embodied in this act. Many of our rich men have not been content with equal protection and equal benefits, but have besought us to make them richer by act of Congress. By attempting to gratify their desires we have in the results of our legislation arrayed section against section, interest against interest, and man against man, in a fearful commotion which threatens to shake the foundations of our Union. It is time to pause in our career to review our principles, and if possible revive that devoted patriotism and spirit of compromise which distinguished the sages of the Revolution and the fathers of our Union. If we can not at once, in justice to interests vested under improvident legislation, make our Government what it ought to be, we can at least take a stand against all new grants of monopolies and exclusive privileges, against any prostitution of our Government to the advancement of the few at the expense of the many, and in favor of compromise and gradual reform in our code of laws and system of political economy.

* Richardson, *Messages and Papers,* II 590–91.

6. Parke Godwin, *Democracy, Constructive and Pacific, 1844**

Thus we have stated that blind competition tends to the formation of gigantic monopolies in every branch of labor; that it depreciates the wages of the working classes; that it excites an endless warfare between human arms, and machinery and capital,—a war in which the weak succumb; that it renders the recurrence of failures, bankruptcies, and commercial crises a sort of endemic disease; and that it reduces the middling and lower classes to a precarious and miserable existence. We have stated, on the authority of authentic documents, that while the few rich are becoming more and more rich, the unnumbered many are becoming poorer. Is anything further necessary to prove that our modern world of industry is a veritable HELL, where disorder, discord, and wretchedness reign, and in which the most cruel fables of the old mythology are more than realized? . . .

What, then, in a world like this, is to be done? The question of questions is this! Either we are to close the shells of our selfishness around us, sinking down into the mire, with stupid indifference, or we are to address ourselves, at once, like noble and true-hearted men, to the solution of the difficulty. The fact of human misery is a broad and glaring one, written in characters of fire and blood across the whole earth. What is to be done with it? We iterate the question.

1. We remark that little or nothing is to be done by any form of political action, that we know of, using the word political only in its common application to the movements of government. And there are two reasons for this; first, that politics have accomplished all that it is required of them to accomplish; and second, that their sphere is so limited, that they cannot be made to touch the source of the evil. We wish to say nothing here against any of our great political parties; but we do assert that the doctrines of either of them, carried out to the hearts' content of the most sanguine advocates of them would achieve nothing in the way of social reform. . . . It is now more than half a century since the controversies of our politics began, and it would require the sharpest optics to discover in what particular they had advanced. There has been infinite labor with no progress. The same questions have been argued and reargued, without coming to a decision. We have heard speech after speech, we have seen election after election; the bar-rooms have resounded with appeals; the streets have re-echoed with clamorings; now this faction has triumphed, and now that; victory and defeat have alternated more swiftly than the changes of the moon; legislatures and senates have met, and Presidents have fulminated; yet does it not appear, after all this noise and commotion—after all this everlasting talk and expense, that we are at all nearer to a conclusion, in these days of John Tyler, than we were in the days of Thomas Jefferson. If any one would be impressed with this view, let him compare the daily newspapers of the two epochs; he will find that with the change of a few names and dates, the articles of one might well answer for the pages of the other. Our long discussion seems to have been afflicted with the curse of perpetual barrenness. This protracted struggle, this ever re-

* Parke Godwin, *Democracy, Constructive and Pacific* (New York, 1844), 21ff.

newed debate, has resulted, when all is told, to the net quotient—zero.

But let us not be understood as saying that there has been no progress in American society. God forbid! How could we say it, when we know that the mighty muscles of the human hand, the mighty powers of the human mind and heart, have been at work? How could we say it, when giant miraculous Labor has been felling the forests, and turning the glebe, and whirling the spinning jennies, and putting down its thoughts in words and deeds; when the spires of an hundred thousand schoolhouses point to the skies; when the fires of truth and self-sacrifice have glowed in many more thousand breasts; when the noblest aspirations were ascending from millions of noble souls? Yes, we thank God, there has been progress: but it has not been by means of, so much as in spite of, our politics. We mean that our politics has never been thorough enough to touch the root of our social distress. It has now no vitality. All the sap has dried out and withered from our discussions. The old straw has been thrashed and rethrashed until it is reduced to the merest impalpable powder—out of which nothing can be made, not even snuff strong enough to tickle a grown man's nostrils. Something deeper— more searching, more comprehensive, more true—is wanting, to raise us from the slough into which we have lamentably fallen.

2. Our help, if any is to come to us, is to be found in the better adjustment of our social relations. The vice for which we seek a remedy is in the heart of society, not its extremities; and it is to the heart that we must apply the cure. What that cure may be, is partly indicated by the whole tenor of this essay. We have shown that capital and labor are at open war. The field of industry, in all its branches, is an eternal field of battle. Either capital tyrannizes over labor, or labor, driven to extremes, rises in insurrection against its oppressor. One or the other of these effects inevitably follows the working of the system of unrestrained competition. How obvious the suggestion, then, that this competition must be brought to an end? It we can introduce peace, where there was before war—if we can make a common feeling where there was before antagonism and hatred—if we can discover a mode of causing men to work for each other instead of against each other—then, we say, we have advanced a most important step toward the solution of the problem.

Now, the power which is able to effect this change, which can turn opposition into accord, divergence into convergence, contest into cooperation, is the principle of the ORGANIZATION OF INDUSTRY ON THE BASIS OF A UNION OF INTERESTS. . . .

The three productive elements of society, the three sources of its wealth, the three wheels of industrial mechanism, are Capital, Labor, and Talent. Is it not conceivable that these three powers could be wisely combined so as to be made to work together, that these three wheels could be made to roll into each other with a beautiful harmony? Can we not suppose that for the anarchical strife of blind competition; that for the war of capital against capital, labor against labor, workman against workman and against machinery; that, for general disorder, the universal shock of productive forces, and the destruction of values in so many contrary movements, might be substituted the productive combination and useful employment of all these forces? Most assuredly such an arrangement can be supposed; and why not accomplished? At any rate, does it not become our first and most imperative duty to seek out the conditions of industrial reconciliation and peace?

There is no radical antagonism in the nature of these things; there is no eternal and necessary repulsion between the various elements of production. The frightful combats of capital against capital, of capital against labor and talent, of laborer against laborer, of masters against workmen and workmen against masters, of each against all and all against each, is not a remorseless and inexorable condition of the life of humanity. They pertain only to the actual mechanism of industry, to the system of chaotic and unregulated competition, to that false liberty of whose triumphs we have boasted with such hollow and ill-timed joy. A better and truer mechanism, a nobler organic liberty, to which these awful evils do not adhere, can be found. The wisdom of man is able to discover, if it has not already under God discovered, an outlet to this labyrinth of suffering—a pathway upward from this dark, disordered, howling abyss.

This is what we mean by true democracy—a state in which the highest rights and interests of man shall be the means and appliances of a full development; and this Democracy, constructive and pacific in its character, becomes the object for which every benevolent and conscientious man should labor. . . . Look to it, O ye people! . . .

It is a series of co-operations that we propose, as the means of our social reform. It is not a mere league on the part of the followers of a particular calling—it is not a treaty of amity between the members of distinct classes —not the promiscuous commingling of all branches of trade, that we vindicate; but it is the voluntary union of the whole of Humanity, on definite and scientific grounds. We contend for the solidarity of the race in organic forms; we desire the universal association of man, according to an universal principle. we aim at the thorough reorganization, not of a segment, but of the whole of society, on a basis of individual independence and freedom, and collective harmony and progress.

7. Dorothea L. Dix, *Memorial to the New York Legislature, 1844**

Gentlemen—

Your attention is solicited to the condition of many indigent and pauper insane persons in the county-houses of this State elsewhere. Your petitioner asks to present their wants and claims, regarding this unfortunate class, not as being properly the charge of those towns and counties where their lot may have fallen, but as Wards of the

State, made so by the most terrible calamity that can assail human nature —a shattered intellect, a total incapacity for self-care and self-government.

Notwithstanding the liberal appropriations for the relief of this class by the establishment of the State curative asylum at Utica, large numbers are yet unprovided for. Many whose cases offer every hope of recovery, if brought

* Dorothea Lynde Dix, *Memorial to the Honorable the Legislature of the State of New York* (Albany, 1844), pp. 3–4, 43, 48–49, 54–55, 56–59.

under remedial treatment, are sinking in the prime of life into irrecoverable insanity; others, whose condition exhibits nothing to encourage hope of benefit from being placed in a curative asylum, are permitted to fall into states of the most shocking and brutalizing degradation—pitiable objects, at once sources of greatest discomfort to all brought within their vicinity, and exposed to exciting irritation from the reckless sports of the idle and vicious. But this is not the darkest view of their condition; these most unfriended and wretched beings are often subject to more horrible circumstances. Fidelity to my cause compels me, however revolting the topic, to speak more explicitly. I state, therefore, that both idiots and insane women are exposed to the basest vice, and become mothers without consciousness of maternity, and without capacity in any way to provide for their offspring, or to exercise those cares which are instinctive with the lowest brute animals. Is this a condition of things to be tolerated in a Christian land, in the very heart of a community claiming to take rank for elevation of moral principles and high-minded justice? I am persuaded it is unnecessary to dwell upon this subject; it must be enough that these evils are known to exist, for legislation to guard against their continuance. It may be well to say that the broadest evidence, sustained by appalling facts, can be adduced, substantiating these monstrous offences. Special details here would be out of place; suffice it, that an investigating committee, though governed by no nice sensibilities, would shrink before half their task should be accomplished.

I will not consume time by narrating individual histories, which, however they might rouse your indignation, or awaken your sensibilities, will, I believe, not be needed to strengthen a cause so evidently claiming your very

serious consideration and efficient action. I shall, as briefly as possible, refer to those institutions in the State, where are found both sufficient and defective provision for all classes of the insane, that from such statements you may determine what additional establishments are required. . . .

The *town poor* of South Hempstead, of whom there were but fifteen, at the time of my visit in December, were "sold," "bid off," "or let," to a resident in the town, the landlord of a miserable tavern. This man was addicted to intemperance, and found favor with the paupers by small allowances of rum, with additions of snuff and tobacco. I went to his house and asked to see the family making at the same time the usual inquiries. He replied surlily, that they lived at some distance from his own house, that he had not much to do with them, that his wife knew about them all. He professed not to know either their numbers, age or condition. The wife came, but her information was equally insufficient, and I directed to be taken to the house where the poor lived; which was distant about one-eighth of a mile from the tavern. This was a small building of one story, in a state of wretched dilapidation. The fifteen inmates of various ages, of both sexes, and various colors, presented a spectacle of squalid neglect, and one might say of poverty also: dirty in person and apparel, in rooms equally exceptionable; the little provision for lodging, was of the worst description. One miserable creature, whether colored or white, crazy or idiotic, I could not clearly make out, was rolled in some ragged, dirty blankets in a bunk in a horrible state of neglect. An aged black woman whose limbs were enveloped in a quantity of rags, to serve the place both of shoes and stockings, was feebly trying to quiet the cries of a young child. The only sufficient supplies about the place for the wants of life were food and air, and even here, there was of the last too much, pouring in through the holes, and broken windows, and floors. Confusion, disorder, and wretched life characterized the place. I was told that the mistress came down almost every day to see them, but her visits were followed it seemed by no very wholesome household arrangements. The history of the town's poor of South Hempstead, for years past has been worse rather than better than it is at the present time. *One dollar* per week is paid for each of the poor; provisions in this quarter are cheap, and rents moderate. . . .

Permit me, briefly, to refer to the prominent defects of the present county-house system throughout the State.

These institutions are *compound* and *complex* in their plans and objects. They are at one and the same time, *alms-houses*, or retreats for the aged, the invalid, and helpless poor: *houses of correction* for the vicious and abandoned; *asylums for orphaned and neglected children; receptacles for the insane and imbecile;* extensive *farming,* and more limited *manufacturing establishments.* Beside, in addition to being *mixed establishments,* they are not, one in ten or twenty counties, built in reference to these various objects. They are not planned to secure division and classification of the inmates. They afford insufficient accommodations, both in "the day rooms," and in the lodging apartments; not being constructed with a view to securing convenient arrangement or sound health. They are almost universally deficient in hospitals, or rooms especially appropriated to the sick, and to invalids. They do not guard against the indiscriminate association of the children with the adult poor. The education of these children, with rare exceptions, is conducted on a very

defective plan. The alms-house schools, so far as I have learnt from frequent inquiries, are not inspected by official persons, who visit and examine the other schools of the county. The moral and religious instruction of the poor at large, in these institutions is either attended to at remote and uncertain intervals, or entirely neglected. The scriptural text, that to "the poor the gospel is preached," that "good news of glad tidings," appears to have failed on its application to alms-houses. "We cannot afford it," says one; "our subscriptions and donations are even now burthensome in the support of foreign missions, to Asia and the South Sea islands." "We have not time," say others, "we have in our town been wholly engaged, for the last six months, by a revival." "Why do you not visit those degraded beings at your alms-house, and try to reclaim them to goodness and virtue?" "Oh, I have no time for such things. I am an active member and secretary of the Moral Reform Society." "How can you refrain from interposing in behalf of those poor fettered maniacs, wearing out a terrible life in chains, shut out from the light of the beautiful sky, and pining in friendless neglect?" "I assure you I have quite as much as I can do to work for the Anti-Slavery Fair. I detest all abuses and oppressions, and have devoted myself to the cause of emancipation in the slave-holding States." "And I," said another, "must lecture on freedom, and justice, and human rights. We at the north must be zealous to rouse the citizens of the southern States from their apathy to the claims of suffering humanity." These, and such like answers, to often renewed questionings, are given continually; and to me they are evidence of our proneness to overlook the discharge of duties "nigh at hand;" and to forget that "the good example" is better than the "reiterated precept." Here *at home,* for a long time, have we ample fields of labor: to teach the gospel of the blessed Jesus by *word* and *life;* to enlighten ignorance; to stay the tide of vicious pauperism; to succor the friendless, support the feeble; to visit the afflicted; to raise the depressed; to lessen human suffering, and elevate human aims; to redress wrongs; rectify abuses; unloose the chains of the maniac and bring release to those who pine in dark cells and dreary dungeons; having plucked the beam from our own eye, we can with a less pharisaical spirit, direct our efforts to clearing the mental vision of neighbor.

I have referred to some of the most obvious defects of county-houses. Considering the compound objects of these, it is surprising that so much good is found in them. It is to be remembered that knowledge is the growth of a tedious experience. The evils to which I have alluded, are felt and acknowledged by all those brought into direct acquaintance with the subject. Greatly too much is required, both of the masters and mistresses of county-houses Few men and women possess such varied and rare gifts as are called into exercise, in conducting these institutions. . . .

It is remarked by a writer who has become distinguished for efforts to lessen the privations of the afflicted, and to secure protection for suffering humanity, that "with regard to paupers at least, the duty of the State is clear and imperative, and this should be the duty of every Christian government, to provide the best *means for the cure of the curable,* and to *take kind care* of the incurable." The duty of society, besides being urged by every consideration of humanity, will be seen to be more imperative, if we consider that insanity is, in many cases, the result of imperfect or vicious social institutions and observances. We have not space to allude to all these; but among

them are revolutions, party strife, unwise and capricious legislation, causing commercial speculations and disasters; false standards of worth and rank, undue encouragement of the propensities and passions, social rivalry, social intemperance; some fashions and conventional usages; religious and political excitement. These, and many other causes for which society is in fault, are productive of a large proportion of the cases of insanity which exist in its bosom. But if to these we add the still larger number which arise from ignorance of the natural laws, which ignorance society should enlighten, we can fairly lay at its door almost all the cases of insanity which occur. I have advanced the claim of the insane to be received as *wards of the State.* . . .

Whatever deliberation this subject may receive, whatever conclusions may be reached, I will indulge the hope that these will embrace a permanent mode of relief. The great seal of your State, which bears that somewhat aspiring device, the *rising Sun,* the *Heaven-bright sky,* the *lofty mountain,* the *flowing river,* the *fertile plain,* and a motto that should not have been assumed but by minds stayed to highest purposes; nor retained, but by those whose lofty principles sanction its use, —your State seal is to me the pledge that you will not delay to remedy those corroding moral evils, to which I have asked your attention; that you will not be satisfied with having commenced a good and noble work, but that you will go forward to complete and perfect your system. I solicit your action *now,* on the various ground of expediency, of justice, of humanity, of duty to yourselves, of duty to your families, of duty to your neighbor, and your fellow citizens, of your duty to the Most High God, who, in ordaining that the "poor should never cease out of the land," at the same time ordained that nations, not less than individuals, should find sanctification in the exercise of the higher charities, and the ennobling acts of life.

I am told that the world is selfish, that men seek only outward aggrandizement and temporal prosperity. I assuredly see much of this, but society would cease to exist if liberality and enlarged principles of action did not more prevail. I discover that negligence and folly, vice and crime, sweep widely and fearfully; but I cannot be blind to the fact that there must be a greater amount of care and reflection, of purity and integrity, else the fabric of social life would fall in ruins, and the intellectual become subservient to animal life.

In view, then, of the ascendency of the more elevated principles of humanity, I renewedly solicit your action now upon the subject under consideration. I might recommend this on the low ground of expediency, and prove by numerical calculations that present complete and efficient plans would at no distant time be the cheapest. But while a fit and wise economy ought to be studied, I cannot suppose that you will, in consulting the mere saving of dollars and cents to your State treasury, lose sight of that justice and humanity which most ennoble human nature, and which should be your governing motives; these involve also the highest responsibilities. God, in giving to you understanding above the brute creation, and immortal capacities, has revealed that there is a treasury whose wealth does not fail, where riches may be garnered for the harvest of eternity.

Provide asylums which shall meet the whole necessities of your State; give to your sister States an example yet wanting, of complete and sufficient institutions for each of these afflicted classes of the insane, and pause only till degradation and suffering are guarded against, so far as human care

and human kindness may prevent the one or diminish the other. It will be said that much already has been done for these poor miserables. I know it, and that is why I expect still larger benefits to reach them. It is *because* men have begun, not only to discover evils but to apply remedies; it is because there is a clearer comprehension upon these subjects, that I appeal to you untroubled by distrust. It has now been learned by experience how much of human suffering may be diminished, how many ills may be obliterated, how much that has been deficient may be supplied, how much that has been wrong may be redressed. No, I will not believe that it is in New-York I am to find statesmen and legislators, who will return to their constituents and say to them that their decisions have stayed the sacred cause of humanity, and checked the work of justice and mercy. Am I importunate? Go, look on such scenes as I have witnessed in your State these last three months; you will forget all in zealously devising plans to heal these great distresses. Am I importunate? Importunity finds justification in acquaintance with the diverse and unfailing resources of this vast State, which open to energetic and vigorous enterprize the way to unprecedented prosperity. Except perverse in the extremest sense, except blinded by the most sullen self-will, except disqualified by the rashest movements, New-York cannot but be the Empire State in that wealth which is computed by ample treasures of gold and silver, as well as from its permanent advantages from natural position. It is hardly possible that prosperity should here suffer more than temporary interruption—a mote crossing the disc of your rising sun—a feeble striving upon a little surface, of your deep flowing river—a passing cloud, shutting out for a moment your sky-reaching mountain. Look around you, is it not true what I say? Look abroad, is not that real which I show? And if true, if real, if you are, in the adoption of your State-seal ambitious, without being vain-glorious; if you are great, without conceit; if you are just, without speciousness; if your noble motto is not a bitter satire upon your acts, then am I more than justified in the confidence, transcending hope, which inspires me while urging the claims of the most dependent, and most miserable portions of the community. Now, amidst the many acts, the various deliberations which consume time in our stately Capitol, consecrate a portion to the highest, most enduring interests—to perpetuating the truest glory of people aspiring to glory—the truest prosperity of a people eager to be prosperous—the truest good of a people emulous to advance!

8. HORACE MANN, *Education a Communal Concern, 1842**

Eduction derives arguments for its support from a more comprehensive range of considerations than ever united their advocacy for any other human interest. Health, freedom, wisdom, virtue, time, eternity, plead in its behalf. Some causes have reference to temporal interests; some to eternal;—education embraces both.

The view which invests education with the awful prerogative of projecting its consequences forward through the whole length of the illimitable future, will not be objected to by the champions of any religious creed. Those who believe that the destiny of the human soul is irrevocably fixed for weal or woe by its state or condition when its exit from life is made,—who believe that, as it is then sanctified, or unregenerate, it must go out from this world, through an opposite avenue, and into an opposite eternity,—will equally believe and maintain the tendency of intellectual and moral guidance, or neglect, especially during the impressible period of youth, to turn its course into the broad, or into the narrow way. Those, also, who believe that, although the soul should enter the spiritual world "unhouselled, unanointed, unannealed," yet that it will not be cut off from hope, but will be allowed to pass through other cycles of probation, . . . will of course believe and maintain that, the lighter the burden of sin which weighs it down, at its entrance into another life, the sooner will its recuperative energies enable it to rise from its guilty fall, and to ascend to the empyrean of perfect happiness. There is still another class, who interpret the Scriptures to promise universal beatitude to the whole human race. . . . They maintain that the soul leaves every earthly impurity in the foul tabernacle of flesh . . . and at once springs aloft to be robed in garments of purity. But even they do not suppose that the spirit, though ransomed and cleansed by omnipotent grace, can overleap the immense moral spaces it has lost, and at once engage in the services of the upper temple, with that seraphic ardor which burns in bosoms, where its flame had been kindled while yet on earth. . . .

In regard to Intellectual Education, no man can offer a single reason for arresting its progress, and confining it

* Horace Mann, "To Our Patrons," *The Common School Journal*, IV (January 1, 1842) , 4–9.

where it now is, which would not be equally available for reducing its present amount. He who would degrade the intellectual standing of Massachusetts to the level of Ireland, would degrade Ireland to the level of interior Africa, or of the Batta Islands. Nor could even the rank of savage life claim any immunity from still lower debasement. In the "lowest deep," there would be some whose selfishness would demand the opening of a still "lower deep." There would be no halting post until the race had reached the limits of degradation in troglodytes and monkeys, and the godlike faculty of reason had been lost in the mechanism of animal instinct. The useful and elegant arts that minister to the comfort of man, and gladden his eye with beauty; poetry and eloquence that ravish the soul; philosophy that comprehends the workmanship of the heavens, and reads, in the present condition of the earth, as in the leaves of a book, the records of myriads of ages gone by; language by which we are taught by all the generations that are past, and by which we may teach all the generations that are to come;—all these would be sunk in oblivion, and all the knowledge possessed by the descendants of Bacon, and Newton, and Franklin, would be to chatter and mow, to burrow in a hole, and crack nuts with the teeth. Such is the catastrophe to which we should come, could those prevail, who would make the present horizon of human knowledge stationary.

Physical Education is not only of great importance on its own account, but, in a certain sense, it seems to be invested with the additional importance of both intellectual and moral; because, although we have frequent proofs, that there may be a human body without a soul, yet, under our present earthly conditions of existence, there cannot be a human soul without a body. The statue must lie prostrate, without a pedestal; and, in this sense, the pedestal is as important as the statue.

The present generation is suffering incalculably under an ignorance of physical education. It is striving to increase the number of pleasurable sensations, without any knowledge of the great laws of health and life, and thus defeats its own object. The sexes, respectively, are deteriorating from their fathers, and especially from their mothers, in constitutional stamina. . . . . Under the modern hothouse system, the puny and feeble are saved. They grow up without strength, passing from the weakness of childhood to that of age, without taking the vigor of manhood in their course. By the various appliances of art, indeed, the stooping frame can be kept upright and the shrunken be rounded out, into the semblance of humanity. But these cheats give no internal, organic force. Though the arts of bolstering up the human figure, and of giving to its unsightly angles the curvilinear forms of grace, should grow into science, and its practice should be the most lucrative of professions, yet not one element of genuine beauty or dignity will be thereby gained. Such arts can never bestow elasticity and vigor upon the frame, nor suffuse "the human face divine" with the roseate hues of health. The complexion will still be wan, the pulse feeble, the motions languid. The eye will have no fire. The imagination will lose its power to turn all light into rainbows. The intellect will never be sufficiently expanded to receive *a system of truths,* and single truths cut out from their connections, and adopted without reference to kindred truths, always mislead. The affections will fall, like Lucifer, from the upper, to fasten upon objects, in the nether sphere. In a word, the forces of the soul will retreat from the fore-head to the hindhead, and the brow, that "dome of thought, and palace of the soul," will be narrow and "villainously low"; for it is here that Nature sets her signet, and stamps her child a philosopher or a cretin. Here she will not suffer her signatures to be counterfeited, for neither tailors nor mantua-makers can insert their cork or padding beneath the tables of the skull.

We have now pointed, as with the finger and rapidly, towards those grand relations in which mankind stand to the cause of education. These relations lie all around us. They connect us with the universe of matter, and with the universe of mind; and hence the necessity of our possessing knowledge, for it is only by knowledge that we can adjust ourselves to the objects to which we are related. These truths also point to the future; and hence the necessity that we should regulate our conduct according to them, for every act of life is a step carrying us further towards, or further from, the goal of our being.

To promote this object, at once so comprehensive and so enduring, is among the first duties of governments; it is also among the first duties of individuals. It is the duty of the great and powerful, in their broad sphere of action; and it is no less the duty of the humble and obscure, in their narrower circle. Let every one contribute "according to his ability."

The labor of another year, in endeavoring to advance the well-being of our fellow-men, through enlightenment, and the impulse of higher motives, is the mite which we propose to cast into the "treasury" of the Lord. We ask others to cast in of their abundance. We ask all to receive into their minds the great idea of social improvement, to contemplate, and strive to imbody in human form, the sublime law of progression,—the possibility and the practicability of an ever-upward ascension in the scale of being. The race can be made happier and better than it is. There are innumerable sufferings which spring from ignorance. This, knowledge will dispel, and relieve multitudes who are now tormented with unnecessary and gratuitous pain. There are innumerable sufferings springing from fountains of perverted feeling, which have no necessary existence, which are no part of the inevitable lot of humanity. These, like the debasing customs of savage life, like the foul superstitions and idolatries of paganism, can be cast off, as a garment which we have outgrown. There are ten thousand existing causes of misery and crime, which need not be reproduced and perpetuated in the coming generation. Many, nay, most, of the burdens which mankind have borne, which we now bear, may be lightened, before they are cast upon our successors. Save, O, save the myriads of innocent beings who are just landing upon the shores of time; —save them from the contaminations of the world into which they are sent; teach not their unpolluted lips to utter curses, nor their hands to uphold injustice, nor their feet to wander in forbidden paths. Even those who take the darkest views of human nature, and who proclaim the most fearful auguries concerning its ultimate destiny,—even they will admit that the young are less vicious than the old; that childhood had a simplicity and an ingenuousness which intercourse with the world corrupts and debauches. They will admit that there is a guilelessness, an uncalculating affection, a sensibility to wrong, in the breasts of the young, which the arts and customs of the world deprave and harden. It is we, who by our ignorances, and our apathy, by our parsimony and our pride, create in them diseases which even the brute creation do not suffer, because they do not abuse the natures which God has given them. Why should we, who, in our considerate moments, would not punish even the wretch suspected of crime, until guilt is fastened upon him by indubitable proof, and who, even then, profess to pity him, as he meets the just retributions of a violated law,—why should we lead children astray by our evil customs and practices, and bring down upon them those penalties, which, in the self-executing law of God, will assuredly follow transgression? To punish the innocent has been regarded with abhorrence and execration in all ages of the world; but to tempt innocence to the commission of those offences which incur punishment, is far more cruel, because guilt is infinitely worse than the punishment which avenges it. Why should innocent childhood be tormented with pains not of its own procuring,—with pains which the follies and the vices of ancestors seem to have prepared, and made ready against its coming? Why should the new-born generations be ushered into a world worse than themselves; to breathe in physical and moral contaminations which they did not scatter; to die of maladies engendered by those who should have been their protectors and guardian spirits?

It is in our power to rescue children from these calamities. It is in our power to guard them from the contagion of guilt, from that subtilest of poisons, an evil example. They can be restrained from entering paths where others have fallen and perished. No rude child of ignorance, left to himself in the wild wilderness where he was born, ever reached to a thousandth part of that depravity, which has been achieved as a common thing, by those whose birthplace was in a land of boasted civilization. Civilization, then, has not accomplished its object. It has given more power than rectitude,—the ability to perform great things without that moral sovereignty, before which

the greatest and grandest achievements stand condemned, if not consecrated by goodness.

And here we would inquire what sphere of patriotic exertion is left open for the lover of his country, but the sphere of improving the rising generation through the instrumentality of a more perfect and efficient system for their education? We call our fathers *patriots,* because they loved their country and made sacrifices for its welfare. But what was their country? A vast tract of wilderness territory did not constitute it. It was not unconscious, insentient plains, or rivers, or mountains, however beautifully and majestically they might spread, or flow, or shine, beneath the canopy of heaven. Their country was chiefly their descendants, the human beings who were to throng these vast domains, the sentient, conscious natures which were to live here,—and living, to enjoy or suffer. The question with them was, whether this should be a land of liberty or bondage, of light or darkness, of religion or superstition. It was to redeem and elevate the millions who, in the providence of God, should people these wide-spreading realms, that they engaged in a cause where those who suffered death seemed to suffer least, where the survivors most challenge our sympathy. But we have no battles to fight by land or sea, against a foreign foe. We have no fathers, or brothers, or sons, in the camp, suffering cold, and hunger, and nakedness. We have no edifice of government to rear, with exhausting study and anxiety. These labors are done and ended, and we have entered into the rich inheritance. What, then, shall we do that we may be patriotic? How shall our love of country, if any we have, be made manifest? How, but by laboring for our descendants,—not in the same way, but with the same fidelity, as our fathers labored for us? Otherwise, there is no moral consanguinity between ourselves and them. Otherwise, we are not of their blood, but gentiles and heathens, boasting a lineage which our acts and lives belie. It is mockery to say, "We have Abraham to our father," while we perform the deeds of pagans. The only sphere, then, left open for our patriotism, is the improvement of our children,—not the few, but the many; not a part of them, but all. This is but one field of exertion, but it opens an infinite career; for the capacities of mankind can go on developing, improving, perfecting, as long as the cycles of eternity revolve. For this improvement of the race, a high, a generous, an expansive education is the true and efficient means. There is not a good work which the hand of man has ever undertaken, which his heart has ever conceived, which does not require a good education for its helper. There is not an evil afflicting the earth, which can be extirpated, until the auxiliary of education shall lend its mighty aid. If an angel were to descend from heaven to earth, on an errand of mercy and love, he would hasten to accomplish his mission by illuminating the minds and purifying the hearts of children. The Saviour took little children in his arms and blessed them; he did not, by any miraculous exertion of power, bar up all passages to sin and error, and at once make mankind the passive recipients of perfection. He left it for us to be agents and co-workers with him in their redemption. He gave to us, not so much the boon of being blessed, as the more precious, the heavenly boon of blessing others. For this end, an instrument has been put into our hands, fully adequate to the accomplishment of so divine a purpose. We have the power to train up children in accordance with those wise and benign laws which the Creator has stamped upon their physical, their intellectual, and their moral nature; and of this stewardship we must assuredly give account. May it be rendered with joy, and not with sorrow!

9. Thomas Wentworth Higginson, *The Eccentricities of Reformers, 1899**

"Oh, why," said an exhausted American wife to her husband, a moderate reformer, "why do the insane so cling to you?" This tendency of every reform to surround itself with a fringe of the unreasonable and half-cracked is really to its credit, and furnishes one of its best disciplines. Those who are obliged by conscience to disregard the peace and proprieties of the social world, in the paths of reform, learn by experience what a trial they are to their friends by observing what tortures they themselves suffer from those who go a few steps farther. They learn self-control by exercising moderation toward those who have lost that quality. . . .

The early anti-slavery meetings in particular were severely tested in respect to patience by those who might almost be called professional lunatics, as for instance Father Lamson, Abby Folsom (Emerson's "flea of conventions"), and G. W. F. Mellen. Lamson's white habiliments and white beard seemed almost like a stage make-up for the situation; and Abby Folsom's "Interminable scroll" (Emerson again), with her shrill climax of all remarks, "It's the capitalists!" seemed like the

* Thomas Wentworth Higginson, *Contemporaries* (Boston, [1899]), pp. 329–41.

rehearsal of a play. Yet it is not quite fair to assume that the patience of the abolitionists was invariable. There were times when it gave way: and I have seen Abby Folsom led from the hall, courteously but decisively, by Wendell Phillips on the one side and a man yet living on the other,—she still denouncing the capitalists as she reluctantly came towards the door. To the occasional policeman present, for whom the abolitionists themselves seemed as much lunatics as their allies, the petty discrimination of putting out only the craziest must have appeared an absurdity; Wendell Phillips at that very meeting had to explain the real distinction, —namely, that he and his friends were not the object of persecution because they were crazy, but because they were known not to be.

Another striking figure on the platform, who always attracted the disapproval of the profane, was Charles Burleigh, who wore not merely long curls on his shoulders, but also a long and rather ill-trimmed beard,—in a beardless period,—and had distinctly that Christ-like look which is often to be found in large gatherings of reformers. Lowell, who was one of the early beard-converts, used to be amused in going about the streets with Burleigh, a much taller man, to find himself pointed out with a sort of subsidiary emphasis, as if he were a young neophyte accompanying his father confessor. Burleigh was undoubtedly one of the ablest men in the anti-slavery conventions. Lowell, in one of his letters, describes him as "looking like one of the old apostles who had slept in the same room with a Quaker who had gone off in the morning with his companion's appropriate costume, leaving him to accommodate himself as best he might to the straight collar and the single breast of the fugitive." He belonged to a gifted family, two of his brothers being poets, and he himself

was a man of singular power in speech, with a rich and mellow voice, a benignant manner and an extremely clear and logical mind; had he also possessed humor, he would have been one of the most effective of orators. His eloquence had every essential except this, as his personal appearance had every quality of distinction but neatness.

Another man of peculiar bearing was Henry C. Wright, whose whim was never to address the presiding officer as "Mr. Chairman," but only as "Chairman," and whose erect figure and commanding voice, with the frequent recurrence of an occasional and imperious "Now, Chairman!" gave him a weight of manner which his matter did not always confirm. He had been in early life a Congregational minister, and had lost his parish, it was said, for the unclerical act (in those days) of swimming across the Connecticut River. His papers and his journals, which were profuse, are now in the Harvard College Library, and will one day, no doubt, furnish ample and quaint materials for the historian of the "Comeouters" of that day. Another noticeable person on the platform was Nathaniel Peabody Rogers, the New Hampshire editor, a man of noble and beautiful character, whose journalism had a spice and zest which would now command a market on merely professional grounds; but who was a Non-resistant of non-resistants, and would, if he could have had his way, have conducted the meetings without president, secretary, or any restrictions on debate. He out-Garrisoned Garrison on this and other points, and they at last parted company, to their mutual regret. He had one of those faces of utter benignity which always surprised Southern visitors to the anti-slavery conventions, they usually expecting to find upon the platform a set of scowling stage villains.

Another picturesque and even eccentric feature upon the anti-slavery platform was the group of the Hutchinson family, raven-haired and keen-eyed as a group of Bohemians, tall and stalwart youths surrounding their rosebud of a sister, Abby. They, too, had a melo dramatic look, with their wide collars and long locks; they put immense fire and fury into "The Car Emancipation" and their other anti-slavery songs. As years went on, they broke up into detached groups, extending into the second generation. The story of these experiences has been told entertainingly in a book by one of the family. Four of the brothers used to give village concerts, in which they adapted themselves to each place they visited, using local "gags" to an extent which brought out screams of laughter. I was present on one occasion, in a country town, when they had refused an encore, but when it finally had to be conceded on the special appeal of a venerable citizen; and they selected for performance one of their most absurd songs:—

> "O potatoes they grow small
>   Over there!
> O potatoes they grow small,
> 'Cos they plants 'em in the fall,
> And they eats 'em, tops and all,
>   Over there."

A muffled chuckle began in all parts of the audience, and swelled to a tumult of applause incomprehensible to me till I afterwards learned that the venerable gentleman in question was known as "Small Potatoes," from an unlucky gift of a basket of such inadequate vegetables to some donation fund.

Whether the hit was wholly accidental on the part of the Hutchinsons I never knew, and the impression on the audience was soon changed when one of the brothers, who had before given evidences of insanity, came forward to make a speech to the audience, lecturing them especially on the undue love of money. He spoke to them courageously and tenderly, like a troubled father, though he still looked young;

and at last said, with infinite pity, "If you wish for money, you can have it from me," and began taking silver coins from his pockets and tossing them among the audience, where they were at first eagerly picked up by boys, and then left untouched, while the spectators seemed awed and spell-bound. I never shall forget the anxious and patient look with which the brothers watched him with their large dark eyes, not, however, interfering; and even when he had emptied his pockets and turned to a box containing the receipts taken at the door, and began to throw half-dollars and quarter-dollars from that, saying to them, "May I?" they only nodded gravely, leaving him to himself. It all recalled descriptions of the reverence given by untaught persons to the acts of the insane. He soon stopped and the music was resumed, the money being honestly collected afterwards and brought back to his brothers. This member of the household finally committed suicide, after a long period during which his disordered mind evidently played with the thought of it, getting all ready for it just at the hour when he knew he should be interrupted, as, for instance, by men coming to the barn to feed the cattle; but finally he went too far. The career of the whole family was a curious instance of the sporadic appearance of a quality akin to genius in certain households, a trait which is familiar to every student of life in New England farming towns.

Parker Pillsbury's "Acts of the Anti-Slavery Apostles" is a storehouse of facts as to the decidedly extreme attitude taken for a time by himself, Stephen Foster, Henry C. Wright, and others, of whom it could be said, as Garrison wrote to his wife about one of these, "He is remarkably successful in raising the spirit of mobocracy wherever he goes. I could wish," he adds, "that brother ——— would exercise more judgment and discretion in the presentation of his views; but it is useless to reason with him, with any hope of altering his course, as he is firmly persuaded that he is pursuing the very best course." It was during one of these mobs that Lucy Stone, urging the men who had spoken to retire from the hall through a back door, was met by them with the question, "Who will protect you?" "This gentleman will protect me," said the sweet-voiced woman, taking the arm of the ringleader of the mob as he sprang on the platform. "Yes, I will," he said, after one look at her serene face; and he piloted her safely out. So clear, however, was the conviction of these especial leaders as to the necessity of very strong statements that one excellent Quaker woman offered this resolution at the tenth anniversary meeting of the Massachusetts Anti-Slavery Society, January 28, 1842: "Resolved, That the sectarian organizations called churches are combinations of thieves, robbers, adulterers, pirates, and murderers, and as such form the bulwarks of American slavery." What she meant was simply what James G. Birney had meant in his tract, "The American Churches the Bulwarks of American Slavery"; but these specifications which she made, though logically consistent, raised natural antagonism in thousands of honest minds.

It must be remembered, on the other hand, that this was a period, even in New England, of Negro pews, Negro cars, and even Negro stages. I can myself recall an instance, about 1840, when a colored woman was ejected from a stage on what is now Massachusetts Avenue, near the Cambridge Common; and Negro cars were often provided, even on Massachusetts railways, from which the white companions of such Negroes were forcibly put out, as were the colored people from white men's cars, even if they had first-class tickets.

With the curious inconsistency of those times, an exception was made if the colored people were servants of whites. These outrages were particularly noticeable on the Eastern Railroad, of which a Quaker was the superintendent. In one number of "The Liberator" (xii. 56) there is a travelers' directory of the various railroads, indicating whether they do or do not have Negro cars. Police justices refused to punish assaults by railroad employees even on white passengers who had resisted or condemned these outrages. Under these circumstances, much was to be pardoned to the spirit of liberty.

The woman suffrage movement, involving as it did a more immediate and personal test of daily habits than the anti-slavery reform, carried with it, naturally, its own fringe of oddities. The mere fact that it coincided with the period of the Bloomer costume would have secured this; for, while it required some mental ability to lengthen one's range of thoughts, it needed none at all to shorten one's skirts. The dress, so far from being indelicate, was scrupulously and almost prudishly modest, and those who wore it would have been dismayed and horrified by the modern bathing-dress; but it brought, as I can personally testify, more discomfort to the speakers of the other sex than any trials of a platform, since the ladies who wore it had often to be escorted home through the irreverent population of a city. But, apart from this, the mere radicalism of the agitation naturally appealed to a certain number of the unbalanced, and the movement had to bear the burden.

This came over me vividly for the first time when attending a Woman's Rights meeting—this being the early designation of the enterprise—in Philadelphia. The gathering was large, and the gallery audience was made up, in a considerable degree, of young medical students, many of these being Southerners and ripe for fun. Just after the meeting had been called to order, a man of quiet appearance came to me and said, "Is Miss Ora Noon present?" Struck by the oddity of the name,—which I have slightly modified in telling this story,—I asked him why he wished to know, and he said that she was a medical student, and some friends from out of town had arrived and wished to see her. "Will you not call for her?" he said; and I, becoming still more suspicious, referred the matter to James Mott, who was just passing. He recognized the name at once, to my great relief, called for her aloud with his usual grave dignity, and a young girl of rather odd appearance got up, made her way to the door, and went out with her friends. After a little tittering, the audience composed itself and we heard no more of the incident. But that night after returning to the hospitable home of the Motts, I was told the whole story of Ora Noon.

She was, it appeared, the daughter of a Southern slaveholder, and was to inherit Negroes on coming of age. She had formed a great desire to study medicine, to which her father was vehemently opposed. After several unsuccessful efforts, she attacked him again on her twentieth birthday and requested, as a birthday gift, his assent to her wish. He still refusing, she coolly said: "Very well; in another year I shall be of age,

and shall come into possession of my own property. I shall then sell my slaves, and this will give the means for my course of medical study." The father laughed at so absurd a proposal; the subject rested for a year, and on the eve of her twenty-first birthday she announced the purpose again. The father at last surrendered, made her promise not to sell her slaves, and counted out to her the money for her first year at Philadelphia. This being in her hands she quietly said: "Tomorrow I shall emancipate my slaves, instead of selling them"; and she did it. She went to Philadelphia, knowing nobody, secured a boarding-place, bought a pair of pistols, a season ticket to the pistol-gallery, and a similar ticket to a leading theatre; and thus began her professional preparations. She proved a most successful student, and led, in spite of the above little eccentricities, an irreproachable life; her sucess at the pistol gallery perhaps helping to protect from any disrespect inspired by her habitual presence at the theatre. It is all a curious illustration of the erratic tendency sometimes visible, just at first, on each step in the emancipation of any class. Very probably the later demeanor of Miss Ora Noon was one of scrupulous decorum; and she may never have needed to employ her pistols against anything more formidable than clay pigeons.

10. HENRY GEORGE, *Progress and Poverty, 1879**

THE PROBLEM

The present century has been marked by a prodigious increase in wealth-producing power. The utilization of steam and electricity, the introduction of improved processes and

labor-saving machinery, the greater subdivision and grander scale of production, the wonderful facilitation of exchanges, have multiplied enormously the effectiveness of labor.

At the beginning of this marvellous

* Henry George, *Progress and Poverty* (New York, 1881), pp. 3–8, 254–59, 265–66, 295, 489–96.

era it was natural to expect, and it was expected, that labor-saving inventions would lighten the toil and improve the condition of the laborer; that the enormous increase in the power of producing wealth would make real poverty a thing of the past. Could a man of the last century—a Franklin or a Priestley—have seen, in a vision of the future, the steamship taking the place of the sailing vessel, the railroad train of the wagon, the reaping machine of the scythe, the threshing machine of the flail; could he have heard the throb of the engines that in obedience to human will, and for the satisfaction of human desire, exert a power greater than that of all the men and all the beasts of burden of the earth combined; could he have seen the forest tree transformed into finished lumber—into doors, sashes, blinds, boxes or barrels, with hardly the touch of a human hand; the great workshops where boots and shoes are turned out by the case with less labor than the old-fashioned cobbler could have put on a sole; the factories where under the eye of a girl, cotton becomes cloth faster than hundreds of stalwart weavers could have turned it out with their hand-looms; could he have seen steam hammers shaping mammoth shafts and mighty anchors, and delicate machinery making tiny watches; the diamond drill cutting through the heart of the rocks, and coal oil sparing the whale; could he have realized the enormous saving of labor resulting from improved facilities of exchange and communication— sheep killed in Australia eaten fresh in England, and the order given by the London banker in the afternoon executed in San Francisco in the morning of the same day; could he have conceived of the hundred thousand improvements which these only suggest, what would he have inferred as to the social condition of mankind?

It would not have seemed like an inference; further than the vision went it would have seemed as though he saw; and his heart would have leaped and his nerves would have thrilled, as one who from a height beholds just ahead of the thirst-stricken caravan the living gleam of rustling woods and the glint of laughing waters. Plainly, in the sight of the imagination, he would have beheld these new forces elevating society from its very foundations, lifting the very poorest above the possibility of want, exempting the very lowest from anxiety for the material needs of life; he would have seen these slaves of the lamp of knowledge taking on themselves the traditional curse, these muscles of iron and sinews of steel making the poorest laborer's life a holiday, in which every high quality and noble impulse could have scope to grow.

And out of these bounteous material conditions he would have seen arising, as necessary sequences, moral conditions realizing the golden age of which mankind always dreamed. Youth no longer stunted and starved; age no longer harried by avarice; the child at play with the tiger; the man with the muck-rake drinking in the glory of the stars! Foul things fled, fierce things tame; discord turned to harmony! For how could there be greed where all had enough? How could the vice, the crime, the ignorance, the brutality, that spring from poverty and the fear of poverty, exist where poverty had vanished? Who should crouch where all were freemen; who oppress where all were peers?

More or less vague or clear, these have been the hopes, these the dreams born of the improvements which give this wonderful era its preëminence. They have sunk so deeply into the popular mind as radically to change the currents of thought, to recast creeds and displace the most fundamental conceptions. The haunting visions of higher possibilities have not merely gathered splendor and vividness, but their direction has changed —instead of seeing behind the faint tinges of an expiring sunset, all the glory of the daybreak has decked the skies before.

It is true that disappointment has followed disappointment, and that discovery, and invention after invention, have neither lessened the toil of those who most need respite, nor brought plenty to the poor. But there have been so many things to which it seemed this failure could be laid, that faith has hardly weakened. We have better appreciated the difficulties to be overcome; but not the less trusted that the tendency of the times was to overcome them.

Now, however, we are coming into collision with facts which there can be no mistaking. From all parts of the civilized world come complaints of industrial depression; of labor condemned to involuntary idleness; of capital massed and wasting; of pecuniary distress among business men; of want and suffering and anxiety among the working classes. All the dull, deadening pain, all the keen, maddening anguish, that to great masses of men are involved in the words "hard times," have afflicted the world. This state of things, common to communities differing so widely in situation, in political institutions, in fiscal and financial systems, in density of population and in social organization, can hardly be accounted for by local causes. There is distress where large standing armies are maintained, but there is also distress where the standing armies are nominal; there is distress where protective tariffs stupidly and wastefully hamper trade, but there is also distress where trade is nearly free; there is distress where autocratic government yet prevails, but there is also

distress where political power is wholly in the hands of the people; in countries where paper is money, and in countries where gold and silver are the only currency. Evidently, beneath all such things as these, we must infer a common cause.

That there is a common cause, and that it is either what we call material progress or something closely connected with material progress, becomes more than an inference when it is noted that the phenomena we class together and speak of as industrial depression are but intensifications of phenomena which always accompany material progress, and which show themselves more clearly and strongly as material progress goes on. . . .

It is to the newer countries—that is, to the countries where material progress is yet in its earlier stages—that laborers emigrate in search of higher wages, and capital flows in search of higher interest. It is in the older countries—that is to say, the countries where material progress has reached later stages—that widespread destitution is found in the midst of the greatest abundance. Go into one of the communities where Anglo-Saxon vigor is just beginning the race of progress; where the machinery of production and exchange is yet rude and inefficient; where the increment of wealth is not yet great enough to enable any class to live in ease and luxury; where the best house is but a cabin of logs or a cloth and paper shanty, and the richest man is forced to daily work— and though you will find an absence of wealth and all its concomitants, you will find no beggars. There is no luxury, but there is no destitution. No one makes an easy living, nor a very good living; but every one *can* make a living, and no one able and willing to work is oppressed by the fear of want.

But just as such a community realizes

the conditions which all civilized communities are striving for, and advances in the scale of material progress—just as closer settlement and a more intimate connection with the rest of the world, and greater utilization of labor-saving machinery, make possible greater economies in production and exchange, and wealth in consequence increases, not merely in the aggregate, but in proportion to population—so does poverty take a darker aspect. Some get an infinitely better and easier living, but others find it hard to get a living at all. The "tramp" comes with the locomotive, and almshouses and prisons are as surely the marks of "material progress" as are costly dwellings, rich warehouses, and magnificent churches. Upon streets lighted with gas and patrolled by uniformed policemen, beggars wait for the passer-by, and in the shadow of college, and library, and museum, are gathering the more hideous Huns and fiercer Vandals of whom Macaulay prophesied.

This fact—the great fact that poverty and all its concomitants show themselves in communities just as they develop into the conditions toward which material progress tends—proves that the social difficulties existing wherever a certain stage of progress has been reached, do not arise from local circumstances, but are, in some way or another, engendered by progress itself.

And, unpleasant as it may be to admit it, it is at last becoming evident that the enormous increase in productive power which has marked the present century and is still going on with accelerating ratio, has no tendency to extirpate poverty or to lighten the burdens of those compelled to toil. It simply widens the gulf between Dives and Lazarus, and makes the struggle for existence more intense. The march of invention has clothed mankind with powers of which a century ago the boldest imagination could not have dreamed. But in factories where labor-saving machinery has reached its most wonderful development, little children are at work; wherever the new forces are anything like fully utilized, large classes are maintained by charity or live on the verge of recourse to it; amid the greatest accumulations of wealth, men die of starvation, and puny infants suckle dry breasts, while everywhere the greed of gain, the worship of wealth, shows the force of the fear of want. The promised land flies before us like the mirage. The fruits of the tree of knowledge turn as we grasp them to apples of Sodom that crumble at the touch. . . .

THE PERSISTENCE OF POVERTY

The great problem, of which recurring seasons of industrial depression are but peculiar manifestations, is now, I think, fully solved, and the social phenomena which all over the civilized world appall the philanthropist and perplex the statesman, which hang with clouds the future of the most advanced races, and suggest doubts of the reality and ultimate goal of what we have fondly called progress, are now explained.

The reason why, is spite of the increase of productive power, wages constantly tend to a minimum which will give but a bare living, is that, with increase in productive power, rent tends to even greater increase, thus producing a constant tendency to the forcing down of wages. . . .

The simple theory which I have outlined (if indeed it can be called a theory which is but the recognition of the most obvious relations) explains this conjunction of poverty with wealth, of low wages with high productive power, of degradation amid enlightenment, of virtual slavery in political liberty. It harmonizes, as results flowing from a general and inexorable law, facts otherwise most perplexing, and exhibits the sequence and relation between phenomena that without reference to it are diverse and contradictory. . . . It explains why improvements which increase the productive power of labor and capital increase the reward of neither. It explains what is commonly called the conflict between labor and capital, while proving the real harmony of interest between them. It cuts the last inch of ground from under the fallacies of protection, while showing why free trade fails to benefit permanently the working classes. It explains why want increases with abundance, and wealth tends to greater and greater aggregations. . . . It explains the vice and misery which show themselves amid dense population, without attributing to the laws of the All-Wise and All-Beneficent defects which belong only to the short-sighted and selfish enactments of men. . . .

But so simple and so clear is this truth, that to see it fully once is always to recognize it. There are pictures which, though looked at again and again, present only a confused labyrinth of lines or scroll work—a landscape, trees, or something of the kind —until once the attention is called to the fact that these things make up a face or a figure. This relation, once recognized, is always afterward clear.

It is so in this case. In the light of this truth all social facts group themselves in an orderly relation, and the most diverse phenomena are seen to spring from one great principle.

It is not in the relations of capital and labor; it is not in the pressure of population against subsistence, that an explanation of the unequal development of our civilization is to be found. The great cause of inequality in the distribution of wealth is inequality in the ownership of land. The ownership of land is the great fundamental fact which ultimately determines the social,

the political, and consequently the intellectual and moral condition of a people. And it must be so. For land is the habitation of man, the storehouse upon which he must draw for all his needs, the material to which his labor must be applied for the supply of all his desires; for even the products of the sea cannot be taken, the light of the sun enjoyed, or any of the forces of nature utilized, without the use of land or its products. On the land we are born, from it we live, to it we return again—children of the soil as truly as is the blade of grass or the flower of the field. Take away from man all that belongs to land, and he is but a disembodied spirit. Material progress cannot rid us of our dependence upon land; it can but add to the power of producing wealth from land; and hence, when land is monopolized, it might go on to infinity without increasing wages or improving the condition of those who have but their labor. It can but add to the value of land and the power which its possession gives. Everywhere, in all times, among all peoples, the possession of land is the base of aristocracy, the foundation of great fortunes, the source of power. As said the Brahmins, ages ago—

"To whomsoever the soil at any time belongs, to him belong the fruits of it. White parasols and elephants mad with pride are the flowers of a grant of land." . . .

THE TRUE REMEDY

We have traced the unequal distribution of wealth, which is the curse and menace of modern civilization to the institution of private property in land. . . . As long as this institution exists no increase in productive power can permanently benefit the masses; but, on the contrary, must tend to still further depress their condition. . . .

There is but one way to remove an evil—and that is, to remove its cause.

Poverty deepens as wealth increases, and wages are forced down while productive power grows, because land, which is the source of all wealth and the field of all labor, is monopolized. To extirpate poverty, to make wages what justice commands they should be, the full earnings of the laborer, we must therefore substitute for the individual ownership of land a common ownership. Nothing else will go to the cause of the evil—in nothing else is there the slighest hope.

This, then, is the remedy for the unjust and unequal distribution of wealth in modern civilization . . . : *We must make land common property.*

This truth involves both a menace and a promise. It shows that the evils arising from the unjust and unequal distribution of wealth, which are becoming more and more apparent as modern civilization goes on, are not incidents of progress, but tendencies which must bring progress to a halt; that they will not cure themselves, but, on the contrary, must, unless their cause is removed, grow greater and greater, until they sweep us back into barbarism. . . . But it also shows that these evils are not imposed by natural laws; that they spring solely from social maladjustments which ignore natural laws, and that in removing their cause we shall be giving an enormous impetus to progress.

The poverty which in the midst of abundance, pinches and embrutes men, and all the manifold evils which flow from it, springs from a denial of justice. In permitting the monopolization of the natural opportunities which nature freely offers to all, we have ignored the fundamental law of justice—for so far as we can see, when we view things upon a large scale, justice seems to be the supreme law of the universe. But by sweeping away this injustice and asserting the rights of all men to natural opportunities, we shall conform

ourselves to the law—we shall remove the great cause of unnatural inequality in the distribution of wealth and power; we shall abolish poverty; tame the ruthless passions of greed; . . . give new vigor to invention and a fresh impulse to discovery; . . . and make tyranny and anarchy impossible.

The reform I have proposed accords with all that is politically, socially, or morally desirable. It has the qualities of a true reform, for it will make all other reforms easier. What is it but the carrying out in letter and spirit of the truth enunciated in the Declaration of Independence—the "self-evident" truth that is the heart and soul of the Declaration—*"That all men are created equal; that they are endowed by their Creator with certain inalienable rights; that among them are life, liberty, and the pursuit of happiness."*

These rights are denied when the equal right to land—on which and by which men alone can live—is denied. Equality of political rights will not compensate for the denial of the equal right to the bounty of nature. Political liberty, when the equal right to land is denied, becomes, as population increases and invention goes on, merely the liberty to compete for employment at starvation wages. This is the truth that we have ignored. And so there come beggars in our streets and tramps on our roads; and poverty enslaves men who we boast are political sovereigns; and want breeds ignorance that our schools cannot enlighten; and citizens vote as their masters dictate; and the demagogue usurps the part of the statesman; and gold weighs in the scales of justice; and in high places sit those who do not pay to civic virtue even the compliment of hypocrisy; and the pillars of the republic that we thought so strong already bend under an increasing strain.

We honor Liberty in name and in form. We set up her statues and sound her praises. But we have not fully trusted her. And with our growth so grow her demands. She will have no half service!

Liberty! it is a word to conjure with, not to vex the ear in empty boastings. For Liberty means Justice, and Justice is the natural law—the law of health and symmetry and strength, of fraternity and co-operation.

They who look upon Liberty as having accomplished her mission when she has abolished hereditary privileges and given men the ballot, who think of her as having no further relations to the everyday affairs of life, have not seen her real grandeur—to them the poets who have sung of her must seem rhapsodists, and her martyrs fools! As the sun is the lord of life, as well as of light; as his beams not merely pierce the clouds, but support all growth, supply all motion, and call forth from what would otherwise be a cold and inert mass all the infinite diversities of being and beauty, so is liberty to mankind. It is not for an abstraction that men have toiled and died; that in every age the witnesses of Liberty have stood forth, and the martyrs of Liberty have suffered.

We speak of Liberty as one thing, and of virtue, wealth, knowledge, invention, national strength and national independence as other things. But, of all these, Liberty is the source, the mother, the necessary condition. She is to virtue what light is to color; to wealth what sunshine is to grain; to knowledge what eyes are to sight. She is the genius of invention, the brawn of national independence. Where Liberty rises, there virtue grows, wealth increases, knowledge expands, invention multiplies human powers, and in strength and spirit the freer nation rises among her neighbors as Saul amid his brethren—taller and fairer. Where Liberty sinks, there virtue fades, wealth diminishes, knowledge is forgotten, invention ceases, and empires once mighty in arms and arts become a helpless prey to freer barbarians!

Only in broken gleams and partial light has the sun of Liberty yet beamed among men, but all progress hath she called forth.

Liberty came to a race of slaves crouching under Egyptian whips, and led them forth from the House of Bondage. She hardened them in the desert and made of them a race of conquerors. The free spirit of the Mosaic law took their thinkers up to heights where they beheld the unity of God, and inspired their poets with strains that yet phrase the highest exaltations of thought. Liberty dawned on the Phoenician coast, and ships passed the Pillars of Hercules to plow the unknown sea. She shed a partial light on Greece, and marble grew to shapes of ideal beauty, words became the instruments of subtlest thought, and against the scanty militia of free cities the countless hosts of the Great King broke like surges against a rock. She cast her beams on the four-acre farms of Italian husbandmen, and born of her strength a power came forth that conquered the world. They glinted from shields of German warriors, and Augustus wept his legions. Out of the night that followed her eclipse, her slanting rays fell again on free cities, and a lost learning revived, modern civilization began, a new world was unveiled; and as Liberty grew, so grew art, wealth, power, knowledge, and refinement. In the history of every nation we may read the same truth. It was the strength born of Magna Charta that won Crécy and Agincourt. It was the revival of Liberty from the despotism of the Tudors that glorified the Elizabethan age. It was the spirit that brought a crowned tyrant to the block that planted here the seed of a mighty tree. It was the energy of ancient freedom that, the moment it had gained unity, made Spain the mightiest power of the world, only to fall to the lowest depth of weakness when tyranny succeeded liberty. See, in France, all intellectual vigor dying under the tyranny of the Seventeenth Century to revive in splendor as Liberty awoke in the Eighteenth, and on the enfranchisement of French peasants in the Great Revolution, basing the wonderful strength that has in our time defied defeat.

Shall we not trust her?

In our time, as in times before, creep on the insidious forces that, producing inequality, destroy Liberty. On the horizon the clouds begin to lower. Liberty calls to us again. We must follow her further; we must trust her fully. Either we must wholly accept her or she will not stay. It is not enough that men should vote; it is not enough that they should be theoretically equal before the law. They must have liberty to avail themselves of the opportunities and means of life; they must stand on equal terms with reference to the bounty of nature. Either this, or Liberty withdraws her light! Either this, or darkness comes on, and the very forces that progress has evolved turn to powers that work destruction. This is the universal law. This is the lesson of the centuries. Unless its foundations be laid in justice the social structure cannot stand.

Our primary social adjustment is a denial of justice. In allowing one man to own the land on which and from which other men must live, we have made them his bondsmen in a degree which increases as material progress goes on. This is the subtle alchemy that in ways they do not realize is extracting from the masses in every civilized country the fruits of their weary toil; that is instituting a harder and more hopeless slavery in place of that which has been destroyed; that is bringing political despotism out of political

freedom, and must soon transmute democratic institutions into anarchy.

It is this that turns the blessings of material progress into a curse. It is this that crowds human beings into noisome cellars and squalid tenement houses; that fills prisons and brothels; that goads men with want and consumes them with greed; that robs women of the grace and beauty of perfect womanhood; that takes from little children the joy and innocence of life's morning.

Civilization so based cannot continue. The eternal laws of the universe forbid it. Ruins of dead empires testify and the witness that is in every soul answers, that it cannot be. It is something grander that Benevolence, something more august than Charity—it is Justice herself that demands of us to right this wrong. Justice that will not be denied; that cannot be put off—Justice that with the scales carries the sword. Shall we ward the stroke with liturgies and prayers? Shall we avert the decrees of immutable law by raising churches when hungry infants moan and weary mothers weep?

Though it may take the language of prayer, it is blasphemy that attributes to the inscrutable decrees of Providence the suffering and brutishness that come of poverty; that turns with folded hands to the All-Father and lays on Him the responsibility for the want and crime of our great cities. We degrade the Everlasting. We slander the Just One. A merciful man would have better ordered the world; a just man would crush with his foot such an ulcerous ant-hill! It is not the Almighty, but we who are responsible for the vice and misery that fester amid our civilization. The Creator showers upon us his gifts— more than enough for all. But like swine scrambling for food, we tread them in the mire—tread them in the mire, while we tear and rend each other!

In the very centers of our civilization

to-day are want and suffering enough to make sick at heart whoever does not close his eyes and steel his nerves. Dare we turn to the Creator and ask Him to relieve it? Supposing the prayer were heard, and at the behest with which the universe sprang into being there should glow in the sun a greater power; new virtue fill the air; fresh vigor the soil; that for every blade of grass that now grows two should spring up, and the seed that now increases fifty-fold should increase a hundred-fold! Would poverty be abated or want relieved? Manifestly no! Whatever benefit would accrue would be but temporary. The new powers streaming through the material universe could be utilized only through land.

This is not merely a deduction of political economy; it is a fact of experience. We know it because we have seen it. Within our own times, under our very eyes, that Power which is above all, and in all, and through all; that Power of which the whole universe is but the manifestation; that Power which maketh all things, and without which is not anything made that is made, has increased the bounty which men may enjoy, as truly as though the fertility of nature had been increased. Into the mind of one came the thought that harnessed steam for the service of mankind. To the inner ear of another was whispered the secret that compels the lightning to bear a message round the globe. In every direction have the laws of matter been revealed; in every department of industry have arisen arms of iron and fingers of steel, whose effect upon the production of wealth has been precisely the same as an increase in the fertility of nature. What has been the result? Simply that land owners get all the gain. . . .

Can it be that the gifts of the Creator may be thus misappropriated with impunity? Is it a light thing that labor should be robbed of its earnings while greed rolls in wealth—that the many should want while the few are surfeited? Turn to history, and on every page may be read the lesson that such wrong never goes unpunished; that the Nemesis that follows injustice never falters nor sleeps! Look around to-day. Can this state of things continue? May we even say, "After us the deluge!" Nay; the pillars of the state are trembling even now, and the very foundations of society begin to quiver with pent-up forces that glow underneath. The struggle that must either revivify, or convulse in ruin, is near at hand, if it be not already begun.

The fiat has gone forth! With steam and electricity, and the new powers born of progress, forces have entered the world that will either compel us to a higher plane or overwhelm us, as nation after nation, as civilization after civilization, have been overwhelmed before. It is the delusion which precedes destruction that sees in the popular unrest with which the civilized world is feverishly pulsing, only the passing effect of ephemeral causes. Between democratic ideas and the aristocratic adjustments of society there is an irreconcilable conflict. Here in the United States, as there in Europe, it may be seen arising. We cannot go on permitting men to vote and forcing them to tramp. We cannot go on educating boys and girls in our public schools and then refusing them the right to earn an honest living. We cannot go on prating of the inalienable rights of man and then denying the inalienable right to the bounty of the Creator. Even now, in old bottles the new wine begins to ferment, and elemental forces gather for the strife!

But if, while there is yet time, we turn to Justice and obey her, if we trust Liberty and follow her, the dangers that now threaten must disappear, the forces that now menace will turn to agencies of elevation. Think of the powers now wasted; of the infinite fields of knowledge yet to be explored; of the possibilities of which the wondrous inventions of this century give us but a hint. With want destroyed; with greed changed to noble passions; with the fraternity that is born of equality taking the place of the jealousy and fear that now array men against each other; with mental power loosed by conditions that give to the humblest comfort and leisure; and who shall measure the heights to which our civilization may soar? Words fail the thought! It is the Golden Age of which poets have sung and high-raised seers have told in metaphor! It is the glorious vision which has always haunted man with gleams of fitful splendor. It is what he saw whose eyes at Patmos were closed in a trance. It is the culmination of Christianity—the City of God on earth, with its walls of jasper and its gates of pearl! It is the reign of the Prince of Peace!

11. Edward Bellamy, *The Wastes of Individual Enterprise, 1887**

The wastes which resulted from leaving the conduct of industry to irresponsible individuals, wholly without mutual understanding or concert, were mainly four: first, the waste by mistaken undertakings; second, the waste from the competition and mutual hostility of those engaged in industry; third, the waste by periodical gluts and crises, with the consequent interruptions of industry; fourth, the waste from idle capital and labor, at all times. Any one of these four great leaks, were all the others stopped, would suffice to make the difference between wealth and poverty on the part of a nation.

Take the waste by mistaken undertakings, to begin with. In your day the production and distribution of commodities being without concert or organization, there was no means of knowing just what demand there was for any class of products, or what was the rate of supply. Therefore, any enterprise by a private capitalist was always a doubtful experiment. The projector having no general view of the field of industry and consumption, such as our government has, could never be sure either what the people wanted, or what arrangements other capitalists were making to supply them. In view of this, we are not surprised to learn that the chances were considered several to one in favor of the failure of any given business enterprise, and that it was common for persons who at last succeeded in making a hit to have failed repeatedly. If a shoemaker, for every pair of shoes he succeeded in completing, spoiled the leather of four or five pair, besides losing the time spent on them, he would stand about the same chance of getting rich as your contemporaries did with their system of private enterprise, and its average of four or five failures to one success.

The next of the great wastes was that from competition. The field of industry was a battlefield as wide as the world, in which the workers wasted, in assailing one another, energies which, if expended in concerted effort, . . . would have enriched all. As for mercy or quarter in this warfare, there was absolutely no suggestion of it. To

* Edward Bellamy, *Looking Backward 2000–1887* (Boston, 1889), pp. 229–35.

deliberately enter a field of business and destroy the enterprises of those who had occupied it previously, in order to plant one's own enterprise on their ruins, was an achievement which never failed to command popular admiration. Nor is there any stretch of fancy in comparing this sort of struggle with actual warfare, so far as concerns the mental agony and physical suffering which attended the struggle, and the misery which overwhelmed the defeated and those dependent on them. Now nothing about your age is, at first sight, more astounding to a man of modern times than the fact that men engaged in the same industry, instead of fraternizing as comrades and colaborers to a common end, should have regarded each other as rivals and enemies to be throttled and overthrown. This certainly seems like sheer madness, a scene from bedlam. But more closely regarded, it is seen to be no such thing. Your contemporaries, with their mutual throat-cutting, knew very well what they were at. The producers of the nineteenth century were not, like ours, working together for the maintenance of the community, but each solely for his own maintenance at the expense of the community. If, in working to this end, he at the same time increased the aggregate wealth, that was merely incidental. It was just as feasible and as common to increase one's private hoard by practices injurious to the general welfare. One's worst enemies were necessarily those of his own trade, for, under your plan of making private profit the motive of production, a scarcity of the article he produced was what each particular producer desired. It was for his interest that no more of it should be produced than he himself could produce. To secure this consummation as far as circumstances permitted, by killing off and discouraging those engaged in his line of industry, was his constant ef-

fort. When he had killed off all he could, his policy was to combine with those he could not kill, and convert their mutual warfare into a warfare upon the public at large by cornering the market, as I believe you used to call it, and putting up prices to the highest point people would stand before going without the goods. The day dream of the nineteenth century producer was to gain absolute control of the supply of some necessity of life, so that he might keep the public at the verge of starvation, and always command famine prices for what he supplied. This, Mr. West, is what was called in the nineteenth century a system of production. I will leave it to you if it does not seem, in some of its aspects, a great deal more like a system for preventing production. Some time when we have plenty of leisure I am going to ask you to sit down with me and try to make me comprehend, as I never yet could, though I have studied the matter a great deal, how such shrewd fellows as your contemporaries appear to have been in many respects ever came to entrust the business of providing for the community to a class whose interest it was to starve it. I assure you that the wonder with us is, not that the world did not get rich under such a system, but that it did not perish outright from want. This wonder increases as we go on to consider some of the other prodigious wastes that characterized it.

Apart from the waste of labor and capital by misdirected industry, and that from the constant bloodletting of your industrial warfare, your system was liable to periodical convulsions, overwhelming alike the wise and unwise, the successful cut-throat as well as his victim. I refer to the business crises at intervals of five to ten years, which wrecked the industries of the nation, prostrating all weak enterprises and crippling the strongest, and were followed by long periods, often of many years, of so-called dull times, during which the capitalists slowly re-gathered their dissipated strength while the laboring classes starved and rioted. Then would ensue another brief season of prosperity, followed in turn by another crisis and the ensuing years of exhaustion. As commerce developed, making the nations mutually depend-ent, these crises became world-wide, while the obstinacy of the ensuing state of collapse increased with the area affected by the convulsions, and the consequent lack of rallying centres. In proportion as the industries of the world multiplied and became complex, and the volume of capital involved was increased, these business cata-clysms became more frequent, till, in the latter part of the nineteenth cen-tury, there were two years of bad times to one of good, and the system of in-dustry, never before so extended or so imposing, seemed in danger of collaps-ing by its own weight. After endless

discussions, your economists appear by that time to have settled down to the despairing conclusion that there was no more possibility of preventing or controlling these crises than if they had been drouths or hurricanes. It only remained to endure them as necessary evils, and when they had passed over to build up again the shattered struc-ture of industry, as dwellers in an earthquake country keep on rebuilding their cities on the same site. . . .

The causes of the trouble inherent in . . . [the] industrial system . . . were in its very basis, and must needs be-come more and more maleficent as the business fabric grew in size and com-plexity. One of these causes was the lack of any common control of the different industries, and the consequent impossibility of their orderly and co-ordinate development. It inevitably resulted from this lack that they were continually getting out of step with one another and out of relation with the demand.

12. HENRY A. WALLACE, *An Economic Bill of Rights, 1945**

For the second time in twenty-five years America has proved her capacity to meet the challenge of total war. Twice in twenty-five years we have amazed the whole world—and ourselves—with our daring conception of what America could do when forced to war. We have astonished a grateful world by the stupendous number of planes, tanks and guns rolling off our assembly lines; with the bridge of ships we have erected across the oceans; by the over-whelming force with which America has turned the scales of battle.

Thus has America met the challenge of war—with boldness, courage and

determination. Thus has America be-come the symbol—the world over—for the dynamic force of a free people fighting for a free world.

But what of the peacetime problems here at home which will follow the successful conclusion of this war? Is America prepared to meet the chal-lenge of these peacetime problems as it has twice met the challenge of war? Shall we approach the problems of peace with the same boldness of con-ception, the same courage and deter-mination as we have approached the problems of war?

In the answer to these questions lies

* *The New York Times*, January 26, 1945.

the future of America. To anyone who has faith in America the answer is clear. The American people are prepared to meet the problems of peace in the same inspiring way that they have met the problems of war. The American people are resolved that we shall insure that the youth of this nation will never again be called upon to fight in another war.

And the American people are equally resolved that when our boys return home from this war they shall come back to the brightest possible, the freest possible, the finest possible place on the face of this earth—to a place where all persons, regardless of race, color, creed or place of birth, shall live in peace, honor and dignity—free from want and free from fear.

To do otherwise would betray the faith of every soldier, every worker, every business man, every farmer in this country, who is giving his best for America.

In determining the course of action we should pursue after the war it is well for America to pause and take stock of her capacities. For America's capacities should be the measure of America's future.

America's known capacities are not difficult to calculate. We are now producing goods and services to the gigantic total of $200,000,000,000 a year with 52,000,000 workers and 12,000,000 soldiers. In simple language that means that today America is producing nearly twice as much as she had ever produced before the war. But an enormous part of the goods and services we are producing today does not find its way into the American home. No, it represents the ships, the guns, the planes and tanks we are using to fight this war.

But I know, and you know, that if we can produce a huge flow of ships and guns and planes and tanks, we can also produce an abundance of houses and cars and clothing and provide education and recreation and the other good things of life for all Americans.

And I know, and you know, that when our boys return home from the war and are again able to put their power into the stream of peacetime production, America's capacity to produce will be even greater than it is today. Yes, much greater than today, even when we remember that some of our returning soldiers will prefer to resume their education; that some older people will begin a retirement, delayed to participate in war work, and that many women will give up their jobs in favor of homemaking.

Making full allowance for these groups, the fact remains that America will have the capacity after the war for producing houses, cars, clothing, education, recreation and all of the good things of life on a scale that staggers the imagination. That is what America can and will do if we have the courage and vision to give her the chance.

But to accomplish this task of utilizing our full productive capacity year after year, it is childish to think that this can be accomplished by a small segment of business and finance, even though that small segment consists of the giants of industry and the tycoons of American finance.

Nor can this be accomplished by throwing crumbs to 20,000 business enterprises out of a total of over 3,000,000 struggling small businesses in the United States. Why, an America geared to that limited conception of our capacity will find itself faced with millions of unemployed. The same people who set their sights too low for war are now asking the American people to set their sights too low for prosperity. They do not grasp the strength and the spirit of America.

Nor do any of us think for a minute

that there is any quack remedy or cure-all that can be automatically applied. The sober facts are that genuine progress will be achieved only through concrete plans and a real effort.

In the President's message to Congress last year and this year he set forth eight self-evident economic truths as representing a second Bill of Rights under which a new basis of security and prosperity can be established for all—regardless of station, race or creed.

America led the world in establishing political democracy. It must lead the world once more in strengthening and extending political democracy by firmly establishing economic democracy. Let us not forget the painful lessons of the rise of fascism. Let us remember that political democracy is at best insecure and unstable without economic democracy. Fascism thrives on domestic economic insecurity, as well as on lack of or divided resistance to external aggression. Fascism is not only an enemy from without, it is also potentially an enemy from within.

We now must establish an economic bill of rights, not only out of common decency, but also to insure the preservation of our political freedoms. We must accord to this economic bill of rights the same dignity—the same stature—in our American tradition as that we have accorded to the original Bill of Rights.

The key to making this economic bill of rights a part of the American way of life . . . is the wholehearted recognition by all our people of the simple fact that in America the future of the American worker lies in the well-being of American private enterprise; and the future of American private enterprise lies in the well-being of the American worker. The greatest single thing that this war has demonstrated on the home front is that when the American worker and the American business man and the American

farmer work together as one team, there are no limits on what America can accomplish.

But to work together as a team, . . . there must be a common goal. In this war that goal has been the defeat of our enemies in the shortest possible period of time. In the peace to come the goal must be the well-being of America. . . .

To the extent that private enterprise grows in strength, the economic bill of rights grows in reality—and to the extent that the economic bill of rights grows in reality, American private enterprise grows in strength. Thus all the measures which are suggested in this program for the implementation of the economic bill of rights are at the same time designed to make American capitalism and private enterprise work in the same great manner in peace as it has worked in war. . . .

The first economic right is "the right to a useful and remunerative job in the industries, or shops, or farms, or mines of the nation."

To assure the full realization of this right to a useful and remunerative job, an adequate program must provide America with sixty million productive jobs. We must have more jobs than workers; not more workers than jobs. Only with more jobs than workers can every man be guaranteed a job with good wages and decent working conditions. This requires private enterprise working at expanded capacity.

This necessary expansion of our peacetime productive capacity will require new facilities, new plants and new equipment

It will require large outlays of money which should be raised through normal investment channels. But while private capital should finance this expansion program, the Government should recognize its responsibility for sharing part of any special or abnormal risk of loss attached to such financing.

Therefore I propose that the Government guarantee the lender against the special and abnormal risks which may be involved in achieving our objective. This will provide new and expanding industry with plenty of private credit at reasonable interest rates. Through this program we shall merely be extending to the financing of old and new business the principles which have proved so successful in our experience with the V loans, T loans and the Federal Housing Administration loans.

A comprehensive investment program dedicated to expanding the peacetime productive capacity of America is the very essence of the American way of raising our standard of living. We build the plants for greater production so that all of us may share in their greater output. But greater output is not our only benefit from this plant expansion.

In fact, our benefits also include the wages paid to the labor employed in building these plants, in constructing the machinery to be used in the plants and in operating the plants after they are erected. These payments as wages all contribute to the nation's buying power, so that as a nation we shall have more money with which to buy the goods produced by these expanded plants.

As a matter of fact, a comprehensive investment program of this character could make possible $20,000,000,000 of new private investment each year. Why, just the job of building these plants and the machinery for them would give America 5,000,000 more jobs a year than we had in this work before the war. And this does not include the workers who would be needed to operate these plants after they are built.

In a nutshell, then, if we are going to have remunerative jobs for all, we must have an expanded private industry capable of hiring millions more men. I propose that the Government do its part in helping private enterprise finance this expansion of our industrial plant. It will be privately owned, privately operated and privately financed, but the Government will share with the private investor the unusual and abnormal financial risks which may be involved in getting started.

But, in providing jobs for everyone, we shall not only have to increase demand for our industrial and agricultural production here at home but also abroad. Some parts of our industrial and agricultural production demand a high level of foreign trade to be efficient and prosperous.

This is particularly true in our heavy equipment industries whose output will be needed. The foreign demand for such farm commodities as cotton, tobacco and wheat will also be great if other countries have the opportunity to buy. We therefore must take steps, in cooperation with other countries, to see that international trade and investment is resumed promptly on a sound basis.

This Administration has pioneered in the direction of international economic collaboration with its reciprocal trade program and the establishment of the export-import bank. It has again taken the lead in suggesting international monetary stabilization and sound international investment measures—measures that are a fundamental prerequisite to healthy foreign trade and commerce. . . .

With Congressional approval of this program and with our program of jobs for all in this country—the foreign trade of the United States can be trebled after the war. This increase in our foreign trade should mean 3,000,000 more jobs after the war than we had before the war.

Nor are the benefits of the increased

foreign trade and investment confined to increasing our prosperity. I want to emphasize that such cooperative measures for expanding international trade and investment are at the same time the economic foundation for a lasting peace. A prosperous world will be a world free of both economic and political aggression.

There is one further phase of this program of providing jobs for all which must be made an integral part of any long-range program. That is the task of seeing to it that there are not just jobs for all next year—or for the year after that. No, we are talking about jobs for all as a permanent part of our American way of life.

But it is inevitable, however, that an economy of free enterprise like ours will have some fluctuation in the number of jobs it can provide. Adjustments in employment are an essential part of an expanding free economy, and for these minor fluctuations, we provide unemployment insurance. But we must not allow such fluctuations ever to deteriorate into panic or depression. We cannot again be caught in that vicious downward spiral of unemployment, wage cuts and stagnated business.

Whenever the number of gainfully employed in this country falls below 57,000,000 our Government should take prompt steps to see that new jobs are made available to keep the total from falling significantly below that figure. This is the floor below which we must not allow employment to fall.

The basic function of your Government in taking care of any such slack in jobs is to see to it that private enterprise is assisted until it can absorb this slack. This is entirely possible. During the war the Federal, State and local Governments have found it necessary to put aside the construction of roads, buildings and public facilities to the value of many billions of dol-

lars. We have a need, too, for vast programs of the type exemplified by TVA.

Some of this construction will have to be undertaken immediately after the war. A good deal of it, however, can be postponed so that its construction could be timed with periods when the volume of employment that industry, commerce and agriculture can offer begins to fall. We must have a reservoir of planned and approved Federal, State and local projects ready to be tapped. And when employment falls below this floor of 57,000,000 jobs, this reservoir of planned and approved public works should be opened up to provide more jobs and take up the slack.

Such useful and essential public works should not produce Government or "relief" jobs, however. No, they should produce private jobs. This is possible if we insist that this construction be done by private firms under contract with the Government; private firms employing labor at the prevailing rate of wages and under standard labor conditions.

This assurance of a reserve of private jobs through constructive public works when needed to take up the slack will have a profound effect on the whole direction of our economy. In fact, the knowledge that Government accepts this responsibility of maintaining a floor under jobs will act as an immense stabilizing force on the whole economy.

The second economic right is "the right to earn enough to provide food and clothing and recreation."

America must remain pre-eminently the land of high wages and efficient production. Every job in America must provide enough for a decent living.

During the war we have been compelled to hold down wage increases that might have provoked runaway inflation. With all the arms and war materials we were producing, there was only a limited amount of consumption goods available. Increasing wages without increasing the amount of goods available to the consumer would have been an open invitation to inflation.

However, the end of the war, even the end of the war in Europe, will change this picture. Then there will be more goods available for America to buy, and it is only good common sense to see that the workman is paid enough to buy these goods.

The gains made by labor during the war must be retained in full. After the last war, as part of the process of returning to "normalcy," the slogan "Labor must be deflated" was adopted. This must not happen again. This time we must make sure that wage rates are not reduced when the wartime demand for labor is diverted into peacetime channels. We must make sure that the labor market is not broken by unemployment and wage slashes.

American labor should be assured that there are not going to be any wage cuts after this war. What is even more important—when the worker's hours are cut back to peacetime levels a real attempt must be made to adjust wage rates upward.

And wages should be constantly increased as the productivity of industry is increased. An expanding American economy can continue to expand only if the increased productivity is divided equitably between business and the worker. In fact—you know, and I know, that unless the worker does get his share of America's increased production in the form of increased wages and unless business gets its share in the form of increased profits—neither will prosper and all, business men, wage-earners and farmers, will lose.

But an increase in wages is not the only benefit the American worker should secure from increased productivity. He should also benefit in the form of shorter hours of work, in the form of increased leisure and opportunities for healthful recreation. Thus increased wages and shorter hours go hand-in-hand in solving the prosperity problem the American way.

There is one further aspect of the wage-earner's problem that I would like to comment on. That is his aspiration for an annual wage or guaranteed annual income from his job. It is a terribly important part of any real attempt to implement America's economic bill of rights. The size of the wage-earner's pay envelope is important —vitally important to American prosperity. But we all know that it is equally important to know how many pay envelopes he gets during a year. I would like to see him get a guaranteed minimum annual wage and I think the time has come for America to begin tackling this most difficult problem.

Now this goal cannot be attained overnight. It cannot be achieved in a manner to harm business Nor can it be achieved with the same speed in every business.

But we can start on the job of giving labor an annual wage. We can do a lot if we all will only agree that it is a problem business and labor must solve and if we all approach the problem with a genuine desire to succeed. And Government must do its part too. It must aid business in stabilizing its labor needs so that the burden of an annual wage will not be uneconomical. This, in my opinion, is the American way to bring about the annual wage, and I have confidence in the American way of doing things.

The third economic right is "the right of every farmer to raise and sell his products at a rate which will give him and his family a decent living."

American farmers now have by far the largest farm income in history. This is their due reward for the greatest agricultural production in history. We must assure the farmers that there will always be a market for all their output at good prices.

Concretely we should maintain an adequate floor on farm prices and thereby assure the farmer against the dangers of falling prices for his products. Our farm program must be one of expansion rather than curtailment. With jobs for all at good wages and with foreign markets greatly expanded, the farmer will be able to sell at good prices all that he can raise.

But this is not all. The farmer's income must have stability. To that end there should be established a comprehensive Federal crop insurance program which will secure the farmer against the hazards of crop failure.

To this must be added concrete steps to raise the standards of living on the farm and in the rural areas. We need a complete program of new and modernized homes and farm buildings. We must press forward with rural electrification and improvement. Only in this way can we bring to the rural communities modern facilities for decent and healthful living.

The fourth economic right is "the right of every business man, large and small, to trade in an atmosphere of freedom from unfair competition and domination by monopolies at home and abroad."

Our economic bill of rights, like our political Bill of Rights, is based on freedom of enterprise—freedom of enterprise not merely and exclusively for the few, but broadly and inclusively for the many. The political Bill of Rights insured the destruction of special prerogatives and privileges. The economic bill of rights will insure the destruction of special economic prerogatives and privileges.

No special class of business deserves to be the spoiled darling of Government. The American people have no interest in preserving the vested interests and monopolistic privileges of greedy big business. The interest of the American people lies in using the resources of the country to achieve a prosperous America, prosperous for all business, large and small, and for all the people.

We must break through the barriers of monopoly and international cartels that stand in the way of a healthy expansion of free enterprise.

We must overcome the monopolistic frame of mind which thinks of business in terms of restricted output at high prices per unit. We must pass on to workers and consumers the benefits of technological progress and large-scale production. Free enterprise in the American tradition can flourish only by doing a large volume of business at a small profit per unit.

We must protect free enterprise against monopolies and cartels through continued vigorous enforcement of the anti-trust laws. Private enterprise yields its full advantage to the consuming public and to other business only when it is genuinely free and competitive. He is a sinister enemy of free enterprise who pays lip-service to competition but also labels every anti-trust prosecution a "persecution."

Our economy has important new expanding sectors in air transport, frequency modulation, television, and fibers, plastics and many other fields. These new expanding business areas in particular must be kept free of the constricting hand of monopoly. There must be a place in these new business areas—as everywhere in our economy— for enterprising small firms. It is from these new and small firms that the great industries of the future will grow. We need new industries and new firms to have industrial progress and we must not permit them to be stifled by monopoly.

The fifth economic right is "the right of every family to a decent home."

Concretely, we should adopt a housing program looking toward the construction, through private enterprise, of 2,000,000 housing units a year and ridding this country of its urban and rural slums. We need to build at least 15,000,000 new housing units if we are to eliminate all our slums and substandard dwellings. The right to a home is meaningless when that home is a hovel. We cannot afford slums.

A well-housed America must have modern homes—homes with all the latest electrical and mechanical equipment which will eliminate the drudgery of household work. To the fullest extent possible we must be a land of home owners, and to that end we must assure every family an opportunity for home ownership by making certain that there is available private credit on terms which will reduce the down payment and cut by one-third the monthly cost of buying homes.

New residential construction and the modernization of America's homes alone can provide jobs for 4,000,000 people a year. This is 2,000,000 more than the maximum amount engaged in such work prior to the war.

The sixth economic right is "the right to adequate medical care and the opportunity to achieve and enjoy good health."

As Selective Service has revealed, too large a proportion of our younger men now fall below reasonable health standards. This is a warning signal to America with respect to that state of health of all segments of our population. This condition calls for immediate and drastic action.

We cannot permit the health of our people to be impaired by poverty or lack of medical and hospital facilities. I say to you that your Federal and State Governments have just as much responsibility for the health of their people as they have for providing them with education and police and fire protection. Health and adequate medical and hospital care are not luxuries. They are basic necessities to which all are entitled.

We must see that medical attention is available to all the people. But this health program must be achieved in the American way. Every person should have the right to go to the doctor and hospital of their own choosing. The Federal and State Governments should work hand in hand in making health insurance an integral part of our Social Security program just as old age and unemployment benefits are today.

We need more hospitals and doctors. We should make sure that such facilities are available and that we build hospitals in every community, rural and urban, that does not now have such facilities for all of its people.

Never again can we afford the waste of poor health in America because of poverty or inadequate facilities. And I say to you now that this program will prove in the long run to be a saving to America.

We must not be content to provide medical attention for people after they become sick. We must implement and extend our knowledge of maximum health as well as preventions of sickness. The Govenment should appropriate needed funds to finance a greatly expanded program of medical research in private and public institutions.

The seventh economic right is "the right to adequate protection from the economic fears of old age, sickness, accident and unemployment."

We must assure people who are disabled and temporarily unemployed that they will be taken care of adequately. We must assure them that they will not be in want because of loss of income during this period of compulsory unemployment. We cannot neglect these groups without incurring serious dangers to the stability of our whole economy.

A broader Social Security program will be needed after the war. Old Age Insurance should be adequate to provide all of our older men and women with the means for decent living. Our present old age benefits are definitely inadequate. A decent, self-respecting old age Social Security program should be deemed to be a right, not a charity, a right springing from the years of service each person delivers to the sum total of a better America.

An adequate Social Security program will, of itself, by adding to the spendable purchasing power available to the people and by placing a floor on consumption, add more than 2,000,000 jobs a year.

The eighth economic right is "the right to a good education."

We must have an educated and informed America. Even now most of our rural areas and some of our urban areas are poorly provided with schools. Our teachers are underpaid. Our schools are badly understaffed. We need more schools and at least 500,000 more teachers.

Through Federal aid to poorer communities for the development of locally controlled educational programs we propose to equalize and extend educational opportunities through the land. We propose to provide facilities for technical and higher education for all qualified young men and women without regard to their financial means. In this America, the pioneer of free education, the right to technical and higher education should be as universal as the right to a secondary school education.

This is the kind of program that can provide jobs, economic security and rising standards of living for all Americans —regardless of race, color or creed. Our democracy can be a living force only if it means the good life for all the people.

The millions of productive jobs that this program will bring are jobs in private enterprise. They are jobs based on the expanded demand for the output of our economy for consumption and investment. And this program need place no real burden on the Federal budget, notwithstanding the reduction in taxes which must come after the war.

On the contrary, a program of this character can provide America with a national income of such a size that it will be possible to reduce the tax rates still further on personal incomes, on business profits and on consumption, and still collect enough tax revenues to meet the needs of the Government, including orderly retirement of the national debt.

These should be our immediate goals, once final victory over our enemies has been achieved.

Now there are those who say that these goals are the dream of a "man willing to jeopardize the country's future with untried ideas and idealistic schemes." These people think they are the realists.

Actually, these are the persons of limited vision and stunted imagination. These people are of the same breed as these "sound business men" who haggled over pennies in the purchase of strategic stockpiles before the war, only to leave the materials for the Japs to use against us. Those are people who will fight against enemies, waging total war, by pinching pennies. These people think the same as those who said the President was dreaming when he declared in 1940 that the American people would produce 50,000 planes in one year. Do these Monday-morning quarterbacks have that great faith in the American people, and in their way of life, which is required in order to understand the meaning of America?

I am confident, however, that the

great majority of the American people share the same great faith in America and in the American way of doing things which I have expressed here. We know our way and the road ahead is straight and broad, although there are many hills which we must climb. The program which I have set forth is only the first milestone, for the capacity of the American way of life in the years to come is beyond the vision of man. The American system of free enterprise is the best the world has ever known, and through it we can obtain, God willing, the best that this world has to offer.

13. The Editors of *Fortune, The Tranformation of American Capitalism, 1951**

Fifty years ago American capitalism seemed to be what Marx predicted it would be and what all the muckrakers said it was—the inhuman offspring of greed and irresponsibility, committed by its master, Wall Street, to a long life of monopoly. It seemed to provide overwhelming proof of the theory that private ownership could honor no obligation except the obligation to pile up profits. It was, indeed, close to the capitalism that Andrei Vishinsky today keeps on denouncing so laboriously and humorlessly. And it was the capitalism that millions of people abroad and many even at home, to the immense aid and comfort of the Communists, still think American capitalism is.

But American capitalism today is actually nothing of the kind. There has occurred a great transformation, of which the world as a whole is as yet unaware, the speed of which has outstripped the perception of the historians, the commentators, the writers of business books—even many businessmen themselves. No important progress whatever can be made in the understanding of America unless the nature of this transformation is grasped and the obsolete intellectual stereotypes discarded.

Many evidences of the transformation are at hand, though they have never yet been drawn together into what is very urgently needed—a restatement of capitalistic theory in modern American terms. Take, for example, the all-pervasive character of American capitalism, as stressed in The American Way of Life. There has been a vast dispersion of ownership and initiative, so that the capitalist system has become intimately bound in with the political system and takes nourishment from its democratic roots. What might be called the influence of Main Street has become vastly more important than the control of Wall Street. U. S. capitalism is *popular* capitalism, not only in the sense that it has popular support, but in the deeper sense that the people as a whole participate in it and use it.

But perhaps the transformation can best be understood by looking at what has happened to "Big Business," which once was supposed to have controlled the economy from its headquarters in Wall Street. The fact is that Wall Street no longer wields much power over Big Business, which in turn is far from being the most powerful sector of the economy. For economic power boils down to the ability to decide who makes what and who gets what and in what proportions, and business alone

* Article by the editors of *Fortune*, February, 1951. Courtesy of *Fortune Magazine*.

no longer decides this. "The class struggle in America," writes Professor Clair Wilcox in the *Harvard Business Review*, "is not a struggle between the proletariat and the bourgeoisie. It is a struggle between functional groups possessing concentrated power—a struggle to control the products of industry." These groups, as Professor Wilcox describes them, are Big Labor, Big Agriculture, Big Little Business, and Big Business. Of them all, Big Business, if only because it is subject to the most pressure, exercises its power with a strong and growing sense of responsibility. It has led the way to the formation of a kind of capitalism that neither Karl Marx nor Adam Smith ever dreamed of.

At the bottom of the change is simple morality, which has concerned the U.S. throughout its history, sometimes to the point of fanaticism. "The American," H. L. Mencken once said, "save in moments of conscious and swiftly lamented deviltry, casts up all ponderable values, including the value even of beauty, in terms of right and wrong." Like the European who described moral indignation as suppressed envy, Mencken scorned it as the mark of the peasant; and the American's capacity for moral indignation *has* resulted in many "uncivilized" excesses like prohibition. But it has also made him the most omnivorous reformer in history. Karl Marx based his philosophy on the fatalistic assumption that what he described as the inherent defects of capitalism are above the will of men to affect them. It has remained for the history of U. S. capitalism, beginning as early as the 1870's, to show that the moral convictions of men can change the course of capitalistic development . . .

During the 1920's popular demand for reform was almost nonexistent. For one thing, the scorn of some of the nation's most effective writers made preoccupation with moral issues unfashionable if not ludicrous. For another, business seemed to be doing fine, and seemed to deserve not reform but praise. As the immensely popular *Saturday Evening Post* demonstrated in almost every issue, as Herbert Hoover himself phrased it, "The slogan of progress is changing from the full dinner pail to the full garage."

The catastrophe of depression blasted this dream. The shocked and angry people, seeing their livelihood disappear, put the Right to Life above the other rights. Their natural tendency to blame the bust on those who only yesterday were taking credit for having started an eternal boom was strengthened by revelations such as those of the Pecora congressional investigation into Wall Street financial practices. So they embraced the latter-day Populism of the New Deal, and demanded that something be done. Writers and intellectuals took up the cudgels. Some were merely inclined to condemn what they had for so long condemned, but many tried to find out how and why it had happened, and how to keep it from happening again.

Many of the ensuing reforms survived. Immediately after the Pecora investigation, Congress passed a law divorcing investment banking from deposit banking. And a year later it passed the well-intentioned Securities Exchange Act, which put the Stock Exchange under federal regulation, gave the Federal Reserve Board authority to limit speculative margins, required all officers and stockholders of big companies to report their dealings in their companies' securities, and created the Securities and Exchange Commission to watch over the investment market.

Other attempts at reform were less successful. NRA, for example, went to a well-deserved death. As for the famed Temporary National Economic Committee, much of what it investigated was beside the point by the time it was in print—and not only because of the impending war. Even while the committee was mulling over the power of big business, and the intellectuals were in full cry on the trail of finance capitalism, business initiative had been dispersed among hundreds of enterprises; business power in the aggregate found itself confronted by the rising power of the unions on the one hand, the farmers on the other; and Wall Street had ceased to be a valid symbol of great tyranny.

The decline of Wall Street actually began long before the reforms of the New Deal. It began when corporations grew rich and independent. . . . Wall Street did not feel the change at first. In the boom of the 1920's the issue of new securities passed the $500-million-a-year mark, and a rich time was had by all. But even then the bulk of the Street's effort was going into the buying and selling of old issues (and new issues of holding companies that used the money to buy old issues), the promotion of dubious foreign bonds, and the lending of money at, say, 7 per cent for the speculative purchase of stock paying, say, 5 per cent. And even then corporations were putting up to ten times as much money into their reserves as all companies were raising in new stocks and bonds. And the depression hit the Street's new-issue function even harder than it hit the trading function. High income taxes and the growing corporate practice of financing new issues through insurance and trust companies trimmed the new-issue business almost to the vanishing point.

Except as its opinions still influence investment policies, Wall Street today exerts only a fraction of the power it once wielded. Industry now plows back 60 per cent of its profits, as against 30 per cent in the 1920's, and the bulk of the money used in capital formation comes from corporate earning or from internal sources such as depreciation. The largest brokerage house on the Street, accounting for 10 per cent of the stock trading on the Stock Exchange, is Merrill Lynch, Pierce, Fenner & Beane, 90 per cent of whose customers are small-fry out-of-towners. . . .

And where, in this regrouping of U. S. economic power, do we find the sense of responsibility that ought to go with the power if the nation is to increase its productivity? Labor, with a few exceptions, does not yet show much of it, and agriculture shows even less. The only place it can be found in any force is in the individual business enterprise, which now has the initiative that might have remained in Wall Street had not the transformation taken place.

One of the two chief characteristics of big modern enterprise is that it is run by hired management. As Berle and Means put it, the power inherent in the control of the "active property" —the plant, organization and good will—has superseded the power inherent in "passive property"—the stocks and bonds. Even companies whose owners are managers may be described as management-run. The Ford company, for example, behaves not as an organization solely dedicated to earning the maximum number of dollars for the Ford family, but as an organization dedicated first of all to its own perpetuation and growth.

The other chief characteristic of the big modern enterprise is that management is becoming a profession. This means, to begin with, that a professional manager holds his job primarily because he is good at it. Often he has begun at the bottom and worked his way up by sheer merit. Or more often he has been carefully and even scientifically chosen from a number of bright and appropriately educated young men, put through an executive-training course, and gradually insinuated into the activities for which he shows the most talent. Since even at the top he generally functions as a member of a committee rather than as a final authority, his talents are so well balanced that none of them protrude excessively. He lives on what he makes, and even when he is well paid he doesn't have much left after taxes. Generally he is gregarious, and usually he is not a colossal "personality." But if he is not a General MacArthur, neither is he a Mr. Milquetoast. And if he is expected not to give arbitrary orders, he is also expected not to take them. In most well-run big enterprises, an executive is by definition a man who would object officially to a policy decision he disapproved.

More important, the manager is becoming a professional in the sense that like all professional men he has a responsibility to society as a whole. This is not to say that he no longer needs good, old-fashioned business sense. He does, and more than ever. The manager is responsible primarily to his company as a profit-earning mechanism, and current talk about the corporation as a non-profit institution is more than a little naïve. . . .

But the great happy paradox of the profit motive in the American system is that management, precisely because it is in business to make money years on end, cannot concentrate exclusively on making money here and now. To keep on making money years on end, it must, in the words of Frank Abrams, Chairman of the Standard Oil Company of New Jersey, "conduct the affairs of the enterprise in such a way as to maintain an *equitable* and *working balance* among the claims of the various directly interested groups —stockholders, employees, customers,

and the public at large." . . . The corporate manager . . . is part of a group that enjoys power only so long as it does not abuse it—in other words, precisely so long as it does not exercise power the way men and groups of men used to before the capitalistic transformation. . . .

One of the most pressing concerns of almost every large company today is what people are going to think about it. Board meetings often turn into self-examination sessions, with managers defending or explaining their actions as if before accusing judges. Ot a recent board meeting of a large consumer-goods company, the president rose up and remarked that the foremen had in effect built up a block between management and labor, and that management was mostly at fault. Fully two hours were devoted to soul-searching and discussion. There was also the matter of closing an old mill in a small town. Not only was the specific situation explored thoroughly, but the history of other similar cases was brought up. This problem was solved, after a full hour's discussion, by the decision to move a storage plant into the town and thus absorb nearly all the displaced employees. As one executive remarked, "At least half our time was taken up with discussing the repercussions of what we propose to do. And this is what the boys who write the books call the managerial revolution."

What may set a new high in business' concern with fundamental values and questions is a current project of Corning Glass Works, which is celebrating its centennial in 1951. On the premise that "As long as there are men making and operating machines, there will be a humanistic problem as well as a scientific and technological problem in an industrial society," Corning has joined the American Council of Learned Societies in sponsoring a conference on "Living in Industrial Civilization." The conference was held in May, 1951, at the Corning Glass Center, and attended by academicians and men of affairs from all over the world. They discussed such topics as Work and Human Values; Leisure and Human Values; the Individual's Sense of Community; Confidence in Life.

Nothing perhaps is more indicative of the corporation's awareness of its responsibilities than the growth of public-relations "programs." Although many of them are hardly more than publicity campaigns, more and more managers understand tolerably well that good business public relations is good performance publicly appreciated, because adequately communicated. Now the mere comprehension of a moral axiom, as all parents know, does not guarantee its observance. But its constant iteration does make the subject more and more acutely aware of its importance, and thus eventually influences his behavior. As Paul Garret of G. M. has been saying for years, "Our program is finding out what people like, doing more of it; finding out what people don't like, doing less of it."

All of which should not be interpreted to mean that business is already rolling us down the six-lane, high-speed highway to economic paradise. We have concerned ourselves here with the pace-setters of American management, and do not presume to imply that all managers and all other companies are doing as well. Many still give precedence to the big, quick profit. Many incline to regard the stockholder mainly as a convenient personification of the profit goal, labor as a lamentably sensitive kind of commodity, and the customer as the man who gets rolled. Like many a labor and agricultural leader, these businessmen try to increase their share of the national product regardless of their contribution to that product. What Professor Wilcox calls Big (or organized) Little Business, for example, is responsible for or protected by most of the fair-trade laws, licensing systems, local bidding laws, and other legal devices that maintain prices independently of the market.

Big Business, too, has something to answer for. Just how much power it has, for example, to fix prices, and to what extent it uses or abuses that power are right now the subjects of much expert contention. Some economists maintain that "Oligopoly is by all evidence the ruling market form in the modern economy"—i.e., since the nation's corporate assets are concentrated in a relatively few companies, the market is made up of a few sellers, who can administer prices. Other economists, attacking the statistics on which such conclusions are based, maintain that only 20 per cent of the national income is provided by unregulated oligopoly, and that an analysis of competition in terms of market realities, which nobody has yet completed, will show that the American economy is becoming more, not less, competitive. It is to be hoped that such an important analysis will be undertaken soon. But whatever its results, it is not likely to reveal that business, socially speaking, has yet attained perfection.

What counts, however, is that certain business leaders *are* setting the pace, and *are* being followed. What counts is that the old concept that the owner has a right to use his property just the way he pleases has evolved into the belief that ownership carries social obligations, and that a manager is a trustee not only for the owner but for society as a whole. Such is the Transformation of American Capitalism. In all the world there is no more hopeful economic phenomenon.

VII

* *

Democracy and the Consent of the Governed

JOHN WILLIAM GARDNER

foundation executive, taught psychology before entering foundation work.

He has been president of the Carnegie Corporation of New York and Carnegie Foundation for the Advancement of Teaching since 1955.

He was born in Los Angeles in 1912. He received an A.B. degree in 1935 and an A.M. in 1936 from Stanford University, and a Ph.D. from the University of California in 1938. From 1936 to 1942 he taught psychology at California, Connecticut College, and Mount Holyoke College.

Mr. Gardner served with the Federal Communications Commission in Washington in 1942 and 1943. He was in the Marine Corps from 1943 to 1946.

He became a staff member of the Carnegie Corporation of New York in 1946.

John W. Gardner ✳✳✳ Can We Count on More Dedicated People?

Critics are saying that we have lost our devotion to American ideals. They are saying that the individual American has lost his faith, his discipline and his vitality. They are saying that he is a spoiled, demanding, overfed oaf who cares for nothing but his own creature comforts and diversion.

I don't believe it.

But something is wrong. At a moment in our history when we need all our sense of purpose and capacity for sustained effort, we seem in danger of losing our bearings, of surrendering to a "cult of easiness."

Why? Others have tried to explain our failures at the level of national policy and leadership. Such explanations are undoubtedly helpful. It is my intention, however, to explore the question as it touches the citizen.

Our national problems have become so complex that it is not easy for the individual to see what he can do about them. The tasks facing the frontiersmen two centuries ago may have been grim, but they were also obvious. Each man knew what he must do. But what can a man of today do about inflation, about international organization, about the balance of trade? There are answers to these questions, but they are not self-evident. The individual American—busy earning a living, repapering the dining room, getting the children off to school, paying the bills—doesn't hear one clear call to action. He hears a jumble of outcries and alarms, of fanfares and dirges, of voices crying "Hurry!" and voices crying "Wait!" Meanwhile he has problems of his own.

The men who founded this nation knew that in a world largely hostile to the idea of freedom, a free society would have to prove that it is capable of, and worthy of, survival. The requirement is unchanged today. Free societies must prove their ability to make good on their promises and to keep alive their cherished values. And they must prove their vigor, their capacity to practice the disciplined virtues. Above all, they must prove their capacity to achieve excellence.

The free society is still the exceptional society, and the world is still full of people who believe that men need masters. The survival of the idea for which this nation stands is not inevitable. It may survive if enough Americans care enough.

It would be easier to grasp that truth if we weren't so blessedly comfortable. Part of our problem is how to stay awake on a full stomach. Since the beginning of time most humans have had to work hard either because subsistence demanded it or because their taskmasters required it. Now we don't have to work very hard to stay alive; and free people have no taskmasters. With such release from outward pressures, free men may make the fatal mistake of thinking that no effort is required of them.

Nothing could be more dangerous to our future. Free men must be quick to understand the kinds of effort that are required to keep their society vital and strong. If they have the wisdom to demand much of themselves, their society will flourish. But a free society that refuses to exert itself will not last long. And freedom alone won't save it.

Americans have many differing ideas about the appropriate goals for our society. That is as it should be. But we do have shared aims. And our hope of greatness as a nation lies in these shared aims. No people in history ever lifted itself above the normal trajectory without a widely shared "vision of greatness."

Some people say that we are uncertain of our shared aims. Some say we're drifting because we've achieved everything we ever wanted. Both statements are dead wrong. To say that we are confused is one way of evading the difficult tasks before us. We are not really in doubt about the more serious of our shared aims. We know what they are. We know that they are difficult. And we know that we have not achieved them.

Are examples needed?

We want peace with justice. We want a world that doesn't live under the fear of the bomb, a world that acknowledges the rule of law, a world in which no nation can play bully and no nation need live in fear. How many Americans would disagree with that purpose? Is it easy? Have we come close to achieving it? Read your morning paper.

We want freedom. We don't think man was born to have someone else's foot on his neck—or someone else's hand over his mouth. We want freedom at home and we want a world in which freedom is possible. Who would disagree with that as a national aim? Who would call it easy? Who would say we've achieved it?

We believe in the dignity and worth of the individual, and it has always been our unshakable purpose to protect and preserve that dignity.

We believe that every person should be enabled to achieve the best that is in him, and we are the declared enemies of disease, ignorance, poverty and all other conditions which stunt the individual and prevent such fulfillment.

We believe in equality before the law, in equal political suffrage, and —dearest of all to Americans—equality of opportunity. "We may not all hit home runs," the saying goes, "but every man should have his chance at bat."

Those are only some of the more obvious goals we are committed to as Americans. Have we gone as far as we should in achieving them? Are all our problems solved? Look around.

In the world at large we see the threat of universal destruction. We see great nations striving fiercely to prove that free societies are outmoded. We see underdeveloped lands stirring out of their ancient sleep, poised between chaos and orderly development, listening indiscriminately to those who would help them and those who would use them.

At home we see—despite our impressive achievements in human welfare —still too many children trapped in poverty and ignorance; too many talents blighted by lack of opportunity; too many men and women who never achieve their full potential; racial and religious prejudice in the South and in the North; the invasion of personal freedom by government and by large organizations; juvenile delinquency and social disintegration in the big cities; corruption and the misuse of power; and creeping mediocrity in every phase of our national life.

Is this a fair picture of our nation? Of course not. Our achievements in providing a better life for Americans are astounding to other societies. We may be deeply proud of what we've accomplished. But smugness and complacency do not look good on us. Our historic attitude has been pride in what we've accomplished and impatience that we haven't accomplished more. Let's not change now.

Obviously we don't agree on how to deal with our major problems. As free Americans we will argue that question right to the door of the polling booth.

But we know what the problems are and agree on our more important aims. So what is lacking? The answer is simple: We lack leadership on the part of our leaders, and commitment on the part of every American. I want to talk about the matter of individual "commitment."

The establishment of a durable peace, the strengthening of a free society, the enrichment of the traditions on which freedom depends —these cannot be achieved by aimless or listless men. All our wisdom, all our talent and vitality, all our steadfastness will be needed if we wish to attain these goals. Can we count on an ample supply of dedicated Americans?

The answer must be conditional. If—as a nation—we understand, expect and honor dedication, the supply will be ample. But if we assume that dedicated men are exceedingly rare and probably a little foolish, the supply will be low. It is unfortunately true that Americans have to some degree lost the habit of asking for or expecting devoted action. Long continued, such failure to expect dedication can have only one outcome: we shall eventually lose the capacity for it.

Of course every line of behavior has its pathology, and there is a pathology of dedication. People sometimes commit themselves to vicious or criminal goals. Or their commitment to worthy goals becomes so fanatical that they destroy as much as they create. And there is the "true believer" who surrenders himself to a mass movement or to dogmatic beliefs in order to escape the responsibilities of freedom. A free society does not invite that kind of allegiance. It wants only one kind of devotion—the devotion of free, rational, responsible individuals.

It is my conviction that free and responsible individuals are proud to offer such devotion if given the opportunity. People would rather work hard for something they believe in than enjoy a pampered idleness. They would rather sacrifice their comfort for an honored objective than pursue endless diversions. It is a mistake to speak of dedication as a sacrifice. Every man knows that there is exhilaration in intense effort applied toward a meaningful end. The religious precept that you must lose yourself to find yourself is no less true at the secular level. No one who has observed the devoted scientist in his laboratory can doubt the spiritual rewards of such work. The same is true of anyone who is working toward goals that represent the highest values of his society.

We fall into the error of thinking that happiness necessarily involves ease, diversion, tranquillity—a state in which all of one's wishes are satisfied. For most people happiness is not to be found in this vegetative state but in striving toward meaningful goals. The dedicated person has not achieved all of his goals. His life is the endless pursuit of goals, some of them unattainable. He may never have time to surround himself with luxuries. He may often be tense, worried, fatigued. He has little of the leisure one associates with the storybook conception of happiness.

But he has found a more meaningful happiness. The truth is that happiness in the sense of total gratification is not a state to which man can aspire. It is for the cows, possibly for the birds, but not for us.

We want meaning in our lives. When we raise our sights, strive for excellence, and dedicate ourselves to the highest goals of our society, we are enrolling in an ancient and meaningful cause: the age-long struggle of man to realize the best that is in him. Man reaching toward the most exalted goals he can conceive, man striving impatiently and restlessly for excellence has produced great religious insights, created great art, penetrated secrets of the universe and set standards of conduct which give meaning to the phrase "the dignity of man." On the other hand, man without standards, man with his eyes on the ground has proven over and over, in every society, at every period in history, that humans can be lower than the beasts, sunk in ignorance, morally and ethically blind, living a life devoid of meaning.

The task we face as a nation of keeping our ideals alive is partly a question of leadership. Even in a democracy leaders must lead. If our citizens are to recapture a sense of mission with respect to the purposes we care the most about, our leaders must have the capacity and the vision to ask for it. It is hard to expect an upsurge of devotion to the common good in response to leaders who lack the moral depth to understand such devotion—or the courage to evoke it, or the stature to merit the response which follows. One of the great tasks of leadership is to help a society achieve the best that is in it.

But it takes more than leadership to preserve the ideals of a free society. The values we cherish will not survive without the constant attention of the ordinary citizen. Unlike the Pyramids, the monuments of the spirit will not stand untended. They must be nourished in each generation by the allegiance of believing men and women. The fact that millions have died violent deaths while defending individual freedom does not ensure survival of that principle if we cease paying our tithes of devotion. Every free man, in his work and in his family life, in his public behavior and in the secret places of his heart, should see himself as a builder and maintainer of the ideals of his society. Individual Americans —truck drivers and editors, grocers and senators, beauty operators and ballplayers—can contribute to the greatness and strength of a free society, or they can help it to die.

How does one contribute to the greatness and strength of a free society? That is a question to which there are many true answers. One answer is —pursue excellence! Those who are most devoted to a democratic society must be precisely the ones who insist that free men are capable of the highest standards of performance, that a free society can be a great society in the richest sense of that phrase. The idea for which this nation stands will not survive if the highest goal free men can set themselves is an amiable mediocrity.

At the simplest level, the pursuit of excellence means an increased concern for competence on the part of the individual. Keeping a free society free—and vital and strong—is no job for the half-educated and the slovenly. In a society of free men competence is a primary duty. The man who does his job well tones up the whole society. And the man who does a slovenly job—whether he is a janitor or a judge, a surgeon or a technician—lowers the tone of the society. So do the chiselers of high and low degree, the sleight-of-hand artists who know how to gain an advantage without honest work. They are the regrettable burdens of a free society.

But excellence implies more than competence. It implies a striving for the highest standards in every phase of life. We need individual excellence in all its forms, in every kind of creative endeavor, in political life, in education, in industry—in short, universally. And, not least, we need excellence in standards of individual conduct.

The words for Americans to live by are these: If you believe in a free society, be worthy of a free society. You don't need to quit your job and enroll as a missionary in Africa to prove your dedication. Stay where you are and do a better job, be a better citizen, live a better life. Every good man strengthens society. In this day of sophisticated judgments on man and society, that is a notably unfashionable thing to say, but it is true. Men of integrity, by their very existence, rekindle the belief that as a people we can live above the level of moral squalor. We need that belief, for a cynical community is a corrupt community. More than any other form of government, democracy requires a certain optimism concerning mankind. The best argument for democracy is the existence of men who justify that optimism. It follows that one of the best ways to serve democracy is to be that kind of man. When you see such men and women, tip your hat and bow. The future of our civilization is in their hands.

Can People Make Their Own Political Decisions?

The American polity proved extraordinarily flexible in permitting the nation to reconcile divergent points of view and to take positive action while yet protecting the rights and interests of those who might be adversely affected. It was able to do so by slowly developing the means through which the operations of government were accompanied by the consent of the governed. Ultimately the state claimed to represent the will of the majority; but even then it preferred to act with the acquiescence of the minority rather than by coercion. Consent was thus the core of American democracy.

All these assumptions rested on the premise that the people who were members of the polity were competent to arrive at valid political decisions. Yet, in our own times, as Dr. Gardner points out, national problems have become so complex that it is not easy for an individual to see what he can do about them. Increasingly the average man looks to his leaders for guidance; but in a democracy, the quality of effective leadership depends upon the capacity of the citizens to follow. It is therefore of the utmost importance to consider the question, with which Americans often wrestled in the past, of how far the people can be trusted with the power of political decision.

The ideas and practices of American democracy developed slowly. Yet almost from the start, political institutions rested on a basis of consent of the governed. This was a result of the conditions of settlement which subtly modified inherited conceptions of political obedience.

In the seventeenth century, there seemed to be no question that it was the business of the rulers to rule and of the people to obey. John Winthrop (1588–1649) clearly set that proposition forth in the defense of his actions as Governor of Massachusetts in 1645. Yet, even in that very forceful statement, the magistrate acknowledged that the source of his authority lay in the consent of those over whom he governed (1).

Moreover, Winthrop's claim to unbounded authority quickly became anachronistic. Eighteenth-century developments tended to emphasize the dependence upon consent and to restrain the powers of the rulers. The Revolution thus was the culmination of a process that had actually begun much earlier. The separation from England did, however, stimulate a great deal of thought on the nature of political allegiance. John Adams (1735–1826), a young Massachusetts lawyer, who was later to become second President of the United States, was driven by the approach of independence to probe the meaning of consent in his consideration of the form that a new government would take (2). Alexander Hamilton (1757–1804), John Jay (1745–1829), and James Madison (1751–1836), the authors of the Federalist Papers, an influential series of articles advocating the adoption of the Constitution, also considered the necessity for balance and consent in the polity at a later stage in the development of the federal union (3).

Within the generally accepted consensus that emerged after 1789, there was room for a good deal of division of opinion. The more conservative Americans criticized the inclination of the mob to take the law into its own hands; and the more radical objected to any efforts to restrain the will of the majority. But there was widespread agreement on fundamental principles in the early nineteenth century, as was evident in the thoughtful statements on equality by the novelist James Fenimore Cooper (1789–1851), (4).

The decades that followed did not shake the faith in government by consent. Indeed, the most penetrating criticism of the concept came not through the denial of the necessity for consent but through extreme assertions of it. For it was possible to push the idea so far as to give every man an effective veto and thus to deprive the government of the power to act at all. Henry D. Thoreau (1817–62), for instance, gave primacy to the rights of the individual conscience even when it led to an outright defiance of the state (see below, page 489).

But this position was not widely held. Americans more generally agreed that orderly democratic government was the last best hope of men on earth and were willing to accept the rule of law even when it ran counter to its own interests and ideas. The great exception was the crisis which led to the bloody test of civil war. Abraham Lincoln (1809–65) fully understood this issue. The eloquent statement in his first Inaugural Address (5), delivered while the shadow of war already hung over the country, set it forth clearly. A little later, the poet Walt Whitman (1819–92) celebrated the virtues of popular rule, although fully conscious of the deficiences of the common man as citizen (6).

The closing decades of the nineteenth century were troubled times for orderly government. Americans then faced unprecedented problems in the wake of expansion and industrialization. Ignorant politicians often yielded to the temptations of unscrupulous men who sought to further their own interests by corrupting the government processes. The local boss, the venal judge, the bought legislature were all too common. In revulsion, some Americans expressed doubt about the very premises of democracy. Henry Adams (1838–1918), the brilliant scion of a distinguished family, was thoroughly disillusioned with the Washington political situation of the last quarter of the century, and etched its portrait in bitter tones in his anonymous novel, "Democracy" (7). George Ade (1866–1944) mocked the relative reversal of standards in business and politics (8). And the iconoclastic critic H. L. Mencken (1880–1956) expressed disgust with the total hypocrisy of political democracy (9).

Yet, more thoughtful men understood, as Lincoln had, that for all its faults democracy was the only means of assuring government by consent. The poet Carl Sandburg (1878–) wrote of his faith in the capacity of the people to find their own way (10); and the philosopher John Dewey (1859–1952) continued to insist that there was no feasible alternative to the methods of democracy (11). Only thus could men remain free and yet work together.

1. JOHN WINTHROP, *On Liberty, 1645**

The great questions that have troubled the country, are about the authority of the magistrates and the liberty of the people. It is yourselves who have called us to this office, and being called by you, we have our authority from God, in way of an ordinance, such as hath the image of God eminently stamped upon it, the contempt and violation whereof hath been vindicated with examples of divine vengeance. I entreat you to consider, that when you choose magistrates, you take them from among yourselves, men subject to like passions as you are. Therefore when you see infirmities in us, you should reflect upon your own, and that would make you bear the more with us, and not be severe censurers of the failings of your magistrates, when you have continual experience of the like infirmities in yourselves and others. We account him a good servant, who breaks not his covenant. The covenant between you and us is the oath you have taken of us, which is to this purpose, that we shall govern you and judge your causes by the rules of God's laws and our own, according to our best skill. When you agree with a workman to build you a ship or house, etc., he undertakes as well for his skill as for his faithfulness, for it is his profession, and you pay him for both. But when you call one to be a magistrate, he doth not profess nor undertake to have sufficient skill for that office, nor can you furnish him

with gifts, etc., therefore you must run the hazard of his skill and ability. But if he fail in faithfulness, which by his oath he is bound unto, that he must answer for. If it fall out that the case be clear to common apprehension, and the rule clear, also, if he transgress here, the error is not in the skill, but in the evil of the will: it must be required of him. But if the case be doubtful, or the rule doubtful, to men of such understanding and parts as your magistrates are, if your magistrates should err here, yourselves must bear it.

For the other point concerning liberty, I observe a great mistake in the country about that. There is a two-fold liberty, natural (I mean as our nature is now corrupt) and civil or federal. The first is common to man with beasts and other creatures. By this, man, as he stands in relation to man simply, hath liberty to do what he lists; it is a liberty to evil as well as to good. This liberty is incompatible and inconsistent with authority, and cannot endure the least restraint of the most just authority. The exercise and maintaining of this liberty makes men grow more evil, and in time to be worse than brute beasts: *We are all the worse for freedom.* This is that great enemy of truth and peace, that wild beast, which all the ordinances of God are bent against, to restrain and subdue it. The other kind of liberty I call civil or federal; it may also be

* Robert C. Winthrop, *Life and Letters of John Winthrop* (Boston, 1869), II, 339–42.

termed moral, in reference to the covenant between God and man, in the moral law, and the politic covenants and constitutions amongst men themselves. This liberty is the proper end and object of authority, and cannot subsist without it; and it is a liberty to that only which is good, just, and honest. This liberty you are to stand for, with the hazard (not only of your goods, but) of your lives, if need be. Whatsoever crosseth this, is not authority, but a distemper thereof. This liberty is maintained and exercised in a way of subjection to authority; it is of the same kind of liberty wherewith Christ hath made us free. The woman's own choice makes such a man her husband; yet being so chosen, he is her lord, and she is to be subject to him, yet in a way of liberty, not of bondage; and a true wife accounts her subjection her honor and freedom, and would not think her condition safe and free, but in her subjection to her husband's authority. Such is the liberty of the church under the authority of Christ, her king and husband; his yoke is so easy and sweet to her as a bride's ornaments; and if through forwardness or wantonness, etc., she shake it off, at any time, she is at no rest in her spirit,

until she take it up again; and whether her lord smiles upon her, and embraceth her in his arms, or whether he frowns, or rebukes, or smites her, she apprehends the sweetness of his love in all, and is refreshed, supported, and instructed by every such dispensation of his authority over her. On the other side, ye know who they are that complain of this yoke and say, let us break their bands, etc., we will not have this man to rule over us. Even so, brethren, it will be between you and your magistrates. If you stand for your natural corrupt liberties, and will do what is good in your own eyes, you will not endure the least weight of authority, but will murmur, and oppose, and be always striving to shake off that yoke; but if you will be satisfied to enjoy such civil and lawful liberties, such as Christ allows you, then will you quietly and cheerfully submit unto that authority which is set over you, in all the administrations of it, for your good. Wherein, if we fail at any time, we hope we shall be willing (by God's assistance) to hearken to good advice from any of you, or in any other way of God; so shall your liberties be preserved, in upholding the honor and power of authority amongst you.

2. JOHN ADAMS, *Thoughts on Government, 1776**

We ought to consider what is the end of government before we determine which is the best form. Upon this point all speculative politicians will agree, that the happiness of society is the end of government, as all divines and moral philosophers will agree that the happiness of the individual is the end of man. From this principle it will follow, that the form of government which communicates

ease, comfort, security, or, in one word, happiness, to the greatest number of persons, and in the greatest degree, is the best.

All sober inquirers after truth, ancient and modern, pagan and Christian, have declared that the happiness of man, as well as his dignity, consists in virtue. Confucius, Zoroaster, Socrates, Mahomet, not to mention authorities really sacred, have agreed in this.

* John Adams, *Works* (C. F. Adams, ed.; Boston, 1851), IV, 193–200.

If there is a form of government, then, whose principle and foundation is virtue, will not every sober man acknowledge it better calculated to promote the general happiness than any other form?

Fear is the foundation of most governments; but it is so sordid and brutal a passion, and renders men in whose breasts it predominates so stupid and miserable, that Americans will not be likely to approve of any political institution which is founded on it.

Honor is truly sacred, but holds a lower rank in the scale of moral excellence than virtue. Indeed, the former is but a part of the latter, and consequently has not equal pretensions to support a frame of government productive of human happiness.

The foundation of every government is some principle or passion in the minds of the people. The noblest principles and most generous affections in our nature, then, have the fairest chance to support the noblest and most generous models of government.

A man must be indifferent to the sneers of modern Englishmen, to mention in their company the names of Sidney, Harrington, Locke, Milton, Nedham, Neville, Burnet, and Hoadly. No small fortitude is necessary to confess that one has read them. The wretched condition of this country, however, for ten or fifteen years past, has frequently reminded me of their principles and reasonings. They will convince any candid mind, that there is no good government but what is republican. That the only valuable part of the British constitution is so; because the very definition of a republic is "an empire of laws, and not of men." That, as a republic is the best of governments, so that particular arrangement of the powers of society, or, in other words, that form of government which is best contrived to secure an impartial and exact execution of the laws, is the best of republics.

Of republics there is an inexhaustible variety, because the possible combinations of the powers of society are capable of innumerable variations.

As good government is an empire of laws, how shall your laws be made? In a large society, inhabiting an extensive country, it is impossible that the whole should assemble to make laws. The first necessary step, then, is to depute power from the many to a few of the most wise and good. But by what rules shall you choose your representatives? Agree upon the number and qualifications of persons who shall have the benefit of choosing, or annex this privilege to the inhabitants of a certain extent of ground.

The principal difficulty lies, and the greatest care should be employed, in constituting this representative assembly. It should be in miniature an exact portrait of the people at large. It should think, feel, reason, and act like them. That it may be the interest of this assembly to do strict justice at all times, it should be an equal representation, or, in other words, equal interests among the people should have equal interests in it. Great care should be taken to effect this, and to prevent unfair, partial, and corrupt elections. Such regulations, however, may be better made in times of greater tranquillity than the present; and they will spring up themselves naturally, when all the powers of government come to be in the hands of the people's friends. At present, it will be safest to proceed in all established modes, to which the people have been familiarized by habit.

A representation of the people in one assembly being obtained, a question arises, whether all the powers of government, legislative, executive, and judicial, shall be left in this body?

I think a people cannot be long free, nor ever happy, whose government is in one assembly. My reasons for this opinion are as follows:—

1. A single assembly is liable to all the vices, follies, and frailties of an individual; subject to fits of humor, starts of passion, flights of enthusiasm, partialities, or prejudice, and consequently productive of hasty results and absurd judgments. And all these errors ought to be corrected and defects supplied by some controlling power.

2. A single assembly is apt to be avaricious, and in time will not scruple to exempt itself from burdens, which it will lay, without compunction, on its constituents.

3. A single assembly is apt to grow ambitious, and after a time will not hesitate to vote itself perpetual. This was one fault of the Long Parliament; but more remarkably of Holland, whose assembly first voted themselves from annual to septennial, then for life, and after a course of years, that all vacancies happening by death or otherwise, should be filled by themselves, without any application to constitutents at all.

4. A representative assembly, although extremely well qualified, and absolutely necessary, as a branch of the legislative, is unfit to exercise the executive power, for want of two essential properties, secrecy and despatch.

5. A representative assembly is still less qualified for the judicial power, because it is too numerous, too slow, and too little skilled in the laws.

6. Because a single assembly, possessed of all the powers of government, would make arbitrary laws for their own interest, execute all laws arbitrarily for their own interest, and adjudge all controversies in their own favor.

But shall the whole power of legislation rest in one assembly? Most of the foregoing reasons apply equally to prove that the legislative power ought to be more complex: to which we may add, that if the legislative power is wholly in one assembly, and the executive in another, or in a single person, these two powers will oppose and encroach upon each other, until the contest shall end in war, and the whole power, legislative and executive, be usurped by the strongest.

The judicial power, in such case, could not mediate, or hold the balance between the two contending powers, because the legislative would undermine it. And this shows the necessity, too, of giving the executive power a negative upon the legislative, otherwise this will be continually encroaching upon that.

To avoid these dangers, let a distinct assembly be constituted, as a mediator between the two extreme branches of the legislature, that which represents the people, and that which is vested with the executive power.

Let the representative assembly then elect by ballot, from among themselves or their constituents, or both, a distinct assembly, which, for the sake of perspicuity, we will call a council. It may consist of any number you please, say twenty or thirty, and should have a free and independent exercise of its judgment, and consequently a negative voice in the legislature.

These two bodies, thus constituted, and made integral parts of the legislature, let them unite, and by joint ballot choose a governor, who, after being stripped of most of those badges of domination, called prerogatives, should have a free and independent exercise of his judgment, and be made also an integral part of the legislature. This, I know, is liable to objections; and, if you please, you may make him only president of the council, as in Connecticut. But as the governor is to be invested with the executive power, with consent of council, I thing he ought to have a negative upon the legislative. If he is annually elective, as he ought to be, he will always have so much reverence and affection for the people, their representatives and counsellors, that, although you give him an independent exercise of his judgment, he will seldom use it in opposition to the two houses, except in cases the public utility of which would be conspicuous; and some such cases would happen.

In the present exigency of American affairs, when, by an act of Parliament, we are put out of the royal protection, and consequently discharged from our allegiance, and it has become necessary to assume government for our immediate security, the governor, lieutenant-governor, secretary, treasurer, commissary, attorney-general, should be chosen by joint ballot of both houses. And these and all other elections, especially of representatives and counsellors, should be annual, there not being in the whole circle of the sciences a maxim more infallible than this, "where annual elections end, there slavery begins."

These great men, in this respect, should be, once a year,

Like bubbles on the sea of matter borne,
They rise, they break, and to that sea return.

This will teach them the great political virtues of humility, patience, and moderation, without which every man in power becomes a ravenous beast of prey.

This mode of constituting the great offices of state will answer very well for the present; but if by experiment it should be found inconvenient, the legislature may, at its leisure, devise other methods of creating them, by elections of the people at large, as in Connecticut, or it may enlarge the term for which they shall be chosen to seven years, or three years, or for life, or make any other alterations which the society shall find productive of its ease, its safety, its freedom, or, in one word, its happiness.

A rotation of all offices, as well as of representatives and counsellors, has many advocates, and is contended for with many plausible arguments. It would be attended, no doubt, with many advantages; and if the society has a sufficient number of suitable characters to supply the great number of vacancies which would be made by such a rotation, I can see no objection to it. These persons may be allowed to serve for three years, and then be excluded three years, or for any longer or shorter term.

Any seven or nine of the legislative council may be made a quorum, for doing business as a privy council, to advise the governor in the exercise of the executive branch of power, and in all acts of state.

The governor should have the command of the militia and of all your armies. The power of pardons should be with the governor and council.

Judges, justices, and all other officers, civil and military, should be nominated and appointed by the governor, with the advice and consent of council, unless you choose to have a government more popular; if you do, all officers, civil and military, may be chosen by joint ballot of both houses; or, in order to preserve the independence and importance of each house, by ballot of one house, concurred in by the other. Sheriffs should be chosen by the freeholders of counties; so should registers of deeds and clerks of counties.

All officers should have commissions, under the hand of the governor and seal of the colony.

The dignity and stability of government in all its branches, the morals of the people, and every blessing of society depend so much upon an upright and skillful administration of justice, that the judicial power ought to be distinct from both the legislative and executive, and independent upon both, that so it may be a check upon both, as both should be checks upon that. The judges, therefore, should be always men of learning and experience in the laws, of exemplary morals, great patience, calmness, coolness, and attention. Their minds should not be distracted with jarring interests; they should not be dependent upon any man, or body of men. To these ends, they should hold estates for life in their offices; or, in other words, their commissions should be during good behavior, and their salaries ascertained and established by law. For misbehavior, the grand inquest of the colony, the house of representatives, should impeach them before the governor and council, where they should have time and opportunity to make their defence; but, if convicted, should be removed from their offices, and subjected to such other punishment as shall be thought proper.

A militia law, requiring all men, or with very few exceptions besides cases of conscience, to be provided with arms and ammunition, to be trained at certain seasons; and requiring counties, towns, or other small districts, to be provided with public stocks of ammunition and intrenching utensils, and with some settled plans for transporting provisions after the militia, when marched to defend their country against sudden invasions; and requiring certain districts to be provided with field-pieces, companies of matrosses, and perhaps some regiments of light-horse, is always a wise institution, and, in the present circumstances of our country, indispensable.

Laws for the liberal education of youth, especially of the lower class people, are so extremely wise and useful, that, to a humane and generous mind, no expense for this purpose would be thought extravagant.

The very mention of sumptuary laws will excite a smile. Whether our countrymen have wisdom and virtue enough to submit to them, I know not, but the happiness of the people might be greatly promoted by them, and a revenue saved sufficient to carry on this war forever. Frugality is a great revenue, besides curing us of vanities, levities, and fopperies, which are real antidotes to all great, manly, and warlike virtues.

But must not all commissions run in the name of a king? No. Why may they not as well run thus, "The colony of   to A. B. greeting," and be tested by the governor?

Why may not writs, instead of running in the name of the king, run thus, "The colony of   to the sheriff," &c., and be tested by the chief justice?

Why may not indictments conclude, "against the peace of the colony of   and the dignity of the same"?

A constitution founded on these principles introduces knowledge among the people, and inspires them with a conscious dignity becoming freemen; a general emulation takes place, which causes good humor, sociability, good manners, and good morals to be general. That elevation of sentiment inspired by such a government, makes the common people brave and enterprising. That ambition which is inspired by it makes them sober, industrious, and frugal. You will find among them some elegance, perhaps, but more solidity; a little pleasure, but a great deal of business; some politeness, but more civility. If you compare such a country with the regions of domination, whether monarchical or aristocratical, you will fancy yourself in Arcadia or Elysium.

If the colonies should assume governments separately, they should be left entirely to their own choice of the forms; and if a continental constitution should be formed, it should be a congress, containing a fair and adequate representation of the colonies, and its authority should sacredly be confined to these cases, namely, war, trade, disputes between colony and colony, the post-office, and the unappropriated lands of the crown, as they used to be called.

These colonies, under such forms of government, and in such a union, would be unconquerable by all the monarchies of Europe.

You and I, my dear friend, have been sent into life at a time when the greatest lawgivers of antiquity would have wished to live. How few of the human race have ever enjoyed an opportunity of making an election of government, more than of air, soil, or climate, for themselves or their children! When, before the present epocha, had three millions of people full power and a fair opportunity to form and establish the wisest and happiest government that human wisdom can contrive? I hope you will avail yourself and your country of that extensive learning and indefatigable industry which you possess, to assist her in the formation of the happiest governments and the best character of a great people. For myself, I must beg you to keep my name out of sight; for this feeble attempt, if it should be known to be mine, would oblige me to apply to myself those lines of the immortal John Milton, in one of his sonnets:—

"I did but prompt the age to quit their
     clogs
By the known rules of ancient liberty,
When straight a barbarous noise
     environs me
Of owls and cuckoos, asses, apes, and
     dogs."

3. [JAMES MADISON] FEDERALIST PAPERS, *Factions, Union and Consent in a Republic, 1787**

Among the numerous advantages promised by a well-constructed Union, none deserves to be more accurately developed than its tendency to break and control the violence of faction. The friend of popular governments never finds himself so much alarmed for their character and fate, as when he contemplates their propensity to this dangerous vice. He will not fail, therefore, to set a due value on any plan which . . . provides a proper cure for it. . . .

By a faction, I understand a number of citizens, whether amounting to a majority or minority of the whole, who are united and actuated by some common impulse of passion, or of interest, adverse to the rights of other citizens, or to the permanent and aggregate interests of the community.

There are two methods of curing the mischiefs of faction: the one, by removing its causes; the other, by controlling its effects.

There are again two methods of removing the causes of faction: the one, by destroying the liberty which is essential to its existence; the other, by giving to every citizen the same opin-

* *Federalist Papers* (E. G. Bourne, ed.; New York, 1901), I, 62 ff., 256 ff.

ions, the same passions, and the same interests.

It could never be more truly said than of the first remedy, that it was worse than the disease. Liberty is to faction what air is to fire, an aliment without which it instantly expires. But it could not be less folly to abolish liberty, which is essential to political life, because it nourishes faction, than it would be to wish the annihilation of air, which is essential to animal life, because it imparts to fire its destructive agency.

The second expedient is as impracticable as the first would be unwise. As long as the reason of man continues fallible, and he is at liberty to exercise it, different opinions will be formed. As long as the connection subsists between his reason and his self-love, his opinions and his passions will have a reciprocal influence on each other; and the former will be objects to which the latter will attach themselves. The diversity in the faculties of men, from which the rights of property originate, is not less an insuperable obstacle to a uniformity of interests. The protection of these faculties is the first object of government. From the protection of different and unequal faculties of acquiring property, the possession of different degrees and kinds of property immediately results; and from the influence of these on the sentiments and views of the respective proprietors, ensues a division of the society into different interests and parties.

The latent causes of faction are thus sown in the nature of man; and as we see them everywhere brought into different degrees of activity, according to the different circumstances of civil society. A zeal for different opinions concerning religion, concerning government, and many other points, as well of speculation as of practice; an attachment to different leaders ambitiously contending for pre-eminence and power; or to persons of other descriptions whose fortunes have been interesting to the human passions, have, in turn, divided mankind into parties, inflamed them with mutual animosity, and rendered them much more disposed to vex and oppress each other than to co-operate for their common good. So strong is this propensity of mankind to fall into mutual animosities, that where no substantial occasion presents itself, the most frivolous and fanciful distinctions have been sufficient to kindle their unfriendly passions and excite their most violent conflicts. But the most common and durable source of factions has been the various and unequal distribution of property. Those who hold and those who are without property have ever formed distinct interests in society. Those who are creditors, and those who are debtors, fall under a like discrimination. A landed interest, a manufacturing interest, a mercantile interest, a moneyed interest, with many lesser interests, grow up of necessity in civilized nations, and divide them into different classes, actuated by different sentiments and views. The regulation of these various and interfering interests forms the principal task of modern legislation, and involves the spirit of party and faction in the necessary and ordinary operations of the government.

No man is allowed to be a judge in his own cause, because his interest would certainly bias his judgment, and, not improbably, corrupt his integrity. With equal, nay with greater reason, a body of men are unfit to be both judges and parties at the same time; yet what are many of the most important acts of legislation, but so many judicial determinations, not indeed concerning the rights of single persons, but concerning the rights of large bodies of citizens? And what are the different classes of legislators but advocates and parties to the causes which they determine? Is a law proposed concerning private debts? It is a question to which the creditors are parties on one side and the debtors on the other. Justice ought to hold the balance between them. Yet the parties are, and must be, themselves the judges; and the most numerous party, or, in other words, the most powerful faction must be expected to prevail. Shall domestic manufactures be encouraged, and in what degree, by restrictions on foreign manufacturers? are questions which would be differently decided by the landed and the manufacturing classes, and probably by neither with a sole regard to justice and the public good. The apportionment of taxes on the various descriptions of property is an act which seems to require the most exact impartiality; yet there is, perhaps, no legislative act in which greater opportunity and temptation are given to a predominant party to trample on the rules of justice. Every shilling with which they overburden the inferior number, is a shilling saved to their own pockets.

It is in vain to say that enlightened statesmen will be able to adjust these clashing interests, and render them all subservient to the public good. Enlightened statesmen will not always be at the helm. Nor, in many cases, can such an adjustment be made at all without taking into view indirect and remote considerations, which will rarely prevail over the immediate interest which one party may find in disregarding the rights of another or the good of the whole.

The inference to which we are brought is, that the *causes* of faction cannot be removed, and that relief is only to be sought in the means of controlling its *effects*.

If a faction consists of less than a majority, relief is supplied by the republican principle, which enables the majority to defeat its sinister views by regular vote. It may clog the administration, it may convulse the society; but it will be unable to execute and mask its violence under the forms of the Constitution. When a majority is included in a faction, the form of popular government, on the other hand, enables it to sacrifice to its ruling passion or interest both the public good and the rights of other citizens. To secure the public good and private rights against the danger of such a faction, and at the same time to preserve the spirit and the form of popular government, is then the great object to which our inquiries are directed. Let me add that it is the great desideratum by which this form of government can be rescued from the opprobrium under which it has so long labored, and be recommended to the esteem and adoption of mankind.

By what means is this object attainable? Evidently by one of two only. Either the existence of the same passion or interest in a majority at the same time must be prevented, or the majority, having such coexistent passion or interest, must be rendered, by their number and local situation, unable to concert and carry into effect schemes of oppression. If the impulse and the opportunity be suffered to coincide, we well know that neither moral nor religious motives can be relied on as an adequate control. They are not found to be such on the injustice and violence of individuals, and lose their efficacy in proportion to the number combined together, that is, in proportion as their efficacy becomes needful.

From this view of the subject it may be concluded that a pure democracy, by which I mean a society consisting of a small number of citizens, who assemble and administer the government in person, can admit of no cure for the mischiefs of faction. A common passion or interest will, in almost every case, be felt by a majority of the whole; a communication and concert result from the form of government itself; and there is nothing to check the inducements to sacrifice the weaker party or an obnoxious individual. Hence it is that such democracies have ever been spectacles of turbulence and contention; have ever been found incompatible with personal security, or the rights of property; and have in general been as short in their lives as they have been violent in their deaths. Theoretic politicians, who have patronized this species of government, have erroneously supposed that by reducing mankind to a perfect equality in their political rights, they would at the same time be perfectly equalized and assimilated in their possessions, their opinions, and their passions.

A republic, by which I mean a government in which the scheme of representation takes place, opens a different prospect, and promises the cure for which we are seeking. Let us examine the points in which it varies from pure democracy, and we shall comprehend both the nature of the cure and the efficacy which it must derive from the union.

The two great points of difference between a democracy and a republic are: First, the delegation of the government, in the latter, to a small number of citizens elected by the rest; secondly, the greater number of citizens, and greater sphere of country, over which the latter may be extended.

The effect of the first difference is, on the one hand, to refine and enlarge the public views, by passing them through the medium of a chosen body of citizens, whose wisdom may best discern the true interest of their country, and whose patriotism and love of justice will be least likely to sacrifice it to temporary or partial considerations. Under such a regulation, it may well happen that the public voice, pronounced by the representatives of the people, will be more consonant to the public good than if pronounced by the people themselves, convened for the purpose. On the other hand, the effect may be inverted. Men of factious tempers, of local prejudices, or of sinister designs, may by intrigue, by corruption, or by other means, first obtain the suffrages, and then betray the interests of the people. The question resulting is, whether small or extensive republics are most favorable to the election of proper guardians of the public weal; and it is clearly decided in favor of the latter by two obvious considerations.

In the first place, it is to be remarked that, however small the republic may be, the representatives must be raised to a certain number, in order to guard against the cabals of a few; and that, however large it may be, they must be limited to a certain number, in order to guard against the confusion of a multitude. Hence, the number of representatives in the two cases not being in proportion to that of the two constituents, and being proportionally greater in the small republic, it follows that, if the proportion of fit characters be not less in the large than in the small republic, the former will present a greater option, and consequently a greater probability of a fit choice.

In the next place, as each representative will be chosen by a greater number of citizens in the large than in the small republic, it will be more difficult for unworthy candidates to practise with success the vicious arts by which elections are too often carried; and the suffrages of the people being more free, will be more likely to centre in men who possess the most attractive merit and the most diffusive and established characters.

It must be confessed that in this, as in most other cases, there is a mean, on both sides of which inconveniences will be found to lie. By enlarging too much the number of electors, you render the representatives too little acquainted with all their local circumstances and lesser interests; as by reducing it too much, you render him unduly attached to these, and too little fit to comprehend and pursue great and national objects. The federal Constitution forms a happy combination in this respect; the great and aggregate interests being referred to the national, the local and particular to the State legislatures.

The other point of difference is, the greater number of citizens and extent of territory which may be brought within the compass of republican than of democratic government; and it is this circumstance principally which renders factious combinations less to be dreaded in the former than in the latter. The smaller the society, the fewer probably will be the distinct parties and interests composing it; the fewer the distinct parties and interests, the more frequently will a majority be found of the same party; and the smaller the number of individuals composing a majority, and the smaller the compass within which they are placed, the more easily will they concert and execute their plans of oppression. Extend the sphere and you take in a greater variety of parties and interests; you make it less probable that a majority of the whole will have a common motive to invade the rights of other citizens; or if such a common motive exists, it will be more difficult for all who feel it to discover their own strength, and to act in unison

with each other. Besides other impediments, it may be remarked that, where there is a consciousness of injust or dishonorable purposes, communication is always checked by distrust in proportion to the number whose concurrence is necessary. . . .

The . . . question . . . offers itself . . . , whether the general form and aspect of the government be strictly republican. It is evident that no other form would be reconcilable with the genius of the people of America; with the fundamental principles of the Revolution; or with that honorable determination which animates every votary of freedom, to rest all our political experiments on the capacity of mankind for self-government. If the plan of the convention, therefore, be found to depart from the republican character, its advocates must abandon it as no longer defensible.

What, then, are the distinctive characters of the republican form? Were an answer to this question to be sought, not by recurring to principles, but in the application of the term by political writers, to the constitutions of different States, no satisfactory one would ever be found. Holland, in which no particle of the supreme authority is derived from the people, has passed almost universally under the denomination of a republic. The same title has been bestowed on Venice, where absolute power over the great body of the people is exercised, in the most absolute manner, by a small body of hereditary nobles. Poland, which is a mixture of aristocracy and of monarchy in their worst forms, has been dignified with the same appellation. The government of England, which has one republican branch only, combined with an hereditary aristocracy and monarchy, has, with equal impropriety, been frequently placed on the list of republics. These examples, which are nearly as dissimilar to each other as to a genuine republic, show the extreme inaccuracy with which the term has been used in political disquisitions.

If we resort for a criterion to the different principles on which different forms of government are established, we may define a republic to be, or at least may bestow that name on, a government which derives all its powers directly or indirectly from the great body of the people, and is administered by persons holding their offices during pleasure, for a limited period, or during good behavior. It is *essential* to such a government that it be derived from the great body of the society, not from an inconsiderable proportion, or a favored class of it; otherwise a handful of tyrannical nobles, exercising their oppressions by a delegation of their powers, might aspire to the rank of republicans, and claim for their government the honorable title of republic. It is *sufficient* for such a government that the persons administering it be appointed, either directly or indirectly, by the people; and that they hold their appointments by either of the tenures just specified; otherwise every government in the United States,

as well as every other popular government that has been or can be well organized or well executed, would be degraded from the republican character. According to the constitution of every State in the Union, some or other of the officers of government are appointed indirectly only by the people. According to most of them, the chief magistrate himself is so appointed. And according to one, this mode of appointment is extended to one of the coordinate branches of the legislature. According to all the constitutions, also, the tenure of the highest office is extended to a definite period, and in many instances, both within the legislative and executive departments, to a period of years. According to the provisions of most of the constitutions, again, as well as according to the most respectable and received opinions on the subject, the members of the judiciary department are to retain their offices by the firm tenure of good behavior.

On comparing the Constitution planned by the convention with the standard here fixed, we perceive at once that it is, in the most rigid sense, conformable to it.

4. James Fenimore Cooper, *Distinctive American Principles, 1838**

Distinctive American principles as properly refer to the institutions of the states as to those of the Union. A correct notion of the first cannot be formed without keeping the latter constantly in view.

The leading distinctive principle of this country, is connected with the fact that all political power is strictly a trust, granted by the constituent to

the representative. These representatives possess different duties, and as the greatest check that is imposed on them, while in the exercise of their offices, exists in the manner in which the functions are balanced by each other, it is of the last importance that neither class trespass on the trusts that are not especially committed to its keeping.

* James Fenimore Cooper, *The American Democrat* (Cooperstown, N.Y., 1838; reprinted New York, 1931), pp. 21–28.

The machinery of the state being the same in appearance, in this country and in that from which we are derived, inconsiderate commentators are apt to confound their principles. In England, the institutions have been the result of those circumstances to which time has accidentally given birth. The power of the king was derived from violence, the monarch, before the act of succession, in the reign of Queen Anne, claiming the throne in virtue of the conquest by William, in 1060. In America, the institutions are the result of deliberate consultation, mutual concessions, and design. In England, the people may have gained by diminishing the power of the king, who first obtained it by force; but, in America, to assail the rightful authority of the executive, is attacking a system framed by the constituencies of the states, who are virtually the people, for their own benefit. No assault can be made on any branch of this government, while in the exercise of its constitutional duties, without assaulting the right of the body of the nation, which is the foundation of the whole polity.

In countries, in which executive power is hereditary, and clothed with high prerogatives, it may be struggling for liberty to strive to diminish its influence; but, in this republick, in which the executive is elective, has no absolute authority in framing the laws, serves for a short period, is responsible, and has been created by the people, through the states, for their own purposes, it is assailing the rights of that people, to attempt in any manner to impede its legal and just action.

It is a general law in politics, that the power most to be distrusted, is that which, possessing the greatest force, is the least responsible. Under the constitutional monarchies of Europe, (as they exist in theory, at least,) the king, besides uniting in his single person all the authority of the executive, which includes a power to make war, create peers, and unconditionally to name to all employments, has an equal influence in enacting laws, his veto being absolute; but, in America, the executive, besides being elective, is stripped of most of these high sources of influence, and is obliged to keep constantly in view the justice and legality of his acts, both on account of his direct responsibilities, and on account of the force of public opinion.

In this country, there is far more to apprehend from congress, than from the executive, as is seen in the following reasons:—Congress is composed of many, while the executive is one, bodies of men notoriously acting with less personal responsibilities than individuals; congress has power to enact laws, which it becomes the duty of the executive to see enforced, and the really legislative authority of a country is always its greatest authority; from the decisions and constructions of the executive, the citizen can always appeal to the courts for protection, but no appeal can lie from the acts of congress, except on the ground of unconstitutionality; the executive has direct personal responsibilities under the laws of the land, for any abuses of his authority, but the member of congress, unless guilty of open corruption, is almost beyond personal liabilities.

It follows that the legislature of this country, by the intention of the constitution, wields the highest authority under the least responsibility, and that it is the power most to be distrusted. Still, all who possess trusts, are to be diligently watched, for there is no protection against abuses without responsibility, nor any real responsibility, without vigilance.

Political partisans, who are too apt to mistake the impulses of their own hostilities and friendships for truths, have laid down many false principles on the subject of the duties of the executive. When a law is passed, it goes to the executive for execution, through the executive agents, and, at need, to the courts for interpretation. It would seem that there is no discretion vested in the executive concerning the constitutionality of a law. If he distrusts the constitutionality of any law, he can set forth his objections by resorting to the veto; but it is clearly the intention of the system that the whole legislative power, in the last resort, shall abide in congress, while it is necessary to the regular action of the government, that none of its agents, but those who are especially appointed for that purpose, shall pretend to interpret the constitution, in practice. The citizen is differently situated. If he conceive himself oppressed by an unconstitutional law, it is his inalienable privilege to raise the question before the courts, where a final interpretation can be had. By this interpretation the executive and all his agents are equally bound to abide. This obligation arises from the necessity of things, as well as from the nature of the institutions. There must be somewhere a power to decide on the constitutionality of laws, and this power is vested in the supreme court of the United States, on final appeal.

When called on to approve a law, even though its principle should have been already pronounced on by the courts, the executive is independent. He is now a legislator, and can disregard all other constructions of the constitution, but those dictated by his own sense of right. In this character, to the extent of his veto-power, he is superior to the courts, which have cognizance of no more than each case as it is presented for their consideration. The president may approve of a law that the court has decided to be unconstitutional in principle, or he may veto a law that the court has decided

to be constitutional in principle. The legislator himself, is compelled to submit to the interpretation of the court, however different his own views of the law may have been in passing it, but as soon as he comes to act again as a legislator, he becomes invested with all his own high duties and rights. The court cannot make the constitution, in any case; it only interprets the law. One court may decide differently from another, and instances often occur in which the same judges see reason to change their own decisions, and it would be, to the last degree, inexpedient, to give the court an authority beyond the necessity of the circumstances.

Although the court can render a law null, its power does not extend beyond the law already passed. Congress may re-enact it, as often as it please, and the court will still exercise its reason in rejecting it. This is the balance of the constitution, which invites inquiry, the constituencies of the states holding a legal authority to render that constitutional which the courts have declared to be unconstitutional, or vice versa, by amendments to the instrument itself; the supremacy of the court being merely temporary, conditional, and growing out of expediency and necessity.

It has been said that it is a vital principle of this government, that each of its branches should confine itself to the particular duties assigned it by the constitution, and in no manner exceed them. Many grave abuses have already arisen from losing sight of this truth, and there is danger that the whole system will be perverted from its intention, if not destroyed, unless they are seasonably corrected. Of these, the most prevalent, the one most injurious to the public service, that which has been introduced the most on foreign and the least on American principles, is the practice of using the time and influence of the legislatures, for the purpose of acting on the public mind, with a view to affect the elections. The usage has already gained so much footing, as seriously to impede the course of legislation.

This is one of the cases, in which it is necessary to discriminate between the distinctive principles of our own government, and those of the government of the country from which we are derived. In England, by the mode in which the power of the executive has been curtailed, it is necessary that the ministerial contests should be conducted in the legislative bodies, but, in this country, such a course cannot be imitated, without the legislators' assuming an authority that does not belong to them, and without dispossessing the people, in some measure, of their rights. He who will examine the constitution for the powers of congress, will find no authority to pass resolutions on, or to waste the time, which is the property of the public, in discussing the matters, on which, after all, congress has no power to decide. This is the test of legislative authority. Congress cannot properly even discuss a subject, that congress cannot legally control, unless it be to ascertain its own powers. In cases that do not admit of question, this is one of the grossest abuses of the institutions, and ought to be classed with the usurpations of other systems.

There is a feeling connected with this subject, that it behooves every upright citizen cautiously to watch. He may be opposed to the executive, for instance, as a partyman, and yet have an immediate representative in congress, of his own particular way of thinking; and it is a weakness of humanity, under such circumstances, for one to connect himself most directly with his own immediate candidate, and to look on his political opponent with distrust. The jealousy created by this feeling, induces unreflecting men to imagine that curbing their particular representatives, in matters of this nature, is curtailing their own rights, and disposes them to defend what is inherently wrong, on personal motives.

Political systems ought to be, and usually are, framed on certain great and governing principles. These principles cannot be perverted, or lost sight of, without perverting, or rendering nugatory the system itself; and, under a popular government, in an age like this, far more is to be apprehended from indirect attacks on the institutions, than from those which are direct. It is usual to excuse these departures from the right on the plea of human propensities, but human institutions are framed expressly to curb such propensities, and no truth is more salutary than that which is contained in the homely saying, that "law makers should not be law breakers."

It is the duty of the citizen to judge of all political acts on the great principles of the government, and not according to his own political partialities, or prejudices. His own particular representative is no more a representative of the people, than the representative of any other man, and one branch of the government is no more representative than another. All are to keep within their respective spheres, and it may be laid down as a governing maxim of the institutions, *that the representative who exceeds his trusts, trespasses on the rights of the people.*

All comparisons between the powers of the British parliament and those of congress are more than useless, since they are bodies differently constituted, while one is absolute, and the other is merely a special trustee for limited and defined objects.

In estimating the powers of congress,

there is a rule that may be safely confided in, and which has been already hinted at. The powers of congress are express and limited. That body, therefore, can have no right *to pass resolutions* other than those which affect their own police, or, in a moral sense, even to make speeches, except on subjects on which *they have a right to pass laws.* The instant they exceed these limits, they exceed the bounds of their delegated authority. By applying this simple test to their proceedings, any citizen may, in ordinary cases, ascertain how far the representatives of the nation abuse their trusts.

Liberty is not a matter of words, but a positive and important condition of society. Its greatest safeguards, after placing its foundations on a popular base, is in the checks and balances imposed on the public servants, and all its real friends ought to know that the most insidious attacks, are made on it by those who are the largest trustees of authority, in their efforts to increase their power.

The government of the United States has three branches. The executive, the legislative and the judicial. These several branches are independent of each other, though the first is intended to act as a check on the second, no law or resolution being legal that is not first submitted to the president for his approval. This check, however, does not render the first an integral part of the legislature, as laws and resolutions may be passed without his approval, by votes of two thirds.

In most constitutional monarchies, the legislatures, being originally secondary powers, were intended as checks on the action of the crown, which was possessed of the greatest, and, by consequence, of the most dangerous authority; whereas, the case is reversed in America, the executive using his veto as a check on congress. Such is the intention of the constitution, though the tactics of party, and the bitterness of opposition, have endeavored to interpret the instrument differently, by appealing to the ancient prejudices derived from England.

5. ABRAHAM LINCOLN, *First Inaugural Address, 1861**

Fellow-citizens of the United States:

In compliance with a custom as old as the government itself, I appear before you to address you briefly, and to take in your presence the oath prescribed by the Constitution of the United States to be taken by the President "before he enters on the execution of his office."

I do not consider it necessary at present for me to discuss those matters of administration about which there is no special anxiety or excitement.

Apprehension seems to exist among the people of the Southern States that by the accession of a Republican administration their property and their peace and personal security are to be endangered. There has never been any reasonable cause for such apprehension. Indeed, the most ample evidence to the contrary has all the while existed and been open to their inspection. It is found in nearly all the published speeches of him who now addresses you. I do but quote from one of those speeches when I declare that "I have no purpose, directly or

* Richardson, *Messages and Papers*, VI, 5–12.

indirectly, to interfere with the institution of slavery in the States where it exists. I believe that I have no lawful right to do so, and I have no inclination to do so." Those who nominated and elected me did so with full knowledge that I had made this and many similar declarations, and had never recanted them. And, more than this, they placed in the platform for my acceptance, and as a law to themselves and to me, the clear and emphatic resolution which I now read:

Resolved, That the maintenance inviolate of the rights of the States, and especially the right of each State to order and control its own domestic institutions according to its own judgment exclusively, is essential to that balance of power on which the perfection and endurance of our political fabric depend; and we denounce the lawless invasion by armed force of the soil of any State or Territory, no matter under what pretext, as among the gravest of crimes.

I now reiterate these sentiments; and, in doing so, I only press upon the public attention the most conclusive evidence of which the case is susceptible, that the property, peace, and security of no section are to be in any wise endangered by the now incoming administration. I add, too, that all the protection which, consistently with the Constitution and the laws, can be given, will be cheerfully given to all the States when lawfully demanded, for whatever cause—as cheerfully to one section as to another.

There is much controversy about the delivering up of fugitives from service or labor. The clause I now read is as plainly written in the Constitution as any other of its provisions:

No person held to service or labor in one State, under the laws thereof, escaping into another, shall in consequence of any law or regulation therein be discharged from such service or labor, but shall be delivered up on claim of the party to whom such service or labor may be due.

It is scarcely questioned that this provision was intended by those who made it for the reclaiming of what we call fugitive slaves; and the intention of the lawgiver is the law. All members of Congress swear their support to the whole Constitution—to this provision as much as to any other. To the proposition, then, that slaves whose cases come within the terms of this clause "shall be delivered up," their oaths are unanimous. Now, if they would make the effort in good temper, could they not with nearly equal unanimity frame and pass a law by means of which to keep good that unanimous oath?

There is some difference of opinion whether this clause should be enforced by national or State authority; but surely that difference is not a very material one. If the slave is to be surrendered, it can be of but little consequence to him or to others by which authority it is done. And should anyone in any case be content that his oath shall go unkept on a merely unsubstantial controversy as to how it shall be kept?

Again, in any law upon this subject, ought not all the safeguards of liberty known in civilized and humane jurisprudence to be introduced, so that a free man be not, in any case, surrendered as a slave? And might it not be well at the same time to provide by law for the enforcement of that clause in the Constitution which guarantees that "the citizens of each State shall be entitled to all privileges and immunities of citizens in the several States"?

I take official oath today with no mental reservations, and with no purpose to construe the Constitution or laws by any hypercritical rules. And while I do not choose now to specify particular acts of Congress as proper to be enforced, I do suggest that it will be much safer for all, both in official and private stations, to conform to and abide by all those acts which stand unrepealed, than to violate any of them, trusting to find impunity in having them held to be unconstitutional.

It is seventy-two years since the first inauguration of a President under our National Constitution. During that period fifteen different and greatly distinguished citizens have, in succession, administered the executive branch of the government. They have conducted it through many perils, and generally with great success. Yet, with all this scope of precedent, I now enter upon the same task for the brief constitutional term of four years under great and peculiar difficulty. A disruption of the Federal Union, heretofore only menaced, is now formidably attempted.

I hold that, in contemplation of universal law and of the Constitution, the Union of these States is perpetual. Perpetuity is implied, if not expressed in the fundamental law of all national governments. It is safe to assert that no government proper ever had a provision in its organic law for its own termination. Continue to execute all the express provisions of our National Constitution, and the Union will endure forever—it being impossible to destroy it except by some action not provided for in the instrument itself.

Again, if the United States be not a government proper, but an association of States in the nature of contract merely, can it, as a contract, be peaceably unmade by less than all the parties who made it? One party to a contract may violate it—break it, so to speak—but does it not require all to lawfully rescind it?

Descending from these general principles, we find the proposition that in legal contemplation the Union is perpetual confirmed by the history of the Union itself. The Union is much older than the Constitution. It was formed, in fact, by the Articles of Association in 1774. It was matured and continued by the Declaration of Independence in 1776. It was further matured, and the faith of all the then thirteen states expressly plighted and engaged that it should be perpetual, by the Articles of Confederation in 1778. And finally, in 1787, one of the declared objects for ordaining and establishing the Constitution was "to form a more perfect Union."

But if destruction of the Union by one or by a part only of the states be lawfully possible, the Union is *less* perfect than before the Constitution, having lost the vital element of perpetuity.

It follows from these views that no state upon its own mere motion can lawfully get out of the Union; that resolves and ordinances to that effect are legally void, and that acts of violence within any state or states against the authority of the United States are insurrectionary or revolutionary, according to circumstances.

I therefore consider that in view of the Constitution and the laws the Union is unbroken, and to the extent of my ability I shall take care, as the Constitution itself expressly enjoins upon me, that the laws of the Union be faithfully executed in all the states. Doing this I deem to be only a simple duty on my part; and I shall perform it so far as practicable unless my rightful masters, the American people, shall withhold the requisite means or in some authoritative manner direct the contrary. I trust this will not be regarded as a menace, but only as the declared purpose of the Union that it *will* constitutionally defend and maintain itself.

In doing this, there needs to be no bloodshed or violence, and there shall be none unless it be forced upon the national authority. The power confided to me will be used to hold, occupy, and possess the property and places belonging to the government and to collect the duties and imposts; but, beyond what may be necessary for these objects, there will be no invasion, no using of force against or among the people anywhere. Where hostility to the United States in any interior locality, shall be so great and so universal as to prevent competent resident citizens from holding the federal offices, there will be no attempt to force obnoxious strangers among the people for that object. While the strict legal right may exist in the government to enforce the exercise of these offices, the attempt to do so would be so irritating and so nearly impracticable withal, that I deem it better to forgo for the time the uses of such offices.

The mails, unless repelled, will continue to be furnished in all parts of the Union. So far as possible the people everywhere shall have that sense of perfect security which is most favorable to calm thought and reflection. The course here indicated will be followed unless current events and experience shall show a modification or change to be proper, and in every case and exigency my best discretion will be exercised according to circumstances actually existing, and with a view and a hope of a peaceful solution of the national troubles and the restoration of fraternal sympathies and affections.

That there are persons in one section or another who seek to destroy the Union at all events, and are glad of any pretext to do it, I will neither affirm nor deny; but if there be such, I need address no word to them. To those, however, who really love the Union may I not speak?

Before entering upon so grave a matter as the destruction of our national fabric, with all its benefits, its memories, and its hopes, would it not be wise to ascertain precisely why we do it? Will you hazard so desperate a step while there is any possibility that any portion of the ills you fly from have no real existence? Will you, while the certain ills you fly to are greater than all the real ones you fly from—will you risk the commission of so fearful a mistake?

All profess to be content in the Union if all constitutional rights can be maintained. Is it true, then, that any right, plainly written in the Constitution, has been denied? I think not. Happily the human mind is so constituted that no party can reach to the audacity of doing this. Think, if you can, of a single instance in which a plainly written provision of the Constitution has ever been denied. If by the mere force of numbers a majority should deprive a minority of any clearly written constitutional right, it might, in a moral point of view, justify revolution—certainly would if such a right were a vital one. But such is not our case. All the vital rights of minorities and of individuals are so plainly assured to them by affirmations and negations, guarantees and prohibitions, in the Constitution, that controversies never arise concerning them. But no organic law can ever be framed with a provision specifically applicable to every question which may occur in practical administration. No foresight can anticipate, nor any document of reasonable length contain, express provisions for all possible questions. Shall fugitives from labor be surrendered by national or by state authority? The Constitution does not expressly say. *May* Congress prohibit slavery in the territories? The Constitution does not expressly say. *Must* Congress protect slavery in the territories? The Constitution does not expressly say.

From questions of this class spring all our constitutional controversies, and we divide upon them into majorities and minorities. If the minority will not acquiesce, the majority must, or the government must cease. There is no other alternative, for continuing the government is acquiescence on one side or the other. If a minority in such case will secede rather than acquiesce, they make a precedent which in turn will divide and ruin them, for a minority of their own will secede from them whenever a majority refuses to be controlled by such minority. For instance, why may not any portion of a new confederacy a year or two hence arbitrarily secede again, precisely as portions of the present Union now claim to secede from it? All who cherish disunion sentiments are now being educated to the exact temper of doing this.

Is there such perfect identity of interests among the states to compose a new union as to produce harmony only and prevent renewed secession?

Plainly the central idea of secession is the essence of anarchy. A majority held in restraint by constitutional checks and limitations, and always changing easily with deliberate changes of popular opinions and sentiments, is the only true sovereign of a free people. Whoever rejects it does of necessity fly to anarchy or to despotism. Unanimity is impossible. The rule of a minority, as a permanent arrangement, is wholly inadmissible; so that, rejecting the majority principle, anarchy, or despotism in some form is all that is left.

I do not forget the position assumed by some that constitutional questions are to be decided by the Supreme Court, nor do I deny that such decisions must be binding in any case upon the parties to a suit as to the object of that suit, while they are also entitled to very high respect and consideration

in all parallel cases by all other departments of the government. And while it is obviously possible that such decision may be erroneous in any given case, still the evil effect following it, being limited to that particular case, with the chance that it may be overruled and never become a precedent for other cases, can better be borne than could the evils of a different practice. At the same time the candid citizen must confess that if the policy of the government, upon vital questions affecting the whole people, is to be irrevocably fixed by decisions of the Supreme Court, the instant they are made, in ordinary litigation between parties in personal actions, the people will have ceased to be their own rulers, having to that extent practically resigned their government into the hands of that eminent tribunal. Nor is there in this view any assault upon the court or the judges. It is a duty from which they may not shrink to decide cases properly brought before them, and it is no fault of theirs if others seek to turn their decisions to political purposes.

One section of our country believes slavery is right, and ought to be extended, while the other believes it is wrong, and ought not to be extended. This is the only substantial dispute. The fugitive-slave clause of the Constitution, and the law for the suppression of the foreign slave-trade, are each as well enforced, perhaps, as any law can ever be in a community where the moral sense of the people imperfectly supports the law itself. The great body of the people abide by the dry legal obligation in both cases, and a few break over in each. This, I think, cannot be perfectly cured; and it would be worse in both cases after the separation of the sections than before. The foreign slave-trade, now imperfectly suppressed, would be ultimately revived, without restriction, in one section, while fugitive slaves, now only partially surrendered, would not be surrendered at all by the other.

Physically speaking, we cannot separate. We cannot remove our respective sections from each other, nor build an impassable wall between them. A husband and wife may be divorced, and go out of the presence and beyond the reach of each other; but the different parts of our country cannot do this. They cannot but remain face to face, and intercourse, either amicable or hostile, must continue between them. Is it possible, then, to make that intercourse more advantageous or more satisfactory after separation than before? Can aliens make treaties easier than friends can make laws? Can treaties be more faithfully enforced between aliens than laws can among friends? Suppose you go to war, you cannot fight always; and when, after much loss on both sides, and no gain on either, you cease fighting, the identical old questions as to terms of intercourse, are again upon you.

This country, with its institutions, belongs to the people who inhabit it. Whenever they shall grow weary of the existing government, they can exercise their constitutional right of amending it, or their revolutionary right to dismember or overthrow it. I cannot be ignorant of the fact that many worthy and patriotic citizens are desirous of having the National Constitution amended. While I make no recommendation of amendments, I fully recognize the rightful authority of the people over the whole subject, to be exercised in either of the modes prescribed in the instrument itself; and I should, under existing circumstances, favor rather than oppose a fair opportunity being afforded the people to act upon it. I will venture to add that to me the convention mode seems preferable, in that it allows amendments to originate with the people them-

selves, instead of only permitting them to take or reject propositions originated by others not especially chosen for the purpose, and which might not be precisely such as they would wish to either accept or refuse. I understand a proposed amendment to the Constitution—which amendment, however, I have not seen—has passed Congress, to the effect that the Federal Government shall never interfere with the domestic institutions of the States, including that of persons held to service. To avoid misconstruction of what I have said, I depart from my purpose not to speak of particular amendments so far as to say that, holding such a provision to now be implied constitutional law, I have no objection to its being made express and irrevocable.

The chief magistrate derives all his authority from the people, and they have conferred none upon him to fix terms for the separation of the States. The people themselves can do this also if they choose; but the executive, as such, has nothing to do with it. His duty is to administer the present government, as it came to his hands, and to transmit it, unimpaired by him, to his successor.

Why should there not be a patient confidence in the ultimate justice of the people? Is there any better or equal hope in the world? In our present differences is either party without faith of being in the right? If the Almighty Ruler of Nations, with his eternal truth and justice, be on your side of the North, or on yours of the South, that truth and that justice will surely prevail by the judgment of this great tribunal of the American people.

By the frame of the government under which we live, this same people have wisely given their public servants but little power for mischief; and have, with equal wisdom, provided for the return of that little to their own hands at very short intervals. While the people retain their virtue and vigilance, no administration, by any extreme of wickedness or folly, can very seriously injure the government in the short space of four years.

My countrymen, one and all, think calmly and well upon this whole subject. Nothing valuable can be lost by taking time. If there be an object to hurry any of you in hot haste to a step which you would never take deliberately, that object will be frustated by taking time; but no good object can be frustated by it. Such of you as are now dissatisfied, still have the old Constitution unimpaired, and, on the sensitive point, the laws of your own framing under it; while the new administration will have no immediate power, if it would, to change either. If it were admitted that you who are dissatisfied hold the right side in the dispute, there still is no single good reason for precipitate action. Intelligence, patriotism, Christianity, and a

firm reliance on Him who has never yet forsaken this favored land, are still competent to adjust in the best way all our present difficulty.

In your hands, my dissatisfied fellow-countrymen, and not in mine, is the momentous issue of civil war. The government will not assail you. You can have no conflict without being yourselves the aggressors. You have no oath registered in heaven to destroy the government, while I shall have the most solemn one to "preserve, protect, and defend it."

I am loath to close. We are not enemies, but friends. We must not be enemies. Though passion may have strained, it must not break our bonds of affection. The mystic chords of memory, stretching from every battlefield and patriot grave to every living heart and hearthstone all over this broad land, will yet swell the chorus of the Union when again touched, as surely they will be, by the better angels of our nature.

6. WALT WHITMAN, *Democratic Vistas, 1871**

As to the political section of Democracy, which introduces and breaks ground for further and vaster sections, few probably are the minds, even in these republican States, that fully comprehend the aptness of that phrase, "THE GOVERNMENT OF THE PEOPLE, BY THE PEOPLE, FOR THE PEOPLE," which we inherit from the lips of Abraham Lincoln; a formula whose verbal shape is homely wit, but whose scope includes both the totality and all the minutiae of the lesson.

The People! Like our huge earth itself, which, to ordinary scansion, is full of vulgar contradictions and of-

fence, man, viewed in the lump, displeases, and is a constant puzzle and affront to the merely educated classes. The rare, cosmical, artist mind, lit with the Infinite, alone confronts his manifold and oceanic qualities—but taste, intelligence, and culture (so called) have been against the masses, and remain so. There is plenty of glamour about the most damnable crimes and hoggish meannesses, special and general, of the feudal and dynastic world over there, with its *personnel* of lords and queens and courts, so well-dress'd and so handsome. But the People are ungram-

* Walt Whitman, *Collected Works*, II, 71–79.

matical, untidy, and their sins gaunt and ill-bred.

Literature, strictly consider'd, has never recognized the People, and, whatever may be said, does not today. Speaking generally, the tendencies of literature, as hitherto pursued, have been to make mostly critical and querulous men. It seems as if, so far, there were some natural repugnance between a literary and professional life and the rude rank spirit of the democracies. There is, in later literature, a treatment of benevolence, a charity business, rife enough it is true; but I know nothing more rare, even in this country, than a fit scientific estimate and reverent appreciation of the People—of their measureless wealth of latent power and capacity, their vast, artistic contrasts of lights and shades —with, in America, their entire reliability in emergencies, and a certain breadth of historic grandeur, of peace or war, far surpassing all the vaunted samples of book-heroes, or any *haut ton* coteries, in all the records of the world.

The movements of the late secession war, and their results, to any sense that studies well and comprehends them, show that popular democracy, whatever its faults and dangers, practically justifies itself beyond the proudest claims and wildest hopes of its enthusiasts. Probably no future age can know, but I well know, how the gist of this fiercest and most resolute of the world's warlike contentions resided exclusively in the unnamed, unknown rank and file; and how the brunt of its labor of death was, to all essential purposes, volunteered. The People, of their own choice, fighting, dying for their own idea, insolently attack'd by the seccession-slave-power, and its very existence imperil'd. Descending to detail, entering any of the armies, and mixing with the private soldiers, we see and have seen august spectacles. We

have seen the alacrity with which the American-born populace, the peaceablest and most good-natured race in the world, and the most personally independent and intelligent, and the least fitted to submit to the irksomeness and exasperation of regimental discipline, sprang, at the first tap of the drum, to arms—not for gain, nor even glory, nor to repel invasion—but for an emblem, a mere abstraction—for the life, *the safety of the flag*. We have seen the unequal'd docility and obedience of these soldiers. We have seen them tried long and long by hopelessness, mismanagement, and by defeat; have seen the incredible slaughter toward or through which the armies (as at first Fredericksburg, and afterward at the Wilderness), still unhesitatingly obey'd orders to advance. We have seen them in trench, or crouching behind breastwork, or tramping in deep mud, or amid pouring rain or thick-falling snow, or under forced marches in hottest summer (as on the road to get to Gettysburg)—vast suffocating swarms, divisions, corps, with every single man so grimed and black with sweat and dust, his own mother would not have known him—his clothes all dirty, stain'd and torn, with sour, accumulated sweat for perfume —many a comrade, perhaps a brother, sun-struck, staggering out, dying, by the roadside, of exhaustion—yet the great bulk bearing steadily on, cheery enough, hollow-bellied from hunger, but sinewy with unconquerable resolution.

We have seen this race proved by wholesale, by drearier, yet more fearful tests—the wound, the amputation, the shatter'd face or limb, the slow hot fever, long impatient anchorage in bed, and all the forms of maiming, operation, and disease. Alas! America have we seen, though only in her early youth, already to hospital brought. There have we watch'd these soldiers, many of them only boys in years—mark'd their decorum, their religious nature and fortitude, and their sweet affection. Wholesale, truly. For at the front, and through the camps, in countless tents, stood the regimental, brigade, and division hospitals; while everywhere amid the land, in or near cities, rose clusters of huge, white-wash'd, crowded, one-story wooden barracks; and there ruled agony with bitter scourge, yet seldom brought a cry; and there stalk'd death by day and night along the narrow aisles between the rows of cots, or by the blankets on the ground, and touch'd lightly many a poor sufferer, often with blessed, welcome touch.

I know not whether I shall be understood, but I realize that it is finally from what I learn'd personally mixing in such scenes that I am now penning these pages. One night in the gloomiest period of the war, in the Patent-office hospital in Washington city, as I stood by the bedside of a Pennsylvania soldier, who lay, conscious of quick approaching death, yet perfectly calm, and with noble, spiritual manner, the veteran surgeon, turning aside, said to me, that though he had witness'd many, many deaths of soldiers, and had been a worker at Bull Run, Antietam, Fredericksburg, etc., he had not seen yet the first case of a man or boy that met the approach of dissolution with cowardly qualms or terror. My own observation fully bears out the remark.

What have we here, if not, towering above all talk and argument, the plentifully-supplied, last-needed proof of democracy, in its personalities? Curiously enough, too, the proof on this point comes, I should say, every bit as much from the South, as from the North. Although I have spoken only of the latter, yet I deliberately include all. Grand, common stock! to me the accomplish'd and convincing growth,

prophetic of the future; proof undeniable to sharpest sense, of perfect beauty, tenderness and pluck, that never feudal lord, nor Greek, nor Roman breed, yet rival'd. Let no tongue ever speak in disparagement of the American races, North or South, to one who has been through the war in the great army hospitals.

Meantime, general humanity (for to that we return, as, for our purposes, what it really is, to bear in mind) has always, in every department, been full of perverse maleficence, and is so yet. In downcast hours the soul thinks it always will be—but soon recovers from such sickly moods. I myself see clearly enough the crude, defective streaks in all the strata of the common people; the specimens and vast collections of the ignorant, the credulous, the unfit and uncouth, the incapable, and the very low and poor. The eminent person just mention'd sneeringly asks whether we expect to elevate and improve a nation's politics by absorbing such morbid collections and qualities therein. The point is a formidable one, and there will doubtless always be numbers of solid and reflective citizens who will never get over it. Our answer is general, and is involved in the scope and letter of this essay. We believe the ulterior object of political and all other government (having, of course, provided for the police, the safety of life, property, and for the basic statute and common law, and their administration, always first in order), to be among the rest, not merely to rule, to repress disorder, etc., but to develop, to open up to cultivation, to encourage the possibilities of all beneficent and manly outcroppage, and of that aspiration for independence, and the pride and self-respect latent in all characters. (Or, if there be exceptions, we cannot, fixing our eyes on them alone, make theirs the rule for all.)

I say the mission of government,

henceforth, in civilized lands, is not repression alone, and not authority alone, not even of law, nor by that favorite standard of the eminent writer, the rule of the best men, the born heroes and captains of the race (as if such ever, or one time out of a hundred, get into the big places, elective or dynastic) —but higher than the highest arbitrary rule, to train communities through all their grades, beginning with individuals and ending there again, to rule themselves. What Christ appear'd for in the moral-spiritual field for human-kind, namely, that in respect to the absolute soul, there is in the possession of such by each single individual, something so transcendent, so incapable of gradations (like life), that, to that extent, it places all beings on a common level, utterly regardless of the distinctions of intellect, virtue, station, or any height or lowliness whatever—is tallied in like manner, in this other field, by democracy's rule that men, the nation, as a common aggregate of living identities, affording in each a separate and complete subject for freedom, worldly thrift and happiness, and for a fair chance for growth, and for protection in citizenship, etc., must, to the political extent of the suffrage or vote, if no further, be placed, in each and in the whole, on one broad, primary, universal, common platform.

The purpose is not altogether direct; perhaps it is more indirect. For it is not that democracy is of exhaustive account in itself. Perhaps, indeed, it is (like Nature), of no account in itself. It is that, as we see, it is the best, perhaps only, fit and full means, formulater, general caller-forth, trainer, for the million, not for grand material personalities only, but for immortal souls. To be a voter with the rest is not so much; and this, like every institute, will have its imperfections. But to become an enfranchised man, and now, impediments removed, to stand and start without humiliation, and equal with the rest; to commence, or have the road clear'd to commence, the grand experiment of development, whose end (perhaps requiring several generations), may be the forming of a full-grown man or woman—that *is* something. To ballast the State is also secured, and in our times is to be secured, in no other way.

We do not (at any rate I do not), put it either on the ground that the People, the masses, even the best of them, are, in their latent or exhibited qualities, essentially sensible and good —nor on the ground of their rights; but that good or bad, rights or no rights, the democratic formula is the only safe and preservative one for coming times. We endow the masses with the suffrage for their own sake, no doubt; then, perhaps still more, from another point of view, for community's sake. Leaving the rest to the sentimentalists, we present freedom as sufficient in its scientific aspect, cold as ice, reasoning, deductive, clear and passionless as crystal.

7. HENRY ADAMS, *A People's Politician, 1880**

Ratcliffe looked the character of Prime Minister sufficiently well at this moment. He would have held his own, at a pinch, in any Court, not merely in Europe but in India or China, where dignity is still expected of gen-

* Henry Adams, *Democracy* (New York: Holt, Rinehart and Winston, Inc., 1908), pp. 307–10, 350–55, 356–57, 357–58.

tlemen. Excepting for a certain coarse and animal expression about the mouth, and an indefinable coldness in the eye, he was a handsome man and still in his prime. Every one remarked how much he was improved since entering the Cabinet. He had dropped his senatorial manner. His clothes were no longer congressional, but those of a respectable man, neat and decent. His shirts no longer protruded in the wrong places, nor were his shirt-collars frayed or soiled. His hair did not stray over his eyes, ears, and coat, like that of a Scotch terrier, but had got itself cut. Having overheard Mrs. Lee express on one occasion her opinion of people who did not take a cold bath every morning, he had thought it best to adopt this reform, although he would not have had it generally known, for it savoured of caste. He made an effort not to be dictatorial and to forget that he had been the Prairie Giant, the bully of the Senate. In short, what with Mrs. Lee's influence and what with his emancipation from the Senate chamber with its code of bad manners and worse morals, Mr. Ratcliffe was fast becoming a respectable member of society whom a man who had never been in prison or in politics might safely acknowledge as a friend.

Mr. Ratcliffe was now evidently bent upon being heard. After chatting for a time with some humour on the President's successes as a man of fashion, he changed the subject to the merits of the President as a statesman, and little by little as he spoke he became serious and his voice sank into low and confidential tones. He plainly said that the President's incapacity had now become notorious among his followers; that it was only with difficulty his Cabinet and friends could prevent him from making a fool of himself fifty times a day; that all the party leaders who had occasion to deal with

him were so thoroughly disgusted that the Cabinet had to pass its time in trying to pacify them; while this state of things lasted, Ratcliffe's own influence must be paramount; he had good reason to know that if the Presidential election were to take place this year, nothing could prevent his nomination and election; even at three years' distance the chances in his favour were at least two to one; and after this exordium he went on in a low tone with increasing earnestness, while Mrs. Lee sat motionless as the statue of Agrippina, her eyes fixed on the ground:

"I am not one of those who are happy in political life. I am a politician because I cannot help myself; it is the trade I am fittest for, and ambition is my resource to make it tolerable. In politics we cannot keep our hands clean. I have done many things in my political career that are not defensible. To act with entire honesty and self-respect, one should always live in a pure atmosphere, and the atmosphere of politics is impure. Domestic life is the salvation of many public men, but I have for many years been deprived of it. I have now come to that point where increasing responsibilities and temptations make me require help." . . .

Thus it was that, having read the letter once in order to learn what was in it, he turned back, and slowly read it again in order to gain time. Then he replaced it in its envelope, and returned it to Mrs. Lee, who, with equal calmness, as though her interest in it were at an end, tossed it negligently into the fire, where it was reduced to ashes under Ratcliffe's eyes.

He watched it burn for a moment, and then turning to her, said, with his usual composure, "I meant to have told you of that affair myself. I am sorry that Mr. Carrington has thought proper to forestall me. No doubt he has his own motives for taking my character in charge."

"Then it is true!" said Mrs. Lee, a little more quickly than she had meant to speak.

"True in its leading facts; untrue in some of its details, and in the impression it creates. During the Presidential election which took place eight years ago last autumn, there was, as you may remember, a violent contest and a very close vote. We believed (though I was not so prominent in the party then as now), that the result of that election would be almost as important to the nation as the result of the war itself. Our defeat meant that the government must pass into the blood-stained hands of rebels, men whose designs were more than doubtful, and who could not, even if their designs had been good, restrain the violence of their followers. In consequence we strained every nerve. Money was freely spent, even to an amount much in excess of our resources. How it was employed I will not say. I do not even know, for I held myself aloof from these details, which fell to the National Central Committee of which I was not a member. The great point was that a very large sum had been borrowed on pledged securities, and must be repaid. The members of the National Committee and certain senators held discussions on the subject, in which I shared. The end was that towards the close of the session the head of the committee, accompanied by two senators, came to me and told me that I must abandon my opposition to the Steamship Subsidy. They made no open avowal of their reasons, and I did not press for one. Their declaration, as the responsible heads of the organization, that certain action on my part was essential to the interests of the party, satisfied me. I did not consider myself at liberty to persist in a mere private opinion in regard to a measure about which I recognized the extreme likelihood of my being in error. I accordingly reported the bill, and voted for it, as did a large majority of the party. Mrs. Baker is mistaken in saying that the money was paid to me. If it was paid at all, of which I have no knowledge except from this letter, it was paid to the representative of the National Committee. I received no money. I had nothing to do with the money further than as I might draw my own conclusions in regard to the subsequent payment of the campaign debt."

Mrs. Lee listened to all this with intense interest. Not until this moment had she really felt as though she had got to the heart of politics, so that she could, like a physician with his stethoscope, measure the organic disease. Now at last she knew why the pulse beat with such unhealthy irregularity, and why men felt an anxiety which they could not or would not explain. Her interest in the disease overcame her disgust at the foulness of the revelation. To say that the discovery gave her actual pleasure would be doing her injustice; but the excitement of the moment swept away every other sensation. She did not even think of herself. Not until afterwards did she fairly grasp the absurdity of Ratcliffe's wish that in the face of such a story as this, she should still have vanity enough to undertake the reform of politics. And with his aid too! The audacity of the man would have seemed sublime if she had felt sure that he knew the difference between good and evil, between a lie and the truth; but the more she saw of him, the surer she was that his courage was mere moral paralysis, and that he talked about virtue and vice as a man who is colour-blind talks about red and green; he did not see them as she saw them; if left to choose for himself he would have nothing to guide him. Was it politics that had caused this atrophy of the moral senses by disuse? Meanwhile, here she sat face to face with a moral lunatic, who had not even enough sense of humour to see the absurdity of his own request, that she should go out to the shore of this ocean of corruption, and repeat the ancient *rôle* of King Canute, or Dame Partington with her mop and her pail. What was to be done with such an animal?

The bystander who looked on at this scene with a wider knowledge of facts, might have found entertainment in another view of the subject, that is to say, in the guilelessness of Madeleine Lee. With all her warnings she was yet a mere baby-in-arms in the face of the great politician. She accepted his story as true, and she thought it as bad as possible; but had Mr. Ratcliffe's associates now been present to hear his version of it, they would have looked at each other with a smile of professional pride, and would have roundly sworn that he was, beyond a doubt, the ablest man this country had ever produced, and next to certain of being President. They would not, however, have told their own side of the story if they could have helped it, but in talking it over among themselves they might have assumed the facts to have been nearly as follows: that Ratcliffe had dragged them into an enormous expenditure to carry his own State, and with it his own re-election to the Senate; that they had tried to hold him responsible, and he had tried to shirk the responsibility; that there had been warm discussions on the subject; that he himself had privately suggested recourse to Baker, had shaped his conduct accordingly, and had compelled them, in order to save their own credit, to receive the money. . . .

"Mrs. Lee," said he, with harsh emphasis and dogmatic tone, "there are conflicting duties in all the transactions of life, except the simplest. However we may act, do what we may, we must violate some moral obligation. All that can be asked of us is that we should guide ourselves by what we think the highest. At the time this affair occurred, I was a Senator of the United States. I was also a trusted member of a great political party which I looked upon as identical with the nation. In both capacities I owed duties to my constituents, to the government, to the people. I might interpret these duties narrowly or broadly. I might say: Perish the government, perish the Union, perish this people, rather than that I should soil my hands! Or I might say, as I did, and as I would say again: Be my fate what it may, this glorious Union, the last hope of suffering humanity, shall be preserved. . . .

"You ought not to blame me—you cannot blame me justly. It is to your sense of justice I appeal. Have I ever concealed from you my opinions on this subject? Have I not on the contrary always avowed them? Did I not here, on this very spot, when challenged once before by this same Carrington, take credit for an act less defensible than this? Did I not tell you then that I had even violated the sanctity of a great popular election and reversed its result? That was my sole act! In comparison with it, this is a trifle! Who is injured by a steamship company subscribing one or ten hundred thousand dollars to a campaign fund? Whose rights are affected by it? Perhaps its stock holders receive one dollar a share in dividends less than they otherwise would. If they do not complain, who else can do so?"

8. George Ade, *The Mislaid Ambition, 1900**

One of the Most Promising Boys in a Graded School had a Burning Ambition to be a Congressman. He loved Politics and Oratory. When there was a Rally in Town he would carry a Torch and listen to the Spellbinder with his Mouth open.

The Boy wanted to grow up and wear a Black String Tie and a Bill Cody Hat and walk stiff-legged, with his Vest unbuttoned at the Top, and be Distinguished.

On Friday Afternoons he would go to School with his Face scrubbed to a shiny pink and his Hair roached up on one side, and he would Recite the Speeches of Patrick Henry and Daniel Webster and makes Gestures.

When he Graduated from the High School he delivered an Oration on "The Duty of the Hour," calling on all young Patriots to leap into the Arena and with the Shield of Virtue quench the rising Flood of Corruption. He said that the Curse of Our Times was the Greed for Wealth, and he pleaded for Unselfish Patriotism among those in High Places.

He boarded at Home for a while without seeing a chance to jump into the Arena, and finally his Father worked a Pull and got him a Job with a Steel Company. He proved to be a Handy Young Man, and the Manager sent Him out to make Contracts. He stopped roaching his Hair, and he didn't give the Arena of Politics any serious Consideration except when the Tariff on Steel was in Danger.

In a little while he owned a few Shares, and after that he became a Director. He joined several Clubs and began to enjoy his Food. He drank a Small Bottle with his Luncheon each Day, and he couldn't talk Business un-

less he held a Scotch High Ball in his Right Hand.

With the return of Prosperity and the Formation of the Trust and the Whoop in all Stocks he made so much Money that he was afraid to tell the Amount.

His Girth increased—he became puffy under the Eyes—you could see the little blue Veins on his Nose.

He kept his Name out of the Papers as much as possible, and he never gave Congress a Thought except when he talked to his Lawyer of the Probable Manner in which they would Evade any Legislation against Trusts. He took two Turkish Baths every week and wore Silk Underwear. When an Eminent Politician would come to his Office to shake him down he would send out Word by the Boy in Buttons that he had gone to Europe. That's what he thought of Politics.

One day while rummaging in a lower Drawer in his Library, looking for a Box of Poker Chips, he came upon a Roll of Manuscript and wondered what it was. He opened it and read how it was the Duty of all True Americans to hop into the Arena and struggle unselfishly for the General Good. It came to him in a Flash—this was his High School Oration!

Then suddenly he remembered that for several Years of his Life his consuming Ambition had been—to go to Congress!

With a demoniacal Shriek he threw himself at full length on a Leather Couch and began to Laugh.

He rolled off the Sofa and tossed about on a $1,200 Rug in a Paroxysm of Merriment.

His Man came running into the Library and saw the Master in Con-

---

* George Ade, *More Fables* (Chicago, 1900), pp. 61–68.

vulsions. The poor Trust Magnate was purple in the Face.

They sent for a Great Specialist, who said that his Dear Friend had ruptured one of the smaller Arteries, and also narrowly escaped Death by Apoplexy.

He advised Rest and Quiet and the avoidance of any Great Shock.

So they took the High School Oration and put it on the Ice, and the Magnate slowly recovered and returned to his nine-course Dinners.

MORAL: *Of all Sad Words of Tongue or Pen, the Saddest are these, "It Might Have Been."*

9. H. L. MENCKEN, *Notes on Democracy, 1926**

Democracy came into the Western World to the tune of sweet, soft music. There was, at the start, no harsh bawling from below; there was only a dulcet twittering from above. Democratic man thus began as an ideal being, full of ineffable virtues and romantic wrongs—in brief, as Rousseau's noble savage in smock and jerkin, brought out of the tropical wilds to shame the lords and masters of the civilized lands. The fact continues to have important consequences to this day. It remains impossible, as it was in the Eighteenth Century, to separate the democratic idea from the theory that there is a mystical merit, an esoteric and ineradicable rectitude, in the man at the bottom of the scale —that inferiority, by some strange magic, becomes a sort of superiority— nay, the superiority of superiorities. Everywhere on earth, save where the enlightenment of the modern age is confessedly in transient eclipse, the movement is toward the completer and more enamoured enfranchisement of the lower orders. Down there, one hears, lies a deep, illimitable reservoir of righteousness and wisdom, unpolluted by the corruption of privilege. What baffles statesmen is to be solved by the people, instantly and by a sort of seraphic intuition. Their yearnings are pure; they alone are capable of a perfect patriotism; in them is the only hope of peace and happiness on this lugubrious ball. The cure of the evils of democracy is more democracy! . . .

So much for the theory. It seems to me, and I shall here contend, that all the known facts lie flatly against it— that there is actually no more evidence for the wisdom of the inferior man, nor for his virtue, than there is for the notion that Friday is an unlucky day. There was, perhaps, some excuse for believing in these phantasms in the days when they were first heard of in the world, for it was then difficult to put them to the test, and what cannot be tried and disproved has always had a lascivious lure for illogical man. But now we know a great deal more about the content and character of the human mind than we used to know, both on high levels and on low levels, and what we have learned has pretty well disposed of the old belief in its congenital intuitions and inherent benevolences. It is, we discover, a function, at least mainly, of purely physical and chemical phenomena, and its development and operation are subject to precisely the same natural laws which govern the development and operation, say, of the human nose or lungs. There are minds which start out with a superior equipment, and proceed to high and arduous deeds; there are

* H. L. Mencken, *Notes on Democracy* (New York: Alfred A. Knopf, Inc., 1926), pp. 3–4, 9–11, 43–50, 147–48, 195–206. Copyright 1926 by Alfred A. Knopf, Inc., and reprinted by permission.

minds which never get any further than a sort of insensate sweating, like that of a kidney. We not only observe such differences; we also begin to chart them with more or less accuracy. Of one mind we may say with some confidence that it shows an extraordinary capacity for function and development —that its possessor, exposed to a suitable process of training, may be trusted to acquire the largest body of knowledge and the highest skill at ratiocination to which *Homo sapiens* is adapted. Of another we may say with the same confidence that its abilities are sharply limited—that no conceivable training can move it beyond a certain point. In other words, men differ inside their heads as they differ outside. There are men who are naturally intelligent and can learn, and there are men who are naturally stupid and cannot. . . .

All the revolutions in history have been started by hungry city mobs. The fact is, indeed, so plain that it has attracted the notice even of historians, and some of them deduce from it the doctrine that city life breeds a love of liberty. It may be so, but certainly that love is not visible in the lower orders. I can think of no city revolution that actually had liberty for its object, in any rational sense. The ideas of freedom that prevail in the world to-day were first formulated by country gentlemen, aided and abetted by poets and philosophers, with occasional help from an eccentric king. One of the most valid of them—that of free speech—was actually given its first support in law by the most absolute monarch of modern times, to wit, Frederick the Great. When the city mob fights it is not for liberty, but for ham and cabbage. When it wins, its first act is to destroy every form of freedom that is not directed wholly to that end. And its second is to butcher all professional libertarians. If Thomas Jefferson had been living in Paris in 1793 he would have made an even narrower escape from the guillotine than Thomas Paine made.

The fact is that liberty, in any true sense, is a concept that lies quite beyond the reach of the inferior man's mind. He can imagine and even esteem, in his way, certain false forms of liberty—for example, the right to choose between two political mountebanks, and to yell for the more obviously dishonest—but the reality is incomprehensible to him. And no wonder, for genuine liberty demands of its votaries a quality he lacks completely, and that is courage. The man who loves it must be willing to fight for it; blood, said Jefferson, is its natural manure. More, he must be able to *endure* it—an even more arduous business. Liberty means self-reliance, it means resolution, it means enterprise, it means the capacity for doing without. The free man is one who has won a small and precarious territory from the great mob of his inferiors, and is prepared and ready to defend it and make it support him. All around him are enemies, and where he stands there is no friend. He can hope for little help from other men of his own kind, for they have battles of their own to fight. He has made of himself a sort of god in his little world, and he must face the responsibilities of a god, and the dreadful loneliness. Has *Homo boobiens* any talent for this magnificent self-reliance? He has the same talent for it that he has for writing symphonies in the manner of Ludwig van Beethoven, no less and no more. That is to say, he has no talent whatsoever, nor even any understanding that such a talent exists. Liberty is unfathomable to him. He can no more comprehend it than he can comprehend honour. What he mistakes for it, nine times out of ten, is simply the banal right to empty hallelujahs upon his oppressors. He is an ox whose last proud, defiant gesture is to lick the butcher behind the ear. . . .

Thus the lower orders of men, however grandiloquently they may talk of liberty today, have actually had but a short and highly deceptive experience of it. It is not in their blood. The grandfathers of at least half of them were slaves, and the great-grandfathers of three-fourths, and the great-great-grandfathers of seven-eighths, and the great-great-great-grandfathers of practically all. The heritage of freedom belongs to a small minority of men, descended, whether legitimately or by adultery, from the old lords of the soil or from the patricians of the free towns. It is my contention that such a heritage is necessary in order that the concept of liberty, with all its disturbing and unnatural implications, may be so much as grasped—that such ideas cannot be implanted in the mind of man at will, but must be bred in as all other basic ideas are bred in. The proletarian may mouth the phrases, as he did in Jefferson's day, but he cannot take in the underlying realities, as was also demonstrated in Jefferson's day. What his great-great-grandchildren may be capable of I am not concerned with here; my business is with the man himself as he now walks the world. Viewed thus, it must be obvious that he is still incapable of bearing the pangs of liberty. They make him uncomfortable; they alarm him; they fill him with a great loneliness. There is no high adventurousness in him, but only fear. He not only doesn't long for liberty; he is quite unable to stand it. What he longs for is something wholly different, to wit, security. He needs protection. He is afraid of getting hurt. All else is affectation, delusion, empty words.

The fact, as we shall see, explains many of the most puzzling political phenomena of so-called free states. The great masses of men, though theoretically free, are seen to submit supinely to oppression and exploitation of a hundred abhorrent sorts. Have they no means of resistance? Obviously they have. The worst tyrant, even under democratic plutocracy, has but one throat to slit. The moment the majority decided to overthrow him he would be overthrown. But the majority lacks the resolution; it cannot imagine taking the risk. So it looks for leaders with the necessary courage, and when they appear it follows them slavishly, even after their courage is discovered to be mere buncombe and their altruism only a cloak for more and worse oppressions. Thus it oscillates eternally between scoundrels, or, if you would take them at their own valuation, heroes. Politics becomes the trade of playing upon its natural poltroonery—of scaring it half to death, and then proposing to save it. There is in it no other quality of which a practical politician, taking one day with another, may be sure. Every theoretically free people wonders at the slavishness of all the others. But there is no actual difference between them. . . .

Whenever the liberties of *Homo vulgaris* are invaded and made a mock of in a gross and contemptuous manner, as happened, for example, in the United States during the reign of Wilson, Palmer, Burleson and company, there are always observers who marvel that he bears the outrage with so little murmuring. Such observers only display their unfamiliarity with the elements of democratic science. The truth is that the common man's love of liberty, like his love of sense, justice and truth, is almost wholly imaginary. As I have argued, he is not actually happy when free; he is uncomfortable, a bit alarmed, and intolerably lonely. He longs for the warm, reassuring smell of the herd, and is willing to take the herdsman with it. Liberty is not a thing for such as he. He cannot enjoy it rationally himself, and he can think of it in others only as something to be taken away from them. It is, when it becomes a reality, the exclusive possession of a small and disreputable minority of men, like knowledge, courage and honour. A special sort of man is needed to understand it, nay, to stand it—and he is inevitably an outlaw in democratic societies. The average man doesn't want to be free. He simply wants to be safe. . . .

Whether or not democracy is destined to survive in the world until the corruptible puts on incorruption and the immemorial Christian dead leap out of their graves, their faces shining and their yells resounding—this is something, I confess, that I don't know, nor is it necessary, for the purposes of the present inquiry, that I venture upon the hazard of a guess. My business is not prognosis, but diagnosis. I am not engaged in therapeutics, but in pathology. That simple statement of fact, I daresay, will be accepted as a confession, condemning me out of hand as unfit for my task, and even throwing a certain doubt upon my *bona fides*. For it is one of the peculiar intellectual accompaniments of democracy that the concept of the insoluble becomes unfashionable—nay, almost infamous. To lack a remedy is to lack the very license to discuss disease. The causes of this are to be sought, without question, in the nature of democracy itself. It came into the world as a cure-all, and it remains primarily a cure-all to this day. Any boil upon the body politic, however vast and raging, may be relieved by taking a vote; any flux of blood may be stopped by passing a law. The aim of government is to repeal the laws of nature, and re-enact them with moral amendments. War becomes simply a device to end war. The state, a mystical emanation from the mob, takes on a transcendental potency, and

acquires the power to make over the father which begat it. Nothing remains inscrutable and beyond remedy, not even the way of a man with a maid. It was not so under the ancient and accursed systems of despotism, now happily purged out of the world. They, too, I grant you, had certain pretensions of an homeric gaudiness, but they at least refrained from attempts to abolish sin, poverty, stupidity, cowardice, and other such immutable realities. Mediaeval Christianity, which was a theological and philosophical *apologia* for those systems, actually erected belief in that immutability into a cardinal article of faith. The evils of the world were incurable: one put off the quest for a perfect moral order until one got to heaven, *post mortem*. There arose, in consequence, a scheme of checks and balances that was consummate and completely satisfactory, for it could not be put to a test, and the logical holes in it were chinked with miracles. But no more. Today the Holy Saints are deposed. Now each and every human problem swings into the range of practical politics. The worst and oldest of them may be solved facilely by travelling bands of lady Ph.D.'s, each bearing the mandate of a Legislature of kept men, all unfaithful to their protectors.

Democracy becomes a substitute for the old religion, and the antithesis of it: the Ku Kluxers, though their reasoning may be faulty, are not far off the facts in their conclusion that Holy Church is its enemy. It shows all the magical potency of the great systems of faith. It has the power to enchant and disarm; it is not vulnerable to logical attack. I point for proof to the appalling gyrations and contortions of its chief exponents. Read, for example, the late James Bryce's "Modern Democracies." Observe how he amasses incontrovertible evidence that democracy doesn't work—and then concludes with a stout declaration that it does. Or, if his two fat volumes are too much for you, turn to some school reader and give a judicious perusal to Lincoln's Gettysburg Address, with its argument that the North fought the Civil War to save self-government to the world!—a thesis echoed in falsetto, and by feebler men, fifty years later. It is impossible, by any device known to philosophers, to meet doctrines of that sort; they obviously lie outside the range of logical ideas. There is, in the human mind, a natural taste for such hocus-pocus. It greatly simplifies the process of ratiocination, which is unbearably painful to the great majority of men. What dulls and baffles the teeth may be got down conveniently by an heroic gulp. No doubt there is an explanation here of the long-continued popularity of the dogma of the Trinity, which remains unstated in plain terms after two thousand years. And no doubt the dogma of Transubstantiation came under fire in the Reformation because it had grown too simple and comprehensible—because even the Scholastic philosophy had been unable to convert its plain propositions into something that could be believed without being understood. Democracy is shot through with this delight in the incredible, this banal mysticism. One cannot discuss it without colliding with preposterous postulates, all of them cherished like authentic hairs from the whiskers of Moses himself. I have alluded to its touching acceptance of the faith that progress is illimitable and ordained of God—that every human problem, in the very nature of things, may be solved. There are corollaries that are even more naïve. One, for example, is to the general effect that optimism is a virtue in itself—that there is a mysterious merit in being hopeful and of glad heart, even in the presence of adverse and immovable facts. This curious no-

tion turns the glittering wheels of Rotary, and is the motive power of the political New Thoughters called Liberals. Certainly the attitude of the average American Liberal toward the so-called League of Nations offered superb clinical material to the student of democratic psychopathology. He began by arguing that the League would save the world. Confronted by proofs of its fraudulence, he switched to the doctrine that believing in it would save the world. So later on, with the Washington Disarmament Conference. The man who hopes absurdly, it appears, is in some fantastic and gaseous manner a better citizen than the man who detects and exposes the truth. Bear this sweet democratic axiom clearly in mind. It is, fundamentally, what is the matter with the United States.

As I say, my present mandate does not oblige me . . . to prove here that democracy is too full of evils to be further borne. On the contrary, I am convinced that it has some valuable merits, not often described, and I shall refer to a few of them presently. All I argue is that its manifest defects, if they are ever to be got rid of at all, must be got rid of by examining them realistically—that they will never cease to afflict all the more puissant and exemplary nations so long as discussing them is impeded by concepts borrowed from theology. As for me, I have never encountered any actual evidence, convincing to an ordinary jury, that *vox populi* is actually *vox Dei*. The proofs, indeed, run the other way. The life of the inferior man is one long protest against the obstacles that God interposes to the attainment of his dreams, and democracy, if it is anything at all, is simply one way of getting 'round these obstacles. Thus it represents, not a jingling echo of what seems to be the divine will, but a raucous defiance of it. To that extent, perhaps, it is truly civilized, for civilization, as I have argued elsewhere, is best described as an effort to remedy the blunders and check the cruel humours of the Cosmic Kaiser. But what is defiant is surely not official, and what is not official is open to examination.

For all I know, democracy may be a self-limiting disease, as civilization itself seems to be. There are obvious paradoxes in its philosophy, and some of them have a suicidal smack. It offers John Doe a means to rise above his place beside Richard Roe, and then, by making Roe his equal, it takes away the chief unsufructs of the rising. I here attempt no pretty logical gymnastics: the history of democratic states is a history of disingenuous efforts to get rid of the second half of that dilemma. There is not only the natural yearning of Doe to use and enjoy the superiority that he has won; there is also the natural tendency of Roe, as an inferior man, to acknowledge it. Democracy, in fact, is always inventing class distinctions, despite its theoretical abhorrence of them. The baron has departed, but in his place stand the grand goblin, the supreme worthy archon, the sovereign grand commander. Democratic man, as I have remarked, is quite unable to think of himself as a free individual; he must belong to a group, or shake with fear and loneliness—and the group, of course, must have its leaders. It would be hard to find a country in which such brummagem serene highnesses are revered with more passionate devotion than they get in the United States. The distinction that goes with mere office runs far ahead of the distinction that goes with actual achievement. A Harding is regarded as genuinely superior to a Halsted, no doubt because his doings are better understood. But there is a form of human striving that is understood by democratic man even better than Harding's, and that is the striv-

ing for money. Thus the plutocracy, in a democratic state, tends to take the place of the missing aristocracy, and even to be mistaken for it. It is, of course, something quite different. It lacks all the essential characters of a true aristocracy: a clean tradition, culture, public spirit, honesty, honour, courage—above all, courage. It stands under no bond of obligation to the state; it has no public duty; it is transient and lacks a goal. Its most puissant dignitaries of to-day came out of the mob only yesterday—and from the mob they bring all its peculiar ignobilities. As practically encountered, the plutocracy stands quite as far from the *honnête homme* as it stands from the Holy Saints. Its main character is its incurable timorousness; it is for ever grasping at the straws held out by demagogues. Half a dozen gabby Jewish youths, meeting in a back room to plan a revolution—in other words, half a dozen kittens preparing to upset the Matterhorn—are enough to scare it half to death. Its dreams are of banshees, hobgoblins, bugaboos. The honest, untroubled snores of a Percy or a Hohenstaufen are quite beyond it.

The plutocracy, as I say, is comprehensible to the mob because its aspirations are essentially those of inferior men: it is not by accident that Christianity, a mob religion, paves heaven with gold and precious stones, i.e., with money. There are, of course, reactions against this ignoble ideal among men of more civilized tastes, even in democratic states, and sometimes they arouse the mob to a transient distrust of certain of the plutocratic pretensions. But that distrust seldom arises above mere envy, and the polemic which engenders it is seldom sound in logic or impeccable in motive. What it lacks is aristocratic disinterestedness, born of aristocratic security. There is no body of opinion behind it that is, in the strictest sense, a free opinion. Its chief exponents, by some divine irony, are pedagogues of one sort or another— which is to say, men chiefly marked by their haunting fear of losing their jobs. Living under such terrors, with the plutocracy policing them harshly on one side and the mob congenitally suspicious of them on the other, it is no wonder that their revolt usually peters out in metaphysics, and that they tend to abandon it as their families grow up, and the costs of heresy become prohibitive. The pedagogue, in the long run, shows the virtues of the Congressman, the newspaper editorial writer or the butler, not those of the aristocrat. When, by any chance, hc persists in contumacy beyond thirty, it is only too commonly a sign, not that he is heroic, but simply that he is pathological. So with most of his brethren of the Utopian Fife and Drum Corps, whether they issue out of his own seminary or out of the wilderness They are fanatics; not statesmen. Thus politics, under democracy, resolves itself into impossible alternatives. Whatever the label on the parties, or the war cries issuing from the demagogues who lead them, the practical choice is between the plutocracy on the one side and a rabble of preposterous impossibilities on the other. One must either follow the New York *Times,* or one must be prepared to swallow Bryan and the Bolsheviki. It is a pity that this is so. For what democracy needs most of all is a party that will separate the good that is in it theoretically from the evils that beset it practically, and then try to erect that good into a workable system. What it needs beyond everything is a party of liberty. It produces, true enough, occasional libertarians, just as despotism produces occasional regicides, but it treats them in the same drum-head way. It will never have a party of them until it invents and installs a genuine aristocracy, to breed them and secure them.

10. Carl Sandburg, *The People Will Live On, 1936**

The people will live on.
The learning and blundering people will live on.
    They will be tricked and sold and again sold
And go back to the nourishing earth for rootholds,
    The people so peculiar in renewal and comeback,
    You can't laugh off their capacity to take it.
The mammoth rests between his cyclonic dramas.

The people so often sleepy, weary, enigmatic,
is a vast huddle with many units saying:
    "I earn my living.
    I make enough to get by
    and it takes all my time.
    If I had more time
    I could do more for myself
    and maybe for others.

* From *The People, Yes* by Carl Sandburg, copyright 1936, by Harcourt, Brace and World, Inc., and used with their permission.

I could read and study
and talk things over
and find out about things.
It takes time.
I wish I had the time."

The people is a tragic and comic two-face:
hero and hoodlum: phantom and gorilla twist-
ing to moan with a gargoyle mouth: "They
buy me and sell me . . . it's a game . .
sometime I'll break loose . . . "
    Once having marched
    Over the margins of animal necessity,
    Over the grim line of sheer subsistence
      Then man came
    To the deeper rituals of his bones,
    To the lights lighter than any bones,
    To the time for thinking things over,
    To the dance, the song, the story,
    Or the hours given over to dreaming,
      Once having so marched.

Between the finite limitations of the five senses
and the endless yearnings of man for the beyond
the people hold to the humdrum bidding of work and
    food
while reaching out when it comes their way
for lights beyond the prison of the five senses,
for keepsakes lasting beyond any hunger or death.
    This reaching is alive.
The panderers and liars have violated and smutted it.
    Yet this reaching is alive yet
    for lights and keepsakes.
      The people know the salt of the sea
      and the strength of the winds
      lashing the corners of the earth.
      The people take the earth
      as a tomb of rest and a cradle of hope.
      Who else speaks for the Family of Man?
      They are in tune and step
      with constellations of universal law.

      The people is a polychrome,
      a spectrum and a prism
      held in a moving monolith,
      a console organ of changing themes,
      a clavilux of color poems
      wherein the sea offers fog
      and the fog moves off in rain
      and the labrador sunset shortens
      to a nocturne of clear stars
      serene over the shot spray
      of northern lights.

      The steel mill sky is alive.
      The fire breaks white and zigzag
      shot on a gun-metal gloaming.

Man is a long time coming.
Man will yet win.
Brother may yet line up with brother:

This old anvil laughs at many broken hammers.
  There are men who can't be bought.
  The fireborn are at home in fire.
  The stars make no noise.
  You can't hinder the wind from blowing.
  Time is a great teacher.
  Who can live without hope?
In the darkness with a great bundle of grief
  the people march.
In the night, and overhead a shovel of stars **for**
  keeps, the people march:
                              "Where to? What next?"

11. JOHN DEWEY, *Democracy and the Experts, 1927**

A negative phase of the earlier argument for political democracy has largely lost its force. For it was based upon hostility to dynastic and oligarchic aristocracies, and these have largely been reft of power. The oligarchy which now dominates is that of an economic class. It claims to rule, not in virtue of birth and hereditary status, but in virtue of ability in management. . . . Consequently the shoe is now on the other foot It is argued that the check upon the oppressive power of this particular oligarchy lies in an intellectual aristocracy, not in appeals to an ignorant, fickle mass whose interests are superficial and trivial, and whose judgments are saved from incredible levity only when weighted down by heavy prejudice.

It may be argued that the democratic movement was essentially transitional. It marked the passage from feudal institutions to industrialism, and was coincident with the transfer of power from landed proprietors, allied to churchly authorities, to captains of industry, under conditions which involved an emancipation of the masses from legal limitations which had previously hemmed them in. But, so it is contended in effect, it is absurd to convert this legal liberation into a dogma which alleges that release from old oppressions confers upon those emancipated the intellectual and moral qualities which fit them for sharing in regulation of affairs of state. The essential fallacy of the democratic creed, it is urged, is the notion that a historic movement which effected an important and desirable release from restrictions is either a source or a proof of capacity in those thus emancipated to rule, when in fact there is no factor common in the two things. The obvious alternative is rule by those intellectually qualified, by expert intellectuals.

This revival of the Platonic notion that philosophers should be kings is the more taking because the idea of experts is substituted for that of philosophers, since philosophy has become

* John Dewey, *The Public and Its Problems* (New York; Holt, Rinehart and Winston, Inc.), [1927], pp. 203–11.

something of a joke, while the image of the specialist, the expert in operation, is rendered familiar and congenial by the rise of the physical sciences and by the conduct of industry. A cynic might indeed say that the notion is a pipe-dream, a revery entertained by the intellectual class in compensation for an impotence consequent upon the divorce of theory and practice, upon the remoteness of specialized science from the affairs of life: the gulf being bridged not by the intellectuals but by inventors and engineers hired by captains of industry. One approaches the truth more nearly when one says that the argument proves too much for its own cause. If the masses are as intellectually irredeemable as its premise implies, they at all events have both too many desires and too much power to permit rule by experts to obtain. The very ignorance, bias, frivolity, jealousy, instability, which are alleged to incapacitate them from share in political affairs, unfit them still more for passive submission to rule by intellectuals. Rule by an economic class may be disguised from the masses; rule by experts could not be covered up. It could be made to work only if the intellectuals became the willing tools of big economic interests. Otherwise they would have to ally themselves with the masses, and that implies, once more, a share in government by the latter.

A more serious objection is that expertness is most readily attained in specialized technical matters, matters of administration and execution which postulate that general policies are already satisfactorily framed. It is assumed that the policies of the experts are in the main both wise and benevolent, that is, framed to conserve the genuine interests of society. The final obstacle in the way of any aristocratic rule is that in the absence of an articulate voice on the part of the masses, the best do not and cannot remain the best, the wise cease to be wise. It is impossible for high-brows to secure a monopoly of such knowledge as must be used for the regulation of common affairs. In the degree in which they become a specialized class, they are shut off from knowledge of the needs which they are supposed to serve.

The strongest point to be made in behalf of even such rudimentary political forms as democracy has already attained, popular voting, majority rule and so on, is that to some extent they involve a consultation and discussion which uncover social needs and troubles. This fact is the great asset on the side of the political ledger. De Tocqueville wrote it down almost a century ago in his survey of the prospects of democracy in the United States. Accusing a democracy of a tendency to prefer mediocrity in its elected rulers, and admitting its exposure to gusts of passion and its openness to folly, he pointed out in effect that popular government is educative as other modes of political regulation are not. It forces a recognition that there are common interests, even though the recognition of *what* they are is confused; and the need it enforces of discussion and publicity brings about some clarification of what they are. The man who wears the shoe knows best that it pinches and where it pinches, even if the expert shoemaker is the best judge of how the trouble is to be remedied. Popular government has at least created public spirit even if its success in informing that spirit has not been great.

A class of experts is inevitably so removed from common interests as to become a class with private interests and private knowledge, which in social matters is not knowledge at all. The ballot is, as often said, a substitute for bullets. But what is more significant is that counting of heads compels prior recourse to methods of discussion, consultation and persuasion, while the essence of appeal to force is to cut short resort to such methods. Majority rule, just as majority rule, is as foolish as its critics charge it with being. But it never is *merely* majority rule. As a practical politician, Samuel J. Tilden, said a long time ago: "The means by which a majority comes to be a majority is the more important thing": antecedent debates, modification of views to meet the opinions of minorities, the relative satisfaction given the latter by the fact that it has had a chance and that next time it may be successful in becoming a majority. Think of the meaning of the "problem of minorities" in certain European states, and compare it with the status of minorities in countries having popular government. It is true that all valuable as well as new ideas begin with minorities, perhaps a minority of one. The important consideration is that opportunity be given that idea to spread and to become the possession of the multitude. No government by experts in which the masses do not have the chance to inform the experts as to their needs can be anything but an oligarchy managed in the interests of the few. And the enlightenment must proceed in ways which force the administrative specialists to take account of the needs. The world has suffered more from leaders and authorities than from the masses.

The essential need, in other words, is the improvement of the methods and conditions of debate, discussion and persuasion. That is *the* problem of the public. We have asserted that this improvement depends essentially upon freeing and perfecting the processes of inquiry and of dissemination of their conclusions. Inquiry, indeed, is a work which devolves upon experts. But their expertness is not shown in framing and executing policies, but in discovering and making known the facts upon which the former depend. They are technical experts in the sense that scientific investigators and artists manifest *expertise*. It is not necessary that the many should have the knowledge and skill to carry on the needed investigations; what is required is that they have the ability to judge of the bearing of the knowledge supplied by others upon common concerns.

It is easy to exaggerate the amount of intelligence and ability demanded to render such judgments fitted for their purpose. In the first place, we are likely to form our estimate on the basis of present conditions. But indubitably one great trouble at present is that the data for good judgment are lacking; and no innate faculty of mind can make up for the absence of facts. Until secrecy, prejudice, bias, misrepresentation, and propaganda as well as sheer ignorance are replaced by inquiry and publicity, we have no way of telling how apt for judgment of social policies the existing intelligence of the masses may be. It would certainly go much further than at present. In the second place, *effective* intelligence is not an original, innate endowment. No matter what are the differences in native intelligence (allowing for the moment that intelligence can be native), the actuality of mind is dependent upon the education which social conditions effect. Just as the specialized mind and knowledge of the past is embodied in implements, utensils, devices and technologies which those of a grade of intelligence which could not produce them can now intelligently use, so it will be when currents of public knowledge blow through social affairs.

The level of action fixed by *embodied* intelligence is always the important thing. In savage culture a superior man will be superior to his fellows, but his knowledge and judgment will lag in many matters far behind that of an inferiorly endowed person in an advanced civilization. Capacities are limited by the objects and tools at hand. They are still more dependent upon the prevailing habits of attention and interest which are set by tradition and institutional customs. Meanings run in the channels formed by instrumentalities of which, in the end, language, the vehicle of thought as well as of communication, is the most important. A mechanic can discourse of ohms and amperes as Sir Isaac Newton could not in his day. Many a man who has tinkered with radios can judge of things which Faraday did not dream of. It is aside from the point to say that if Newton and Faraday were now here, the amateur and mechanic would be infants beside them. The retort only brings out the point: the difference made by different objects to think of and by different meanings in circulation. A

more intelligent state of social affairs, one more informed with knowledge, more directed by intelligence, would not improve original endowments one whit, but it would raise the level upon which the intelligence of all operates. The height of this level is much more important for judgment of public concerns than are differences in intelligence quotients. As Santayana has said: "Could a better system prevail in our lives a better order would establish itself in our thinking. It has not been for want of keen senses, or personal genius, or a constant order in the outer world, that mankind has fallen back repeatedly into barbarism and superstition. It has been for want of good character, good example, and good government." The notion that intelligence is a personal endowment or personal attainment is the great conceit of the intellectual class, as that of the commercial class is that wealth is something which they personally have wrought and possess.

VIII

* *

Equality in a Melting Pot
of People

ALBERT WOHLSTETTER

forty-six, is associate director of projects at the Rand Corporation.

Since 1951 he has conducted studies for the Rand Corporation on the problem of deterring general war and the vulnerability of retaliatory forces. From 1956 to 1959 he was chairman of the strategic air power group of the Rand Corporation, dealing with problems of both offense and defense.

He was scientific adviser to the United States delegation at Geneva during the 1958 discussions with the Russians on the prevention of surprise attack. He has also been a consultant to the State Department.

Mr. Wohlstetter was educated in the New York public schools and Columbia University. In World War II he was a research associate at the National Bureau of Economic Research, a consultant to the War Production Board and an official of Atlas Aircraft Products.

Albert Wohlstetter ✳✳✳✳ No Highway to High Purpose

When we ask ourselves what has happened to our national purpose, we sound vaguely as if, in a moment of absent-mindedness, we had mislaid it. In fact, our first self-conscious impulse is to see where we may have left it. Shall we look in the Constitution? Will we perhaps find it in something Lincoln or Woodrow Wilson said? What our Founding Fathers have said remains important and inspiring. Still, neglect of their teachings cannot be the whole story, for in the last decade or so, while our purpose is said to have been ebbing, their teachings have been less neglected than in preceding times.

Nonetheless, if the nation-wide questioning of national purpose evokes uneasy stirrings, it is for this very reason useful. It indicates that we are in trouble, that a further questioning and debate are in order. But the limitation of the questions raised so far is that they ask for very general answers, for a statement of ends without any explicit weighing of means or costs. They sometimes seem to imply, therefore, that our difficulties are not really complex, deep, or particular, and that they can be solved by a simple reaffirmation—and of some one thing at that. To ask for our national purpose suggests that there is one high overriding aim waiting ready-made, if not to be found by leafing through some documents, perhaps to be revealed effortlessly as in a dream, "the American dream." Even the word "mission," frequently used in discussions of national purpose, connotes revealed truth rather than working programs to be won by hard analysis of what we want and what we can do and the efforts needed. While we may talk about national purpose in the singular, the first thing to observe about our aims is that we have many of them. They are connected; some depend on others; many conflict. Obviously two aims may conflict when each represents the interests of a different group. But even ends which the nation as a whole can be said to share oppose other accepted national ends.

Take "the common defense"—a purpose of nationhood recognized by

407

the Founding Fathers, and even more critical today. We all want to avoid getting killed in a missile raid. On the other hand, most of us would like to see an increase in our present enjoyments. Yet reducing the chance of our demolition is at odds with getting the utmost in production of civilian goods and services. Deciding to reduce the risk that we may have no future at all is only an extreme form of the choice between present and future enjoyments—a choice we make in the everyday act of saving—and there is a growing public recognition of the importance of that choice.

There are other conflicts. We want to make the new nations of the world more stable and help them abolish poverty by technical innovation —but innovation means change and instability. We would like to increase democracy everywhere, but this conflicts with our desire not to interfere with the internal affairs of other nations. We hope to propagate the peaceable uses of science and technology, but in doing so we spread information about methods of destruction. We want to defend the independent non-Communist countries but this increases the hostility of the Communist world. In all these matters our desires are complex and partially conflicting.

To make fundamental choices, we must understand specific means as well as general ends. Today we need to learn about intricate and uncertain matters, like missiles and their implications. We must contemplate some extremely unpleasant possibilities, just because we want to avoid them and achieve something better. Nobody, however, likes to think about anything unpleasant, even to avoid it. And so the crucial problem of thermonuclear war is frequently dispatched with the label "War is unthinkable"— which, translated freely, means we don't want to think about it. But a purpose hammered out of connected and partially conflicting desires has to be the product of reflection and choice, and if the problems are profound the choice, once made, calls for exertion. There is, unfortunately, no highway leading to high purpose.

We cannot resolve the conflict of ends by the simple device of choosing *one* and ignoring all the others. This is true even of such important ends as reducing the risk of annihilation, a fact which explains the almost universal disparagement of "mere survival" as a national goal. We want much more than simply to survive. To preserve and extend democracy inside our own boundaries and in other parts of the world is not just a nice thought; it is vital. If we did not take these goals seriously, physical survival might be easy. We could reduce the danger of thermonuclear attack on the United States by giving the Communists free anything they want to take by aggression. In fact, several eminent non-Communist Englishmen have suggested this alternative for our consideration. In rejecting it, however, we need not sound excessively disdainful about the value of keeping alive. Physical survival is necessary to achieve our other widely shared purposes, even though it is not enough.

When we have tended in the past to fix on one goal to the exclusion of others, we have in effect been evading the responsibility for taking greater pains. Since World War II our policy has been notable for both an extreme reluctance to call for national effort and a wild oscillation from one purpose to another, rather than a steady stress on some combination of goals.

For example, we have gone from supporting emergency economic aid for our allies to concentrating on their defense so exclusively that most economic aid had to be represented as "defense support." We have swung from unilateral disarmament—and a neglect of the Communist threat —to rearmament and even to a conception that negotiations with the Communists are futile, if not treasonable, and that liberation of the satellites should come first. In recoil from this extreme and out of sheer fatigue, many of us have staked enormous hopes on the possibility of concluding broad agreements with the Russians soon, and our resolution to defend parts of the free world against Communist aggression has become subject to doubt. Now the ghost of Paris has displaced the Spirit of Camp David and the Spirit of Geneva, and we may fear another emotional swing.

Throughout all these swings since the war, our wish for cheap answers concealed from us the depth of our problems. We adopted a technical assistance program as an inexpensive substitute for American capital to develop backward countries. A defense of our allies was based on nuclear threat rather than on matching the nonnuclear forces of our antagonists. Collections of gadgetry were hopefully supposed to provide a defense of our cities at modest cost. And now there has been a stripping of our air defense and a search undertaken for a method of deterring war with a minimum of effort and a maximum of hope. For some, negotiations with the Russians were a laborsaving gadget to achieve stability at even lower defense levels. But the tremendous political and technical revolutions that rack the world today exclude any cheap or single solution. We may fear that our achievements are menaced by the need to make an effort. I think this is wrong. They are threatened by the risks involved in failing to make an effort.

We have deep troubles, crises that call for resolution and leadership. It is worth saying, however, especially since laments about the "quality of American life" have become a ritual, that there are very large areas in our society which do not call for leadership and common purposes.

There may indeed be a crisis in American culture, as some of the contributors to this debate believe. I am not sure. Myself, I don't care for tail fins or Elvis or advertising jingles or even Coca-Cola, but I doubt that their popularity is a national danger. An immense sea of mediocrity surrounds but has not submerged poets such as Robert Lowell and Elizabeth Bishop, artists of the order of Alexander Calder, the choreographers Martha Graham and George Balanchine, and an abundance of excellent architects—Mies van der Rohe, Eero Saarinen, Gorden Bunshafte, Marcel Breuer, Walter Gropius, Richard Neutra, and many others. New York concert halls offer an extraordinary range of music from ancient to modern that is unmatched in Paris, London, or Rome. The audience for the best in art, music, and literature may be limited, but so far it always has been, and I am more impressed than some with the wide accessibility of great works made possible by the long playing record and the paperback. Perhaps, as Pablo Casals has said, when good music is easy to hear it can successfully compete with rock 'n' roll.

However, if it cannot, I doubt that anything our leaders have to say will help much. Whatever their differences on domestic and foreign policy, Mr. Truman's and Mr. Eisenhower's comments on contemporary art are similarly unflattering and would lead us nowhere I want to go. In any case I don't think we should all be going to the same place. In the area of our private enjoyments we can dispense with a single voice speaking for America.

There are, however, critical points at which private aims become a public concern. For example, as individuals we decide where to live, where to work, and how to travel to and from work; but if multiplied a millionfold without public guidance these decisions are not likely to be compatible at all. In fact they have brought about intolerable congestion and an urban sprawl desired by no one. Again, we are being forced to recognize that even individual decisions about where to eat or whom to serve in restaurants or to transport in buses are an urgent common concern. Clearly we must put high on our agenda a large extension of freedom and equality of opportunity especially to American minorities: the Negro, the Puerto Rican, the Indian, and the Asian. Such a domestic purpose is worthy in its own right, and it also bears an obvious relation to our foreign policy. Race prejudice at home is an enormous handicap to any nation aspiring to lead a non-Communist world that is largely colored.

And foreign policy plays an increasingly important role in the American political scene. Most Americans seem to agree on the need for foreign economic and military aid. The growing recognition that our national ends must be international in scope is a sign of increasing national maturity. To disperse the benefits of technology, to expand the forces of production so as to end poverty, and at the same time to extend political freedom and self-government in the world—these are great aspirations. As aspirations, they appear in the United Nations charter, which was signed without embarrassment by some of freedom's sworn enemies. To bring them down from the level of pious benevolence to something concrete enough to deserve the name of purpose requires the evolution of detailed and consistent policies. And we face enormous problems in assisting the non-Communist countries in their economic and political self-development, if at the same time we want to help them to remain free of Communist domination.

For a candid look at the "free world" suggests that the phrase, if not a euphemism, has a circumscribed meaning. It means "free from the domination of the Communist bloc" and covers nations with a tremendous variety of political institutions, ranging from those few that have an effective multiparty system and a considerable popular control to a very large number of authoritarian regimes. The truth is that in the world today there are only a few local enclaves of representative democracy.

In much of Latin America, more than a century after liberation from Spain and Portugal, dictatorships succeed one another and representative government, though symbolized in many constitutions, is an unrealized ideal. And colonialism in Africa and Asia prepared its subjects no better for democratic self-rule. While the technological revolutions under way will bring tremendous changes, few nations have institutions that permit internal shifts in political power without violence, and the time when such institutions will be general is a long way off. Even more remote is a world government ensuring that revolutionary shifts in power among nations can take place without violence.

Today many influential people believe that disarmament is the shortest path to world government as well as the only hope of avoiding a world-wide nuclear war. I believe that arms control may achieve very useful ends, but only if its limitations are understood. No arms agreement in prospect will bring us within shouting distance of world government. And while some agreed arrangements might add a little more stability to our present uneasy peace, others could make the balance even more precarious.

An examination of some of the great and complex issues of war, peace, and arms control will show why defining national purposes will take much hard thought and produce no panacea. We tend emotionally to associate peace and all that is good with treaties and international arrangements, just as we associate war and all that is bad with arms. But our emotions mislead us in these simple equations. The principal goal of American arms today is to avoid war by deterring aggression. And history is replete with international agreements which have actually encouraged aggression.

Still it would be unfortunate if, reacting from our excessive wishfulness before the recent Summit meeting, we now considered realistic agreements neither possible nor useful. For agreements might slow the increase or dispersion of a military technology that favored aggression rather than defense. They might limit the size of various military forces, or their method and area of operation, or provide information as to their whereabouts. By such devices agreements might lower the likelihood of war being started deliberately or as the result of an "accident" or misunderstanding. They could reduce aggressive capabilities or provide warning of an actual aggression or reassurance that no aggression is under way, and so make mutual deterrence more reliable.

Useful agreements are possible because not all our interests conflict with those of our opponents. But our mutual interests are limited, and any realistic agreement is likely to be a limited one and to contain safeguards against violation. There is no magic in agreement. In almost every year from the end of World War I to the start of World War II, the United States, England, and France negotiated international agreements to limit armaments. But neglected controls and penalties. And their zeal was hardly diminished by the overt violations of these agreements by the Japanese, the Germans, and the Italians. The chronicle makes instructive reading today. Only a few months after the Japanese troops in 1931 opened their offensive in Manchuria, sixty nations met in a General Disarmament Conference which, in time, drafted plans to limit warships, to abolish submarines and, ultimately, to eliminate military aircraft. On March 7, 1936, Germany reoccupied the Rhineland, violating the Versailles and Locarno Treaties; scarcely two weeks later, a treaty for the limitation of naval arms was signed at London by seven powers. On July 7, 1937, the Japanese invaded China; ten days later the English concluded bilateral agreements with Germany and the U.S.S.R. And so it went up to the eve of the war. It is not too much to say that, for the Western powers in the interval between World War I and World War II, the international treaties were little more than formal records of their decisions to cut their own national budgets. The treaties were rationalizations for unilateral disarmament.

While it is true that arms have never staved off war indefinitely, the same must be said for arms limitations agreements. An agreement cannot be taken as either good or bad without an examination of its contents. If both sides are wary, the arrangements instituted are likely to be better for both sides than was the *status quo* before the agreement; and, more important, living up to the agreement will be better than violating it.

It is often claimed that the enormous dangers of the nuclear age should make agreement easier now. They may make agreement more urgent, but in crucial respects it is harder. A wishful and careless plan would be much more dangerous than before the last war. Nuclear weapons offer an enormous advantage to the aggressor. They make retaliation much harder to achieve, thus giving no automatic assurance that an aggressor will be punished. Even a partial disarmament, if one-sided, could invite the debacle. And *total* disarmament, in spite of its rhetorical usefulness, is really understood by both sides to be out of the question in a world of divided sovereignties. In such a world, if one side were totally disarmed the concealment of even a few nuclear weapons by the other side would enable it to dominate. It is a hard truth that for the foreseeable future arms control arrangements can only complement national defenses.

Both sides recognize implicitly that some arms arrangements might worsen the chance of peace. The Russians fear that Western proposals for inspection will furnish the West with intelligence usable in aggression. The West on the other hand fears (correctly) that, in the absence of adequate inspection, the Russians would be free to violate agreements secretly and so obtain the means to dominate. Enthusiasts for agreement suggest, all too easily, that the current arms negotiators in Geneva are mad, or simply lacking in common sense. But the negotiators are not mad or senseless. To devise agreements that reduce rather than increase the possibilties for aggression take great inventiveness and sober study. A realistic arms control arrangement has to be founded on a mutual interest and a recognition that this mutuality is only partial. The West is quite right in saying that agreements should not be based on faith. If both sides had real faith, no agreement would be necessary. It would be more nearly accurate to say that sound arms control arrangements can be based only on an explicit and precise mutual distrust.

The best reason for any specific arms agreement is to reduce the risk of war. For us the most trivial, almost frivolous, motive for agreement is to reduce a nation's defense budget—that is, the level of effort. But there is no evidence that a mutually useful agreement would permit less effort. Not counting the large cost of an adequate control system, any realistic agreement for reduction is one area is likely to call for increased effort in others. Nuclear disengagement in Europe, for example, might increase the stability of the peace, but it would require the reversal of our NATO military policy and a new emphasis on nonnuclear forces.

On no subject has discussion been more confused and inconsistent than on the above-mentioned level of American effort. On the one hand we are told that Americans are fat, self-indulgent, undisciplined, and at the highest peak of material prosperity. On the other, we hear the customary references to the "crushing economic burden of the arms race." As fortresses are invariably "impregnable," risks "calculated," and disarmament "moral," so the burden of the arms race is always "crushing." There have been direful predictions since the end of World War II that an attempt to defend ourselves will turn America into a garrison state. But our defense budget has varied from 40% to 5% to 15% and down again to 9% of our gross national product, and our experience offers little confirmation for such fears. Whether or not Americans and Western Europeans are self-indulgent, they were never richer, and they consume more each year. The U.S. government has estimated that our gross national product will increase from $500 billion to $750 billion in the next decade.

The most important implication of our great prosperity and rate of increase in productive power is that we can afford larger efforts for economic development, for reducing the risks of thermonuclear war, and for protecting the political independence and self-development of the non-Communist world. Furthermore we may be able to do it with only a modest sacrifice. In fact, I know of no responsible proposals for meeting these goals that have called for any reduction in our peak level of spending for immediate enjoyment. The widely discussed defense program recommended by the Rockefeller Brothers Fund, for example, could easily be accommodated by the growth in our gross national product predicted by the government—with no decrease in consumer spending but only a temporary slowing in the rate of its growth.

Would the American public make this mild "sacrifice?" That seems to me to depend on what the public thinks the sacrifice is for. Rather too much has been made of the frivolity and self-indulgence of the fat American public. An analysis of consumer expenditures hardly sustains the claim. Consumers have increased their spending for such sober purposes as medical care and education faster than the rise in their incomes and faster than the increase in spending for recreation or for the iniquitous tail fins. None of this seems foolish. In particular there is no reason to believe that Americans would not make a greater effort to accomplish their major purposes if they understood that the risks of *not* making such an effort were large and the rewards for effort were great. But I doubt that the public of this country was ever less informed on matters directly affecting its life and death. On the contrary, at each great crisis the public has been reassured that no further effort is required.

Leaders of opinion have a large responsibility here to inform the public and widen discussion. The great issues of war and peace deserve to be treated candidly and objectively, without wishfulness or hysteria. It is not only the politicians who have been deficient in these respects. In my view, the scientists also have performed poorly. They have been bitterly divided and both extremes have tended to use the authority of science rather than its method—to be wishful and impassioned rather than objective. What is needed is sober thought about the concrete problems of extending democracy inside our own country, of helping the economic and political self-development of other countries, and of negotiating without illusion to settle differences with our antagonists while maintaining the military strength to discourage their use of force.

These are tall orders. They cannot be filled quickly, or finally, or by means of some semiautomatic gadget, or in one heroic burst of energy. Nor will the answer come to us in a dream. I suspect that in the wide range of activities we must undertake, dreaming will require the least discipline and the least attention to diet. Our problem is more like that of training for a steep, rocky climb. If, as we are told, America is no longer a youth, we may yet hope to exploit the advantages of maturity: strength, endurance, judgment, responsibility, freedom from the extremes of optimism and pessimism—and steadiness of purpose.

A purpose is not the same thing as a wish. Or a dream. Or even a mission. But one fundamental purpose of a democracy is the exercise of reasoned choice, the conscious shaping of events. Even setbacks would be more meaningful if—to use Hamilton's phrase—instead of being ruled by "accident," we could govern ourselves by "reflection and choice." If the hard problems of our time stir us to more reflective choice, then they will have helped us fulfill one important purpose of a democratic society.

Can a Variety of Peoples Remain Equal in Freedom?

Among the critical points at which private aims become a public concern, Wohlstetter points out, is the extension of equality to the underprivileged American minorities. The Negro, the Puerto Rican, the Indian, and the Asian suffer under disabilities that create serious social tensions; and race prejudice at home is an enormous handicap in foreign policy.

This is no new problem. During much of its past, the United States was a nation of strangers; and it labored under the strains created by the efforts of diverse men to learn to live together.

That it was a democracy only complicated the matter. Since the political system functioned by securing the consent of the governed, it was necessary to achieve some degree of consensus among the conflicting interests in the country. That, in turn, was premised upon the assumption that there were sufficiently broad ranges of common interests among all Americans to give them a similar point of view.

Yet the population of the United States was composed of men of many different origins. Ethnic differences did not of themselves disappear in the course of migration. Irishmen, Negroes, Scots, Jews, and Englishmen, as well as their children, remained recognizably distinct from one another for a long period. Americans were therefore frequently compelled to consider the meanings of equality—the extent to which all these people by virtue of their residence in the nation were fully a part of it.

In the seventeenth century, the need for population produced a welcoming attitude toward all men who could help meet the challenge of the wilderness. That receptive mood persisted through the whole period when expansion remained characteristic of American society. As the idea of citizenship became clear in the eighteenth century, it seemed appropriate that all who participated in building the country should be equally citizens.

Even under British rule, the Americans liberalized the naturalization proceedings, far beyond the practice of the mother country; and George III's interference with immigration was one of the grievances of the Declaration of Independence. With the separation from England, the open attitude toward newcomers became national policy. The immigration of Europeans was not restricted until well into the twentieth century; and despite occasional outbursts of hostility as in the Alien and Sedition Act, the Know-Nothing movement, and the American Protective Association, the conception of equality of treatment remained unchallenged.

Down through the nineteenth century, the unresolved problem of American society was that of the Negro. Not only was the black man clearly set off from the rest of the population by color and by deep cultural differences; his situation was complicated by his position as a slave and, even after freedom, by economic and social inferiority. The problem of his proper place and of the extent to which he was endowed with the rights of other men remained a troubling one down to our own times.

These attitudes were amply reflected in the writing and thinking of the Americans who confronted the problem. Earnest humanitarians like John Woolman (see above, page 299) objected to the institution of slavery. Judge Samuel Sewall (1652–1730) of Massachusetts could not reconcile such servitude with the Christian conception of the brotherhood of man (1). And many, like the poet and journalist William Cullen Bryant (1794–1878), enthusiastically regarded the diversity of American life as the source of the nation's cultural strength (2).

Yet there was a persistent desire, particularly in the South, but not confined to it, to make an exception of the Negro. But the black man could be excluded from the privileges of other Americans only by denying some of the basic assumptions of a free society. William J. Grayson (1788–1863), a South Carolina congressman, for example, was driven to maintaining that the position of the slave was superior to that of the northern free laborer (3). A similar point of view was set forth by George Fitzhugh (1806–1881) in the argument that a society based on slavery was superior to one that rested on free institutions (4). It was doubtful, however, that most Southerners were willing to accept those extreme positions.

The Civil War ended the institution of slavery, but it did not resolve the problems created by the Negroes' anomalous situation. George Washington Cable (1844–1925), a native of New Orleans and a former Confederate soldier, was among the minority of the men of his section who wished justice to be done for the freed Negro (5). But for three quarters of a century, racist doctrines and political and social divisions kept the Negro within his restricted and inferior position. Indeed, the overtones of prejudice affected other groups as well; the weight of discrimination, although to a lesser degree, in time fell also upon the shoulders of Asiatics, Southern Europeans, Slavs, and Jews.

The turn of the tide came in the 1940's. The great war against Germany and Japan compelled Americans to re-examine the extent to which prejudice was reconcilable with their ideals. The European disaster revealed the ultimate consequences of racism. And the necessity of dealing upon equal terms with the colored peoples who formed a large part of the world's population led to a decisive change in attitudes. A Commission on Civil Rights appointed by President Harry S. Truman in 1947 pointed to the necessity for recognition of the fundamental equality of rights among all Americans (6). The same President's Commission on Immigration and Naturalization in 1952 reveoled the inequitable basis of existing immigration law (7). And, on May 17, 1954, the Supreme Court handed down a unanimous opinion in the case of "Brown v. The Board of Education of Topeka" which held that segregation deprived Negro students of the equal rights guaranteed to them by the Constitution (8).

The consequences of these shifting points of view have only just begun to emerge. In 1956, a social historian, Oscar Handlin (1915–) examined some of the possible results (9). A great Southerner, novelist William Faulkner (1897–), in an eloquent speech to the youth of Japan pointed to some of the implications for the people of his section (10). And James Baldwin 1924–), a brilliant young Negro writer, in a sensitive short story examined some of the meanings of color for the men of his race (11). These are factors in a situation that will continue to trouble Americans for years to come.

1. SAMUEL SEWALL, *The Selling of Joseph, 1700**

Forasmuch as Liberty *is in real value next unto* Life: *None ought to part with it themselves, or deprive others of it, but upon most mature consideration.*

The numerousness of slaves at this day in the Province, and the uneasiness of them under their slavery, hath put many upon thinking whether the foundation of it be firmly and well laid; so as to sustain the vast weight that is built upon it. It is most certain that all men, as they are the sons of *Adam,* are co-heirs; and have equal Right unto Liberty, and all other outward comforts of life. GOD *hath given the Earth* (with all its Commodities) *unto the Sons of* Adam . . . *and hath made of one blood, all nations of men, for to dwell on all the face of the earth, and hath determined the times before appointed, and the bounds of their habitation: that they should seek the Lord. Forasmuch then as we are the Offspring of GOD &c.* . . . Now although the title given by the last *ADAM,* doth infinitely better mens estates, respecting GOD and themselves; and grants them a most beneficial and inviolable lease under the broad seal of heaven, who were before only Tenants at Will: yet through the indulgence of GOD to our first parents after the fall, the outward estate of all and every of their children, remains the same, as to one another. So that originally, and naturally, there is no such thing as slavery. *Joseph* was

rightfully no more a slave to his brethren, than they were to him: and they had no more authority to *sell* him, than they had to *slay* him. And if *they* had nothing to do to sell him; the Ishmaelites bargaining with them, and paying down twenty pieces of silver, could not make a Title. Neither could *Potiphar* have any better interest in him than the *Ishmaelites* had . . . . For he that shall in this case plead *Alteration of Property,* seems to have forfeited a great part of his own claim to humanity. There is no proportion between twenty pieces of silver, and LIBERTY. The commodity itself is the claimer. If *Arabian* gold be imported in any quantities, most are afraid to meddle with it, though they might have it at easy rates; lest if it should have been wrongfully taken from the owners, it should kindle a fire to the consumption of their whole estate. 'Tis pity there should be more caution used in buying a horse, or a little lifeless dust; than there is in purchasing men and women: whenas they are the offspring of GOD, and their Liberty is more precious than all gold.

And seeing GOD hath said, *He that stealeth a man and selleth him, or if he be found in his hand, he shall surely be put to death.* . . , this law being of everlasting equity, wherein man stealing is ranked amongst the most atrocious of capital Crimes: what louder cry can there be made of

* "Diary of Samuel Sewall," Massachusetts Historical Society, *Collections*, Series V, Vol. VI (1879), pp. 16n–20n.

that Celebrated Warning, "*Caveat Emptor!*"

And all things considered, it would conduce more to the welfare of the province, to have white servants for a term of years, than to have slaves for life. Few can endure to hear of a Negro's being made free; and indeed they can seldom use their freedom well; yet their continual aspiring after their forbidden liberty, renders them unwilling servants. And there is such a disparity in their conditions, color & hair, that they can never embody with us, and grow up into orderly families, to the peopling of the land: but still remain in our Body Politick as a kind of extravasat blood. As many Negro men as there are among us, so many empty places there are in our train bands, and the places taken up of men that might make husbands for our daughters. And the sons and daughters of *New England* would become more like *Jacob,* and *Rachel,* if this slavery were thrust quite out of doors. Moreover it is too well known what temptations masters are under, to connive at the Fornication of their slaves; lest they should be obliged to find them wives, or pay their Fines. It seems to be practically pleaded that they might be lawless; 'tis thought much of, that the law should have satisfaction for their thefts, and other immoralities; by which means, *Holiness to the Lord,* is more rarely engraven upon this sort of servitude. It is likewise most lamentable to think, how in taking Negroes out of *Africa,* and selling of them here, that which GOD has joyned together men do boldly rend asunder; men from their country, husbands from their wives, parents from their children. How horrible is the uncleanness, mortality, if not murder, that the ships are guilty of that bring great crouds of these miserable men, and women. Methinks,

when we are bemoaning the barbarous usage of our friends and kinsfolk in *Africa;* it might not be unseasonable to enquire whether we are not culpable in forcing the Africans to become slaves amongst our selves. And it may be a question whether all the benefit received by *Negro* slaves, will balance the accompt of cash laid out upon them; and for the redemption of our own enslaved friends out of *Africa.* Besides all the persons and estates that have perished there.

Obj. 1. *These Blackamores are of the Posterity* of Cham, and *therefore are under the Curse of Slavery.* . . .

Answ. Of all offices, one would not beg this; *viz.* Uncall'd for, to be an executioner of the vindictive wrath of God; the extent and duration of which is to us uncertain. If this ever was a commission; how do we know but that it is long since out of date? Many have found it to their cost, that a prophetical denunciation of judgment against a person or people, would not warrant them to inflict that evil. If it would, *Hazael* might justify himself in all he did against his Master, and the *Israelites.* . . .

But it is possible that by cursory reading, this text may have been mistaken. For *Canaan* is the Person cursed three times over without the mentioning of *Cham.* Good expositors suppose the curse entail'd on him, and that this prophesie was accomplished in the extirpation of the *Canaanites,* and in the servitude of the *Gibeonites.* Whereas the blackmores are not descended of *Canaan,* but of *Cush.* . . . *Princes shall come out of Egypt* [Misraim], *Ethiopia* [Cush] *shall soon stretch out her hands unto God.* Under which Names, all *Africa* may be comprehended; and their Promised Conversion ought to be prayed for. . . . *Can the Ethiopian change his skin?* This shows that Black men are the posterity of *Cush:* Who time out of mind have been distinguished by their color. . . .

Obj. 2. *The Nigers are brought out of a Pagan Country, into places where the Gospel is Preached.*

Answ. Evil must not be done, that good may come of it. The extraordinary and comprehensive benefit accruing to the Church of God, and to *Joseph* personally, did not rectify his brethrens sale of him.

Obj. 3. *The* Africans *have wars one with another: Our Ships bring lawful captives taken in those wars.*

Answ. For ought is known, their wars are much such as were between *Jacob's* Sons and their Brother *Joseph.* If they be between town and town; provincial, or national: every war is upon one side unjust. An unlawful war can't make lawful captives. And by receiving, we are in danger to promote, and partake in their barbarous cruelties. I am sure, if some gentlemen should go down to the Brewsters to take the air, and fish: and a stronger party from *Hull* should surprise them, and sell them for slaves to a ship outward bound: they would think themselves unjustly dealt with; both by sellers and buyers. And yet 'tis to be feared, we have no other kind of title to our *Nigers. Therefore all things whatsoever ye would that men should do to you, do ye even so to them: for this is the Law and the Prophets.* . . .

Obj. 4. Abraham *had servants bought with his money, and born in his house.*

Answ. Until the circumstances of *Abraham's* purchase be recorded, no argument can be drawn from it. In the mean time, charity obliges us to conclude, that he knew it was lawful and good.

It is observable that the *Israelites* were strictly forbidden the buying or selling one another for slaves. . . . And GOD gaged His Blessing in lieu of any loss they might conceipt they suffered thereby. . . . And since the partition wall is broken down, inordinate self love should likewise be demolished. GOD expects that Christians should be of a more ingenuous and benign frame of spirit. Christians should carry it to all the world, as the Israelites were to carry it one towards another. And for men obstinately to persist in holding their neighbors and brethren under the rigor of perpetual bondage, seems to be no proper way of gaining assurance that God has given them spiritual freedom. Our Blessed Savior has altered the measures of the ancient love-song, and set it to a most excellent new tune, which all ought to be ambitious of learning. . . . These Ethiopians, as black as they are; seeing they are the sons and daughters of the first *Adam,* the brethren and sisters of the last ADAM, and the offspring of GOD; they ought to be treated with a respect agreeable.

2. WILLIAM CULLEN BRYANT, *Variety of Character in America, 1825**

Whoever will take the pains to pursue this subject a little into its particulars will be surprised at the infinite variety of forms of character which spring up under the institutions of our country. Religion is admitted on

* [William Cullen Bryant], "[Review of] *Redwood*," *North American Review,* XX (1825), 253–56.

all hands to be a mighty agent in moulding the human character; and, accordingly, with the perfect allowance and toleration of all religions, we see among us their innumerable and diverse influences upon the manners and temper of our people. Whatever may be his religious opinions, no one is restrained by fear of consequences from avowing them, but is left to nurse his peculiarities of doctrine into what importance he pleases. The Quaker is absolved from submission to the laws in those particulars which offend his conscience, the Moravian finds no barriers in the way of his work of proselytism and charity, the Roman Catholic is subjected to no penalty for pleasing himself with the magnificent ceremonial of his religion, and the Jew worships unmolested in his synagogue. In many parts of our country we see communities of that strange denomination, the Shakers, distinguished from their neighbors by a garb, a dialect, an architecture, a way of worship, of thinking, and of living, as different as if they were in fact of a different origin, instead of being collected from the families around them. In other parts we see small neighborhoods of the Seventh Day Baptists, retaining their simplicity of manners and quaintness of language delivered down from their fathers. Here we find the austerities of puritanism preserved to this day, there the rights and doctrines of the Church of England are shown in their effect on the manners of the people, and yet in another part of the country springs up a new and numerous sect, who wash one another's feet and profess to revive the primitive habits of the apostolic times.

It is in our country also that these differences of character, which grow naturally out of geographical situation, are least tampered with and repressed by political regulations. The adventurous and roving natives of our sea-coasts and islands are a different race of men from those who till the interior, and the hardy dwellers of our mountainous districts are not like the inhabitants of the rich plains that skirt our mighty lakes and rivers. The manners of the Northern States are said to be characterized by the keenness and importunity of their climate, and those of the Southern to partake of the softness of theirs. In our cities you will see the polished manners of the European capitals, but pass into the more quiet and unvisited parts of the country, and you will find men whom you might take for the first planters of our colonies. The descendants of the Hollanders have not forgotten the traditions of their fathers, and the legends of Germany are still recited, and the ballads of Scotland still sung, in settlements whose inhabitants derive their origin from those countries. It is hardly possible that the rapid and continual growth and improvement of our country, a circumstance wonderfully exciting to the imagination and altogether unlike anything witnessed in other countries, should not have some influence in forming our national character. At all events, it is a most fertile source of incident. It does for us in a few short years what in Europe is a work of centuries. The hardy and sagacious native of the Eastern States settles himself in the wilderness by the side of the emigrant from the British Isles; the pestilence of the marshes is braved and overcome; the bear and wolf and catamount are chased from their haunts; and then you see cornfields and roads and towns springing up as if by enchantment. In the mean time pleasant Indian villages, situated on the skirts of their hunting-grounds, with their beautiful green plats for dancing and martial exercises, are taken into the bosom of our extending population, while new States are settled and cities founded far beyond them. Thus a great deal of history is crowded into a brief space. Each little hamlet, in a few seasons, has more events and changes to tell of, than a European village can furnish in a course of ages.

But, if the writer of fictitious history does not find all the variety he wishes in the various kinds of our population, descended, in different parts of our country, from ancestors of different nations, and yet preserving innumerable and indubitable tokens of their origin, if the freedom with which every man is suffered to take his own way, in all things not affecting the peace and good order of society, does not furnish him with a sufficient diversity of characters, employments, and modes of life, he has yet other resources. He may bring into his plots men, whose characters and manners were formed by the institutions and modes of society in the nations beyond the Atlantic, and he may describe them faithfully, as things which he has observed and studied. If he is not satisfied with indigenous virtue, he may take for the model of his characters men of whom the old world is not worthy, and whom it has cast out from its bosom. If domestic villany be not dark enough for his pictures, here are fugitives from the justice of Europe come to prowl in America. If the coxcombs of our own country are not sufficiently exquisite, affected, and absurd, here are plenty of silken fops from the capitals of foreign kingdoms. If he finds himself in need of a class of men more stupid and degraded than are to be found among the natives of the United States, here are crowds of the wretched peasantry of Great Britain and Germany, flying for refuge from intolerable suffering, in every vessel that comes to our shores. Hither, also, resort numbers of that order of men who, in foreign countries, are called the middling class, the most valuable part of the communities they leave, to enjoy a moderate affluence, where the abuses and exactions of a distempered system of government cannot reach them to degrade them to the condition of the peasantry. Our country is the asylum of the persecuted preachers of new religions and the teachers of political doctrines which Europe will not endure; a sanctuary for dethroned princes and the consorts of slain emperors. When we consider all these innumerable differences of character, native and foreign, this infinite variety of pursuits and objects, this endless diversity and change of fortunes, and behold them gathered and grouped into one vast assemblage in our own country, we shall feel little pride in the sagacity or the skill of that native author, who asks for a richer or wider field of observation.

3. WILLIAM J. GRAYSON, *The Joys of Slavery, 1854**

How small the choice, from cradle to the grave,
Between the lot of Hireling and of Slave!
To each alike applies the stern decree,
That man shall labour; whether bond or free,
For all that toil, the recompense we claim—

* William J. Grayson, *The Hireling and Slave* (Charleston, S.C., 1854) , pp. 19–55.

Food, fire, a home and clothing—is the same.
   The manumitted serfs of Europe find
Unchanged this sad estate of all mankind;
What blessing to the churls has freedom proved,
What want supplied, what task or toil removed?
Hard work and scanty wages still their lot,
In youth o'erlaboured, and in age forgot,
The mocking boon of freedom they deplore,
In wants, cares, labours never known before.
   Free but in name—the slaves of endless toil,
In Britain still they turn the stubborn soil,
Spread on each sea her sails for every mart,
Ply in her cities every useful art;
But vainly may the Peasant toil and groan,
To speed the plough in furrows not his own;
In vain the art is plied, the sail is spread,
The daily work secures no daily bread;
With hopeless eye, the pauper Hireling sees
The homeward sail swell proudly to the breeze,
Rich fabrics, wrought by his unequalled hand,
Borne by each breeze to every distant land;
Unbounded wealth, propitious seasons yield,
And bounteous harvests crown the smiling field;
The streams of wealth that foster pomp and pride,
No food nor shelter for his wants provide,
He fails to win, by toil intensely hard,
The bare subsistence—labour's least reward.
   In squalid hut —a kennel for the poor,
Or noisome cellar, stretched upon the floor,
His clothing rags, of filthy straw his bed,
With offal from the gutter daily fed,
Thrust out from Nature's board, the Hireling lies—
No place for him that common board supplies,
No neighbor helps, no charity attends,
No philanthropic sympathy befriends;
None heed the needy wretch's dying groan,
He starves unsuccor'd, perishes unknown.
   These are the miseries, such the wants, the cares,
The bliss that freedom for the serf prepares;
Vain in his skill in each familiar task,
Capricious Fashion shifts her Protean mask,
His ancient craft gives work and bread no more,
And want and death sit scowling at his door.
   Close by the hovel, with benignant air,
To lordly halls illustrious crowds repair—
The Levite tribes of Christian love that show
No care nor pity for a neighbor's woe;
Who meet, each distant evil to deplore,
But not to clothe or feed their country's poor;
They waste no thought on common wants or pains,
On misery hid in filthy courts and lanes,
On alms that ask no witnesses but Heaven,
By pious hands to secret suffering given;
Their's the bright sunshine of the public eye,
The pomp and circumstance of charity,

The crowded meeting, the repeated cheer,
The sweet applause of prelate, prince or peer,
The long report of pious trophies won
Beyond the rising or the setting sun,
The mutual smile, the self-complacent air,
The laboured speech and Pharisaic prayer,
Thanksgivings for their purer hearts and hands,
Scorn for the publicans of other lands,
And soft addresses—Sutherland's delight,
That gentle dames at pious parties write—
These are the cheats that vanity prepares,
The soft deceits of her seductive fairs,
When Exeter expands her portals wide,
And England's saintly coteries decide
The proper nostrum for each evil known
In every land on earth, except their own,
But never heed the sufferings, wants, or sins,
At home, where all true charity begins.
   There, unconcerned, the philanthropic eye
Beholds each phase of human misery;
Sees the worn child compelled in mines to slave
Through narrow seams of coal, a living grave,
Driven from the breezy hill, the sunny glade,
By ruthless hearts, the drudge of labour made,
Unknown the boyish sport, the hour of play,
Stript of the common boon, the light of day,
Harnessed like brutes, like brutes to tug and strain
And drag, on hands and knees, the loaded wain:
There crammed in huts, in reeking masses thrown,
All moral sense and decency unknown,
With no restraint, but what the felon knows,
With the sole joy, that beer or gin bestows,
To gross excess and brutalizing strife,
The drunken Hireling dedicates his life:
Three women prostitute themselves for bread,
Mothers rejoice to find their infants dead,
Childhood bestows no childish sports or toys,
Age, neither reverence nor repose enjoys,
Labour, with hunger, wages ceaseless strife,
And want and suffering only end with life;
In crowded huts, contagious ills assail,
Insidious typhus and its plagues prevail;
Gaunt famine prowls around his pauper prey,
And daily sweeps his ghastly hosts away;
Unburied corses taint the summer air,
And crime and outrage revel with despair.
   Or—from their humble homes and native land
Forced by a landlord's pitiless command,
Far, in ungenial climes, condemned to roam,
That sheep may batten in the peasant's home—
The pauper exiles, from the hill that yields
One parting look on their abandoned fields,
Behold with tears, no manhood can restrain,
Their ancient hamlet level'd with the plain:
They go, a squalid band, unhoused, unfed,

The sky their only roof, the ditch their bed,
In crowded ships, new miseries to find,
More hideous still than those they left behind;
Grim Chol'ra thins their ranks, ship fevers sweep
Their livid tythes of victims to the deep;
The sad survivors, on a foreign shore,
The double loss of homes and friends deplore,
And beg a stranger's bounty to supply
The food and shelter that their homes deny.

   Yet homebred misery, such as this, imparts
Nor grief, nor care, to philanthropic hearts;
The tear of sympathy forever flows,
Though not for Saxon or for Celtic woes;
The hireling white, without a pitying eye,
Or helping hand, at home may starve and die;
But that the distant black may softlier fare,
Eat, sleep and play, exempt from toil and care,
All England's meek philanthropists unite,
With frantic eagerness, harangue and write,
By purchased tools, diffuse distrust and hate,
Sow factions strife, in each dependent State,
Cheat with delusive lies the public mind,
Invent the cruelties, they fail to find,
Slander, in pious garb, with prayer and hymn,
And blast a people's fortune for a whim.

   Cursed by these factious arts, that take the guise
Of charity, to cheat the good and wise,
The bright Antilles see, from year to year,
Their harvests fail, their fortunes disappear;
The cane no more its golden treasure yields;
Unsightly weeds deform the fertile fields;
The Negro freeman—thrifty while a slave,
Becomes a helpless drone or crafty knave,
Each effort to improve his nature foils;
Begs, steals, or sleeps and starves, but never toils,
For savage sloth, mistakes the freedom won,
And ends, the mere barbarian he begun. . . .

   Taught by the Master's efforts, by his care,
Fed, clothed, protected, many a patient year,
From trivial numbers now to millions grown,
With all the Whiteman's useful arts their own,
Industrious, docile, skilled in wood and field,
To guide the plough, the sturdy axe to wield,
The Negroes schooled by Slavery embrace
The highest portion of the Negro race;
And none the savage native will compare,
Of barbarous Guinea, with its offspring here.

   If bound to daily labour while he lives,
His is the daily bread that labour gives;
Guarded from want, from beggary secure,
He never feels what Hireling crowds endure,
Nor knows, like them, in hopeless want to crave,
For wife and child, the comforts of the slave,
Or the sad thought that, when about to die,

He leaves them to the world's cold charity,
And sees them forced to seek the poor-house door—
The last, sad, hated refuge of the poor.
    Still Europe's pious coteries sigh and groan
Note our defects, yet never see their own,
Grieve that the Slave is never taught to write,
And reads no better than the Hireling White;
Do their own ploughmen no instruction lack,
Have whiter clowns more knowledge than the Black?
Has the French peasant, or the German boor,
Of learning's treasure any larger store;
Have Ireland's millions, flying from the rule
Of those who censure, ever known a school?
A thousand years, and Europe's wealth impart
No means to mend the Hireling's head or heart;
They build no schools to teach the pauper White,
Their toiling millions neither read nor write;
Whence then the idle clamour when they rave
For schools and teachers for the distant Slave?
    And why the soft regret, the coarse attack,
If Justice punish the offending Black?
Are Whites not punished?—When Utopian times
Shall drive from Earth all miseries and crimes,
And teach the World the art to do without
The cat, the gauntlet, and the brutal knout,
Banish the halter, galley, jails and chains,
And strip the law of penalties and pains;
Here too, offence and wrong they may prevent,
And Slaves, with Hirelings, need no punishment:
'Till then, what lash of Slavery will compare
With the dread scourge that British soldiers bear?
What gentle rule, in Britain's Isle, prevails,
How rare her use of gibbets, stocks and jails!
How much humaner, than a master's whip,
Her penal colony and convict ship!
Whose code of law can darker pages show,
Where blood for smaller misdemeanors flow?
The triffling theft or trespass that demands,
For slaves, light penance from a master's hands,
Where Europe's milder punishments are known,
Incur the penalty of death alone.
    And yet the Master's lighter rule ensures
More order than the sternest code secures;
No mobs of factious workmen gather here,
No strikes we dread, no lawless riots fear;
Nuns, from their convent driven, at midnight fly,
Churches, in flames, ask vengeance from the sky,
Seditious schemes in bloody tumults end,
Parsons incite, and Senators defend,
But not where slaves their easy labours ply,
Safe from the snare, beneath a Master's eye;
In useful tasks engaged, employed their time,
Untempted by the demagogue to crime,
Secure they toil, uncursed their peaceful life,

With freedom's hungry broils and wasteful strife,
No want to goad, no faction to deplore,
The Slave escapes the perils of the poor.

● ● ●

And yet the life, so unassailed by care,
So blest with moderate work, with ample fare,
With all the good the pauper Hireling needs,
The happier Slave on each plantation leads;
Safe from harassing doubts and annual fears,
He dreads no famine, in unfruitful years;
If harvests fail from inauspicious skies,
The Master's providence his food supplies;
No paupers perish here for want of bread,
Or lingering live, by foreign bounty fed;
No exiled trains of homeless peasants go,
In distant climes, to tell their tales of woe;
Far other fortune, free from care and strife,
For work, or bread, attends the Negro's life,
And Christian Slaves may challenge as their own,
The blessings claimed in fabled states alone—
The cabin home, not comfortless, though rude,
Light daily labour, and abundant food,
The sturdy health, that temperate habits yield,
The cheerful song, that rings in every field,
The long, loud laugh, that freemen seldom share,
Heaven's boon to bosoms unapproached by care,
And boisterous jest and humour unrefined,
That leave, though rough, no painful sting behind;
While, nestling near, to bless their humble lot,
Warm social joys surround the Negro's cot,
The evening dance its merriment imparts,
Love, with his rapture, fills their youthful hearts,
And placid age, the task of labour done,
Enjoys the summer shade, the winter's sun,
And, as through life no pauper want he knows,
Laments no poorhouse penance at its close.
His too the Christian privilege to share
The weekly festival of praise and prayer;
For him the Sabbath shines with holier light,
The air is balmier, and the sky more bright;
Winter's brief suns with warmer radiance glow,
With softer breath the gales of autumn blow,
Spring with new flowers more richly strews the ground,
And summer spreads a fresher verdure round;
The early shower is past; the joyous breeze
Shakes patt'ring rain drops from the rustling trees,
And with the sun, the fragrant offerings rise,
From Nature's censers to the bounteous skies;
With cheerful aspect, in his best array,
To the far forest church he takes his way;
With kind salute the passing neighbor meets,
With awkward grace the morning traveller greets,
And joined by crowds, that gather as he goes,
Seeks the calm joy the Sabbath morn bestows.

4. GEORGE FITZHUGH, *Cannibals All, 1857**

The moral philosophy of our age (which term we use generically to include Politics, Ethics, and Economy, domestic and national) is deduced from the existing relations of men to each other in free society, and attempts to explain, to justify, to generalize and regulate those relations. If that system of society be wrong, and its relations false, the philosophy resulting from it must partake of its error and falsity. On the other hand, if our current philosophy be true, slavery must be wrong, because that philosophy is at war with slavery. No successful defence of slavery can be made, till we succeed in refuting or invalidating the principles on which free society rests for support or defence. The world, however, is sick of its philosophy; and the Socialists have left it not a leg to stand on. In fact, it is, in all its ramifications, a mere expansion and application of Political Economy—and Political Economy may be summed up in the phrase, "Laissez Faire," or "Let Alone." A system of unmitigated selfishness pervades and distinguishes all departments of ethical, political, and economic science. The philosophy is partially true, because selfishness, as a rule of action and guide of conduct, is necessary to the existence of man, and of all other animals. But it should not be, with man especially, the only rule and guide; for he is, by nature, eminently social and gregarious. His wants, his weakness, his appetites, his affections compel him to look without, and beyond self, in order to sustain self. The eagle and the owl, the lion and the tiger are not gregarious, but solitary and self-supporting. They practice political economy because 'tis adapted to their natures. But men and beavers, herds, bees, and ants require a different philosophy, another guide of conduct. The Bible (independent of its authority) is [by] far man's best guide, even in this world. Next to it, we would place Aristotle. But all books written four hundred or more years ago, are apt to yield useful instruction, whilst those written since that time will generally mislead. We mean, of course, books on moral science. We should not be far out in saying that no book on physics written more than four hundred years ago is worth reading, and none on morals written within that time. The Reformation, which effected much of practical good, gave birth to a false philosophy, which has been increasing and ramifying until our day, and now threatens the overthrow of all social institutions. The right of Private Judgment led to the doctrine of Human Individuality, and a Social Contract to restrict that individuality. Hence, also, arose the doctrines of Laissez Faire, free competition, human equality, freedom of religion, of speech and of the press, and universal liberty. The right of Private Judgment, naturally enough, leads to the right to act on that judgment, to the supreme sovereignty of the indivdual, and the abnegation of all government. No doubt the Reformation resulted from the relaxation of feudalism and the increased liberties of mind and body which men had begun to relish and enjoy. We have no quarrel with the Reformation, as such, for reform was needed, nor with all of the philosophy that has been deduced from it; but it is the excess of reform, and the excessive applications of that philosophy, to which we

* George Fitzhugh, *Cannibals All! or Slaves without Masters* (Richmond, Va., 1857; reprinted, Cambridge, Mass., 1960), pp. 52–54, 65–67, 69, 204–6.

object. Man is selfish, as well as social; he is born a part and member of society, born and lives a slave of society; but he has also natural individual rights and liberties. What are his obligations to society, what his individual rights, what position he is entitled to, what duties he should fulfill depend upon a thousand ever-changing circumstances, in the wants and capacities of the individual, and in the necessities and well-being of the society to which he belongs. Modern philosophy treats of men only as separate monads or individuals; it is, therefore, always partly false and partly true; because, whilst man is always a limb or member of the Being, Society, he is also a Being himself, and does not bear to society the mere relation which the hand or the foot does to the human body. *We* shall propose no new philosophy, no universal and unerring principles or guide in place of those which we assail. A Moral Pathology, which feels its way in life, and adapts itself to circumstances as they present themselves, is the nearest approach to philosophy which it is either safe or wise to attempt. All the rest must be left to Religion, to Faith, and to Providence. This inadequacy of philosophy has, in all ages and nations, driven men to lean on religious faith for support.

Mobs, secret associations, insurance companies, and social and communistic experiments are striking features and characteristics of our day, outside of slave society. They are all attempting to supply the defects of regular governments, which have carried the Let Alone practice so far that one-third of mankind are let alone to indulge in such criminal immoralities as they please, and another third to starve. Mobs (*vide* California) supply the deficiencies of a defective police, and insurance companies and voluntary unions and associations afford that security and protection which government, under the lead of political economy, has ceased to render.

A lady remarked to us, a few days since, "that society was like an army, in which the inferior officers were as necessary as the commander-in-chief. Demoralization and insubordination ensue if you dispense with sergeants and corporals in an army, and the same effects result from dispensing with guardians, masters, and heads of families in society." We don't know whether she included the ladies in her ideas of the heads of families; protesting against such construction of her language, we accept and thank her for her illustration. Rev'd Nehemiah Adams has a similar thought in his admirable work, *A South-side View of Slavery,* which we regret is not before us. On some public occasion in Charleston, he was struck with the good order and absence of all dissipation, and very naïvely asked where was their mob. He was informed that "they were at work." He immediately perceived that slavery was an admirable police institution, and moralizes very wisely on the occasion. Slavery is an indispensable police institution—especially so to check the cruelty and tyranny of vicious and depraved husbands and parents. Husbands and parents have, in theory and practice, a power over their subjects more despotic than kings; and the ignorant and vicious exercise their power more oppressively than kings. Every man is not fit to be king, yet all must have wives and children. Put a master over them to check their power, and we need not resort to the unnatural remedies of woman's rights, limited marriages, voluntary divorces, and free love, as proposed by the abolitionists.

Mr. Carlyle says, "Among practical men the idea prevails that government can do nothing but 'keep the peace.' They say all higher tasks are unsafe for it, impossible for it, and, in fine, not necessary for it or for us. Truly, it is high time that same beautiful notion of No-Government should take itself away. The world is daily rushing towards wreck whilst it lasts. If your government is to be constituted anarchy, what issue can it have? Our own interest in such government is, that it would be kind enough to cease and go its way before the inevitable wreck."

The reader will excuse us for so often introducing the thoughts and words of others. We do so not only for the sake of their authority, but because they express our own thoughts better than we can express them ourselves. In truth, we deal out our thoughts, facts, and arguments in that irregular and desultory way in which we acquired them. We are no regular built scholar—have pursued no "royal road to mathematics," nor to anything else. We have, by observation and desultory reading, picked up our information by the wayside, and endeavored to arrange, generalize, and digest it for ourselves. To learn "to forget" is almost the only thing we have labored to learn. We have been so bored through life by friends with dyspeptic memories, who never digest what they read because they never forget it, who retain on their intellectual stomachs in gross, crude, undigested, and unassimilated form everything they read, and retail and repeat it in that undigested form to every good-natured listener; we repeat, that we have been so bored by friends with good memories that we have resolved to endeavor to express what was useful out of facts, and then to throw the facts away. A great memory is a disease of the mind, which we are surprised no medical writer has noticed. The lunatic asylum should make provision for those affected with this disease; for, though less dangerous, they are far more troublesome and annoying than any other class of lunatics. Learning, observation, reading,

are only useful in the general, as they add to the growth of the mind. Undigested and unforgotten, they can no more have this effect, than undigested food on the stomach of a dyspeptic can add to his physical stature. We thought once this thing was original with us, but find that Say pursued this plan in writing his Political Economy. He first read all the books he could get hold of on this subject, and then took time to forget them, before he began to write.

We will not trouble the reader further, for the present, with our egotisms or our arguments, but refer him to the whole of Carlyle's *Latter-Day Pamphlets* to prove that "the world is too little governed," and, therefore, is going to wreck.

We promised to write no more in this chapter; but, like Parthos, when "we have an idea," we want to give others the benefit of it. We agree with Mr. Jefferson that all men have natural and inalienable rights. To violate or disregard such rights, is to oppose the designs and plans of Providence, and cannot "come to good." The order and subordination observable in the physical, animal, and human world show that some are formed for higher, others for lower stations—the few to command, the many to obey. We conclude that about nineteen out of every twenty individuals have "a natural and inalienable right" to be taken care of and protected, to have guardians, trustees, husbands, or masters; in other words, they have a natural and inalienable right to be slaves. The one in twenty are as clearly born or educated or some way fitted for command and liberty. Not to make them rulers or masters is as great a violation of natural right as not to make slaves of the mass. A very little individuality is useful and necessary to society—much of it begets discord, chaos and anarchy.

An unexplored moral world stretches

out before us, and invites our investigation; but neither our time, our abilities, nor the character of our work, will permit us to do more than glance at its loveliness.

It is pleasing, however, to turn from the world of political economy, in which "might makes right," and strength of mind and of body are employed to oppress and exact from the weak, to that other and better, and far more numerous world, in which weakness rules, clad in the armor of affection and benevolence. It is delightful to retire from the outer world, with its competitions, rivalries, envyings, jealousies, and selfish war of the wits, to the bosom of the family, where the only tyrant is the infant—the greatest slave the master of the household. You feel at once that you have exchanged the keen air of selfishness, for the mild atmosphere of benevolence. Each one prefers the good of others to his own, and finds most happiness in sacrificing selfish pleasures, and ministering to others' enjoyments. The wife, the husband, the parent, the child, the son, the brother and the sister, usually act towards each other on scriptural principles. The infant, in its capricious dominion over mother, father, brothers and sisters, exhibits, in strongest colors, the "strength of weakness," the power of affection. The wife and daughters are more carefully attended by the father, than the sons, because they are weaker and elicit more of his affection.

The dependent exercise, because of their dependence, as much control over their superiors, in most things, as those superiors exercise over them. Thus, and thus only, can conditions be equalized. This constitutes practical equality of rights, enforced not by human, but by divine law. Our hearts bleed at the robbing of a bird's nest; and the little birds, because they are weak, subdue our strength and command our care. We love and cherish the rose, and sympathize with the lily which some wanton boy has bruised and broken. Our faithful dog shares our affections, and we will risk our lives to redress injustice done him.

Man is not all selfish. "Might does not always make right." Within the family circle, the law of love prevails, not that of selfishness.

But, besides wife and children, brothers and sister, dogs, horses, birds and flowers—slaves, also, belong to the family circle. Does their common humanity, their abject weakness and dependence, their great value, their ministering to our wants in childhood, manhood, sickness and old age, cut them off from that affection which everything else in the family elicits? No; the interests of master and slave are bound up together, and each in his appropriate sphere naturally endeavors to promote the happiness of the other.

The humble and obedient slave exercises more or less control over the most brutal and hard-hearted master. It is an invariable law of nature, that weakness and dependence are elements of strength, and generally sufficiently limit that universal despotism, observable throughout human and animal nature. The moral and physical world is but a series of subordinations, and the more perfect the subordination, the greater the harmony and happiness. Inferior and superior act and react on each other through agencies and media too delicate and subtle for human apprehensions; yet, looking to usual results, man should be willing to leave to God what God only can regulate. Human law cannot beget benevolence, affection, maternal and paternal love; nor can it supply their places; but it may, by breaking up the ordinary relations of human beings, stop and disturb the current of these finer feelings of our nature. It may abolish slavery; but it can never create between the capitalist and the laborer, between the employer and employed, the kind and affectionate relations that usually exist between master and slave.

5. GEORGE W. CABLE, *The Freedman's Case, 1885**

We need to go back to the roots of things and study closely, analytically, the origin, the present foundation, the rationality, the rightness, of those sentiments surviving in us which prompt an attitude qualifying in any way peculiarly the black man's liberty among us. . . .

First, then, what are these sentiments? Foremost among them stands the idea that he is of necessity an alien. He was brought to our shores a naked, brutish, unclean, captive, pagan savage, to be and remain a kind of connecting link between man and the beasts of burden. The great changes to result from his contact with a superb race of masters were not taken into account. As a social factor he was intended to be as purely zero as the brute at the other end of his plow-line. The occasional mingling of his blood with that of the white man worked no change in the sentiment; one, two, four, eight, multiplied upon or divided into zero, still gave zero for the result. Generations of American nativity made no difference; his children and children's children were born in sight of our door, yet the old notion held fast. He increased to vast numbers, but it never wavered. He accepted our dress, language, religion, all the fundamentals of our civilization, and became forever expatriated from his own land; still he remained, to us, an alien. Our sentiment went blind. It did not see that gradually, here by force and there by choice, he was fulfilling a host of conditions that earned at least a solemn moral right to that naturalization which no one at first had dreamed of giving him. Frequently he even bought back the freedom of which he had been robbed, became a tax-payer, and at times an educator of his children at his own expense; but the old idea of alienism passed laws to banish him, his wife, and children by thousands from the State, and threw him into loathsome jails as a common felon, for returning to his native land.

It will be wise to remember that these were the acts of an enlightened, God-fearing people, the great mass of whom have passed beyond all earthly accountability. They were our fathers. I am the son and grandson of slaveholders. These were their faults; posterity will discover ours; but these things must be frankly, fearlessly taken into account if we are ever to understand the true interests of our peculiar state of society.

Why, then, did this notion, that the man of color must always remain an alien, stand so unshaken? We may readily recall how, under ancient systems, he rose not only to high privileges, but often to public station and power. Singularly, with us the trouble lay in a modern principle of liberty. The whole idea of American government rested on all men's equal, inalienable right to secure their life, liberty, and the pursuit of happiness

* George W. Cable, *The Silent South* (New York, 1885), pp. 6–11, 15–20.

by governments founded in their own consent. Hence, our Southern forefathers, shedding their blood, or ready to shed it, for this principle, yet proposing in equal good conscience to continue holding the American black man and mulatto and quadroon in slavery, had to anchor that conscience, their conduct, and their laws in the conviction that the man of African tincture was, not by his master's arbitrary assertion merely, but by nature and unalterably, an alien. If that hold should break, one single wave of irresistible inference would lift our whole Southern social fabric and dash it upon the rocks of Negro emancipation and enfranchisement. How was it made secure? Not by books, though they were written among us from every possible point of view, but, with the mass of our slave-owners, by the calm hypothesis of a positive, intuitive knowledge. To them the statement was an axiom. They abandoned the methods of moral and intellectual reasoning, and fell back upon this assumption of a God-given instinct, nobler than reason, and which it was an insult to a freeman to ask him to prove on logical grounds.

Yet it was found not enough. The slave multiplied. Slavery was a dangerous institution. Few in the South to-day have any just idea how often the slave plotted for his freedom. Our Southern ancestors were a noble, manly people, springing from some of the most highly intelligent, aspiring, upright, and refined nations of the modern world; from the Huguenot, the French Chevalier, the Old Englander, the New Englander. Their acts were not always right; whose are? But for their peace of mind they had to believe them so. They therefore spoke much of the Negro's contentment with that servile condition for which nature had designed him. Yet there was no escaping the knowledge that we dared not trust the slave caste with any power that could be withheld from them. So the perpetual alien was made also a perpetual menial, and the belief became fixed that this, too, was nature's decree, not ours.

Thus we stood at the close of the Civil War. There were always a few Southerners who did not justify slavery, and many who cared nothing whether it was just or not. But what we have described was the general sentiment of good Southern people. . . .

This perpetuation of the alien, menial relation tended to perpetuate the vices that naturally cling to servility, dense ignorance and a hopeless separation from true liberty; and as we could not find it in our minds to blame slavery with this perpetuation, we could only assume as a further axiom that there was, by nature, a disqualifying moral taint in every drop of Negro blood. The testimony of an Irish, German, Italian, French, or Spanish beggar in a court of justice was taken on its merits; but the colored man's was excluded by law wherever it weighed against a white man. The colored man was a prejudged culprit. The discipline of the plantation required that the difference between master and slave be never lost sight of by either. It made our master caste a solid mass, and fixed a common masterhood and subserviency between the ruling and the serving race. Every one of us grew up in the idea that he had, by birth and race, certain broad powers of police over any and every person of color.

All at once the tempest of war snapped off at the ground every one of these arbitrary relations, without removing a single one of the sentiments in which they stood rooted. . . .

[Now the slave] is virtually freed by the consent of his master, but the master retaining the exclusive right to define the bounds of his freedom.

Many everywhere have taken up the idea that this state of affairs is the end to be desired and the end actually sought in reconstruction as handed over to the States. I do not charge such folly to the best intelligence of any American community; but I cannot ignore my own knowledge that the average thought of some regions rises to no better idea of the issue. The belief is all too common that the nation, having aimed at a wrong result and missed, has left us of the Southern States to get now such other result as we think best. I say this belief is not universal. There are those among us who see that America has no room for a state of society which makes its lower classes harmless by abridging their liberties, or, as one of the favored class lately said to me, has "got 'em so they don't give no trouble." There is a growing number who see that the one thing we cannot afford to tolerate at large is a class of people less than citizens; and that every interest in the land demands that the freedman be free to become in all things, as far as his own personal gifts will lift and sustain him, the same sort of American citizen he would be if, with the same intellectual and moral calibre, he were white.

Thus we reach the ultimate question of fact. Are the freedman's liberties suffering any real abridgment? The answer is easy. The letter of the laws, with a few exceptions, recognizes him as entitled to every right of an American citizen; and to some it may seem unimportant that there is scarcely one public relation of life in the South where he is not arbitrarily and unlawfully compelled to hold toward the white man the attitude of an alien, a menial, and a probable reprobate, by reason of his race and color. One of the marvels of future history will be that it was counted a small matter, by a majority of our nation, for six mil-

lions of people within it, made by its own decree a component part of it, to be subjected to a system of oppression so rank that nothing could make it seem small except the fact that they had already been ground under it for a century and a half.

Examine it. It proffers to the freedman a certain security of life and property, and then holds the respect of the community, that dearest of earthly boons, beyond his attainment. It gives him certain guarantees against thieves and robbers, and then holds him under the unearned contumely of the mass of good men and women. It acknowledges in constitutions and statutes his title to an American's freedom and aspirations, and then in daily practice heaps upon him in every public place the most odious distinctions, without giving ear to the humblest plea concerning mental or moral character. It spurns his ambition, tramples upon his languishing self-respect, and indignantly refuses to let him either buy with money, or earn by any excellence of inner life or outward behavior, the most momentary immunity from these public indignities even for his wife and daughters. Need we cram these pages with facts in evidence, as if these were charges denied and requiring to be proven? They are simply the present avowed and defended state of affairs peeled of its exteriors.

Nothing but the habit, generations old, of enduring it could make it endurable by men not in actual slavery. We were whites of the South to remain every way as we are, and our six million blacks to give place to any sort of whites exactly their equals, man for man, in mind, morals, and wealth, provided only that they had tasted two years of American freedom, and were this same system of tyrannies attempted upon them, there would be as bloody an uprising as this continent has ever seen. We can say this quietly. There is not a scruple's weight of present danger. These six million freedmen are dominated by nine million whites immeasurably stronger than they, backed by the virtual consent of thirty odd millions more. Indeed, nothing but the habit of oppression could make such oppression possible to a people of the intelligence and virtue of our Southern whites, and the invitation to practice it on millions of any other than the children of their former slaves would be spurned with a noble indignation.

Suppose, for a moment, the tables turned. Suppose the courts of our Southern States, while changing no laws requiring the impaneling of jurymen without distinction as to race, etc., should suddenly begin to draw their thousands of jurymen all black, and well-nigh every one of them counting not only himself, but all his race, better than any white man. Assuming that their average of intelligence and morals should be not below that of jurymen as now drawn, would a white man, for all that, choose to be tried in one of those courts? Would he suspect nothing? Could one persuade him that his chances of even justice were all they should be, or all they would be were the court not evading the law in order to sustain an outrageous distinction against him because of the accidents of his birth? Yet only read white man for black man, and black man for white man, and that— I speak as an eye-witness—has been the practice for years, and is still so to-day; an actual emasculation, in the case of six million people both as plaintiff and defendant, of the right of trial by jury.

In this and other practices the outrage falls upon the freedman. Does it stop there? Far from it. It is the first premise of American principles that whatever elevates the lower stratum of the people lifts all the rest, and whatever holds it down holds all down. For twenty years, therefore, the nation has been working to elevate the freedman. It counts this one of the great necessities of the hour. It has poured out its wealth publicly and privately for this purpose. It is confidently hoped that it will soon bestow a royal gift of millions for the reduction of the illiteracy so largely shared by the blacks. Our Southern States are and for twenty years have been, taxing themselves for the same end. The private charities alone of the other States have given twenty millions in the same good cause. Their colored seminaries, colleges, and normal schools dot our whole Southern country, and furnish our public colored schools with a large part of their teachers. All this and much more has been or is being done in order that, for the good of himself and everybody else in the land, the colored man may be elevated as quickly as possible from all the debasements of slavery and semi-slavery to the full stature and integrity of citizenship. And it is in the face of all this that the adherent of the old régime stands in the way to every public privilege and place—steamer landing, railway platform, theatre, concert-hall, art display, public library, public school, court-house, church, everything—flourishing the hot branding-iron of ignominious distinctions. He forbids the freedman to go into the water until he is satisfied that he knows how to swim, and for fear he should learn hangs mill-stones about his neck. This is what we are told is a small matter that will settle itself. Yes, like a roosting curse, until the outraged intelligence of the South lifts its indignant protest against this stupid firing into our own ranks.

6. PRESIDENT'S COMMITTEE ON CIVIL RIGHTS, *The Essential Rights, 1947**

The men who founded our Republic, as those who have built any constitutional democracy, faced the task of reconciling personal liberty and group authority, or of establishing an equilibrium between them. In a democratic state we recognize that the common interest of the people must be managed by laws and procedures established by majority rule. But a democratic majority, left unrestrained, may be as ruthless and tyrannical as were the earlier absolute monarchs. Seeing this clearly, and fearing it greatly, our forefathers built a constitutional system in which valued personal liberties, carefully enumerated in a Bill of Rights, were placed beyond the reach of popular majorities. Thus the people permanently denied the federal government power to interfere with certain personal rights and freedoms.

Freedom, however, as we now use the term, means even more than the traditional "freedoms" listed in our Bill of Rights—important as they are. . . .

Four basic rights have seemed important to this Committee and have influenced its labors. We believe that each of these rights is essential to the well-being of the individual and to the progress of society.

1. *The right to safety and security of the person.*—Freedom can exist only where the citizen is assured that his person is secure against bondage, lawless violence, and arbitrary arrest and punishment. Freedom from slavery in all its forms is clearly necessary if all men are to have equal opportunity to use their talents and to lead worthwhile lives. Moreover, to be free, men must be subject to discipline by society only for commission of offenses clearly defined by law and only after trial by due process of law. Where the administration of justice is discriminatory, no man can be sure of security. Where the threat of violence by private persons or mobs exists, a cruel inhibition of the sense of freedom of activity and security of the person inevitably results. Where a society permits private and arbitrary violence to be done to its members, its own integrity is inevitably corrupted. It cannot permit human beings to be imprisoned or killed in the absence of due process of law without degrading its entire fabric.

2. *The right to citizenship and its privileges.*—Since it is a purpose of government in a democracy to regulate the activity of each man in the interest of all men, it follows that every mature and responsible person must be able to enjoy full citizenship and have an equal voice in his government. Because the right to participate in the political process is customarily limited to citizens there can be no denial of access to citizenship based upon race, color, creed, or national origin. Denial of citizensip for these reasons cheapens the personality of those who are confined to this inferior status and endangers the whole concept of a democratic society.

To deny qualified citizens the right to vote while others exercise it is to do violence to the principle of freedom and equality. Without the right to vote, the individual loses his voice in the group effort and is subjected to rule by a body from which he has been excluded. Likewise, the right of the individual to vote is important to

* President's Committee on Civil Rights, *To Secure These Rights* (Washington, D.C., 1947).

the group itself. Democracy assumes that the majority is more likely as a general rule to make decisions which are wise and desirable from the point of view of the interests of the whole society than is any minority. Every time a qualified person is denied a voice in public affairs, one of the components of a potential majority is lost, and the formation of a sound public policy is endangered.

To the citizen in a democracy, freedom is a precious possession. Accordingly, all able-bodied citizens must enjoy the right to serve the nation and the cause of freedom in time of war. Any attempt to curb the right to fight in its defense can only lead the citizen to question the worth of the society in which he lives. A sense of frustration is created which is wholly alien to the normal emotions of a free man. In particular, any discrimination which, while imposing an obligation, prevents members of minority groups from rendering full military service in defense of their country is for them a peculiarly humiliating badge of inferiority. The nation also suffers a loss of manpower and is unable to marshal maximum strength at a moment when such strength is most needed.

3. *The right to freedom of conscience and expression.*—In a free society there is faith in the ability of the people to make sound, rational judgments. But such judgments are possible only where the people have access to all relevant facts and to all prevailing interpretations of the facts. How can such judgments be formed on a sound basis if arguments, viewpoints, or opinions are arbitrarily suppressed? How can the concept of the marketplace of thought in which truth ultimately prevails retain its validity if the thought of certain individuals is denied the right of circulation? The Committee reaffirms our tradition that freedom of expression may be curbed by

law only where the danger to the well-being of society is clear and present.

Our forefathers fought bloody wars and suffered torture and death for the right to worship God according to the varied dictates of conscience. Complete religious liberty has been accepted as an unquestioned personal freedom since our Bill of Rights was adopted. We have insisted only that religious freedom may not be pleaded as an excuse for criminal or clearly antisocial conduct.

4. *The right to equality of opportunity.*—It is not enough that full and equal membership in society entitles the individual to an equal voice in the control of his government; it must also give him the right to enjoy the benefits of society and to contribute to its progress. The opportunity of each individual to obtain useful employment, and to have access to services in the fields of education, housing, health, recreation and transportation, whether available free or at a price, must be provided with complete disregard for race, color, creed and national origin. Without this equality of opportunity the individual is deprived of the chance to develop his potentialities and to share the fruits of society. The group also suffers through the loss of the contributions which might have been made by persons excluded from the main channels of social and economic activity. . . .

THE RIGHT TO EMPLOYMENT

A man's right to an equal chance to utilize fully his skills and knowledge is essential. The meaning of a job goes far beyond the paycheck. Good workers have a pride in the organization for which they work and feel satisfaction in the jobs they are doing. A witness before a congressional committee has recently said:

Discrimination in employment damages lives, both the bodies and the minds, of those discriminated against and those who discriminate. It blights and perverts that healthy ambition to improve one's standard of living which we like to say is peculiarly American. It generates insecurity, fear, resentment, division and tension in our society. . . .

Discrimination is most acutely felt by minority group members in their inability to get a job suited to their qualifications. Exclusions of Negroes, Jews, or Mexicans in the process of hiring is effected in various ways—by newspaper advertisements requesting only whites or gentiles to apply, by registration or application blanks on which a space is reserved for "race" or "religion," by discriminatory job orders placed with employment agencies, or by the arbitrary policy of a company official in charge of hiring. . . .

Discrimination in hiring has forced many minority workers into low-paying and often menial jobs such as common laborer and domestic servant. This has done much to bring about the situation reported by the Bureau of the Census in 1940—

Striking differences between the occupations of whites and Negroes were shown in 1940 census statistics. Farmers, farm laborers, and other laborers constituted 62.2 percent of all employed Negro men and only 28.5 percent of all employed white men. Only about 5 percent of all employed Negro men, compared with approximately 30 percent of employed white men, were engaged in professional, semiprofessional, proprietary, managerial, and clerical or sales occupations. Skilled craftsmen represented 15.6 per cent of employed white men and only 4.4 per cent of employed Negro men. More than half of the Negro craftsmen were mechanics, carpenters, painters, plasterers and cement finishers, and masons. . . .

THE RIGHT TO PUBLIC SERVICES AND ACCOMMODATIONS

Services supplied by the government should be distributed in a non-discriminatory way. Activities financed by the public treasury should serve the whole people; they cannot, in consonance with the democratic principle, be used to advance the welfare of a portion of the population only. Moreover, many privately-owned and operated enterprises should recognize a responsibility to sell to all who wish to buy their services. They cannot be permitted to confine their benefits to a selected clientele. This is particularly true of those private businesses which hold franchises from the state or enjoy a monopoly status. Even when no franchise has been granted, and competition exists, certain private businesses because of the essential character of the services they render should serve all comers. It has been made clear to the Committee that unfortunately, many public services, supplied by both government and private business, do not reach all persons on an equality of access basis. . . .

Segregation has become the cornerstone of the elaborate structure of discrimination against some American citizens. Theoretically this system simply duplicates educational, recreational and other public services, according facilities to the two races which are "separate but equal." In the Committee's opinion this is one of the outstanding myths of American history for it is almost always true that while indeed separate, these facilities are far from equal. Throughout the segregated public institutions, Negroes have been denied an equal share of tax-supported services and facilities. So far as private institutions are concerned, there is no specific legal disability on the right of Negroes to develop equal institutions of their own. However, the economic, social, and indirect legal obstacles to this course are staggering. . . .

In any event we believe that not even the most mathematically precise equality of segregated institutions can properly be considered equality under the law. No argument or rationalization can alter this basic fact: a law which forbids a group of American citizens to associate with other citizens in the ordinary course of daily living creates inequality by imposing a caste status on the minority group.

If reason and history were not enough to substantiate the argument against segregation, recent experiences further strengthen it. For these experiences demonstrate that segregation is an obstacle to establishing harmonious relationships among groups. They prove that where the artificial barriers which divide people and groups from one another are broken, tension and conflict begin to be replaced by co-operative effort and an environment in which civil rights can thrive. . . .

More than 400 merchant seamen were asked a series of indirect questions which were then built into an "Index of Prejudice against Negroes." The results reported by Ira N. Brophy in the *Public Opinion Quarterly* (Winter, 1945–46) were surprising. They demonstrated that whether a man had been born in the North or the South was not important in determining whether he was prejudiced against Negroes. The extent of his education and the jobs he had held before he went to sea were not important. What was important was whether the men were members of unions with tolerant policies toward Negroes; how many trips to sea a man had made; how many times he had been under enemy fire; and how many times he had been to sea with Negroes. Here again what determined whether a white man was prejudiced against Negroes was the kind and amount of

experience he had had with them. Where there was contact with Negroes on an equal footing in a situation of mutual dependence and common effort prejudice declined. . . .

The Committee is not convinced that an end to segregation in education or in the enjoyment of public services essential to people in a modern society would mean an intrusion upon the private life of the individual. In a democracy, each individual must have freedom to choose his friends and to control the pattern of his personal and family life. But we see nothing inconsistent between this freedom and a recognition of the truth that democracy also means that in going to school, working, participating in the political process, serving in the armed forces, enjoying government services in such fields as health and recreation, making use of transportation and other public accommodation facilities, and living in specific communities and neighborhoods, distinctions of race, color, and creed have no place. . . .

GOVERNMENT'S RESPONSIBILITY FOR SECURING THE RIGHTS

The National Government of the United States must take the lead in safeguarding the civil rights of all Americans. We believe that this is one of the most important observations that can be made about the civil rights problem in our country today. We agree with words used by the President, in an address at the Lincoln Memorial in Washington in June, 1947:

We must make the Federal Government a friendly, vigilant defender of the rights and equalities of all Americans. . . . Our National Government must show the way.

It is essential that our rights be preserved against the tyrannical actions of public officers. Our forefathers saw the need for such protection when they gave us the Bill of Rights as a safeguard against arbitrary government. But this is not enough today. We need more than protection of our rights against government; we need protection of our rights against private persons or groups, seeking to undermine them. In the words of the President:

> We cannot be content with a civil liberties program which emphasizes only the need of protection against the possibility of tyranny by the Government. . . . We must keep moving forward, with new concepts of civil rights to safeguard our heritage. The extension of civil rights today means not protection of the people against the Government, but protection of the people by the Government.

There are several reasons why we believe the federal government must play a leading role in our efforts as a nation to improve our civil rights record.

First, many of the most serious wrongs against individual rights are committed by private persons or by local public officers. In the most flagrant of all such wrongs—lynching—private individuals, aided upon occassion by state or local officials, are the ones who take the law into their own hands and deprive the victim of his life. The very fact that these outrages continue to occur, coupled with the fact that the states have been unable to eliminate them, points clearly to a strong need for federal safeguards.

Second, it is a sound policy to use the idealism and prestige of our whole people to check the wayward tendencies of a part of them. It is true that the conscience of a nation is colored by the moral sense of its local communities. Still, the American people have traditionally shown high national regard for civil rights, even though the record in many a community has been far from good. We should not fail to make use of this in combating civil rights violations. The local community must be encouraged to set its own house in order. But the need for leadership is pressing. That leadership is available in the national government and it should be used. We cannot afford to delay action until the most backward community has learned to prize civil liberty and has taken adequate steps to safeguard the rights of every one of its citizens.

Third, our civil rights record has growing international implications. These cannot safely be disregarded by the government at the national level which is responsible for our relations with the world, and left entirely to government at the local level for proper recognition and action. Many of man's problems, we have been learning, are capable of ultimate solution only through international cooperation and action. The subject of human rights, itself, has been made a major concern of the United Nations. It would indeed be ironical if in our own country the argument should prevail that safeguarding the rights of the individual is the exclusive, or even the primary concern of local government. . . .

Fourth, the steadily growing tendency of the American people to look to the national government for the protection of their civil rights is highly significant. This popular demand does not by itself prove the case for national government action. But the persistent and deep-felt desire of the American citizen for federal action safeguarding his civil rights is neither a request for spoils by a selfish pressure group, nor is it a shortsighted and opportunistic attempt by a temporary majority to urge the government into a dubious or unwise course of action. It is a demand rooted in the folkways of the people, sound in instinct and reason, and impossible to ignore. The American people are loyal to the institutions of local self-government, and distrust highly centralized power. But we have never hesitated to entrust power and responsibility to the national government when need for such a course of action has been demonstrated and the people themselves are convinced of that need.

Finally, the national government should assume leadership in our American civil rights program because there is much in the field of civil rights that it is squarely responsible for in its own direct dealings with millions of persons. It is the largest single employer of labor in the country. More than two million persons are on its payroll. The freedom of opinion and expression enjoyed by these people is in many ways dependent upon the attitudes and practices of the government. By not restricting this freedom beyond a point necessary to insure the efficiency and loyalty of its workers, the government, itself, can make a very large contribution to the effort to achieve true freedom of thought in America. By scrupulously following fair employment practices, it not only sets a model for other employers to follow, but also directly protects the rights of more than two million workers to fair employment.

The same is true of the armed forces. Their policies are completely determined by the federal government. That government has the power, the opportunity and the duty to see that discrimination and prejudice are completely eliminated from the armed services, and that the American soldier or sailor enjoys as full a measure of civil liberty as is commensurate with military service.

The District of Columbia and our dependent areas are under the immediate authority of the national government. By safeguarding civil rights in these areas, it can protect several million people directly, and encourage the states and local communities throughout the country to do likewise. Finally, through its extensive public services, the national government is the largest single agency in the land endeavoring to satisfy the wants and needs of the consumer. By making certain that these services are continuously available to all persons without regard to race, color, creed or national origin, a very important step toward the elimination of discrimination in American life will have been taken.

Leadership by the federal government in safeguarding civil rights does not mean exclusive action by that government. There is much that the states and local communities can do in this field, and much that they alone can do. The Committee believes that Justice Holmes' view of the states as 48 laboratories for social and economic experimentation is still valid. The very complexity of the civil rights problem calls for much experimental, remedial action which may be better undertaken by the states than by the national government. Parallel state and local action supporting the national program is highly desirable. It is obvious that even though the federal government should take steps to stamp out the crime of lynching, the states cannot escape the responsibility to employ all of the powers and resources available to them for the same end. Or again, the enactment of a federal fair employment practice act will not render similar state legislation unnecessary.

In certain areas the states must do far more than parallel federal action. Either for constitutional or administrative reasons, they must remain the primary protectors of civil rights. This is true of governmental efforts to control or outlaw racial or religious discrimination practiced by privately supported public-service institutions such as schools and hospitals, and of places of public accommodation such as hotels, restaurants, theaters, and stores.

Furthermore, government action alone, whether federal, state, local, or all combined, cannot provide complete protection of civil rights. Everything that government does stems from and is conditioned by the state of public opinion. Civil rights in this country will never be adequately protected until the intelligent will of the American people approves and demands that protection. Great responsibility, therefore, will always rest upon private organizations and private individuals who are in a position to educate and shape public opinion. The argument is sometimes made that because prejudice and intolerance cannot be eliminated through legislation and government control we should abandon that action in favor of the long, slow, evolutionary effects of education and voluntary private efforts. We believe that this argument misses the point and that the choice it poses between legislation and education as to the means of improving civil rights is an unnecessary one. In our opinion, both approaches to the goal are valid, and are, moreover, essential to each other.

It may be impossible to overcome prejudice by law, but many of the evil discriminatory practices which are the visible manifestations of prejudice can be brought to an end through proper government controls. At the same time, it is highly desirable that efforts be made to understand more fully the causes of prejudice and to stamp them out. These efforts will necessarily occupy much time and can in many instances best be made by private organizations and individuals.

7. PRESIDENT'S COMMISSION ON IMMIGRATION, *America—A Land of Immigrants, 1952**

In a short period of human history the people of the United States built this country from a wilderness to one of the most powerful and prosperous nations in the world. The people who built America were 40 million immigrants who have come since the *Mayflower,* and their descendants. We are still a vigorous and growing nation, and the economic, social and other benefits available to us, the descendants of immigrant forebears, are constantly expanding.

One remarkable national development testifies to the wisdom of our early and continuing belief in immigration. One of the causes of the American Revolution, as stated in the Declaration of Independence, was the fact that England hindered free immigration into the colonies.

Our growth as a nation has been achieved, in large measure, through the genius and industry of immigrants of every race and from every quarter of the world. The story of their pursuit of happiness is the saga of America. Their brains and their brawn helped to settle our land, to advance our agriculture, to build our industries, to develop our commerce, to produce new inventions and, in general, to make us the leading nation that we now are.

Immigration brought wealth to the United States, many billions of dollars.

* President's Commission on Immigration and Naturalization, *Whom We Shall Welcome* [Washington, D.C., 1952], pp. 23–32.

The immigrants did not bring this wealth in their baggage—many arrived penniless and in debt—but in their skills, their trades, and their willingness to work. In his testimony to the Commission, Dr. Louis I. Dublin, statistician and second vice president of the Metropolitan Life Insurance Co., pointed out that a young adult immigrant of 18 years today is worth to the Nation at least $10,000, since that is what it costs to raise the average American. The average net worth of such a person to the economy of the United States falls between $30,000 and $80,000, depending on his potential earning power. Throughout our history immigrants have in this way represented additional wealth to our country.

Scarcely one aspect of our American economy, culture, or development can be discussed without reference to the fundamental contribution of immigrants. No roster of leading Americans in business, science, arts, and the professions could be complete without the names of many immigrants. In our history the following aliens may be mentioned, among many, who became outstanding industrialists: Andrew Carnegie (Scot), in the steel industry; John Jacob Astor (German), in the fur trade; Michael Cudahy (Irish), of the meat-packing industry; the Du Ponts (French), of the munitions and chemical industry; Charles L. Fleischmann (Hungarian), of the yeast business; David Sarnoff (Russian), of the radio industry; and William S. Knudsen (Danish), of the automobile industry.

Immigrant scientists and inventors are likewise too numerous to list in detail. Among those whose genius has benefited the United States are Albert Einstein (German), in physics; Michael Pupin (Serbian), in electricity; Enrico Fermi (Italian), in atomic research; John Ericsson (Swedish), who

invented the ironclad ship and the screw propeller; Giusseppe Bellanca (Italian), and Igor Sikorsky (Russian), who made outstanding contributions to airplane development; John A. Udden (Swedish), who was responsible for opening the Texas oil fields; Lucas P. Kyrides (Greek), industrial chemistry; David Thomas (Welsh), who invented the hot blast furnace; Alexander Graham Bell (Scot), who invented the telephone; Conrad Huber (Russian), who invented the flashlight; and Otto Mergenthaler (German), who invented the linotype machine.

Many of our leading musicians, actors, motion-picture producers, and others in the arts are foreign-born. Law, medicine, education, literature, research, organized labor, and journalism are only a few other of the innumerable fields benefited by outstanding immigrants. Any such list can only be a sample of how much immigrants have enriched the America which granted them hospitality and welcome.

The encouragement of immigration was part of the tradition of the United States and one of the reasons why it became a great and powerful nation. Immigration to the United States has come from virtually every corner of the globe. The greater part of it, however, came from Europe. It is especially interesting to note that the major impulses to come to the United States from the various countries of Europe were passing phenomena, rising at certain stages of the economic or political life in their homelands, and then subsiding. The sources of American immigration shifted with the changing of needs, both in the United States and in the countries of origin. Each generation, even each decade, brought a changing pattern of immigration. . . .

The earliest mass migrations were drawn from the English, Scots, and Scot-Irish people of the British Isles.

Colonial immigration of such Britons was supplanted in numbers in the period 1820—60 by migration from Ireland, but the most acute migration fever had passed in Ireland by the end of the 1850's. Immigration from west and southwest Germany became important in this period, and with the opening up of eastern Germany total German immigration was the dominant stream from 1860 to 1890. In these years Scandinavia vied with Ireland in numbers of immigrants. But the crest of this "new" migration from Germany and Scandinavia was passed in the 1860's and gave way to another "new" migration dominated by immigrants from Italy, Austria-Hungary, and Russia.

The emigration fever spread across the European continent from west to east and from north to south. Thus up to 1890 Italian migration to America came largely from the more economically advanced north of Italy. After 1890 Italian migration came increasingly from the south. The main founts of immigration from Austria were in chronological sequence—first, the more developed Bohemia; second, the relatively backward Carinthia and Tyrol; and then, after 1900, Galicia (especially Poles and Jews). Only in the last stages did the movement include substantial numbers of Ukrainians from remote eastern Galicia.

Migration from Hungary and other east European countries was first composed of the minorities most in touch with the West. The distinctive feature of the emigration from Russia which was the last major country of European emigration was its non-Russian ethnic character. Emigration from Russia was firstly made up of peoples culturally most closely in contact with the West, that is, the Jews of the towns, the Baltic peoples, the Poles, and, finally, the Ukrainians.

Thus, by the time of the first World War, the area of Europe from which migrants were drawn had spread to include almost the whole of the continent. The sources of heaviest migration have moved across Europe in a widened circle from the center of first migration in northwest Europe to the latest in southern and southeastern Europe. There was always a clear correlation between immigration and economic conditions in the United States. In the periods of unrestricted immigration, the volume of immigration rose during prosperity but rapidly disappeared in times of depression when it would have contributed to unemployment. . . . Immigrants came when they were needed and stayed away when they were not. Before quota restrictions were imposed, immigration was large in periods of full employment, small in times of unemployment.

The great depression of the 1930's began almost a decade after the passage of restrictive immigration legislation. The unemployment of the 1930's therefore could hardly be attributed to immigration. On the contrary, a number of distinguished economists believe the restriction of immigration to have been one cause of the depression. Throughout American history rapid increase of population had provided a constantly expanding market for our products. The decline in population growth incident to reduction of immigration and to the declining birth rate in the 1920's removed one factor contributing to our expanding economy.

During the depression, quota restrictions were of no significance—even the small quotas for Southern and Eastern Europe were unfilled. As in the earlier periods, with or without quotas and restrictive devices, prospective immigrants had no incentive or desire to come to this country in time of depression. In fact, in the depression years from 1931 through 1936, a total of 240,000 more aliens left than were admitted. The Commission finds no evidence that immigration either caused or aggravated the depression.

Historically speaking, therefore, immigration has supplied much of the brain and sinew, the human resources that have created our nation. It has come when and where manpower was in demand to build up America and to raise its standard of living, but it has not, of itself, caused depression and unemployment. The new immigrant has helped to enrich the native descendants of earlier immigration.

In reviewing the history of debates on the problem of immigration, the Commission was impressed by the fact that those opposing immigration appear to have been influenced in this view by a pessimistic outlook regarding the future economic growth of the United States. The nation was barely founded before a Congressman rose to say on the floor of the House of Representatives in 1797 that while a liberal immigration policy was satisfactory when the country was new and unsettled, now that the United States had reached maturity and was fully populated, further immigration should be stopped.

However, such views have continued throughout our history. In 1921, the Immigration Committee of the House of Representatives again recommended complete termination of all immigration. By the 1920's there was widespread fear that the country could not profitably absorb immigration in the volume received before World War I. The territorial frontier was gone. The country was "filled up" in the sense that good agricultural land was almost fully occupied and under cultivation. The economy was rapidly becoming industrialized, a "mature" economy was emerging, and therefore, it was

argued, immigration had to be drastically curtailed.

With the 1921 Quota Act, originally designed for a 1-year emergency, there began a wholly new departure in American law: a limitation on the number of immigrants that could be admitted into the United States. The Immigration Act of 1924 not only carried into permanent law the concept of a limitation on numbers, but also initiated the formula of selection on the basis of race and nationality. The Immigration and Nationality Act of 1952 continued and strengthened the same principles.

The onset of the depression in 1929 seemed to validate the views of those who feared that economic maturity meant the end of economic growth in the United States. This did not prove to be the case.

Our economy has expanded by leaps and bounds. Our gross national product in 1924 of $140 billion (in 1951 dollars) grew to $329 billion in 1951; foreign exports of goods expanded from $6.5 billion (1951 dollars) in 1924 to $15 billion in 1951; manufacturing production increased by 140 percent, and agricultural output by 51 percent between 1924 and 1951. Our farmers had an average per capita income from farming of only $302 in 1924 (in terms of 1951 purchasing power), which rose to $760 per capita in 1951. These are but a few examples of growth since the 1920's, and of the dynamic nature of our economy.

This economic expansion required an expanding labor force. The demands were met, as in the past, partly through natural growth and partly from migration. The labor force increased from 41.2 million in 1920 to 66 million in 1951. When the normal sources of European immigration were substantially cut off by our legislation of the 1920's, our industries had to seek other sources of labor. This they found in three ways: (1) by enormous migration from our own rural areas in the United States; (2) by increased immigration from Puerto Rico, the West Indies, and the non-quota countries of the Western Hemisphere; and (3) by special legislation providing for temporary immigration from neighboring countries.

During World War II, and after, many hundreds of thousands of workers were drawn from the farms to man the factories and other establishments of our urban centers. Since 1940 over one and a half million southern Negroes moved to the cities of the North and West to fill the manpower shortages. The Negro population of the North and West more than doubled through this migration. But this was not enough. This source of manpower had to be supplemented by some 200,000 Puerto Ricans, and other West Indians. Quite aside from the movements of native white people in the United States, there were nearly 2 million total migrants who moved into the northern and western States from these internal sources in the decade 1940-50, and the movement continues unabated.

During the same period there was a net foreign immigration of one and a half million people that went chiefly to the industrial areas of the country. Thus, the total migration to the North and West from the South and from abroad during the forties was at least as large as the net immigration in the decade 1890-1900, the third largest decade of European immigration in our history. In other words, the northern cities continued to need immigrants but had to get them mainly from elsewhere than Europe.

But even this was not enough to meet the demands of our growing economy. Congress also found it necessary to enact special immigration legislation admitting certain groups of im-migrants temporarily to meet the manpower shortages, both in agricultural and nonagricultural employment.

As a result of acute labor shortages in agriculture during World War II, special programs for recruitment of seasonal and temporary workers from Western Hemisphere countries were undertaken by intergovernmental agreements. Large numbers of aliens were involved in these programs, both during the war and after. The greatest number of Mexican farm workers legally in the United States for this purpose at any one time during World War II was 67,860 around August 1, 1944. As many as 21,000 Jamaicans and 6,000 Bahamans, as well as small numbers of Canadians and other North Americans, entered the United States under similar programs from time to time during this period. After the war, and under a law enacted in 1948, this recruitment of immigrant agricultural workers was continued on a peacetime basis. During the year 1951, some 191,000 Mexican nationals were admitted temporarily for agricultural work. Even this movement of immigrants, authorized by Congress, is overshadowed by the illegal entry each year of over half million Mexican "wetbacks."

Specific agricultural activities have sometimes received explicit Congressional exemption from restrictive immigration provisions. Two enactments have authorized the granting of special quota immigration visas to skilled sheepherders, to be charged against future quotas. Under 1950 legislation, 250 were permitted to enter, of whom 125 were admitted during the fiscal year 1951. Another statute in 1952 authorized the admision of 500 more sheepherders.

In the original 1948 Displaced Persons Act, Congress provided a 40 percent preference for agricultural labor, a further indication of Congressional recognition of immigration as a potential source of agricultural manpower.

During the war a manpower gap also appeared in the nonagricultural occupations. A total of 135,283 Mexican nationals worked on railroads in the United States from May 1943 to August 1945. More might have been used, but the Mexican government imposed a maximum ceiling of 75,000 who could be permitted in this country at any particular time. During the fiscal year 1951 some 10,000 Canadian woodsmen were permitted entry into Maine, Vermont, New Hampshire, and New York to fill a need for manpower not otherwise available.

Another example of the use of immigration to meet labor shortages can be seen in the United States Department of Labor's certifications for waiver of the contract labor provisions of the pre-1952 immigration act. Such waivers were based on the unavailability of similar domestic labor. In the 7-year period from 1946 to 1952 there were 11,028 certifications, in addition to Canadian woodsmen. These certifications covered a total of 448 different occupations, many of which appeared year after year in this 7-year period.

In the light of this experience under the restrictive limitations on immigration under the laws in effect since 1924, the Commission finds that immigration continues to be what it has always been in our history, a source of necessary manpower. Despite the efforts to change this situation by shutting off immigration from its customary sources, the American economy still continues to demand some form of immigration to meet the manpower demands of a growing and vigorous nation.

8. The Supreme Court, *Desegregation in the Public Schools, 1954**

These cases come to us from the States of Kansas, South Carolina, Virginia, and Delaware. They are premised on different facts and different local conditions, but a common legal question justifies their consideration together in this consolidated opinion.

In each of the cases, minors of the Negro race, through their legal representatives, seek the aid of the courts in obtaining admission to the public schools of their community on a nonsegregated basis. In each instance, they had been denied admission to schools attended by white children under laws requiring or permitting segregation according to race.

This segregation was alleged to deprive the plaintiffs of the equal protection of the laws under the Fourteenth Amendment. In each of the cases other than the Delaware case, a three-judge Federal District Court denied relief to the plaintiffs on the so-called "Separate but Equal" doctrine announced by this court in Plessy *v.* Ferguson, 163 U.S. 537.

Under that doctrine, equality of treatment is accorded when the races are provided substantially equal facilities, even though these facilities be separate. In the Delaware case, the Supreme Court of Delaware adhered to that doctrine, but ordered that the

* *Brown et al.* v. *Board of Education of Topeka et al.*, 347 U.S. 483 (1954).

plaintiffs be admitted to the white schools because of their superiority to the Negro schools.

The plaintiffs contend that segregated public schools are not "equal" and cannot be made "equal," and that hence, they are deprived of the equal protection of the laws. Because of the obvious importance of the question presented, the Court took jurisdiction. Argument was heard in the 1952 term, and reargument was heard this term on certain questions propounded by the Court.

Reargument was largely devoted to the circumstances surrounding the adoption of the Fourteenth Amendment in 1868. It covered, exhaustively, consideration of the Amendment in Congress, ratification by the states, then existing practices in racial segregation, and the views of proponents and opponents of the Amendment.

This discussion and our own investigation convince us that, although these sources cast some light, it is not enough to resolve the problem with which we are faced.

At best, they are inconclusive. The most avid proponents of the postwar Amendments undoubtedly intended them to remove all legal distinctions among "all persons born or naturalized in the United States."

Their opponents, just as certainly, were antagonistic to both the letter and the spirit of the Amendments and wished them to have the most limited effect. What others in Congress and the State Legislature had in mind cannot be determined with any degree of certainty.

An additional reason for the inclu-sive nature of the Amendment's history, with respect to segregated schools, is the status of public education at that time. In the South, the movement toward free common schools, supported by general taxation, had not yet taken hold. Education of white children was largely in the hands of private groups. Education of Negroes was almost non-existent, and practically all of the race was illiterate. In fact, any education of Negroes was forbidden by law in some states.

Today, in contrast, many Negroes have achieved outstanding success in the arts and sciences as well as in the business and professional world. It is true that public education has already advanced further in the North, but the effect of the Amendment on Northern States was generally ignored in the Congressional debates.

Even in the North, the conditions of public education did not approximate those existing today. The curriculum was usually rudimentary; ungraded schools were common in rural areas; the school term was but three months a year in many states; and compulsory school attendance was virtually unknown.

As a consequence, it is not surprising that there should be so little in the history of the Fourteenth Amendment relating to its intended effect on public education.

In the first cases in this court construing the Fourteenth Amendment, decided shortly after its adoption, the court interpreted it as proscribing all state-imposed discriminations against the Negro race.[1]

---

[1] Slaughter-house cases, 16 Wall. 36, 67–72 (1873); Strauder *v.* West Virginia, 100 U.S. 303, 307–08 (1879):
"It ordains that no state shall deprive any person of life, liberty, or property, without due process of law, or deny to any person within its jurisdiction the equal protection of the laws. What is this but declaring that the law in the states shall be the same for the black as for the white; that all persons, whether colored or white, shall stand equal before the laws of the states, and, in regard to the colored race, for whose protection the Amendment was primarily designed, that no discrimination shall be made against them by law because of their color?

"The words of the Amendment, it is true, are prohibitory, but they contain a necessary implication of a positive immun-

The doctrine of "Separate but Equal" did not make its appearance in this court until 1896 in the case of Plessy *v.* Ferguson, supra, involving not education but transportation.[2]

American courts have since labored with the doctrine for over half a century. In this court, there have been six cases involving the "Separate but Equal" doctrine in the field of public education.

In Cumming *v.* County Board of Education, 175 U. S. 528, and Gong Lum *v.* Rice, 275 U. S. 78, the validity of the doctrine itself was not challenged.[3] In most recent cases, all on the graduate school level, inequality was found in that specific benefits enjoyed by white students were denied to Negro students of the same educational qualifications. Missouri ex rel. Gaines *v.* Canada, 305 U. S. 337; Sipuel *v.* Oklahoma, 332 U. S. 331; Sweatt *v.* Painter, 339 U. S. 629; McLaurin *v.* Oklahoma State Regents, 339 U. S. 637.

In nine of these cases it was necessary to re-examine the doctrine to grant relief to the Negro plaintiff. And in Sweatt *v.* Painter, supra, the court expressly reserved decision on the question whether Plessy *v.* Ferguson should be held inapplicable to public education.

In the instant cases, that question is directly presented. Here, unlike Sweatt *v.* Painter, there are findings below that the Negro and white schools involved have been equalized, or are being equalized, with respect to buildings, curricula, qualifications and salaries of teachers, and other "tangible" factors.[4]

Our decision, therefore, cannot turn on merely a comparison of these tangible factors in the Negro and white schools involved in each of the cases. We must look instead to the effect of segregation itself on public education.

In approaching this problem, we cannot turn the clock back to 1868, when the Amendment was adopted, or even to 1896, when Plessy *v.* Ferguson was written. We must consider public education in the light of its full development and its present place in

---

ity, or right, most valuable to the colored race—the right to exemption from unfriendly legislation against them distinctively as colored—exemption from legal discriminations, implying inferiority in civil society, lessening the security of their enjoyment of the rights which others enjoy, and discriminations which are steps toward reducing them to the condition of a subject race."

See also Virginia *v.* Rives, 100 U.S. 313, 318 (1879); ex parte Virginia, 100 U.S. 339, 344–345 (1879).

[2] The doctrine apparently originated in Roberts *v.* City of Boston, 59 Mass., 198, 206 (1849), upholding school segregation against attack as being violative of a state constitutional guarantee of equality. Segregation in Boston public schools was eliminated in 1855. Mass. Acts 1855, C. 256. But elsewhere in the North segregation in public education has persisted until recent years. It is apparent that such segregation has long been a nation-wide problem, not merely one of sectional concern.

[3] In the Cumming case, Negro taxpayers sought an injunction requiring the defendant school board to discontinue the operation of a high school for white children until the board resumed operation of a high school for Negro children.

Similarly in the Gong Lum case, the plaintiff, a child of Chinese descent, contended that the state authorities had misapplied the doctrine by classifying him with Negro children and requiring him to attend a Negro school.

[4] In the Kansas case, the court below found substantial equality as to all such factors, 98 F. Supp. 797, 798.

In the South Carolina case, the court below found that the defendants were proceeding "promptly and in good faith to comply with the court's decree." 103 F. Supp. 920, 921.

In the Virginia case, the court below noted that the equalization program was already "afoot and progressing" (103 F. Supp. 337, 341); since then, we have been advised in the Virginia Attorney General's brief on reargument, that the program has now been completed.

In the Delaware case, the court below similarly noted that the state's equalization program was well under way. 91 A 2d 137, 149.

American life throughout the nation. Only in this way can it be determined if segregation in public schools deprives these plaintiffs of the equal protection of the laws.

Today, education is perhaps the most important function of state and local governments. Compulsory school attendance laws and the great expenditures for education both demonstrate our recognition of the importance of education to our democratic society. It is required in the performance of our most basic public responsibilities, even service in the armed forces. It is the very foundation of good citizenship.

Today, it is a principal instrument in awakening the child to cultural values, in preparing him for later professional training, and in helping him to adjust normally to his environment.

In these days, it is doubtful that any child may reasonably be expected to succeed in life if he is denied the opportunity of an education. Such an opportunity, where the state has undertaken to provide it, is a right which must be made available to all on equal terms.

We come then to the question presented: Does segregation of children in public schools solely on the basis of race, even though the physical facilities and other "tangible" factors may be equal, deprive the children of the minority group of equal educational opportunities? We believe that it does.

In Sweatt *v*. Painter, supra, in finding that a segregated law school for Negroes could not provide them equal educational opportunities, this court relied in large part on "those qualities which are incapable of objective measurement but which make for greatness in a law school."

In McLaurin *v*. Oklahoma State Regents, supra, the court, in requiring that a Negro admitted to a white graduate school be treated like all other students, again resorted to intangible considerations: ". . . his ability to study, engage in discussions and exchange views with other students, and, in general, to learn his profession."

Such considerations apply with added force to children in grade and high schools. To separate them from others of similar age and qualifications solely because of their race generates a feeling of inferiority as to their status in the community that may affect their hearts and minds in a way unlikely ever to be undone.

The effect of this separation on their educational opportunities was well stated by a finding in the Kansas case by a court which nevertheless felt compelled to rule against the Negro plaintiffs:

"Segregation of white and colored children in public schools has a detrimental effect upon the colored children. The impact is greater when it has the sanction of the law; for the policy of separating the races is usually interpreted as denoting the inferiority of the Negro group.

"A sense of inferiority affects the motivation of a child to learn. Segregation with the sanction of law, therefore, has a tendency to retard the educational and mental development of Negro children and to deprive them of some of the benefits they would receive in a racially integrated school system."[5]

Whatever may have been the extent of psychological knowlege at the time of Plessy *v*. Ferguson, this finding is amply supported by modern authority.

[5] A similar finding was made in the Delaware case:
"I conclude from the testimony that in our Delaware society, state-imposed segregation in education itself results in the Negro children, as a class, receiving educational opportunities which are substantially inferior to those available to white children otherwise similarly situated." 87 A, 2d 862, 865.

Any language in Plessy *v.* Ferguson contrary to this finding is rejected.

We conclude that in the field of public education the doctrine of "Separate but Equal" has no place. Separate educational facilities are inherently unequal. Therefore, we hold that the plaintiffs and others similarly situated for whom the actions have been brought are, by reason of the segregation complained of, deprived of the equal protection of the laws guaranteed by the Fourteenth Amendment. This disposition makes unnecessary any discussion whether such segregation also violates the Due Process Clause of the Fourteenth Amendment.

Because these are class actions, because of the wide applicability of this decision, and because of the great variety of local conditions, the formulation of decrees in these cases presents problems of considerable complexity. On

reargument, the consideration of appropriate relief was necessarily subordinated to the primary question—the constitutionality of segregation in public education.

We have now announced that such segregation is a denial of the equal protection of the laws. In order that we may have the full assistance of the parties in formulating decrees, the cases will be restored to the docket, and the parties are requested to present further argument on Questions 4 and 5 previously propounded by the court for the reargument this term.[6]

The Attorney General of the United States is again invited to participate. The Attorneys General of the states requiring or permitting segregation in public education will also be permitted to appear as amici curiae upon request to do so by September 15, 1954, and submission of briefs by October 1, 1954.

[6] "4. Assuming it is decided that segregation in public schools violates the Fourteenth Amendment

" (A) Would a decree necessarily follow providing that within the limits set by normal geographic school districting, Negro children should forthwith be admitted to schools of their choice, or

" (B) May this court, in the exercise of its equity powers, permit an effective gradual adjustment to be brought about from existing segregated systems to a system not based on color distinctions?

"On the assumption on which Questions 4 (A) and (B) are based, and assuming further that this court will exercise its equity powers to the end described in

Question 4 (B),

" (A) Should this court formulate detailed decrees in these cases;

" (B) If so, what specific issues should the decrees reach;

" (C) Should this court appoint a special master to hear evidence with a view to recommending specific terms for such decrees;

" (D) Should this court remand to the courts of first instance with directions to frame decrees in these cases, and if so, what general directions should the decrees of this court include and what procedures should the court of first instance follow in arriving at the specific terms of more detailed decrees?"

9. OSCAR HANDLIN, *Where Equality Leads, 1956**

The public debate on desegregation has dealt largely with the shadow of the issue rather than with its substance. Not states' rights or federalism or the control of education, but some other,

gnawing fear—rarely expressed—lies behind the violence of the protest against the Supreme Court's decision. The dread lest desegregation open the way to a contaminating race mixture is the

* Oscar Handlin, "Where Equality Leads," *Atlantic Monthly,* CXCVIII (November, 1956), 50-54. Copyright 1956 by Oscar Handlin.

fundamental anxiety that troubles many white Southerners; it is the nightmare that drives men to disregard the law in Tennessee and Texas and Alabama.

It is fruitless to argue details with the victim in the grip of a nightmare. He will not be convinced that his views of race are false, or that his understanding of his own history is faulty. The images that rouse his anxiety, illusory though they be, have their own reality and will not disappear through the simple demonstration of their irrationality. It may help, however, to expose the nightmare for what it is: a figment of the mind needlessly frightened of the future.

The haunting specter of racial amalgamation corresponds to nothing in the world of actuality. It is rather the product of three profound misconceptions. The men frightened by it mistake the meaning of the Supreme Court's decision of 1954. They misjudge the probable consequences of desegregation on both whites and blacks. And, most important, their conjectures as to what results will follow upon more intimate contact between Negroes and other Americans in the schools run counter to all the available evidence.

The significance of the Court's decision will become clear only when it is viewed in the light of the history of segregation since the end of the Civil War. Conscious of the complexity of the problem of emancipation, the men who carried through the Reconstruction programs were anxious not only to free the slave but also to safeguard his future civic rights. That was the purpose of the Fourteenth Amendment, which made the Negroes citizens and which forbade the states to abridge their privileges and immunities or to deny them the equal protection of the law. To prevent any discrimination on the ground of race or previous con-

dition of servitude, Congress enacted a series of civil rights acts, designed to guarantee that equality. As a result, there was a slow but perceptible improvement in the status of the Negro in the first two decades after the peace. That was true in education as in other matters.

Only in the 1880s did segregation emerge as a defined pattern of social behavior. Segregation was not directed simply at the schools; it aimed to create a mode of life that would establish the distinct inferiority of the Negro by setting him apart in every important activity—in the school as elsewhere.

In the face of the new departure the courts were cautious. The mandate of the Fourteenth Amendment was clear, but the supporters of segregation argued that they had no intention of negating it. It was possible, they insisted, to provide separate but equal facilities in education as in transportation and in the other spheres where the two races had contact. In 1896, in the famous case of *Plessy v. Ferguson,* the Supreme Court accepted that contention, assuming that the privileges guaranteed by the Fourteenth Amendment would still be assured under a segregated regime. The decision affirmed the right of the Negroes to equality, but it accepted the argument that equality could be attained through separateness.

When the Supreme Court reviewed this issue in 1954, it had almost sixty years of experience on the basis of which to test the validity of that argument. Its unanimous decision was that the pattern of separate treatment, as it had developed, had not brought equality of treatment to the Negro. This was a question of fact and not of law. No serious observer of the Southern scene has denied that the educational facilities supplied to the black citizens of the Southern states were markedly inferior to those of the whites. Indeed, in many vital respects the Negro's relative situation had actually deteriorated since 1896. Those who had affirmed the compatibility of segregation and equality had not in those decades of opportunity made it work.

The Court was therefore compelled to review the findings of *Plessy v. Ferguson.* If separateness did not bring the equality guaranteed by the Fourteenth Amendment, then the laws establishing the segregated system were unconstitutional, for they fixed the Negro in an inferior place and thus deprived him of the rights guaranteed by the Amendment.

But that was all the Court said. Its findings were purely negative. It did not go on to any positive injunction laying down a line of action to be followed. Instead, it left the various states free gradually to develop a variety of adjustments that would meet the clear constitutional obligation to provide equal treatment for all citizens regardless of race.

Whether the Southern states are to proceed in good conscience to do so is the only question now at issue. Were it considered with entire good will by all Southerners as it is by the majority, a variety of conceivable answers might emerge. For the Supreme Court by no means affirmed, as the extremists sometimes imply, that total, immediate integration was the only acceptable alternative. Men freed of violence and of the emotional hatreds of the past ought to be able to develop a number of different solutions to a problem that varies widely from place to place.

The Court did not hold thus that only a single unified school system would meet the requirements of equal treatment. It did not, for instance, intend to limit or bar private schools, or forms of separation that are purely voluntary. Catholics who choose to

attend parochial schools are still free to do so; and any groups of whites or Negroes who wish to withdraw to educational systems of their own are not depriving themselves or others of constitutional rights, so long as that withdrawal is purely voluntary.

By the same token, the Court did not rule against selection genuinely based on criteria other than race. It will still be possible to send boys to one school, girls to another, to set apart students specially interested in music or science, and to single out the retarded for special treatment. Indeed, the Court's decision insisted only that the element of racial compulsion be removed, and it left a considerable range of alternatives available to those who wish to adapt themselves to the conditions it created. In the years to come, good sense and tolerance will undoubtedly encourage the majority of Americans to explore these alternatives. The results will vary widely according to the local conditions of each community.

Desegregation therefore does not necessarily involve the emergence of a single, all-inclusive, integrated type of school, unless the students and their parents choose to have it do so. The question then arises: what will the parents choose?

On this point, many opponents of desegregation fall into an ingenious contradiction. They are prone to argue that the Southern Negro is content with the situation as it is; only the outside agitator seeks a change. Yet they are violently hostile to the suggestion that the colored man be given freedom of choice, for in their innermost hearts they fear he would demand to be taken into the white school. They thus maintain that the Negro desires no change but would change if he could! They are wrong on both counts. The truth is that the Negro's attitude is not abstract, but a concomitant of the surrounding circumstances. He is totally committed neither to segregation nor to integration. He prefers one or the other as it forms a favorable part of his whole life.

Any parent—white or black—who confronts the choice of a school for his child thinks not in terms of slogans or even of general principles. He thinks rather in terms of very concrete considerations. Which institution will best equip the boy or girl for a desirable career? Where will he be most likely to be happy, to find friends, to acquire an understanding of himself and of his culture? The ultimate answers will vary greatly, for they depend not upon theory, but upon the background of the parents and their situation in the communities in which they live.

Under conditions of genuine equality, Negroes have thus shown the inclination to continue to attend schools preponderantly made up of members of their own race. In 1949, for instance, an Indiana state law prohibited the segregation which theretofore prevailed in some schools, including those of the city of Evansville. The result was not the mass rush to the white schools that some Hoosiers had anticipated. The overwhelming majority of Evansville Negroes—over 90 per cent—continued to attend their own schools. On the other hand, there is no doubt that the colored people of Clinton, Tennessee, or Clay, Kentucky, who braved obloquy, boycott, and the danger of violence to do so, preferred to send their children to integrated schools.

Integration is not an end in itself but a means to an end. Black parents, like white, hope that education will give their boys and girls the best possible preparation for life. They resent the compulsion to attend Negro schools, unequal to the white, that will forever burden their children with handicaps and label them indelibly with the stigma of inferiority. They will not resent schools that are genuinely equal and that bear no imputation of inferiority, no matter what their racial composition. Indeed, under some circumstances, they may actually find their children more comfortable in such schools with those who share a common cultural and social background.

There will necessarily be substantial regional and communal differences in adjustment. In the great metropolitan cities, residential and housing patterns already separate the population along ethnic, social, and economic, as well as racial lines. The schools which draw their students from the homogeneous neighborhoods in which they are situated reflect the composition of the area as a matter of course. Classes in Bronzeville and Harlem are predominantly Negro, just as those in East Boston are Italian and those in Hamtramck are Polish. Only in rare instances are such schools likely to contain a completely mixed and heterogeneous student body. In smaller cities there is less scope for such adjustments. The elementary schools may reflect neighborhood differences. But if there is only one high school in town it will have to accommodate all the students eligible to attend it.

The greatest problem will no doubt exist in rural regions which enjoy a minimum of flexibility. There the segregated school has been least convenient and most expensive; and there it most often produced the types of inferiority that the Supreme Court condemned. It may be that no solution other than integration in the general school system will do justice to the dozen Negro families of Clinton, Tennessee. But the fact that integration is sought there does not mean it will be sought everywhere.

The experience of the colleges has been instructive in this regard. Desegregation began sooner in higher than in elementary education. Yet it has not produced a hegira from the Negro to the white institutions. The Universities of Texas and of North Carolina now admit colored students, but relatively few choose to attend in preference to their own excellent colleges. The consciousness that they are free to choose destroys the imputation of inferiority.

The fact is that there are no grounds for the belief that a mass intermingling of the races would everywhere immediately follow the end of compulsory segregation. On the contrary, all the available evidence sustains the belief that genuine equality and freedom of choice within the latitude of the Court's decision would permit a variety of experiments that could cope with the problem and creatively resolve it.

The inability to act rationally in these matters is grounded in the fear that the new school contacts between blacks and whites will produce a higher degree of racial mixture than in the past. This is the crux of the matter.

Yet there is not a shred of evidence to support the contention that desegregation will hasten amalgamation. There are good grounds for expecting rather that widened equality may retard the trend in that direction.

The assertion that the white race in the United States has maintained its purity through three centuries of history flies completely in the face of the facts. Let us beg the question of whether it is even possible to speak of a pure race; and let us assume that the "whites" are one race and the "blacks" another. Still it is demonstrable that the "blood" of the one group has long since been crossed with that of the other. In the nature of the case, the number of Negroes who have passed into the white group is not ascertainable; estimates range as high as 30,000

a year. Whatever the number, the trend has been substantial since the eighteenth century; and those who have "passed," with their progeny, must form a considerable element of the total population.

The evidence of white strains among the Negroes is more visible. Almost 3,000,000 Americans are mulattoes; and many more, whose skin color is darker, have nevertheless some degree of mixed paternity. Careful studies have shown that between 70 and 90 per cent of the Negroes of the United States have at least one known white ancestor; the number without some such strain in their heritage must be small indeed. Racial intermixture was begun when the slaves were first brought into this country in the North and in the South; it was not prevented by the existence of slavery; nor has the persistence of segregation slowed it down.

The apparent difference between the United States and South America is primarily one of definition and attitude. In the United States, a man is a Negro, whatever his color, if he has any known Negro ancestor. In Brazil, and elsewhere in Latin America, color is determined by the preponderant strain. Thus in the United States a man with one Negro great-grandparent would be colored; in Brazil he would be white. In the United States his marriage to a white would be an intermarriage and would earn the opprobrium of the prejudiced; in Brazil it would not. Otherwise, the difference shrinks to one of degree.

In any case, intermarriage has been a negligible factor in causing race mixture. The law forbids it in many parts of the country; and where it is legal the number of unions so consummated is small. In Northern cities, where such marriages are most likely to occur, they form only between 3 and 5 per cent of those in which Negroes are involved. Expressed in terms of the percentage of white marriages, they would make but an infinitesimal fraction. It is not thus that the blood strains have in the past been crossed.

Furthermore, all of our data indicate that the growth of equality between the races does not increase the rate of intermarriage. There are communities in Ontario, in northern Michigan, and in western Massachusetts where whites have lived side by side with Negroes for more than a hundred years. No segregation there has kept apart the children of the two races. Yet the two groups have nevertheless maintained their identity and separateness. Wherever statistics measure the rate of intermarriage, they deny rather than confirm the fear that equality stimulates intermarriage. In Boston, for instance, the percentage has fallen steadily since 1900 as the position of the Negroes has improved.

This is exactly what might be anticipated in view of the character of American marriage and of the factors that generally influence the choice of partners in it. Concealed in the Southern view is the curious assumption that, given freedom of choice, men and women would tend to select mates of the opposite race, for this, clearly, is a purely voluntary matter; mere propinquity forces no one into love. All the evidence points in the opposite direction. Marriages are usually formed among individuals of common cultural, social, and religious backgrounds—even where race does not intrude. Take a large city high school, where boys and girls of diverse antecedents mix without distinction of race, creed, or national origins. Ten years after graduation, the former students will have sorted themselves out in marriages with the partners closest to themselves in color, religion, and antecedents. This, after all, is a process by which the family is extended across the generations; and those who enter upon it

have in mind not only their own emotions but also the feelings of their parents and relatives as well as of the children who will come of it. In the absence of compelling forces to the contrary, opportunity and inclination will alike lead to marriage within some existing group.

All the scholarly investigations of the intermarriages which have actually occurred confirm this conclusion. Such marriages are most likely to involve the lower social classes and individuals whose own family ties are weak. Generally it is the black man who marries a white woman whose status is inferior to his own. (Many such unions were effected by servicemen abroad.) The white man who takes a black wife is likely to be foreign-born, detached from any group of his own, and without binding social ties. Significantly a large percentage of those who enter upon such unions are divorced or widowed, people whose earlier attempts at marriage had failed.

It is important in this connection to remember that the upper social groups among the Negroes have always frowned upon interracial marriages precisely because these groups, although closest to the whites, were prosperous and stable in their own family life. Frederick Douglass thus lost a good deal of his popularity when he took a white wife; and W. E. B. DuBois, in *Dusk of Dawn,* describes his own mixed emotions as he gave up courting a colored girl because she looked quite white and he feared the inference that he was marrying outside the race.

Does it not follow then that segregation, which established the inferiority of the Negro and prevents him from attaining a stable personal and family life, actually magnifies the incentive to seek the escape of intermarriage? On the other hand, any measure, like desegregation, which widens opportunities and increases the scope of equality also increases the stability of Negro family life, heightens self-respect, and thus indirectly diminishes the incentives toward intermarriage.

It is not surprising, therefore, to find a subtle change in the attitudes of Negroes with the improvement of their status in the past thirty years. There was a time when colored people were so depressed by the sense of their own inferiority that they accepted unquestioningly all the white man's standards. Their own habits and tastes, like their blackness, were inherently degrading; and success and happiness went to those who could most closely model themselves upon the dominant race. There was a premium upon "marrying light" even though within the group, because that most closely approximated the standards of the whites.

With the Negro's achievement of some degree of stability and the restoration of his self-confidence, there has been a significant change, even since Gunnar Myrdal noticed it in 1944. Rejecting the notion of his own inferiority, the Negro has ceased to take the white as the determining model. He has come to value the standards and tastes of his own group and often actually to take pride in his color. Not a few are unwilling to "pass" even though their pigmentation is pale enough to permit them to do so. The girl who holds the cake of soap in the *Ebony* advertisement is black; and she is pretty to those who see her because she is black. The era of the hair straightener is coming to an end. The notion that Negroes are eager to marry whites is a delusion born of the white's own vanity and of his ignorance of the real sentiments of his fellow Americans of another color.

The experience of schools in which segregation has come to an end amply confirms these judgments. The circum-

stances vary widely according to the conditions and traditions of the communities in which the adjustment occurs. In the Southern colleges, Negroes, once admitted, have generally enjoyed a minimum of social contact with white students. Elsewhere the relationship between the races has extended beyond the classroom to the formal social activities conducted under school auspices. But even when the boy and girl of different colors dance together at the senior prom, they do not think of dating. They hesitate, as does the Methodist with the Catholic, because courtship and marriage involve an altogether different order of considerations.

The obsession with the unreal dangers of intermarriage has unfortunately obscured the true source of race mixture in the past and in the present. The white ancestors of the mulattoes and of the Negroes of varying degrees of lightness of skin were not married to blacks. These are the progeny of relationships outside wedlock; and miscegenation, not intermarriage, has, in the United States, been the mode of infusing the black with the white strain in our society. Furthermore, miscegenation under these terms was the direct product of the inferiority of Negro women. Whatever has tended to increase that inferiority has increased the rate of miscegenation. Whatever diminishes it lowers the rate. In that sense, segregation actually is indirectly more conducive to the mixture of races than is desegregation.

Through much of the nineteenth century, white men who kept black concubines suffered no loss of social esteem thereby. Until the Civil War, the women were their property, and no control limited the treatment accorded them. In most of the Southern states miscegenation was no crime, although intermarriage was.

Concubinage began to decline after the Civil War. It hardly exists now. It was extirpated by the liberation of the Negroes, which removed their women from the absolute power of the masters.

Less formal sexual relations between white men and black women, however, were long thereafter tolerated in many parts of the South. They were facilitated by the disorganization of Negro family life and by the simple brute fact that blacks were incapable of protecting their daughters and sisters against the aggressions of those who had once been their masters. The law and the mores were alike acquiescent. There are authentic, if scarcely credible, instances of respectable white businessmen who warned off the Negro preacher who wished to strengthen the morals of the women in his flock.

Insofar as that can be measured, the incidence of interracial sexual intercourse seems also to have declined perceptibly in the last forty years. It has fallen off precisely because the Negro now sees the prospect of leading a decent family life and because he himself has grown in self-respect and in the power to resist. The transformation in the general conception of what the law and the practices of society owe him is the most important element in that change.

If we strengthen the trend toward equality of opportunity and of rights, then we strengthen also the elements of cohesion and order in the Negro's own life. If we weaken that trend and perpetuate his inferiority, then we weaken also the fabric of his family life and leave him a loose, helpless, and potentially disorderly element in our society. Desegregation, which opens doors to full participation in citizenship, will have the former effect. Segregation, our experience has shown us, will have the latter.

In the perspective of centuries, amalgamation may or may not be desirable. The question is unreal and irrelevant. Our problem is immediate; and in the perspective of the next few decades the creation of a school system that segregates none of our children against their will and offers all of them equal treatment can only help us all.

Our democratic society has an abundance of room for a plurality of social types and social groups. If we can but free ourselves of the habit of thinking in terms of the absolutes of total conformity and amalgamation on the one hand and of total separateness and segregation on the other, we shall find our institutions flexible enough to accommodate a variety of solutions among which individuals will be able to make their own personal choices. It was the virute of the Supreme Court to have understood that, and in its decision to have laid a foundation for constructive development in the future. And it is the insistence upon thinking of the nightmare of amalgamation as the only alternative to segregation that is most likely to perpetuate the tensions that all Americans should dread.

10. WILLIAM FAULKNER, *To the Youth of Japan, 1955**

A hundred years ago, my country, the United States, was not one economy and culture, but two of them, so opposed to each other that ninety-five

* Robert A. Jelliffe, *Faulkner at Nagano* (Tokyo: Kenkyusha Ltd. [1956]), pp. 185–88.

years ago they went to war against each other to test which one should prevail. My side, the South, lost that war, the battles of which were fought not on neutral ground in the waste of the ocean, but in our own homes, our gardens, our farms, as if Okinawa and Guadalcanal had been not islands in the distant Pacific but the precincts of Honshu and Hokkaido. Our land, our homes were invaded by a conqueror who remained after we were defeated; we were not only devastated by the battles which we lost, the conqueror spent the next ten years after our defeat and surrender despoiling us of what little war had left. The victors in our war made no effort to rehabilitate and reestablish us in any community of men or of nations.

But all this is past; our country is one now. I believe our country is even stronger because of that old anguish since that very anguish taught us compassion for other peoples whom war had injured. I mention it only to explain and show that Americans from my part of America at least can understand the feeling of the Japanese young people of today that the future offers him nothing but hopelessness, with nothing any more to hold or believe in. Because the young people of my country during those ten years must have said in their turn: "What shall we do now? Where shall we look for the future? Who can tell us what to do, how to hope and believe?"

I would like to think that there was someone there at that time too, to speak to them out of what little experience and knowledge a few more years might have added to what he had, to reassure them that man is tough, that nothing, nothing—war, grief, hopelessness, despair—can last as long as man himself can last; that man himself will prevail over all his anguishes, provided he will make the effort to; make the effort to believe in

man and in hope—to seek not for a mere crutch to lean on, but to stand erect on his own feet by believing in hope and in his own toughness and endurance.

I believe that is the only reason for art—for the music, the poetry, the painting—which man has produced and is still ready to dedicate himself to. That art is the strongest and most durable force man has invented or discovered with which to record the history of his invincible durability and courage beneath disaster, and to postulate the validity of his hope.

I believe it is war and disaster which remind man most that he needs a record of his endurance and toughness. I think that that is why after our own disaster there rose in my country, the South, a resurgence of good writing, writing of a good enough quality that people in other lands began to talk of a "regional" Southern literature until even I, a countryman, have become one of the first names in our literature which the Japanese people want to talk to and listen to.

I believe that something very like that will happen here in Japan within the next few years—that out of your disaster and despair will come a group of writers whom all the world will want to listen to, who will speak not a Japanese truth but a universal truth.

Because man's hope is in man's freedom. The basis of the universal truth which the writers speak is freedom in which to hope and believe, since only in liberty can hope exist—liberty and freedom not given man as a free gift but as a right and a responsibility to be earned if he deserves it, is worthy of it, is willing to work for it by means of courage and sacrifice, and then to defend it always.

And that Freedom must be complete freedom for all men; we must choose now not between color and color nor between kind and kind nor between ideology and ideology. We must choose simply between being slave and being free. Because the day is past now when we can choose a little of each. We cannot choose a freedom established on a hierarchy of freedom, on a caste system of degree of equality like military rank. We think of the world today as being a helpless battleground in which two mighty forces face each other in the form of two irreconcilable ideologies. I do not believe they are two ideologies. I believe that only one of them is an ideology because the other is simply a human belief that no government shall exist immune to the check of the consent of the governed; that only one of them is a political state or ideology, because the other one is simply a mutual state of man mutually believing in mutual liberty, in which politics is merely one more of the clumsy methods to make and hold good that condition in which all men shall be free. A clumsy method, until we have found something better, as most of the mechanics of social democracy creak and rattle. But until we find a better, democracy will do, since man is stronger and tougher and more enduring than even his mistakes and blundering.

11. James Baldwin, *The Search for Identity, 1953*[*]

From all available evidence no black man had ever set foot in this tiny Swiss village before I came. I was told before arriving that I would probably be a "sight" for the village; I took this to mean that people of my complexion were rarely seen in Switzerland, and also that city people are always something of a "sight" outside of the city. It did not occur to me—possibly because I am an American—that there could be people anywhere who had never seen a Negro.

It is a fact which cannot be explained on the basis of the inaccessibility of the village. The village is very high, but it is only four hours from Milan and three hours from Lausanne. It is true that it is virtually unknown. Few people making plans for a holiday would elect to come here. On the other hand, the villagers are able, presumably, to come and go as they please —which they do: to another town at the foot of the mountain, with a population of approximately five thousand, the nearest place to see a movie or go to the bank. In the village there is no movie house, no bank, no library, no theater; very few radios, one jeep, one station wagon; and, at the moment, one typewriter, mine, an invention which the woman next door to me here had never seen. There are about six hundred people living here, all Catholic—I conclude this from the fact that the Catholic church is open all year round, whereas the Protestant chapel, set off on a hill a little removed from the village, is open only in the summertime when the tourists arrive. There are four or five hotels, all closed now, and four or five *bistros,* of which, however, only two do any business during the winter. These two do not do a great deal, for life in the village seems to end around nine or ten o'clock. There are a few stores, butcher, baker, *épicerie,* a hardware store, and a money-changer—who cannot change travelers' checks, but must send them down to the bank, an operation which takes two or three days. There is something called the *Ballet Haus,* closed in the winter and used for God knows what, certainly not ballet, during the summer. There seems to be only one schoolhouse in the village, and this for the quite young children; I suppose this to mean that their older brothers and sisters at some point descend from these mountains in order to complete their education—possibly, again, to the town just below. The landscape is absolutely forbidding, mountains towering on all four sides, ice and snow as far as the eye can reach. In this white wilderness, men and women and children move all day, carrying washing, wood, buckets of milk or water, sometimes skiing on Sunday afternoons. All week long boys and young men are to be seen shoveling snow off the rooftops, or dragging wood down from the forest in sleds.

The village's only real attraction, which explains the tourist season, is the hot spring water. A disquietingly high proportion of these tourists are cripples, or semi-cripples, who come year after year—from other parts of Switzerland, usually—to take the waters. This lends the village, at the height of the season, a rather terrifying air of sanctity, as though it were a lesser Lourdes. There is often something beautiful, there is always something awful, in the spectacle of a person who has lost one of his faculties, a faculty he never questioned until it was gone, and who struggles to recover it. Yet people remain people, on crutches or indeed on deathbeds; and wherever I passed, the first summer I was here, among the native villagers, or among the lame, a wind passed with me—of astonishment, curiosity, amusement, and outrage. That first

summer I stayed two weeks and never intended to return. But I did return in the winter, to work; the village offers, obviously, no distractions whatever and has the further advantage of being extremely cheap. Now it is winter again, a year later, and I am here again. Everyone in the village knows my name, though they scarcely ever use it, knows that I come from America—though, this, apparently, they will never really believe: black men come from Africa—and everyone knows that I am the friend of the son of a woman who was born here, and that I am staying in their chalet. But I remain as much a stranger today as I was the first day I arrived, and the children shout *Neger! Neger!* as I walk along the streets.

It must be admitted that in the beginning I was far too shocked to have any real reaction. In so far as I reacted at all, I reacted by trying to be pleasant—it being a great part of the American Negro's education long before he goes to school) that he must make people "like" him. This smile-and-the-world-smiles-with-you routine worked about as well in this situation as it had in the situation for which it was designed, which is to say that it did not work at all. No one, after all, can be liked whose human weight and complexity cannot be, or has not been, admitted. My smile was simply another unheard-of phenomenon which allowed them to see my teeth—they did not, really, see my smile and I began to think that, should I take to snarling, no one would notice any difference. All of the physical characteristics of the Negro which had caused me, in America, a very different and almost forgotten pain were nothing less than miraculous—or infernal—in the eyes of the village people. Some thought my hair was the color of tar, that it had the texture of wire, or the texture of cotton. It was jocularly suggested that I might let it all grow long and make myself a winter coat. If I sat in the sun for more than five minutes some daring creature was certain to come along and gingerly put his fingers on my hair, as though he were afraid of an electric shock, or put his hand on my hand, astonished that the color did not rub off. In all of this, in which it must be conceded there was yet no suggestion that I was human: I was simply a living wonder.

I knew that they did not mean to be unkind, and I know it now; it is necessary, nevertheless, for me to repeat this to myself each time that I walk out of the chalet. The children who shout *Neger!* have no way of knowing the echoes this sound raises in me. They are brimming with good humor and the more daring swell with pride when I stop to speak with them. Just the same, there are days when I cannot pause and smile, when I have no heart to play with them; when, indeed, I mutter sourly to myself, exactly as I muttered on the streets of a city these children have never seen, when I was no bigger than these children are now: *Your* mother was a *nigger*. Joyce is right about history being a nightmare—but it may be the nightmare from which no one *can* awaken. People are trapped in history and history is trapped in them.

There is a custom in the village—I am told it is repeated in many villages—of "buying" African natives for the purpose of converting them to Christianity. There stands in the church all year round a small box with a slot for money, decorated with a black figurine, and into this box the villagers drop their francs. During the *carnaval* which precedes Lent, two village children have their faces blackened—out of which bloodless darkness their blue eyes shine like ice—and fantastic horsehair wigs are placed on their blond heads; thus disguised, they solicit among the villagers for money for the missionaries in Africa. Between the box in the church and the blackened children, the village "bought" last year six or eight African natives. This was reported to me with pride by the wife of one of the *bistro* owners and I was careful to express astonishment and pleasure at the solicitude shown by the village for the souls of black folks. The *bistro* owner's wife beamed with a pleasure far more genuine than my own and seemed to feel that I might now breathe more easily concerning the souls of at least six of my kinsmen.

I tried not to think of these so lately baptized kinsmen, of the price they themselves would pay, and said nothing about my father, who having taken his own conversion too literally, never, at bottom, forgave the white world (which he described as heathen) for having saddled him with a Christ in whom, to judge at least from their treatment of him, they themselves no longer believed. I thought of white men arriving for the first time in an African village, strangers there, as I am a stranger here, and tried to imagine the astounded populace touching their hair and marveling at the color of their skin. But there is a great difference between being the first white man to be seen by Africans and being the first black man to be seen by whites. The white man takes the astonishment as tribute, for he arrives to conquer and to convert the natives, whose inferiority in relation to himself is not even to be questioned; whereas I, without a thought of conquest, find myself among a people whose culture controls me, has even, in a sense, created me, people who have cost me more in anguish and rage than they will ever know, who yet do not even know of my existence.

The astonishment with which I might have greeted them, should they have stumbled into my African village a few hundred years ago, might have rejoiced their hearts. But the astonishment with which they greet me today can only poison mine.

And this is so despite everything I may do to feel differently, despite my friendly conversations with the *bistro* owner's wife, despite their three-year-old son who has at last become my friend, despite the *saluts* and *bonsoirs* which I exchange with people as I walk, despite the fact that I know that no individual can be taken to task for what history is doing, or has done. I say that the culture of these people controls me—but they can scarcely be held responsible for European culture. America comes out of Europe, but these people have never seen America, nor have most of them seen more of Europe than the hamlet at the foot of their mountain. Yet, they move with an authority which I shall never have, and they regard me, quite rightly, not only as a stranger in their village but as a suspect latecomer, bearing no credentials, to everything they have—however unconsciously—inherited.

For this village, even were it incomparably more remote and incredibly more primitive, is the West, the West onto which I have been so strangely grafted. These people cannot be, from the point of view of power, strangers anywhere in the world: they have made the modern world, in effect, even if they do not know it. The most illiterate among them is related, in a way that I am not, to Dante, Shakespeare, Michelangelo, Aeschylus, Da Vinci, Rembrandt, and Racine; the cathedral at Chartres says something to them which it cannot say to me, as indeed would New York's Empire State Building, should anyone here ever see it. Out of their hymns and dances come Beethoven and Bach. Go back a few centuries and they are in their full glory—but I am in Africa, watching the conquerors arrive.

The rage of the disesteemed is personally fruitless, but it is also absolutely inevitable; this rage, so generally discounted, so little understood even among the people whose daily bread it is, is one of the things that makes history. Rage can only with difficulty, and never entirely, be brought under the domination of the intelligence and is therefore not susceptible to any arguments whatever. This is a fact which ordinary representatives of the *Herrenvolk,* having never felt this rage and being unable to imagine it, quite fail to understand. Also, rage cannot be hidden, it can only be dissembled. This dissembling deludes the thoughtless, and strengthens rage, and adds to rage, contempt. There are, no doubt, as many ways of coping with the resulting complex of tensions as there are black men in the world, but no black man can hope ever to be entirely liberated from this internal warfare—rage, dissembling, and contempt having inevitably accompanied his first realization of the power of white men. What is crucial here is that, since white men represent in the black man's world so heavy a weight, white men have for black men a reality which is far from being reciprocal; and hence all black men have toward all white men an attitude which is designed, really, either to rob the white man of the jewel of his naïveté, or else to make it cost him dear.

The black man insists, by whatever means he finds at his disposal, that the white man cease to regard him as an exotic rarity and recognize him as a human being. This is a very charged and difficult moment, for there is a great deal of will power involved in the white man's naïveté. Most people are not naturally reflective any more than they are naturally malicious, and the white man prefers to keep the black man at a certain human remove because it is easier for him thus to preserve his simplicity and avoid being called to account for crimes committed by his forefathers, or his neighbors. He is inescapably aware, nevertheless, that he is in a better position in the world than black men are, nor can he quite put to death the suspicion that he is hated by black men therefore. He does not wish to be hated, neither does he wish to change places; at this point in his uneasiness he can scarcely avoid having recourse to those legnds which having recourse to those legends which men, the most usual effect of which is that the white man finds himself enmeshed, so to speak, in his own language which describes hell, as well as the attributes which lead one to hell, as being as black as night.

Every legend, moreover, contains its residuum of truth, and the root func tion of language is to control the universe by describing it. It is of quite considerable significance that black men remain, in the imagination, and in overwhelming numbers in fact, beyond the disciplines of salvation; and this despite the fact that the West has been "buying" African natives for centuries. There is, I should hazard, an instantaneous necessity to be divorced from this so visibly unsaved stranger, in whose heart, moreover, one cannot guess what dreams of vengeance are being nourished; and, at the same time, there are few things on earth more attractive than the idea of the unspeakable liberty which is allowed the unredeemed. When, beneath the black mask, a human being begins to make himself felt one cannot escape a certain awful wonder as to what kind of human being it is. What one's imagination makes of other people is dictated, of course, by the laws of one's own personality and

it is one of the ironies of black-white relations that, by means of what the white man imagines the black man to be, the black man is enabled to know who the white man is.

I have said, for example, that I am as much a stranger in this village today as I was the first summer I arrived, but this is not quite true. The villagers wonder less about the texture of my hair than they did then, and wonder rather more about me. And the fact that their wonder now exists on another level is reflected in their attitudes and in their eyes. There are the children who make those delightful, hilarious, sometimes astonishingly grave overtures of friendship in the unpredictable fashion of children; other children, having been taught that the devil is a black man, scream in genuine anguish as I approach. Some of the older women never pass without a friendly greeting, never pass, indeed, if it seems that they will be able to engage me in conversation; other women look down or look away or rather contemptuously smirk. Some of the men drink with me and suggest that I learn how to ski—partly, I gather, because they cannot imagine what I would look like on skis—and want to know if I am married, and ask questions about my *métier*. But some of the men have accused *le sale nègre*—behind my back—of stealing wood and there is already in the eyes of some of them that peculiar, intent, paranoiac malevolence which one sometimes surprises in the eyes of American white men when, out walking with their Sunday girl, they see a Negro male approach.

There is a dreadful abyss between the streets of this village and the streets of the city in which I was born, between the children who shout *Neger!* today and those who shouted *Nigger!* yesterday—the abyss is experience, the American experience. The syllable hurled behind me today expresses, above all, wonder; I am a stranger here. But I am not a stranger in America and the same syllable riding on the American air expresses the war my presence has occasioned in the American soul.

For this village brings home to me this fact: that there was a day, and not really a very distant day, when Americans were scarcely Americans at all but discontented Europeans, facing a great unconquered continent and strolling, say, into a marketplace and seeing black men for the first time. The shock this spectacle afforded is suggested, surely, by the promptness with which they decided that these black men were not really men but cattle. It is true that the necessity on the part of the settlers of the New World of reconciling their moral assumptions with the fact—and the necessity—of slavery enhanced immensely the charm of this idea, and it is also true that this idea expresses, with a truly American bluntness, the attitude which to varying extents all masters have had toward all slaves.

But between all former slaves and slave-owners and the drama which begins for Americans over three hundred years ago at Jamestown, there are at least two differences to be observed. The American Negro slave could not suppose, for one thing, as slaves in past epochs had supposed and often done, that he would ever be able to wrest the power from his master's hands. This was a supposition which the modern era, which was to bring about such vast changes in the aims and dimensions of power, put to death; it only begins, in unprecedented fashion, and with dreadful implications, to be resurrected today. But even had this supposition persisted with undiminished force, the American Negro slave could not have used it to lend his condition dignity, for the reason that this supposition rests on another: that the slave in exile yet remains related to his past, has some means—if only in memory—of revering and sustaining the forms of his former life, is able, in short, to maintain his identity.

This was not the case with the American Negro slave. He is unique among the black men of the world in that his past was taken from him, almost literally, at one blow. One wonders what on earth the first slave found to say to the first dark child he bore. I am told that there are Haitians able to trace their ancestry back to African kings, but any American Negro wishing to go back so far will find his journey through time abruptly arrested by the signature on the bill of sale which served as the entrance paper for his ancestor. At the time—to say nothing of the circumstances—of the enslavement of the captive black man who was to become the American Negro, there was not the remotest possibility that he would ever take power from his master's hands. There was no reason to suppose that his situation would ever change, nor was there, shortly, anything to indicate that his situation had ever been different. It was his necessity, in the words of E. Franklin Frazier, to find a "motive for living under American culture or die." The identity of the American Negro comes out of this extreme situation, and the evolution of this identity was a source of the most intolerable anxiety in the minds and the lives of his masters.

For the history of the American Negro is unique also in this: that the question of his humanity, and of his rights therefore as a human being, became a burning one for several generations of Americans, so burning a question that it ultimately became one of those used to divide the nation. It is out of this argument that the venom of the epithet *Nigger!* is derived. It is an argument which Europe has never had, and hence Europe quite sincerely fails to understand how or why the argument arose in the first place, why its effects are so frequently disastrous and always so unpredictable, why it refuses until today to be entirely settled. Europe's black possessions remained—and do remain—in Europe's colonies, at which remove they represented no threat whatever to European identity. If they posed any problem at all for the European conscience, it was a problem which remained comfortingly abstract: in effect, the black man, *as a man,* did not exist for Europe. But in America, even as a slave, he was an inescapable part of the general social fabric and no American could escape having an attitude toward him. Americans attempt until today to make an abstraction of the Negro, but the very nature of these abstractions reveals the tremendous effects the presence of the Negro has had on the American character.

When one considers the history of the Negro in America it is of the greatest importance to recognize that the moral beliefs of a person, or a people, are never really as tenuous as life—which is not moral—very often causes them to appear; these create for them a frame of reference and a necessary hope, the hope being that when life has done its worst they will be enabled to rise above themselves and to triumph over life. Life would scarcely be bearable if this hope did not exist. Again, even when the worst has been said, to betray a belief is not by any means to have put oneself beyond its power; the betrayal of a belief is not the same thing as ceasing to believe. If this were not so there would be no moral standards in the world at all. Yet one must also recognize that morality is based on ideas and that all ideas are dangerous— dangerous because ideas can only lead

to action and where the action leads no man can say. And dangerous in this respect: that confronted with the impossibility of remaining faithful to one's beliefs, and the equal impossibility of becoming free of them, one can be driven to the most inhuman excesses. The ideas on which American beliefs are based are not, though Americans often think so, ideas which originated in America. They came out of Europe. And the establishment of democracy on the American continent was scarcely as radical a break with the past as was the necessity, which Americans faced, of broadening this concept to include black men.

This was, literally, a hard necessity. It was impossible, for one thing, for Americans to abandon their beliefs, not only because these beliefs alone seemed able to justify the sacrifices they had endured and the blood that they had spilled, but also because these beliefs afforded them their only bulwark against a moral chaos as absolute as the physical chaos of the continent it was their destiny to conquer. But in the situation in which Americans found themselves, these beliefs threatened an idea which, whether or not one likes to think so, is the very warp and woof of the heritage of the West, the idea of white supremacy.

Americans have made themselves notorious by the shrillness and the brutality with which they have insisted on this idea, but they did not invent it; and it has escaped the world's notice that those very excesses of which Americans have been guilty imply a certain, unprecedented uneasiness over the idea's life and power, if not, indeed, the idea's validity. The idea of white supremacy rests simply on the fact that white men are the creators of civilization (the present civilization, which is the only one that matters; all previous civilizations are simply "contributions" to our own) and are therefore civilization's guardians and defenders. Thus it was impossible for Americans to accept the black man as one of themselves, for to do so was to jeopardize their status as white men. But not so to accept him was to deny his human reality, his human weight and complexity, and the strain of denying the overwhelmingly undeniable forced Americans into rationalizations so fantastic that they approached the pathological.

At the root of the American Negro problem is the necessity of the American white man to find a way of living with the Negro in order to be able to live with himself. And the history of this problem can be reduced to the means used by Americans—lynch law and law, segregation and legal acceptance, terrorization and concession—either to come to terms with this necessity, or to find a way around it, or (most usually) to find a way of doing both these things at once. The resulting spectacle, at once foolish and dreadful, led someone to make the quite accurate observation that "the Negro-in-America is a form of insanity which overtakes white men."

In this long battle, a battle by no means finished, the unforeseeable effects of which will be felt by many future generations, the white man's motive was the protection of his identity; the black man was motivated by the need to establish an identity. And despite the terrorization which the Negro in America endured and endures sporadically until today, despite the cruel and totally inescapable ambivalence of his status in his country, the battle for his identity has long ago been won. He is not a visitor to the West, but a citizen there, an American; as American as the Americans who despise him, the Americans who fear him, the Americans who love him

—the Americans who became less than themselves, or rose to be greater than themselves by virtue of the fact that the challenge he represented was inescapable. He is perhaps the only black man in the world whose relationship to white men is more terrible, more subtle, and more meaningful than the relationship of bitter possessed to uncertain possessor. His survival depended, and his development depends, on his ability to turn his peculiar status in the Western world to his own advantage and, it may be, to the very great advantage of that world. It remains for him to fashion out of his experience that which will give him sustenance, and a voice.

The cathedral at Chartres, I have said, says something to the people of this village which it cannot say to me; but it is important to understand that this cathedral says something to me which it cannot say to them. Perhaps they are struck by the power of the spires, the glory of the windows; but they have known God, after all, longer than I have known him, and in a different way, and I am terrified by the slippery bottomless well to be found in the crypt, down which heretics were hurled to death, and by the obscene, inescapable gargoyles jutting out of the stone and seeming to say that God and the devil can never be divorced. I doubt that the villagers think of the devil when they face a cathedral because they have never been identified with the devil. But I must accept the status which myth, if nothing else, gives me in the West before I can hope to change the myth.

Yet, if the American Negro has arrived at his identity by virtue of the absoluteness of this estrangement from his past, American white men still nourish the illusion that there is some means of recovering the European innocence, of returning to a state in which black men do not exist. This is one of the greatest errors Americans can make. The identity they fought so hard to protect has, by virtue of that battle, undergone a change: Americans are as unlike any other white people in the world as it is possible to be. I do not think, for example, that it is too much to suggest that the American vision of the world—which allows so little reality, generally speaking, for any of the darker forces in human life, which tends until today to paint moral issues in glaring black and white—owes a great deal to the battle waged by Americans to maintain between themselves and black men a human separation which could not be bridged. It is only now beginning to be borne in on us—very faintly, it must be admitted, very slowly, and very much against our will—that this vision of the world is dangerously inaccurate; and perfectly useless. For it protects our moral high-mindedness at the terrible expense of weakening our grasp of reality. People who shut their eyes to reality simply invite their own destruction, and anyone who insists on remaining in a state of innocence long after that innocence is dead turns himself into a monster.

The time has come to realize that the inter-racial drama acted out on the American continent has not only created a new black man, it has created a new white man, too. No road whatever will lead Americans back to the simplicity of this European village where white men still have the luxury of looking on me as a stranger. I am not, really, a stranger any longer for any American alive. One of the things that distinguishes Americans from other people is that no other people has ever been so deeply involved in the lives of black men, and vice versa. This fact faced, with all its implications, it can be seen that the history of the American Negro problem is not merely shameful, it is also something of an achievement. For even when the worst has been said, it must also be added that the perpetual challenge posed by this problem was always, somehow, perpetually met. It is precisely this black-white experience which may prove of indispensable value to us in the world we face today. This world is white no longer, and it will never be white again.

IX

****

Freedom and Human Rights

Walter Lippmann

special writer for the New York *Herald Tribune,* is known not only as an editor and journalist, but as a thoughtful critic of American life.

Born in New York City in 1889, Mr. Lippmann graduated from Harvard University in 1910. After a period of free-lancing, he joined the *New Republic,* when it was founded in 1914; and then went to the New York *World,* becoming its editor in 1929.

He was assistant to the Secretary of War, 1917; acted as Colonel E. M. House's secretary in preparing data for the Paris Peace Conference; and was a captain in U.S. Army Military Intelligence during the war.

Mr. Lippmann is the author of many books, including *The Communist World and Ours, The Public Philosophy, Isolation and Alliances,* and *The Cold War.* He is a regular contributor to many magazines.

Walter Lippmann ✳✳✳✳ National Purpose

In a rather special sense Americans have always been a purposeful nation. For the country is settled by the descendants of people who pulled up their roots in the old societies, and crossed the wide ocean for a purpose. Always they came with a sense that they would make for themselves a better life in a new world. They believed that they had new work to do and that all who saw their example would be enlightened and inspired by it.

The bond of American union has not been piety and reverence for the past but a conviction of purpose and of the destiny it would bring for posterity. America has always been not only a country but a dream. There has always been a general and unquestioned belief that here on this soil there would be demonstrated to mankind the blessings of freedom: as the shackles and servitudes of the past were put away, there would arise a great and glorious society.

And so, until very recently at least, we have looked upon it as in the nature of things that for America nothing is finished, that this is a young nation still in the beginnings of its career in the world. From this sense of purpose and of the American destiny we have drawn energy and confidence. Americans have been a nation of exuberant optimists, sniffing the air with a buoyant feeling that it is the early morning and that it is good to be alive. Evil and the perversities of fate and the burdens of mortality were not more than obstacles to be gotten at and overcome.

There were no insoluble human problems. At the worst, there were problems that it might take a generation or two to master. It never occurred to Americans to ask whether they were going to "survive." They had just begun to live. Nor did they worry about the consequences of becoming rich, fat, lazy, self-indulgent, self-centered, and beset with the illusion that the present can be made to last forever. For they were not yet rich and they had to work hard for a living.

If, as so many of us think today, we are now without such a general and inspired sense of national purpose, where shall we look for the cause and the remedy?

The cause of the vacancy is, I believe, this: we have reached a point in our internal development and in our relations with the rest of the world where we have fulfilled and outlived most of what we used to regard as the program of our national purposes.

We are rather like a man whose purpose it is to cross the continent, and having started from New York he has gotten to Chicago. Which way shall he go then? There is more than one way to cross the continent, and until he has chosen which way and then has worked out the intermediate stops, he will remain in Chicago, feeling worried and without a sense of direction and of clear purpose.

As I see it, the American people today are like the man who got to Chicago, and needs a new road map to show him the way from there on.

In this century, the sense of national purpose has been a composite wrought under three innovating Presidents, under Theodore Roosevelt, Woodrow Wilson, and Franklin Roosevelt. They led the country on the road which it has taken for some fifty years—since America emerged as a great power in the world, and since here at home it has become an ever more industrialized and urbanized society.

Time has passed and history has not stood still. The Roosevelt-Wilson-Roosevelt formulae and policies and programs no longer fit the character of the world Americans are now concerned with, the world as it has developed since the second World War. We are now waiting to be shown the way into the future. We are waiting for another innovator in the line of the two Roosevelts and Wilson.

The innovator for whom the country is waiting will not come with a new revelation of the ultimate ends and commitments of our society. The ultimate ends are fixed. They are lasting and they are not disputed. The nation is dedicated to freedom. It is dedicated to the rights of man and to government with the consent of the governed. The innovation, which is now beginning, will be in the means, in the policies and programs and measures, by which the ultimate ends of our free society can be realized in the world today.

My thesis is that to affirm the ultimate ends—as every public man does in almost every speech—is not a substitute for, is not the equivalent of declaring our national purpose and of leading the nation. These affirmations are like standing up when the *Star-Spangled Banner* is played, and then doing nothing further about anything. They beg the question, which is not whither the nation should go, but how it should get there.

The remedy, then, will not be found in the restatement of our ideals, however resounding the rhetoric. It will be found in the innovation of the political formulae, the concrete measures, the practical programs, by which our ideals can be realized in the greatly changed world we now live in. I feel sure that innovators will appear with the new generation that is rising to power. For it is not the nation which is old, but only its leaders.

Broadly speaking, there have been two great epochs in our history, each with its own dominant national purpose. The first epoch extended from the middle of the eighteenth century down through the nineteenth. Beginning with the colonial wars of the eighteenth century and then with the founding of the Republic, the central national purpose of the American people was to open up the continental territory, to consolidate that territory firmly within the American union, and to make the territory invulnerably secure as against all other powers.

In the pursuit of this national purpose, the American colonists fought the French and the Indians. The independent American nation fought the British and the Spanish and the Mexicans and the Indians. It fought a great and terrible Civil War to preserve the union of its territory. Officially, it may be said that this epoch, during which the national purpose was to consolidate the national territory, ended in 1890, when the last of our thirty-seven wars with the Indians was concluded.

After the turn of the century, the original national American purpose having been fulfilled, a new epoch began. It began, we may say, with Theodore Roosevelt's recognition that the United States was no longer a sheltered and semidependent nation but that, having settled the continental territory, it had become one of the great powers. Theodore Roosevelt, who was a far-seeing innovator, saw too that the United States was no longer a rural nation of independent farmers. Increasingly, it was becoming an industrial society inhabited by great corporations which exercised power that often challenged the authority of the established government itself.

The innovation begun by Theodore Roosevelt was carried further by Woodrow Wilson. Wilson accepted reluctantly the burden of our being a great power. When he was forced into the first World War, he attempted to define a national purpose which would reduce the burden of being a great power. He began by declaring that the world must be made safe for democracy and ended by demanding that it become democratic.

This has proved to be an aspiration rather than a purpose and a policy and a program. For had it become a national purpose, the nation would have found itself committed to a perpetual crusade and, therefore, to perpetual war. Nevertheless, the aspiration, though it is quite unrealizable in a very great part of the world, has become an element of the American conscience. Even when we feel compelled to subsidize some of our more primitive clients, the Wilsonian ideology makes us uneasy and embarrassed.

When Franklin Roosevelt became President, he found himself, rather unexpectedly, confronted with the breakdown of the established economic order. Contrary also to his hope and to his expectations, he was confronted with the rise of a new thing in modern history—the monster of the totalitarian state. Necessity became the mother of invention. It demanded the improvisation of a new national purpose in domestic and in foreign affairs. The innovations of Roosevelt were a grand improvisation.

From the New Deal, particularly from the second phase of it when Roosevelt turned from a planned economy to a compensated economy, the present generation of Americans have inherited the formulae of their political actions. They have inherited the compensated economy and the welfare state, and no serious person in either party would now propose to repeal and undo them.

In foreign affairs, the country learned in the second World War that it was no longer one among many great powers but that in fact it was the leading power upon which the whole Western world depended for its security and for leadership. This is a burden and a responsibility and a danger and a demand upon our resources and a test of our wisdom which the first Roosevelt and Wilson never anticipated, which the second Roosevelt began to be aware of from about the middle of the war to the time of his death.

In the fifteen years which have passed since the end of the second World War, the condition of mankind has changed more rapidly and more deeply than in any other period within the experience of the American people. There has been a swift and radical change in the balance of power in the world. Among the masses of the people in the underdeveloped countries there is in all the continents a mounting revolution. There is a radical change in the technology of war and in the technology of industry. There is in the United States and in the advanced countries a great and threatening agglomeration of people in cities. There is a menacing increase in the population of the world. There is a development of the mass media of communication which, because it marks a revolution in popular education and in the presentation of information, and in the very nature of debate and deliberation, is affecting profoundly the assumptions of the older democratic system.

Nobody, it is fair to say, not the most sensitive and knowing among us, is as yet able to realize fully what all these changes mean and to point out specifically and with sufficient clarity how this country should deal with them. But what we do know is that the formulations of national purpose which were made in the first half of this century are now inadequate. In part we have fulfilled them. In part we have outlived them. In part they have become irrelevant because of the unexpected changes in the condition of things. In part they are out of focus. All in all, they do not now mobilize our energies.

Necessity will again be the mother of invention, and in the time to come we shall close the gap which now exists between the new realities and the old formulations of our national purpose. I do not presume to anticipate the innovators for whom we are waiting. But there is already visible, it seems to me, the shape of the land across which the innovators must lead the nation.

Thus, for the first time in American experience we are confronted with a rival power which denies the theory and the practice of our society, and has forced upon us a competition for the leadership of the world. This challenge coincides with the radically new fact that the oceans have ceased to be our ramparts and that our land is no longer invulnerable.

As there is no chance that our immensely formidable rival will disarm or disappear, we shall have to live in the same world with him. We shall have to solve problems which did not exist for Wilson and for the two Roosevelts. We shall have to devise ways of protecting our vital interests, which are world-wide, and we shall have to do this without precipitating an insoluble crisis that would generate an inevitable war. This will demand a deep reformulation of our foreign policy, which has hitherto been, and in a great part still is, addressed to a very different world situation. It will demand a re-education of American opinion, not only when it yearns for the lost innocence of our old isolation but also when it plunges into a new globalism which supposes that we are omnipotent, and averts its eyes from the hard reality of the power of the Communist bloc.

We know, of course, that the challenge is a broad one. The competition is in the whole field of national power. It is a competition not only in military power but in all forms of power, the power to produce wealth and the power to use wealth for education, for the advancement of science, and for public as well as private ends.

On our success in achieving military security by arms and by an astute diplomacy depends our national existence. Our ability to meet the whole challenge depends upon our success in learning to use our growing wealth for something more than more and more private satisfaction. It depends upon our being able and willing to use it for imponderable and immaterial ends, like science and education and the public amenities.

To use increments of our growing wealth wisely and prudently for public and immaterial ends: that is the goal, so I believe, toward which our national purpose will now be directed. We have to pay for defense, and there can be no serious dispute that we must pay for it. But we have also to be able and willing to pay for the things which cannot be consumed privately, such as the education of children, the development of beautiful cities, and the advancement of knowledge. We have to be able and willing to pay for what is, to put it briefly, civilization itself.

At bottom, we have to do these things because they need to be done, because they have to be done, and because they are supremely worth doing. Even if we were not challenged, we would need to do them for their own sake. We would need to do them even if the Soviet Union and the whole Communist orbit were still where they were fifty years ago.

But now we are in fact challenged, and because of that we must do these civilized things, not only to make a better life for ourselves but in order to mobilize the power to avoid a much worse life. Were there no great rival and challenger, we might dawdle along, we might indulge in a growing private affluence while we suffered a declining national greatness. But for us there is no choice but to respond to the challenge, even though this demands that we change many of our cherished dogmas and harden ourselves to a sterner way of life. For our freedom and our system of democratic government are not likely to survive just because we believe in them and enjoy them. We shall have to prove that with them and through them we can satisfy the needs of our people and be equal to the challenge of the time we live in.

Western freedom will not survive just because it is a noble ideal. In the age we live in it will survive if, and I think only if, we can take freedom down with us into the hurly-burly of the competition and conflict and prove that a free society can make itself the good society.

I should like to add a postscript to express a personal feeling about the challenge we face and the response we must make. It is that with all the danger and trouble and worry it causes us, the Soviet challenge may yet prove to have been a blessing in disguise. For without it, what would become of us if we felt that we were invulnerable, if our influence in the world were undisputed, if we had no need to prove that we can rise above a comfortable, tranquil self-satisfaction?

We would, I feel sure, slowly deteriorate and fall apart, having lost our great energies because we did not exercise them, having lost our daring because everything was so warm and so comfortable and so cozy. We would then have entered into the decline which has marked the closing period in the history of so many societies—when they have gotten everything they wanted, when they have come to think that there is no great work to be done, and that the purpose of life is to hold on and stay put. For then the night has come and they doze off and they begin to die.

How Can the Individual Guard His Freedom?

In all the choices that Americans were compelled to make as their institutions developed they were aided by a widely accepted criterion, that the end of social action was the furtherance of the welfare of the individual. That sense of purpose, early in their history, led to the belief that there were matters in which the state was not competent to interfere. Within certain areas the citizen was presumed to be free from any coercion by the state or by other agencies. The exact boundaries of those areas might be subject to dispute, but that there were limits beyond which the government might not trespass was, after the eighteenth century, not subject to dispute.

In our own times, it has often been difficult to define those limits. The challenges to society are so severe, and the concentration of large amounts of power in the hands of the government is so great, that the proper boundaries seem almost to have receded out of sight. In an emergency, scruples tend to be forgotten; and we have unfortunately been living under a succession of emergencies for a half century.

Yet, as Walter Lippmann points out, the nation has been dedicated to freedom, and whatever innovations will be called for in the future ought to be applied in a context that preserves the ultimate ends of a free society. In passing judgment on these matters, it will be helpful to recall some of the considerations that moved earlier Americans in their thinking about the nature of individual rights.

It was significant that at the very start of settlement, the colonists sometimes found it useful to set down statements of their liberties. Under the conditions of the New World, where customary restraints could not be relied upon, explicit formulations were desirable. So, in 1641, the government of the Massachusetts Bay Colony approved a statement of the body of liberties of the people which was intended to guide the operations of their polity (1). This, like the charters of many colonies, spelled out the terms under which the rulers could act, but it did not deny that those terms could themselves be changed by the authorities. In the text, each formulation of a liberty is qualified by the assumption that action by the General Court could modify it.

The further step to the belief that some rights were inherent in the nature of man and not subject to interference even by legitimate use of power came in the eighteenth century. Ultimately that idea would be phrased in concepts of natural rights derived from the Enlightenment. But in America it gained strength from practical conditions that emphasized the freedom of the individual, that minimized convention and habit, and encouraged nonconformity. Benjamin Franklin (1706–90), for instance, seemed to mock accepted moral values in his account of Polly Baker's speech (2). By the same token, a good deal of the force of the rhetoric of Patrick Henry (1736–99) was derived from its appeal to the liberty of the individual (3).

The sentiment that the citizen ought to be free from restraint was particularly strong when it came to matters of conscience. It was fed, no doubt, by the actual religious diversity of the colonies which made any kind of establishment suspect, but also by a deep conviction that beliefs ought to be free from restraint. Thomas Jefferson (1743–1826), who described the actual state of religious liberty in Virginia by the time of the Revolution, was not content with what had been achieved in practice and sought additional constitutional guarantees (4). Such assurance came in the bill of rights attached to the various state and federal constitutions of which Virginia's is representative (5).

In the nineteenth century there were few serious challenges to the liberties thus defined except from Southerners, like Fitzhugh, obsessed by the defense of slavery (see above, pages 427–431). Indeed, the problems of those hundred years were more likely to lead to extreme statements of the rights of the individual, such as those of Henry D. Thoreau (1817–62), whose essay on civil disobedience made each man the ultimate judge of the appropriateness of government action (6). Although few Americans were willing to take that radical position, most retained a deep sympathy for the dissenting individual. They saw, as Mark Twain (1835–1910) did, that conscience might sometimes conflict with the law (7); and with the poet, Emily Dickinson (1830–86), they were unwilling to assent always and totally to the dictates of the majority (8).

The great challenge to individual rights came in the twentieth century during, and shortly after, the two great wars that challenged the security of the

American Republic. The fact that the country was in danger and that major sacrifices were being demanded of all the people seemed to justify a restriction of free expression in the interests of national unity. Censorship, the prosecution of radicals, and the fear of any kind of nonconformity were new features of American life in this period. In his notable dissent, Justice Oliver Wendell Holmes (1841–1935) pointed to the dangers of these measures and suggested a standard by which the government might preserve its own safety and yet leave individual liberties intact (9).

Successive periods of tension, however, led to growing demands for conformity. Given the perils of the times, it seemed dangerous to permit the diversities that had heretofore been tolerated in American society. There were always some who protested. In an eloquent brief, the distinguished constitutional lawyer Louis Marshall (1856–1929) argued that a state law which restrained the operations of parochial schools was unconstitutional (10).

World War II created similar crises and evoked similar defenses of individual liberties. Dean Eugene B. Rostow of the Yale Law School (1913–) pointed out the tragic consequences of the internment of the Japanese-Americans (11). And Supreme Court Justice William O. Douglas (1898–) exposed the dangers of repressive postwar attitudes (12). There thus remains a broad area within which the line is still undefined between the power of the community to act and the right of the individual to his liberty. The definition of that line will surely constitute a major problem of the future.

1. *The Massachusetts Body of Liberties, 1641**

The free fruition of such liberties immunities and privileges as humanity, civility, and Christianity call for as due to every man in his place and proportion without impeachment and infringement hath ever been and ever will be the tranquillity and stability of churches and commonwealths. And the denial or deprival thereof, the disturbance if not the ruin of both.

We hold it therefore, our duty and safety whilst we are about the further establishing of this government to collect and express all such freedoms as for present we foresee may concern us, and our posterity after us, and to ratify them with our solemn consent.

We do therefore this day religiously and unanimously decree and confirm these following rights, liberties and privileges concerning our churches and civil state to be respectively, impartially, and inviolably enjoyed and observed throughout our jurisdiction forever.

1. No man's life shall be taken away, no man's honor or good name shall be stained, no man's person shall be arrested, restrained, banished, dismembered, nor any ways punished, no man shall be deprived of his wife or children, no man's goods or estate shall be taken away from him, nor any way indamaged under color of law or countenance of authority, unless it be by virtue or equity of some

* Massachusetts Historical Society, *Collections,* Third Series, Vol. VIII (1843), pp. 216–37.

express law of the country warranting the same, established by a General Court and sufficiently published, or in case of the defect of a law in any particular case by the word of God. And in capital cases, or in cases concerning dismembering or banishment according to that word to be judged by the General Court.

2. Every person within this jurisdiction, whether inhabitant or foreigner shall enjoy the same justice and law, that is general for the plantation, which we constitute and execute one towards another without partiality or delay.

3. No man shall be urged to take any oath or subscribe any articles, covenants or remonstrance, of a public and civil nature, but such as the General Court hath considered, allowed, and required.

4. No man shall be punished for not appearing at or before any civil assembly, court, council, magistrate, or officer, nor for the omission of any office or service, if he shall be necessarily hindered by any apparent act or providence of God which he could neither foresee nor avoid. . . .

5. No man shall be compelled to any public work or service unless the press be grounded upon some act of the General Court, and have reasonable allowance therefore.

6. No man shall be pressed in person to any office, work, wars or other public service, that is necessarily and sufficiently exempted by any natural or personal impediment, as by want of years, greatness of age, defect of mind, failing of senses, or impotence of limbs.

7. No man shall be compelled to go out of the limits of this plantation upon any offensive wars which this Commonwealth or any of our friends or confederates shall voluntarily undertake. But only upon such vindictive

and defensive wars on our own behalf or the behalf of our friends and confederates as shall be enterprised by the counsel and consent of a Court general, or by authority derived from the same.

8. No man's cattle or goods of what kind soever shall be pressed or taken for any public use or service, unless it be by warrant grounded upon some act of the General Court, nor without such reasonable prices and hire, as the ordinary rates of the country do afford. . . .

9. No monopolies shall be granted or allowed amongst us, but of such new inventions that are profitable to the country, and that for a short time. . . .

11. All persons which are of the age of 21 years, and of right understanding and memories, whether excommunicate or condemned shall have full power and liberty to make their wills and testaments, and other lawful alienations of their lands and estates.

12. Every man whether inhabitant or foreigner, free or not free shall have liberty to come to any public court, council, or town meeting, and either by speech or writing to move any lawful, seasonable, and material question, or to present any necessary motion, complaint, petition, bill or information, whereof that meeting hath proper cognisance, so it be done in convenient time, due order, and respective manner. . . .

16. Every inhabitant that is an householder shall have free fishing and fowling in any great ponds and bays, coves and rivers, so far as the sea ebbs and flows within the precincts of the town where they dwell, unless the free men of the same town or the General Court have otherwise appropriated them, provided that this shall not be extended to give leave to any man to

come upon others' property without their leave.

17. Every man of or within this jurisdiction shall have free liberty, notwithstanding any civil power to remove both himself, and his family at their pleasure out of the same, provided there be no legal impediment to the contrary.

18. No man's person shall be restrained or imprisoned by any authority whatsoever, before the law hath sentenced him thereto, if he can put in sufficient security, bail or mainprise, for his appearance, and good behavior in the meantime, unless it be in crimes capital, and contempts in open court, and in such cases where some express act of court doth allow it. . . .

26. Every man that findeth himself unfit to plead his own cause in any court shall have liberty to employ any man against whom the court doth not except, to help him, provided he give him no fee or reward for his pains. This shall not exempt the party himself from answering such questions in person as the court shall think meet to demand of him. . . .

29. In all actions at law it shall be the liberty of the plaintiff and defendant by mutual consent to choose whether they will be tried by the bench or by a jury, unless it be where the law upon just reason hath otherwise determined. The like liberty shall be granted to all persons in criminal cases. . . .

33. No man's person shall be arrested, or imprisoned upon execution or judgment for any debt or fine, if the law can find competent means of satisfaction otherwise from his estate, and if not his person may be arrested and imprisoned where he shall be kept at his own charge, not the plaintiff's till satisfaction be made, unless the court that had cognizance of the cause or some superior court shall otherwise provide. . . .

42. No man shall be twice sentenced by civil justice for one and the same crime, offense, or trespass.

43. No man shall be beaten with above 40 stripes, nor shall any true gentleman, nor any man equal to a gentleman be punished with whipping, unless his crime be very shameful, and his course of life vicious and profligate. . . .

45. No man shall be forced by torture to confess any crime against himself nor any other unless it be in some capital case, where he is first fully convicted by clear and sufficient evidence to be guilty, after which if the cause be of that nature, that it is very apparent there be other conspirators, or confederates with him, then he may be tortured, yet not with such tortures as be barbarous and inhumane. . . .

58. Civil authority hath power and liberty to see the peace, ordinances and rules of Christ observed in every church according to his word. So it be done in a civil and not in an ecclesiastical way.

59. Civil authority hath power and liberty to deal with any church member in a way of civil justice, notwithstanding any church relation, office or interest.

60. No church censure shall degrade or depose any man from any civil dignity, office, or authority he shall have in the commonwealth. . . .

62. Any shire or town shall have liberty to choose their deputies whom and where they please for the General Court. So be it they be free men, and have taken their oath of fealty, and inhabiting in this jurisdiction. . . .

67. It is the constant liberty of the free men of this plantation to choose yearly at the Court of Election out of the freemen all the general officers of this jurisdiction. If they please to discharge them at the day of election

by way of vote. They may do it without showing cause. But if at any other General Court, we hold it due justice, that the reasons thereof be alleged and proved. By general officers we mean, our governor, deputy governor, assistants, treasurer, general of our wars. And our admiral at sea, and such as are or hereafter may be of the like general nature.

68. It is the liberty of the freemen to choose such deputies for the General Court out of themselves, either in their own towns or elsewhere as they judge fittest. And because we cannot foresee what variety and weight of occasions may fall into future consideration, and what counsels we may stand in need of, we decree. That the deputies (to attend the General Court in the behalf of the country) shall not any time be stated or enacted, but from Court to Court, or at the most but for one year, that the country may have an annual liberty to do in that case what is most behoofeful for the best welfare thereof.

69. No General Court shall be dissolved or adjourned without the consent of the major part thereof. . . .

77. In all cases wherein any freeman is to give his vote, be it in point of election, making constitutions and orders or passing sentence in any case of judicature or the like, if he cannot see reason to give it positively one way or another, he shall have liberty to be silent, and not pressed to a determined vote.

78. The general or public treasure or any part thereof shall never be expended but by the appointment of a General Court, nor any shire treasure, but by the appointment of the freemen thereof, nor any town treasure but by the freemen of that township. . . .

89. If any people of other nations professing the true Christian religion shall flee to us from the tyranny or oppression of their persecutors, or from famine, wars, or the like necessary and compulsory cause, they shall be entertained and succored amongst us, according to that power and prudence, god shall give us. . . .

91. There shall never be any bond slavery, villinage or captivity amongst us unless it be lawful captives taken in just wars, and such strangers as willingly sell themselves or are sold to us. And these shall have all the liberties and Christian usages which the law of god established in Israel concerning such persons doth morally require. This exempts none from servitude who shall be judged thereto by authority. . . .

94. *Capital Laws*

(1) If any man after legal conviction shall have or worship any other god, but the lord god, he shall be put to death.

(2) If any man or woman be a witch, (that is hath or consulteth with a familiar spirit,) they shall be put to death.

(3) If any person shall blaspheme the name of god, the father, Son or Holy Ghost, with direct, express, presumptuous or high handed blasphemy, or shall curse god in the like manner, he shall be put to death. . . .

(12) If any man shall conspire and attempt any invasion, insurrection, or public rebellion against our commonwealth, or shall endeavor to surprise any town or towns, fort or forts therein, or shall treacherously and perfidiously attempt the alteration and subversion of our frame of polity or government fundamentally, he shall be put to death.

95. *A Declaration of the Liberties the Lord Jesus hath given to the Churches.*

(1) All the people of god within this jurisdiction who are not in a church way, and be orthodox in judgment, and not scandalous in life,

shall have full liberty to gather themselves into a church estate. Provided they do it in a Christian way, with due observation of the rules of Christ revealed in his word.

(2) Every church hath full liberty to exercise all the ordinances of god, according to the rules of scripture.

(3) Every church hath free liberty of election and ordination of all their officers from time to time, provided they be able, pious and orthodox.

(4) Every church hath free liberty of admission, recommendation, dismission, and expulsion, or deposal of their officers, and members, upon due cause, with free exercise of the discipline and censures of Christ according to the rules of his word.

2. Benjamin Franklin, *Polly Baker's Speech, 1747* *

The Speech of Miss Polly Baker before a Court of Judicature, at Connecticut near Boston in New England; where she was prosecuted the fifth time, for having a Bastard Child: Which influenced the Court to dispense with her Punishment, and which induced one of her Judges to marry her the next Day—by whom she had fifteen Children.

"May it please the honourable bench to indulge me in a few words: I am a poor, unhappy woman, who have no money to fee lawyers to plead for me, being hard put to it to get a living. I shall not trouble your honours with long speeches; for I have not the presumption to expect that you may, by any means, be prevailed on to deviate in your Sentence from the law, in my favour. All I humbly hope is, that your honours would charitably move the governor's goodness on my behalf, that my fine may be remitted. This is the fifth time, gentlemen, that I have been dragg'd before your court on the same account; twice I have paid heavy fines, and twice have been brought to publick punishment, for want of money to pay those fines. This may have been agreeable to the laws, and I don't dispute it; but since laws are sometimes unreasonable in themselves, and therefore repealed; and others bear too hard on the subject in particular circumstances, and therefore there is left a power somewhere to dispense with the execution of them; I take the liberty to say, that I think this law, by which I am punished, both unreasonable in itself, and particularly severe with regard to me, who have always lived an inoffensive life in the neighbourhood where I was born, and defy my enemies (if I have any) to say I ever wrong'd any man, woman, or child. Abstracted from the law, I cannot conceive (may it please your honours) what the nature of my offense is. I have brought five fine children into the world, at the risque of my life; I have maintain'd them well by my own industry, without burthening the township, and would have done it better, if it had not been for the heavy charges and fines I have paid. Can it be a crime (in the nature of things, I mean) to add to the king's subjects, in a new country, that really wants people? I own it, I should think it rather a praiseworthy than a punishable action. I have debauched

* Benjamin Franklin, *Writings* (A. H. Smyth, ed.; New York, 1905), II, 463–67.

no other woman's husband, nor enticed any other youth; these things I never was charg'd with; nor has any one the least cause of complaint against me, unless, perhaps, the ministers of justice, because I have had children without being married, by which they have missed a wedding fee. But can this be a fault of mine? I appeal to your honours. You are pleased to allow I don't want sense; but I must be stupified to the last degree, not to prefer the honourable state of wedlock to the condition I have lived in. I always was, and still am willing to enter into it; and doubt not my behaving well in it, having all the industry, frugality, fertility, and skill in economy appertaining to a good wife's character. I defy any one to say I ever refused an offer of that sort: on the contrary, I readily consented to the only proposal of marriage that ever was made me, which was when I was a virgin, but too easily confiding in the person's sincerity that made it, I unhappily lost my honour by trusting to his; for he got me with child, and then forsook me.

"That very person, you all know, he is now become a magistrate of this country; and I had hopes he would have appeared this day on the bench, and have endeavoured to moderate the Court in my favour; then I should have scorn'd to have mentioned it; but I must now complain of it, as unjust and unequal, that my betrayer and undoer, the first cause of all my faults and miscarriages (if they must be deemed such), should be advanced to honour and power in this government that punishes my misfortunes with stripes and infamy. I should be told, 'tis like, that were there no act of Assembly in the case, the precepts of religion are violated by my transgressions. If mine is a religious offense, leave it to religious punishments. You

have already excluded me from the comforts of your church communion. Is not that sufficient? You believe I have offended heaven, and must suffer eternal fire: Will not that be sufficient? What need is there then of your additional fines and whipping? I own I do not think as you do, for, if I thought what you call a sin was really such, I could not presumptuously commit it. But, how can it be believed that heaven is angry at my having children, when to the little done by me towards it, God has been pleased to add his divine skill and admirable workmanship in the formation of their bodies, and crowned the whole by furnishing them with rational and immortal souls?

"Forgive me, gentlemen, if I talk a little extravagantly on these matters; I am no divine, but if you, gentlemen, must be making laws, do not turn natural and useful actions into crimes by your prohibitions. But take into your wise consideration the great and growing number of batchelors in the country, many of whom, from the mean fear of the expences of a family, have never sincerely and honourably courted a woman in their lives; and by their manner of living leave unproduced (which is little better than murder) hundreds of their posterity to the thousandth generation. Is not this a greater offense against the publick good than mine? Compel them, then, by law, either to marriage, or to pay double the fine of fornication every year. What must poor young women do, whom customs and nature forbid to solicit the men, and who cannot force themselves upon husbands, when the laws take no care to provide them any, and yet severely punish them if they do their duty without them; the duty of the first and great command of nature and nature's God, *encrease and multiply;* a duty, from the steady performance of which nothing has been able to deter me, but for its sake I have hazarded the loss of the publick esteem, and have frequently endured publick disgrace and punishment; and therefore ought, in my humble opinion, instead of a whipping, to have a statue erected to my memory."

3. PATRICK HENRY, *Liberty or Death, 1775* *

Mr. President, it is natural to man to indulge in the illusions of hope. We are apt to shut our eyes against a painful truth and listen to the song of that syren, till she transforms us into beasts. Is this the part of wise men, engaged in a great and arduous struggle for liberty? Are we disposed to be of the number of those, who having eyes, see not, and having ears, hear not, the things which so nearly concern their temporal salvation? For my part, whatever anguish of spirit it may cost, I am willing to know the whole truth; to know the worst, and to provide for it.

I have but one lamp by which my feet are guided; and that is the lamp of experience. I know of no way of judging of the future but by the past. And judging by the past, I wish to know what there has been in the conduct of the British ministry for the last ten years, to justify those hopes with which gentlemen have been pleased to solace themselves and the house? Is it that insidious smile with which our petition has been lately received? Trust it not, sir; it will prove a snare to your feet. Suffer not yourselves to be betrayed with a kiss. Ask yourselves how this gracious reception of our petition comports with those warlike preparations which cover our waters and darken our land. Are fleets and armies necessary to a work of love and reconciliation? Have we shown ourselves so unwilling to be reconciled, that force must be called in to win back our love? Let us not deceive ourselves, sir. These are the implements of war and subjugation, the last arguments to which kings resort.

I ask gentlemen, sir, what means this martial array, if its purpose be not to force us to submission? Can gentlemen assign any other possible motive for it? Has Great Britain any enemy in this quarter of the world, to call for all this accumulation of navies and armies? No, sir, she has none. They are meant for us; they can be meant for no other. They are sent over to bind and rivet upon us those chains, which the British ministry have been so long forging. And what have we to oppose to them? Shall we try argument? Sir, we have been trying that for the last ten years. Have we any thing new to offer upon the subject? Nothing. We have held the subject up in every light of which it is capable; but it has been all in vain. Shall we resort to entreaty and humble supplication? What terms shall we find, which have not been already exhausted? Let us not, I beseech you, sir, deceive ourselves longer. Sir, we have done every thing that could be done, to avert the storm which is now coming on. We have petitioned, we have remonstrated, we have supplicated, we have prostrated ourselves before the throne, and have implored its interposition to arrest the tyrannical hands of the ministry and parliament. Our petitions have been slighted; our

* Patrick Henry, *Life, Correspondence and Speeches* (W. W. Henry, ed.; New York, 1891), I, 262–66.

remonstrances have produced additional violence and insult; our supplications have been disregarded; and we have been spurned, with contempt, from the foot of the throne. In vain, after these things, may we indulge the fond hope of peace and reconciliation. There is no longer any room for hope. If we wish to be free, if we mean to preserve inviolate those inestimable privileges for which we have been so long contending, if we mean not basely to abandon the noble struggle in which we have been so long engaged, and which we have pledged ourselves never to abandon, until the glorious object of our contest shall be obtained, we must fight! —I repeat it, sir, we must fight!! An appeal to arms and to the God of Hosts is all that is left us!

They tell us, sir, that we are weak, unable to cope with so formidable an adversary. But when shall we be stronger? Will it be the next week or the next year? Will it be when we are totally disarmed, and when a British guard shall be stationed in every house? Shall we gather strength by irresolution and inaction? Shall we acquire the means of effectual resistance by lying supinely on our backs, and hugging the delusive phantom of hope, until our enemies shall have bound us hand and foot? Sir, we are not weak, if we make a proper use of those means which the God of nature hath placed in our power. Three millions of people, armed in the holy cause of liberty, and in such a country as that which we possess, are invincible by any force which our enemy can send against us. Besides, sir, we shall not fight our battles alone. There is a just God who presides over the destinies of nations, and who will raise up friends to fight our battles for us. The battle, sir, is not to the strong alone; it is to the vigilant, the active, the brave. Besides, sir, we have no election. If we were base enough to desire it, it is now too late to retire from the contest. There is no retreat, but in submission and slavery! Our chains are forged. Their clanking may be heard on the plains of Boston! The war is inevitable—and let it come!! I repeat it, sir, let it come!!!

It is in vain, sir, to extenuate the matter. Gentlemen may cry, peace, peace—but there is no peace. The war is actually begun! The next gale that sweeps from the north will bring to our ears the clash of resounding arms! Our brethren are already in the field! Why stand we here idle? What is it that gentlemen wish? What should they have? Is life so dear, or peace so sweet, as to be purchased at the price of chains and slavery? Forbid it, Almighty God! I know not what course others may take; but as for me, give me liberty, or give me death!

4. THOMAS JEFFERSON, *Religious Freedom in Virginia, 1782**

The Anglicans retained full possession of the country about a century. Other opinions began then to creep in, and the great care of the government to support their own church, having begotten an equal degree of indolence in its clergy, two-thirds of the people had become dissenters at

* Thomas Jefferson, "Notes on Virginia," *Writings* (Paul L. Ford, ed.; New York, 1894), III, 262–68.

the commencement of the present revolution. The laws indeed were still oppressive on them, but the spirit of the one party had subsided into moderation, and of the other had risen to a degree of determination which commanded respect.

The present state of our laws on the subject of religion is this. The convention of May, 1776, in their declaration of rights, declared it to be a truth, and a natural right, that the exercise of religion should be free; but when they proceeded to form on that declaration the ordinance of government, instead of taking up every principle declared in the Bill of Rights, and guarding it by legislative sanction, they passed over that which asserted our religious rights, leaving them as they found them. The same convention, however, when they met as a member of the general assembly in October, 1776, repealed all *acts of Parliament* which had rendered criminal the maintaining any opinions in matters of religion, the forbearing to repair to church, and the exercising any mode of worship; and suspended the laws giving salaries to the clergy, which suspension was made perpetual in October, 1779. Statutory oppressions in religion being thus wiped away, we remain at present under those only imposed by the common law or by our own acts of assembly. . . .

Our rulers can have authority over such natural rights only as we have submitted to them. The rights of conscience we never submitted, we could not submit. We are answerable for them to our God. The legitimate powers of government extend to such acts only as are injurious to others. But it does me no injury for my neighbor to say there are twenty gods or no god. It neither picks my pocket nor breaks my leg. If it be said, his testimony in a court of justice cannot be relied on, reject it then, and be the

stigma on him. Constraint may make him worse by making him a hypocrite, but it will never make him a truer man. It may fix him obstinately in his errors but will not cure them. Reason and free inquiry are the only effectual agents against error. Give a loose to them, they will support the true religion, by bringing every false one to their tribunal, to the test of their investigation. They are the natural enemies of error and of error only. Had not the Roman government permitted free inquiry, Christianity could never have been introduced. Had not free inquiry been indulged, at the era of the Reformation, the corruptions of Christianity could not have been purged away. If it be restrained now, the present corruptions will be protected, and new ones encouraged. Was the government to prescribe to us our medicine and diet, our bodies would be in such keeping as our souls are now. Thus in France the emetic was once forbidden as a medicine, and the potato as an article of food. Government is just as infallible, too, when it fixes systems in physics. Galileo was sent to the Inquisition for affirming that the earth was a sphere; the government had declared it to be as flat as a trencher, and Galileo was obliged to abjure his error. This error however at length prevailed, the earth became a globe, and Descartes declared it was whirled round its axis by a vortex. The government in which he lived was wise enough to see that this was no question of civil jurisdiction, or we should all have been involved by authority in vortices. In fact, the vortices have been exploded, and the Newtonian principle of gravitation is now more firmly established, on the basis of reason, than it would be were the government to step in and to make it an article of necessary faith. Reason and experiment have been indulged, and error has fled before them. It is error alone which needs the support of government. Truth can stand by itself. Subject opinion to coercion; whom will you make your inquisitors? Fallible men; men governed by bad passions, by private as well as public reasons. And why subject it to coercion? To produce uniformity. But is uniformity of opinion desirable? No more than of face and stature. Introduce the bed of Procrustes then, and, as there is danger that the large men may beat the small, make us all of a size, by lopping the former and stretching the latter. Difference of opinion is advantageous in religion. The several sects preform the office of a *Censor morum* over each other. Is uniformity attainable? Millions of innocent men, women, and children, since the introduction of Christianity, have been burned, tortured, fined, imprisoned; yet we have not advanced one inch toward uniformity. What has been the effect of coercion? To make one half the world fools, and the other half hypocrites. To support roguery and error all over the earth. Let us reflect that it is inhabited by a thousand millions of people. That these profess probably a thousand different systems of religion. That ours is but one of that thousand. That if there be but one right, and ours that one, we should wish to see the 999 wandering sects gathered into the fold of truth. But against such a majority we cannot effect this by force. Reason and persuasion are the only practicable instruments. To make way for these, free inquiry must be indulged; and how can we wish others to indulge it while we refuse it ourselves. But every state, says an inquisitor, has established some religion. No two, say I, have established the same. Is this a proof of the infallibility of establishments? Our sister-states of Pennsylvania and New York, however, have long subsisted without any establishment at all. The experiment was new and doubtful when they made it. It has answered beyond conception. They flourish infinitely. Religion is well supported; of various kinds, indeed, but all good enough; all sufficient to preserve peace and order; or if a sect arises whose tenets would subvert morals, good sense has fair play and reasons and laughs it out of doors without suffering the state to be troubled with it. They do not hang more malefactors than we do. They are not more disturbed with religious dissensions. On the contrary, their harmony is unparalleled and can be ascribed to nothing but their unbounded tolerance, because there is no other circumstance in which they differ from every nation on earth. They have made the happy discovery that the way to silence religious disputes is to take no notice of them. Let us too give this experiment fair play and get rid, while we may, of those tyrannical laws. It is true, we are as yet secured against them by the spirit of the times. I doubt whether the people of this country would suffer an execution for heresy or a three years' imprisonment for not comprehending the mysteries of the Trinity. But is the spirit of the people an infallible, a permanent reliance? Is it government? Is this the kind of protection we receive in return for the rights we give up? Besides, the spirit of the times may alter, will alter. Our rulers will become corrupt, our people careless. A single zealot may commence persecutor, and better men be his victims. It can never be too often repeated that the time for fixing every essential right on a legal basis is while our rulers are honest and ourselves united. From the conclusion of this war we shall be going downhill. It will not then be necessary to resort every moment to the people for support. They will be forgotten, therefore, and their rights disregarded. They will forget themselves, but in the sole faculty of making money, and will never think of uniting to effect a due respect for their rights. The shackles, therefore, which shall not be knocked off at the conclusion of this war will remain on us long, will be made heavier and heavier, till our rights shall revive or expire in a convulsion.

5. *The Virginia Bill of Rights, 1776**

SECTION 1. That all men are by nature equally free and independent, and have certain inherent rights, of which, when they enter into a state of society, they cannot, by any compact, deprive or divest their posterity; namely, the enjoyment of life and liberty, with the means of acquiring and possessing property, and pursuing and obtaining happiness and safety.

SEC. 2. That all power is vested in, and consequently derived from, the people; that magistrates are their trustees and servants, and at all times amenable to them.

SEC. 3. That government is, or ought to be, instituted for the common benefit, protection, and security of the people, nation, or community; of all the various modes and forms of government, that is best which is capable of producing the greatest degree of happiness and safety, and is most effectually secured against the danger of maladministration; and that, when any government shall be found inadequate or contrary to these purposes, a majority of the community hath an indubitable, inalienable, and indefeasible right to reform, alter, or abolish it, in such manner as shall be judged most conducive to the public weal.

SEC. 4. That no man, or set of men, are entitled to exclusive or separate emoluments or privileges from the community, but in consideration of public services; which, not being descendible, neither ought the offices of magistrate, legislator, or judge to be hereditary.

SEC. 5. That the legislative and executive powers of the State should be separate and distinct from the judiciary; and that the members of the two first may be restrained from oppression, by feeling and participating the burdens of the people, they should at fixed periods, be reduced to a private station . . . and the vacancies be supplied by frequent, certain, and regular elections. . . .

SEC. 6. That elections of members to serve as representatives of the people, in assembly, ought to be free; and that all men, having sufficient evidence of permanent common interest with, and attachment to, the community, have the right of suffrage. . . .

SEC. 7. That all power of suspending laws, or the execution of laws, by any authority, without consent of the representatives of the people, is injurious to their rights, and ought not to be exercised.

SEC. 8. That in all capital or criminal prosecutions a man hath a right to demand the cause and nature of his accusation, to be confronted with the accusers and witnesses, to call for evidence in his favor, and to a speedy trial by an impartial jury . . . ; nor can he be compelled to give evidence against himself; that no man be de-

* Poore, *Federal and State Constitutions*, II, 1908–9.

prived of his liberty, except by the law of the land or the judgment of his peers.

SEC. 9. That excessive bail ought not to be required, nor excessive fines imposed, nor cruel and unusual punishments inflicted.

SEC. 10. That general warrants, whereby an officer or messenger may be commanded to search suspected places without evidence of a fact committed, or to seize any person or persons not named, or whose offense is not particularly described and supported by evidence, are grievous and oppressive, and ought not to be granted.

SEC. 11. That in controversies respecting property, and in suits between man and man, the ancient trial by jury is preferable to any other. . . .

SEC. 12. That the freedom of the press is one of the great bulwarks of liberty, and can never be restrained but by despotic governments.

SEC. 13. That a well-regulated militia . . . is the proper . . . defense of a free state; that standing armies, in time of peace, should be avoided, as dangerous to liberty; and that in all cases the military should be under strict subordination to, and governed by, the civil power. . . .

SEC. 16. That religion, or the duty which we owe to our Creator, and the manner of discharging it, can be directed only by reason and conviction, not by force or violence; and therefore all men are equally entitled to the free exercise of religion, according to the dictates of conscience; and that it is the mutual duty of all to practice Christian forebearance, love, and charity towards each other.

6. HENRY D. THOREAU, *On Civil Disobedience, 1849**

I heartily accept the motto,—"That government is best which governs least"; and I should like to see it acted up to more readily and systematically. Carried out, it finally amounts to this, which also I believe,—"That government is best which governs not at all"; and when men are prepared for it, that will be the kind of government which they will have. Government is at best but an expedient; but most governments are usually, and all governments are sometimes, inexpedient. The objections which have been brought against a standing army, and they are many and weighty, and deserve to prevail, may also at last be brought against a standing government. The standing army is only an arm of the standing government. The government itself, which is only the mode which the people have chosen to execute their will, is equally liable to be abused and perverted before the people can act through it. Witness the present Mexican war, the work of comparatively a few individuals using the standing government as their tool; for, in the outset, the people would not have consented to this measure.

This American government,—what is it but a tradition, though a recent one, endeavoring to transmit itself unimpaired to posterity, but each instant losing some of its integrity? It has not the vitality and force of a single living man; for a single man can bend it to his will. It is a sort of wooden gun to

* H. D. Thoreau, "Resistance to Civil Government," *Aesthetic Papers* (Elizabeth P. Peabody, ed.; Boston, 1849), pp. 189–211.

the people themselves; and, if ever they should use it in earnest as a real one against each other, it will surely split. But it is not the less necessary for this; for the people must have some complicated machinery or other, and hear its din, to satisfy that idea of government which they have. Governments show thus how successfully men can be imposed on, even impose on themselves, for their own advantage. It is excellent, we must all allow; yet this government never of itself furthered any enterprise, but by the alacrity with which it got out of its way. *It* does not keep the country free. *It* does not settle the West. *It* does not educate. The character inherent in the American people has done all that has been accomplished; and it would have done somewhat more, if the government had not sometimes got in its way. For government is an expedient by which men would fain succeed in letting one another alone; and, as has been said, when it is most expedient, the governed are most let alone by it. Trade and commerce, if they were not made of India rubber, would never manage to bounce over the obstacles which legislators are continually putting in their way; and, if one were to judge these men wholly by the effects of their actions, and not partly by their intentions, they would deserve to be classed and punished with those mischievous persons who put obstructions on the railroads.

But, to speak practically and as a citizen, unlike those who call themselves no-government men, I ask for, not at once no government, but *at once* a better government. Let every man make known what kind of government would command his respect, and that will be one step toward obtaining it.

After all, the practical reason why, when the power is once in the hands of the people, a majority are permitted, and for a long period continue, to rule, is not because they are most likely to be in the right, nor because this seems fairest to the minority, but because they are physically the strongest. But a government in which the majority rule in all cases cannot be based on justice, even as far as men understand it. Can there not be a government in which majorities do not virtually decide right and wrong, but conscience?—in which majorities decide only those questions to which the rule of expediency is applicable? Must the citizen ever for a moment, or in the least degree, resign his conscience to the legislator? Why has every man a conscience, then? I think that we should be men first, and subjects afterward. It is not desirable to cultivate a respect for the law, so much as for the right. The only obligation which I have a right to assume, is to do at any time what I think right. It is truly enough said, that a corporation has no conscience; but a corporation of conscientious men is a corporation *with* a conscience. Law never made men a whit more just; and, by means of their respect for it, even the well-disposed are daily made the agents of injustice. A common and natural result of an undue respect for law is, that you may see a file of soldiers, colonel, captain, corporal, privates, powder-monkeys and all, marching in admirable order over hill and dale to the wars, against their wills, aye, against their common sense and consciences, which makes it very steep marching indeed, and produces a palpitation of the heart. They have no doubt that it is a damnable business in which they are concerned; they are all peaceably inclined. Now, what are they? Men at all? or small moveable forts and magazines, at the service of some unscrupulous man in power? . . .

The mass of men serve the State

thus, not as men mainly, but as machines, with their bodies. They are the standing army, and the militia, jailers, constables, *posse comitatus*, &c. In most cases there is no free exercise whatever of the judgment or of the moral sense; but they put themselves on a level with wood and earth and stones; and wooden men can perhaps be manufactured that will serve the purpose as well. Such command no more respect than men of straw, or a lump of dirt. They have the same sort of worth only as horses and dogs. Yet such as these even are commonly esteemed good citizens. Others, as most legislators, politicians, lawyers, ministers, and officeholders, serve the State chiefly with their heads; and, as they rarely make any moral distinctions, they are as likely to serve the devil, without intending it, as God. A very few, as heroes, patriots, martyrs, reformers in the great sense, and *men,* serve the State with their consciences also, and so necessarily resist it for the most part; and they are commonly treated by it as enemies. . . .

How does it become a man to behave toward this American government to-day? I answer that he cannot without disgrace be associated with it. I cannot for an instant recognize that political organization as *my* government which is the *slave's* government also.

All men recognize the right of revolution; that is, the right to refuse allegiance to and to resist the government, when its tyranny or its inefficiency are great and unendurable. But almost all say that such is not the case now. But such was the case, they think, in the Revolution of '75. If one were to tell me that this was a bad government because it taxed certain foreign commodities brought to its ports, it is most probable that I should not make an ado about it, for I can do without them: all machines have their friction; and possibly this does enough good to counterbalance the evil. At any rate, it is a great evil to make a stir about it. But when the friction comes to have its machine, and oppression and robbery are organized, I say, let us not have such a machine any longer. In other words, when a sixth of the population of a nation which has undertaken to be the refuge of liberty are slaves, and a whole country is unjustly overrun and conquered by a foreign army, and subjected to military law, I think that it is not too soon for honest men to rebel and revolutionize. What makes this duty the more urgent is the fact that the country so overrun is not our own, but ours is the invading army. . . .

Does any one think that Massachusetts does exactly what is right at the present crisis? . . . Practically speaking, the opponents to a reform in Massachusetts are not a hundred thousand politicians at the South, but a hundred thousand merchants and farmers here, who are more interested in commerce and agriculture than they are in humanity, and are not prepared to do justice to the slave and to Mexico, *cost what it may.* I quarrel not with far-off foes, but with those who, near at home, coöperate with, and do the bidding of, those far away, and without whom the latter would be harmless. We are accustomed to say, that the mass of men are unprepared; but improvement is slow, because the few are not materially wiser or better than the many. It is not so important that many should be as good as you, as that there be some absolute goodness somewhere; for that will leaven the whole lump. There are thousands who are *in opinion* opposed to slavery and to the war, who yet in effect do nothing to put an end to them; who, esteeming themselves children of Washington and Franklin, sit down with their hands in their pockets, and say that they know not what to do, and do nothing; who even postpone the question of freedom to the question of free-trade, and quietly read the prices-current along with the latest advices from Mexico, after dinner, and, it may be, fall asleep over them both. What is the price-current of an honest man and patriot to-day? They hesitate, and they regret, and sometimes they petition; but they do nothing in earnest and with effect. They will wait, well disposed, for others to remedy the evil, that they may no longer have it to regret. At most, they give only a cheap vote, and a feeble countenance and Godspeed, to the right, as it goes by them. There are nine hundred and ninety-nine patrons of virtue to one virtuous man. But it is easier to deal with the real possessor of a thing than with the temporary guardian of it.

All voting is a sort of gaming, like checkers or backgammon, with a slight moral tinge to it, a playing with right and wrong, with moral questions; and betting naturally accompanies it. The character of the voters is not staked. I cast my vote, perchance, as I think right; but I am not vitally concerned that that right should prevail. I am willing to leave it to the majority. Its obligation, therefore, never exceeds that of expediency. Even voting *for the right* is *doing* nothing for it. It is only expressing to men feebly your desire that it should prevail. A wise man will not leave the right to the mercy of chance, nor wish it to prevail through the power of the majority. There is but little virtue in the action of masses of men. When the majority shall at length vote for the abolition of slavery, it will be because they are indifferent to slavery, or because there is but little slavery left to be abolished by their vote. *They* will then be the only slaves. Only *his* vote can hasten the abolition of slavery who asserts his own freedom by his vote. . . .

It is not a man's duty, as a matter of course, to devote himself to the eradication of any, even the most enormous wrong; he may still properly have other concerns to engage him; but it is his duty, at least, to wash his hands of it, and, if he gives it no thought longer, not to give it practically his support. If I devote myself to other pursuits and contemplations, I must first see, at least, that I do not pursue them sitting upon another man's shoulders. I must get off him first, that he may pursue his contemplations too. See what gross inconsistency is tolerated. I have heard some of my townsmen say, "I should like to have them order me out to help put down an insurrection of the slaves, or to march to Mexico;—see if I would go;" and yet these very men have each, directly by their allegiance, and so indirectly, at least, by their money, furnished a substitute. The soldier is applauded who refuses to serve in an unjust war by those who do not refuse to sustain the unjust government which makes the war; is applauded by those whose own act and authority he disregards and sets at naught; as if the state were penitent to that degree that it hired one to scourge it while it sinned, but not to that degree that it left off sinning for a moment. Thus, under the name of Order and Civil Government, we are all made at last to pay homage to and support our own meanness. After the first blush of sin comes its indifference; and from immoral it becomes, as it were, *un*moral, and not quite unnecessary to that life which we have made. . . .

How can a man be satisfied to entertain an opinion merely, and enjoy *it?* Is there any enjoyment in it, if his opinion is that he is aggrieved? If you are cheated out of a single dollar by your neighbor, you do not rest satisfied with knowing that you are cheated, or with saying that you are cheated, or even with petitioning him to pay you your due; but you take effectual steps at once to obtain the full amount, and see that you are never cheated again. Action from principle,—the perception and the performance of right,—changes things and relations; it is essentially revolutionary, and does not consist wholly with any thing which was. It not only divides states and churches, it divides families; aye, it divides the *individual,* separating the diabolical in him from the divine.

Unjust laws exist: shall we be content to obey them, or shall we endeavor to amend them, and obey them until we have succeeded, or shall we transgress them at once? Men generally, under such a government as this, think that they ought to wait until they have persuaded the majority to alter them. They think that, if they should resist, the remedy would be worse than the evil. But it is the fault of the government itself that the remedy *is* worse than the *evil. It* makes it worse. Why is it not more apt to anticipate and provide for reform? Why does it not cherish its wise minority? Why does it cry and resist before it is hurt? Why does it not encourage its citizens to be on the alert to point out its faults, and *do* better than it would have them? Why does it always crucify Christ, and excommunicate Copernicus and Luther, and pronounce Washington and Franklin rebels?

One would think, that a deliberate and practical denial of its authority, was the only offence never contemplated by government; else, why has it not assigned its definite, its suitable and proportionate penalty? If a man who has no property refuses but once to earn nine shillings for the State, he is put in prison for a period unlimited by any law that I know, and determined only by the discretion of those who placed him there; but if he should steal ninety times nine shillings from the State, he is soon permitted to go at large again.

If the injustice is part of the necessary friction of the machine of government, let it go, let it go: perchance it will wear smooth,—certainly the machine will wear out. If the injustice has a spring, or a pulley, or a rope, or a crank, exclusively for itself, then perhaps you may consider whether the remedy will not be worse than the evil; but if it is of such a nature that it requires you to be the agent of injustice to another, then, I say, break the law. Let your life be a counter friction to stop the machine. What I have to do is to see, at any rate, that I do not lend myself to the wrong which I condemn. . . .

I do not hesitate to say, that those who call themselves Abolitionists should at once effectually withdraw their support, both in person and property, from the government of Massachusetts and not wait till they constitute a majority of one, before they suffer the right to prevail through them. I think that it is enough if they have God on their side, without waiting for that other one. Moreover, any man more right than his neighbors constitutes a majority of one already.

I meet this American government, or its representative, the state government, directly, and face to face, once a year—no more—in the person of its tax-gatherer; this is the only mode in which a man situated as I am necessarily meets it; and it then says distinctly, Recognize me; and the simplest, most effectual, and, in the present posture of affairs, the indispensablest mode of treating with it on this head, of expressing your little satisfaction with and love for it, is to deny it then. My civil neighbor, the tax-gatherer, is the very man I have to deal with,—for it is, after all, with men and not with parchment that I quarrel,—and he has voluntarily chosen to be an agent of the government. How shall he ever know well what he is and does as an officer of the government, or as a man, until he is obliged to consider whether he shall treat me, his neighbor, for whom he has respect, as a neighbor and well-disposed man, or as a maniac and disturber of the peace, and see if he can get over this obstruction to his neighborliness without a ruder and more impetuous thought or speech corresponding with his action. I know this well, that if one thousand, if one hundred, if ten men whom I could name,—if ten *honest* men only,—aye, if *one* HONEST man, in this State of Massachusetts, *ceasing to hold slaves,* were actually to withdraw from this copartnership, and be locked up in the county jail therefor, it would be the abolition of slavery in America. For it matters not how small the beginning may seem to be: what is once well done is done forever. But we love better to talk about it: that we say is our mission. Reform keeps many scores of newspapers in its service, but not one man. If my esteemed neighbor, the State's ambassador, who will devote his days to the settlement of the question of human rights in the Council Chamber, instead of being threatened with the prisons of Carolina, were to sit down the prisoner of Massachusetts, that State which is so anxious to foist the sin of slavery upon her sister,—though at present she can discover only an act of inhospitality to be the ground of a quarrel with her,—the Legislature would not wholly waive the subject the following winter.

Under a government which imprisons any unjustly, the true place for a just man is also a prison. The proper place today, the only place which Massachusetts has provided for her freer and less depending spirits, is in her prisons, to be put out and locked out of the State by her own act, as they have already put themselves out by their principles. . . . A minority is powerless while it conforms to the majority; it is not even a minority then; but it is irresistible when it clogs by its whole weight. If the alternative is to keep all just men in prison, or give up war and slavery, the State will not hesitate which to choose. If a thousand men were not to pay their tax bills this year, that would not be a violent and bloody measure, as it would be to pay them, and enable the State to commit violence and shed innocent blood. This is, in fact, the definition of a peaceable revolution if such is possible. . . .

I have contemplated the imprisonment of the offender, rather than the seizure of his goods,—though both will serve the same purpose,—because they who assert the purest right, and consequently are most dangerous to a corrupt State, commonly have not spent much time in accumulating property. To such the State renders comparatively small service, and a slight tax is wont to appear exorbitant, particularly if they are obliged to earn it by special labor with their hands. . . .

When I converse with the freest of my neighbors, I perceive that, whatever they may say about the magnitude and seriousness of the question, and their regard for the public tranquillity, the long and the short of the matter is, that they cannot spare the protection of the existing government, and they dread the consequences to their property and families of disobedience to it. For my own part, I should not like to think that I ever rely on the protection of the State. . . . No: until I want the protection of Massachusetts to be extended to me in some distant southern port, where my liberty is endangered, or until I am bent solely on building up an estate at home by peaceful enterprise, I can afford to refuse allegiance to Massachusetts, and her right to my property and life. It costs me less in every sense to incur the penalty of disobedience to the State, than it would to obey. I should feel as if I were worth less in that case.

Some years ago, the State met me in behalf of the church, and commanded me to pay a certain sum toward the support of a clergyman whose preaching my father attended, but never I myself. "Pay it," it said, "or be locked up in the jail." I declined to pay. But, unfortunately, another man saw fit to pay it. I did not see why the schoolmaster should be taxed to support the priest, and not the priest the schoolmaster; for I was not the State's schoolmaster, but I supported myself by voluntary subscription. I did not see why the lyceum should not present its tax-bill, and have the State to back its demand, as well as the church. However, at the request of the selectmen, I condescended to make some such statement as this in writing:—"Know all men by these presents, that I, Henry Thoreau, do not wish to be regarded as a member of any incorporated society which I have not joined." This I gave to the town-clerk; and he has it. The State, having thus learned that I did not wish to be regarded as a member of that church, has never made a like demand on me since; though it said that it must adhere to its original presumption that time. If I had known how to name them, I should then have signed off in detail from all the societies which I never signed on to; but I did not know where to find a complete list.

I have paid no poll-tax for six years. I was put into a jail once on this account, for one night; and, as I stood considering the walls of solid stone, two or three feet thick, the door of wood and iron, a foot thick, and the iron grating which strained the light, I could not help being struck with the foolishness of that institution which treated me as if I were mere flesh and blood and bones, to be locked up. I wondered that it should have concluded at length that this was the best use it could put me to, and had never thought to avail itself of my services in some way. I saw that, if there was a wall of stone between me and my townsmen, there was a still more difficult one to climb or break through, before they could get to be as free as I was. I did not for a moment feel confined, and the walls seemed a great waste of stone and mortar. I felt as if I alone of all my townsmen had paid my tax. They plainly did not know how to treat me, but behaved like persons who are underbred. In every threat and in every compliment there was a blunder; for they thought that my chief desire was to stand the other side of that stone wall. I could not but smile to see how industriously they locked the door on my meditations, which followed them out again without let or hinderance, and *they* were really all that was dangerous. As they could not reach me, they had resolved to punish my body; just as boys, if they cannot come at some person against whom they have a spite, will abuse his dog. I saw that the State was half-witted, that it was timid as a lone woman with her silver spoons, and that it did not know its friends from its foes, and I lost all my remaining respect for it, and pitied it.

Thus the State never intentionally confronts a man's sense, intellectual or moral, but only his body, his senses. It is not armed with superior wit or honesty, but with superior physical strength. I was not born to be forced. I will breathe after my own fashion. Let us see who is the strongest. What force has a multitude? They only can force me who obey a higher law than I. They force me to become like themselves. I do not hear of *men* being *forced* to live this way or that by masses of men. What sort of life were that to live? When I meet a government which says to me, "Your money or your life," why should I be in haste to give it my money? It may be in a great strait, and not know what to do: I cannot help that. It must help itself; do as I do. It is not worth the while to snivel about it. I am not responsible for the successful working of the machinery of society. I am not the son of the engineer. I perceive that, when an acorn and a chestnut fall side by side, the one does not remain inert to make way for the other, but both obey their own laws, and spring and grow and flourish as best they can, till one, perchance, overshadows and destroys the other. If a plant cannot live according to its nature, it dies; and so a man. . . .

I have never declined paying the highway tax, because I am as desirous of being a good neighbor as I am of being a bad subject; and, as for supporting schools, I am doing my part to educate my fellow-countrymen now. It is for no particular item in the tax-bill that I refuse to pay it. I simply wish to refuse allegiance to the State, to withdraw and stand aloof from it effectually. I do not care to trace the course of my dollar, if I could, till it buys a man, or a musket to shoot one with,—the dollar is innocent,—but I am concerned to trace the effects of my allegiance. In fact, I quietly declare war with the State, after my fashion, though I will still make what use and get what advantage of her I can, as is usual in such cases.

If others pay the tax which is demanded of me, from a sympathy with the State, they do but what they have already done in their own case, or rather they abet injustice to a greater extent than the State requires. If they pay the tax from a mistaken interest in the individual taxed, to save his property or prevent his going to jail, it is because they have not considered wisely how far they let their private feelings interfere with the public good.

This, then, is my position at present. But one cannot be too much on his guard in such a case, lest his action be biassed by obstinacy, or an undue regard for the opinions of men. Let him see that he does only what belongs to himself and to the hour. . . .

I do not wish to quarrel with any man or nation. I do not wish to split hairs, to make fine distinctions, or set myself up as better than my neighbors. I seek rather, I may say, even an excuse for conforming to the laws of the land. I am but too ready to conform to them. Indeed I have reason to suspect myself on this head; and each year, as the tax-gatherer comes round, I find myself disposed to review the acts and position of the general and state governments, and the spirit of the people, to discover a pretext for conformity. I believe that the State will soon be able to take all my work of this sort out of my hands, and then I shall be no better a patriot than my fellow-countrymen. Seen from a lower point of view, the Constitution, with all its faults, is very good; the law and the courts are very respectable; even this State and this American government are, in many respects, very admirable and rare things, to be thankful for, such as a great many have described them; but seen from a point of view a little higher, they are what I have described them; seen from a higher still, and the highest, who shall say what they are, or that they are worth looking at or thinking of at all?

However, the government does not concern me much, and I shall bestow the fewest possible thoughts on it. It is not many moments that I live under a government, even in this world. If a man is thought-free, fancy-free, imagination-free, that which *is not* never for a long time appearing *to be* to him, unwise rulers or reformers cannot fatally interrupt him.

I know that most men think differently from myself; but those whose lives are by profession devoted to the study of these or kindred subjects, content me as little as any. Statesmen and legislators, standing so completely within the institution, never distinctly and nakedly behold it. They speak of moving society, but have no resting-place without it. They may be men of a certain experience and discrimination, and have no doubt invented ingenious and even useful systems, for which we sincerely thank them; but all their wit and usefulness lie within certain not very wide limits. They are wont to forget that the world is not governed by policy and expediency. Webster never goes behind government, and so cannot speak with authority about it. His words are wisdom to those legislators who contemplate no essential reform in the existing government; but for thinkers, and those who legislate for all time, he never once glances at the subject. I know of those whose serene and wise speculations on this theme would soon reveal the limits of his mind's range and hospitality. . . . Notwithstanding his special acuteness and ability, he is unable to take a fact out of its merely political relations, and behold it as it lies absolutely to be disposed of by the intellect,—what, for instance, it behoves a man to do here in America to-day with regard to slavery, but ventures, or is driven, to make some such desperate answer as the following, while professing to speak absolutely, and as a private man,—from which what new and singular code of social duties might be inferred?—"The manner," says he, "in which the government of those States where slavery exists are to regulate it, is for their own consideration, under their responsibility to their constituents, to the general laws of propriety, humanity, and justice, and to God. Associations formed elsewhere, springing from a feeling of humanity, or other cause, have nothing whatever to do with it. They have never received any encouragement from me, and they never will.

They who know of no purer sources of truth, who have traced up its stream no higher, stand, and wisely stand, by the Bible and the Constitution, and drink at it there with reverence and humility; but they who behold where it comes trickling into this lake or that pool, gird up their loins once more, and continue their pilgrimage toward its fountainhead.

No man with a genius for legislation has appeared in America. They are rare in the history of the world. There are orators, politicians, and eloquent men, by the thousand; but the speaker has not yet opened his mouth to speak who is capable of settling the much vexed questions of the day. We love eloquence for its own sake, and not for any truth which it may utter, or any heroism it may inspire. Our legislators have not yet learned the comparative value of free-trade and of freedom, of union, and of rectitude, to a nation. They have no genius or talent for comparatively humble questions of taxation and finance, commerce and manufactures and agriculture. If we were left solely to the wordy wit of legislators in Congress for our guidance, uncorrected by the seasonable experience and the effectual complaints of the people, America would not long retain her rank among the nations. For eighteen hundred years, though perchance I have no right to say it, the New Testament has been written; yet where is the legislator who has wisdom and practical talent enough to avail himself of the light which it sheds on the science of legislation?

The authority of government, even

such as I am willing to submit to,—for I will cheerfully obey those who know and can do better than I, and in many things even those who neither know nor can do so well,—is still an impure one: to be strictly just, it must have the sanction and consent of the governed. It can have no pure right over my person and property but what I concede to it. The progress from an absolute to a limited monarchy, from a limited monarchy to a democracy, is a progress toward a true respect for the individual. Even the Chinese philosopher was wise enough to regard the individual as the basis of the empire. Is a democracy, such as we know it, the last improvement possible in government? Is it not possible to take a step further towards recognizing and organizing the rights of man? There will never be a really free and enlightened State until the State comes to recognize the individual as a higher and independent power, from which all its own power and authority are derived, and treats him accordingly. I please myself with imagining a State at last which can afford to be just to all men, and to treat the individual with respect as a neighbor; which even would not think it inconsistent with its own repose if a few were to live aloof from it, not meddling with it, nor embraced by it, who fulfilled all the duties of neighbors and fellowmen. A State which bore this kind of fruit, and suffered it to drop off as fast as it ripened, would prepare the way for a still more perfect and glorious State, which also I have imagined, but not yet anywhere seen.

7. Mark Twain, *Conscience, 1884**

Jim said it made him all over trembly and feverish to be so close to freedom. Well, I can tell you it made me all over trembly and feverish, too, to hear him, because I begun to get it through my head that he *was* most free—and who was to blame for it? Why, *me*. I couldn't get that out of my conscience, no how nor no way. It got to troubling me so I couldn't rest; I couldn't stay still in one place. It hadn't ever come home to me before, what this thing was that I was doing. But now it did; and it stayed with me, and scorched me more and more. I tried to make out to myself that *I* warn't to blame, because *I* didn't run Jim off from his rightful owner; but it warn't no use, conscience up and says, every time, "But you knowed he was running for his freedom, and you could 'a' paddled ashore and told somebody." That was so—I couldn't get around that no way. That was where it pinched. Conscience say to me, "What had poor Miss Watson done to you that you could see her nigger go off right under your eyes and never say one single word? What did that poor old woman do to you that you could treat her so mean? Why, she tried to learn you your book, she tried to learn you your manners, she tried to be good to you every way she knowed how. *That's* what she done."

I got to feeling so mean and so miserable I most wished I was dead. I fidgeted up and down the raft, abusing myself to myself, and Jim was fidgeting up and down past me. We neither of us could keep still. Every

* Mark Twain, *Adventures of Huckleberry Finn* (first printed, 1884; New York, 1912), pp. 125–30.

time he danced around and says, "Dah's Cairo!" it went through me like a shot, and I thought if it *was* Cairo I reckoned I would die of miserableness.

Jim talked out loud all the time while I was talking to myself. He was saying how the first thing he would do when he got to a free state he would go to saving up money and never spend a single cent, and when he got enough he would buy his wife, which was owned on a farm close to where Miss Watson lived; and then they would both work to buy the two children, and if their master wouldn't sell them, they'd get an Ab'litionist to go and steal them.

It most froze me to hear such talk. He wouldn't ever dared to talk such talk in his life before. Just see what a difference it made in him the minute he judged he was about free. It was according to the old saying, "Give a nigger an inch and he'll take an ell." Thinks I, this is what comes of my not thinking. Here was this nigger, which I had as good as helped to run away, coming right out flat-footed and saying he would steal his children— children that belonged to a man I didn't even know; a man that hadn't ever done me no harm.

I was sorry to hear Jim say that, it was such a lowering of him. My conscience got to stirring me up hotter than ever, until at last I says to it, "Let up on me—it ain't too late yet— I'll paddle ashore at the first light and tell." I felt easy and happy and light as a feather right off. All my troubles was gone. I went to looking out sharp for a light, and sort of singing to myself. By and by one showed. Jim sings out; "We's safe, Huck, we's safe! Jump up and crack yo' heels! Dat's de good ole Cairo at las', I jis knows it!"

I says:

"I'll take the canoe and go and see, Jim. It mightn't be, you know."

He jumped and got the canoe ready, and put his old coat in the bottom for me to set on, and give me the paddle; and as I shoved off, he says:

"Pooty soon I'll be a-shout'n' for joy, en I'll say, it's all on accounts o' Huck; I's a free man, en I couldn't ever ben free ef it hadn't ben for Huck; Huck done it. Jim won't ever forgit you, Huck; you's de bes' fren' Jim's ever had, en you's de *only* fren' ole Jim's got now."

I was paddling off, all in a sweat to tell on him; but when he says this, it seemed to kind of take the tuck all out of me. I went along slow then, and I warn't right down certain whether I was glad I started or whether I warn't. When I was fifty yards off, Jim says:

"Dah you goes, de ole true Huck; de on'y white genlman dat ever kep' his promise to ole Jim."

Well, I just felt sick. But I says, I *got* to do it—I can't get *out* of it. Right then along comes a skiff with two men in it with guns, and they stopped and I stopped. One of them says:

"What's that yonder?"

"A piece of raft," I says.

"Do you belong on it?"

"Yes, sir."

"Any men on it?"

"Only one, sir."

"Well, there's five niggers run off tonight up yonder, above the head of the bend. Is your man white or black?"

I didn't answer up prompt. I tried to, but the words wouldn't come. I tried for a second or two to brace up and out with it, but I warn't man enough—hadn't the spunk of a rabbit. I see I was weakening; so I just give up trying, and up and says:

"He's white."

"I reckon we'll go and see for ourselves."

"I wish you would," says I, "because it's pap that's there, and maybe you'd help me tow the raft ashore where the light is. He's sick—and so is mam and Mary Ann."

"Oh, the devil! we're in a hurry, boy. But I s'pose we've got to. Come, buckle to your paddle, and let's get along."

I buckled to my paddle and they laid to their oars. When we had made a stroke or two, I says:

"Pap'll be mighty much obleeged to you, I can tell you. Everybody goes away when I want them to help me tow the raft ashore, and I can't do it by myself."

"Well, that's infernal mean. Odd, too. Say, boy, what's the matter with your father?"

"It's the—a—the—well, it ain't anything much."

They stopped pulling. It warn't but a mighty little ways to the raft now. One says:

"Boy, that's a lie. What *is* the matter with your pap? Answer up square now, and it'll be the better for you."

"I will, sir, I will, honest—but don't leave us, please. It's the—the—Gentlemen, if you'll only pull ahead, and let me heave you the headline, you won't have to come a-near the raft—please do."

"Set her back, John, set her back!" says one. They backed water. "Keep away boy—keep to looard. Confound it, I just expect the wind has blowed it to us. Your pap's got the smallpox, and you know it precious well. Why didn't you come out and say so? Do you want to spread it all over?"

"Well," says I, a-blubbering, "I've told everybody before, and they just went away and left us."

"Poor devil, there's something in that. We are right down sorry for you, but we—well, hang it, we don't want the smallpox, you see. Look here, I'll tell you what to do. Don't you try to land by yourself, or you'll smash everything to pieces. You float along down about twenty miles, and you'll come to a town on the left-hand side of the river. It will be long after sunup then, and when you ask for help you tell them your folks are all down with chills and fever. Don't be a fool again, and let people guess what is the matter. Now we're trying to do you a kindness; so you just put twenty miles between us, that's a good boy. It wouldn't do any good to land yonder where the light is—it's only a wood-yard. Say, I reckon your father's poor, and I'm bound to say he's in pretty hard luck. Here, I'll put a twenty dollar gold piece on this board, and you get it when it floats by. I feel mighty mean to leave you; but my kingdom! it won't do to fool with smallpox, don't you see?"

"Hold on, Parker," says the man, "here's a twenty to put on the board for me. Good-by, boy; you do as Mr. Parker told you, and you'll be all right." . . .

They went off and I got aboard the raft, feeling bad and low, because I knowed very well I had done wrong, and I see it warn't no use for me to try to learn to do right; a body that don't get *started* right when he's little ain't got no show—when the pinch comes there ain't nothing to back him up and keep him to his work, and so he gets beat. Then I thought a minute, and says to myself, hold on; s'pose you'd a done right and give Jim up, would you felt better than what you do now? No, says I, I'd feel bad—I'd feel just the same way I do now. Well, then, says I, what's the use you learning to do right when it's troublesome to do right and ain't no trouble to do wrong, and the wages is just the same? I was stuck. I couldn't answer that. So I reckoned I wouldn't bother no more about it, but after this always do whichever come handiest at the time.

8. Emily Dickinson, *Much Madness, 1862**

> Much madness is divinest sense
> To a discerning eye;
> Much sense the starkest madness.
> 'Tis the majority
> In this, as all, prevails.
> Assent, and you are sane;
> Demur,—you're straightway dangerous,
> And handled with a chain.

*Emily Dickinson, *Poems,* p. 24.

9. Oliver W. Holmes, Jr., *Dissent in the Abrams Case, 1919**

This indictment is founded wholly upon the publication of two leaflets which I shall describe in a moment. The first count charges a conspiracy pending the war with Germany to publish abusive language about the form of government of the United States, laying the preparation and publishing of the first leaflet as overt acts. The second count charges a conspiracy pending the war to publish language intended to bring the form of government into contempt, laying the preparation and publishing of the two leaflets as overt acts. The third count alleges a conspiracy to encourage resistance to the United States in the same war and to attempt to effectuate the purpose by publishing the same leaflets. The fourth count lays a conspiracy to incite curtailment of production of things necessary to the prosecution of the war and to attempt to accomplish it by publishing the second leaflet to which I have referred.

The other leaflet, headed "Workers—Wake Up," with abusive language says that America together with the Allies will march for Russia to help the Czecho-Slovaks in their struggle against the Bolsheviki, and that this time the hypocrites shall not fool the Russian emigrants and friends of Russia in America. It tells the Russian emigrants that they now must spit in the face of false military propaganda by which their sympathy and help to the prosecution of the war have been called forth and says that with the money they have lent or are going to lend "they will make bullets not only for the Germans but also for the Workers' Soviets of Russia," and further, "Workers in the ammunition factories, you are producing bullets, bayonets, cannon, to murder not only the Germans but also your dearest, best, who are in Russia fighting for freedom." It then appeals to the same Russian emigrants at some length not to consent to the "inquisitionary expedition to Russia," and says that the destruction of the Russian revolution is "the politics of the march on Russia." The leaflet winds up by saying "Workers, our reply to this barbaric intervention has to be a general strike!" and after a few words on the spirit of revolution, exhortations not to be afraid, and some usual tall talk,

* *Abrams et al.* v. *United States,* 250 U.S. (1919), 616 ff.

ends "Woe unto those who will be in the way of progress. Let solidarity live! The Rebels."

No argument seems to me necessary to show that these pronunciamentos in no way attack the form of government of the United States, or that they do not support either of the first two counts. What little I have to say about the third count may be postponed until I have considered the fourth. With regard to that it seems too plain to be denied that the suggestion to workers in ammunition factories that they are producing bullets to murder their dearest, and the further advocacy of a general strike, both in the second leaflet, do urge curtailment of production of things necessary to the prosecution of the war within the meaning of the Act of May 16, 1918 . . . amending §3 of the earlier Act of 1917. But to make the conduct criminal that statute requires that it should be "with intent by such curtailment to cripple or hinder the United States in the prosecution of the war." It seems to me that no such intent is proved.

I am aware of course that the word intent as vaguely used in ordinary legal discussion means no more than knowledge at the time of the act that the consequences said to be intended will ensue. Even less than that will satisfy the general principle of civil and criminal liability. A man may have to pay damages, may be sent to prison, at common law might be hanged, if at the time of his act he knew facts from which common experience showed that the consequences would follow, whether he individually could foresee them or not. But, when words are used exactly, a deed is not done with intent to produce a consequence unless that consequence is the aim of the deed. It may be obvious, and obvious to the actor, that the consequence will follow, and he may be liable for it even if he forgets it, but

he does not do the act with intent to produce it unless the aim to produce it is the proximate motive of the specific act, although there may be some deeper motive behind.

It seems to me that this statute must be taken to use its words in a strict and accurate sense. They would be absurd in any other. A patriot might think that we were wasting money on aeroplanes, or making more cannon of a certain kind than we needed, and might advocate curtailment with success, yet even if it turned out that the curtailment hindered and was thought by other minds to have been obviously likely to hinder the United States in the prosecution of the war, no one would hold such conduct a crime. I admit that my illustration does not answer all that might be said but it is enough to show what I think and to let me pass to a more important aspect of the case. I refer to the First Amendment to the Constitution that Congress shall make no law abridging the freedom of speech.

I never have seen any reason to doubt that the questions of law that alone were before this Court in the cases of *Schenck, Frohwerk* and *Debs,* were rightly decided. I do not doubt for a moment that by the same reasoning that would justify punishing persuasion to murder, the United States constitutionally may punish speech that produces or is intended to produce a clear and imminent danger that it will bring about forthwith certain substantive evils that the United States constitutionally may seek to prevent. The power undoubtedly is greater in time of war than in time of peace because war opens dangers that do not exist at other times.

But as against dangers peculiar to war, as against others, the principle of the right to free speech is always the same. It is only the present danger of immediate evil or an intent to bring it about that warrants Congress in setting a limit to the expression of opinion where private rights are not concerned. Congress certainly cannot forbid all effort to change the mind of the country. Now nobody can suppose that the surreptitious publishing of a silly leaflet by an unknown man, without more, would present any immediate danger that its opinions would hinder the success of the Government arms or have any appreciable tendency to do so. Publishing these opinions for the very purpose of obstructing, however, might indicate a greater danger and at any rate would have the quality of an attempt. So I assume that the second leaflet, if published for the purpose alleged in the fourth count, might be punishable. But it seems pretty clear to me that nothing less than that would bring these papers within the scope of this law.

An actual intent in the sense that I have explained is necessary to constitute an attempt, where a further act of the same individual is required to complete the substantive crime, for reasons given in *Swift & Co. v. United States,* 196 U.S. 375, 396. It is necessary where the success of the attempt depends upon others, because if that intent is not present the actor's aim may be accomplished without bringing about the evils sought to be checked. An intent to prevent interference with the revolution in Russia might have been satisfied without any hindrance to carrying on the war in which we were engaged.

I do not see how anyone can find the intent required by the statute in any of the defendants' words. The second leaflet is the only one that affords even a foundation for the charge, and there, without invoking the hatred of German militarism expressed in the former one, it is evident from the beginning to the end that the only object of the paper is to help Russia and stop American intervention there against the popular government—not to impede the United States in the war that it was carrying on. To say that two phrases taken literally might import a suggestion of conduct that would have interference with the war as an indirect and probably undesired effect seems to me by no means enough to show an attempt to produce that effect.

I return for a moment to the third count. That charges an intent to provoke resistance to the United States in its war with Germany. Taking the clause in the statute that deals with that in connection with the other elaborate provisions of the Act, I think that resistance to the United States means some forcible act of opposition to some proceeding of the United States in pursuance of the war. I think the intent must be the specific intent that I have described and for the reasons that I have given, I think that no such intent was proved or existed in fact. I also think that there is no hint at resistance to the United States as I construe the phrase.

In this case sentences of twenty years' imprisonment have been imposed for the publishing of two leaflets that I believe the defendants had as much right to publish as the Government has to publish the Constitution of the United States now vainly invoked by them. Even if I am technically wrong and enough can be squeezed from these poor and puny anonymities to turn the color of legal litmus paper; I will add, even if what I think the necessary intent were shown; the most nominal punishment seems to me all that possibly could be inflicted, unless the defendants are to be made to suffer not for what the indictment alleges but for the creed that they avow—a creed that I believe to be the creed of ignorance and immaturity when honestly held, as I see no reason to doubt that it was held here, but which, although made the subject of examination at the trial, no one has a right even to consider in dealing with the charges before the Court.

Persecution for the expression of opinions seems to me perfectly logical. If you have no doubt of your premises or your power and want a certain result with all your heart you naturally express your wishes in law and sweep away all opposition. To allow opposition by speech seems to indicate that you think speech impotent, as when a man says that he has squared the circle, or that you do not care wholeheartedly for the result, or that you doubt either your power or your premises.

But when men have realized that time has upset many fighting faiths, they may come to believe even more than they believe the very foundations of their own conduct that the ultimate good desired is better reached by free trade in ideas—that the best test of truth is the power of the thought to get itself accepted in the competition of the market, and that truth is the only ground upon which their wishes safely can be carried out. That, at any rate, is the theory of our Constitution. It is an experiment, as all life is an experiment. Every year if not every day we have to wager our salvation

upon some prophecy based upon imperfect knowledge. While that experiment is part of our system I think that we should be eternally vigilant against attempts to check the expression of opinions that we loathe and believe to be fraught with death, unless they so imminently threaten immediate interference with the lawful and pressing purposes of the law that an immediate check is required to save the country.

I wholly disagree with the argument of the Government that the First Amendment left the common law as to seditious libel in force. History seems to me against the notion. I had conceived that the United States through many years had shown its repentance for the Sedition Act of 1798 by repaying fines that it imposed. Only the emergency that makes it immediately dangerous to leave the correction of evil counsels to time warrants making any exception to the sweeping command, "Congress shall make no law . . . abridging the freedom of speech." Of course I am speaking only of expressions of opinion and exhortations, which were all that were uttered here, but I regret that I cannot put into more impressive words my belief that in their conviction upon this indictment the defendants were deprived of their rights under the Constitution of the United States.

10. Louis Marshall, *Freedom from Intolerance, 1925**

Analysis of Statute

An analysis of the legislative act which is challenged will be useful, for the purpose of ascertaining and measuring its effect. The statute makes it a misdemeanor for "any parent, guardian, or other person" having control or charge or custody of a child under

* Brief in *Pierce* v. *The Society of the Sisters*, 268 U.S. 510 (1925) in Charles Reznikoff, ed., *Louis Marshall: Champion of Liberty* (Philadelphia: The Jewish Publication Society of America, 1957), II, 957–67. Reprinted with the permission of The American Jewish Committee and The Jewish Publication Society of America.

the age of sixteen years and of the age of eight years or over, to "fail or neglect or refuse to send such child to a public school for a period of time a public school shall be held during the current year" in the district in which the child resides.

This language is all-embracing. It relates to *any parent,* guardian or other person, and to *any child* between the age of eight and sixteen years, and makes the attendance of such child at a public school, as distinguished from a private or parochial school, of so obligatory a nature that the failure, neglect or refusal to send the child to such school becomes a criminal act, "each day's failure to send such child to a public school" constituting a separate offense.

This act is not a compulsory education law, the statutes of Oregon containing adequate provisions to require the attendance of all children within the state at a public or private school, or at the home of the parent or guardian. It proceeds upon the clearly expressed theory of compulsory attendance at a public school. This is emphasized by the exceptions contained in the act, whereby it is provided that certain children "shall not be required to attend *public schools.*" They relate:

(a) To any child who is abnormal, subnormal or physically unable to attend school.

(b) To any child who has completed the eighth grade in accordance with the provisions of the state course of study.

(c) To children of certain ages who reside at a considerable distance from a public school, unless transportation to and from school is supplied by the school district, in which event the exemption from attendance at public school is not to apply.

(d) To any child taught by its parent or a private teacher such subjects as are usually taught in the first eight years in a public school. This is coupled with the condition that before such child can be taught by a parent or private teacher the parent or teacher must receive express permission from the county superintendent to teach. The child is required to report to the superintendent, or to some other person designated by him, at least once every three months, and to take an examination in the work covered. If the county superintendent shall determine that the child is not being properly taught he is to order the parent, guardian, or other person, to send the child to the public school for the remainder of the school year.

It is to be noted that the exception relating to children receiving private instruction is confined to cases where the parent or a private teacher gives the instruction. That eliminates instruction in private or parochial schools.

The Effect of the Statute

The manifest effect of this legislation, therefore, is to forbid instruction otherwise than in the public schools and by parents or private teachers under conditions set forth in the statute, and under the unlimited control of the county school superintendent, or of the person designated by him, and subject to his sole determination as to whether the parent or private teacher may instruct and as to whether or not proper instruction is given by them. This necessarily means the elimination of private and parochial schools, since it would be physically impossible for children of tender years, after having taken the course prescribed in the public schools, to attend any private or parochial school for the purpose of receiving instruction.

Prior to the passage of this act, under the law of Oregon parents were permitted to have their children taught in a private school. (Act of February 25, 1889, Chapter 1; Act of

February 27, 1901, Section 1; Act of February 23, 1907, Section 1, subdivision a.) By the latest of these acts children were not required to attend public schools if taught in a private or parochial school for a period of time equal to that required in the public schools.

The Act of 1923 thus renders unlawful what previously had been lawful, not only pursuant to express enactment of the Legislature, but also according to the unquestioned practice of the citizens of Oregon from the days when it was still a territory.

In fact the public school has been a recent creation, dating from the middle of the nineteenth century. Prior to that time the only existing schools were private, parochial or denominational. Except in a few states, even at the present time, but few institutions of higher learning are public in character. They are conducted by private corporations, and to a large extent by institutions operated under denominational auspices. Many of our greatest universities were called into existence by religious bodies, and some of them are still conducted and managed by such bodies.

The Act under review is at present confined to the education of children between the ages of eight and sixteen years. If this legislation is valid, then it can be extended so as to include not only all minors, but all persons, regardless of age. It might limit the right of any person to secure an education except by attending a public institution. The right to choose the medium whereby an education is to be received is taken away, not only from the parent or guardian of the pupil or student, but also from the pupil or student himself. It matters not whether the public institution in the district in which the person for whom an education is sought or who seeks an education resides, may be of an inferior type or may be conducted by inefficient or temperamentally disqualified teachers. It matters not if a private or parochial school which has acquired a reputation for excellence and thoroughness, is conducted in the district. It matters not if personal or conscientious reasons exist which would lead to a preference for education in a private or parochial school rather than in a public school, or that the parents, or the children themselves, desire that instruction shall be given in a religious atmosphere. The statute categorically declares that the public school alone shall minister to the educational needs of the pupil, that the wishes of the parents and of the pupil shall be disregarded under penalty of fine and imprisonment.

This obligation to attend the public school is limited for the period of time during which a public school is held during a current year in the district. Consequently if, as has been the case in many parts of the country, particularly in the rural districts, the public schools in the district were to give instruction for four months only, and in the same district there were maintained a private or parochial school whose instruction covered nine months of the year, the parents would nevertheless be required to send their children to the public school during the four months of the duration of its courses.

It is not a sufficient answer to say that when the public school closes they might send their children to the private or parochial school for the remaining five months. It requires no stretch of the imagination to recognize the fact that it would be a practical impossibility, without entirely disrupting the system of the private or parochial school, to accept pupils thus situated; and it would be likewise impossible for the pupils, unless especially gifted, to keep up with the courses in the private or parochial school.

Referring to the exceptions contained in the Act, it is evident that the power that created them can repeal them, and, therefore, the dispensation given to a child that has completed the eighth grade from further attendance at the public school, may be withdrawn, as may be likewise the permission to parents and private teachers to give instruction to a child even on compliance with the drastic conditions upon which the exercise of such right at present depends.

The arbitrary character of the conditions accompanying the privilege given to parents and private teachers to instruct a child, practically destroys the right. Parents, however enlightened and however well qualified to teach their children, and private teachers possessed of intelligence and experience, would have to subject themselves to the unfettered discretion of the county school superintendents, whose interests, predilections and prejudices are bound up in the public school system, of which they form a part and to the extension of which they necessarily are inclined.

This legislation is clearly calculated to confer upon the public schools a monopoly of education. That necessarily would tend to the suppression of all religious instruction, the importance of which cannot be minimized. Under our system of government the State is powerless, as it should be, to give religious instruction. That is a right and a duty which rests upon parents, upon the churches and the synagogues. If private, parochial and denominational schools are, however, to be deprived of the right to educate the children, and the parents are forbidden to send their children to such schools, then we shall be in precisely the same situation as that which now

exists in Russia. There it is strictly forbidden to give religious instruction of any kind to children until they reach the age of eighteen years.

Fundamentally, therefore, the questions in these cases are: May liberty to teach and to learn be restricted? Shall such liberty be dependent on the will of the majority? Shall such majority be permitted to dictate to parents and to children where and by whom instruction shall be given? If such power can be asserted, then it will lead inevitably to the stifling of thought. If the will of a temporary majority may thus control, then it is conceivable that it may prohibit the teaching of science, of the classics, of modern languages and literature, of art, and of nature study. A majority might reach the conclusion that the teaching of the Darwinian theory, or of the philosophy of Kant or Spinoza, or the ideas of Montesquieu, or of Jeremy Bentham, or of John Stuart Mill, or of Emerson, should be prohibited. In some parts of this country a majority, if it possessed the power, would unquestionably limit instruction in the public schools to the Three R's. New York has recently witnessed an attempt to eliminate from the handbooks of history used in the public schools, any references to England which were not to its discredit, and any reference to America which, although truthful, did not indicate that it had at all times been immune to criticism.

Recognizing in the main the great merit of our public school system, it is nevertheless unthinkable that public schools alone shall, by legislative compulsion rather than by their own merits, be made the only medium of education in this country. Such a policy would necessarily lead to their deterioration. The absence of the right of selection would at once lower the standards of education. If the children of the country are to be educated upon a dead level of uniformity and by a single method, then eventually our nation would consist of mechanical Robots and standardized Babbitts.

On the theory which seeks to eliminate private and parochial schools, the Legislature might as well compel all of the inhabitants of the land to subscribe to the same newspaper, to attend the same church, to become members of the same political party, and to join the same lodge. Indeed, it would be less of an invasion of liberty to do any of these things than to say to parents that, regardless of their ambitions and aspirations for their children, regardless of the love and affection which they bear to them, regardless of their conscientious beliefs respecting the duty which they owe for the ethical, moral and religious rearing of their children, the State may come in and take away from them that sacred right and the performance of the duty which they conscientiously believe that they owe to their children and to future generations. Our children do not belong to the State. As a rule the poorest of parents are better qualified to take care of their children than the best politician or professional agitator could possibly be.

The Arguments Advanced in Favor of This Legislation

The arguments by the proponents of this measure submitted to the voters of Oregon prior to the election of November 7, 1922, are illuminating. It is stated that "the inspiration for this Act" is a resolution adopted by the Supreme Council A. A. S. Rite for the Southern Jurisdiction of the United States, by the Grand Lodge of Oregon F. & A. M., and by the Imperial Council A. A. O. Nobles Mystic Shrine. The resolution proclaims the belief of these councils "in the free and compulsory education of the children of our nation in public primary schools supported by public taxation, upon which all children shall attend and be instructed in the English language only without regard to race or creed, as the only sure foundation for the perpetuation and preservation of our free institutions guaranteed by the Constitution of the United States."

This is scarcely the statement of a reason. It is an opinion by a group of private individuals, representing their personal preferences and evidently prepared to effectuate them by compulsory proceedings. Apparently they are seeking to compel those of various races and creeds to submit to their compulsory methods. They do not take into account the conscientious convictions of others, who, though willing to contribute their share of the taxation imposed for the support of public schools, are so strong in their preference for private or parochial schools as to pay out of their own pockets, and not out of the public treasury, the cost of the education received by their children at such schools.

Certainly those who are ready to make this sacrifice, if such it may be called, are not indifferent to the cause of education, or to the public welfare, or to the future happiness of their own children. Nor are they hostile to our free institutions or to the guaranties of the Constitution because by their conduct they demonstrate their devotion to those guaranties of liberty which are enshrined in our organic law.

The solitary argument presented in this Official Pamphlet in favor of this legislation (Appendix I to Appellee's Brief, pp. 24, 25), contains the following additional statements:

(a) "Our nation supports the public school for the sole purpose of self-preservation."

That is a fallacy. The nation does not support the public schools at all. The taxpayers in the various localities render such support. We may frankly concede that it is for the public welfare; but that is subserved by private, parochial and religious schools, and by the instruction given by parents and private teachers as well. The aggregate of all of them constitutes the contribution by the public in its entirety to the cause of education.

The nation is no more preserved by the public school than it is by the other agencies. The Fathers of the Republic and a large proportion of our finest citizens never attended a public school, and today a large number of the best examplars of Americanism have received and are receiving their education outside of public schools. In fact, in the City of New York the accommodations afforded by our public schools are inadequate to provide properly for the children of school age, and they are required to attend on part time or to seek instruction in private and parochial schools.

Under the Oregon statute, however inadequate the facilities of the public schools may be, attendance at private and parochial schools, however superior their accommodations and their instruction may be, is practically prohibited.

(b) "The assimilation and education of our foreign-born citizens in the principles of our government, the hopes and inspiration of our people, are best secured by and through attendance of all children in our public schools."

There is no foundation in truth for this statement. The private and parochial schools which exist throughout the country are conducted on the same patriotic lines as are our public schools. Those who are in responsible management and the teaching faculties are just as alive to the necessity of instilling the principles of our government in foreign and native born citizens alike, as are those in charge of our public schools. They are men and women of education and culture who have devoted themselves to the sacred duty of educating the young, and who by their conduct have evinced the same patriotism as actuates the average citizen of the United States.

The assimilation, so-called, of our foreign born citizens is advanced rather than retarded by the private, parochial and religious schools. It is in such schools as these, of which many shining examples are to be found in every large community in the northern and eastern parts of the United States, that special efforts are made not only to educate the foreign born citizen, but the immigrant, in the fundamental principles of our government; and it may be said without exaggeration that our foreign born citizens frequently have a better understanding of the principles of our government than is possessed by many of our native born citizens. They have better opportunity to appreciate the differences between our form of government and that prevailing in the countries in which they were born, and they devote themselves with greater intensity to an understanding of those principles than is the case with many a descendant of the elder population.

(c) "We must now halt those, coming to our country, from forming groups, establishing schools, and thereby bringing up their children in an environment often antagonistic to the principles of our government."

The legislation of recent years has halted immigration into the United States, even though much of our growth and prosperity, as well as many other gifts, as recently pointed out by Dr. Charles W. Eliot, has been due to immigration.

There is no such thing as the creation by the newer population of an environment antagonistic to the principles of our government. Whatever their environment may be, their children cannot be distinguished from those who have long abided here, and they participate in everything that tends to the maintenance of the fundamental principles of our Federal and State governments. They have proven it by their devotion to our institutions both in times of peace and war, and have supplied their full quotas to the armies of the Republic.

(d) "Mix those with prejudices in the public school melting pot for a few years while their minds are plastic, and finally bring out the finished product—a true American."

That is a mere figure of speech, which cannot stand the test of analysis. There is no such thing as a melting pot, anthropologically speaking. If there were, it would be a misfortune. However much iron and copper and lead and zinc and gold and silver may be mixed, the net result is a product which possesses none of the virtues of the original metals and is utterly useless. Far better would it be to purify and refine the original metals, for then their individual values would be enhanced. The difficulty with prejudices, even in the public schools, is that they are frequently aggravated by contact and collision. Among the advantages of private and parochial schools is the fact that there prejudices are apt to be mitigated. At all events they are not stimulated in a truly religious atmosphere or in a genuine cultural environment.

(e) "The permanency of this nation rests in the education of its youth in our public schools, where they will be correctly instructed in the history of our country and the aims of our government, and in those fundamental principles of freedom and democracy, reverence and righteousness, where all shall stand upon one common level."

This is mere truculent rhetoric. Education, of course, contributes to the progress of a nation, but whether such education should be sought exclusively in public schools rather than in private and parochial schools which are equally good or better, so far as thoroughness is concerned, is seriously questioned.

What is meant by the statement that the youth will be "correctly instructed in the history of our country and the aims of our government," etc.? Is it intended to say that it is only in the public school that accuracy is found? The proof to the contrary is overwhelming. Is it implied that it is only the teachers in our public schools who understand "the history of our country and the aims of our government and the fundamental principles of freedom and democracy?" That is obviously an unsound theory.

Chapter 115 of the General Laws of Oregon for 1921, recognized no difference in this regard between the teachers in the public and in the private and parochial schools. The teachers in the former were required to subscribe an oath or affirmation that they would support the Constitution of the State of Oregon and the laws enacted thereunder and would teach by precept and example respect for the flags of the United States and of the State of Oregon, and reverence for law and order and undivided allegiance to the government of our country. The teachers in the private and parochial schools and in academies, colleges, universities, and other institutions of learning, were likewise required to take the same oath or affirmation of allegiance "as that prescribed for public school teachers." Is it to be inferred that the teachers in private and parochial schools were less mindful of their oaths than the teachers in public schools?

There is nothing in the public school which is culturally superior to the private, parochial and religious schools; nor can it be said that the teachers are possessed of moral or intellectual or other qualities which make them the superiors of the men and women who have in the past taught and are now teaching in private and parochial schools. Is it intended to say that those who are wedded to the principles of freedom to such an extent that they are ready to lay down their lives for it, are not correctly instructed in the fundamental principles of freedom?

And the final suggestion, that the youth in our public schools will be more correctly instructed in "reverence and righteousness" than they are in private, parochial or religious schools, is an unequalled specimen of grim humor.

All of these statements combined lead to the conclusion in the minds of those responsible for this species of argumentation, that by the education of the youth of the nation in our public schools "all shall stand upon one common level." By that doubtless is meant the dead level of uniformity. God forbid that that shall be the case! Everything that is interesting or inspiring or elevating would depart out of our national life if all of the mountain peaks were to disappear, and our horizon would be that of a boundless, monotonous and unvarying prairie.

(f) "When every parent in our land has a child in our public school, then and only then will there be united interest in the growth and higher efficiency of our public schools."

What is to prevent the attainment of such higher efficiency, which evidently implies that that stage of efficiency has not been reached so long

as there are children in the land who receive their education in private and parochial schools? Does efficiency depend upon numbers? Is it not the fact that the efficiency of many of our public schools has been hampered by the very fact that classes are too large, and that proper discipline cannot be maintained because of such numbers? Can it not be fairly said that so far as efficiency is concerned the highest achievement has thus far been witnessed in our private schools, as to which it was conceded by Mr. Claxton, former United States Commissioner of Education, that "the private schools and colleges have been the salvation of our public schools," and that "these private institutions have their place in our educational system; they prevent it from becoming autocratic and arbitrary and encourage its growth along new lines."

(g) "Our children must not under any pretext, be it based upon money, creed or social status, be divided into antagonistic groups, cliques or cults there to absorb the narrow views of life as they are taught."

Here those who send their children to private and parochial schools because of their creed are charged with constituting antagonistic groups and as absorbing "narrow views of life." In other words, parents who are anxious for the future welfare and happiness of their children and who seek to dedicate them to moral, ethical and religious principles, are denounced for sending their children to private and parochial schools, because, forsooth, the views of life which they there absorb are characterized as "narrow."

What does that mean but an attempt on the part of the protagonists for this law to sit in judgment upon their fellow-citizens whose ideals differ from theirs? How does such a mental attitude differ from that which prevailed when governments sought to enforce uniformity of religious beliefs and punished nonconformists as criminals? With the most extraordinary ingenuousness they look upon those of other cults as striving "not for the good of the whole but for the supremacy of themselves." What about the cult of those who adopted the resolutions which are described as "the inspiration for the Act," of those who are seeking to force the youth of this country into the public schools and to destroy private and parochial schools, regardless of the wishes of parents and guardians and of the various religious elements in our population?

This is a demonstration of the evils of intolerance and of the dangers inherent in this legislation, which undermines the fundamental concepts of liberty and which has the inevitable tendency of carrying us back to those evil days which preceded the adoption of our American Constitution.

The noble words uttered by the President [Coolidge] on his inauguration a few days ago, redeclare the great truth which is ignored in this legislation:

"The fundamental precept of liberty is toleration. We cannot permit any inquisition either within or without the law or apply any religious test to the holding of office. The mind of America must be forever free."

11. EUGENE ROSTOW, *Our Worst Wartime Mistake, 1945**

The conception of the war power under the American Constitution rests on the experience of the Revolution and the Civil War. It rests on basic political principles which men who had endured those times of trouble had fully discussed and carefully set forth. The chief architects of the conception were men of affairs who had participated in war, and had definite and well-founded ideas about the role of the professional military mind in the conduct of war.

The first and dominating principle of the war power under the Constitution is that the Commander-in-Chief of the armed forces must be a civilian, elected and not promoted to his office. In no other way can the subordination of the military to the civil power be assured. And in every democracy, the relationship between civil and military power is the crucial issue—the issue on which its capacity to survive in time of crisis ultimately depends.

The second principle governing the war power in a democracy is that of responsibility. Like every other officer of government, soldiers must answer for their decisions to the nation's system of law, and not to the Chief of Staff alone. Where military decisions lead to conflicts between individuals and authority—as in the Japanese exclusion program—the courts must adjudicate them. It is essential to every democratic value in society that official action, taken in the name of the war power, should be held to standards of responsibility under such circumstances. The courts have not in the past, and should not now, declare such problems to be beyond the reach of judicial review. The present Sup-

* Eugene Rostow, "Our Worst Wartime Mistake," *Harper's Magazine*, CXCI (September, 1945), 193–201, by permission of Eugene V. Rostow, Professor of Law, Yale University.

reme Court is dominated by the conviction that in the past judicial review has unduly limited the freedom of administrative action. But surely the right answer to bad law is good law, rather than no law at all. The court must review the exercise of military power in a way which permits ample freedom to the executive, yet assures society as a whole that appropriate standards of responsibility have been met.

The issue for judicial decision in these cases is not lessened or changed by saying that the war power includes any steps required to win the war. The problem is still one of judgment as to what helps win a war. Who is to decide whether there was a sensible reason for doing what was done? Is it enough for the general to say that when he acted, he honestly thought it was a good idea to do what he did?

Unless the courts require a showing, in cases like these, of an intelligible relationship between means and ends, society has lost its basic protection against the abuse of military power. The general's good intentions must be irrelevant. There should be evidence in court that his military judgment had a suitable basis in fact.

The history of this question in the Supreme Court is unmistakable. The earlier decisions of the court had vigorously asserted that "what are the allowable limits of military discretion, and whether or not they have been overstepped in a particular case, are judicial questions"; and that there must be evidence enough to satisfy the court as to the need for the action taken. They had made it clear that the law is not neutral in such issues, but has a positive preference for protecting civil rights where possible, and a long-standing suspicion of the military mind when acting outside its own sphere.

Yet in the Japanese-American cases there was literally no evidence what-ever by which the court might test the responsibility of General DeWitt's action. Dozens of Supreme Court decisions had said that the court would not pass on serious constitutional questions without a record before it, establishing the essential facts. Those cases were all ignored. One hundred thousand persons were sent to concentration camps on a record which wouldn't support a conviction for stealing a dog.

The earlier cases not only established the rule that there must be an independent judicial examination of the justification for a military act. They went much further. They declared a simple rule-of-thumb as a guide in handling cases involving military discretion, in which the military undertook to arrest, hold, or try people. So long as the civil courts were open and functioning, the Supreme Court had previously held, there could be no military necessity for allowing generals to hold, try, or punish people. The safety of the country could be thoroughly protected against treason, sabotage, and like crimes by ordinary arrest and trial in the civil courts, unless the courts were shut by riot, invasion, or insurrection.

That was the moral of the great case of *Ex Parte Milligan,* decided in 1866. *Ex Parte Milligan* is a monument in the democratic tradition, and until now it has been the animating force in this branch of our law. To be sure, there is a tendency nowadays to treat *Ex Parte Milligan* as outmoded, as if new methods of "total" warfare made the case an anachronism; but those who take this view have forgotten the circumstances of the Civil War, when fifth columns, propaganda, sabotage, and espionage were rife.

Ex Parte Milligan illustrates the point. Milligan was convincingly charged with active participation in a fifth column plot worthy of Hitler. A group of armed and determined men planned to seize federal arsenals at Columbus, Indianapolis, and at three points in Illinois, and then to release Confederate prisoners of war held in those states. Thus they would create a Confederate army behind the Union lines in Tennessee. Milligan and his alleged co-conspirators acted in Indiana, Missouri, Illinois, and in other border states. Their strategy had a political arm. The Union was to be split politically, and a Northwest Confederation was to be declared, friendly to the South, and embracing six states. This was not an idle dream. It was sponsored by a well-financed society, the Sons of Liberty, thought to have 300,000 members, many of them rich and respectable, and the planned uprising would coincide with the Chicago convention of the Democratic Party, which was then sympathetic to abandoning the war and recognizing the Confederacy.

The unanimous court which freed Milligan for civil trial was a court of fire-eating Unionists. Mr. Justice Davis, who wrote for the majority, was one of President Lincoln's closest friends. The Chief Justice, who wrote for the concurring minority, was a valiant supporter of the war, whatever his shortcomings in other respects. Yet the court had no difficulty in freeing Milligan, and facing down the outcry provoked by the decision.

The court held in Milligan's case that it was unconstitutional to try him before a military commission, rather than a court of law. There was little doubt of his guilt. But it was beyond the powers of the military to measure or punish it. . . .

Yet in the cases of the Japanese-Americans the Supreme Court held the precedent of *Ex Parte Milligan* inapplicable. The reasoning is extraordinarily dangerous. The Japanese-Americans, the court said, were detained by a civilian agency, not by the Army. The program was not exclusively a matter for military administration, and it was enforceable under a statute by ordinary criminal remedies. Therefore, it did not present the question of the power of military tribunals to conduct trials under the laws of war.

But the Japanese-Americans were ordered detained by a general, purporting to act on military grounds. The military order was enforceable, on pain of imprisonment. While a United States marshal, rather than a military policeman, assured obedience to the order, the ultimate sanction behind the marshal's writ is the same as that of the military police: the bayonets of United States troops. It is hardly a ground for distinction that the general's command was backed by the penalty of civil imprisonment, or that he obtained civilian aid in running the relocation camps. The starting point for the entire program was a military order, which had to be obeyed.

In *Ex Parte Milligan* the Supreme Court had said that the military could not constitutionally arrest, nor could a military tribunal constitutionally try, civilians charged with treason and conspiracy to destroy the state by force, at a time when the civil courts were open and functioning. Yet under the plan considered in the Japanese-American cases, people not charged with crime are imprisoned without even a military trial, on the ground that they have the taint of Japanese blood. It would seem clear that if it is illegal to arrest and confine people after an unwarranted military trial, it is surely even more illegal to arrest and confine them without any trial at all. But the Supreme Court says that the issues of the *Milligan* case were not involved in this case because the evacuees were committed to camps by military orders, not by military tribunals, and because their jailers did not wear uniforms!

There are, then, two basic constitutional problems concealed in the court's easy dismissal of *Ex Parte Milligan:* the arrest, removal, and confinement of persons without trial, pending examination of their loyalty; and the indefinite confinement of persons found to be disloyal. On both counts, at least as to citizens, the moral of *Ex Parte Milligan* is plain.

As for the Japanese *aliens* involved in the evacuation program, the constitutional problem is different. In time of war, the government possesses great powers over enemy aliens, which are to be exercised, the courts say, for the "single purpose" of preventing enemy aliens from aiding the enemy. They may be interned if dangerous and their property in the United States may be taken into custody. Yet they are entitled to our general constitutional protections and individual liberty—to trial by jury, the writ of habeas corpus, and the other basic rights of the person. Is it permissible to intern all the Japanese who live on the West Coast, but to allow German and Italian aliens, and Japanese who live elsewhere, general freedom? Surely the control and custody of enemy aliens in wartime should be reasonably equal and even-handed.

The Japanese exclusion program rests on five propositions of the utmost potential menace:

1. Protective custody, extending over three or four years, is a permitted form of imprisonment in the United States.

2. Political opinions, not criminal acts, may contain enough danger to justify such imprisonment.

3. Men, women, and children of a given racial group, both Americans and resident aliens, can be presumed to possess the kind of dangerous ideas which require their imprisonment.

4. In time of war or emergency the military—perhaps without even the concurrence of the legislature—can decide what political opinions require imprisonment, and which groups are infected with them.

5. The decision of the military can be carried out without indictment, trial, examination, jury, the confrontation of witnesses, counsel for the defense, the privilege against self-incrimination, or any of the other safeguards of the Bill of Rights.

The idea of punishment only for individual criminal behavior is basic to all systems of civilized law. A great principle was never lost so casually. Mr. Justice Black's comment was weak to the point of impotence: "Hardships are a part of war, and war is an aggregation of hardships." It was an answer in the spirit of cliché: "Don't you know there's a war going on?" It ignores the rights of citizenship, and the safeguards of trial practice which have been the historical attributes of liberty.

12. WILLIAM O. DOUGLAS, *The Black Silence of Fear, 1952**

There is an ominous trend in this nation. We are developing tolerance only for the orthodox point of view on world affairs, intolerance for new or different approaches. Orthodoxy normally has stood in the path of

* *The New York Times Magazine,* January 13, 1952. Copyright 1952 by William O. Douglas, reprinted by permission of the author.

change. Orthodoxy was always the stronghold of the status quo, the enemy of new ideas—at least new ideas that were disturbing. He who was wedded to the orthodox view was isolated from the challenge of new facts.

The democratic way of life rejects standardized thought. It rejects orthodoxy. It wants the fullest and freest discussion, within peaceful limits, of all public issues. It encourages constant search for truth at the periphery of knowledge.

We as a people have probably never lived up to that standard in any of our communities. But it has been an ideal toward which most of our communities have strived. We have over the years swung from tolerance to intolerance and back again. There have been eras of intolerance when the views of minorities have been suppressed. But there probably has not been a period of greater intolerance than we witness today.

To understand this, I think one has to leave the country, go into the back regions of the world, lose himself there, and become absorbed in the problems of the peoples of different civilizations. When he returns to America after a few months he probably will be shocked. He will be shocked not at the intentions or purposes or ideals of the American people. He will be shocked at the arrogance and intolerance of great segments of the American press, at the arrogance and intolerance of many leaders in public office, at the arrogance and intolerance reflected in many of our attitudes toward Asia. He will find that thought is being standardized, that the permissible area for calm discussion is being narrowed, that the range of ideas is being limited, that many minds are closed to the receipt of any ideas from Asia.

This is alarming to one who loves his country. It means that the philosophy of strength through free speech is being forsaken for the philosophy of fear through repression.

That choice in Russia is conscious. Under Lenin the ministers and officials were encouraged to debate, to advance new ideas and criticisms. Once the debate was over, however, no dissension or disagreement was permitted. But even that small degree of tolerance for free discussion that Lenin permitted disappeared under Stalin. Stalin maintains a tight system of control, permitting no free speech, no real clash in ideas, even in the inner circle. We are, of course, not emulating either Lenin or Stalin. But we are drifting in the direction of repression, drifting dangerously fast.

What is the cause of this drift? What are the forces behind it? It is only a drift, for certainly everything in our tradition would make the great majority of us reject that course as a conscious choice.

The drift goes back, I think, to the fact that we carried over to days of peace the military approach to world affairs. Diplomacy, certainly in our relations with Asia, took a back seat. The military approach conditioned our thinking and our planning. The military, in fact, determined our approach to the Asians and their problems. That has been a great tragedy in Asia. And the tragedy to us at home has been about as great.

Military thinking continued to play a dominant role in our domestic affairs. The conspiratorial role of Soviet communism in the world scene was apparent to all who could read. This conspiratorial role of Soviet communism was, of course, backed by Russia's military strength. We, therefore, had to be strong in a military sense to hold off Russia. But we soon accepted the military role as the dominant one. We thought of Asia in terms of military bases, not in terms of people and their aspirations. We wanted the starving people of Asia to choose sides, to make up their minds whether they were for us or against us, to cast their lot with us and against Russia.

We did not realize that to millions of these people the difference between Soviet dictatorship and the dictatorship under which they presently live is not very great. We did not realize that in some regions of Asia it is the Communist party that has identified itself with the so-called reform program, the other parties being mere instruments for keeping a ruling class in power. We did not realize that the choice between democracy and communism is not, in the eyes of millions of illiterates, the critical choice it is for us.

We forgot that democracy in many lands is an empty word; that the appeal is hollow when made to illiterate people living at the subsistence level. We asked them to furnish staging grounds for a military operation whose outcome, in their eyes, had no perceptible relation to their own welfare. Those who rejected our overtures must be Communists, we said. Those who did not fall in with our military plans must be secretly aligning with Russia, we thought. This was the result of our military thinking, of our absorption in military affairs. In Asia it has brought us the lowest prestige in our existence.

The military effort has been involving more and more of our sons, more and more of our budget, more and more of our thinking. The military policy has so completely absorbed our thoughts that we have mostly forgotten that our greatest strength, our enduring power is not in guns, but in ideas. Today in Asia we are identified not with ideas of freedom, but with guns. Today at home we are thinking

less and less in terms of defeating communism with ideas, more and more in terms of defeating communism with military might.

The concentration on military means has helped to breed fear. It has bred fear and insecurity partly because of the horror of atomic war. But the real reason strikes deeper. In spite of our enormous expenditures, we see that Soviet imperialism continued to expand and that the expansion proceeds without the Soviets firing a shot. The free world continues to contract without a battle for its survival having been fought. It becomes apparent, as country after country falls to Soviet imperialistic ambitions, that military policy alone is a weak one; that military policy alone will end in political bankruptcy and futility. Thus fear mounts.

Fear has many manifestations. The Communist threat inside the country has been magnified and exalted far beyond its realities. Irresponsible talk by irresponsible people has fanned the flames of fear. Accusations have been loosely made. Character assassinations have become common. Suspicion has taken the place of good-will. Once we could debate with impunity along a wide range of inquiry. Once we could safely explore to the edges of a problem, challenge orthodoxy without qualms, and run the gamut of ideas in search of solutions to perplexing problems. Once we had confidence in each other. Now there is suspicion. Innocent acts become tell-tale marks of disloyalty. The coincidence that an idea parallels Soviet Russia's policy for a moment of time settles an aura of suspicion around a person.

Suspicion grows until only the orthodox idea is the safe one. Suspicion grows until only the person who loudly proclaims that orthodox view, or who, once having been a Communist, has been converted, is trustworthy. Competition for embracing the new orthodoxy increases. Those who are unorthodox are suspect. Everyone who does not follow the military policymakers is suspect. Everyone who voices opposition to the trend away from diplomacy and away from political tactics takes a chance. Some who are opposed are indeed "subversive." Therefore, the thundering edict commands that all who are opposed are "subversive." Fear is fanned to a fury. Good and honest men are pilloried. Character is assassinated. Fear runs rampant.

Fear even strikes at lawyers and the bar. Those accused of illegal Communist activity—all presumed innocent, of course, until found guilty—have difficulty getting reputable lawyers to defend them. Lawyers have talked with me about it. Many are worried. Some could not volunteer their services, for if they did they would lose clients and their firms would suffer. Others could not volunteer because if they did they would be dubbed "subversive" by their community and put in the same category as those they would defend. This is a dark tragedy.

Fear has driven more and more men and women in all walks of life either to silence or to the folds of the orthodox. Fear has mounted—fear of losing one's job, fear of being investigated, fear of being pilloried. This fear has stereotyped our thinking, narrowed the range of free public discussion, and driven many thoughtful people to despair. This fear has even entered universities, great citadels of our spiritual strength, and corrupted them. We have the spectacle of university officials lending themselves to one of the worst witch hunts we have seen since early days.

This fear has affected the youngsters. Youth has played a very important role in our national affairs. It has usually been the oncoming generation—full of enthusiasm, full of idealism,

full of energy—that has challenged its elders and the status quo. It is from this young group that the country has received much of its moral power. They have always been prone to question the stewardship of their fathers, to doubt the wisdom of traditional practices, to explode clichés, to quarrel with the management of public affairs.

Youth—like the opposition party in a parliamentary system—has served a powerful role. It has cast doubts on our policies, challenged our inarticulate major premises, put the light on our prejudices, and exposed our inconsistencies. Youth has made each generation indulge in self-examination.

But a great change has taken place. Youth is still rebellious; but it is largely holding its tongue. There is the fear of being labeled a "subversive" if one departs from the orthodox party line. That charge—if leveled against a young man or young woman—may have profound effects. It may ruin a youngster's business or professional career. No one wants a Communist in his organization nor anyone who is suspect.

And so the lips of the younger generation have become more and more sealed. Repression of ideas has taken the place of debate. There may not be a swelling crowd of converts to the orthodox, military view. But the voice of the opposition is more and more stilled; and youth, the mainstay in early days of the revolt against orthodoxy, is largely immobilized.

This pattern of orthodoxy that is shaping our thinking has dangerous implications. No one man, no one group can have the answer to the many perplexing problems that today confront the management of world affairs. The scene is a troubled and complicated one. The problems require the pooling of many ideas, the exposure of different points of view, the hammering out in public discussions of the pros and cons of this policy or of that.

There are few who know first hand the conditions in the villages of Asia, the South Pacific, South America, and Africa. There are few who really know the powerful forces operating from the grass roots in those areas—forces that are reflected in the attitudes of the men who head up the Governments in those countries. But unless we know those attitudes, we cannot manage intelligently. Unless we know, we will waste our energies and our resources. Unless we know, we are not in position to win even political alliances of an enduring nature. Unless we are eager to know, unless we invite a flood of information on these problems, unless we encourage every avenue of approach to them, we will live and act in ignorance.

There are those who think that our present policy toward Asia will lead to disaster—for us. There are those who believe that in Asia we are fast becoming the symbol of what the people of Asia fear and hate. There are those who believe that the most effective bases we can get in Asia are bases in the hearts of Asia's millions, not bases on their lands. There are those who believe that we must substitute a political for a military strategy in Asia; that when there is a cease-fire in Korea, we must make a political settlement with Red China; that if we apply to China the attitude we are now brilliantly exploiting in Yugoslavia, we can manage to make Soviet imperialism crumble.

There are those who are deeply opposed, many of whom put that issue beyond the pale of discussion. There are even some who make the crucial test of one's loyalty or sanity his acceptance or rejection of our present policy toward Asia.

The question of our Asian policy illustrates the need for a wide range of free public discussion. Asia poses probably the most critical issues of the day. Certain it is that if Asia, like China, is swept into the political orbit of Soviet Russia, the Soviets will then command or be able to immobilize— *the bulk of the people of the world —the bulk of the wealth of the world.*

If that happens, it is doubtful if we, with all our atomic bombs, could even win a war.

The great danger of this period is not inflation, nor the national debt, nor atomic warfare. The great, the critical danger is that we will so limit or narrow the range of permissible discussion and permissible thought that we will become victims of the orthodox school. If we do, we will lose flexibility. We will lose the capacity for expert management. We will then become wedded to a few techniques, to a few devices. They will define our policy and at the same time limit our ability to alter or modify it. Once we narrow the range of thought and discussion, we will surrender a great deal of our power. We will become like the man on the toboggan who can ride it but who can neither steer it nor stop it.

The mind of man must always be free. The strong society is one that sanctions and encourages freedom of thought and expression. When there is that freedom, a nation has resiliency and adaptability. When freedom of expression is supreme, a nation will keep its balance and stability.

Our real power is our spiritual strength, and that spiritual strength stems from our civil liberties. If we are true to our traditions, if we are tolerant of a whole market place of ideas, we will always be strong. Our weakness grows when we become intolerant of opposing ideas, depart from our standards of civil liberties, and borrow the policeman's philosophy from the enemy we detest.

That has been the direction of our drift. It is dangerous to the morale of our people; it is destructive of the influence and prestige of our country. We have lost much of our resiliency, much of our inventive genius. The demands of orthodoxy already have begun to sap our strength—and to deprive us of power. One sees it from far-off Asia. From Asia one sees an America that is losing its humanity, its idealism, and its Christian character.

From Asia one sees an America that is strong and rich and powerful, and yet crippled and ineffective because of its limited vision.

When we view this problem full face we are following the American tradition. The times demand a renaissance in freedom of thought and freedom of expression, a renaissance that will end the orthodoxy that threatens to devitalize us.

X

* *

America and the Wider World

Archibald MacLeish

poet, won the Bollingen Prize for Poetry in 1953 and Pulitzer Prizes in 1932, 1953, and 1959.

His works include *The Pot of Earth,* published in 1925; *Frescoes for Mr. Rockefeller's City,* 1933; *Collected Poems 1917–1952; Union Pacific—a Ballet,* 1934; *Land of the Free,* 1938; *America Was Promises,* 1939; *Freedom Is the Right to Choose,* 1951; and *J. B.,* 1957.

Mr. MacLeish was born in Glencoe, Illinois, in 1892. He received an A.B. degree at Yale in 1915, an LL.B. at Harvard in 1919, and a Litt.D. from Yale in 1939.

He was Librarian of Congress from 1939 to 1944 and Assistant Secretary of State in 1944-45. He was chairman of the American delegation to the first general conference of the United Nations Educational, Scientific, and Cultural Organization at Paris in 1946.

Archibald MacLeish ✳✳✳ We Have Purpose . . , We All Know It

That something has gone wrong in America most of us know. We are richer than any nation before us. We have more Things in our garages and kitchens and cellars than Louis Quatorze had in the whole of Versailles. We have come nearer to the suppression of grinding poverty than even the nineteenth-century Utopians thought seriously possible. We have wiped out many of the pests and scourges which afflicted humanity. We have lengthened men's lives and protected their infancy. We have advanced science to the edges of the inexplicable and hoisted our technology to the sun itself.

We are in a state of growth and flux and change in which cities flow out into countryside and countryside moves into cities and new industries are born and old industries vanish and the customs of generations alter and fathers speak different languages from their sons. In brief, we are prosperous, lively, successful, inventive, diligent—but, nevertheless and nothwithstanding, something is wrong and we know it.

The trouble seems to be that we don't feel right with ourselves or with the country. It isn't only the Russians. We have outgrown the adolescent time when everything that was wrong with America was the fault of the Russians and all we needed to do to be saved was to close the State Department and keep the Communists out of motion pictures. It isn't just the Russians now: it's ourselves. It's the way we feel about ourselves as Americans. We feel that we've lost our way in the woods, that we don't know where we are going—if anywhere.

I agree—but I still feel that the diagnosis is curious, for the fact is, of course, that we *have* a national purpose—the most precisely articulated national purpose in recorded history—and that we all know it. It is the purpose put into words by the most lucid mind of that most lucid century, the 18th, and adopted on the Fourth of July in 1776 as a declaration of the existence and national intent of a new nation.

Not only is it a famous statement of purpose: it is also an admirable statement of purpose. Prior to July 4, 1776, the national purpose of nations had been to dominate: to dominate at least their neighbors and rivals and, wherever possible, to dominate the world. The American national purpose was the opposite: to liberate from domination; to set men free.

*All m*en, to Thomas Jefferson, were created equal. *All* men were endowed by their Creator with certain inalienable rights. Among these rights were life, liberty, and the pursuit of happiness. It was the existence of these rights which justified American independence from King George and justified also the revolution which would have to be fought for that independence. It was the existence of these rights which would provide a foundation for the government to be established when independence was secure.

We not only *have* a national purpose: we have a national purpose of such aspiration, such potentiality, such power of hope that we refer to it —or used to—as the American Dream. We were dedicated from our beginnings to the proposition that we existed not merely to exist but to be free, and the dedication was real in spite of the fact that it took us three generations and a bloody war to practice our preachment within our own frontiers. It was real in spite of the fact that its practice is still a delusion in numerous pockets of hypocrisy across the nation.

To be free is not, perhaps, a political program in the modern sense, but from the point of view of a new nation it may be something better. The weakness of political programs—Five Year Plans and the like—is that they can be achieved. But human freedom can never be achieved because human freedom is a continuously evolving condition. It is infinite in its possibilities—as infinite as the human soul which it enfranchises. The nation which seeks it and persists in its search will move through history as a ship moves on a compass course toward a constantly opening horizon.

And America did move steadily on before it lost headway in the generation in which we live. The extraordinary feel of liveness which the Americans communicated, whether agreeably or not, to their early European visitors came from that sense of national expectation. We were never a very philosophical people politically after Jefferson and his contemporaries left us. We were practical men who took instruction from the things we saw and heard and did. But the purpose defined in our Declaration was a reality to us notwithstanding. It gave us *aim* as the continent gave us *scope*, and the old American character with its almost anarchic passion for idiosyncrasy and difference was the child of both. Those Missouri militiamen Parkman describes in *The Oregon Trail* slogging their way West to the war with Mexico, each in his own rig and each in his own way, could have constituted an army nowhere else. When, at Sacramento, a drunken officer commanded his company to halt and a private yelled "Charge!" the company charged, knocking five times their number of Mexicans out of prepared entrenchments. The anarchy didn't matter because they were all headed in the same direction and the name of that direction was West—or freedom. They had a future in common and they had a purpose in common and the purpose was the enfranchisement of men—of all men—to think for themselves, speak for themselves, govern themselves, pursue happiness for themselves, and so become themselves.

Why then do we need to rediscover what our national purpose is? Because the words of the Declaration in its superb housing in the National Archives have become archival words, words out of history? Because the Bill of Rights of the American Constitution belongs, like the Magna Carta, in an airtight case? No one who reads the newspapers could think so. There has never been a time when courts and Congress devoted more of their attention to the constitutional guarantees of individual freedom than they do today, and as for the Declaration of Independence, its language is more alive in the middle of the twentieth century than it was in the middle of the nineteenth or even when it was written. It is not Communism, however Communism may attempt to exploit them, which has begotten the new nations of Asia and Africa or the new nationalistic stirrings in South America and the Caribbean and even in Europe. The Marxist dream is a dream of economic machinery, not of living men: of a universal order and system, not a proliferation of nationalities. No, the dream which has set the jungle and the cane on fire is different and older. It is Thomas Jefferson's dream—the dream which he and his contemporaries believed would change the world. It *is* changing the world —and not later than one might expect. Two hundred years is a short time in the history of institutions.

If the American Dream is out of date today it is out of date only in America—only in America and in the Communist countries in which the political police have extinguished it. But is it really out of date in America? Is its power to direct and draw us really so faint that we are lost in the blaze of our own prosperity and must enlist the aid of learned men to tell us where the future lies? That, I think, is a question for debate in these discussions.

Have we lost our sense of purpose or have we merely lost touch with it? Have we rejected the arduous labor to which our beginnings committed us? Or are we merely confused and bewildered by the volcanic upheavals which have changed the landscapes of our lives? Or is it neither rejection nor confusion? Is it nothing more than the flatulence and fat of an overfed people whose children prepare at the milk-shake counter for coronary occlusions in middle age? Are we simply too thick through the middle to dream?

I doubt for myself that we have rejected the American Dream or have even thought of rejecting it. There are minorities, of course, who have little enthusiasm for the actualities of the American commitment to freedom, but this is largely because they do not understand what the struggle it culminated was all about. Certain areas on the fringes of Europe were preserved by their geographical location from the necessity of living through the crisis of the Western mind which we call the Reformation, and American stock from these areas tends to find the master-mistress idea of the American Revolution—the idea which raised it from a minor war for independence to a world event—incomprehensible if not actually misguided. It is not a question of religion. Catholics from the heart of the European continent understand Jefferson as well as any Protestant. It is a question of geography. Men and women whose ancestors were not obliged to fight the battle for or against freedom of conscience cannot for the life of them understand why censorship should be considered evil or why authority is not preferable to freedom.

But all this does not add up to a rejection of the American dedication to liberty—the American dedication to the enfranchisement of the human spirit. The Irish Catholics, who are among the most persistent and politically powerful advocates of increasing censorship in the U.S., and who are brought up to submit to clerical authority in matters which the American tradition reserves to the individual conscience, are nevertheless among the most fervent of American patriots. And if their enthusiasm for freedom of the mind is restrained, their passion for freedom of the man is glorious. Only if a separate system of education should be used to perpetuate the historical ignorance and moral obtuseness on which fear of freedom of the mind is based would the danger of the rejection of the American Dream from this quarter become serious. As for the rest, the only wholehearted rejection comes from the Marxists with their curiously childish notion that it is more realistic and more intelligent to talk about economic machinery than about men. But the Marxists, both Mr. Hoovers to the contrary notwithstanding, have no perceptible influence on American opinion.

I cannot believe that we have *rejected* the purpose on which our Republic was founded. Neither can I believe that our present purposelessness results from our economic fat and our spiritual indolence. It is not because we are too comfortable that the dream has left us. It is true, I suppose, that we eat better—at least more—than any nation ever has. It is true too that there are streaks of American fat, some of it very ugly fat, and that it shows most unbecomingly at certain points in New York and Miami and along the California coast. But the whole country is not lost in a sluggish, sun-oiled sleep beneath a beach umbrella, dreaming of More and More. We have our share, and more than our share, of mink coats and prestige cars and expense account restaurants and oil millionaires, but America is not made of such things as these. We are an affluent society but we are not affluent to the point of spiritual sloth.

Most American young women, almost regardless of income, work harder in their homes and with their children than their mothers or their grandmothers had to. For one thing, domestic servants have all but disappeared and no machine can cook a meal or mind a baby. For another, there are more babies than there have been for generations. For still another, the rising generation is better educated than its parents were and more concerned with the serious business of life— the life of the mind. To watch your daughter-in-law taking care of her own house, bringing up four children, running the Parent-Teacher Association, singing in the church choir, and finding time nevertheless to read the books she wants to read and hear the music she wants to hear and see the plays she can afford to, is a salutary thing. She may think more about machines and gadgets than you ever did but that is largely because there are more machines and gadgets to think about. No one who has taught, as I have been doing for the past ten years, can very seriously doubt that the generation on the way up is more intelligent than the generation now falling back. And as for the materialism about which we talk so much, it is worth remembering that the popular whipping boy of the moment among the intelligent young is precisely "Madison Avenue," that mythical advertising copy writer who is supposed to persuade us to wallow in cosmetics and tail-fin cars. We may be drowning in Things, but the best of our sons and daughters like it even less than we do.

What then has gone wrong? The answer, I submit, is fairly obvious and will be found where one would expect to find it: in the two great wars which have changed so much beside. The first world war altered not only our position in the world but our attitude toward ourselves and toward our business as a people. Having won a war to "make the world safe for democracy," we began to act as though democracy itself had been won as though there was nothing left for us to do but enjoy ourselves: make money in the stock market, gin in the bathtub, and whoopee in the streets. The American journey had been completed. The American goal was reached. We had emerged from the long trek westward to find ourselves on the Plateau of Permanent Prosperity. We were *there!* It took the disaster of 1929 and the long depression which followed to knock the fantasy out of our heads but the damage had been done. We had lost touch with the driving force of our own history.

The effect of the second war was different—and the same. The second war estranged us from our genius as a people. We fought it because we realized that our dream of human liberty could not survive in the slave state Hitler was imposing on the world. We won it with no such illusions as had plagued us twenty-five years before: there was another more voracious slave state behind Hitler's. But though we did not repeat the folly of the '20s we repeated the delusion of the '20s. We acted again as though freedom were an accomplished fact. We no longer thought of it as safe but we made a comparable mistake: we thought of it as something which could be protected by building walls around it, by "containing" its enemy.

But the truth is, of course, that freedom is never an accomplished fact. It is always a process. Which is why the drafters of the Declaration spoke of the *pursuit* of happiness: they knew their Thucydides and therefore knew that "the secret of happiness is freedom and the secret of freedom, courage." The only way freedom can be defended is not by fencing it in but by enlarging it, exercising it. Though we did defend freedom by exercising it through the Marshall Plan in Europe, we did not, for understandable reasons involving the colonial holdings of our allies, defend freedom by exercising it in Asia and Africa where the future is about to be decided.

The results have been hurtful to the world and to ourselves. How hurtful they have been to the world we can see in Cuba, where a needed and necessary and hopeful revolution against an insufferable dictatorship appears to have chosen the Russian solution of its economic difficulties rather than ours. We have tried to explain that ominous fact to ourselves in the schoolgirl vocabulary of the McCarthy years, saying that Castro and his friends are Communists. But whether they are or not—and the charge is at least unproved—there is no question whatever of the enormous popular support for their regime and for as much of their program as is now known. Not even those who see Communist conspiracies underneath everyone else's bed have contended that the Cuban people were tricked or policed in their enthusiasm for their revolution. On the contrary the people appear to outrun the government in their eagerness for the new order. What this means is obvious. What this means is that the wave of the future, to the great majority of Cubans, is the Russian wave, not the American. That fact, and its implications for the rest of Latin America, to say nothing of Africa and Asia, is the fact we should be looking at, hard and long. If the Russian purpose seems more vigorous and more promising to the newly liberated peoples of the world than the American purpose, then we have indeed lost the "battle for men's minds" of which we talk so much.

As for ourselves, the hurt has been precisely the loss of a sense of national purpose. To engage, as we have over the past fifteen years, in programs having as their end and aim not action to further a purpose of our own but *counter*action to frustrate a purpose of the Russians is to invite just such a state of mind. A nation cannot be sure even of its own identity when it finds itself associated in country after country—as we have most recently in South Korea and Turkey—with regimes whose political practices are inimical to its own.

What, then, is the issue in this debate? What is the problem? Not to *discover* our national purpose but to *exercise* it. Which means, ultimately, to exercise it for its own sake, not for the defeat of those who have a different purpose. There is all the difference in the world between strengthening the enemies of our enemies because they are against what we are against, and supporting the hopes of mankind because we too believe in them, because they are our hopes also. The fields of action in the two cases may be the same: Africa and Asia and Latin America. The tools of action—military assistance and above all economic and industrial and scientific aid—may look alike. But the actions will be wholly different. The first course of action surrenders initiative to the Russians and accepts the Russian hypothesis that Communism is the new force moving in the world. The second asserts what is palpably true, that the new force moving in the world is the force we set in motion, the force which gave us, almost two centuries ago, our liberating mission. The first is costly, as we know. The second will be more costly still. But the second, because it recaptures for the cause of freedom the initiative which belongs to it and restores to the country the confidence it has lost, is capable of succeeding. The first, because it can never be anything but a policy of resistance, can only continue to resist and to accomplish nothing more.

There are those, I know, who will reply that the liberation of humanity, the freedom of man and mind, is nothing but a dream. They are right. It is. It is the American dream.

How Can National Purposes Be Attained beyond the National Borders?

The definition of a national purpose in a society as complex as that of the United States was never simple. The problem was compounded by the necessity for taking account of what Americans meant by nation and also of what their assumptions were about the character of man and the universe in which he lived. All these problems were intimately bound up with the way in which Americans defined their goals.

In addition, in the historical experience of the United States, the very conception of a national purpose demanded that Americans think of themselves in relation to the rest of the world. Every speculation as to why they were where they were was tied to attitudes toward the civilizations from which they had migrated. Any visions of the future were related to attitudes toward the lands beyond their own borders. In that sense American thought was rarely isolationist. If the society that Americans were building was indeed to be a city upon a hill, a model for imitation by other peoples, then the citizens of the Republic were certainly obliged to take into consideration the welfare of other men as well as their own.

Never has that obligation been more pressing than now. Confusion about the extent to which the American dream of a free society, Archibald MacLeish points out, has been hurtful to the world and to ourselves. The very security of the United States has depended upon its success in resolving these problems. And in confronting them it will be helpful to consider the various forms taken in the past by American interests overseas.

The men of the Revolutionary generation who brought the Republic into being had no doubt that the cause of America was the cause of all mankind. Many of them fully expected that Europeans would, in short order, follow the precedent set in 1776 and overthrow their own monarchs. It was in that vein that the poet Joel Barlow (1754–1812) addressed his letter to the people of Piedmont, advising them to revolt against their rulers as the Americans and the French already had (1). The overturn of the old regime in Europe proved not so easy a matter, however; and for the time being, most Americans concluded with George Washington that they had best maintain their neutrality (see above, pages 304–309). While preserving a close interest in the events of Europe in the first half of the nineteenth century, it seemed more strategic to concentrate upon developments in the Western Hemisphere, where the weight of the past was less oppressive.

The Monroe Doctrine enunciated in that spirit formed the basis for the developing conception of manifest destiny. By the second quarter of the nineteenth century it seemed self-evident to most Americans that their nation was destined to spread across the whole of the North American continent. John L. O'Sullivan (1813–95), a New York Democratic politician and editor, became a forceful exponent of this idea. The United States, he explained, was the great nation of the future, destined to bring within its fold the people of the rest of the hemisphere while extending to them the blessings of liberty (2). The conception of America as a mother of republics to which the future belonged was also an inspiration to Walt Whitman (1819–92), whose faith in the likeness of all men convinced him that all would move in the same direction (3).

It was significant that the conviction that the United States was inevitably to expand persisted on through to the end of the nineteenth century. But it subtly changed its form and its emphasis. The writings of Josiah Strong (see above, page 57), while still animated by a missionary attitude toward the outer world, already showed the belief in the superiority of the Americans and in the inferiority of the lesser folk over whom they were to rule. At the end of the century that conviction was strengthened by the racist feeling that innate biological differences set apart superior and inferior people. Economic and military motives then also led some Americans to seek expansion through imperialism. The result was the transformation of the conception of America from that of an equal, bearing freedom, into that of a benevolent but superior ruler. The influence of racist and imperialist ideas was strikingly illustrated in the thinking of Senator Albert J. Beveridge (1862–1927), a progressive in politics yet an exponent of colonialism abroad (4). The personal popularity and the idealistic motives of President Theodore Roosevelt (1858–1919) further spread the conception of the strenuous life of conquest as a peculiar obligation of the United States (5).

Yet imperialism never dominated American thinking. A strong humanitarian countercurrent always made the very idea of colonies objectionable. The poet Vachel Lindsey (1879-1931) spoke nostalgically of the earlier conception of American mission (6). And President Woodrow Wilson (1856–1924), confronted by the crisis of World War I, attempted to state the conditions of peace in idealistic terms that assigned the United States a prominent role in the future rational conduct of world affairs (7).

Woodrow Wilson's hopes were to be frustrated in the 1920's. But before the end of the next decade the signs of a second great war were already on the horizon. The poet Archibald MacLeish (1892–) then ironically commented on the apathy of Americans to their heritage (8). Yet, even then, there were indications both of a continuing sense of responsibility and also of the widespread faith of people throughout the world in the Americans. Wendell L. Willkie (1892-1944), Republican presidential candidate in 1940, movingly described this sentiment as he encountered it in an extensive global tour in 1942 (9).

The leadership of the great alliance that fought the Germans and the Japanese after 1941 strengthened that conception of responsibility. Americans therefore accepted more readily than in 1918 the burdens of restoring the peace. General George C. Marshall (1880–1959), then Secretary of State, announced a plan to aid the economies of the devastated countries that was markedly influential in restoring the prosperity of the free world (10). And President Dwight D. Eisenhower (1890–) in his second Inaugural Address continued to speak the hope for American leadership in bringing peace to the world (11). It had become evident by then that American national purposes could not be achieved simply within the confines of the United States. In the long run it would be necessary to think of that purpose in its world perspective.

1. JOEL BARLOW, *Letter to the People of Piedmont, 1792**

A number of imperious circumstances, of which you have been rather the victims than the authors, have for many centuries inverted the order of things, and deprived you of those advantages which ought to attend your situation. I am a stranger in this part of the world; Italy is known to me only from its history, and your present condition only from distant observation and report. It is not probable that I shall ever have the pleasure of seeing you or any part of your country. You must, therefore, acquit me of entertaining any desire to mislead you, as I can have no possible interest in addressing you this letter, but the interest the human heart naturally takes in uttering the truth on a very important subject. You are my fellow-creatures; as such I love you, and cherish the ties which ought to be mutual between us. You are in a condition which appears to me to call upon you to burst the bands of slavery; in this view, I am ready to hail you as brothers, and wish to aid you in your work.

I presume in the first place, and I think I am not deceived, that you are discontented with your present situation. I believe you are convinced that you cannot be happy, as a people, while the powers of your government remain as they now are, as relative to the church, the state, and the army. If this be true, you must wish for a change; provided such change can be within your power, and provided you are convinced that it would be for your advantage. Let us examine these two points; whether you are able to effect a revolution in your government; and if you are, whether you would be benefited by it.—For it is not my wish to hurry you into measures, of which you cannot see the issue, and for which you are not prepared.

I. *Are you able to effect a revolution in your government?*

The question need never be asked of any people, when considered with reference to themselves only, without regard to their neighbours. A whole people is essentially sovereign. They

*Joel Barlow, *A Letter Addressed to the People of Piedmont . . . . Translated from the French by the Author* (London, 1795).

can at all times do as they please with
their own affairs, unless they are over-
powered by surrounding nations. It is
the people who support the government as it now is; and the same sovereign people can at any time change its
form, and support it in whatever manner it shall please them best. The
question has no difficulty in it, but
when viewed with reference to the
interest which other governments may
have in preventing a revolution in
their neighborhood.

The enquiry, pursued in this connection, becomes more extensive; especially when applied to a country of
small dimensions, and to a nation less
powerful than some of its neighbours.
Such is Piedmont. Had you been called
upon seven years ago to look into your
affairs, and take the government into
your own hands, you must have considered it as a dangerous experiment.
Even supposing the weight of your
sufferings to have been as great then
as they are now, and supposing you had
been possessed of the same information which you have since drawn from
the progress of liberty in Europe, it
would scarcely have been prudent for
you to have engaged in so daring an
enterprise. All the tyrants in your
neighbourhood would have brought forward their armies of slaves to crush
the rebellion. The French court would
have been, at that time, as much your
enemy as the French nation is now
your friend. And the house of Austria,
with all the subdivisions of its power
in Italy, posted at your gates, would
have united with that of Bourbon, to
have guaranteed your king in every
possible extent of his oppression.

Under these disadvantages your struggles for liberty might have been vain;
they might even have produced a
new injury, instead of relieving you
from the old. But the ground is now
changed; the duty you owe to yourselves is clearly pointed out by the

natural current of events; and the work
you have to do, in establishing a perfect and undisturbed liberty, is in my
opinion much easier than you imagine.
France is at this time, not only the
most powerful nation in Europe, but
when engaged, as she now is, in
defence of liberty, she is a match for
all the other powers of Europe, when
united in defence of tyranny. France is
now your natural friend, the friend of
all people and the enemy of all tyrants.
She is indeed the only friend you have
as a nation in this part of the world.
France has brought liberty to your
doors; and she invites you, in the name
of all that is dear to you as men, in
the name of all that can bind you to
the interests of human nature in general, to accept the blessing at her
hands. She has done more; she has
taught you and all other people how
public happiness is to be acquired and
preserved. She has addressed herself
to the great principles of reason which
are common to all men; she has cleared
away the mass of prejudice, of false
doctrine, of superstition in the science
of morals; a mass which the complicated abuses of tyranny, continued for
many centuries, had accumulated on
the human mind. She has laid down
and clearly defined the rights and
duties of man and of citizens, explained the great doctrine of equality,
the true design of government, the
nature of the trust to be reposed in
public officers, as servants of the people, by whom they are created and by
whom they are paid. She has taught
you a great practical truth, which is
too consoling to be rejected, and too
clear to be called in question, *that you
are the sovereigns in your own country;* that you have not, that you cannot have a master, unless you choose
to give up your reason, and renounce
the character of men; that for any
man to call himself your sovereign is
a blasphemy against God the sovereign

of nature, and against men the proprietors of the earth.

Obligations of gratitude are due to the French nation from you, and from every people in Europe. She has conquered liberty for all men, and laid the foundation for universal public felicity. Other nations have only to build the superstructure, of which the model is given them in the constitution of this great republic.

But let us not amuse ourselves with words, nor rest the argument on theoretical principles, however incontestible they may be. Let us speak of facts that are passing before our eyes, and call to mind the events of the great year that is now drawing to a close. You have seen the principal tyrants and the most formidable armies of Europe, combined and marching in full career of promised victory against the liberties of France.—These armies after sweeping over half of Europe and famishing whole countries in their way to the French frontiers, have there been cut to pieces by a handful of freemen, and driven out of their country. Liberty has marched on the heels of the fugitives; the arch tyrant of Austria, at the head of this fatal conspiracy of kings, has lost the finest part of his dominions; many of the subaltern princes of the empire have lost the whole of theirs, and are now beggars abroad among their brother brigands, who are in expectation of the same inevitable fate. The standard of liberty has reached the borders of the Rhine by the miscarriage of the same combination which has brought it to the summit of the Alps. . . .

Under these circumstances, we need no longer enquire whether you are able to effect a revolution; the more natural question is, are you able to resist it? It is true, the French have renounced all ideas of conquest, and have declared that they will never make war against the liberty of any people.

But you will observe that this principle contains in itself a declaration of war against all tyrants who are hostile to the liberty of France; especially against those whose vicinity renders them dangerous to the internal peace of the new republic, by fostering its fugitive traitors, and being the centre of new conspiracies against the rights of man. The court of Turin comes under this description. It is hostile to the liberties of France; it has been so from the beginning; the nature of its external connections and of its internal constitution requires that it should be so to the end. The court of Turin must, therefore, be overturned; the government of your country must be changed, and its powers restored to you, to whom they naturally belong.

This is a simple view of facts, which may serve to indicate the present crisis of your affairs, of which it is proper that you should be apprised; that by a due consideration of the causes you may not be astonished at the effects. I make known to you my opinion, with all the frankness that the solemnity of the subject demands; and it seems almost impossible that you should fail to turn the consequences to your advantage.

II. The more important question to be discussed is, Whether you will be benefited by a revolution in your government?

Many of you will doubtless consider this enquiry as superfluous, because your condition can scarcely be rendered worse, and the means of rendering it better are so obvious that they cannot escape the slightest observation. But those of you who are accustomed to reflect on the principles of liberty will pardon the simplicity of the enquiry, in favour of the great mass of the people whom it is our duty to instruct. There has been so much falsehood and folly imposed on that class of mankind, in order to debase and brutalize their minds to the level of their condition, that their ignorance has become preternatural; it is almost necessary to begin their instruction by informing them that they are human creatures. But, citizen of Italy, defendants of Brutus and Cato, this state of degradation is not the condition designed for man. The God of equal liberty has allotted you a different birthright; you are now invited to reclaim your inheritance, to take possession of your portion among your brethren, to enjoy it in peace, and restore harmony to the great family of men.

You have been fatally misinformed with respect to the nature of the French revolution, and the events that have attended it. Your religious teachers and your political masters have an interest in deceiving you. They unite their efforts for this purpose; they blind your eyes, as you blind the eyes of a mill-horse, that he may not see his harness, nor consider the weight he draws. If the mill-horse could know that he has only a feeble child for a conductor, and that he is made to go constantly round in the same small circle, so that he cannot hope to come nearer his journey's end; especially if he could look into the neighbouring fields and see the other horses enjoying their liberty, he would soon revolt against his little despot, he would grow discouraged with the same unpromising round of fatigue, and refuse to do his work. It is for this reason that you blind his eyes. My friends, the same arts are used with you. The clergy and the nobles of your country, with a man at their head whom they call a king, do nothing but live upon your labours. They cannot support their luxury by any other means than by keeping you constantly at work. They know that if you were to be informed of their weakness and of your own strength, you would refuse to be their drudges. They are sensible that the moment you open

your eyes, you will see that they are but men, that all men are equal in their rights, that they have no more right or power to be kings and lords over you, than you have to be kings and lords over them; and that in consequence of this, you would immediately overturn that abominable system of public robbery which they call a government, and establish a new and equal government, which should secure to every man the fruits of his own labours, protect the innocent, punish the guilty, and instruct every member of society in his duties and rights.

This is precisely what the people of France have done; and the performance of this great work, so necessary to the happiness of mankind, is called the French revolution. It is the knowledge of this revolution which your court and clergy wish to conceal from you lest you should follow the example. They prevent the French newspapers from coming into your country; they forbid the reading of all books that treat of this revolution, and all conversation on that or any other political subject; they have shut up the popular theatres at Turin, and left open none but that of the nobility, from which the citizens are excluded; they have suppressed the great university of that capital, called the *University of the Provinces,* which used to bring students from all parts of Italy, and a considerable emolument to the town; they have doubled the number of their spies, and increased the powers of the police.

All this to keep you ignorant of the French revolution, that you may not be disposed to follow the example. Observe the insult offered to your understanding. If the example were bad, your good sense would teach you to shun it; it would need only to be known, to be despised; and it ought to be explained to all people, that they might learn to avoid such a dangerous innovation. If it be good, it ought to be taught by your teachers, and imitated by all the world. But be assured that the very caution they use to prevent your coming to the knowledge of the fact, is a proof that such a revolution would be an advantage to you and a disadvantage to them.

But this is not all; they have invented a thousand falsehoods to supply the place of truth. They have told you lies, in order to excite your enmity against your best friends, and to rouse you to war against those principles which ought to be as dear to you as to the French; because they are the principles of equal liberty and national happiness, applicable to all people. . . .

You have heard it likewise asserted that the French revolution has been marked with cruelty and murder. This is unfortunately true. But it has likewise been marked with treachery, with bribery, with perjury, with all the complicated wiles of expiring despotism. All the cruelty, all the crimes of every name or denomination, that have attended this revolution, have proceeded from royalty, the adherents of royalty, and the refractory priests. The court of Versailles had been for ages a school of falsehood and deceit; and the execution of the penal laws served as a public exhibition of torture, to familiarize the people with the most sanguinary punishments. If the court of Turin and the laws of Piedmont are any better, it is happier for you; you will have the less wickedness to combat in the course of your revolution. But I fear in some respects they are worse. These circumstances in France has trained up in all parts of the king-

dom a numerous class of men versed in every art of treachery and perfidy. In this situation of things the great mass of the people, who are naturally honest and good, set themselves seriously to work in the business of the revolution; which might have been carried on with the greatest harmony; as it had nothing in view but the welfare of the whole. But these deceitful men, being enemies of the revolution, and finding that they could not oppose it by open force, assumed the mask of patriotism, and brought themselves into places of trust in every department of the legislative and executive power. The effect of this was that these good people found themselves deceived and betrayed in every stage of their affairs, from the beginning of the revolution in 1789, till the tenth of August, 1792. Being surrounded by traitors, and not knowing whom to trust even with the execution of their own vengeance, it was natural and sometimes necessary that they should assume this terrible task upon themselves. In some instances indeed this popular vengeance has been ill directed, and has fallen on innocent heads. But these instances are rare.

The limits, I prescribe to my letter, will not allow of my entering into details on a subject so intricate and extensive. This, however, may be relied on as an undeniable truth, that nothing is more human, generous and just, than the general spirit of the revolution; and whatever particular acts, may seem to contravene these principles, those acts are chargeable upon its enemies, and not upon its friends.

2. John L. O'Sullivan, *The Great Nation of Futurity, 1839**

The American people having derived their origin from many other nations, and the Declaration of National Independence being entirely based on the great principle of human equality, these facts demonstrate at once our disconnected position as regards any other nation; that we have, in reality, but little connection with the past history of any of them and still less with all antiquity, its glories, or its crimes. On the contrary, our national birth was the beginning of a new history, the formation and progress of an untried political system, which separates us from the past and connects us with the future only; and so far as regards the entire development of the natural rights of man, in moral, political, and national life, we may confidently assume that our country is destined to be *the great nation* of futurity.

It is so destined, because the principle upon which a nation is organized fixes its destiny, and that of equality is perfect, is universal. It presides in all the operations of the physical world, and it is also the conscious law of the soul—the self-evident dictate of morality, which accurately defines the duty of man to man, and consequently man's rights as man. Besides, the truthful annals of any nation furnish abundant evidence that its happiness, its greatness, its duration, were always proportionate to the democratic equality in its system of government.

How many nations have had their decline and fall because the equal rights of the minority were trampled on by the despotism of the majority; or the interests of the many sacrificed to the aristocracy of the few; or the rights and interests of all given up to the monarchy of one? These three kinds of government have figured so frequently and so largely in the ages that have passed away that their history, through all time to come, can only furnish a resemblance. Like causes produce like effects, and the true philosopher of history will easily discern the principle of equality, or of privilege, working out its inevitable result. The first is regenerative, because it is natural and right; the latter is destructive to society, because it is unnatural and wrong.

What friend of human liberty, civilization, and refinement can cast his view over the past history of the monarchies and aristocracies of antiquity, and not deplore that they ever existed? What philanthropist can contemplate the oppressions, the cruelties, and injustice inflicted by them on the masses of mankind and not turn with moral horror from the retrospect?

America is destined for better deeds. It is our unparalleled glory that we have no reminiscences of battlefields, but in defense of humanity, of the oppressed of all nations, of the rights of conscience, the rights of personal enfranchisement. Our annals describe no scenes of horrid carnage, where men were led on by hundreds of thousands to slay one another, dupes and victims to emperors, kings, nobles, demons in the human form called heroes. We have had patriots to defend our homes, our liberties, but no aspirants to crowns or thrones; nor have the American people ever suffered themselves to be led on by wicked ambition to depopulate the land, to spread desolation far and

* *The United States Magazine and Democratic Review*, VI (November, 1839), 2–6.

wide, that a human being might be placed on a seat of supremacy.

We have no interest in the scenes of antiquity, only as lessons of avoidance of nearly all their examples. The expansive future is our arena and for our history. We are entering on its untrodden space with the truths of God in our minds, beneficent objects in our hearts, and with a clear conscience unsullied by the past. We are the nation of human progress, and who will, what can, set limits to our onward march? Providence is with us, and no earthly power can. We point to the everlasting truth on the first page of our national declaration, and we proclaim to the millions of other lands that "the gates of hell"—the powers of aristocracy and monarchy—"shall not prevail against it."

The far-reaching, the boundless future, will be the era of American greatness. In its magnificent domain of space and time, the nation of many nations is destined to manifest to mankind the excellence of divine principles; to establish on earth the noblest temple ever dedicated to the worship of the Most High—the Sacred and the True. Its floor shall be a hemisphere—its roof the firmament of the star-studded heavens, and its congregation a Union of many Republics, comprising hundreds of happy millions, calling, owning no man master, but governed by God's natural and moral law of equality, the law of brotherhood—of "peace and good will amongst men. . . ."

Yes, we are the nation of progress, of individual freedom, of universal enfranchisement. Equality of rights is the cynosure of our union of states, the grand exemplar of the correlative equality of individuals; and, while truth sheds its effulgence, we cannot retrograde without dissolving the one and subverting the other. We must onward to the fulfilment of our mission—to the entire development of the principle of our organization—freedom of conscience, freedom of person, freedom of trade and business pursuits, universality of freedom and equality. This is our high destiny, and in nature's eternal, inevitable decree of cause and effect we must accomplish it. All this will be our future history, to establish on earth the moral dignity and salvation of man—the immutable truth and beneficence of God. For this blessed mission to the nations of the world, which are shut out from the lifegiving light of truth, has America been chosen; and her high example shall smite unto death the tyranny of kings, hierarchs, and oligarchs and carry the glad tidings of peace and good will where myriads now endure an existence scarcely more enviable than that of beasts of the field. Who, then, can doubt that our country is destined to be *the great nation* of futurity?

3. WALT WHITMAN, *Thou Mother with Thy Equal Brood, 1872**

1

Thou Mother, with thy equal brood,
Thou varied chain of different States, yet one identity only,
A special song before I go I'd sing o'er all the rest,
For thee, the future.

* Walt Whitman, *Complete Writings* (New York, 1902), II, 235–42.

I'd sow a seed for thee of endless Nationality,
I'd fashion thy ensemble including body and soul,
I'd show away ahead thy real Union, and how it may
        be accomplish'd.

The paths to the house I seek to make,
But leave to those to come the house itself.

Belief I sing, and preparation;
As Life and Nature are not great with reference to the
        present only,
But greater still from what is yet to come,
Out of that formula for thee I sing.

2

As a strong bird on pinions free,
Joyous, the amplest spaces heavenward cleaving,
Such be the thought I'd think of thee America,
Such be the recitative I'd bring for thee.

The conceits of the poets of other lands I'd bring thee not,
Nor the compliments that have served their turn so long,
Nor rhyme, nor the classics, nor perfume of foreign court or indoor
        library;
But an odor I'd bring as from forests of pine in Maine, or breath
        of an Illinois prairie,
With open airs of Virginia or Georgia or Tennessee, or from Texas
        uplands, or Florida's glades,
Or the Saguenay's black stream, or the wide blue spread of Huron,
With presentment of Yellowstone's scenes, or Yosemite,
And murmuring under, pervading all, I'd bring the rustling
        sea-sound,
That endlessly sounds from the two Great Seas of the world.

And for thy subtler sense subtler refrains dread Mother,
Preludes of intellect tallying these and thee, mind-formulas fitted
        for thee, real and sane and large as these and thee,
Thou! mounting higher, diving deeper than we knew, thou
        transcendental Union!
By thee fact to be justified, blended with thought,
Thought of man justified, blended with God,
Through thy idea, lo, the immortal reality!
Through thy reality, lo, the immortal idea!

3

Brain of the New World, what a task is thine,
To formulate the Modern—out of the peerless grandeur of the
        modern,
Out of thyself, comprising science, to recast poems, churches, art,
(Recast, maybe discard them, end them—maybe their work is done,
        who knows?)
By vision, hand, conception, on the background of the mighty
        past, the dead,
To limn with absolute faith the mighty living present.

And yet thou living present brain, heir of the dead, the Old
    World brain,
Thou that lay folded like an unborn babe within its folds so long,
Thou carefully prepared by it so long—haply thou but unfoldest it,
    only maturest it,
It to eventuate in thee—the essence of the bygone time contain'd
    in thee,
Its poems, churches, arts, unwitting to themselves, destined with
    reference to thee;
Thou but the apples, long, long, long a-growing,
The fruit of all the Old ripening to-day in thee.

4

Sail, sail thy best, ship of Democracy,
Of value is thy freight, 'tis not the Present only,
The Past is also stored in thee,
Thou holdest not the venture of thyself alone, not of the Western
    continent alone,
Earth's *résumé* entire floats on thy keel O ship, is steadied by
    thy spars,
With the Time voyages in trust, the antecedent nations sink or
    swim with thee,
With all their ancient struggles, martyrs, heroes, epics, wars, thou
    bear'st the other continents,
Theirs, theirs as much as thine, the destination-port triumphant;
Steer then with good strong hand and wary eye O helmsman, thou
    carriest great companions,
Venerable priestly Asia sails this day with thee,
And royal feudal Europe sails with thee.

5

Beautiful world of new superber birth that rises to my eyes,
Like a limitless golden cloud filling the western sky,
Emblem of general maternity lifted above all,
Sacred shape of the bearer of daughters and sons,
Out of thy teeming womb thy giant babes in ceaseless procession
    issuing,
Acceding from such gestation, taking and giving continual
    strength and life,
World of the real—world of the twain in one,
World of the soul, born by the world of the real alone, led to
    identity, body, by it alone,
Yet in beginning only, incalculable masses of composite precious
    materials,
By history's cycles forwarded, by every nation, language, hither sent,
Ready, collected here, a freer, vast, electric world, to be
    constructed here.
(The true New World, the world of orbic science, morals, literatures
    to come,)
Thou wonder world yet undefined, unform'd, neither do I define
    thee,
How can I pierce the impenetrable blank of the future?
I feel thy ominous greatness evil as well as good,
I watch thee advancing, absorbing the present, transcending the
    past,

I see thy light lighting, and thy shadow shadowing, as if the entire
　　　　globe,
But I do not undertake to define thee, hardly to comprehend thee,
I but thee name, thee prophesy, as now,
I merely thee ejaculate!

Thee in thy future,
Thee in thy only permanent life, career, thy own unloosen'd mind,
　　　　thy soaring spirit,
Thee as another equally needed son, radiant, ablaze, swift-moving
　　　　fructifying all,
Thee risen in potent cheerfulness and joy, in endless great hilarity,
Scattering for good the cloud that hung so long, that weigh'd so
　　　　long upon the mind of man,
The doubt, suspicion, dread, of gradual, certain decadence of man;
Thee in thy larger, saner brood of female, male—thee in thy
　　　　athletes, moral, spiritual, South, North, West, East,
(To thy immortal breasts, Mother of All, thy every daughter, son,
　　　　endear'd alike, forever equal,)
Thee in thy own musicians, singers, artists, unborn yet, but certain,
Thee in thy moral wealth and civilization, (until which thy
　　　　proudest material civilization must remain in vain,)
Thee in thy all-supplying, all-enclosing worship—thee in no
　　　　single bible saviour, merely,
Thy saviours countless, latent within thyself, thy bibles incessant
　　　　within thyself, equal to any, divine as any,
(Thy soaring course thee formulating, not in thy two great wars,
　　　　nor in thy century's visible growth,
But far more in these leaves and chants, thy chants, great Mother!)
Thee in an education grown of thee, in teachers, studies, students,
　　　　born of thee,
Thee in thy democratic fêtes en-masse, thy high original festivals,
　　　　operas, lecturers, preachers,
Thee in thy ultimata, (the preparations only now completed, the
　　　　edifice on sure foundations tied,)
Thee in thy pinnacles, intellect, thought, thy topmost rational joys,
　　　　thy love and godlike aspiration,
In thy resplendent coming literati, thy full-lung'd orators, thy
　　　　sacerdotal bards, kosmic savans,
These! these in thee, (certain to come,) to-day I prophesy.

6

Land tolerating all, accepting all, not for the good alone, all good
　　　　for thee,
Land in the realms of God to be a realm unto thyself,
Under the rule of God to be a rule unto thyself.

(Lo, where arise three peerless stars,
To be thy natal stars my country, Ensemble, Evolution, Freedom,
Set in the sky of Law.)

Land of unprecedented faith, God's faith,
Thy soil, thy very subsoil, all upheav'd,
The general inner earth so long so sedulously draped over, now
　　　　hence for what it is boldly laid bare,
Open'd by thee to heaven's light for benefit or bale.

Not for success alone,
Not to fair-sail unintermitted always,
The storm shall dash thy face, the murk of war and worse than
        war shall cover thee all over,
(Wert capable of war, its tug and trials? be capable of peace, its
        trials,
For the tug and mortal strain of nations come at last in
        prosperous peace, not war;)
In many a smiling mask death shall approach beguiling thee, thou
        in disease shalt swelter,
The livid cancer spread its hideous claws, clinging upon thy
        breasts, seeking to strike thee deep within,
Consumption of the worst, moral consumption, shall rouge thy
        face with hectic,
But thou shalt face thy fortunes, thy diseases, and surmount
        them all,
Whatever they are to-day and whatever through time they may be,
They each and all shall lift and pass away and cease from thee,
While thou, Time's spirals rounding, out of thyself, thyself still
        extricating, fusing,
Equable, natural, mystical Union thou, (the mortal with immortal
        blent,)
Shalt soar toward the fulfilment of the future, the spirit of the
        body and the mind,
The soul, its destinies.

The soul, its destinies, the real real,
(Purport of all these apparitions of the real;)
In thee America, the soul, its destinies,
Thou globe of globes! thou wonder nebulous!
By many a throe of heat and cold convuls'd, (by these thyself
        solidifying,)
Thou mental, moral orb—thou New, indeed new, Spiritual World!
The Present holds thee not—for such vast growth as thine,
For such unparallel'd flight as thine, such brood as thine,
The Future only holds thee and can hold thee.

4. ALBERT J. BEVERIDGE, *Annexation of the Philippines, 1900**

Mr. President, the times call for candor. The Philippines are ours forever, "territory belonging to the United States," as the Constitution calls them. And just beyond the Philippines are China's illimitable markets. We will not retreat from either. We will not repudiate our duty in the archipelago. We will not abandon our opportunity in the Orient. We will not renounce our part in the mission of our race, trustee, under God, of the civilization of the world. And we will move forward to our work, not howling out regrets like slaves whipped to their burdens, but with gratitude for a task worthy of our strength, and thanksgiving to Almighty God that He

* Congressional Record, XXXIII, Pt. 1 (January 9, 1900), 704–12.

has marked us as His chosen people, henceforth to lead in the regeneration of the world.

PHILIPPINES COMMAND THE PACIFIC

This island empire is the last land left in all the oceans. If it should prove a mistake to abandon it, the blunder once made would be irretrievable. If it proves a mistake to hold it, the error can be corrected when we will. Every other progressive nation stands ready to relieve us.

But to hold it will be no mistake. Our largest trade henceforth must be with Asia. The Pacific is our ocean. More and more Europe will manufacture the most it needs, secure from its colonies the most it consumes. Where shall we turn for consumers of our surplus? Geography answers the question. China is our natural customer. She is nearer to us than to England, Germany, or Russia, the commercial powers of the present and the future. They have moved nearer to China by securing permanent bases on her borders. The Philippines gives us a base at the door of all the East.

Lines of navigation from our ports to the Orient and Australia; from the Isthmian Canal to Asia; from all Oriental ports to Australia, converge at and separate from the Philippines. They are a self-supporting, dividend-paying fleet, permanently anchored at a spot selected by the strategy of Providence, commanding the Pacific. And the Pacific is the ocean of the commerce of the future. Most future wars will be conflicts for commerce. The power that rules the Pacific, therefore, is the power that rules the world. And, with the Philippines, that power is and will forever be the American Republic.

VALUE OF CHINA'S TRADE

China's trade is the mightiest commercial fact in our future. Her foreign commerce was $285,738,300 in 1897, of which we, her neighbor, had less than 9 per cent, of which only a little more than half was merchandise sold to China by us. We ought to have 50 per cent, and we will. And China's foreign commerce is only beginning. Her resources, her possibilities, her wants, all are undeveloped. She has only 340 miles of railway. I have seen trains loaded with natives and all the activities of modern life already appearing along the line. But she needs, and in fifty years will have, 20,000 miles of railway.

Who can estimate her commerce, then? That statesman commits a crime against American trade—against the American grower of cotton and wheat and tobacco, the American manufacturer of machinery and clothing—who fails to put America where she may command that trade. Germany's Chinese trade is increasing like magic. She has established ship lines and secured a tangible foothold on China's very soil. Russia's Chinese trade is growing beyond belief. She is spending the revenues of the Empire to finish her railroad into Pekin itself, and she is in physical possession of the imperial province of Manchuria. Japan's Chinese trade is multiplying in volume and value. She is bending her energy to her merchant marine, and is located along China's very coast; but Manila is nearer China than Yokohama is. The Philippines command the commercial situation of the entire East. Can America best trade with China from San Francisco or New York? From San Francisco, of course. But if San Francisco were closer to China than New York is to Pittsburgh, what then? And Manila is nearer Hongkong than Habana is to Washington. And yet American statesmen plan to surrender this commercial throne of the Orient where Providence and our soldiers' lives have placed us. When history comes to write the story of that suggested treason to American supremacy and therefore to the spread of American civilization, let her in mercy write that those who so proposed were merely blind and nothing more.

RESOURCES AND IMMENSE SIZE OF THE ISLANDS

But if they did not command China, India, the Orient, the whole Pacific for purposes of offense, defense, and trade, the Philippines are so valuable in themselves that we should hold them. I have cruised more than 2,000 miles through the archipelago, every moment a surprise at its loveliness and wealth. I have ridden hundreds of miles on the islands, every foot of the way a revelation of vegetable and mineral riches. . . .

CHARACTER OF THE PEOPLE— AGUINALDO

It will be hard for Americans who have not studied them to understand the people. They are a barbarous race, modified by three centuries of contact with a decadent race. The Filipino is the South Sea Malay, put through a process of three hundred years of superstition in religion, dishonesty in dealing, disorder in habits of industry, and cruelty, caprice, and corruption in government. It is barely possible that 1,000 men in all the archipelago are capable of self-government in the Anglo-Saxon sense.

My own belief is that there are not 100 men among them who comprehend what Anglo-Saxon self-government even means, and there are over 5,000,000 people to be governed. I know many clever and highly educated men among them, but there are only three commanding intellects and characters—Arellani [sic], Mabini, and Aguinaldo. Arellano [sic], the chief justice of our supreme court, is a profound lawyer and a brave and incor-

ruptible man. Mabini, who, before his capture, was the literary and diplomatic associate of Aguinaldo, is the highest type of subtlety and the most constructive mind that race has yet produced. Aguinaldo is a clever, popular leader, able, brave, resourceful, cunning, ambitious, unscrupulous, and masterful. He is full of decision, initiative, and authority, and had the confidence of the masses. He is a natural dictator. His ideas of government are absolute orders, implicit obedience, or immediate death. He understands the character of his countrymen. He is a Malay Sylla [sic]; not a Filipino Washington. . . .

WE WILL HOLD IT FAST, AND HOLD IT FOREVER

Here, then, Senators, is the situation. Two years ago there was no land in all the world which we could occupy for any purpose. Our commerce was daily turning toward the Orient, and geography and trade developments made necessary our commercial empire over the Pacific. And in that ocean we had no commercial, naval, or military base. To-day we have one of the three great ocean possessions of the globe, located at the most commanding commercial, naval, and military points in the eastern seas, within hail of India, shoulder to shoulder with China, richer in its own resources than any equal body of land on the entire globe, and peopled by a race which civilization demands shall be improved. Shall we abandon it? That man little knows the common people of the Republic, little understands the instincts of our race, who thinks we will not hold it fast and hold it forever, administering just government by simplest methods. We may trick up devices to shift our burden and lessen our opportunity; they will avail us nothing but delay. We may tangle conditions by applying academic arrangements of self-government to a crude situation; their failure will drive us to our duty in the end. . . .

But, Senators, it would be better to abandon this combined garden and Gibraltar of the Pacific, and count our blood and treasure already spent a profitable loss, than to apply any academic arrangement of self-government to these children. They are not capable of self-government. How could they be? They are not of a self-governing race. They are Orientals, Malays, instructed by Spaniards in the latter's worst estate.

They know nothing of practical government except as they have witnessed the weak, corrupt, cruel, and capricious rule of Spain. What magic will anyone employ to dissolve in their minds and characters those impressions of governors and governed which three centuries of misrule has created? What alchemy will change the oriental quality of their blood and set the self-governing currents of the American pouring through their Malay veins? How shall they, in the twinkling of an eye, be exalted to the heights of self-governing peoples which required a thousand years for us to reach, Anglo-Saxon though we are?

Let men beware how they employ the term "self-government." It is a sacred term. It is the watchword at the door of the inner temple of liberty, for liberty does not always mean self-government. Self-government is a method of liberty—the highest, simplest, best—and it is acquired only after centuries of study and struggle and experiment and instruction and all the elements of the progress of man. Self-government is no base and common thing, to be bestowed on the merely audacious. It is the degree which crowns the graduate of liberty, not the name of liberty's infant class, who have not yet mastered the alphabet of freedom. Savage blood, oriental

blood, Malay blood, Spanish example —are these the elements of self-government?

We must act on the situation as it exists, not as we would wish it. I have talked with hundreds of these people, getting their views as to the practical workings of self-government. The great majority simply do not understand any participation in any government whatever. The most enlightened among them declare that self-government will succeed because the employers of labor will compel their employees to vote as their employer wills and that this will insure intelligent voting. I was assured that we could depend upon good men always being in office because the officials who constitute the government will nominate their successors, choose those among the people who will do the voting, and determine how and where elections will be held.

The most ardent advocate of self-government that I met was anxious that I should know that such a government would be tranquil because, as he said, if anyone criticised it, the government would shoot the offender. A few of them have a sort of verbal understanding of the democratic theory, but the above are the examples of the ideas of the practical workings of self-government entertained by the aristocracy, the rich planters and traders, and heavy employers of labor, the men who would run the government.

PEOPLE INDOLENT—NO COMPETITION
WITH OUR LABOR

Example for decades will be necessary to instruct them in American ideas and methods of administration. Example, example; always example— this alone will teach them. As a race, their general ability is not excellent. Educators, both men and women, to whom I have talked in Cebu and

Luzon, were unanimous in the opinion that in all solid and useful education they are, as a people, dull and stupid. In showy things, like carving and painting or embroidery or music, they have apparent aptitude, but even this is superficial and never thorough. They have facility of speech, too.

The three best educators on the island at different times made to me the same comparison, that the common people in their stupidity are like their caribou bulls. They are not even good agriculturists. Their waste of cane is inexcusable. Their destruction of hemp fiber is childish. They are incurably indolent. They have no continuity or thoroughness of industry. They will quit work without notice and amuse themselves until the money they have earned is spent. They are like children playing at men's work.

No one need fear their competition with our labor. No reward could beguile, no force compel, these children of indolence to leave their trifling lives for the fierce and fervid industry of high-wrought America. The very reverse is the fact. One great problem is the necessary labor to develop these islands—to build the roads, open the mines, clear the wilderness, drain the swamps, dredge the harbors. The natives will not supply it. A lingering prejudice against the Chinese may prevent us from letting them supply it. Ultimately, when the real truth of the climate and human conditions is known, it is barely possible that our labor will go there. Even now young men with the right moral fiber and a little capital can make fortunes there as planters. . . .

DOMINANT NOTES OF OUR FIRST AND SECOND CENTURIES

Mr. President, self-government and internal development have been the dominant notes of our first century; administration and the development of other lands will be the dominant notes of our second century. And administration is as high and holy a function as self-government, just as the care of a trust estate is as sacred an obligation as the management of our own concerns. Cain was the first to violate the divine law of human society which makes of us our brother's keeper. And administration of good government is the first lesson in self-government, that exalted estate toward which all civilization tends.

Administration of good government is not denial of liberty. For what is liberty? It is not savagery. It is not the exercise of individual will. It is not dictatorship. It involves government, but not necessarily self-government. It means law. First of all, it is a common rule of action, applying equally to all within its limits. Liberty means protection of property and life without price, free speech without intimidation, justice without purchase or delay, government without favor or favorites. What will best give all this to the people of the Philippines—American administration, developing them gradually toward self-government, or self-government by a people before they know what self-government means? . . .

Mr. President, this question is deeper than any question of party politics; deeper than any question of the isolated policy of our country even; deeper even than any question of constitutional power. It is elemental. It is racial. God has not been preparing the English-speaking and Teutonic peoples for a thousand years for nothing but vain and idle self-contemplation and self-admiration. No! He has made us the master organizers of the world to establish system where chaos reigns. He has given us the spirit of progress to overwhelm the forces of reaction throughout the earth. He has made us adepts in government that we may administer government among savage and senile peoples. Were it not for such a force as this the world would relapse into barbarism and night. And of all our race He has marked the American people as His chosen nation to finally lead in the regeneration of the world. This is the divine mission of America, and it holds for us all the profit, all the glory, all the happiness possible to man. We are trustees of the world's progress, guardians of its righteous peace. The judgment of the Master is upon us: "Ye have been faithful over a few things; I will make you ruler over many things."

What shall history say of us? Shall it say that we renounced that holy trust, left the savage to his base condition, the wilderness to the reign of waste, deserted duty, abandoned glory, forget our sordid profit even, because we feared our strength and read the charter of our powers with the doubter's eye and the quibbler's mind? Shall it say that, called by events to captain and command the proudest, ablest, purest race of history in history's noblest work, we declined that great commission? Our fathers would not have had it so. No! They founded no paralytic government, incapable of the simplest acts of administration. They planted no sluggard people, passive while the world's work calls them. They established no reactionary nation. They unfurled no retreating flag.

GOD'S HAND IN ALL

That flag has never paused in its onward march. Who dares halt it now —now, when history's largest events are carrying it forward; now, when we are at last one people, strong enough for any task, great enough for any glory destiny can bestow? How comes it that our first century closes with the process of consolidating the American people into a unit just accomplished, and quick upon the stroke of that great hour presses upon us our world opportunity, world duty, and world glory, which none but a people welded into an indivisible nation can achieve or perform?

Blind indeed is he who sees not the hand of God in events so vast, so harmonious, so benign. Reactionary indeed is the mind that perceives not that this vital people is the strongest of the saving forces of the world; that our place, therefore, is at the head of the constructing and redeeming nations of the earth; and that to stand aside while events march on is a surrender of our interests, a betrayal of our duty as blind as it is base. Craven indeed is the heart that fears to perform a work so golden and so noble; that dares not win a glory so immortal.

Do you tell me that it will cost us money? When did Americans ever measure duty by financial standards? Do you tell me of the tremendous toil required to overcome the vast difficulties of our task? What mighty work for the world, for humanity, even for ourselves, has ever been done with ease? Even our bread must we eat by the sweat of our faces. Why are we charged with power such as no people ever knew, if we are not to use it in a work such as no people ever wrought? Who will dispute the divine meaning of the fable of the talents?

Do you remind me of the precious blood that must be shed, the lives that must be given, the broken hearts of loved ones for their slain? And this is indeed a heavier price than all combined. And yet as a nation every historic duty we have done, every achievement we have accomplished, has been by the sacrifice of our noblest sons. Every holy memory that glorifies the flag is of those heroes who have died that its onward march might not be stayed. It is the nation's dearest lives yielded for the flag that makes it dear to us; it is the nation's most precious blood poured out for it that makes it precious to us. That flag is woven of heroism and grief, of the bravery of men and women's tears, of righteousness and battle, of sacrifice and anguish, of triumph and of glory. It is these which make our flag a holy thing. Who would tear from that sacred banner the glorious legends of a single battle where it has waved on land or sea? What son of a soldier of the flag whose father fell beneath it on any field would surrender that proud record for the heraldry of a king? In the cause of civilization, in the service of the Republic anywhere on earth, Americans consider wounds the noblest decorations man can win, and count the giving of their lives a glad and precious duty.

Pray God that spirit never fails. Pray God the time may never come when Mammon and the love of ease shall so debase our blood that we will fear to shed it for the flag and its imperial destiny. Pray God the time may never come when American heroism is but a legend like the story of the Cid, American faith in our mission and our might a dream dissolved, and the glory of our mighty race departed.

And that time will never come. We will renew our youth at the fountain of new and glorious deeds. We will exalt our reverence for the flag by carrying it to a noble future as well as by remembering its ineffable past. Its immortality will not pass, because everywhere and always we will acknowledge and discharge the solemn responsibilities our sacred flag, in its deepest meaning, puts upon us. And so, Senators, with reverent hearts, where dwells the fear of God, the American people move forward to the future of their hope and the doing of His work.

Mr. President and Senators, adopt the resolution offered, that peace may quickly come and that we may begin our saving, regenerating, and uplifting work. Adopt it, and this bloodshed will cease when these deluded children of our islands learn that this is the final word of the representatives of the American people in Congress assembled. Reject it, and the world, history, and the American people will know where to forever fix the awful responsibility for the consequences that will surely follow such failure to do our manifest duty. How dare we delay when our soldiers' blood is flowing?

5. THEODORE ROOSEVELT, *The Strenuous Life, 1899**

As it is with the individual, so it is with the nation. It is a base untruth to say that happy is the nation that has no history. Thrice happy is the nation that has a glorious history. Far better it is to dare mighty things, to win glorious triumphs, even though checkered by failure, than to take rank with those poor spirits who neither enjoy much nor suffer much, because

they live in the gray twilight that knows not victory nor defeat. If in 1861 the men who loved the Union had believed that peace was the end of all things, and war and strife the worst of all things, and had acted up to their belief, we would have saved hundreds of thousands of lives, we would have saved hundreds of millions of dollars. Moreover, besides saving all

*Theodore Roosevelt, "The Strenuous Life," *Works* (New York, 1906), XX, 6–22.

the blood and treasure we then lavished, we would have prevented the heartbreak of many women, the dissolution of many homes, and we would have spared the country those months of gloom and shame when it seemed as if our armies marched only to defeat. We could have avoided all this suffering simply by shrinking from strife. And if we had thus avoided it, we would have shown that we were weaklings, and that we were unfit to stand among the great nations of the earth. Thank God for the iron in the blood of our fathers, the men who upheld the wisdom of Lincoln, and bore sword or rifle in the armies of Grant! Let us, the children of the men who proved themselves equal to the mighty days, let us, the children of the men who carried the great Civil War to a triumphant conclusion, praise the God of our fathers that the ignoble counsels of peace were rejected; that the suffering and loss, the blackness of sorrow and despair, were unflinchingly faced, and the years of strife endured; for in the end the slave was freed, the Union restored, and the mighty American republic placed once more as a helmeted queen among nations.

We of this generation do not have to face a task as that our fathers faced, but we have our tasks, and woe to us if we fail to perform them! We cannot, if we would, play the part of China, and be content to rot by inches in ignoble ease within our borders, taking no interest in what goes on beyond them, sunk in a scrambling commercialism; heedless of the higher life, the life of aspiration, of toil and risk, busying ourselves only with the wants of our bodies for the day, until suddenly we should find, beyond a shadow of question, what China has already found, that in this world the nation that has trained itself to a career of unwarlike and isolated ease is bound, in the end, to go down before other nations which have not lost the manly and adventurous qualities. If we are to be a really great people, we must strive in good faith to play a great part in the world. We cannot avoid meeting great issues. All that we can determine for ourselves is whether we shall meet them well or ill. In 1898 we could not help being brought face to face with the problem of war with Spain. All we could decide was whether we should shrink like cowards from the contest, or enter into it as beseemed a brave and high spirited people; and, once in, whether failure or success should crown our banners. So it is now. We cannot avoid the responsibilities that confront us in Hawaii, Cuba, Porto Rico, and the Philippines. All we can decide is whether we shall meet them in a way that will redound to the national credit, or whether we shall make of our dealings with these new problems a dark and shameful page in our history. To refuse to deal with them at all merely amounts to dealing with them badly. We have a given problem to solve. If we understake the solution, there is, of course, always danger that we may not solve it aright; but to refuse to undertake the solution simply renders it certain that we cannot possibly solve it aright. The timid man, the lazy man, the man who distrusts his country, the over-civilized man, who has lost the great fighting, masterful virtues, the ignorant man, and the man of dull mind, whose soul is incapable of feeling the mighty lift that thrills "stern men with empires in their brains"—all these, of course, shrink from seeing the nation undertake its new duties; shrink from seeing us build a navy and an army adequate to our needs; shrink from seeing us do our share of the world's work, by bringing order out of chaos in the great, fair tropic islands from which the valor of our soldiers and sailors has driven the Spanish flag. These are the men who fear the strenuous life, who fear the only national life which is really worth leading. They believe in that cloistered life which saps the hardy virtues in a nation, as it saps them in the individual; or else they are wedded to that base spirit of gain and greed which recognizes in commercialism the be-all and end-all of national life, instead of realizing that, though an indispensable element, it is, after all, but one of the many elements that go to make up true national greatness. No country can long endure if its foundations are not laid deep in the material prosperity which comes from thrift, from business energy and enterprise, from hard, unsparing effort in the fields of industrial activity; but neither was any nation ever yet truly great if it relied upon material prosperity alone. All honor must be paid to the architects of our material prosperity, to the great captains of industry who have built our factories and our railroads, to the strong men who toil for wealth with brain or hand; for great is the debt of the nation to these and their kind. But our debt is yet greater to the men whose highest type is to be found in a statesman like Lincoln, a soldier like Grant. They showed by their lives that they recognized the law of work, the law of strife; they toiled to win a competence for themselves and those dependent upon them; but they recognized that there were yet other and even loftier duties—duties to the nation and duties to the race.

We cannot sit huddled within our own borders and avow ourselves merely an assemblage of well-to-do hucksters who care nothing for what happens beyond. Such a policy would defeat even its own end; for as the nations grow to have ever wider and wider interests, and are brought into closer and closer contact, if we are to hold our own in the struggle for naval and commercial supremacy, we must build up our power without our own borders. We must build the isthmian canal, and we must grasp the points of vantage which will enable us to have our say in deciding the destiny of the oceans of the East and the West.

So much for the commercial side. From the standpoint of international honor the argument is even stronger. The guns that thundered off Manila and Santiago left us echoes of glory, but they also left us a legacy of duty. If we drove out a medieval tyranny only to make room for savage anarchy, we had better not have begun the task at all. It is worse than idle to say that we have no duty to perform, and can leave to their fates the islands we have conquered. Such a course would be the course of infamy. It would be followed at once by utter chaos in the wretched islands themselves. Some stronger, manlier power would have to step in and do the work, and we would have shown ourselves weaklings, unable to carry to successful completion the labors that great and high-spirited nations are eager to undertake.

The work must be done; we cannot escape our responsibility; and if we are worth our salt, we shall be glad of the chance to do the work—glad of the chance to show ourselves equal to one of the great tasks set modern civilization. But let us not deceive ourselves as to the importance of the task. Let us not be misled by vainglory into underestimating the strain it will put on our powers. Above all, let us, as we value our own self-respect, face the responsibilities with proper seriousness, courage, and high resolve. We must demand the highest order of integrity and ability in our public men who are to grapple with these new problems. We must hold to a rigid accountability those public servants who show unfaithfulness to the interests of the nation or inability to rise to the high level of the new demands upon our strength and our resources.

Of course we must remember not to judge any public servant by any one act, and especially should we beware of attacking the men who are merely the occasions and not the causes of disaster. Let me illustrate what I mean by the army and the navy. If twenty years ago we had gone to war, we should have found the navy as absolutely unprepared as the army. At that time our ships could not have encountered with success the fleets of Spain any more than nowadays we can put untrained soldiers, no matter how brave, who are armed with archaic black-powder weapons, against well-drilled regulars armed with the highest type of modern repeating rifles. But in the early eighties the attention of the nation became directed to our naval needs. Congress most wisely made a series of appropriations to build up a new navy, and under a succession of able and patriotic secretaries, of both political parties, the navy was gradually built up, until its material became equal to its splendid personnel, with the result that in the summer of 1898 it leaped to its proper place as one of the most brilliant and formidable fighting navies in the entire world. We rightly pay all honor to the men controlling the navy at the time it won these great deeds, honor to Secretary Long and Admiral Dewey, to the captains who handled the ships in action, to the daring lieutenants who braved death in the smaller craft, and to the heads of bureaus at Washington who saw that the ships were so commanded, so armed, so equipped, so well engined, as to insure the best results. But let us also keep ever in mind that all of this would not have availed if it had not been for the wisdom of the men who during the preceding fifteen years had built up the navy. Keep

in mind the secretaries of the navy during those years; keep in mind the senators and congressmen who by their votes gave the money necessary to build and to armor the ships, to construct the great guns, and to train the crews; remember also those who actually did build the ships, the armor, and the guns; and remember the admirals and captains who handled battleship, cruiser, and torpedo-boat on the high seas, alone and in squadrons, developing the seamanship, the gunnery, and the power of acting together, which their successors utilized so gloriously at Manila and off Santiago. And, gentlemen, remember the converse, too. Remember that justice has two sides. Be just to those who built up the navy, and, for the sake of the future of the country, keep in mind those who opposed its building up. Read the "Congressional Record." Find out the senators and congressmen who opposed the grants for building the new ships; who opposed the purchase of armor, without which the ships were worthless; who opposed any adequate maintenance for the Navy Department, and strove to cut down the number of men necessary to man our fleets. The men who did these things were one and all working to bring disaster on the country. They have no share in the glory of Manila, in the honor of Santiago. They have no cause to feel proud of the valor of our sea-captains, of the renown of our flag. Their motives may or may not have been good, but their acts were heavily fraught with evil. They did ill for the national honor, and we won in spite of their sinister opposition.

Now, apply all this to our public men of to-day. Our army has never been built up as it should be built up. I shall not discuss with an audience like this the puerile suggestion that a nation of seventy millions of freemen is in danger of losing its liberties from the existence of an army of one hundred thousand men, three-fourths of whom will be employed in certain foreign islands, in certain coast fortresses, and on Indian reservations. No man of good sense and stout heart can take such a proposition seriously. If we are such weaklings as the proposition implies, then we are unworthy of freedom in any event. To no body of men in the United States is the country so much indebted as to the splendid officers and enlisted men of the regular army and navy. There is no body from which the country has less to fear, and none of which it should be prouder, none which it should be more anxious to upbuild.

Our army needs complete reorganization,—not merely enlarging,—and the reorganization can only come as the result of legislation. A proper general staff should be established, and the positions of ordnance, commissary, and quartermaster officers should be filled by detail from the line. Above all, the army must be given the chance to exercise in large bodies. Never again should we see, as we saw in the Spanish war, major-generals in command of divisions who had never before commanded three companies together in the field. Yet, incredible to relate, Congress has shown a queer inability to learn some of the lessons of the war. There were large bodies of men in both branches who opposed the declaration of war, who opposed the ratification of peace, who opposed the upbuilding of the army, and who even opposed the purchase of armor at a reasonable price for the battleships and cruisers, thereby putting an absolute stop to the building of any new fighting-ships for the navy. If, during the years to come, any disaster should befall our arms, afloat or ashore, and thereby any shame come to the United States, remember that the blame will lie upon the men whose names appear upon the roll-calls of Congress on the wrong side of these great questions. On them will lie the burden of any loss of our soldiers and sailors, of any dishonor to the flag; and upon you and the people of this country will lie the blame if you do not repudiate, in no unmistakable way, what these men have done. The blame will not rest upon the untrained commander of untried troops, upon the civil officers of a department the organization of which has been left utterly inadequate, or upon the admiral with an insufficient number of ships; but upon the public men who have so lamentably failed in forethought as to refuse to remedy these evils long in advance, and upon the nation that stands behind those public men.

So, at the present hour, no small share of the responsibility for the blood shed in the Philippines, the blood of our brothers, and the blood of their wild and ignorant foes, lies at the thresholds of those who so long delayed the adoption of the treaty of peace, and of those who by their worse than foolish words deliberately invited a savage people to plunge into a war fraught with sure disaster for them— a war, too, in which our own brave men who follow the flag must pay with their blood for the silly, mock humanitarianism of the prattlers who sit at home in peace.

The army and the navy are the sword and the shield which this nation must carry if she is to do her duty among the nations of the earth —if she is not to stand merely as the China of the western hemisphere. Our proper conduct toward the tropic islands we have wrested from Spain is merely the form which our duty has taken at the moment. Of course we are bound to handle the affairs of our own household well. We must see that there is civic honesty, civic cleanliness, civic good sense in our home administration of city, state, and nation. We must strive for honesty in office, for honesty toward the creditors of the nation and of the individual; for the widest freedom of individual initiative where possible, and for the wisest control of individual initiative where it is hostile to the welfare of the many. But because we set our own household in order we are not thereby excused from playing our part in the great affairs of the world. A man's first duty is to his own home, but he is not thereby excused from doing his duty to the State; for if he fails in this second duty it is under the penalty of ceasing to be a freeman. In the same way, while a nation's first duty is within its own borders, it is not thereby absolved from facing its duties in the world as a whole; and if it refuses to do so, it merely forfeits its right to struggle for a place among the peoples that shape the destiny of mankind.

In the West Indies and the Philippines alike we are confronted by most difficult problems. It is cowardly to shrink from solving them in the proper way; for solved they must be, if not by us, then by some stronger and more manful race. If we are too weak, too selfish, or too foolish to solve them, some bolder and abler people must undertake the solution. Personally, I am far too firm a believer in the greatness of my country and the power of my countrymen to admit for one moment that we shall ever be driven to the ignoble alternative.

The problems are different for the different islands. Porto Rico is not large enough to stand alone. We must govern it wisely and well, primarily in the interest of its own people. Cuba is, in my judgment, entitled ultimately to settle for itself whether it shall be an independent state or an integral portion of the mightiest of republics. But until order and stable liberty are secured, we must remain in the island

to insure them, and infinite tact, judgment, moderation, and courage must be shown by our military and civil representatives in keeping the island pacified, in relentlessly stamping out brigandage, in protecting all alike, and yet in showing proper recognition to the men who have fought for Cuban liberty. The Philippines offer a yet graver problem. Their population includes half-caste and native Christians, warlike Moslems, and wild pagans. Many of their people are utterly unfit for self-government and show no signs of becoming fit. Others may in time become fit but at present can only take part in self-government under a wise supervision, at once firm and beneficent. We have driven Spanish tyranny from the islands. If we now let it be replaced by savage anarchy, our work has been for harm and not for good. I have scant patience with those who fear to undertake the task of governing the Philippines, and who openly avow that they do fear to undertake it, or that they shrink from it because of the expense and trouble; but I have even scanter patience with those who make a pretense of humanitarianism to hide and cover their timidity, and who cant about "liberty" and the "consent of the governed," in order to excuse themselves for their unwillingness to play the part of men. Their doctrines, if carried out, would make it incumbent upon us to leave the Apaches of Arizona to work out their own salvation, and to decline to interfere in a single Indian reservation. Their doctrines condemn your forefathers and mine for ever having settled in these United States.

England's rule in India and Egypt has been of great benefit to England, for it has trained up generations of men accustomed to look at the larger and loftier side of public life. It has been of even greater benefit to India and Egypt. And finally, and most of all, it has advanced the cause of civilization. So, if we do our duty aright in the Philippines, we will add to that national renown which is the highest and finest part of national life, will greatly benefit the people of the Philippine Islands, and, above all, we will play our part well in the great work of uplifting mankind. But to do this work, keep ever in mind that we must show in a very high degree the qualities of courage, of honesty, and of good judgment. Resistance must be stamped out. The first and all-important work to be done is to establish the supremacy of our flag. We must put down armed resistance before we can accomplish anything else, and there should be no parleying, no faltering, in dealing with our foe. As for those in our own country who encourage the foe, we can afford contemptuously to disregard them; but it must be remembered that their utterances are not saved from being treasonable merely by the fact that they are despicable.

When once we have put down armed resistance, when once our rule is acknowledged, then an even more difficult task will begin, for then we must see to it that the islands are administered with absolute honesty and with good judgment. If we let the public service of the islands be turned into the prey of the spoils politician, we shall have begun to tread the path which Spain trod to her own destruction. We must send out there only good and able men, chosen for their fitness, and not because of their partisan service, and these men must not only administer impartial justice to the natives and serve their own government with honesty and fidelity, but must show the utmost tact and firmness, remembering that, with such people as those with whom we are to deal, weakness is the greatest of crimes, and that next to weakness comes lack of consideration for their principles and prejudices.

I preach to you, then, my countrymen, that our country calls not for the life of ease but for the life of strenuous endeavor. The twentieth century looms before us big with the fate of many nations. If we stand idly by, if we seek merely swollen, slothful ease and ignoble peace, if we shrink from the hard contests where men must win at hazard of their lives and at the risk of all they hold dear, then the bolder and stronger peoples will pass us by, and will win for themselves the domination of the world. Let us therefore boldly face the life of strife, resolute to do our duty well and manfully; resolute to uphold righteousness by deed and by word; resolute to be both honest and brave, to serve high ideals, yet to use practical methods. Above all, let us shrink from no strife, moral or physical, within or without the nation, provided we are certain that the strife is justified, for it is only through strife, through hard and dangerous endeavor, that we shall ultimately win the goal of true national greatness.

6. VACHEL LINDSAY, *Abraham Lincoln Walks at Midnight (in Springfield, Illinois), 1915*[*]

It is portentous, and a thing of state
That here at midnight, in our little town

[*]Vachel Lindsay, *Collected Poems* (New York: The Macmillan Company, 1923), pp. 53–54. Copyright 1914 by The Macmillan Company; copyright renewed 1942 by Elizabeth C. Lindsay. Used by permission of The Macmillan Company.

A mourning figure walks, and will not rest,
Near the old court-house pacing up and down,

Or by his homestead, or in shadowed yards
He lingers where his children used to play,
Or through the market, on the well-worn stones
He stalks until the dawn-stars burn away.

A bronzed, lank man! His suit of ancient black,
A famous high top-hat and plain worn shawl
Make him the quaint great figure that men love,
The prairie-lawyer, master of us all.

He cannot sleep upon his hillside now.
He is among us:—as in times before!
And we who toss and lie awake for long
Breathe deep, and start, to see him pass the door.

His head is bowed. He thinks on men and kings.
Yes, when the sick world cries, how can he sleep?
Too many peasants fight, they know not why,
Too many homesteads in black terror weep.

The sins of all the war-lords burn his heart.
He sees the dreadnaughts scouring every main.
He carries on his shawl-wrapped shoulders now
The bitterness, the folly and the pain.

He cannot rest until a spirit-dawn
Shall come;—the shining hope of Europe free:
The league of sober folk, the Workers' Earth,
Bringing long peace to Cornland, Alp and Sea.

It breaks his heart that kings must murder still,
That all his hours of travail here for men
Seem yet in vain. And who will bring white peace
That he may sleep upon his hill again?

7. WOODROW WILSON, *The Conditions of Peace, 1917*[*]

Gentlemen of the Senate: On the eighteenth of December last I addressed an identic note to the governments of the nations now at war, requesting them to state, more definitely than they had yet been stated by either group of belligerents, the terms upon which they would deem it possible to make peace. I spoke on behalf of humanity and of the rights of all neutral nations like our own, many of whose most vital interests the war puts in constant jeopardy. The Central Powers united in a reply which stated merely that they were ready to meet their antagonists in conference to discuss terms of peace. The Entente Powers have replied much more definitely, and have stated, in general terms, indeed, but with sufficient

[*] *Congressional Record*, LIV, Pt. 2 (January 22, 1917), 1741–43.

definiteness to imply details, the arrangements, guarantees, and acts of reparation which they deem to be the indispensable conditions of a satisfactory settlement.

We are that much nearer a definite discussion of the peace which shall end the present war. We are that much nearer the discussion of the international concert which must thereafter hold the world at peace. In every discussion of the peace that must end this war it is taken for granted that the peace must be followed by some definite concert of power, which will make it virtually impossible that any such catastrophe should ever overwhelm us again. Every lover of mankind, every sane and thoughtful man, must take that for granted.

I have sought this opportunity to address you because I thought that I owed it to you, as the council associated with me in the final determination of our international obligations, to disclose to you without reserve the thought and purpose that have been taking form in my mind in regard to the duty of our Government in those days to come when it will be necessary to lay afresh and upon a new plan the foundations of peace among the nations.

It is inconceivable that the people of the United States should play no part in that great enterprise. To take part in such a service will be the opportunity for which they have sought to prepare themselves by the very principles and purposes of their polity and the approved practices of their Government, ever since the days when they set up a new nation in the high and honorable hope that it might in all that it was and did show mankind the way to liberty. They cannot, in honor, withhold the service to which they are now about to be challenged. They do not wish to withhold it. But they owe it to themselves and to the other nations of the world to state the conditions under which they will feel free to render it.

That service is nothing less than this—to add their authority and their power to the authority and force of other nations to guarantee peace and justice throughout the world. Such a settlement cannot now be long postponed. It is right that before it comes this Government should frankly formulate the conditions upon which it would feel justified in asking our people to approve its formal and solemn adherence to a league for peace. I am here to attempt to state those conditions.

The present war must first be ended, but we owe it to candor and to a just regard for the opinion of mankind to say that, so far as our participation in guarantees of future peace is concerned, it makes a great deal of difference in what way and upon what terms it is ended. The treaties and agreements which bring it to an end must embody terms which will create a peace that is worth guaranteeing and preserving, a peace that will win the approval of mankind, not merely a peace that will serve the several interests and immediate aims of the nations engaged.

We shall have no voice in determining what those terms shall be, but we shall, I feel sure, have a voice in determining whether they shall be made lasting or not by the guarantees of a universal covenant, and our judgment upon what is fundamental and essential as a condition precedent to permanency should be spoken now, not afterward, when it may be too late.

No covenant of coöperative peace that does not include the peoples of the new world can suffice to keep the future safe against war, and yet there is only one sort of peace that the peoples of America could join in guaranteeing.

The elements of that peace must be elements that engage the confidence and satisfy the principles of the American governments, elements consistent with their political faith and the practical conviction which the peoples of America have once for all embraced and undertaken to defend.

I do not mean to say that any American Government would throw any obstacle in the way of any terms of peace the Governments now at war might agree upon, or seek to upset them when made, whatever they might be. I only take it for granted that mere terms of peace between the belligerents will not satisfy even the belligerents themselves. Mere agreements may not make peace secure. It will be absolutely necessary that a force be created as a guarantor of the permanency of the settlement so much greater than the force of any nation now engaged or any alliance hitherto formed or projected, that no nation, no probable combination of nations, could face or withstand it. If the peace presently to be made is to endure, it must be a peace made secure by the organized major force of mankind.

The terms of the immediate peace agreed upon will determine whether it is a peace for which such a guarantee can be secured. The question upon which the whole future peace and policy of the world depends is this:—

Is the present war a struggle for a just and secure peace or only for a new balance of power? If it be only a struggle for a new balance of power, who will guarantee, who can guarantee, the stable equilibrium of the new arrangement? Only a tranquil Europe can be a stable Europe. There must be not only a balance of power, but a community of power; not organized rivalries, but an organized common peace.

Fortunately, we have received very explicit assurances on this point. The statesmen of both of the groups of nations, now arrayed against one another, have said, in terms that could not be misinterpreted, that it was no part of the purpose they had in mind to crush their antagonists. But the implication of these assurances may not be equally clear to all, may not be the same on both sides of the water. I think it will be serviceable if I attempt to set forth what we understand them to be.

They imply, first of all, that it must be a peace without victory. It is not pleasant to say this. I beg that I may be permitted to put my own interpretation upon it and that it may be understood that no other interpretation was in my thought. I am seeking only to face realities and to face them without soft concealments. Victory would mean peace forced upon the loser, a victor's terms imposed upon the vanquished. It would be accepted in humiliation, under duress, at an intolerable sacrifice, and would leave a sting, a resentment, a bitter memory, upon which terms of peace would rest, not permanently, but only as upon quicksand.

Only a peace between equals can last; only a peace the very principle of which is equality and a common participation in a common benefit. The right state of mind, the right feeling, between nations, is as necessary for a lasting peace as is the just settlement of vexed questions of territory or of racial and national allegiance.

The equality of nations upon which peace must be founded, if it is to last, must be an equality of rights; the guarantees exchanged must neither recognize nor imply a difference between big nations and small, between those that are powerful and those that are weak. Right must be based upon the common strength, not upon the individual strength, of the nations upon whose concert peace will depend.

Equality of territory, of resources,

there, of course, cannot be; nor any other sort of equality not gained in the ordinary peaceful and legitimate development of the peoples themselves. But no one asks or expects anything more than an equality of rights. Mankind is looking now for freedom of life, not for equipoises of power.

And there is a deeper thing involved than even equality of rights among organized nations. No peace can last, or ought to last, which does not recognize and accept the principle that Governments derive all their just powers from the consent of the governed, and that no right anywhere exists to hand peoples about from sovereignty to sovereignty as if they were property.

I take it for granted, for instance, if I may venture upon a single example, that statesmen everywhere are agreed that there should be a united, independent, and autonomous Poland, and that henceforth inviolable security of life, of worship, and of industrial and social development should be guaranteed to all peoples who have lived hitherto under the power of Governments devoted to a faith and purpose hostile to their own.

I speak of this not because of any desire to exalt an abstract political principle which has always been held very dear by those who have sought to build up liberty in America, but for the same reason that I have spoken of the other conditions of peace, which seem to me clearly indispensable— because I wish frankly to uncover realities. Any peace which does not recognize and accept this principle will inevitably be upset. It will not rest upon the affections or the convictions of mankind. The ferment of spirit of whole populations will fight subtly and constantly against it, and all the world will sympathize. The world can be at peace only if its life is stable, and there can be no stability where the

will is in rebellion, where there is not tranquillity of spirit and a sense of justice, of freedom, and of right.

So far as practicable, moreover, every great people now struggling toward a full development of its resources and of its powers should be assured a direct outlet to the great highways of the sea. Where this cannot be done by the cession of territory it can no doubt be done by the neutralization of direct rights of way under the general guarantee which will assure the peace itself. With a right comity of arrangement no nation need be shut away from free access to the open paths of the world's commerce.

And the paths of the sea must alike in law and in fact be free. The freedom of the seas is the *sine qua non* of peace, equality, and coöperation. No doubt a somewhat radical reconsideration of many of the rules of international practice hitherto sought to be established may be necessary in order to make the seas indeed free and common in practically all circumstances for the use of mankind, but the motive for such changes is convincing and compelling. There can be no trust or intimacy between the peoples of the world without them.

The free, constant, unthreatened intercourse of nations is an essential part of the process of peace and of development. It need not be difficult to define or to secure the freedom of the seas if the Governments of the world sincerely desire to come to an agreement concerning it.

It is a problem closely connected with the limitation of naval armaments and the coöperation of the navies of the world in keeping the seas at once free and safe.

And the question of limiting naval armaments opens the wider and perhaps more difficult question of the limitation of armies and of all programs of military preparation. Difficult and delicate as those questions are, they must be faced with the utmost candor and decided in a spirit of real accommodation if peace is to come with healing in its wings and come to stay.

Peace cannot be had without concession and sacrifice. There can be no sense of safety and equality among the nations if great preponderating armies are henceforth to continue here and there to be built up and maintained. The statesmen of the world must plan for peace and nations must adjust and accommodate their policy to it as they have planned for war and made ready for pitiless contest and rivalry. The question of armaments, whether on land or sea, is the most immediately and intensely practical question connected with the future fortunes of nations and of mankind.

I have spoken upon these great matters without reserve and with the utmost explicitness because it has seemed to me to be necessary if the world's yearning desire for peace was anywhere to find free voice and utterance. Perhaps I am the only person in high authority among all the peoples of the world who is at liberty to speak and hold nothing back. I am speaking as an individual, and yet I am speaking also, of course, as the responsible head of a great Government, and I feel confident that I have said what the people of the United States would wish me to say.

May I not add that I hope and believe that I am, in effect, speaking for liberals and friends of humanity in every nation and of every program of liberty? I would fain believe that I am speaking for the silent mass of mankind everywhere who have as yet had no place or opportunity to speak their real hearts out concerning the death and ruin they see to have come already upon the persons and the homes they hold most dear.

And in holding out the expectation that the people and the Government of the United States will join the other civilized nations of the world in guaranteeing the permanence of peace upon such terms as I have named, I speak with the greater boldness and confidence because it is clear to every man who can think that there is in this promise no breach in either our traditions or our policy as a nation, but a fulfillment rather of all that we have professed or striven for.

I am proposing, as it were, that the nations should with one accord adopt the doctrine of President Monroe as the doctrine of the world: That no nation should seek to extend its policy over any other nation or people, but that every people should be left free to determine its own policy, its own way of development, unhindered, unthreatened, unafraid, the little along with the great and powerful.

I am proposing that all nations henceforth avoid entangling alliances which would draw them into competition of power, catch them in a net of intrigue and selfish rivalry, and disturb their own affairs with influences intruded from without. There is no entangling alliance in a concert of power. When all unite to act in the same sense and with the same purpose, all act in the common interest and are free to live their own lives under a common protection.

I am proposing government by the consent of the governed; that freedom of the seas which in international conference after conference representatives of the United States have urged with the eloquence of those who are the convinced disciples of liberty; and that moderation of armaments which makes of armies and navies a power for order merely, not an instrument of aggression or of selfish violence.

These are American principles, American policies. We can stand for no others. And they are also the principles and policies of forward-looking men and women everywhere, of every modern nation, of every enlightened community. They are the principles of mankind and must prevail.

8. ARCHIBALD MACLEISH, *Brave New World, 1948**

But you, Thomas Jefferson,
You could not lie so still,
You could not bear the weight of stone
On the quiet hill,

You could not keep your green grown peace
Nor hold your folded hand
If you could see your new world now,
Your new sweet land.

There was a time, Tom Jefferson,
When freedom made free men.
The new found earth and the new freed mind
Were brothers then.

There was a time when tyrants feared
The new world of the free.
Now freedom is afraid and shrieks
At tyranny.

Words have not changed their sense so soon
Nor tyranny grown new.
The truths you held, Tom Jefferson,
Will still hold true.

What's changed is freedom in this age.
What great men dared to choose
Small men now dare neither win
Nor lose.

Freedom, when men fear freedom's use
But love its useful name,
Has cause and cause enough for fear
And cause for shame.

We fought a war in freedom's name
And won it in our own.
We fought to free a world and raised
A wall of stone.

Your countrymen who could have built
The hill fires of the free
To set the dry world all ablaze
With liberty—

To burn the brutal thorn in Spain
Of bigotry and hate
And the dead lie and the brittle weed
Beyond the Plate:

Who could have heaped the bloody straw,
The dung of time, to light
The Danube in a sudden flame
Of hope by night—

Your countrymen who could have hurled
Their freedom like a brand
Have cupped it to a candle spark
In a frightened hand.

Freedom that was a thing to use
They've made a thing to save
And staked it in and fenced it round
Like a dead man's grave.

You, Thomas Jefferson,
You could not lie so still,
You could not bear the weight of stone
On your green hill,

You could not hold your angry tongue
If you could see how bold
The old stale bitter world plays new—
And the new world old.

9. WENDELL L. WILLKIE, *One World, 1943**

This war that I saw going on all around the world is, in Mr. Stalin's phrase, a war of liberation. It is to liberate some nations from the Nazi or the Japanese Army, and to liberate others from the threat of those armies. On this much we are all agreed. Are we yet agreed that liberation means more than this? Specifically, are the thirty-one United Nations now fighting together agreed that our common job of liberation includes giving to *all* peoples freedom to govern themselves as soon as they are able, and the economic freedom on which all lasting self-government inevitably rests?

It is these two aspects of freedom, I believe, which form the touchstone of our good faith in this war. I believe

we must include them both in our idea of the freedom we are fighting for. Otherwise, I am certain we shall not win the peace, and I am sure we cannot win the war.

In Chungking, on October 7, 1942, I made a statement to the Chinese and foreign press in which I tried to state some of the conclusions I had reached on my trip around the world. In part, this is what I said:

I have traveled through thirteen countries. I have seen kingdoms, soviets, republics, mandated areas, colonies, and dependencies. I have seen an almost bewildering variety of ways of living and ways of ruling and of being ruled. But I have found certain things common to all

* Wendell L. Willkie, *One World* (New York, 1943), pp. 180 ff. Copyright, 1943 by Wendell L. Willkie. By permission of Simon and Schuster, Inc.

the countries I have visited and to all the ordinary people in those countries with whom I have talked:

They all want the United Nations to win the war.

They all want a chance at the end of the war to live in liberty and independence.

They all doubt, in varying degree, the readiness of the leading democracies of the world to stand up and be counted for freedom for others after the war is over. This doubt kills their enthusiastic participation on our side.

Now, without the real support of these common people, the winning of the war will be enormously difficult. The winning of the peace will be nearly impossible. This war is not a simple, technical problem for task forces. It is also a war for men's minds. We must organize on our side not simply the sympathies but the active, aggressive, offensive spirit of nearly three fourths of the people of the world who live in South America, Africa, eastern Europe, and Asia. We have not done this, and at present are not doing this. We have got to do it. . . .

Men need more than arms with which to fight and win this kind of war. They need enthusiasm for the future and a conviction that the flags they fight under are in bright, clean colors. The truth is that we as a nation have not made up our minds what kind of world we want to speak for when victory comes.

Especially here in Asia the common people feel that we have asked them to join us for no better reason than that Japanese rule would be even worse than Western imperialism. This is a continent where the record of the Western democracies has been long and mixed, but where people—and remember there are a billion of them—are determined no longer to live under foreign control. Freedom and opportunity are the words which have modern magic for the people of Asia, and we have let the Japanese—the most cruel imperi-

alists the modern world has known —steal these words from us and corrupt them to their own uses.

Most of the people in Asia have never known democracy. They may or may not want *our* type of democracy. Obviously all of them are not ready to have democracy handed to them next Tuesday on a silver platter. But they are determined to work out their own destiny under governments selected by themselves.

Even the name of the Atlantic Charter disturbs thoughtful men and women I have been talking to. Do all of those who signed it, these people ask, agree that it applies to the Pacific? We must answer this question with a clear and simple statement of where we stand. And we must begin to sweat over our common problem of translating such a statement into plans which will be concrete and meaningful to the lives of these millions of people who are our allies.

Some of the plans to which such a statement would lead are already clear, I deeply believe, to most Americans:

We believe this war must mean an end to the empire of nations over other nations. No foot of Chinese soil, for example, should be or can be ruled from now on except by the people who live on it. And we must say so *now*, not after the war.

We believe it is the world's job to find some system for helping colonial peoples who join the United Nations' cause to become free and independent nations. We must set up firm timetables under which they can work out and train governments of their own choosing, and we must establish ironclad guarantees, administered by all the United Nations jointly, that they shall not slip back into colonial status.

Some say these subjects should be hushed until victory is won. Exactly the reverse is true. Sincere efforts to find progressive solutions now will bring strength to our cause. Remember, opponents of social change always urge delay because of some present crisis. After the war, the changes may be too little and too late.

We must develop between nations trade and trade routes strong enough to give all peoples the same vested interest in peace which we in America have had.

In the United States, we are being asked to give up temporarily our individual freedom and economic liberty in order to crush the Axis. We must recover this freedom and this liberty after the war. The way to make certain we do recover our traditional American way of life with a rising standard of living for all is to create a world in which all men everywhere can be free.

This statement caused a good deal of comment. Some of it was angry, but for the most part the reaction cheered me greatly. For it confirmed my feeling that the deep drift of public opinion, which works quietly but powerfully, has already moved ahead of many of our leaders on these questions and that it will, before long, push us into the open acknowledgment, before the world, of the beliefs we hold most firmly.

The temptation is great, in all of us, to limit the objectives of a war. Cynically, we may hope that the big words we have used will become smaller at the peace table, that we can avoid the costly and difficult readjustments which will be required to establish and defend real freedom for all peoples.

Many men and women I have talked with from Africa to Alaska asked me the question which has become almost a symbol all through Asia: what about India? Now I did not go to India. I do not propose to discuss that tangled question. But it has one aspect, in the East, which I should report. From Cairo on, it confronted me at every turn. The wisest man in China said to me: "When the aspiration of India for freedom was put aside to some future date, it was not Great Britain that suffered in public esteem in the Far East. It was the United States."

This wise man was not quarreling with British imperialism in India when he said this—a benevolent imperialism, if you like. He does not happen to believe in it, but he was not even talking about it. He was telling me that by our silence on India we have already drawn heavily on our reservoir of good will in the East. People of the East who would like to count on us are doubtful. They cannot ascertain from our attitude toward the problem of India what we are likely to feel at the end of the war about all the other hundreds of millions of Eastern peoples. They cannot tell from our vague and vacillating talk whether or not we really do stand for freedom, or what we mean by freedom.

In China, students who were refugees a thousand miles from their homes asked me if we were going to try to take back Shanghai after the war. In Beirut, Lebanese asked me if their relatives in Brooklyn—one third of all the Lebanese in the world live in the United States—would help to persuade the British and French occupying forces to leave Syria and the Lebanon after the war and let them run their own country.

In Africa, in the Middle East, throughout the Arab world, as well as in China and the whole Far East, freedom means the orderly but scheduled abolition of the colonial system. Whether we like it or not, this is true.

The British Commonwealth of Nations is the world's most spectacular example of such an orderly process. And the success of that great experiment should be immensely encouraging to the United Nations in working out the problems of self-government that lie ahead. For large sections of the world are still governed by the colonial system. Despite the Commonwealth, Great Britain still has numerous colonies, remnants of empire, with little or no self-rule, though the English people, millions of them, at home and throughout the Commonwealth, are working selflessly and with great skill toward reducing these remnants, toward extending the Commonwealth in place of the colonial system.

The English are by no means the only colonial rulers. The French still claim empire in Africa, in Indo-China, in South America, and in islands throughout the world. The Dutch still regard themselves as rulers of large parts of the East Indies and of territories in the West. The Portuguese, the Belgians, and other nations have colonial possessions. And we ourselves have not yet promised complete freedom to all the peoples in the West Indies for whom we have assumed responsibility. Furthermore, we have our domestic imperialisms.

But the world is awake, at last, to the knowledge that the rule of people by other peoples is not freedom, and not what we must fight to preserve.

There will be lots of tough problems ahead. And they will differ in different mandates and different colonies. Not all the peoples of the world are ready for freedom, or can defend it, the day after tomorrow. But today they all want some date to work toward, some assurance that the date will be kept. For the future, they do not ask that we solve their problems for them. They are neither so foolish nor so fainthearted. They ask only for the chance to solve their own problems with economic as well as political co-operation. For the peoples of the world intend to be free not only for their political satisfaction, but also for their economic advancement.

I mentioned among the imperialisms of the world our own domestic imperialisms. This war has opened for us new horizons—new geographical horizons, new mental horizons. We have been a people devoted largely to home enterprise. We have become a people whose first interests are beyond the seas. The names of Russian, Burmese, Tunisian, or Chinese towns command primary attention in our newspapers. The most eagerly seized letters coming into our homes are from our young men in Australia, New Guinea, Guadalcanal, Ireland, or North Africa. Our interests go with their interests, and we may feel certain that when they have battled over the world, they will not return home as provincial Americans. Nor will they find us so. What does all this mean? It means that though we began to grow up with the earlier World War, we are only now changing completely from a young nation of domestic concerns to an adult nation of international interests and world outlook.

A true world outlook is incompatible with a foreign imperialism, no matter how high-minded the governing country. It is equally incompatible with the kind of imperialism which can develop inside any nation. Freedom is an indivisible word. If we want to enjoy it, and fight for it, we must be prepared to extend it to everyone, whether they are rich or poor, whether they agree with us or not, no matter what their race or the color of their skin. We cannot, with good conscience, expect the British to set up an orderly schedule for the liberation of India before we have decided for ourselves to make all who live in America free.

In this war we are allied with four hundred million people of China and we count as our friends three hundred million people of India. Fighting with us are the Filipinos and the natives of Java and the East Indies and of

South Africa. Together, these peoples comprise almost half of the world's population. With none of them have the majority of Americans any ties of race. But we are learning in this war that it is not racial classifications nor ethnological considerations which bind men together; it is shared concepts and kindred objectives.

We are learning that the test of a people is their aim and not their color. Even Hitler's high racial wall has been breached by the recognition of a common purpose with those "honorary Aryans," the Japanese. We, too, have our natural allies. We must, now and hereafter, cast our lot as a nation with all those other peoples, whatever their race or color, who prize liberty as an innate right, both for themselves and for others. We must, now and hereafter, together with those peoples, reject the doctrine of imperialism which condemns the world to endless war.

Let me emphasize once more that race and color do not determine what people are allies and what people are enemies in this struggle. In the East, we have a plain example. Japan is our enemy because of her wanton and barbaric aggression upon weaker nations and because of the imperialistic doctrine by which she seeks to rule and enslave the world. Japan is our enemy because of the treacherous and unprovoked attacks by which she has launched each of her assaults in carrying forward her scheme of conquest.

China is our friend because like us she nourishes no dream of conquest and because she values liberty. She is our ally because, first among the nations, she resisted aggression and enslavement. . . .

It has been a long while since the United States had any imperialistic designs toward the outside world. But we have practiced within our own boundaries something that amounts to race

imperialism. The attitude of the white citizens of this country toward the Negroes has undeniably had some of the unlovely characteristics of an alien imperialism—a smug racial superiority, a willingness to exploit an unprotected people. We have justified it by telling ourselves that its end is benevolent. And sometimes it has been. But so sometimes have been the ends of imperialism. And the moral atmosphere in which it has existed is identical with that in which men—well-meaning men—talk of "the white man's burden."

But that atmosphere is changing. Today it is becoming increasingly apparent to thoughtful Americans that we cannot fight the forces and ideas of imperialism abroad and maintain any form of imperialism at home. The war has done this to our thinking.

Emancipation came to the colored race in America as a war measure. It was an act of military necessity. Manifestly it would have come without war, in the slower process of humanitarian reform and social enlightenment. But it required a disastrous, internecine war to bring this question of human freedom to a crisis, and the process of striking the shackles from the slave was accomplished in a single hour. We are finding under the pressure of this present conflict that long-standing barriers and prejudices are breaking down. The defense of our democracy against the forces that threaten it from without has made some of its failures to function at home glaringly apparent.

Our very proclamations of what we are fighting for have rendered our own inequities self-evident. When we talk of freedom and opportunity for all nations, the mocking paradoxes in our own society become so clear they can no longer be ignored. If we want to talk about freedom, we must mean freedom for others as well as ourselves, and we must mean freedom for everyone inside our frontiers as well as outside. During a war, this is especially important.

The threat to racial and religious, even to political, minority groups springs in wartime from two things—an overzealous mass insistence upon general conformity to majority standards, and the revival under emotional strains of age-old racial and religious distrusts. Minorities then are apt to be charged with responsibility for the war itself, and all the dislocations and discomforts arising from it. They are jealously subjected to scrutiny to determine if they are the recipients of special advantages.

We are all familiar with the process by which, in a war psychology, the unusual is distrusted and anything unorthodox is associated by some people with enemy intriguing. Chauvinists are likely to spring up in any community. There is the instance in our War of 1812 of a young man arrested and held for espionage on the suspicious circumstances that "he carried a long whip and wore an unusual number of buttons on his pantaloons." When affairs go wrong the public, by ancient custom, demands a scapegoat, and the first place to seek one is from a minority.

All this would appear ridiculous in our modern age were it not for the examples of bigotry and persecution we see in countries once presumed to be enlightened, and, even more seriously, were it not for the fact that we are already witnessing a crawling, insidious anti-Semitism in our own country. It will be well to bear in mind continuously that we are fighting today against intolerance and oppression, and that we shall get them in abundance if we lose. If we allow them to develop at home while we are engaging the enemy abroad, we shall have immeasurably weakened our fighting arm.

Our nation is composed of no one race, faith, or cultural heritage. It is a grouping of some thirty peoples possessing varying religious concepts, philosophies, and historical backgrounds. They are linked together by their confidence in our democratic institutions as expressed in the Declaration of Independence and guaranteed by the Constitution for themselves and for their children.

The keystone of our union of states is freedom—freedom for the individual to worship as he chooses, to work as he chooses, and live and rear his children as he chooses. Liberty, if it is to be for all, must be protected by basic safeguards intended to give it the most general diffusion attainable, and none can expect privileges which encroach upon the rights of others. Despite the functionings of our mischievous bureaucracies, and our sometimes excessively enterprising legislatures, and —in deplorable but fortunately isolated instances—the flaring of mob law, we have obtained here in America, in the course of little more than a century and a half of experience and adjustment, the most reasonable expression of freedom that has yet existed in history.

Our success thus far as a nation is not because we have built great cities and big factories and cultivated vast areas, but because we have promoted this fundamental assurance of freedom upon which all our material development has depended, and have tolerated, and learned to use, our diversities.

We remain a relatively new nation. As recently as fifty years ago, more than half our mining and a third of our total manufacturing were carried on by immigrants. More than half of the farm population of some of our leading agricultural states was alien-born. In the formative period of the nation, between 1820 and 1890, more than 15,000,000 newcomers reached our shores, and a still greater number were yet to arrive in the twenty-four years preceding the outbreak of the last war. In other words, we have had two hundred years of reinvigorating immigration which has brought us new blood, new experiences, new ideas. Here was a vast assembly of minority groups which have gone into the welding of a nation. We have created a strong nation because these new arrivals did not have the distractions, under our form of government, of continually opposing and battling one another, but entered as partners into the general upbuilding and consolidation. The height of our civilization, it seems to me, has been reached not by our assembly lines, our inventions, or any of our great factitious development, but by the ability of peoples of varying beliefs and of different racial extractions to live side by side here in the United States with common understanding, respect, and helpfulness.

If we want to see the opposite of this American system, we have merely to look at the military despotism of Hitler and the autocracy of Japan, and the fading dictatorship of Fascist Italy. The story of Germany for the last ten years has been one of racial and religious intolerance that provided a mask behind which a peace-professing dictator lured the people first to minority persecution, then to war. This intolerance gave the German nation the momentary strength of complete regimentation. Actually, it has undermined and weakened the social structure so that when the tide of war turns, collapse is likely to be sudden and complete.

It has always impressed me that, quite apart from any reasons of humanitarianism or justice or any sentiment regarding the protection of the

weak by the strong, it is only common sense to safeguard jealously the rights of minorities. For minorities are rich assets of a democracy, assets which no totalitarian government can afford. Dictatorships must, of necessity, fear and suppress them. But within the tolerance of a democracy, minorities are the constant spring of new ideas, stimulating new thought and action, the constant source of new vigor.

To suppress minority thinking and minority expression would tend to freeze society and prevent progress. For the majority itself is stimulated by the existence of minority groups. The human mind requires contrary expressions against which to test itself.

For now more than ever, we must keep in the forefront of our minds the fact that whenever we take away the liberties of those whom we hate, we are opening the way to loss of liberty for those we love.

Our way of living together in America is a strong but delicate fabric. It is made up of many threads. It has been woven over many centuries by the patience and sacrifices of countless liberty-loving men and women. It serves as a cloak for the protection of poor and rich, of black and white, of Jew and gentile, of foreign- and native-born.

Let us not tear it asunder. For no man knows, once it is destroyed, where or when man will find its protective warmth again.

ONE WORLD

It was only a short time ago—less than a quarter of a century—that the allied nations gained an outstanding victory over the forces of conquest and aggression then led by imperial Germany.

But the peace that should have followed that war failed primarily because no joint objectives upon which it could be based had been arrived at in the minds of the people, and therefore no world peace was possible. The League of Nations was created fullblown; and men and women, having developed no joint purpose, except to defeat a common enemy, fell into capricious arguments about its structural form. Likewise, it failed because it was primarily an Anglo-French-American solution, retaining the old colonial imperialisms under new and fancy terms. It took inadequate account of the pressing needs of the Far East, nor did it sufficiently seek solution of the economic problems of the world. Its attempts to solve the world's problems were primarily political. But political internationalism without economic internationalism is a house built upon sand. For no nation can reach its fullest development alone.

Our own history furnishes, I believe, another clue to our failure. One of our most obvious weaknesses, in the light of what is going on today, is the lack of any continuity in our foreign policy. Neither major party can claim to have pursued a stable or consistent program of international co-operation even during the relatively brief period of the last forty-five years. Each has had its season of world outlook—sometimes an imperialistic one—and each its season of strict isolationism, the Congressional leadership of the party out of power usually, according to accepted American political practice, opposing the program of the party in power, whatever it might be.

For years many in both parties have recognized that if peace, economic prosperity, and liberty itself were to continue in this world, the nations of the world must find a method of economic stabilization and co-operative effort.

These aspirations at the end of the first World War, under the presidency of Woodrow Wilson, produced a program of international co-operation intended to safeguard all nations against military aggression, to protect racial minorities, and to give the oncoming generation some confidence that it could go about its affairs without a return of the disrupting and blighting scourge of war. Whatever we may think about the details of that program, it was definite, affirmative action for world peace. We cannot state positively just how effective it might have proved had the United States extended to it support, influence, and active participation.

But we do know that we tried the opposite course and found it altogether futile. We entered into an era of strictest detachment from world affairs. Many of our public leaders, Democratic and Republican, went about the country proclaiming that we had been tricked, that our ideals had been betrayed, that never again should we allow ourselves to become entangled in world politics which would inevitably bring about another armed outbreak. We were blessed with natural barriers, they maintained, and need not concern ourselves with the complicated and unsavory affairs of an old world beyond our borders.

We shut ourselves away from world trade by excessive tariff barriers. We washed our hands of the continent of Europe and displayed no interest in its fate while Germany rearmed. We torpedoed the London Economic Conference when the European democracies, with France lagging in the rear, were just beginning to recover from the economic depression that had sapped their vitality, and when the instability of foreign exchange remained the principal obstacle to full revival. And in so doing, we sacrificed a magnificent opportunity for leadership in strengthening and rehabilitating the democratic nations, in fortifying them against assault by the forces of aggression which at that very moment were beginning to gather.

The responsibilty for this does not attach solely to any political party. For neither major party stood consistently and conclusively before the American public as either the party of world outlook or the party of isolation. If we were to say that Republican leadership destroyed the League of Nations in 1920, we must add that it was Democratic leadership that broke up the London Economic Conference in 1933. . . .

I am satisfied that the American people never deliberately and intentionally turned their backs on a program for international co-operation. Possibly they would have preferred changes in the precise Versailles covenant, but not complete aloofness from the efforts of other nations. They were betrayed by leaders without convictions who were thinking in terms of group vote catching and partisan advantage.

If our withdrawal from world affairs after the last war was a contributing factor to the present war and to the economic instability of the past twenty years—and it seems plain that it was—a withdrawal from the problems and responsibilities of the world after this war would be sheer disaster. Even our relative geographical isolation no longer exists.

At the end of the last war, not a single plane had flown across the Atlantic. Today that ocean is a mere ribbon, with airplanes making regular scheduled flights. The Pacific is only a slightly wider ribbon in the ocean of the air, and Europe and Asia are at our very doorstep.

America must choose one of three courses after this war: narrow nationalism, which inevitably means the ultimate loss of our own liberty; international imperialism, which means the sacrifice of some other nation's liberty; or the creation of a world in which there shall be an equality of opportunity for every race and every nation. I am convinced the American people will choose, by overwhelming majority, the last of these courses. To make this choice effective, we must win not only the war, but also the peace, and we must start winning it now.

To win this peace three things seem to me necessary—first, we must plan now for peace on a world basis; second, the world must be free, politically and economically, for nations and for men, that peace may exist in it; third, America must play an active, constructive part in freeing it and keeping its peace.

When I say that peace must be planned on a world basis, I mean quite literally that it must embrace the earth. Continents and oceans are plainly only parts of a whole, seen, as I have seen them, from the air. England and America are parts; Russia and China, Egypt, Syria and Turkey, Iraq and Iran are also parts. And it is inescapable that there can be no peace for any part of the world unless the foundations of peace are made secure throughout all parts of the world.

This cannot be accomplished by mere declarations of our leaders, as in an Atlantic Charter. Its accomplishment depends primarily upon acceptance by the peoples of the world. For if the failure to reach international understanding after the last war taught us anything it taught us this: even if war leaders apparently agree upon generalized principles and slogans while the war is being fought, when they come to the peace table they make their own interpretations of their previous declarations. So unless today, while the war is being fought, the people of the United States and of Great Britain, of Russia and of China, and of all the other United Nations, fundamentally agree on their purposes, fine and idealistic expressions of hope such as those of the Atlantic Charter will live merely to mock us as have Mr. Wilson's Fourteen Points. The Four Freedoms will not be accomplished by the declarations of those momentarily in power. They will become real only if the people of the world force them into actuality.

When I say that in order to have peace this world must be free, I am only reporting that a great process has started which no man—certainly not Hitler—can stop. Men and women all over the world are on the march, physically, intellectually, and spiritually. After centuries of ignorant and dull compliance, hundreds of millions of people in eastern Europe and Asia have opened the books. Old fears no longer frighten them. They are no longer willing to be Eastern slaves for Western profits. They are beginning to know that men's welfare throughout the world is interdependent. They are resolved, as we must be, that there is no more place for imperialism within their own society than in the society of nations. The big house on the hill surrounded by mud huts has lost its awesome charm.

Our Western world and our presumed supremacy are now on trial. Our boasting and our big talk leave Asia cold. Men and women in Russia and China and in the Middle East are conscious now of their own potential strength. They are coming to know that many of the decisions about the future of the world lie in their hands. And they intend that these decisions shall leave the peoples of each nation free from foreign domination, free for economic, social and spiritual growth.

Economic freedom is as important as political freedom. Not only must people have access to what other peoples produce, but their own products must in turn have some chance of reaching men all over the world. There will be no peace, there will

be no real development, there will be no economic stability, unless we find the method by which we can begin to break down the unnecessary trade barriers hampering the flow of goods. Obviously the sudden and uncompromising abolition of tariffs after the war could only result in disaster. But obviously, also, one of the freedoms we are fighting for is freedom to trade. I know there are many men, particularly in America, where our standard of living exceeds the standard of living in the rest of the world, who are genuinely alarmed at such a prospect, who believe that any such process will only lessen our own standard of living. The reverse of this is true.

Many reasons may be assigned for the amazing economic development of the United States. The abundance of our national resources, the freedom of our political institutions, and the character of our population have all undoubtedly contributed. But in my judgment the greatest factor has been the fact that by the happenstance of good fortune there was created here in America the largest area in the world in which there were no barriers to the exchange of goods and ideas.

And I should like to point out to those who are fearful one inescapable fact. In view of the astronomical figures our national debt will assume by the end of this war, and in a world reduced in size by industrial and transportation developments, even our present standard of living in America cannot be maintained unless the exchange of goods flows more freely over the whole world. It is also inescapably true that to raise the standard of living of any man anywhere in the world is to raise the standard of living by some slight degree of every man everywhere in the world.

Finally, when I say that this world demands the full participation of a self-confident America, I am only passing on an invitation which the peoples of the East have given us. They would like the United States and the other United Nations to be partners with them in this grand adventure. They want us to join them in creating a new society of independent nations, free alike of the economic injustices of the West and the political malpractices of the East. But as partners in that great new combination they want us neither hesitant, incompetent, nor afraid. They want partners who will not hesitate to speak out for the correction of injustice anywhere in the world.

Our allies in the East know that we intend to pour out our resources in this war. But they expect us now—not after the war—to use the enormous power of our giving to promote liberty and justice. Other peoples, not yet fighting, are waiting no less eagerly for us to accept the most challenging opportunity of all history—the chance to help create a new society in which men and women the world around can live and grow invigorated by independence and freedom.

10. George C. Marshall, *The Marshall Plan, 1947*[*]

In considering the requirements for the rehabilitation of Europe the physical loss of life, the visible destruction of cities, factories, mines and railroads was correctly estimated, but it has become obvious during recent months that this visible destruction was probably less serious than the dislocation of the entire fabric of European economy. For the past ten years conditions have been highly abnormal.

The feverish preparation for war and the more feverish maintenance of the war effort engulfed all aspects of national economies. Machinery has fallen into disrepair or is entirely obsolete. Under the arbitrary and destructive Nazi rule, virtually every possible enterprise was geared into the German war machine. Long-standing commercial ties, private institutions, banks, insurance companies and shipping companies disappeared, through loss of capital, absorption through nationalization or by simple destruction.

In many countries, confidence in the local currency has been severely shaken. The breakdown of the business structure of Europe during the war was complete. Recovery has been seriously retarded by the fact that two years after the close of hostilities a peace settlement with Germany and Austria has not been agreed upon. But even given a more prompt solution of these difficult problems, the rehabilitation of the economic structure of Europe quite evidently will require a much longer time and greater effort than had been foreseen. . . .

The truth of the matter is that Europe's requirements for the next three or four years of foreign food and other essential products——principally from America—are so much greater than her present ability to pay that she must have substantial additional help, or face economic, social and political deterioration of a very grave character.

The remedy lies in breaking the vicious circle and restoring the confidence of the European people in the economic future of their own countries

[*] Secretary of State George C. Marshall, Address, June 6, 1947, *The New York Times,* June 6, 1947, p. 2.

and of Europe as a whole. The manufacturer and the farmer throughout wide areas must be able and willing to exchange their products for currencies, the continuing value of which is not open to question.

Aside from the demoralizing effect on the world at large and the possibilities of disturbances arising as a result of the desperation of the people concerned, the consequences to the economy of the United States should be apparent to all. It is logical that the United States should do whatever it is able to do to assist in the return of normal economic health in the world, without which there can be no political stability and no assured peace.

Our policy is directed not against any country or doctrine but against hunger, poverty, desperation and chaos. Its purpose should be the revival of a working economy in the world so as to permit the emergence of political and social conditions in which free institutions can exist. Such assistance, I am convinced, must not be on a piecemeal basis as various crises develop. Any assistance that this Government may render in the future should provide a cure rather than a mere palliative. . . .

It is already evident that, before the United States Government can proceed much further in its efforts to alleviate the situation and help start the European world on its way to recovery, there must be some agreement among the countries of Europe as to the requirements of the situation and the part those countries themselves will take in order to give proper effect to whatever action might be undertaken by this Government. It would be neither fitting nor efficacious for this Government to undertake to draw up unilaterally a program designed to place Europe on its feet economically. This is the business of the Europeans. The initiative, I think, must come from Europe. The role of this country should consist of friendly aid in the drafting of a European program and of later support of such a program so far as it may be practical for us to do so. The program should be a joint one, agreed to by a number, if not all European nations.

11. DWIGHT D. EISENHOWER, *Second Inaugural Address, 1957**

We live in a land of plenty, but rarely has this earth known such peril as today.

In our nation work and wealth abound. Our population grows. Commerce crowds our rivers and rails, our ships, harbors and highways. Our soil is fertile, our agriculture productive. The air rings with the song of our industry—rolling mills, and blast furnaces, dynamos, dams and assembly lines—the chorus of America the bountiful.

Now this is our home—yet this is not the whole of our world. For our world is where our full destiny lies—with men, of all peoples and all nations, who are or would be free. And for them—and so for us—this is no time of ease or of rest.

In too much of the earth there is want, discord, danger. New forces and new nations stir and strive across the earth, with power to bring, by their fate, great good or great evil to the free world's future.

From the deserts of North Africa to the islands of the South Pacific one-

* *The New York Times,* January 22, 1957.

third of all mankind has entered upon an historic struggle for a new freedom: freedom from grinding poverty. Across all continents, nearly a billion people seek, sometimes almost in desperation, for the skills and knowledge and assistance by which they may satisfy from their own resources, the material wants common to all mankind.

No nation, however old or great, escapes this tempest of change and turmoil. Some, impoverished by the recent World War, seek to restore their means of livelihood. In the heart of Europe, Germany still stands tragically divided. So is the whole continent divided. And so, too, all the world.

The divisive force is international communism and the power that it controls.

The designs of that power, dark in purpose, are clear in practice. It strives to seal forever the fate of those it has enslaved. It strives to break the ties that unite the free. And it strives to capture—to exploit for its own greater power—all forces of change in the world, especially the needs of the hungry and the hopes of the oppressed.

Yet the world of international communism has itself been shaken by a fierce and mighty force; the readiness of men who love freedom to pledge their lives to that love.

Through the night of their bondage, the unconquerable will of heroes has struck with the swift, sharp thrust of lightning. Budapest is no longer merely the name of a city; henceforth it is a new and shining symbol of man's yearning to be free.

Thus across all the globe there harshly blow the winds of change. And we—though fortunate be our lot— know that we can never turn our backs to them.

We look upon this shaken earth, and we declare our firm and fixed purpose—the building of a peace with justice in a world where moral law prevails.

The building of such a peace is a bold and solemn purpose. To proclaim it is easy. To serve it will be hard. And to attain it, we must be aware of its full meaning—and ready to pay its full price.

We know clearly what we seek, and why.

We seek peace, knowing that peace is the climate of freedom. And now, as in no other age, we seek it because we have been warned, by the power of modern weapons, that peace may be the only climate possible for human life itself.

Yet this peace we seek cannot be born of fear alone; it must be rooted in the lives of nations. There must be justice, sensed and shared by all peoples, for, without justice the world can know only a tense and unstable truce.

There must be law, steadily invoked and respected by all nations, for without law, the world promises only such meager justice as the pity of the strong upon the weak. But the law of which we speak, comprehending the values of freedom, affirms the equality of all nations, great and small.

Splendid as can be the blessings of such a peace, high will be its cost; in toil patiently sustained, in help honorably given, in sacrifice calmly borne.

We are called to meet the price of this peace.

To counter the threat of those who seek to rule by force, we must pay the costs of our own needed military strength and help to build the security of others.

We must use our skills and knowledge and, at times, our substance, to help others rise from misery, however far the scene of suffering may be from our shores. For wherever in the world a people knows desperate want, there must appear at least the spark of hope, the hope of progress—or there will surely rise at last the flames of conflict.

We recognize and accept our own deep involvement in the destiny of men everywhere. We are accordingly pledged to honor, and to strive to fortify, the authority of the United Nations. For in that body rests the best hope of our age for the assertion of that law by which all nations may live in dignity.

And beyond this general resolve, we are called to act a responsible role in the world's great concerns or conflicts—whether they touch upon the affairs of a vast region, the fate of an island in the Pacific, or the use of a canal in the Middle East.

Only in respecting the hopes and cultures of others will we practice the equality of all nations. Only as we show willingness and wisdom in giving counsel—in receiving counsel and in sharing burdens, will we wisely perform the work of peace.

For one truth must rule all we think and all we do. No people can live to itself alone. The unity of all who dwell in freedom is their only sure defense.

The economic need of all nations—in mutual dependence—makes isolation an impossibility, not even America's prosperity could long survive if other nations did not prosper. No nation can longer be a fortress, lone and strong and safe. And any people, seeking such shelter for themselves, can now build only their own prison.

Our pledge to these principles is constant, because we believe in their rightness.

We do not fear this world of change. America is no stranger to much of its spirit. Everywhere we see the seeds of the same growth that America itself has known.

The American experiment has, for generations, fired the passion and the courage of millions elsewhere seeking freedom, equality, opportunity. And the American story of material progress has helped excite the longing of all needy people for some satisfaction of their human wants. These hopes that we have helped to inspire, we can help to fulfill.

In this confidence we speak plainly to all peoples.

We cherish our friendship with all nations that are or would be free. We respect, no less, their independence. And, when, in time of want or peril, they ask our help, they may honorably receive it; for we no more seek to buy their sovereignty than we would sell our own. Sovereignty is never bartered among free men.

We honor the aspirations of those nations which, now captive, long for freedom. We seek neither their military alliance nor any artificial imitation of our society. And they can know the warmth of the welcome that awaits them when, as must be, they join again the ranks of freedom.

We honor, no less in this divided world than in a less tormented time, the people of Russia. We do not dread, rather do we welcome, their progress in education and industry.

We wish them success in their demands for more intellectual freedom, greater security before their own laws, fuller enjoyment of the rewards of their own toil. For as such things may come to pass, the more certain will be the coming of that day when our peoples may freely meet in friendship.

And so we voice our hope and our belief that we can help to heal this divided world. Thus may the nations cease to live in trembling before the menace of force. Thus may the weight of fear and the weight of arms be taken from the burdened shoulders of mankind.

Index of Names

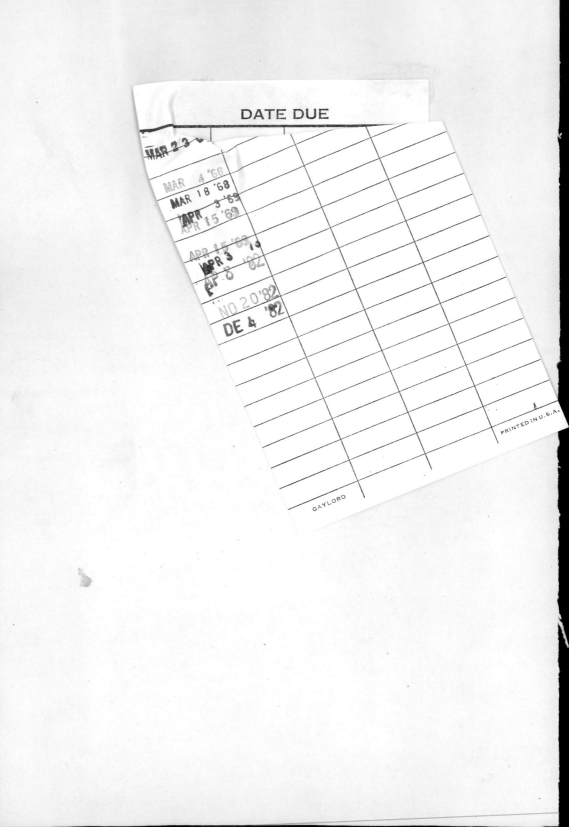

DATE DUE

MAR 4 '68			
MAR 18 '68			
MAR 3 '69			
APR 15 '69			
APR 15 '69			
APR 3 '82			
FE 8 '82			
NO 20'82			
DE 4 '82			

GAYLORD

PRINTED IN U.S.A.